Fodor's 07

ALASKA

Where to Stay and Eat for All Budgets

Must-See Sights and Local Secrets

Ratings You Can Trust

Fodor's Travel Publications New York, Toronto, London, Sydney, Auckland

www.fodors.com

FODOR'S ALASKA 2007
Editor: Heidi Leigh Johansen

Contributing Editors: Felice Aarons, Shannon Kelly
Editorial Production: Tom Holton
Editorial Contributors: Jim Altieri, Carissa Bluestone, Tricia Brown, Dermot Cole, Nick Horton, Ken Marsh, Tom Reale, Bill Sherwonit
Maps: David Lindroth Inc.; Mark Stroud, Moon Street Cartography, *cartographers*; Bob Blake and Rebecca Baer, *map editors*
Design: Fabrizio La Rocca, *creative director*; Guido Caroti, *art director*; Tina Malaney and Chie Ushio, *designers;* Moon Sun Kim, *cover design*; Melanie Marin, *senior picture editor*
Production/Manufacturing: Colleen Ziemba
Cover Photo (Tracy Arm, Fords Terror Wilderness, Tongass Forest): John Hyde

COPYRIGHT

ISBN-10: 1–4000–1715–7

ISBN-13: 978–1–4000–1715–7

ISSN: 0271–2776

SPECIAL SALES

This book is available for special discounts for bulk purchases for sales promotions or premiums. Special editions, including personalized covers, excerpts of existing guides, and corporate imprints, can be created in large quantities for special needs. For more information, write to Special Markets/Premium Sales, 1745 Broadway, MD 6-2, New York, New York 10019, or e-mail specialmarkets@randomhouse.com.

AN IMPORTANT TIP & AN INVITATION

Although all prices, opening times, and other details in this book are based on information supplied to us at press time, changes occur all the time in the travel world, and Fodor's cannot accept responsibility for facts that become outdated or for inadvertent errors or omissions. So **always confirm information when it matters,** especially if you're making a detour to visit a specific place. Your experiences—positive and negative—matter to us. If we have missed or misstated something, **please write to us.** We follow up on all suggestions. Contact the Alaska editor at editors@fodors.com or c/o Fodor's at 1745 Broadway, New York, NY 10019.

PRINTED IN THE UNITED STATES OF AMERICA

10 9 8 7 6 5 4 3 2 1

Be a Fodor's Correspondent

Your opinion matters. It matters to us. It matters to your fellow Fodor's travelers, too. And we'd like to hear it. In fact, we *need* to hear it.

When you share your experiences and opinions, you become an active member of the Fodor's community. That means we'll not only use your feedback to make our books better, but we'll publish your names and comments whenever possible. Throughout our guides, look for "Word of Mouth," excerpts of your unvarnished feedback.

Here's how you can help improve Fodor's for all of us.

Tell us when we're right. We rely on local writers to give you an insider's perspective. But our writers and staff editors—who are the best in the business—depend on you. Your positive feedback is a vote to renew our recommendations for the next edition.

Tell us when we're wrong. We're proud that we update most of our guides every year. But we're not perfect. Things change. Hotels cut services. Museums change hours. Charming cafés lose charm. If our writer didn't quite capture the essence of a place, tell us how you'd do it differently. If any of our descriptions are inaccurate or inadequate, we'll incorporate your changes in the next edition and will correct factual errors at fodors.com *immediately.*

Tell us what to include. You probably have had fantastic travel experiences that aren't yet in Fodor's. Why not share them with a community of like-minded travelers? Maybe you chanced upon a beach or bistro or B&B that you don't want to keep to yourself. Tell us why we should include it. And share your discoveries and experiences with everyone directly at fodors.com. Your input may lead us to add a new listing or highlight a place we cover with a "Highly Recommended" star or with our highest rating, "Fodor's Choice."

Give us your opinion instantly at our feedback center at www.fodors.com/feedback. You may also e-mail editors@fodors.com with the subject line "Alaska Editor." Or send your nominations, comments, and complaints by mail to Alaska Editor, Fodor's, 1745 Broadway, New York, NY 10019.

You and travelers like you are the heart of the Fodor's community. Make our community richer by sharing your experiences. Be a Fodor's correspondent.

Happy traveling!

Tim Jarrell, Publisher

CONTENTS

CLOSEUPS

MAPS

ALASKA IN FOCUS

ABOUT THIS BOOK

Our Ratings

Sometimes you find terrific travel experiences and sometimes they just find you. But usually the burden is on you to select the right combination of experiences. That's where our ratings come in.

As travelers we've all discovered a place so wonderful that its worthiness is obvious. And sometimes that place is so unique that superlatives don't do it justice: you just have to be there to know. These sights, properties, and experiences get our highest rating, **Fodor's Choice,** indicated by orange stars throughout this book.

Black stars highlight sights and properties we deem **Highly Recommended,** places that our writers, editors, and readers praise again and again for consistency and excellence.

By default, there's another category: any place we include in this book is by definition worth your time, unless we say otherwise. And we will.

Disagree with any of our choices? Care to nominate a place or suggest that we rate one more highly? Visit our feedback center at www.fodors.com/feedback.

Budget Well

Hotel and restaurant price categories from ¢ to $$$$ are defined in the opening pages of each chapter. For attractions, we always give standard adult admission fees; reductions are usually available for children, students, and senior citizens. Want to pay with plastic? **AE, D, DC, MC, V** following restaurant and hotel listings indicate whether American Express, Discover, Diners Club, MasterCard, and Visa are accepted.

Restaurants

Unless we state otherwise, restaurants are open for lunch and dinner daily. We mention dress only when there's a specific requirement and reservations only when they're essential or not accepted—it's always best to book ahead.

Hotels

Hotels have private bath, phone, TV, and air-conditioning and operate on the European Plan (aka EP, meaning without meals), unless we specify that they use the Continental Plan (CP, with a Continental breakfast), Breakfast Plan (BP, with a full breakfast), or Modified American Plan (MAP, with breakfast and dinner) or are all-inclusive (AI, including all meals and most activities). We always list facilities but not whether you'll be charged an extra fee to use them, so when pricing accommodations, find out what's included.

Many Listings

- ★ Fodor's Choice
- ★ Highly recommended
- ✉ Physical address
- Directions
- Mailing address
- Telephone
- Fax
- On the Web
- E-mail
- Admission fee
- Open/closed times
- Start of walk/itinerary
- M Metro stations
- Credit cards

Hotels & Restaurants

- Hotel
- Number of rooms
- Facilities
- Meal plans
- ✕ Restaurant
- Reservations
- Dress code
- Smoking
- BYOB
- Hotel with restaurant that warrants a visit

Outdoors

- Golf
- Camping

Other

- Family-friendly
- Contact information
- ⇨ See also
- Branch address
- Take note

WHAT'S WHERE

SOUTHEAST ALASKA	
	Southeast Alaska (also known as the Panhandle or more commonly among Alaskans simply as "Southeast") encompasses the Inside Passage—more than a century ago the traditional route to the Klondike goldfields and today the centerpiece for Alaskan cruises. Juneau, the state's water-locked capital, is here, as well as fishing villages such as Petersburg and Ketchikan, which is known for its totem poles. An onion-dome cathedral accents Sitka, the onetime capital of Russian America. Each fall up to 4,000 eagles gather just outside Haines to feast on salmon at the Alaska Chilkat Bald Eagle Preserve. One of the few places in the world where you can inspect from a short distance massive tidewater glaciers is Glacier Bay National Park. The towns of Southeast Alaska are linked by air and the Alaska Marine Highway (the state ferry system); only Haines, Hyder, and Skagway have road links to "the Outside." If you're not a cruise-ship passenger, visiting towns serviced by the cruise ships can be disconcerting, as the ships disgorge thousands of tourists into these small communities. However, the scenery outside the often-crowded towns is phenomenal: long fjords pierce the mountainous terrain, timbered slopes plunge to the rocky shores, and marine life abounds from tiny seabirds to multiton whales.
ANCHORAGE 	With nearly half the state's population, Anchorage is Alaska's biggest city and the state's only true metropolis. You'll find a varied selection of ethnic restaurants, a performing arts center, theater groups, an opera company, and an orchestra here. The Anchorage Museum of History and Art houses an outstanding collection of historic and contemporary Alaskan art. The Alaska Native Heritage Center celebrates the rich diversity of the state's original inhabitants. At nearby Lake Hood—the largest seaplane base in the world—the Alaska Aviation Heritage Museum preserves examples of rare and restored planes. For all the attractions Anchorage offers, most visitors spend little time here, using it as a jumping-off point for excursions into less-settled parts of the state or merely as a place to catch a plane home. But there's plenty to do and see if you are passing through—and the occasional moose ambling down a city bike trail or a hawk passing through will remind you of the vast stretches of wilderness just outside the city borders.

Alaska
Chukchi Sea
Icy Cape
Barrow
Point Barrow
Point Hope
LISBURNE PENINSULA
NORTH
Arctic Circle
Noatak River
Anaktuvuk Pass
BROOK
CHUKOTKA
Cape Espenberg
Kotzebue
Kobuk River
Bettles
Nunyagmo
Bering Strait
Kotzebue Sound
SEWARD PENINSULA
THE BUSH
Koyukuk
RUSSIA
UNITED STATES
Teller
Taylor
Provideniya
Nome
Tanana
Galena
Manley Hot Springs
Savoonga
River
Norton Sound
Saint Lawrence Island
Unalakleet
MOUNTAINS
Yukon
River
Mt. McKinley 20,320ft
KUSKOKWIM
Takotna
St Marys
Cape Romanzof
YUKON DELTA
Kuskokwim
ALASKA
Saint Matthew Island
Aniak
Bethel
Kenai
Nunivak Island
Soldovia
AHKLUN MTS
River
Iliamna
Kuskokwim Bay
Cook Inlet
1
Homer
Dillingham
Nushagak
Naknek
Cape Newenham
King Salmon
Bristol Bay
Saint Paul Island
Pribilof Islands
Saint George Island
Port Lions
Kodiak
Shelikof Strait
Bering Sea
Port Heiden
PENINSULA
Kodiak Island
ALASKA
Cold Bay
Sand Point
PACIFIC OCEAN
Unimak Island
SEE INSET AT RIGHT
ALEUTIAN ISLANDS
Unalaska
Unalaska Island
Umnak Island
0
200 mi
0
200 km

Beaufort Sea
Harrison Bay
Prudhoe Bay
Deadhorse
Mackenzie Bay
Trans-Alaska Pipeline
Dalton Hwy.
RANGE
Arctic Circle
CANADA
UNITED STATES
Porcupine R.
Fort Yukon
Yukon
River
NORTHWEST TERRITORIES
Livengood
Circle
Steese Hwy.
Chena Hot Springs
Eagle
Fairbanks
INTERIOR
Dawson
Tanana
Alaska River
George Parks Hwy.
RANGE
YUKON TERRITORY
Cantwell
Tok
Hwy
Richardson Hwy.
Slana
Nabesna
SOUTH CENTRAL
Gulkana
Glennallen
Alaska
Chitina
Wasilla
Palmer
McCarthy
Valdez
Copper
Anchorage
Haines Junction
Hwy
Whitehorse
Columbia Glacier
Whittier
Mt. St. Elias 18,008ft
Cordova
Seward
Prince William Sound
KENAI PENINSULA
Skagway
Haines
Yakutat
BRITISH COLUMBIA
COAST MOUNTAINS
Gustavus
Juneau
Glacier Bay National Park & Preserve
Gulf of Alaska
Hoonah
Chichagof Island
Sitka
SOUTHEAST
Petersburg
Baranof Island
Wrangell
Alaska Marine Highway
Ketchikan
Dixon Entrance
Queen Charlotte Islands
Bering Sea
Attu Island
Adak
Atka Island
Unimak Island
Unalaska
Unalaska Island
Umnak Island
ALEUTIAN ISLANDS
200 miles
300 km
Pacific Ocean

WHAT'S WHERE

SOUTH CENTRAL ALASKA 	South Central encapsulates nearly all that the state has to offer: great fishing, hiking, rafting, and wildlife viewing, much of it easily accessible. Using Anchorage as a base, you could spend several vacations in this region and still be left wanting more. Especially well visited are the towns of Seward and Homer on the Kenai Peninsula. Kodiak, 100 mi offshore in the gulf of Alaska, is known as the Emerald Island for its green-carpeted mountains. The biggest terrestrial carnivore on Earth, the Kodiak brown bear, makes its home here. Even areas not readily reachable by road are within a short, easy flight by small plane, and dozens of charter outfits compete for your business. Although the summer crowds can be daunting in some of the most popular spots, a little research and effort can take you to areas where you can experience true wilderness solitude.
THE INTERIOR 	Bounded by the Brooks Range to the north and the Alaska Range to the south, the Interior is home to Mt. McKinley, the highest peak in North America, and to Denali National Park & Preserve, a 6-million-acre home to some of Alaska's best wildlife, scenery, and adventure. The weather is more extreme in the Interior than in the South Central region, with warmer summers and colder winters. Founded in 1901 by a merchant and a prospector, Fairbanks, the state's second-largest city, is quite different from Anchorage: it is smaller and less sophisticated and is considered more rustically "Alaskan." Fairbanks is the gateway to the Far North—the towns of the Arctic and the Bering Coast that are connected mainly by air—and to Canada's Yukon Territory, whose gold-rush history is preserved in such towns as Dawson City and Whitehorse.

THE BUSH

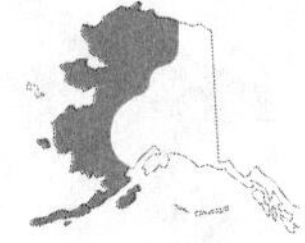

The Bush, more a spirit than a place, is the last frontier of the Last Frontier. Regions not connected by Alaska's road system are considered the Bush. From Nome to Barrow, much of the ground is permanently frozen, and for months at a time the sun never sets—or rises. In the Arctic are the hardy Eskimo people and the Prudhoe Bay oil fields, near Barrow, America's northernmost community. Prospectors still pan for gold on the beach in Nome, where they are occasionally joined by a wandering polar bear. Only one road leads up to the Arctic, the Dalton Highway. Otherwise, the only link between these outposts of civilization is by air or sea—unless you happen to have a sled-dog team, a snowmobile, or a Rollagon (a vehicle specially designed for crossing tundra).

The Bush offers brown-bear viewing in Katmai National Park, steaming volcanoes on the Alaska Peninsula and the Aleutian Islands, and the Bering seacoast's more than 100,000 square mi of watery wilderness. If you're planning an unguided Bush visit, keep in mind the planning and research involved, not to mention the primitive facilities you'll find here. Many of the smaller villages don't have any visitor amenities such as hotels, restaurants, or public transportation. However, if you can get past the logistical barriers, exploring the Bush is true adventuring. You're miles from civilization, without the conveniences of modern life; self-reliance and creativity go a long way in making your stay safe and enjoyable.

QUINTESSENTIAL ALASKA

Seafood & Sourdough

Alaska's primary claim to gastronomic fame is seafood. The rich coastal waters produce prodigious quantities of halibut, salmon, crab, and shrimp, along with such specialties as abalone, sea urchin, herring roe, and sea cucumbers. If you haven't yet tasted fresh Alaskan salmon, do so here—there's nothing quite like a barbecued Copper River king salmon.

Sourdough bread, pastries, and pancakes are a local tradition, dating back to the gold-rush days. Prospectors and pioneers carried a stash of sourdough starter so that they could always whip up a batch of dough in short order. The old-timers became known as sourdoughs, a title that latter-day Alaskans earn by living here for 20 years.

After you return from your outdoor adventure, indulge your cravings with the best of Alaskan culinary delights. Start with sourdough pancakes for breakfast; for lunch go for smoked salmon spread on sourdough bread; top it off with a dinner of fresh halibut and wild-berry cobbler. Then you can consider yourself an honorary Alaska sourdough.

Kayaking

Sea kayaking is big among Alaskans. It was the Aleuts who invented the kayak (or *bidarka*) to fish and hunt sea mammals. When early explorers encountered the Aleuts, they compared them to sea creatures, so at home did they appear on their small ocean craft. Kayaks have the great advantage of portability. More stable than canoes, they also give you a feel for the water and a view from water level. Oceangoing kayakers will find plenty of offshore Alaskan adventures, especially in the protected waters of the Southeast, Prince William Sound, and Kenai Fjords National Park.

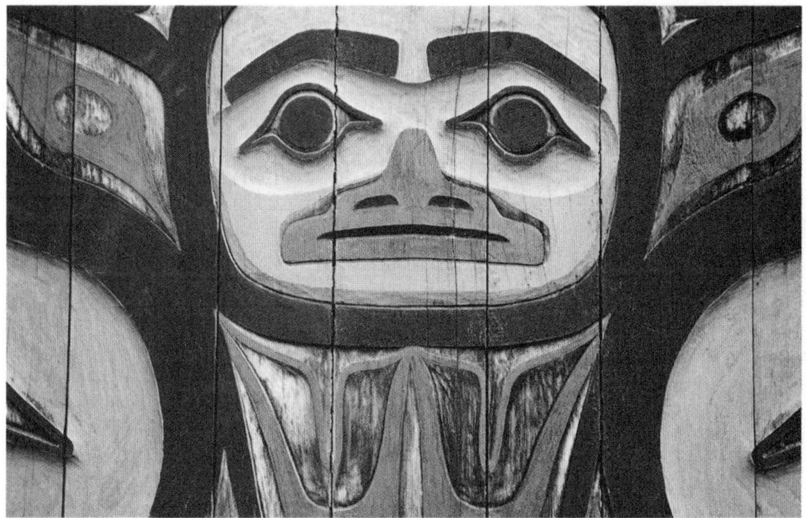

The variety of Alaskan marine life that you can view from a sea kayak is astonishing. It's possible to see whales, seals, sea lions, and sea otters, as well as bird species too numerous to list. Although caution is required when dealing with large stretches of open water, the truly Alaskan experience of self-propelled boating in a pristine ocean environment can be a life-changing thrill. Find more information about kayaking and many other sports in Chapter 1.

Native Crafts

Alaska's rich native culture is reflected in its abundance of craft traditions, from totem poles to intricate baskets and detailed carvings. Many of the native crafts you'll see across the state are results of generations of traditions passed down among tribes; the craft process is usually labor-intensive, using local resources such as rye grasses or fragrant cedar trees.

Each of Alaska's native groups is noted for particular skills. Inuit art includes ivory carvings, spirit masks, dance fans, baleen baskets, and jewelry. Also be on the lookout for mukluks (seal- or reindeer-skin boots). The Tlingit peoples of Southeast Alaska are known for their totem poles, as well as for baskets and hats woven from spruce root and cedar bark. Tsimshian Indians also work with spruce root and cedar bark, and Haida Indians are noted basket makers and carvers. Athabascans specialize in birch-bark creations, decorated fur garments, and beadwork. The Aleut, a maritime people dwelling in the southwest reaches of the state, make grass basketry that is considered among the best in the world. For tips about buying an authentic item, check out *Made in Alaska,* in Chapter 3.

WHEN TO GO

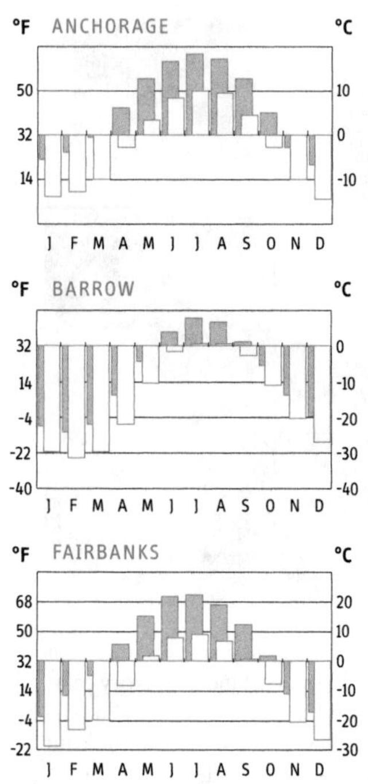

Because Alaska is so enormous, each region experiences a different climate, and seasons come and go at different times of the year. In summer the sun does not set for more than 2½ months in Barrow, north of the Arctic Circle. Even as far south as Juneau, you can see a glow of summertime twilight in the sky at midnight. In winter the situation is reversed, and the sun does not rise for more than two months in Alaska's northernmost regions. Anchorage gets about 5½–6 hours of daylight in mid-December.

Alaska is not a land of perpetual ice and snow—much of the state is snow-free during those long summer days. With fair weather comes an onslaught of tourists and peak-season prices. Summer, particularly late June through July, brings on plagues of mosquitoes. July and August are also the rainiest months throughout South Central and Interior Alaska. Fortunately, in perpetually wet Southeast Alaska, these months are the driest portion of the year. To avoid the summer crowds and prices, go during spring or fall.

Winter is the season for skiing, sledding, ice-skating, dog mushing, ice fishing, and other sports. The long nights are also ideal for viewing the northern lights (aka the aurora borealis). To see the aurora borealis you need a dark night with clear skies, distance from city lights, and sufficient solar activity to set off the stunning drapes of color that dance across the sky. Total darkness means you won't see them in the summer, clear skies usually imply cold temperatures, distance from city lights means you can't sit around your Anchorage hotel room waiting for something to appear, and the whole solar activity thing is a matter of luck. Your best bet is a fall or winter night outside of Fairbanks; Chena Hot Springs Resort is our recommendation for best viewing.

Climate

These charts list the average daily maximum and minimum temperatures for several Alaskan cities.

Forecasts **Weather Channel Connection** (900/932-8437 95¢ per minute from a Touch-Tone phone www.weather.com).

Numbers below vertical bands relate each zone to Greenwich Mean Time (0 hrs).
Local times frequently differ from these general indications, as indicated by light-face numbers on map.

- Anchorage **2**
- Atlanta **20**
- Bogotá **23**
- Buenos Aires **27**
- Caracas **24**
- Chicago **10**
- Dallas **11**
- Denver **8**
- Edmonton **4**
- Halifax **17**
- Honolulu **1**
- Juneau **3**
- Lima **25**
- Los Angeles **7**
- Mexico City **13**
- Miami **21**
- Minneapolis **9**
- Montevideo **28**
- Montréal **16**
- New Orleans **12**
- New York City **18**
- Ottawa **15**
- Rio de Janeiro **30**
- San Francisco **6**
- San José (CR) **22**
- Santiago **26**
- São Paolo **29**
- Toronto **14**
- Vancouver **5**
- Washington, D.C. **19**

IF YOU LIKE

Museums

A superb way to learn about Alaskan history and heritage is to hit any one of these museums, whose exhibits and treasures range from ceremonial blankets and native masks to gold-rush history pieces and Eskimo singing concerts.

- **Alaska Native Heritage Center, Anchorage.** This 26-acre facility celebrates native Alaskan culture. Five village exhibits encircle a small lake, and there are films, dances, and talks by native artisans.
- **Anchorage Museum of History and Art, Anchorage.** In addition to a fine collection of historical items, this museum features contemporary Alaskan art, guided tours, great meals (courtesy of Marx Brothers' Cafe), and a classy gift shop.
- **Living Museum of the Arctic, Kotzebue.** You can experience Eskimo culture firsthand at this unique museum: Listen to a storyteller, watch a ceremonial dance, and bounce high on a blanket toss—an ancient practice whereby hunters were launched high in the air from blankets of walrus or seal hide to scan the seas for game.
- **University of Alaska Museum of the North, Fairbanks.** A must-see for all visitors to the Interior, the museum gives an excellent overview of Alaska's human and natural history, including the state's largest display of gold, and Blue Babe, a mummified steppe bison.

Bicycling

Biking can be a rewarding adventure in accessible parts of the state. The paved-road system is straightforward, and traffic is usually light. However, the road shoulders can be narrow, and people tend to drive fast in rural areas. Unpaved highways are bikable but tougher going. Use caution when it comes to traffic, weather, and wildlife.

- **Anchorage, Alaska.** Anchorage has an excellent bike-trail system. Biking this city is a good way to appreciate its setting as a metropolis perched on the edge of vast wilderness—but beware the occasional furry creature sharing the bike trail with you!
- **Denali National Park & Preserve.** Take your mountain bike on the Alaska Railroad and bike Denali. Although the park road is largely unpaved, it has a good dirt surface and only light traffic. This immense preserve has some of the best wildlife viewing in the state.
- **The Interior.** Mountain biking has become a hot sport here. Fairbanks has miles of scenic bike paths along the Chena River. Most roads have wide shoulders and those incredible Alaska views. Trails used in winter by mushers, snowmobilers, and cross-country skiers are taken over by bikers when the snow melts.
- **Southeast Alaska and the Ferry System.** You can bring your bike on Alaska's ferry system at an extra charge. Use it to explore the Southeast's charming communities and surrounding forests, but come prepared for heavy rain.

Creature Comforts

Alaska isn't only tundra hiking, grizzly-bear watching, and salmon fishing. If you know where to look, it's possible to spend your vacation pampering yourself, enjoying fine dining and a great wine selection, and still experience hearty outdoor adventures in the "real" Alaska.

As with many activities in Alaska, accessibility is a primary consideration. Lodging properties can be divided into those on the road system, and those that require a boat or air journey. In Southeast Alaska many lodges can be reached by boat from a nearby town or village, while properties elsewhere in the state usually require a flight in a small plane.

- **Alaska's Capital Inn, Juneau.** Luxury meets history in this gracious hilltop bed-and-breakfast with upscale services, delicious breakfasts, and period furnishings from the early 1900s.
- **Alyeska Prince Hotel, Girdwood.** An hour south of Anchorage, this luxurious hotel offers plenty of opportunities for spoiling yourself silly. The crown jewel of the resort is the Seven Glaciers Restaurant, a 7-minute tram ride up Mt. Alyeska. There you can enjoy the stunning view of the valley and the namesake glaciers; knowledgeable diners consider the restaurant to be among Alaska's finest.
- **Chena Hot Springs Resort, Chena Hot Springs.** If you are in or near Fairbanks, some thermal soaking is a must. Here you can spend the day enjoying a wide range of outdoor activities, followed by a long soak in the hot springs–warmed hot tubs, topped off by an exceptional dinner.
- **Kachemak Bay Wilderness Lodge, Homer.** Across Kachemak Bay from Homer, and accessible by boat or floatplane, this is a place where you can fill your days with hiking, fishing, guided-boats tours, and sightseeing in a pristine setting, followed by delicious seafood dining. The owners are longtime Alaskans who know how to cater to nature lovers, and the attentive and professional staff can meet your every need.
- **Kenai Princess Wilderness Lodge, Cooper Landing.** Charming bungalows with fireplaces and vaulted ceilings of natural-finish wood make up this sprawling complex on a bluff overlooking the Kenai River. Flightseeing, fishing, and hiking on the nature trail near the lodge are among the possible activities.
- **Pearson's Pond Luxury Inn and Adventure Spa, Juneau.** Yoga in the morning; wine and cheese in the evening; whirlpool tubs with rain showers; private balconies; and a well-stocked breakfast nook—all are among the luxurious amenities that define this B&B, situated on a small pond near Mendenhall Glacier.
- **Seven Seas *Mariner*.** Cordon Bleu cuisine, a luxurious spa, and impeccable service make this all-suites, all-balcony ship a top choice for relaxing in the lap of luxury while cruising amidst dramatic Alaskan scenery.

IF YOU LIKE

Scenic Drives

You'll be hard-pressed to find a drive in Alaska that isn't scenic. Spectacular mountain ranges, sweeping marine panoramas, and mile upon mile of open tundra are possible backdrops. Besides world-class scenery, there's always the potential for wildlife encounters, so the wise motorist is always on the alert for something furry darting—or strolling, in the case of the regal moose—out of the roadside brush. Keep in mind that many roads are not plowed in winter, and heavy rain can create hazardous conditions. To obtain Alaskan road reports, call the State Department of Transportation in Fairbanks. ☎ *907/451–2200.*

- **Glenn Highway, South Central.** Passing between the Chugach and Talkeetna mountains and past numerous glaciers, this highway heading east out of Anchorage is especially scenic in late summer and early fall.
- **Kalifornsky Beach Road, South Central.** Near Soldotna, this 20-mi-long loop off the Sterling Highway is parallel to the coastline along Cook Inlet. The peaks of the Alaska Range are visible, and the active volcanoes Mt. Iliamna and Mt. Redoubt are across the inlet. Boats ply the waters here, and bald eagles and beluga whales are common sights.
- **George Parks Highway, South Central and Interior.** Connecting Fairbanks and Anchorage, and passing by Denali National Park, the George Parks offers views of Mt. McKinley on a clear day. Heading north, the mountain seems to loom over you as you drive toward Talkeetna.
- **Richardson Highway, South Central and Interior.** The first highway built in Alaska, this 364-mi road between Fairbanks and the port of Valdez will offer you farm country, vast tundra, and mountain vistas.
- **Taylor Highway, South Central and Interior.** Winding along mountain ridges and through valleys of the Fortymile River is a 160-mi stretch of narrow, rough, gravel highway. This road will transport you to another era, when gold was the main reason folks from the Lower 48 made it into the Interior. It remains one of the few places to see active mining without leaving the road system.
- **Denali Highway, Interior.** For a rustic drive, try this road between Paxson and Cantwell. The gravel road is 135 mi of semi-tough sledding for highway vehicles; if you've got a well-equipped ride, it's worth the effort. You'll find open tundra, views of the Alaska Range, lakes and streams, and miles of land that moose, caribou, grizzlies, wolves, and numerous species of birds call home sweet home.
- **Dalton Highway, Interior and the Bush.** More than 400 mi of road, the Dalton Highway connects Interior Alaska to the shores of the Arctic Ocean. Winding, exhilarating, and varied, it's a true Alaskan motor trek. Built as a hauling road, there are still plenty of 18-wheelers that will share the highway with you as you cross through the Brooks Range into the Arctic Plains.

ON THE CALENDAR

	Top seasonal events include the Anchorage Fur Rendezvous in February, the Iditarod Trail Sled Dog Race in March, Juneau's Alaska Folk Festival in April, and Sitka's Alaska Day Celebration in October.
WINTER December	The offbeat **Talkeetna Winterfest** (☎ 907/733–2330) combines competitive athletic events in the Wilderness Women Contest, with competitive bidding for eligible mountain-man bachelors at the Bachelor Society Ball. The **Anchorage Film Festival** (☎ 907/338–3690 🌐 www.anchoragefilmfestival.com) screens dozens of independent films in early December.
January	Bethel's **Kuskokwim 300** (☎ 907/543–3300 🌐 www.k300.org) is one of the state's premier sled-dog races. At Seward's **Polar Bear Jump Off** (☎ 907/224–5230 🌐 www.sewardak.org) bare skin meets barely above-freezing water. Spread over two weekends, the **Anchorage Folk Festival** (☎ 907/566–2334 🌐 www.anchoragefolkfestival.org) at the University of Alaska Anchorage features hundreds of performers and workshops.
Mid-January–February	**Sled-Dog Racing** (☎ 907/562–2235) season in Anchorage begins with sprints every weekend.
February	**Tent City Winter Festival** (☎ 800/367–9745 🌐 www.wrangellchamber.org) in Wrangell captures the flavor of Alaska's early days. At the **Cordova Iceworm Festival** (☎ 907/424–7260 🌐 www.iceworm.org) a 140-foot iceworm parades through city streets. Other events include a talent show and fun fair. Participants in the **Yukon Quest International Sled Dog Race** (☎ 907/452–7954 🌐 www.yukonquest.com) mush their way between Whitehorse, the Yukon Territory, and Fairbanks. Anchorage's **Fur Rendezvous** (☎ 907/277–8615 🌐 www.furrondy.net) delivers more than 150 events—from snowshoe softball to the Open World Championship Sled Dog Races.
SPRING March	The **World Ice Art Championships and Winter Carnival** (☎ 907/452–1105 🌐 www.icealaska.com) brings ice artists to downtown Fairbanks. The **Iditarod Trail Sled Dog Race** (☎ 907/376–5155 or 800/545–6874 🌐 www.iditarod.com) starts on the first Saturday in March and

ON THE CALENDAR

	stretches for more than 1,000 mi from Anchorage to Nome. More than 70 dog teams compete in the world's premier sled-dog race. The **Bering Sea Ice Golf Classic** (☎ 907/443–5535 🌐 www.nomealaska.org) is played with orange golf balls on the pack ice of the Bering Sea near Nome during the Iditarod. The seasonal "Nome National Forest" (150 or so abandoned Christmas trees) provides forest cover.
April	The three-day **Camai Dance Festival** (☎ 907/543–1977 🌐 www.bethelarts.com) in Bethel attracts dance groups from throughout Alaska and also from outside the state. The **Alaska Folk Festival** (☎ 907/463–3316 🌐 www.juneau.com/aff) in Juneau is a laid-back mix of music, handmade crafts, and foods. The **Alyeska Spring Carnival** (☎ 907/754–2259 or 800/880–3880 🌐 www.alyeskaresort.com) holds court at the Alyeska Resort & Ski Area, 40 mi southeast of Anchorage. The featured event is the Slush Cup, in which skiers and snowboarders attempt to ski across a slushy pond at the base of the mountain. The **World Free Skiing Championship** (☎ 206/933–2809) lures the world's top daredevil skiers to snowy Thompson Pass near Valdez. It's part of the **Chugach Mountain Festival,** which also includes a mountain-bike race, backcountry ski race, and film festival.
Late April–early May	During the **Copper River Delta Shorebird Festival** (☎ 907/424–7260) in Cordova, see the migration of millions of shorebirds.
May	The **Little Norway Festival** (☎ 907/772–4636 🌐 www.petersburg.org) in Petersburg salutes the town's Scandinavian heritage. The **Kodiak Crab Festival** (☎ 907/486–5557 🌐 www.kodiak.org) brings good food, a parade, a footrace, a survival-suit race, and the blessing of the fleet. **Juneau Jazz & Classics** (☎ 907/463–3378 🌐 www.jazzandclassics.org) features performances by regionally and nationally known classical and jazz musicians over a 10-day period. The **Kachemak Bay Shorebird Festival** (☎ 907/235–7740 🌐 www.homeralaska.org/shorebird.htm) in Homer features talks by bird experts, guided walks, and workshops.
SUMMER June	The **Sitka Summer Music Festival** (☎ 907/747–6774 🌐 www.sitkamusicfestival.org) is a monthlong series of chamber music performances.

	The **Midnight Sun Baseball Game** (☏ 907/451–0095 🌐 www.goldpanners.com) celebrates the longest day of the year, in Fairbanks. The **Last Frontier Theatre Conference** (☏ 907/834–1614) is held every June in Valdez, sponsored by Prince William Sound Community College, and draws nationally recognized playwrights, directors, and actors.
July	The **Mt. Marathon Race** (☏ 907/224–8051 🌐 www.sewardak.org) in Seward is a rugged and often bloody race up the 3,000-foot mountain. The best vantage point is right below the trail's starting line. The **World Eskimo–Indian Olympics** (☏ 907/452–6646 🌐 www.weio.org) in Fairbanks tests participants in such skills as ear pulling, the knuckle hop, and the blanket toss. The popular **KBBI Concert on the Lawn** (☏ 907/235–7721 🌐 www.kbbi.org) transforms Homer with a mini-Woodstock mélange of live bands and good food. The **Talkeetna Moose Dropping Festival** (🌐 www.talkeetnachamber.org/event-moosedropping.html) raises funds for the local historical society. No worries, no moose are dropped during the festival!
August	**Southeast Alaska State Fair** (☏ 907/766–2476 🌐 www.seakfair.org) brings exhibits and music to the Haines Fairgrounds.
Late August–early September	The **Alaska State Fair** (☏ 907/745–4827 or 800/850–3247 🌐 www.alaskastatefair.org) in Palmer is the state's big end-of-summer blowout. Don't miss the famous gargantuan vegetables.
FALL October	The **Alaska Day Celebration** (☏ 907/747–5940 🌐 www.sitka.com) brings out the whole town of Sitka to celebrate October 18, the day the United States acquired Alaska from Russia. The weeklong festival includes a period costume ball and a parade. Held in conjunction with the annual Alaska Federation of Natives convention, the **Quyana Alaska Native Dance Festival** (☏ 907/274–3611 🌐 www.nativefederation.org) in Anchorage provides a taste of the state's native culture.
November	The **Athabascan Old Time Fiddling Festival** (☏ 907/452–1825) enlivens Fairbanks with traditional native music. The **Carrs Great Alaska Shoot-out** (☏ 907/786–1230 🌐 www.shootout.net) takes place at Sullivan Arena in Anchorage, where some of the best college basketball teams in the country compete.

GREAT ITINERARIES

ANCHORAGE TO THE KENAI

2 Days: Welcome to Anchorage!

There's a free shuttle between the North and South terminals of the easy-to-navigate Anchorage International Airport. Once you're settled, take to the streets: explore the fun and somewhat kitschy downtown shops, head to the outdoor markets on the weekend, take in the sights at Ship Creek, and explore one of the city's museums. **Logistics:** Getting to town is a snap (buses, reasonable taxis, and hotel shuttles are your choices for the short ride).

1 Day: Chugach State Park

Anchorage's ½-million-acre backyard wilderness includes glaciers, tundra meadows, forested valleys, and plenty of wildlife. In September, this is one of the best places in the state to see moose. **Logistics:** This is a do-it-yourself park: the only facilities are trailheads, a few basic campgrounds, and picnic areas. A good place to start is 3,350-foot Flattop Mountain, Alaska's most-climbed peak. There's a fantastic viewpoint near the parking lot ($5 parking fee).

2 Days: Seward

Surrounded by lush mountains at the head of Resurrection Bay, Seward is the primary gateway to Kenai Fjords National Park. You can join a coastal wildlife tour, explore the Alaska SeaLife Center, and take a stroll along the waterfront.
Logistics: The spectacular drive south from Anchorage takes about 2 hours on the Seward Highway. Or take the Alaska Railroad.

2–4 Days: The Kenai's Wild Country

Option #1: Kenai Fjords National Park

Tidewater glaciers, Exit Glacier, and ocean life are highlights of this spectacular coastal parkland. **Logistics:** Take a tour from Seward to spot whales. You can also stay in public-use cabins, hike up to the Harding Icefield from Exit Glacier, and travel by kayak out of Miller's Landing.

Option #2: Chugach National Forest

Sprawling across much of the Kenai Peninsula and Prince William Sound, this 6-million-acre area is the country's second-largest national forest. Girdwood, Seward, Cooper Landing, and Cordova offer convenient access points to trailheads and campgrounds as well as visitor services and outfitters. **Logistics:** Stop in the **Seward Ranger District Headquarters** (✉ 334 4th Ave. ☎ 907/224–3374) for trail and hiking info.

Option #3: Kenai National Wildlife Refuge

Covering nearly 2 million acres, the Kenai refuge encompasses part of the vast Harding Icefield as well as rugged peaks and forested lowlands inhabited by moose and bears. **Logistics:** The refuge is enormous, but road access is limited. The Skilak Loop Road between Cooper Landing and Sterling offers a chance to escape traffic. In Soldotna, the visitor center on Ski Hill Road has maps and updates on park conditions.

1–2 Days: Kenai & Soldotna

The sportfishing hubs of South Central, these sister cities lie along the world-famous

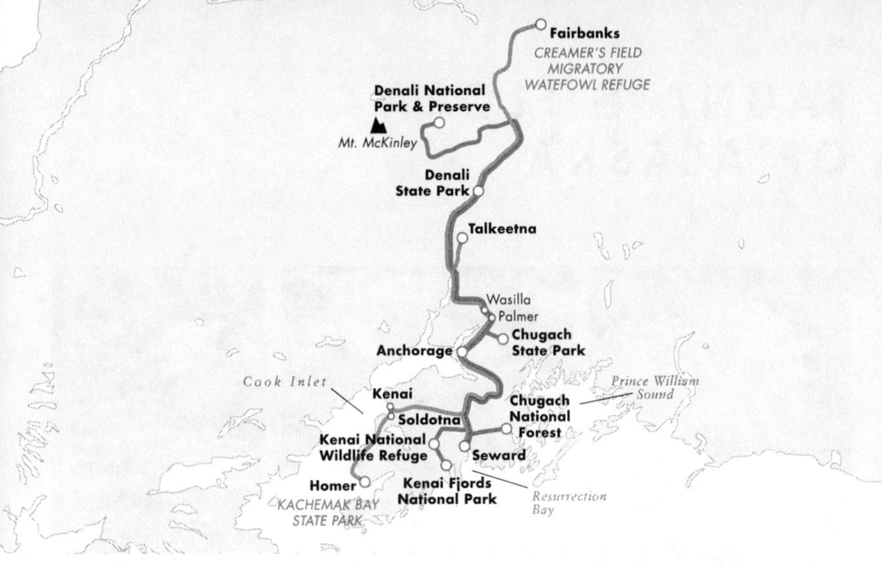

Kenai River. Pacific salmon spawn here each summer, including the mighty king salmon. **Tip:** Or you can dig clams at Clam Gulch, 24 mi south of Soldotna.

1–2 Days: Homer

This end-of-the-road coastal town calls itself the halibut capital of the world, but it also has a thriving community of artists. Take a water taxi to nearby Kachemak Bay State Park and visit the Pratt Museum. **Logistics:** The Sterling highway ends in Homer; it's a 4-hour drive from Anchorage.

ANCHORAGE TO THE INTERIOR

1 day: Talkeetna

Mountaineers congregate at this rural community before flying into the Alaska Range. Book a flightseeing trip here and land on a glacier if you're so inclined. **Tips:** Talkeetna is a one-hour drive north on the Parks Highway from Anchorage. Even if you don't stay at the Talkeetna Alaskan Lodge, stop by to take in the view from the patio.

1–2 Days: "Little Denali"

Denali State Park has some of South Central's best tundra hikes, along the Curry-Kesugi Ridge. The park has spectacular views of Mt. McKinley. **Logistics:** At Byers Lake you can camp or stay in public-use cabins.

2–5 Days: Denali National Park & Preserve

Larger than the state of Massachusetts, Alaska's most famous parkland is a wilderness of high mountains, glacial rivers, forest, and tundra plains. Mt. McKinley rises 20,320 feet into the heavens, while grizzly bears roam alpine meadows and wolves hunt caribou, moose, and Dall sheep. **Logistics:** We highly recommend making shuttle-bus reservations in advance, getting out on the first bus in the morning, and going as far as Fish Creek for the best wildlife viewing.

1–2 Days: Fairbanks

The Golden Heart of Alaska is the starting point for trips into much of northern Bush Alaska. Near town, you can hike the trails in Creamer's Field Migratory Waterfowl Refuge; enjoy exhibits at the Museum of the North; and take a riverboat tour. **Logistics:** Consider taking the scenic Alaska Railroad ride back to Anchorage to catch your flight home. For more information check out www.akrr.com.

FAUNA & FLORA OF ALASKA

FAUNA

Arctic Ground Squirrel

(C)(*Spermophilus parryii*): These yellowish brown, gray-flecked rodents are among Alaska's most common and widespread mammals. Ground squirrels are known for their loud, persistent chatter. They may often be seen standing above their tundra den sites, watching for grizzlies, golden eagles, and weasels.

Arctic Tern

(F)(*Sterna paradisaea*): These are the world's long-distance flying champs; some members of their species make annual migratory flights between the high Arctic and the Antarctic. Sleekly beautiful, the bird has a black cap and striking blood-red bill and feet. They often can be seen looking for small fish in ponds and coastal marshes.

Bald Eagle

(A)(*Haliaeetus leucocephalus*): With a wingspan of 6 to 8 feet, these grand Alaska residents are primarily fish eaters, but they will also take birds or small mammals when the opportunity presents itself. The world's largest gathering of bald eagles occurs in Southeast Alaska each winter, along the Chilkat River near Haines.

Beluga Whale

(B)(*Dephinapterus leucas*): Belugas are gray at birth, blueish gray as adolescents, and white as adults (the word *byelukha* is Russian for "white"). Though they seem to favor fish, belugas' diet includes more than 100 different species, from crabs to squid. They live along much of the coast, from the Beaufort Sea to the Gulf of Alaska.

Black-capped Chickadee

(D)(*Parus atricapillus*): This songbird is one of Alaska's most common residents. As with two close relatives, the chestnut-backed and boreal chickadees, the black-cap gets through the winters by lowering its body temperature at night and shivering through the long hours of darkness.

Caribou

(G)(*Rangifer tarandus*): Sometimes called the "nomads of the north," caribou are long-distance wandering mammals. They are also the most abundant of the state's large mammals; in fact, there are more caribou in Alaska than people! The Western Arctic Caribou Herd alone numbers more than 400,000 members, while the Porcupine Caribou Herd has ranged between 120,000 and 180,000 over the past decades. Another bit of caribou trivia: they are the only members of the deer family in which both sexes grow antlers. Those of bulls may grow up to 5½ feet long with a span of up to 3 feet.

Common Loon

(E)(*Gavia immer*): Some sounds seem to be the essence of wilderness: the howl of the wolf, the hooting of the owl, and the cry of the loon. The common loon is one of five *Gavia* species to inhabit Alaska (the others are the Arctic, Pacific, red-throated, and yellow-billed). Common loons are primarily fish eaters. Excellent swimmers, they are able to stay submerged for up to three minutes.

Common Raven

(*Corvus corax*): A popular character in Alaska native stories, the raven in traditional indigenous culture is both creator and trickster. Entirely black, with a wedge-shaped tail and a heavy bill that helps distinguish it from crows, the raven is Alaska's most widespread avian resident.

Common Redpoll

(*Carduelis flammea*): Even tinier than the chickadee, the common redpoll along with its close cousin, the hoary redpoll (*Carduelis hornemanni*), are among the few birds to inhabit Alaska's Interior year-round. Though it looks a bit like a sparrow, this red-capped, black-bibbed songbird is a member of the finch family.

Dall Sheep

(*Ovis dalli dalli*): One of four wild sheep to inhabit North America, the white Dall is the only one to reside within Alaska. Residents of high alpine areas, the sheep live in mountain chains from the St. Elias Range to the Brooks Range. Though both sexes grow horns, those of females are short spikes, while males grow grand curls that are "status symbols" displayed during mating season.

Dolly Varden

(*Salvelinus malma*): This sleek, flashy fish inhabits lakes and streams throughout Alaska's coastal regions. A member of the char family, it was named after a character in Charles Dickens' novel *Barnaby Rudge* because the brightly colored spots on its sides resemble Miss Dolly Varden's pink-spotted dress and hat. Some members of the species remain in freshwater all their life, while sea-run dollies may live in the ocean for two to five years before returning to spawn.

Golden Eagle

(*Aquila chrysaetos*): With a wingspan of up to 7½ feet, this inland bird can often be spotted spiraling high in the sky, riding thermals. The bird usually nests on cliff faces and feeds upon small mammals and ptarmigan. The plumage of adult birds is entirely dark, except for a golden head. These migratory eagles spend their winters as far away as Kansas and New Mexico.

Great Horned Owl

(*Bubo virginianus*): The best-known of Alaska's several species of owls, and one whose call is a familiar one here. It is a large owl with prominent ear tufts and a white throat with barred markings. Residing in forests from Southeast Alaska to the Interior, it preys on squirrels, hares, grouse, and other birds.

Harbor Seal

(*Phoca vitulina*): Inhabiting shallow marine waters and estuaries along much of Alaska's southern coast, harbor seals may survive up to 30 years in the wild, on a diet of fish, squid, octopus, and shrimp. They, in turn, may be eaten or killed by Orcas, sea lions, or humans. Solitary in the water, harbor seals love company on land, and will gather in large colonies. They weigh up to 250 pounds and range in color from black to white.

Hermit Thrush

(*Catharus guttatus*): Some Alaskans argue that there is no northern song more beautiful than the flutelike warbling of the hermit thrush and its close relative, the Swainson's thrush (*Catharus ustulatus*). The two birds are difficult to tell apart, except for their songs, the hermit's reddish brown tail, and the color of their eye rings. Among the many songbird migrants to visit Alaska each spring, they begin singing in May while seeking mates and defending territories in forested regions of southern and central Alaska.

Horned Puffin

(H)(*Fratercula corniculata*): Named for the black, fleshy projections above each eye, horned puffins are favorites among birders. Included in the group of diving seabirds known as alcids, puffins spend most of their life on water, coming to land only for nesting. They are expert swimmers, using their wings to "fly" underwater and their webbed feet as rudders. Horned puffins have large orange-red and yellow bills. A close relative, the tufted puffin (*Fratercula cirrhata*), is named for its yellow ear tufts.

Top: Dall sheep

Lynx

(*Lynx canadensis*): The lynx is the only wild cat to inhabit Alaska. It's a secretive animal that depends on stealth and quickness. It may kill birds, squirrels, and mice, but the cat's primary prey is the snowshoe hare (*Lepus americanus*), particularly in winter; its population numbers closely follow those of the hare's boom-bust cycles. Large feet and a light body help the lynx run through deep snowpack.

Moose

(*Alces alces gigas*): The moose is the largest member of the deer family, the largest bulls standing 7 feet tall at the shoulders and weighing up to 1,600 pounds. The peak of breeding occurs in late September. Females give birth to calves in late May and early June; twins is the norm. Bulls enter the rut in September, with the most dominant engaging in brutal fights. Though most commonly residents of woodlands, some moose live in or just outside Alaska's cities.

Mountain Goat

(*Oreamnos americanus*): Sometimes confused with Dall sheep, mountain goats inhabit Alaska's coastal mountains. As adults, both males and females have sharp-pointed horns that are short and black (sheep have buff-colored horns). They also have massive chests and comparatively small hindquarters, plus bearded chins.

Musk Ox

(*Ovibos moschatus*): The musk ox is considered an Ice Age relic that survived into the present at least partly because of a defensive tactic: they stand side by side and form rings to fend off predators such as grizzlies and wolves. Unfortunately for the species, that tactic didn't work very well against humans armed with guns. Alaska's last native musk oxen were killed in 1865. Musk oxen from Greenland were reintroduced here in 1930; they now reside on Nunivak Island. The animal's most notable physical feature is its long guard hairs, which form "skirts" that nearly reach the ground. Inupiats called musk ox *oomingmak,* meaning "bearded one." Beneath those coarser hairs is fine underfur called qiviut, which can be woven into warm clothing.

Pacific Halibut

(*Hippoglossus stenolepis*): The halibut is the largest of the flatfish to inhabit Alaska's coastal waters, with females weighing up to 500 pounds. Long-lived "grandmother" halibut may survive 40 years or more, producing millions of eggs each year. Bottom dwellers that feed on fish, crabs, clams, and squid, they range from the Panhandle to Norton Sound. Young halibut generally stay near shore, but older fish have been found at depths of 3,600 feet.

Pacific Salmon

(I)(*Oncorhynchus*): Five species of Pacific salmon spawn in Alaska's waters, including the king, silver, sockeye, pink, and chum. Hundreds of millions of salmon return to the state's streams and lakes each summer and fall, after spending much of their lives in saltwater. They form the backbone of Alaska's fishing industry and draw sportfishers from around the world.

Rainbow Trout

(*Salmo gairdneri*): A favorite of anglers, the rainbow trout inhabits streams and lakes in Alaska's coastal regions. The Bristol Bay region is best known for large 'bows, perhaps because of its huge returns of salmon. Rainbows feed heavily on salmon

Top left: Lynx
Top right: Moose

FAUNA & FLORA OF ALASKA

eggs as well as the deteriorating flesh of spawned-out salmon. Sea-run rainbows, or steelhead, grow even larger after years spent feeding in ocean waters. The state record for steelhead/rainbow trout is 42 pounds, 3 ounces.

Red Fox

(*Vulpes vulpes*): Though it's called the red fox, this species actually has four color phases: red, silver, black, and cross (with a cross pattern on the back and shoulders). An able hunter, the red fox preys primarily on voles and mice, but will also eat hares, squirrels, birds, insects, and berries.

Sandhill Crane

(*Grus canadensis*): The sandhill's call has been described as "something between a French horn and a squeaky barn door." Though others may dispute that description, few would disagree that the crane's calls have a prehistoric feeling. And, in fact, scientists say the species has changed little in the 9 million years since its earliest recorded fossils. Sandhills are the tallest birds to inhabit Alaska; their wingspan reaches up to 7 feet. The gray plumage of adults is set off by a bright red crown. Like geese, they fly in Vs during migratory journeys.

Sea Otter

(K)(*Enhydra lutris*): Sea otters don't depend on blubber to stay warm. Instead, hair trapped in their dense fur keeps their skin dry. Beneath their outer hairs, the underfur ranges in density from 170,000 to one million hairs per square inch. Not surprisingly, the otter takes good care of its coat, spending much of every day grooming. Otters also spend a lot of time eating. In one study, researchers found that adult otters consumed 14 crabs a day, equaling about one-fourth of their body weight.

Sitka Blacktailed Deer

(*Odocoileus hemionus sitkensis*): The Panhandle's rain forest is the primary home of this deer, though it has been transplanted to Prince William Sound and Kodiak. Dark gray in winter, and reddish brown in summer, it's stockier than the whitetails found in the Lower 48. The deer stay at lower elevations during the snowy months of winter, then move up to alpine meadows in summer.

Snowy Owl

(L)(*Nyctea scandiaca*): Inhabiting the open coastal tundra, the snowy owl is found from the western Aleutian Islands to the Arctic. Adults are largely white (though females have scattered light brown spots) though immature birds are heavily marked with brown. Their numbers rise and fall with swings in the population of lemmings, their primary prey. Rather than hoots, the snowy emits loud croaks and whistles.

Steller's Sea Lion

(Q)(*Eumetopias jubatus*): It's ability—and tendency—to roar is what gives the sea lion its name. Because they can rotate their rear flippers and lift their bellies off the ground, sea lions can get around on land much more easily than seals can. They are also much larger, the males reaching up to 9 feet and weighing up to 1,500 pounds. They feed primarily on fish, but will also eat sea otters and seals. They have been designated an endangered species because their populations north of the Panhandle have suffered huge declines.

Walrus

(P)(*Odobenus rosmarus*): The walrus's ivory tusks can be dangerous weapons; there are stories of walruses killing polar bears when attacked. Weighing up to 2 tons, the walrus's primary food—which it detects in water with the help of a bristled muzzle—includes clams, mussels, snails, crabs, and shrimp.

Willow Ptarmigan

(O)(*Lagopus lagopus*): One of three species of ptarmigan (the others are the rock and the white-tailed), the willow is the most widespread. It is also Alaska's state bird, as picked by schoolchildren in a statewide vote. It tends to live in willow thickets, where it both feeds and hides from a variety of predators. Aggressively protective parents, willow ptarmigan have been known to attack humans to defend their young.

Wolf

(*Canis lupus*): The largest and most charismatic of the far North's wild canines, wolves roam throughout all of mainland Alaskan. They form close-knit family packs, which may range from a few animals to more than 30. Packs hunt a variety of prey, from small mammals and birds to caribou, moose, and Dall sheep. They communicate with each other through body language, barks, and howls.

Wolverine

(*Gulo gulo*): Consider yourself lucky if you see a wolverine, because they are among the most secretive animals of the North. They are also fierce predators, with enormous strength and endurance. Denali biologists once reported seeing a wolverine drag a Dall sheep carcass more than 2 mi; an impressive feat, since the sheep likely weighed four times what the wolverine did. They have been known to run 40 mph through snow when chased by hunters. Though they look a lot like bears and have the ferocity of a grizzly, wolverines are in fact the largest members of the weasel family.

Wood Frog

(*Rana sylvatica*): One of the few amphibians to inhabit Alaska, and the only one to live north of the Panhandle, these frogs range as far north as the Arctic, surviving winters through the help of a biochemical change that keeps them in a suspended state, while frozen. Come spring, the bodies revive after thawing. Though they mate and lay eggs in water, wood frogs spend most of their lives on land.

FLORA

Balsam Poplar and Black Cottonwood

(*Populus balsamifera* and *Populus trichocarpa*): These two closely related species sometimes interbreed and are difficult, if not impossible, to tell apart. Mature trees of both species have gray bark that is rough and deeply furrowed. In midsummer they produce cottony seed pods. They also have large, shiny, arrowhead-shaped leaves.

Birch

(*Betula*): Ranging from Kodiak Island to the Brooks Range, birch trees are important members of Alaska's boreal forests. Deciduous trees that prefer well-drained soils, they have white bark and green heart-to-diamond-shaped leaves with sharp points and toothed edges. One species, the paper birch (*Betula papyrifera*), is easily distinguished by its peeling, paperlike bark.

Blueberry

(J)(*Vaccinium*): A favorite of berry pickers, blueberries are found throughout Alaska, except for the farthest northern reaches of the Arctic. They come in a variety of forms, including head-high forest bushes and sprawling tundra mats. Pink, bell-shape flowers bloom in spring and dark blue to almost black fruits begin to ripen in July or August, depending on the locale.

Top: Wood frog

Cow Parsnip

(R)(*Heracleum lanatum*): Also known to some as Indian celery, cow parsnip resides in open forests and meadows. The plant may grow several feet high, with dull green leaves the size of dinner plates; thick, hairy, hollow stalks; and clusters of white flowers. Anyone who harvests—or walks among—this species must take great care. Oils on the stalks, in combination with sunlight, can produce severe skin blistering.

Devil's Club

(N)(*Echinopanax horridum*): This is a prickly shrub that may grow 4 to 8 feet high and forms dense, spiny thickets in forests ranging from the Panhandle to South Central. Hikers need to be wary of this plant: its large, maple-like leaves (which can be a foot or more across) have spines, and needles cover its pale brown trunk. In late summer, black bears enjoy its bright red berries.

Salmonberry

(M)(*Rubus spectabilis*): The salmonberry canes, on which the leaves and fruits grow, may reach 7 feet tall; they grow in dense thickets. The juicy raspberrylike fruits may be either orange or red at maturity; the time of ripening is late June through August.

Spruce

(*Picea*): Three species of spruce grow in Alaska. Sitka spruce (*Picea sitchensis*) is an important member of coastal rain-forest communities; white spruce (*Picea glauca*) prefers dry, well-drained soils in boreal forests that stretch from South Central to the Arctic; black spruce (*Picea mariana*) thrives in wet, boggy areas.

Tall Fireweed

(*Epilobium angustifolium*): The fireweed is among the first plants to reinhabit burn areas and, in the proper conditions it grows well. Found throughout much of Alaska, it's a beautiful plant, with fuchsia flowers that bloom from the bottom to the top of stalks; it's said that the final opening of flowers is a sign that winter is only weeks away. Spring fireweed shoots can be eaten raw or steamed and its blossoms can be added to salads. A related species is dwarf fireweed (*Epilobium latifolium*); also known as "river beauty," it is shorter and bushier.

Wild Prickly Rose

(S)(*Rosa acicularis*): Serrated leaves grow on prickly spines and fragrant, five-petaled flowers begin blooming in late spring. The flowers vary from light pink to dark red. Appearing in late summer and fall, bright red rose hips rich in vitamin C can be harvested for jellies, soups, or pie.

Willow

(*Salix*): An estimated three dozen species of willow grow in Alaska. Some, like the felt-leaf willow (*Salix alaxensis*), may reach tree size; others form thickets; still others, like the Arctic willow (*Salix arctica*), hug the ground in alpine terrain. They often grow thickest in the sub-alpine zone between forest and tundra. Whatever the size, willows produce soft "catkins" (pussy willows), which are actually columns of densely packed flowers without petals. The plant is an important food for many animals, from moose to songbirds.

—Bill Sherwonit

Top left: Gray wolf
Top center: Wolverine
Top right: Sitka spruce

Sports & Wilderness Adventures

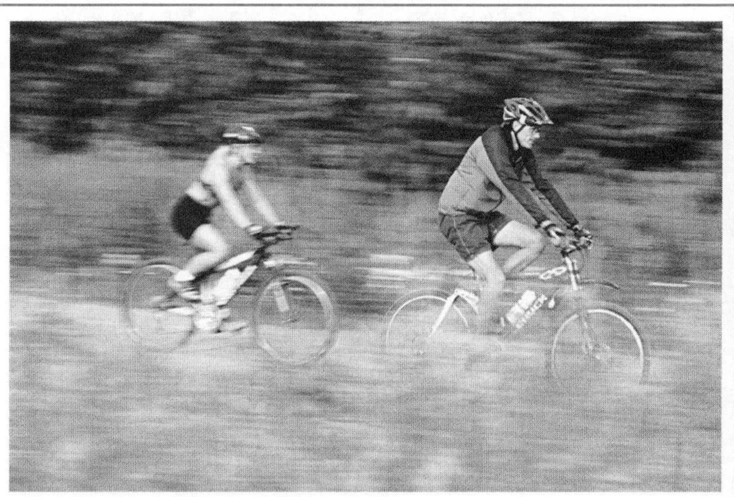

Alaska offers plenty of adventure for travelers on two wheels.

WORD OF MOUTH

"When I was younger, I almost ran off with my lover to Alaska. I always wondered what I missed."

–cigalechanta

"Now that we're back from our two-week Alaska trip, I can say quite honestly that kayaking in Alaska will not disappoint you. The place is magnificent. My best advice is to bring a barrel of money and tons of time!"

–BayouGal

www.fodors.com/forums

Updated by Ken Marsh

Derived from an Aleut word meaning "great land," *Alaska* is a fitting name for the 49th state, the one with more land in parks, wilderness areas, and wildlife refuges than all the other states combined. In fact, about one-third of Alaska's 375 million acres is set aside in protected public lands.

These are lands of prodigious scale and awesome beauty. Four great mountain ranges—the St. Elias, Alaska, Brooks, and Chugach—as well as more than 30 lesser chains sweep through the state. The St. Elias Mountains form the highest coastal range in the world; the Alaska Range contains North America's highest peak (Mt. McKinley, 20,320 feet); the Brooks Range roughly follows the Arctic Circle, and the Chugach arcs through Alaska's most populous region.

Due partly to its relative inaccessibility and frequently demanding climate, most of this extraordinary state has remained largely undeveloped since it was acquired by the United States in 1867. (The United States paid Russia all of $7.2 million—2 cents an acre—for this treasure.) First called Indian Country and then made a district, Alaska became a proper territory in 1912, going on to achieve statehood in 1959.

Alaska's public lands are as varied as they are magnificent; recreational activities include wildlife viewing, hiking, mountain-biking, kayaking, rafting, canoeing, fishing, hunting, mountaineering, skiing, and snowboarding. Road access is limited, however (Alaska averages only 1 mi of road for every 42 sq mi of land; the U.S. average ratio is 1 to 1), and many of these lands must be reached via airplane or boat.

WELCOME TO THE 49TH

Interspersed among Alaska's great mountain ranges are canyons and waterfalls, alpine valleys, salmon-rich rivers, clear lakes, blue glaciers, temperate rain forests, and sweeping, spongy tundra plains. Adding to this wealth are thousands of miles of spectacular tidal coastline. Strap on your boots and prepare yourself for some unforgettable outdoor adventuring!

Even the most-visited parks—Denali National Park & Preserve, Glacier Bay National Park & Preserve, Kenai Fjords National Park, and Chugach State Park—allow backpackers and kayakers abundant opportunities for remote wilderness experiences. Parks closer to roads, and to Anchorage and Fairbanks, tend to draw more visitors, but that does not necessarily translate into the numbers encountered in parks of the Lower 48. Particularly remote and solitary experiences await in some of the state's least-visited places, such as Wood-Tikchik State Park, where one lonely ranger patrols 1.55 million acres, or Aniakchak National Monument & Preserve, south of Katmai, where trekkers can go days or weeks without seeing another human.

PLANNING YOUR ADVENTURE

Trips to Alaska are best planned months, or even a year, in advance, particularly to the most popular destinations, such as Denali and Glacier Bay national parks. Prime time for summer backcountry sports is June through early September. Winter sports are better enjoyed near the end of the season, in March and early April, when longer daylight hours return, temperatures start to rise a bit, and snow conditions are unsurpassed for activities like snowshoeing, skiing, and mushing.

> **NAVIGATING THIS CHAPTER**
>
> Flip through this chapter to find tips on how best to plan your adventure; in-depth descriptions of sports, from kayaking to skiing to biking; as well as our favorite regions and guides for each sport; and finally our best wildlife-viewing advice and experiences. Keep in mind that as you flip through regional chapters in this book, we'll recommend even more local outfitters and guides.

Alaska's wilderness is enormous almost beyond comprehension. Visitors to the farther-flung reaches should come prepared for constantly changing and often harsh weather, difficult or impassable terrains, mosquitoes and gnats, bear encounters, and other backcountry challenges. A keen knowledge of the country, proper clothing, quality camping gear, good physical conditioning, and excellent navigation skills are vital to successful and safe trips. Visitors without extensive wilderness experience can avoid logistical headaches and hazards by hiring local tour guides to provide equipment, direction, and necessary expertise.

Choosing a Trip

Opportunities for outdoor adventures lurk beyond the edge of every Alaska village, port, and city. A day—or a week—of sea kayaking in Prince William Sound may begin, simply enough, a stone's throw from the streets of Whittier, which is a scenic hour's drive south of Anchorage. A much more complex trip, such as a 10-day navigation of the North Fork Koyukuk River, may require a commuter flight from Fairbanks to the remote community of Bettles, and from there a prearranged flight into the headwaters high in the Brooks Range. So the first question is whether you'd like an organized tour or a do-it-yourself trip.

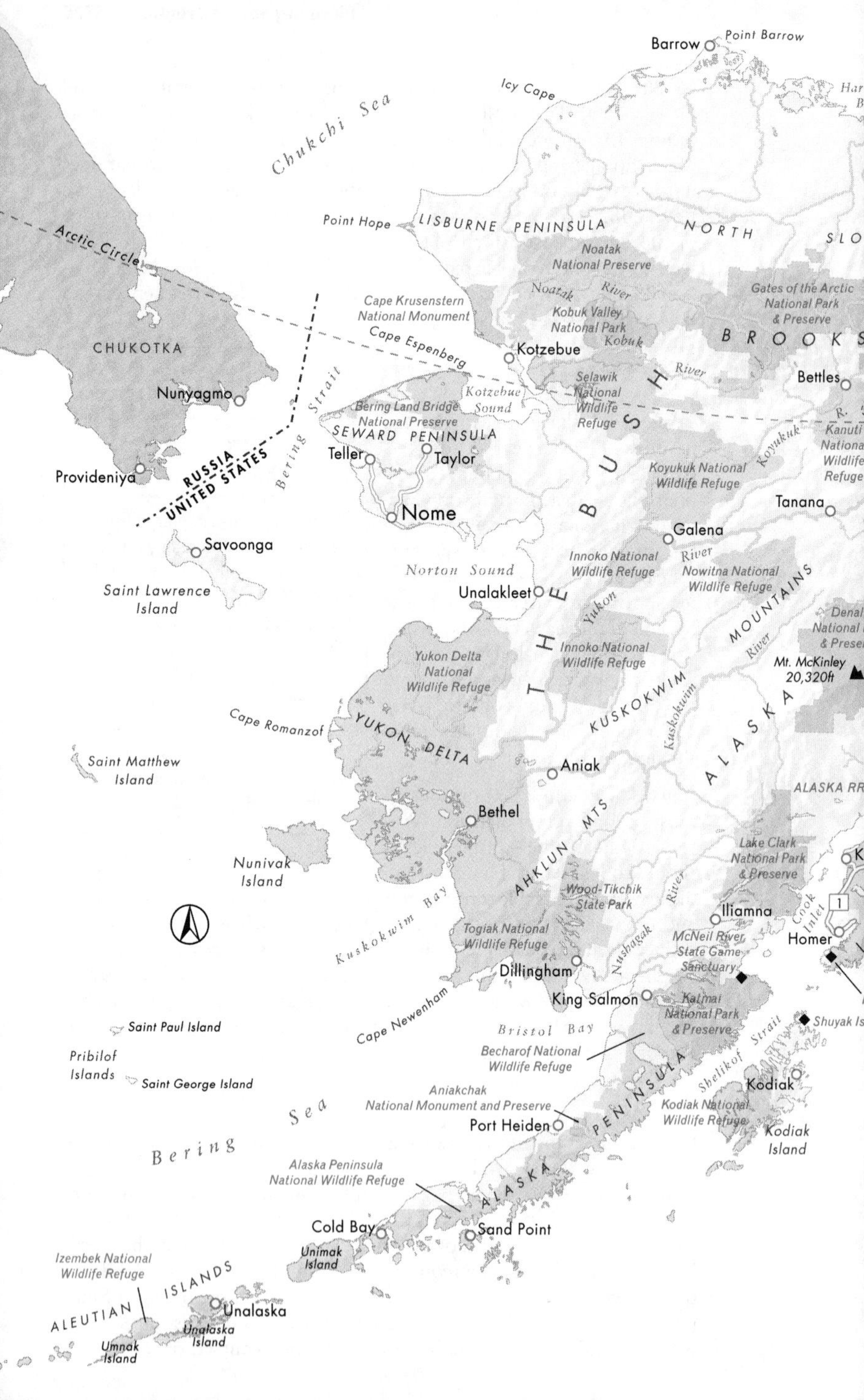

Barrow
Point Barrow
Icy Cape
Chukchi Sea
Point Hope
LISBURNE PENINSULA
NORTH
Arctic Circle
Noatak National Preserve
Noatak River
Gates of the Arctic National Park & Preserve
Cape Krusenstern National Monument
Kobuk Valley National Park
Kobuk River
Cape Espenberg
Kotzebue
BROOKS
CHUKOTKA
Bettles
Selawik National Wildlife Refuge
Kotzebue Sound
Nunyagmo
Bering Strait
Bering Land Bridge National Preserve
SEWARD PENINSULA
Kanuti National Wildlife Refuge
Koyukuk
Teller
Taylor
RUSSIA
UNITED STATES
Provideniya
THE BUSH
Koyukuk National Wildlife Refuge
Tanana
Nome
Galena
Savoonga
Innoko National Wildlife Refuge
Norton Sound
Nowitna National Wildlife Refuge
Saint Lawrence Island
Unalakleet
Yukon
MOUNTAINS
Innoko National Wildlife Refuge
Yukon Delta National Wildlife Refuge
Mt. McKinley 20,320ft
KUSKOKWIM
Kuskokwim River
Cape Romanzof
YUKON DELTA
ALASKA
Saint Matthew Island
Aniak
ALASKA RR
Bethel
AHKLUN MTS
Nunivak Island
Lake Clark National Park & Preserve
Wood-Tikchik State Park
Kuskokwim Bay
Iliamna
1
Cook Inlet
Togiak National Wildlife Refuge
McNeil River State Game Sanctuary
Homer
Nushagak River
Dillingham
King Salmon
Katmai National Park & Preserve
Cape Newenham
Shuyak Is
Saint Paul Island
Bristol Bay
Pribilof Islands
Becharof National Wildlife Refuge
Shelikof Strait
Saint George Island
Kodiak
Aniakchak National Monument and Preserve
Kodiak National Wildlife Refuge
Sea
Port Heiden
Kodiak Island
Bering
PENINSULA
Alaska Peninsula National Wildlife Refuge
ALASKA
Cold Bay
Sand Point
Unimak Island
Izembek National Wildlife Refuge
ALEUTIAN ISLANDS
Unalaska
Unalaska Island
Umnak Island

Alaska Parks & Wildlife Refuges
0
200 mi
0
200 km
Beaufort Sea
Harrison Bay
Prudhoe Bay
Deadhorse
Trans-Alaska Pipeline
Mackenzie Bay
Arctic National Wildlife Refuge
Dalton Hwy.
Arctic Circle
NORTHWEST TERRITORIES
Yukon Flats National Wildlife Refuge
Fort Yukon
White Mountains National Recreation Area
Circle
Livengood
Steese Hwy.
Yukon-Charley Rivers National Preserve
Fairbanks
INTERIOR
Eagle
CANADA
UNITED STATES
Dawson
Tanana
Alaska River
Hwy
George Parks Hwy.
Cantwell
Tok
YUKON TERRITORY
Denali State Park
Richardson Hwy.
Slana
Nabesna
Gulkana
Glennallen
SOUTH CENTRAL
Chitina
McCarthy
Palmer
Chugach State Park
Anchorage
Valdez
Wrangell-Saint Elias National Park & Preserve
Mt. St. Elias 18,008ft
Haines Junction
Hwy
Whitehorse
Alaska
Kenai
Whittier
Columbia Glacier
Cordova
Seward
Prince William Sound
BRITISH COLUMBIA
Skagway
Yakutat
Haines
Chilkat State Park
Kenai Fjords National Park
Kenai National Wildlife Refuge
Kachemak Bay State Park
Glacier Bay National Park & Preserve
Gustavus
Juneau
COAST MOUNTAINS
Hoonah
Gulf of Alaska
Chichagof Island
Admiralty Island National Monument
Sitka
Petersburg
Baranof Island
Wrangell
SOUTHEAST
Alaska Marine Highway
Ketchikan
PACIFIC OCEAN
Misty Fiords National Monument
Dixon Entrance
Queen Charlotte Islands
Not all public and state lands are shown.
Less than 1% of land in Alaska is privately owned.

Before you decide, consider this: What challenges are you reasonably willing and able to embrace? The answer will depend upon many factors, including how much wilderness experience you have, what kind of physical condition you are in, how much time you have, and how much money you can afford to spend on gear and logistics. ■ **TIP→ Remember that the Alaskan wilderness can be as difficult to navigate as it is beautiful; it's far wiser to weigh your options and plan ahead than to step into the last frontier poorly prepared.** Carefully define and evaluate your abilities and then start planning. Be honest with yourself and know when to enlist the services of local guides or outfitters; allowing these professionals to provide vital gear, expertise, and direction can make your adventure safer, more comfortable, and more fulfilling.

RESOURCES With proper planning and the help of local professionals, there's an Alaska trip—and likely many—just for you, no matter your age, physical ability, or level of wilderness savvy. The first step is to obtain a list of outfitters and guides who are permitted to operate in the regions you plan to visit. Such a list is available from the staff of the refuge, forest, or park you plan to visit. When contacting businesses, learn as much as you can about the guides, the nature of the activities they offer, and the area you want to explore. Also be sure to determine how well the guides know the area. Feel free to ask for references. Throughout this book you'll find in-depth information about all of Alaska's regions; contact information and insider tips are provided for every park, refuge, and wildland that we deem worthy of a visit.

STEP LIGHTLY

Ecotourists aim to travel responsibly, taking care to conserve natural environments. Ecotourism typically is smaller scale and involves more education than traditional tourism; often, you are led by guides who know the local natural history and cultures. Itineraries allow you a closer connection to the areas explored. As one Alaskan guide says, "Slow down, take a deep breath, feel where you are." The **International Ecotourism Society** (🌐 www.ecotourism.org) is a great resource.

Here are some top organizations to help you get started:

A state-produced *Alaska Vacation Planner* (which also contains information on ecotourism) can be obtained from the **Alaska Travel Industry Association** (☎ 907/929–2200, 800/862–5275 to order vacation planners 🌐 www.travelalaska.com).

The **Alaska Wilderness Recreation and Tourism Association** (☎ 907/258–3171 🌐 www.awrta.org) can provide information on many businesses and activities across the state.

Recreational Equipment Inc. (☎ 907/272–4565 🌐 www.rei.com) is a great resource for equipment needs.

Larger tour companies will take care of everything for you if you want to just sit back and be guided through a specific part of the state doing a variety of activities. In some cases they also offer shorter tours and activities for independent travelers. Be sure to ask questions about timing and pricing.

Gray Line of Alaska (☎ 206/281–3535 or 800/544–2206 🌐 www.graylinealaska.com).

Princess Cruises and Tours (☎ 800/426–0442 🌐 www.princesslodges.com).

Smaller, independent tour companies and agencies offer, you guessed it, smaller-scale tours and packages; they are good resources for tailor-made Alaskan journeys. See individual sports listed in this chapter for specialized Alaska-based companies.

Alaska Bound (☎ 231/439–3000 or 888/252–5727 🌐 www.alaskabound.com).

Alaska Tour & Travel (☎ 907/245–0200 or 800/208–0200 🌐 www.alaskatravel.com).

Alaska Tours (☎ 907/277–3000 🌐 www.alaskatours.com).

Viking Travel (☎ 907/772–3818 or 800/327–2571 🌐 www.alaskaferry.com).

Money Matters

To reserve a spot, most tour operators require a deposit, with the entire balance due sometime before your starting date. In most cases, if you cancel your reservation, you get at least a partial refund, but policies vary widely. ■ TIP→ **Find out how far in advance you must cancel to get a full refund,** and ask whether any allowances are made for cancellations due to medical emergencies. If cancellation insurance is available, you may want to take it. You'll receive a full refund regardless of the reason for your cancellation.

Taxes are generally not included in the quoted price and can add substantially to the cost of your trip. Depending on the program, you should also ask about gratuities; inquire about which members of the tour personnel customarily get tipped and what the average rate is.

Safety First

In choosing a guide, a primary concern should be safety. A guide should be equipped with proper technical and first-aid gear and should know how to use it.

If you have no experience in the activity, ask what sort of training you'll receive. Explain your own goals and abilities, and be sure to ask about the difficulty of the terrain to be covered; 1 mi across hilly, trail-less tundra may demand the same energy as 2 or 3 mi on a flat, maintained trail. Most guides plan trips so that you'll have time to relax and enjoy the landscape or look for wildlife, but it's a good idea to ask about the travel schedule and number of miles to be covered daily. As a general rule, hikers in good physical condition should be able to travel 2 mi an hour on maintained trails and about 1 mi per hour or less across trail-less terrain. Traveling 5 to 6 mi per day, even on trails, is likely to be tiring for a novice. Be honest with the guide regarding your level of expertise.

The amount of weight you'll be carrying on your back will also influence your traveling ability, especially if you haven't carried a heavy pack before, so determine the amount of gear you'll be required to carry, particularly if you'll be hiking, backpacking, or glacier trekking.

Gear & Weather

Be sure to ask what gear the company will provide. Guides normally provide group gear, such as tents and tarps, and expect you to provide your own personal equipment, such as boots, rain gear, a pack, and a sleeping bag. (In some cases, guides can rent you gear such as sleeping bags or packs.)

EVERYBODY LOVES THE SUNSHINE

In most parts of the state, June through August are considered prime months for summer backcountry trips. July is usually the warmest month. Hope for sunshine, but come prepared for rain, especially in August as the weather starts to change.

Ask about the weather you're likely to encounter. From the temperate rain forests of the Tongass National Forest in Alaska's Southeast to the inland deserts of the Northwest, climates across the state vary greatly. No matter what region you visit, always come prepared for cool, wet weather, even in midsummer. Insect repellent (and sometimes head nets) may be required to ward off mosquitoes, flies, and no-see-ums during all snow-free months. Finally, it's best to go with a small group to minimize impact on the landscape and wildlife; fewer than 10 people is ideal.

Lodging

From beautiful wilderness lodges to remote campsites to spongy tundra with only the stars to look at, your options for lodging in the state are quite varied. Try to keep in mind where you'll be most comfortable and happy going to sleep after a day of adventuring.

Public-Use Cabins

Not all Alaska wilderness trips require the expense of luxury lodges or the sacrifices of tent camping. For between $15 and $65 per night, backcountry travelers can have a million-dollar view and a roof over their heads at one of more than 250 public-use cabins available across the state. Cabin costs and locations depend upon which of five land-management agencies they fall under—the U.S. Forest Service, National Wildlife Refuges, National Park Service, Bureau of Land Management, or Alaska State Parks. Most cabins are remote or semiremote and must be reached by plane, boat, or trail. ■ TIP→ **Almost all must be reserved in advance,** either in person, by mail, or online; in some cases nominal service fees may be charged for cancellations.

Accommodations are rustic; most cabins have bunks or wooden sleeping platforms, tables, heating stoves, outdoor fire pits, outhouses, and, sometimes, skiffs. Agency Web sites offer descriptions of individual cabins, including the number of bunks, types of stoves, and other amenities visitors can expect. Visitors who fly to cabins located on lakes or in coastal areas where skiffs are provided can usually rent outboards and gasoline tanks in the closest town and bring them along.

The most convenient way to shop for public-use cabins is to visit the listings posted online by the agencies that oversee them. Listings for individual cabins include notes on accessibility (you may need to charter a floatplane from the nearest community, paddle a sea kayak, hike, mountain-bike, or travel in on horseback). Logbooks are provided at most cabins; check out entries from previous guests about area hikes, wildlife sightings, and fishing opportunities.

For the central **National Park Service** Web site listing information about the cabins, visit 🌐 www.nps.gov/aplic/cabins.

In order to reserve any public-use cabin, log on to 🌐 www.reserveusa.com or call ☎ 877/444–6777.

Alaska State Parks. More than 50 cabins are maintained over a huge area between Ketchikan and Fairbanks. Some are road accessible; reservations can be made up to six months in advance. Cabins vary in size, with sleeping capacity ranging from three to 10 people. For more information, contact the Department of Natural Resources Public Information Center in Anchorage. ☎ *907/269–8400.*

Bureau of Land Management. Several public-use cabins are located in the White Mountains National Recreation Area near Fairbanks. Cabins can be booked up to 30 days in advance by mail, phone, or in person. For more information, contact the Bureau of Land Management Land Information Center. 📫 *1150 University Ave., Fairbanks 99709-3844* ☎ *907/474–2250.*

National Park Service. Cabins are available in Kenai Fjords National Park, Wrangell–St. Elias National Park, and Yukon–Charley Rivers National Park. ☎ *907/271–2737 in Kenai Fjords, 907/822–5234 in Wrangell–St. Elias, 907/547–2233 in Yukon–Charley.*

National Wildlife Refuges. Eight public-use cabins are located in Kodiak National Wildlife Refuge on Kodiak Island. Cabins can be reached by floatplane or boat only. Reservations are scheduled by a lottery. Applications, which may be mailed or delivered in person, are accepted until the last business day before the drawing date. 📫 *1390 Buskin River Rd., Kodiak 99615* ☎ *907/487–2600.*

U.S. Forest Service. The agency maintains more than 150 cabins in Southeast's Tongass National Forest, and more than 40 in the Chugach National Forest in South Central. Most cabins can be reached only by boat or plane; those accessible by trails are very popular and frequently booked months in advance. Maximum length of stay ranges from three to seven nights in the summer. Cabin reservations may be made up to six months ahead. To reserve cabins or find out about cabin availability, call or check online. ☎ *877/444–6777.*

Wilderness Lodges

If your goal is to really get away from it all, consider booking a remote Alaska wilderness lodge. Some of the most popular are in the river drainages of Bristol Bay, in the secluded bays of Southeast Alaska, along the western edge of Cook Inlet, around Katmai and Lake Clark national parks, and in the Susitna Valley north of Anchorage. Most of these lodges specialize in fishing and/or bear-viewing. Lodges in and near Denali emphasize opportunities to explore the wilderness as well as natural history programs. Activities can also include dog-mushing, hiking, rafting, flightseeing, horseback-riding, and gold-panning.

Lodge stays generally include daily guided trips as well as all meals. Fees can be expensive (daily rates of $300–$900 per person). To learn more about specific lodges in the region you plan to visit, fire up a search engine and shop online. Study individual Web sites and make a list of those most likely to fulfill your requirements. Before making a final decision, e-mail or phone (many lodge operators provide toll-free numbers for clients) with questions about activities offered, prices, gratuities, and what you should expect. ■ TIP→ **You may need to book at least a year in advance for some of the more popular lodges,** though last-minute cancellations can sometimes create openings even late in the season.

For listings of wilderness lodges in all regions of Alaska, including individual Web sites, phone numbers, and general information, visit ⊕ www.travelalaska.com or ⊕ www.alaska.com. As you read through this book, you'll find plenty of recommendations for great wilderness lodges. Below we've listed three options.

Denali Backcountry Lodge. Located in the very heart of Denali National Park & Preserve, this is a true wilderness experience. Meals and before-dinner social hour occur in the main lodge building. Activities for overnight guests include naturalist programs; hiking; fishing; gold-panning; mountain-biking; and, for an extra fee, flightseeing when weather permits. Family-style meals emphasizing Alaskan fare are included in the room rate. ☎ *907/376–1992 or 877/233–6254* ⊕ *www.denalilodge.com.*

Kenai Princess Wilderness Lodge. This "elegantly rustic" complex 45 mi from Seward sits on a bluff overlooking the Kenai River. Paths lead from the main lodge to sweet and spacious bungalows with big beds, a wood-burning fireplace, a sitting area, and a porch. ☎ *907/595–1425 or 800/426–0500* ⊕ *www.princessalaskalodges.com.*

Tutka Bay Wilderness Lodge. Perched among spruces and coastal western hemlocks over Kachemak Bay, this property is accessible via plane or boat. Popular activities include sea-kayaking, sportfishing, birding, bear- and marine wildlife–viewing, and relaxing in the open-air hot tub. ☎ *907/235–3905 or 800/606–3909* ⊕ *www.tutkabaylodge.com.*

Camping

Hundreds of campgrounds, both public and private, are found along Alaska's road system. They typically include sites for both tent and RV camping, with fire pits, latrines, running potable water, picnic benches, and other camping amenities. Most campsites are available on a first-come, first-served basis, so it pays to conduct research in advance when planning road trips.

A HISTORY OF PROTECTION

Alaska's wealth of public lands is no accident. More than 100 million acres were marked for protection in 1980 when President Jimmy Carter signed into law the Alaska National Interest Lands Conservation Act (ANILCA). The act instantly doubled the size of the national park and refuge system in the United States, and tripled the amount of federal lands designated as wilderness. But the process of what many call the most significant land conservation measure in the nation's history was not simple.

When Alaska became a state in 1959, nearly all of its land mass was federally owned. Under the Statehood Act, the new state was allowed to choose 104 million acres to be managed as a revenue base. Of that, 91 million acres have been chosen. As the state began staking land, Alaska's native people argued that lands traditionally belonging to them were being taken. They pointed out that, lacking an act of Congress removing native title, the state land selections were illegal. A resolution came in 1971 when the Alaska Native Claims Settlement Act (ANCSA) granted Alaska's native peoples the right to choose 44 million acres of federal land in Alaska. So far, about 38 million acres have been selected and transferred to native ownership.

Today Alaska's protected federal lands include nearly 55 million acres of national parks, 73 million acres of national wildlife refuges, 25 wild and scenic rivers totaling nearly 2 million acres, and 5.8 million acres of wilderness areas. Along with the federally protected lands established in Alaska by the passage of ANILCA, approximately 3.2 million acres of superb lands are set aside as state parks.

BACKCOUNTRY AND PARKLAND CAMPING If you wish to explore Alaska's vast backcountry wilderness, you will almost certainly have to establish your own campsites (though some parks do have remote tent sites). Before heading into the backcountry, contact the appropriate management agency, such as the state or national park, wildlife refuge, or national forest unit that you'll be visiting for advice or restrictions.

Several variables must be considered whenever camping in the wilderness, including water sources, good drainage (you don't want to end up swamped in heavy rains), protection from high winds, and the presence of any game trails (which in bear country should be avoided). Campers are also advised to practice low-impact camping techniques to minimize damage to the environment. For example: carry out *all* garbage; avoid camping on fragile vegetation; if possible, camp on already established sites; never cut standing trees; wash yourself, your clothes, and your dishes at least 100 feet from water sources; bring a trowel and dig "cat-hole" latrines for human waste at least 100 feet from your camp, water sources, and trails; and burn or carry out toilet paper. When traveling in trail-less areas (particularly tundra), fan out instead of walking single file to avoid trampling vegetation.

Resources Information on roadside camping can be obtained at **Alaska Public Land Information Centers** (www.nps.gov/aplic/center) in Tok, Fairbanks, and Anchorage, and at park, refuge, and national-forest headquarters across the state.

CAR & RV CAMPING RV camping is popular along Alaska's road systems because it allows visitors the freedom to create their own itineraries while traveling and camping in relative comfort. Although many drive their own vehicles up the Alaska Highway from Canada and the Lower 48, others choose to fly or cruise to Alaska and rent SUVs or motor homes once they arrive. Between June and August—peak summer season—motor-home rentals range from $125 to $200 per day, depending upon size and model. To save money, opt for weeklong packages and off-season prices offered by most rental companies, or consider sharing a motor-home rental and costs with friends.

Campgrounds and dump stations—including state, federal, and privately-owned operations—as well as propane services are available in or near almost all communities along Alaska's highway system. State campgrounds provide overnight camping for $10 to $15 per night, depending upon the facility; dump-station use fees are $5. On public lands along remote stretches of highway, pleasant, free camping can sometimes be found in clearings, pull-offs, and old gravel pits.

Resources *The Milepost* (www.themilepost.com) offers mile-by-mile information on all of Alaska's main highways.

The state of Alaska publishes an informative free guide called *RV Tips Trip Information Planning Booklet: A practical guide to campgrounds, dumpstations, and propane services along Alaska's highways.* To view the guide online, go to www.dced.state.ak.us/oed/student_info/pub/rvtips.pdf.

For more information about individual state campgrounds, locations, fees, and services, visit the state **Department of Natural Resources** Web site at www.dnr.state.ak.us/parks/asp/fees.htm.

Equipment

Get the best equipment you can afford; it's a must in Alaska. Quality gear is a good investment, and it can make your trip to Alaska safer and that much more comfortable and enjoyable. TIP→ **Before you go on an organized trip, be sure to ask your guide what gear will be supplied, and what won't.**

The Essential Items

When setting out for a day hike from base camp, it's wise to carry a pack stocked with a few essentials. These include a first-aid kit, including bandages and moleskin; bear spray; a plastic bottle of drinking water; high-energy snacks; a warm sweater or jacket; windproof rain gear, in case the weather suddenly changes (avoid cotton clothing as it

WORD OF MOUTH

"As long as you have a good pair of hiking boots treated with water repellent, you should be fine. We also brought a pair of shoes for walking, and something a bit nicer for going out in the evening."
-Julie304

does not retain body warmth when wet); a disposable lighter; fire starters, such as a candle or heat tab; a flare or flashlight; a knife (preferably a multifunctional pocketknife); a topographical map; toilet paper; sunglasses and sunblock; bug repellent; duct tape, for all kinds of emergencies; and a compass.

COMPASS NOTE

The farther north you travel, the more the compass needle will be skewed upward and to the east of north by several degrees. U.S. Geological Survey maps show this difference between magnetic and true north, called magnetic declination, at the bottom of maps. With these maps you can use your compass accordingly; otherwise, allow for this deviation as you do your compass reading. In many cases, hand-held global-positioning systems may easier to use.

BACKPACKS First decide whether to get a pack with an internal or external frame. If you choose the latter, pick one that balances the pack upright when you set it on the ground; this is a great help in the areas of Alaska that don't have trees. Internal frames are an advantage when going through brush, which is common in Alaska. A rainproof cover for your pack is a good idea, even if it's just a heavy plastic garbage bag (bring extras).

TENTS Because winterlike storms can occur at almost any time of year, a freestanding four-season tent is highly recommended, one that can withstand strong winds and persistent rainfall (or even snow squalls). There are few situations more miserable than being stuck in a battered, leaky tent with a storm raging outside. Tie-down ropes and tent flies are essential items, and mosquito netting is another must.

SLEEPING GEAR For sleeping comfort, bring a sleeping pad to add cushioning and insulation beneath your sleeping bag. Be sure your bag is warm enough for the changing conditions; even in midsummer, nighttime temperatures may fall to the freezing mark, especially in the mountains.

COOKING GEAR Bring a lightweight camping stove with fuel. Firewood may be scarce and what there is may be wet. Burning wood in many parklands is now frowned upon or prohibited in order to protect the surroundings.

Besides a stove, fuel, and matches or butane lighter, necessary cooking items include light but sturdy utensils (for instance, a spoon and fork made of hard plastic); a bowl and mug (drinking plenty of hot beverages is a great way to stay both warm and hydrated); a pot or two for heating water and cooking; a potholder; and a dependable pocketknife. As with other equipment, you'll need to balance quality gear with weight considerations.

After an uphill climb, a hiker enjoys the view of a massive glacier

SPORTS, TOP REGIONS & TOURS

Alaska! It's a gigantic, vibrant state teeming with fish-packed rivers, snow-dusted mountaintops, and massive blue glaciers. Who has a travel wish list that *doesn't* include this state? An Alaska vacation can be as relaxing or adventurous as you choose. Thrill-seekers might check out helicopter skiing in the Chugach Mountains out of Girdwood, Valdez, or Cordova, or rafting in Denali National Park & Preserve. Sea-kayakers will find solitude and abundant marine wildlife in Southeast's Glacier Bay or South Central's Kenai Fjords.

Backcountry adventurers can escape civilization with a sled-dog team in Gates of the Arctic National Park far above the Arctic Circle, or in the Susitna Valley less than a two-hour drive north of Anchorage. The Aleutian and Pribilof islands are bird-watching meccas, while Katmai National Park and Kodiak National Wildlife Refuge are hot spots for bear viewing. An increasing number of trips and tours now make it possible to spend a week or two (or more) learning—and performing—feats from horse packing within sight of Mt. McKinley to hiking or mountain-biking through some of the state's most challenging landscapes. Below you'll find our favorite sports, along with recommended trips and experiences, questions to consider, and suggestions to help you choose the right program. Be sure to check out sections entitled "Sports, the Outdoors & Guided Tours" in all of our regional chapters, from Anchorage to South Central to Southeast, for more details and additional rental and tour options.

UNDERSTATEMENT OF THE YEAR

Calling Alaska "gigantic" is an understatement if ever there was one: If you placed a map of Alaska on top of a map of the lower 48 states, its boundaries would extend from the Canadian border to the Mexican border and from the Atlantic to the Pacific.

Biking

Biking is an excellent way to see Alaska, whether it's on a prearranged tour or an afternoon jaunt on some rented wheels. There are bike-rental shops in larger communities such as Anchorage and Fairbanks;

they frequently offer street maps and can tell you their favorite routes. Alaska's dirt trails, including many found within city parks, promise biking opportunities for cyclists of all abilities, while hundreds of miles of paved trails and highways provide choice touring routes. Whether you plan to grind your way up a dusty mountain path or cruise swiftly along a well-traveled highway, come prepared to handle emergencies. Always carry a basic bicycle repair kit including chain tool, Allen wrenches, spare inner tubes, and tube-repair materials, along with a compact bicycle-tire pump. Bring plenty of fluids (either in water bottles or camel packs), enough food to sustain your energy, and a light jacket or rain shell.

Top Regions & Experiences

Biking is especially popular within the larger cities and along the road systems of South Central and the Interior. Favored touring routes include the unpaved Denali and Taylor highways and McCarthy Road. The Copper River Highway outside of Cordova and some of the less-traveled roads north of Fairbanks also beckon cyclists. Biking is also a fantastic way to explore Southeast's coastal towns via the Alaska Marine Highway System.

SOUTHEAST Biking Southeast Alaska can be an exhilarating if sometimes wet experience. The **Alaska Marine Highway** (🌐 www.ferryalaska.com) charges a fee ($15–$50, depending on your route) if you bring your bike aboard. It's well worth it. Watch for breaching whales aboard the ferry, then stop in small towns to check out Gold Rush history, salmon bakes, and cute boardwalks and B&Bs.

ANCHORAGE & ENVIRONS Alaska's largest metropolis is laced with excellent biking opportunities—some challenging, others easy, all scenic—within and just outside city limits. For a comprehensive guide to mountain biking in the Anchorage area, pick up a copy of *Mountain Bike Anchorage,* by Rosemary Austin. The **Tony Knowles Coastal Trail** is 11 glorious mi of paved trail following the coastline from downtown past Westchester Lagoon. Check out the spectacular views of Mt. Susitna (locally called Sleeping Lady), Cook Inlet, and the Chugach Range. Ride the trail all the way to **Kincaid Park** to enjoy its 40 mi of dirt trails through acres of spruce and birch forest. Keep an eye out for moose! Outside the city limits, our favorite trails are those around **Far North Bicentennial Park** and **Eklutna Lake.**

BIKING TO CRESCENT

The ascent is gradual, but the trek over Crescent Creek Trail, 100 highway mi south of Anchorage, can feel steeper and longer under a hot July sun. In places the trail goes almost vertical, and hairpin switchbacks broken by spruce roots require caution. None of that seems to matter, though, once Crescent Lake appears through the cottonwoods. On a windless afternoon the lake resembles an ice-blue gem surrounded by rocky ridgelines and a great big sky.

KENAI PENINSULA & PRINCE WILLIAM SOUND A short drive from Anchorage, the Kenai Peninsula offers outstanding opportunities for mountain-bikers seeking thigh-busting challenges amid extraordinary scenery. **Crescent Creek Trail** (at Mile 44.9 of Sterling Highway; drive 3 mi to the trailhead at end of gravel road); **Devil's Pass** (at Mile 39.5 of Seward Highway); **Johnson Pass** (at Miles 32.6 and 63.7 of Seward Highway), and the **Resurrection trail systems** offer miles of riding for a wide range of expertise. Cyclists here are subject to highly fickle mountain weather patterns. Also remember that you're never really alone in wild Alaska: be sure to bring along bear spray and bug dope. For maps and descriptions of trails, visit the state Department of Natural Resources Web site at 🌐 www.dnr.state.ak.us/parks/aktrails/ats/ken-ats.htm.

FAIRBANKS Visitors to the Golden Heart City will find plenty of biking opportunities around town. People in these parts are becoming big biking fans—it's a trend that keeps lots of the trails well maintained. The **Back Door Trail** is part of the **Ester Dome Trails system,** which has miles of mountain-biking trails ranging from single tracks to fire roads. Back Door Trail stretches over 8 mi with an 800-foot elevation gain; it's rated by the Fairbanks Cycle Club as easy. To get started, drive west of Fairbanks on Parks Highway; turn right on Old Nenana Highway. Park at Ester Community Park near the firehouse just before the Ester turnoff.

One of our favorite rides, the paved multiuse **Farmers Loop Bike Path** winds through suburbs and farmlands, passing by Creamer's Field Migratory Waterfowl Refuge. The path starts on the University of Alaska campus (at the corner of University and College) and takes you on a loop to the Steese Highway and back to town. The **University Ski Trails** are located on University of Alaska Fairbanks campus (look for the well-marked trailhead and parking lot off Tanana Loop Road). This is pretty good stuff: 15 mi of dirt trails with a 1,500-foot elevation gain.

Resources & Guides

★ **Alaska Backcountry Bike Tours.** Based in Palmer, north of Anchorage, this company offers guided day- and multiday trips; rental options include hard-tail and full-suspension bikes. ☎ *866/354–2453* 🌐 *www.mountainbikealaska.com.*

Alaska Bicycle Adventures. Starting in Anchorage, these multiday touring packages explore South Central and nearby scenic highways. ☎ *907/245–2175* 🌐 *www.alaskabike.com.*

★ **Alaska Bicycle Tours/Sockeye Cycle Company.** Based in Haines, and in summertime in Skagway, these folks specialize in guided bike tours of Southeast and remote sections of Canada's Northwest and Yukon. ☎ *907/766–2869 or 877/292–4154* 🌐 *www.cyclealaska.com.*

★ **Alaska Outdoor Rentals & Guides.** This family-operated Fairbanks business provides bicycle rentals and guided tours of the area. ☎ *907/457–2453* 🌐 *www.akbike.com.*

Backroads. Offering a challenging 8-day trip through South Central, this tried-and-true tour company is worth the investment. ☎ *510/527–1555 or 800/462–2848* 🌐 *www.backroads.com.*

Denali Outdoor Center. This operator, located in Denali National Park & Preserve, offers bicycle rentals and guided tours into the park. ☎ *907/683–1925 or 888/303–1925* 🌐 *www.denalioutdoorcenter.com.*

Downtown Bicycle Rental. Located in downtown Anchorage near the head of the popular Tony Knowles Coastal Trail, this rental shop has large selection of quality bikes and accessories. ☎ *907/279–5293* ⊕ *www.alaska-bike-rentals.com.*

Fairbanks Cycle Club and **Alaska Outdoor Rentals & Guides** can give you information on touring and mountain-biking routes around Fairbanks. ⊕ *www.fairbankscycleclub.org and* ⊕ *www.akbike.com/trailguide.html.*

Lifetime Adventures. Operating out of the state parks campground at Eklutna Lake about 26 mi northeast of Anchorage, Lifetime rents bikes and trailers. They also have a popular Paddle & Pedal package in which you paddle in one direction and pedal your way back. ☎ *907/694–7982 or 800/952–8624* ⊕ *www.lifetimeadventures.net.*

Canoeing

Canoeing opportunities are abundant in this land of three million lakes and 3,000 rivers. Although it's possible to pull off the road and launch at any of hundreds of lakes and streams crossing Alaska's road system, the most easily accessed canoe trail systems with well-marked, maintained portages are found in South Central. Canoes, paddles, and life vests can be rented for $20 to $30 a day from area rental outfits.

> **PEACEFUL PADDLING**
>
> From your canoe seat the world seems a simpler place. The air is still, the lake a reflector of autumn colors and indigo sky. Nearby, a trout rises for a midge, leaving behind a silver wake that brightens as it spreads. A full moon has begun to peek over the mountains to the east—there will be frost in the morning—and you wonder as you paddle quietly back to camp if tonight you'll hear wolves howling.

Lakes and rivers around sea level in South Central are usually ice-free from mid-May through September, while those found at higher elevations and in the Interior and northern regions of the state are more likely to be ice-free from early June to mid-September. Many paddlers find the first couple of weeks after breakup and the final two weeks before freeze-up the most pleasant, for their cool temperatures and lack of mosquitoes and black flies.

Top Regions & Experiences

Three spectacular canoe trail systems are located in South Central, including the **Swan Lake Canoe Trail** and **Swanson River Canoe Trail,** both set in the 1.3-million-acre Kenai National Wildlife Refuge on the Kenai Peninsula, and the **Nancy Lake Canoe Trail** in the Susitna Valley.

NORTH OF ANCHORAGE

The **Nancy Lake Canoe Trail** system is located off the Parks Highway about a 90-minute drive north of Anchorage. The system is managed by Alaska State Parks and features an 8-mi-long chain of lakes. Portages are well-marked with orange, diamond-shaped signs marked with a "P." Wet sections are covered with boardwalk.

Experienced wilderness paddlers seeking some of the continent's most far-flung waters may want to explore systems like the Interior's Fortymile River Trail, Innoko River Trail, or Lower Beaver Creek Water Trails.

KENAI PENINSULA The **Swan Lake Canoe Trail** system includes a 60-mi-long series of lakes and small streams connected by overland portages ranging from a few hundred feet to more than a mile. The system can be entered through any of three trailhead entrances off Swanson River Road outside of Sterling (head out of town on the Sterling Hwy. and turn off at milepost 83.4). Trails are managed by the Kenai National Wildlife Refuge, which accurately describes the landscape as rolling hill country. There are plenty of spruce and birch forests here, plus amazing views of the Kenai Mountains to the east. Portages vary in condition.

The popular **Swanson River Canoe Trail** system, also set within the Kenai National Wildlife Refuge, is 50 mi long. The landscape is as wonderful as that of Swan Lake, with maintained portages ranging from a few hundred feet to more than a mile long. Follow the same driving directions as for Swan Lake out of Sterling.

Resources & Guides

Alaska Canoe & Campground. This outfit rents within Kenai National Wildlife Refuge. ☎ *907/262–2331* 🌐 *www.alaskacanoetrips.com.*

Alaska Department of Natural Resources. Check out the listings of canoe trails throughout the state, along with maps. 🌐 *www.dnr.state.ak.us/parks/aktrails/atstrans.htm.*

★ **Alaska Discovery.** One of the oldest outfits in the state, these folks are based in the Southeast and organize trips in the region and beyond, including a river trip on the Noatak River in the Brooks Range. ☎ *800/586–1911* 🌐 *www.akdiscovery.com.*

Recreational Equipment Inc. The Anchorage outpost rents canoes and accessories. ☎ *907/272–4565* 🌐 *www.rei.com.*

Backcountry Safaris. This Anchorage outfit, with 20 years of experience, has reasonable canoe-rental rates. ☎ *907/222–1632 or 877/812–2159* 🌐 *www.backcountrysafaris.com.*

Fodor'sChoice ★ **Sourdough Outfitters.** Sometimes using inflatable canoes, this company (established 1972) offers paddling trips up north in the Brooks Range. ☎ *907/692–5252* 🌐 *www.sourdoughoutfitters.com.*

Tippecanoe. Canoes can be rented from Tippecanoe Rentals in Willow, north of Anchorage. Call ahead to arrange to have one waiting for you at the Nancy Lake trailhead. ☎ *907/495-6688* 🌐 *www.paddlealaska.com.*

Dogsledding

Decades ago, before snowmobiles and airplanes became mainstays of winter travel here, dog teams provided transportation for rural Alaskans. Some of the finest dog teams in the state hailed from remote native villages. Today, mushing is widely considered Alaska's state sport. It's not for everyone. For one thing, you have to like the cold. You also have to like roughing it. Even the nicest accommodations are only a step or two removed from camping. Most important, you have to like dogs—a lot. Contrary to the romantic image you may have of sled dogs, they're not all cuddly, clean Siberian huskies. Most mushers, including the people who run dogsled tours, take very good care of their dogs, but the dogs are working dogs, not show dogs.

Here are some facts to consider when choosing your trip: on some mushing trips, participants travel by cross-country skiing or snowshoeing, rather than actually mushing, for at least part of the trip; some introduction to these sports is usually included in your orientation. **■ TIP→ If you're not interested in skiing or snowshoeing, make sure you'll be given a sled. It's always smart to get a good idea of how strenuous the outfitter's pace is.** If you're expecting a relaxing vacation, make sure you don't pick an outfitter who will have you doing everything from hitching up the dogs to pitching tents.

Top Regions & Experiences

ANCHORAGE & SOUTH CENTRAL

Notable mushing communities exist in South Central, especially the Mat-Su Valley and Kenai Peninsula. Every year mushers traverse the wilderness between Anchorage and Nome in the famous **Iditarod Trail Sled Dog Race.** Other sprint and long-distance races in the area draw competitors and fans. Among the best are the **World Championship Sled Dog Race** held each February in Anchorage during the Fur Rendezvous celebration. On the Kenai Peninsula, Kasilof (off the Sterling Hwy.) is home to many notable mushers.

FAIRBANKS & THE INTERIOR

The **Open North American Championships** are held every March in Fairbanks. The 1,000-mi-long **Yukon Quest** between Fairbanks and Whitehorse, Yukon, also lures mushers from around the globe. Plenty of local outfitters can set you up for a day-long sled ride, complete with a visit to the kennels.

WOOF

"Hike!" yells a musher as she releases the brake. On command, a team of surprisingly small but amazingly strong huskies charges off, howling with excitement. Of all the wild sporting adventures out there, dogsledding may be the wildest. There's usually enough snow for dogsled runs from late October or November through March or early April.

Resources & Guides

Chugach Express Dog Sled Tours. Year-round mushing tours pass through a valley surrounded by the Chugach Mountains, about an hour's drive south of Anchorage. The one-hour tours include a visit to the kennel of the owner, a former Iditarod musher. ☎ *907/783–2266, 907/783–7669 for reservations* 🌐 *www.chugachexpress.com.*

Cotter Kennels. Operating outside of Fairbanks, at the Chena Hot Springs Resort, these Yukon Quest winner and Iditarod top-three finishers offer dogsled rides in winter and dog cart rides in summer. ☎ *907/451–8104 or 800/478–4681* 🌐 *www.chenahotsprings.com.*

IdidaRide Sled Dog Tours. This family outfit out of Seward on the Kenai Peninsula runs wintertime tours with their Iditarod dogs. ☎ *907/224–8607 or 800/478–3139* 🌐 *www.ididaride.com.*

Plettner Sled Dog Kennels. Lynda Plettner, Iditarod veteran, offers mushing tours through the Mat-Su Valley, with prices starting at $100; reservations required. Summer kennel tours are offered as well. The kennels are located a 90-minute drive north of Anchorage off the Parks Highway. ☎ *877/892–6944* 🌐 *www.plettner-kennels.com.*

Fodor'sChoice ★ **Sourdough Outfitters.** From February through April, 4- to 11-day sledding expeditions are organized within the Gates of the Arctic National Park and the North Slope. The owners provide all camping gear plus special boots, parkas, mittens, and snowshoes. ☎ *907/692–5252* 🌐 *www.sourdoughoutfitters.com.*

Flightseeing

Air-taxi services in all major cities and many smaller communities offer flightseeing tours. Most offer a variety of packages, allowing clients to design their own tours if discussed in advance. The smaller companies are often more flexible, while the multiplane companies can better match plane size to your needs. Prices vary and usually depend upon the size of the plane, number of clients, and length of the tour. As with taxicabs, passengers can often split costs. Generally, a half-hour flightseeing trip will run each person somewhere between $65 and $85, usually with a two- or three-person minimum, depending on aircraft size. Hourly rates, depending on how big the plane is and on how much competition there is in the area, can run from $85 to more than $300. Keep in mind that if there's a drop-off and pick-up involved, you pay for all the time the plane is operating, in both directions. ■ **TIP→ Shop around before committing to any one service; some very good flightseeing bargains are available.**

Flights in smaller planes and helicopters are particularly dependent upon weather. In some cases, clouds may simply obscure certain sites, while bad weather often grounds pilots altogether, forcing tours to be canceled. Ask about cancellation policies if you've paid in advance and never push a pilot do something he or she is reluctant to do; messing up your schedule a bit is a much better option than flying in unsafe conditions.

BIG LAND, BIG SKY

Alaska's vastness defies imagination. Flying is the most efficient—and sometimes most enthralling—way to get around this largely roadless land, home to more pilots per capita than any other state. Savvy residents know that flying is an excellent way to see huge swathes of countryside, so flightseeing tours have flourished in recent decades.

Top Regions & Experiences

SOUTHEAST In Southeast, flightseeing services based in communities surrounding **Misty Fiords National Monument, the Tongass National Forest, Mendenhall Glacier,** and **Glacier Bay National Park & Preserve** offer aerial views of coastal mountain ranges, remote shorelines, glaciers, ice fields, and wildlife. Some

Flightseeing over Mt. McKinley may be one of the most awesome experiences the state has to offer.

even include opportunities to land and fish, or view local wildlife, such brown bears, black bears, sea otters, seals, and whales. Visitors passing through Southeast on cruise lines or via the Alaska Marine Highway System will find flightseeing options in all ports.

ANCHORAGE & SOUTH CENTRAL This area is the state's air-travel hub. Plenty of flightseeing services operating out of city airports and floatplane bases can take you on spectacular tours of **Mt. McKinley, the Chugach Range, Prince William Sound, Kenai Fjords National Park,** and **the Harding Icefield.** Flightseeing services are available in Seward, Homer, Talkeetna, and other South Central communities. Anchorage hosts the greatest number and variety of services, including those operating fixed-wing aircraft, floatplanes, and helicopters.

THE BUSH Why not head to the state's most remote parts in a small plane? Check out scenic **Katmai National Park & Preserve** and the **Valley of 10,000 Smokes,** a volcanic region of steaming calderas and hardened lava moonscapes. Most services are based in the communities of King Salmon or Naknek, which are served by a common airport with jet service from Anchorage.

Resources & Guides

★ **Emerald Air Service.** A company that gets great reviews on Fodors.com, Emerald is based in Homer; they'll take you to remote Southwestern bear country. All-day trips run $550 per person. ☎ *907/235–6993* 🌐 *www.emeraldairservice.com.*

Katmailand. This outfit has concessions at Brooks and Grosvenor lodges in Katmai National Park. ☎ *800/544–0551* 🌐 *www.katmailand.com.*

★ **Rust's Flying Service.** An Anchorage company in business since 1963, Rust's will take you on narrated flightseeing tours of Mt. McKinley and Denali, Columbia Glacier, and Prince William Sound. ☎ *907/243–1595 or 800/544–2299* 🌐 *www.flyrusts.com.*

Southeast Aviation. This Ketchikan-based operation offers floatplane tours of the glaciers and mountains of Misty Fiords National Monu-

HELPFUL WEB SITES

List of Alaska air taxis: 🌐 www.flyalaska.com/directoryp.html. National Transportation Safety Board database to check air-taxi safety records: 🌐 www.ntsb.gov/NTSB/query.asp.

ment. Wildlife sightings are quite common. ☎ *907/225–2900 or 888/359–6478* 🌐 *www.southeastaviation.com.*

Talkeetna Aero Services. These folks are located a two-hour drive north of Anchorage, in the shadow of McKinley; take a twin-engine aerial tour of the mountain. ☎ *907/733–2899, 907/683–2899, or 888/733–2899* 🌐 *www.talkeetna-aero.com.*

Talkeetna Air Taxi. Check out McKinley and environs, then swoop down to a glacier to test your boots. ☎ *907/733–2218 or 800/533–2219* 🌐 *www.talkeetnaair.com.*

WORD OF MOUTH

"In Juneau, we liked seeing Mendenhall Glacier, which is not far from downtown. We also enjoyed the floatplane trip over the Juneau Icefields to Taku Glacier Lodge. There they served king salmon cooked over alder logs."
–sluggo

★ **Wings Airways and Taku Glacier Lodge.** This Juneau-based company specializes in tours of the surrounding ice fields and the Taku Flight & Feast ride, on which a salmon feast awaits you. ☎ *907/586–6275* 🌐 *www.wingsairways.com.*

Glacier Trekking

Roughly 100,000 glaciers flow out of Alaska's mountains, covering 5% of the state. These slow-moving "rivers of ice" concentrate in the Alaska Range, Wrangell Mountains, and the state's major coastal mountain chains: the Chugach, St. Elias, Coast, and Kenai ranges. Alaska's largest glacier, the Bering, covers 2,250 square mi—twice the size of Rhode Island. If you're an adventurous backcountry traveler, glaciers present icy avenues into the remote corners of premier mountain wilderness areas. **■ TIP→ For information about glaciers, flip to *Glaciers: Notorious Landscape Architects* in Chapter 5.**

Glacier terrain includes a mix of ice, rock debris, and often-deep surface snow; sometimes frigid pools of meltwater collect on the surface. Watch out for glacier crevasses. Sometimes hidden by snow, especially in spring and early summer (a popular time for glacier trekking), these cracks in the ice may present life-threatening traps for unwary travelers. Though some are only inches wide, others may be several yards across and hundreds of feet deep. ⚠ **Glacier travel should be attempted only after you've been properly trained. If you haven't been taught proper glacial travel and crevasse-rescue techniques, hire a backcountry guide to provide the necessary gear and expertise.** Some companies offer day or half-day hikes onto glaciers that don't have the same physical demands as longer treks but that still require proper equipment and training. For instance, St. Elias Alpine Guides takes hikers of all ages and abilities on one of its glacier walks.

Top Regions & Experiences

SOUTHEAST In Southeast, visitors to the capital city of Juneau can drive or take the bus to **Mendenhall Glacier,** located on the outskirts of town. This 85-mi-long, 45-mi-wide sheet of ice provides awesome glacier trekking opportunities. Guided tour packages area very good idea for beginners.

Crampon-clad feet meet Alaskan ice—unforgettable.

SOUTH CENTRAL & THE INTERIOR

The mountains outside the state's largest city have their share of glaciers. Among the most popular for trekkers of all abilities is **Matanuska Glacier,** located at Mile 103 off the Glenn Highway (about a 90-minute drive northeast of Anchorage). Anchorage-based guides often use the Matanuska as a training ground for those new to navigating glaciers.

Talkeetna, a two-hour drive north of Anchorage, is a small community famous as the jump-off point to some of the world's greatest and most challenging glacier treks. The town rests a short bush-plane hop from the foot of the Alaska Range, near the base of **Mt. McKinley.** Miles of ice await the most intrepid and experienced trekkers. Local and Anchorage-based guide services offer training and tours into the region.

Far to the east, off the McCarthy Road between Valdez and Glennallen, are the great ice fields of the **Wrangell Mountains.** Experienced outfitters based in the town of McCarthy get newcomers in touch with awesome ice where few outsiders dare visit.

Resources & Guides

Above & Beyond Alaska. If you're in the Juneau area and want to get your glacier fix, these folks offer treks to the popular Mendenhall Glacier. ☎ *907/364–2333* 🌐 *www.beyondak.com.*

Adventure Bound. Based in Juneau, these guides offer all-day summertime trips to Sawyer Glacier within Tracy Arm. ☎ *907/463–2509 or 800/228–3875* 🌐 *www.adventureboundalaska.com.*

Alaska Mountaineering School. Whether it's on mountaineering expeditions to McKinley or less extreme treks into the Alaska Range, this Talkeetna company takes the time to train you before heading out to pristine backcountry. ☎ *907/733–1016* 🌐 *www.climbalaska.org.*

Exposure Alaska. A variety of small-group options, from ice-climbing and short treks on the blue ice of the Matanuska Glacier, to more intense multiday outings from Prince William Sound to Denali, are offered through this Anchorage company. ☎ *907/761–3761 or 800/956–6422* 🌐 *www.exposurealaska.com.*

NorthStar Trekking. A Juneau-based operation specializing in helicopter glacier trekking on the Juneau Icefield, these folks accommodate a broad range of physical abilities. All trips are conducted in small groups, gear provided. Flightseeing tours are also offered. ☎ *907/790–4530* 🌐 *www.glaciertrekking.com.*

Fodor'sChoice ★ **St. Elias Alpine Guides.** Based in the town of McCarthy, within Wrangell–St. Elias National Park, these überexperienced guides conduct day hikes to nearby glaciers and extended glacier treks well beyond. ☎ *907/554–4445 or 888/933–5427* 🌐 *www.steliasguides.com.*

★ **Ultima Thule Outfitters.** Based at a fly-in-only lodge on the Chitina River within Wrangell–St. Elias National Park, Ultima Thule leads guided activities in the surrounding mountains, including alpine and glacier treks. A longtime presence in these parts, they're known for family-style hospitality. ☎ *907/258–0636* 🌐 *www.ultimathulelodge.com.*

Hiking & Backpacking

From Southeast's coastal rain forests and the Interior's historic Yukon River country to the high Arctic tundra, Alaska presents some of the continent's finest landscape for wilderness hiking and backpacking. Or, if remote backcountry is not your preference, it's possible to travel well-maintained and well-marked trails on the edges of Alaska's largest cities and still get a taste of the wild. Many of the trails in road-accessible parklands, refuges, and forests are well maintained and cross terrain that is easy for novice hikers, seniors, and families with children.

BLISS IN BOOTS

In late June and early July, when the sun barely sets in much of Alaska, it's tempting to shoulder your pack and keep on hiking. Around 10 PM the light grows mellow and golden. The birds seem to call all night long. Your boots crunch softly over gravel bars and hillocks. This time of year Alaska rarely sleeps; there will be time for rest when summer is over.

Top Regions & Experiences

Below we've listed some notable exceptions to one rule: Most of Alaska is pristine wilderness, with few or no trails. In such areas it's best to be accompanied by an experienced backcountry traveler who understands the challenges of trail-less wilderness: how to behave in bear country, how to navigate using map and compass techniques, and how to cross glacial streams. ■ **TIP→ For information about hiking Southeast's Chilkoot Trail, flip to *Gold! Gold! Gold!* in Chapter 3.**

SOUTHEAST Virtually all hiking country in the Southeast is part of the 17-million-acre Tongass National Forest, administered by the U.S. Forest Service. It can be wet and steep here, but you also will be walking through temperate rain forest—lush and gorgeous!

FROM ANCHORAGE TO DENALI **Chugach State Park,** along Anchorage's eastern edge, has dozens of trails, many of them suited for day hikes or overnight camping. Across Turnagain Arm, near Hope, hikers can step onto the **Resurrection Pass Trail** which traverses the forests, streams, and mountains of the Chugach National Forest. And though it is best known for its trail-less wilderness, **Denali National Park & Preserve** has some easy-to-hike trails near the park

1

HIKING TERRAINS

RIVERS

Crossing Alaska's rivers requires care. Many are swift, silty streams that are hard to read. They often flow over impermeable bottoms (either rock or permafrost), which means a good rain can raise water levels a matter of feet, not inches, in a surprisingly short time. (For this very reason, avoid pitching tents near streams.) Warm days can also dramatically increase the meltwater from glaciers. Be aware of weather changes that might affect the ease of river crossings. Look for the widest, shallowest place you can find, with many channels. This may entail traveling up- or downstream. A guide who knows the region is invaluable at such times.

A sturdy staff, your own or made from a handy branch, is useful to help you keep your balance and measure the depths of silty water. You should unbuckle your pack when crossing a swift stream. Avoid wearing a long rain poncho; it can catch the water and tip you over. For added stability it may help for two or more people to link arms when crossing.

Hikers debate the best footwear for crossing Alaska's rivers. Some take along sneakers and wear them through the water; others take off their socks so they will remain dry and can comfort cold feet on the opposite shore. But bear in mind that Alaska waters are probably frigid, and the bottom is usually rough; bare feet are not advised.

TUNDRA

Tundra hiking, especially in higher alpine country, can be a great pleasure. In places, the ground is so springy you feel like you're walking on a trampoline. In the Arctic, however, where the ground is underlaid with permafrost, you will probably find the going as wet as it is in the Southeast forests. Summer sunshine melts the top, leaving puddles and marshy spots behind. Comfortable waterproof footgear can help when traversing such landscapes. Tundra travel can require the skill of a ballet dancer if the ground is tufted with tussocks.

FORESTS

Forest trails are hard to maintain and often wet, especially in coastal lowlands, and they may be potholed or blocked with beaver dams. The ground stays soggy much of the time, and brush grows back quickly after it is cut. Especially nasty is devil's club, a large, broad-leafed plant with greenish flowers that eventually become clusters of bright red berries; it's also thickly armored with stinging needles.

entrance, not to mention miles of taiga and tundra waiting to be explored. Nearby "Little Denali"—**Denali State Park**—has the 36-mi-long Kesugi Ridge Trail, within easy reach of the Parks Highway.

FAIRBANKS & THE INTERIOR If you're in the Interior's main hub, definitely check out **Creamer's Field Migratory Waterfowl Refuge** for easy trails and great birding. Some 100 mi east of Fairbanks, the **Pinnell Mountain National Recreation Trail** offers a great three-day hike above the tree line.

Alaska's wide-open tundra and fantastic scenery draws hikers from around the globe.

Resources & Guides

Alaska Mountaineering School. Best known for its McKinley expeditions, this Talkeetna-based company also leads custom-designed backcountry expeditions in the Alaska Range. ☎ *907/733–1016* 🌐 *www.climbalaska.org.*

Fodor'sChoice ★ **Alaska Nature Tours.** This company in Southeast Alaska leads summer hiking trips into the Alaska Chilkat Bald Eagle Preserve near Haines. Other trips include beach walks and rain-forest hikes. ☎ *907/766–2876* 🌐 *www.kcd.com/aknature.*

Alaskan Gourmet Adventures. Fun hiking trips with great guides are on offer with this Anchorage-based operator. ☎ *907/346–1087* 🌐 *www.hikealaska.com.*

★ **Arctic Treks.** These wilderness hiking and backpacking trips, sometimes combined with river floats, explore areas throughout the Arctic region's Brooks Range, including Gates of the Arctic and the Arctic National Wildlife Refuge. ☎ *907/455–6502* 🌐 *www.arctictreksadventures.com.*

Go North Alaska Adventure Travel Center. This is a Fairbanks business with experience since 1991 in organizing Brooks Range tours. ☎ *907/479–7272 or 866/236–7272* 🌐 *www.gonorthalaska.com.*

Fodor'sChoice ★ **St. Elias Alpine Guides.** For more than a quarter century, this outfitter has been leading mountain hikes, nature tours, and extended backpacking expeditions in the St. Elias and Wrangell mountain ranges. ☎ *888/933–5427 or 907/554–4445* 🌐 *www.steliasguides.com.*

Fodor'sChoice ★ **Sourdough Outfitters.** Summer backpacking and river trips galore in the beautiful Brooks Range. ☎ *907/692–5252* 🌐 *www.sourdoughoutfitters.com.*

Horse Packing

To minimize a horse-packing group's impact on the environment, most are limited to 12 riders, and some to just three or four. Most outfits post at least two wranglers for 12 guests, and some bring along another person who serves as cook and/or assistant wrangler. All outfitters who operate on federal lands are required to have a permit.

■ **TIP→ It's a good idea to find out how much time is spent in the saddle each day and how difficult the riding is.** Six hours is a long day in the saddle, and although some outfitters schedule that much, most keep the riding time to about four hours. Most trips move at a walk, but some trot, lope, and even gallop. As with many other guided adventures, special expertise is not required for horse packing, and guides will train you in the basics before setting out.

On trips into the wilderness, expect the food to be straightforward cowboy fare, cooked over a campfire or cookstove. Guides often pull double duty in the kitchen, and often a little help from group members is willingly accepted. If you have any dietary restrictions, make arrangements beforehand. For lodging, don't allow yourself to be surprised: find out what the rooms are like if you're going to be staying in motels or cabins, and if the trip involves camping, ask about the campsites and about shower and latrine arrangements.

Top Regions & Experiences

SOUTH CENTRAL Encompassing more than 13 million acres of mountains, glaciers, and remote river valleys, **Wrangell–St. Elias National Park & Preserve** is wild and raw. There's no better way to absorb the enormity and natural beauty of this region than on horseback. Centuries-old game trails and networks blazed and maintained by contemporary outfitters wind through lowland spruce forests and into wide-open high-country tundra. From there, horses can take you almost anywhere, over treeless ridgelines and to sheltered campsites on the shores of scenic tarns.

Closer to the state's population center in South Central, yet no less magnificent for horse packing, is the Kenai Peninsula. Outfitters here frequently travel the well-groomed mountain trails of the **Chugach National Forest** and **Kenai Mountains.** In both regions, wildlife is abundant: moose, bear, Dall sheep, mountain goats, and wolves are frequently seen. Although overnight cabins are occasionally available, guests should come prepared to camp outdoors.

SADDLE UP!

There are no traffic jams, no overcrowded campgrounds on horse packing vacations. The farther into the wilderness you go, the more untouched and spectacular the landscape. You can also cover a lot more ground with less effort than you can backpacking. Before you book, ask your outfitter for suggestions on appropriate clothing, footwear, and gear.

Resources & Guides

Alaska Horsemen. This Cooper Landing–based company offers multiday pack trips into the Kenai Mountains via Crescent Lake, Resurrection, and other area trail systems. ☎ *907/595–1806 or 800/595–1806* 🌐 *www.alaskahorsemen.com.*

Castle Mountain Outfitters. Based in the Chickaloon, north of Anchorage in Matanuska Valley, this outfitter conducts a variety of trips ranging from guided hour-long horseback rides to one-week expeditions. ☎ *907/745–6427* 🌐 *www.mtaonline.net/~cmoride/index.html.*

D & S Alaskan Trail Rides. Specializing in short rides of Denali State Park, these outfitters are right off the Parks Highway, north of Anchorage. ☎ *907/733–2207, 907/733–2205, or 907/745–2208* 🌐 *www.alaskantrailrides.com.*

Wrangell Outfitters. This husband-wife team from Fairbanks takes visitors on horse packing trips into the heart of Wrangell–St. Elias National Park & Preserve. ☎ *907/479–5343* 🌐 *www.wrangelloutfitters.com.*

River Rafting

So much of Alaska is roadless wilderness that rivers often serve as the best avenues to explore the landscape. This is especially true in several of Alaska's premier parklands and refuges. Here, as elsewhere, rivers are ranked according to their degrees of difficulty. ■ TIP→ **Class I rivers are considered to be easy floats with minimal rapids; at the other extreme, Class VI rivers are extremely dangerous and nearly impossible to navigate. Generally only very experienced river runners should attempt anything above Class II on their own.** Also be aware that river conditions change considerably from season to season and sometimes day to day, so always check ahead to determine a river's current condition. The National Weather Service Alaska–Pacific River Forecast Center keeps tabs on Alaska's most popular streams. The center's Web site (🌐 aprfc.arh.noaa.gov/ak_ahps2.php) provides the latest data on water levels and flow rates, including important flood-stage alerts.

Do-it-yourselfers would be wise to consult two books on Alaska's rivers: *Fast & Cold: A Guide to Alaska Whitewater* (Skyhouse), by Andrew Embick (though intended primarily for white-water kayakers, it has good information for rafters as well), and *The Alaska River Guide: Canoeing, Kayaking, and Rafting in the Last Frontier* (Alaska Northwest Books), by Karen Jettmar.

Fortunately you don't have to be an expert river runner to explore many of Alaska's premier waterways. Experienced rafting companies operate throughout the state. Some outfits emphasize extended wilderness trips and natural-history observations, whereas others specialize in thrilling one-day (or shorter) floats through Class III and IV white water that will get your adrenaline pumping. And some combine a little of both.

Top Regions & Experiences

Never has the term "it's all good" been truer than in the context of river rafting in Alaska. With thousands of rivers to choose from, virtually every region of the state promises prime rafting. Which region and river you float depends largely upon the impetus of your

RIOTOUS RIVERS

From the Southeast Panhandle to the far reaches of the Arctic, Alaska is blessed with an abundance of wild, pristine rivers. The federal government has officially designated more than two dozen Alaska streams as "wild and scenic rivers," but hundreds more would easily qualify. Some meander gently through forests or tundra. Others, fed by glacier runoff, rush wildly through mountains and canyons.

trip. White-water thrill-seekers will find challenging streams tumbling from the mountainous areas of South Central, while rafters interested in sportfishing may choose extended float trips on the gentler salmon- and trout-rich rivers of Southwest. Birders and campers may consider the pristine rivers draining the North Slope of the Brooks Range or Northwest Alaska. Beyond your agenda, though, which river you choose to float should depend upon your rafting and backcountry skills. If there's any question at all, go with an experienced river guide.

SOUTH CENTRAL For those seeking the adrenaline surge of white-water rafting, South Central offers many accessible and affordable options. **Chugach National Forest's Six-Mile River,** about a 90-minute drive south of Anchorage on the Seward Highway, is relished for its Class VI and V white water and spectacular canyon scenery. Options available off the highway system north of Anchorage include the glacial **Eagle** and **Matanuska** rivers, each known for varying degrees of white water.

THE INTERIOR & THE BUSH Heading north out of Anchorage via the Parks Highway, the **Nenana River** flows along the eastern side of Denali National Park & Preserve, offering a variety of conditions ranging from calm to Class III and IV.

Flowing north out of the eastern Brooks Range to the Arctic Ocean, the **Kongakut** and **Hulahula** rivers promise far-flung wilderness adventures. As much as the water, trips here are about seeing the high Arctic tundra landscape and wildlife such as caribou, grizzly bears, musk ox, and thousands of nesting birds.

Resources & Guides

Be certain that the guide gives you a safety talk before going on the water. It's important to know what you should do if you do get flipped out of the raft or if the boat overturns. Also find out what gear and clothing are required. Ask if you'll be paddling or simply riding as a passenger. Reputable rafting companies will discuss all of this, but it never hurts to ask.

★ **Alaska Discovery.** This Juneau-based outfitter leads 9- to 12-day trips down two of North America's wildest rivers, the Tatshenshini and Alsek. The trips begin in Canada and end in Glacier Bay. Check out also the rafting/hiking trips in the Arctic National Wildlife Refuge and Gates of the Arctic. ☎ *800/586–1911* 🌐 *www.akdiscovery.com.*

Alaska Outdoor Adventures. South Central's Six-Mile River and Turnagain Pass are two trips offered by this Whittier-based company. ☎ *907/472–2534 or 877/472–2534* 🌐 *www.akadventures.com.*

Alaska Wildland Adventures. Head down the Kenai River and learn about the surroundings and wildlife with these guides. ☎ *800/478–4100* 🌐 *www.alaskarivertrips.com.*

Chugach Adventure Guides. Right outside of Anchorage, this company has plenty of trips on offers, from Six-Mile River to a Talkeetna four-day float. ☎ *907/783–2004 or 877/783–2004* 🌐 *www.alaskanrafting.com.*

Chugach Outdoor Center. Head to Hope, about a 90-minute drive south of Anchorage, for a broad regional menu ranging from nearby Six-Mile

River's Class IV and V whitewater to the Talkeetna River north of Anchorage and Denali's Nenana River. Van shuttles from Anchorage are available with advance reservations. ☎ *907/277–7238 or 866/277–7238* 🌐 *www.chugachoutdoorcenter.com.*

Denali Raft Adventures. River trips are conducted on the glacially fed, whitewater Nenana River, which skirts the eastern boundary of Denali National Park & Preserve. Trips vary from two-hour scenic floats to all-day white-water canyon trips. ☎ *907/683–2234 or 888/683–2234* 🌐 *www.denaliraft.com.*

Fodor'sChoice ★ **Nova.** On offer with these super-experienced guides: white-water trips down the Matanuska, Chickaloon, and Talkeetna rivers in South Central Alaska; multiday float trips through Wrangell–St. Elias and part-day trips on the Kenai Peninsula's Six-Mile River. White-water ratings range from Class I to Class V. ☎ *907/745–5753 or 800/746–5753* 🌐 *www.novalaska.com.*

Sea-Kayaking

Fodor'sChoice ★ Sea-kayaking can be as thrilling or as peaceful as you want. More stable than a white-water kayak and more comfortable than a canoe, a sea kayak, even one loaded with a week's worth of gear, is maneuverable enough to poke into hidden crevices, explore side bays, and beach on deserted spits of sand. Don't assume, though, that if you've kayaked 10 minutes without tipping over you'll be adequately prepared to circumnavigate Glacier Bay National Park & Preserve. There's a lot to learn, and until you know your way around tides, currents, and nautical charts, you should go with an experienced guide who also knows what and how to pack and where to pitch a tent.

It is important for you to honestly evaluate your tolerance for cold, dampness, and high winds. Nothing can ruin a trip faster than pervasive discomfort. ■ **TIP→ Ask whether the outfitter stocks a variety of boats, so you can experiment until you find the kayak that best fits your weight, strength, ability, and paddling style.**

Top Regions & Experiences

SOUTHEAST This largely roadless coastal region is the setting of North America's last great temperate wilderness. Sometimes called Alaska's Panhandle, this appendage of islands, mainland, and fjords is a sparsely populated, scenic paradise for sea-kayaking. In deep Southeast, Ketchikan is a popular starting point for many sea-kayakers. Set in the heart of the **Tongass National Forest** and well within paddling range of the **Misty Fiords National Monument,** this former logging town is home to several sea-kayaking guides and rental businesses. Ketchikan is also a stop on the Alaska Marine Highway, making it convenient for travelers to simply drive or walk off the state ferry and spend a couple of days exploring local bays and fjords before boarding another ferry.

An equally popular destination for Southeast saltwater paddlers is **Glacier Bay National Park & Preserve.** The hub for this region is Juneau, where kayakers can hop a plane or ferry to the small community of Gustavus, located within the park.

Never fear: It doesn't take long to get the hang of paddling a sea kayak.

SOUTH CENTRAL **Prince William Sound,** with its miles of bays, islands, forests, and glaciers is a big draw for sea-kayakers. Popular ports include Whittier, Cordova, and Valdez. Of the three, Whittier and Valdez are on the state highway system, making them most accessible (Whittier is a one-hour drive south from Anchorage). Guides catering to ocean paddlers are found in all three ports.

Two Kenai Peninsula venues also lure sea-kayakers. About a two-hour drive south of Anchorage, at the terminus of the Seward Highway, **Resurrection Bay** serves up awesome scenery and marine wildlife. Homer, perched over **Kachemak Bay,** at the terminus of the Sterling Highway (a five-hour drive south of Anchorage), is also an excellent spot.

Resources & Guides

Fodor'sChoice ★ **Alaska Discovery.** These experienced guides know Southeast Alaska intimately, and they emphasize skills and safety. Destinations include Tracy Arm, Glacier Bay, Icy Bay, Point Adolphus (for whale-watching), and Admiralty Island (with bear-viewing at Pack Creek). Also check out the inn-to-inn paddling trip through the Kenai Peninsula's Kachemak Bay. ☎ *800/586–1911* 🌐 *www.akdiscovery.com.*

Anadyr Adventures. Prince William Sound comes alive from a sea kayak. See for yourself with Anadyr, based in Valdez. ☎ *907/835–2814 or 800/865–2925* 🌐 *www.anadyradventures.com.*

Prince William Sound Kayak Center. Operating out of Whittier since 1981, this center provides kayak rentals, introductory classes, guided day tours, and escorted trips in Prince William Sound. ☎ *907/276–7235 or 877/472–2452* 🌐 *www.pwskayakcenter.com.*

Southeast Exposure. Over twenty years in the business translates into great trips with this Ketchikan outfit. Their most popular paddle is through Misty Fiords National Monument. ☎ *907/225–8829* 🌐 *www.southeastexposure.com.*

THE STROKES

Anyone who doesn't mind getting a little wet and has an average degree of fitness can be a sea kayaker. The basic stroke is performed in a circular motion with a double-bladed paddle: you pull one blade through the water while pushing forward with the other through the air. Most people pick it up with a minimal amount of instruction. And once you do, off you can go into blissful Alaska waters.

Spirit Walker Expeditions. This veteran Southeast company (based in Gustavus) offers guided wilderness sea-kayaking trips that combine a mix of scenery, wildlife, solitude, and paddling within the Inside Passage. Guides prepare meals, offer instruction, and provide all gear. Beginners are welcome. ☎ *907/697–2266 or 800/529–2537* 🌐 *www.seakayakalaska.com.*

Sunny Cove Sea Kayaking. Extended trips in and around Kenai Fjords National Park involve paddling among icebergs, seals, and seabirds as tidewater glaciers calve in the distance. Day and overnight trips explore Resurrection Bay, near Seward. Tours include equipment, instruction, and meals. ☎ *907/224–8810, 800/770–9119 reservations* 🌐 *www.sunnycove.com.*

Skiing & Snowboarding

Alaska's growing reputation as a great destination for Nordic, downhill, and extreme downhill skiing is well deserved. Three of the state's largest cities—Anchorage, Fairbanks, and Juneau—have nearby ski areas, complete with equipment rentals and ski schools. Many of Alaska's towns have maintained trails for cross-country skiers. Anchorage's trail system is considered among the nation's finest and has hosted world-class races.

For those who are more ambitious, Alaska's wilderness areas present plenty of opportunities, and lots of challenges. Unless you are knowledgeable in winter backcountry travel, camping techniques, and avalanche dangers, the best strategy is to hire a guide when exploring Alaska's backcountry on skis. ■ TIP→ **Given the extremes of Alaska's winters, your primary concern should be safety: be sure your guide has had avalanche-awareness and winter-survival training.** Conditions can change quickly, especially in mountainous areas, and what began as an easy cross-country ski trip can suddenly become a survival saga if you're not prepared for the challenges of an Alaska winter.

Top Regions & Experiences

SOUTHEAST **Eaglecrest** gets high marks for excellent spring skiing. Set 12 mi outside of Juneau, ski season runs December through mid-April. This hill is rarely crowded and the views on a bright day are remarkable.

SOUTH CENTRAL & THE INTERIOR **Alyeska Resort,** located 40 mi south of Anchorage in Girdwood, is Alaska's largest and best-known downhill ski resort. It encompasses 1,000 acres of terrain for all skill levels. Ski rentals are available at the resort. Local ski and snowboard guides teach classes on the mountain and offer helicopter ski and snowboard treks into more remote venues in the nearby Chugach and Kenai ranges.

Closer to Anchorage, two much smaller ski hill operations, **Alpenglow** and **Hilltop,** offer great runs for beginners. Both are also good options when the weather occasionally rules out Alyeska.

Moose Mountain, outside of Fairbanks, is the ski and snowboard draw for visitors to the Interior. More than 1,250 feet of terrain includes every-

Self-propelled exploration in the waters of Prince William Sound, South Central Alaska.

(above) Hiking next to astounding blue glaciers in Glacier Bay National Park & Preserve, Southeast Alaska. (opposite page, top) Colorful autumn tundra in Denali National Park & Preserve, Interior Alaska. (opposite page, bottom) A bull moose enjoying Alaskan waters.

(top) The Alaska Raptor Center in Sitka and the yearly winter gathering of bald eagles at the Alaska Chilkat Bald Eagle Preserve near Haines are good bets for seeing eagles in Southeast Alaska. (bottom) Alaskans call Mt. McKinley by its original name, Denali, which means "the high one." (opposite page) A grizzly bear on the move.

(top) Awe-inspiring views across the waters of Prince William Sound, South Central Alaska. (bottom) Prince William Sound's roaring Steller's sea lions, considered an endangered species west of Cape St. Elias.

(top) A humpback whale breaches in the cold Alaskan waters. (bottom) A hiker's fantasy: gorgeous backdrops and miles of coastline right outside Anchorage in Chugach State Park, South Central Alaska.

(top) Herds of magnificent caribou migrate across Alaska's Arctic every year. (bottom left) A colorful totem pole at the Alaska Native Heritage Center in Anchorage. (bottom right) A bald eagle keeps watch.

thing from bunny slopes to vertical. Best of all, while the city known for frigid winters, the mountain enjoys warmer temperatures.

Resources & Guides

Alaska Mountaineering School. Custom cross-country ski trips of varying lengths and degrees of difficulty can be arranged, primarily through Denali national and state parks, with an emphasis on natural history. ☎ *907/733–1016* 🌐 *www.climbalaska.org.*

Fodor's Choice ★ **Alaska Nature Tours.** This company in Southeast rents ski and snowboard gear and conducts trips into the amazing Alaska Chilkat Bald Eagle Preserve near Haines. ☎ *907/766–2876* 🌐 *www.alaskanaturetours.net.*

Chugach Powder Guides. This decade-old helicopter-ski and snowcat operation focuses on backcountry skiing and snowboarding in the Chugach Range out of Girdwood and Seward. ☎ *907/783–4354* 🌐 *www.chugachpowderguides.com.*

Sportfishing

Fodor's Choice ★ Five species of Pacific salmon (king, silver, sockeye, pink, and chum) spawn in Alaska's innumerable rivers and creeks, alongside rainbow trout, cutthroat trout, steelhead, arctic char, sheefish, Dolly Varden char, arctic grayling, northern pike, and lake trout, among other freshwater species. Salmon are also caught in saltwater, along with halibut, lingcod, many varieties of rockfish (locally called snapper or sea bass), and salmon sharks that can weigh more than 800 pounds.

Alaska's salmon sharks aren't the only sport fish capable of reaching huge proportions: the world-record king salmon, weighing 97¼ pounds, was caught in the Kenai River, and halibut exceeding 300—and occasionally 400—pounds are annually caught in Pacific Ocean waters. Even so, some anglers will tell you that bigger isn't necessarily better. Sockeyes, medium-weight salmon averaging 6 to 8 pounds, are considered by many to be the best tasting and best fighting, pound for pound, of any fish. And though the sail-finned arctic grayling commonly weighs a pound or less, its willingness to rise for dry flies makes it a favorite among fly fishermen.

■ TIP→ **Be aware that sportfishing regulations vary widely from area to area. Licenses are required for both fresh- and saltwater fishing.** To learn more about regulations, contact the **Alaska Department of Fish and Game.** (☎ 907/465–4180 sportfishing seasons and regulations, 907/465–2376 licenses 🌐 www.adfg.state.ak.us). To purchase a fishing license online, visit the state of Alaska Web site (🌐 www.admin.adfg.state.ak.us/license).

> **GONE FISHIN'**
>
> Famous for streams rich in salmon, trophy-size trout and char, and sizable saltwater catches, Alaska is an angler's paradise. It's one thing to have so many fish-packed rivers to choose from; it's an added bonus that the backdrop, as you cast your line, is some of the most stunning scenery in the world.

Top Regions & Experiences

Roadside fishing for salmon, trout, char, pike, and grayling is available in **South Central** and **Interior Alaska.**

CLOSE UP

Important Wilderness Safety Tips

PREPARATION & ORGANIZATION

Be sure you're in good physical shape before venturing into backcountry. Avoid traveling alone. If your experience in Alaska's outdoors is limited, travel with a guide. Prepare yourself for the type of landscape you'll be visiting. If you are traveling by boat along the coast, bring a tide book. If backpacking overland, know in advance whether you'll have to cross large glacial rivers. Always pay close attention to the weather. When you're hiking in any protected land, check in and out with a ranger. Leave an itinerary and the names of people to call in case of an emergency with at least one person. Be as specific as you can about your destination and estimated date of return.

MAPS

Use maps (preferably 1 inch: 1 mi maps published by the U.S. Geological Survey) and a compass at the very minimum. Cell phones usually don't work in remote wilderness areas. Other options for emergency use are electronic locator devices, global positioning systems, and handheld aviation radios.

WEATHER

Alaska's rugged terrains are prone to constantly changing weather. Always be prepared for storms and winterlike conditions. Also be prepared for unexpected delays. One of the most common phrases used by pilots in Alaska is "weather permitting." Never "push" the weather; every year, people die in aviation, boating, and overland accidents because they want to get home on schedule despite dangerously stormy conditions.

STAY FOUND

Prevention is the way to go in the wild. That means planning hiking routes carefully, carrying detailed maps, and knowing how to operate your compass or handheld GPS unit. Other precautions include leaving a detailed itinerary with family or park rangers. If you do get lost, those you've notified in town will know when and where to start looking. It's also smart to carry a whistle.

HYPOTHERMIA

Hypothermia, the lowering of the body's core temperature, is an ever-present threat in Alaska's wilderness. Wear warm clothing (in layers) when the weather is cool and/or wet; this includes a good wind- and waterproof parka or shell, warm head- and hand gear, and waterproof or water-resistant boots. Eat regularly to maintain energy and drink enough liquids to stay properly hydrated.

The onset of hypothermia can be recognized by the following symptoms: shivering, accelerated heartbeat, and goose bumps; this may be followed by clumsiness, slurred speech, disorientation, and unconsciousness. In the extreme, it can result in death. If you notice any of these symptoms in yourself or your traveling companion, stop, add layers of clothing, light a fire or camp stove, and warm yourself; a cup of tea or any hot fluid also helps. Avoid alcohol, which only speeds hypothermia and impairs judgment. If your clothes are wet, change immediately. Be sure to put on a warm hat (most of the body's heat is lost through the head) and gloves. If there are only two of you, stay together: a person with hypothermia should never be left alone.

WATER SAFETY

Alaska's waters, even its wildest rivers and lakes, often carry *Giardia*, locally called beaver fever, a parasite that can cause diarrhea and sap your strength. Boil your drinking water in the backcountry or treat it with iodine tablets.

Utter bliss: fishing pole, rubber boots, and a quiet morning.

In fact, Alaska's best-known salmon stream, the **Kenai River,** parallels the Sterling Highway. But in most of the state, prime fishing waters can be reached only by boat or air. Not surprisingly, hundreds of fishing charters and dozens of sportfishing lodges operate statewide, attracting anglers from around the world. **Southwest Alaska,** in particular, is known for its fine salmon, trout, and char fishing, but many of its best spots are remote and expensive to reach.

SOUTHEAST This huge coastal region is renowned for its outstanding sportfishing for salmon, rockfish, and halibut. Charters operate out of all main ports and the action is frequently so good that catching a limit is almost a given. Splendid scenery is guaranteed. Streams in this region also offer fine angling for steelhead, cutthroat trout, rainbow trout, and Dolly Varden. The waters of **Prince of Wales Island** are especially popular among steelhead, salmon, and trout anglers, with the Karta and Thorne rivers among the favorites.

SOUTH CENTRAL & THE INTERIOR Alaska lives up to its reputation for angling excellence in South Central. From the hub of Anchorage, the Seward and Sterling highways provide access to the world-famous spots on the Kenai Peninsula. Anglers seeking rainbow trout, Dolly Varden, and salmon will do no better than the **Kenai River.** This dream stream—tinted an opaque emerald from glacial runoff—serves up fine fishing from ice-out in spring to freeze-up in late fall. The **Russian River,** a tributary which joins the upper Kenai River near Cooper Landing, is a dashing mountain stream that runs crystal-clear—except when its chock-full of red salmon from mid-June through August. Other fine Kenai Peninsula streams include **Quartz Creek, Deep Creek,** and **Anchor River.** Many excellent trout and salmon guides are based in the Kenai River towns of Cooper Landing, Sterling, Soldotna, and Kenai.

Saltwater angling out of the ports of **Whittier, Seward,** and **Homer** is legendary for king, pink, and silver salmon as well as for rockfish, lingcod, and huge halibut. Charter operators are available in most ports, offering half-day and full-day fishing trips.

North of Anchorage, the Parks Highway courses through the **Mat-Su Valley,** a scenic piece of wilderness backed by Mt. McKinley and veined with fine streams. Five species of salmon, rainbow trout, Dolly Varden, grayling, northern pike, and lake trout are among the draws here. Some of the most popular Parks Highway streams include **Willow, Sheep, Montana,** and **Clear** creeks. Fishing guides based in Wasilla, Houston, Willow, and Talkeetna offer riverboat and fly-in trips. Remember that salmon runs are seasonal. Kings run late-May through mid-July, and silvers run from mid-July through August. And don't forget the lakes; scores of them brim with trout, landlocked salmon, arctic char, and grayling. Cast for them from canoes or float tubes on calm summer afternoons.

THE BUSH The most popular Bush sportfishing region is roadless **Southwest,** home of the richest salmon runs in the world. Along with huge schools of red salmon, kings, silvers, chums, and pinks, anglers will find trophy rainbow trout, Dolly Varden, arctic grayling, and arctic char. Many anglers fish with guides based out of remote fishing lodges located on rivers and lakes. Others do it themselves, arranging for bush planes to drop them off in headwater streams, then floating the river in rafts, fishing along the way until reaching a pre-arranged pick-up point.

Resources, Guides & Charters

When hiring a guide, ask what species are likely to be caught, catch limits, and any special equipment or clothing needs. Normally, all necessary fishing gear is provided and the guides will teach you the appropriate fishing techniques. In some cases, catch-and-release ethics may be emphasized. Prime time for saltwater fishing is July through mid-August; for river trips, mid-June through September.

Alaska Fishing Online. This Web resource provides listings of fishing charter services, air-taxi operators, and angling lodges around the state. Browse listings by region, and be sure to shop around for the best price. Also, ask plenty of questions to ensure you find the outfit best suited to your needs. 🌐 *www.alaskafishing.com.*

Alaska River Adventures. These Cooper Landing-based guides take small groups fishing throughout the region, with self-professed "well-seasoned old pros." ☎ *907/595–2000 or 888/836–9027* 🌐 *www.alaskariveradventures.com.*

Alaska Wildland Adventures. Just north of Anchorage, in Girdwood, these folks offer an all-women's fly-fishing adventure. ☎ *907/783–2928 or 800/334–8730* 🌐 *www.alaskawildland.com.*

Alaskan Fishing Adventures. Anglers are guided in several areas of the Kenai Peninsula, including Resurrection Bay, Cook Inlet, and the Kenai River, home of the famous Kenai king salmon that may weigh 90 pounds. Among the other species they catch are halibut, sockeye and silver salmon, and rainbow trout. Boats have a four-person limit on rivers, six-person limit on saltwater. ☎ *800/548–3474* 🌐 *www.alaskanfishing.com.*

Central Charter Booking Agency. In Homer, this company can arrange fishing trips in outer Kachemak Bay and Lower Cook Inlet, areas known for excellent halibut fishing. Boat sizes vary considerably; some have a six-person limit, whereas others can take up to 16 passengers. ☎ *907/235–7847 or 800/478–7847* 🌐 *www.centralcharter.com.*

The Fish House. Operating out of Seward since 1974, this booking agency represents dozens of Resurrection Bay and Kenai Peninsula fishing charters and can hook you up for half-day or full-day charters. ☎ *907/224–3674 or 800/257–7760* 🌐 *www.thefishhouse.net.*

Great Alaska Adventure Lodge. Fishing packages are run out of this Kenai River lodge. Trips with expert guides include fly-in fish camps, river floats, and saltwater charters. Stories are traded at happy hour in the lodge. ☎ *907/262–4515 in summer, 360/697–6454 in winter, 800/544–2261 year-round* 🌐 *www.greatalaska.com.*

ALASKA'S TOP FISH & THEIR SOURCES

SPECIES	COMMON NAME	WHERE FOUND
Arctic Char (F, S)	Char	*SC, SW, NW, I, A*
Arctic Grayling (F)	Grayling	*SE, SC, SW, NW, I, A*
Brook Trout (F)	Brookie	*SE*
Burbot (F)	Lingcod	*SC, I, SW, NW, A*
Chinook Salmon (F, S)	King	*SE, SC, SW, I*
Chum Salmon (F, S)	Dog	*SE, SC, SW, NW, I*
Coho Salmon (F, S)	Silver	*SE, SC, SW, NW, I*
Cutthroat Trout (F, S)	Cutt	*SE, SC*
Dolly Varden (F, S)	Dolly	*SE, SC, SW, NW, I, A*
Lake Trout (F)	Laker	*SC, SW, NW, I, A*
Northern Pike (F)	Northern	*SC, SW, NW, I*
Pacific Halibut (S)	'But	*SE, SC, SW, NW*
Pink Salmon (F, S)	Humpy	*SE, SC, SW, NW*
Smelt (F, S)	Hooligan	*SE, SC, SW, NW, I, A*
Rainbow Trout (F)	'Bow	*SE, SC, SW, I*
Sheefish (F)	Shee, Inconnu	*NW, I*
Sockeye Salmon (F, S)	Red	*SE, SC, SW, NW, I*
Steelhead (F, S)	Steelie	*SE, SC, SW*

(F) = *Freshwater* (S) = *Saltwater* (F, S) = *Freshwater and Saltwater* A = *Arctic*
SC = *South Central* I = *Interior* SE = *Southeast* NW = *Northwest* SW = *Southwest*

ENJOYING ALASKA'S WILDLIFE

Unique for its vast reserves of protected wilderness, Alaska is rich in a huge range of wildlife. Stunning natural beauty serves as a backdrop wherever you venture here. Alaska's 375 million acres support more than 800 species of animals including mammals, birds, and fish. The 105 different mammals range from whales to shrews (Alaska's shrews are the smallest of North America's land mammals, weighing ⅒ ounce). Some 475 species of birds range from hummingbirds to bald eagles, including species found nowhere else in North America. Migrant birds come here annually from every continent and many islands to take advantage of Alaska's rich breeding and rearing grounds in its wetlands, rivers, shores, and tundra. Among the 430 different kinds of fish—including five kinds of salmon—some weigh more than 400 pounds (halibut) whereas others more commonly weigh less than a pound (arctic grayling).

The largest numbers of animals can be seen during periods of migration. The state is strategically positioned for creatures that migrate vast distances. Some birds, for instance, fly from the southern tip of South America to nest and rear their young on sandbars in Alaska's wild rivers. Others travel from parts of Asia to thrive in Alaska's summers. The arctic tern comes here all the way from Antarctica. Sea mammals congregate in great numbers in the waters of Prince William Sound, the Panhandle, the Gulf of Alaska, and the Bering, Beaufort, and Chukchi seas. Hundreds of thousands of caribou move across the Arctic, including the Porcupine herd (named after the Porcupine River), which travels between Canada and Alaska. Anadromous fish by the millions swim up Alaska's rivers, returning unerringly to the waters where they were born.

Bears live in virtually every part of the state, and though they are often solitary, it is not unusual to see a sow with cubs. In some areas bears gather in large numbers to feed upon rich runs of salmon. Several world-class bear-viewing areas from Southeast to Southwest Alaska attract visitors. Moose abound in the wetter country of the Southeast, as well as in forested portions of South Central and Interior Alaska. Caribou wander over the tundra country of the Arctic, sub-Arctic, and South Central. The coastal mountains of Southeast and South Central harbor mountain goats, and the mountains of the South Central, Interior, and Arctic regions are home to white Dall sheep. Wolves and lynx, though more rarely seen, live in many parts of the Southeast, South Central, Interior, and Arctic regions, and if you're lucky, a wolf may dash across the road in front of you, or a smaller mammal, such as a red fox or snowshoe hare, may watch you when you're rafting or even when you're traveling on wheels.

Strategies for Spotting Wildlife

Know what you're looking for. Have some idea of the habitat the wildlife you seek thrives in. Season and time of day are critical. Many animals are nocturnal and best viewed during twilight, which during summer in Alaska's northern regions can last all night. In the winter, large creatures such as moose and caribou can be spotted from far away, as their dark bodies stand out against the snow. It is also possible to track animals after a fresh snowfall. You may have only a few hours of sunlight each day during which you can look for wildlife in winter, and in northern Alaska, there won't be any direct sunlight at all during the winter months.

Be careful. Keep a good distance, especially with animals that can be dangerous. Whether you're on foot or in a vehicle, don't get too close. A pair of good binoculars or a spotting scope is well worth the expense and extra weight. Don't get too close to or touch wildlife (and, if you're traveling with pets, keep them leashed). **Move slowly,** stop often, look, and listen. The exception is when you see a bear; let the animal know you're there with noise. Avoid startling an animal and risking a dangerous confrontation, especially with a sow bear with cubs or a cow moose with calf.

Keep your hat on if you are in territory where arctic terns, gulls, or pomarine jaegers nest, often around open alpine or tundra lakes and tarns. These species are highly protective of their nests and young and are skillful dive-bombers. Occasionally, they connect with human heads, and the results can be painful.

Be prepared to wait; patience often pays off. And if you're an enthusiastic birder or animal watcher, **be prepared to hike over some rough terrain** to reach the best viewing vantage. **Respect and protect** both the animal you're watching and its habitat. Don't chase or harass the animals. The willful act of harassing an animal is punishable in Alaska by a $1,000 fine. This includes flushing birds from their nests and purposely frightening animals with loud noises.

Don't disturb or surprise the animals, which also applies to birds' eggs, the young, the nests, and such habitats as beaver dams. It's best to let the animal discover your presence quietly, if at all, by keeping still or moving slowly (except when viewing bears or moose). If you accidentally disturb an animal, limit your viewing time and leave as quietly as possible. **Don't use a tape recorder or any device** to call a bird or to attract other animals if you're in bear country, as you might call a hungry bear. And **don't feed animals,** as any creature that comes to depend on humans for food almost always comes to a sorry end. Both state and federal laws prohibit the feeding of wild animals.

Top Regions & Experiences

Even those traveling by car in Alaska have abundant opportunity to spot wildlife. For those traveling by boat, the **Alaska Marine Highway,** the route plied by Alaska's state ferries, passes through waters rich with fish, sea mammals, and birds. Throughout the Southeast, ferries often provide sightings of whales, porpoises, and sea otters, and virtually always of bald eagles. In **Kenai Fjords National Park,** tour boats enable you to view sea mammals and seabirds. Smaller boats and touring vessels are found in such places as **Glacier Bay National Park & Preserve,** an especially good place to spot humpback whales, puffins, seals, shorebirds, and perhaps a black or brown bear. **Denali National Park & Preserve** is known worldwide for its wildlife; you are likely to see grizzlies, moose, Dall sheep, caribou, foxes, golden eagles, and even wolves. The **Alaska Chilkat Bald Eagle Preserve** hosts the world's largest gathering of bald eagles each fall and winter. And Dall sheep that inhabit **Chugach State Park** can often be seen along the Seward Highway south of Anchorage.

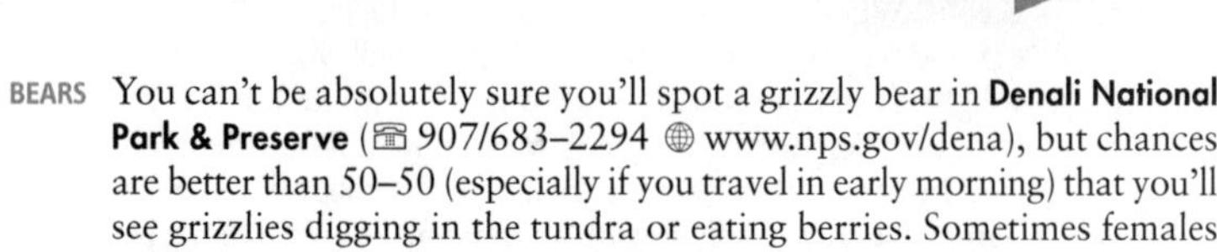

For a more in-depth look at bears, head to
Welcome to Bear Country in Chapter 7

BEARS You can't be absolutely sure you'll spot a grizzly bear in **Denali National Park & Preserve** (☎ 907/683–2294 🌐 www.nps.gov/dena), but chances are better than 50–50 (especially if you travel in early morning) that you'll see grizzlies digging in the tundra or eating berries. Sometimes females even nurse their cubs within sight of the park road. Talk with the staff at the visitor center near the park entrance when you arrive.

Katmai National Park (☎ 907/246–3305 🌐 www.nps.gov/katm), on the Alaska Peninsula, has an abundance of bears, on average more than one brown bear per square mile, among the highest densities of any region in North America. In July, when the salmon are running up Brooks River, bears concentrate around Brooks River Falls, resulting in a great view of these animals as they fish, and the spectacle of hundreds of salmon leaping the falls.

Kodiak National Wildlife Refuge (☎ 907/487–2600 or 888/408–3514 🌐 kodiak.fws.gov), on Kodiak Island, is an excellent place to see brown bears, particularly along salmon-spawning streams.

The **McNeil River State Game Sanctuary,** on the Alaska Peninsula, hosts the world's largest gathering of brown bears (as many as 70 have been counted at one time at McNeil Falls) and thus affords unsurpassed photographic opportunities. Peak season, when the local salmon are running, is early June through mid-August. Much-sought-after reservations are available by a lottery conducted in March by the **Alaska Department of Fish and Game** (☎ 907/267–2182 🌐 www.wc.adfg.state.ak.us/mcneil/index.cfm).

At **Pack Creek,** on Admiralty Island in Southeast, you'll see brown bears fishing for spawning salmon—pink, chum, and silver. To get here, you can fly (air charter) or take a boat from Juneau. If you time your visit to coincide with the salmon runs in July and August, you will almost surely see bald eagles. Permits are required to visit during the peak bear-viewing period; contact **Admiralty Island National Monument** (☎ 907/586–8790 🌐 www.fs.fed.us/r10/tongass/districts/admiralty/packweb/packhome.html).

The **Silver Salmon Creek Lodge** (☎ 888/872–5666 🌐 www.silversalmoncreek.com) conducts a bear-viewing program along the shores of western Cook Inlet, near Lake Clark National Park, with lodging, meals, and guide services for both bear viewing and sportfishing.

BIRDS If you come on your own, try the following sure and easily accessed bets for bird spotting. In **Anchorage,** walk around Potter Marsh or Westchester Lagoon or along the Tony Knowles Coastal Trail and keep your eye out for shorebirds, waterfowl, and the occasional bald eagle. Songbird enthusiasts are likely to see many species in town or neighboring Chugach State Park. The **Anchorage Audubon Society** (☎ 907/338–2473

Continued on page 77

KEEPERS OF THE DEEP:
A LOOK AT ALASKA'S WHALES

It's unforgettable: a massive, barnacle-encrusted humpback breaches skyward from the placid waters of an Alaskan inlet, shattering the silence with a thundering display of grace, power, and beauty. Welcome to Alaska's coastline.

(top) A breaching humpback (left) An Orca whale

Alaska's cold, nutrient-rich waters offer a bounty of marine life that's matched by few regions on earth. Eight species of whales frequent the state's near-shore waters, some migrating thousands of miles each year to partake of Alaska's marine buffet. The state's most famous cetaceans (the scientific classification of marine mammals that includes whales, dolphins, and porpoises) are the humpback whale, the gray whale, and the Orca (a.k.a. the killer whale).

Best Regions to View Whales

Whales can be viewed throughout the world; after all, they are migratory animals. But thanks to its pristine environment, diversity of cetacean species, and jaw-dropping beauty, Alaska is perhaps the planet's best whale-watching locale.

From April through October, humpbacks visit many of Alaska's coastal regions, including the Bering Sea, the Aleutian Islands, and Prince William Sound. The **Inside Passage,** though, is the best place to see them: it's home to a migratory population of up to 600 humpbacks. Good bets for whale-viewing include taking a trip on the **Alaska Marine Highway,** spending time in **Glacier Bay National Park,** or taking a day cruise out of any of Southeast's main towns. While most humpbacks return to

Mutually curious!

Hawaiian waters in the winter, some spend the whole year in Southeast Alaska.

Gray whales favor the coastal waters of the Pacific, which terminate in the Bering Sea. Their healthy population—some studies estimate that 30,000 gray whales populate the west coast of North America—make

THE HUMPBACK: Musical, Breaching Giant

Humpbacks' flukes allow them to breach so effectively that they can propel two-thirds of their massive bodies out of the water.

Known for their spectacular breaching and unique whale songs, humpbacks are captivating. Most spend their winters in the balmy waters off the Hawaiian Islands, where females, or sows, give birth. Come springtime, humpbacks set off on a 3,000-mile swim to their Alaskan feeding grounds.

Southeast Alaska is home to one of the world's only groups of bubble-net feeding humpbacks. Bubble-netting is a cooperative hunting technique in which one humpback circles below a school of baitfish while exhaling a "net" of bubbles, causing the fish to gather. Other humpbacks then feed at will from the deliciously dense group of fish.

The Song of the Humpback

All whale species communicate sonically, but the humpback is the most musical. During mating season, males emit haunting, songlike calls that can last for up to 30 minutes at a time. Most scientists attribute the songs to flirtatious, territorial, or competitive behaviors.

QUICK FACTS:

Scientific name: *Megaptera novaeangliae*

Length: Up to 50 feet

Weight: Up to 90,000 pounds (45 tons)

Coloring: Dark blue to black, with barnacles and knobby, lighter-colored flippers

Life span: 30 to 40 years

Reproduction: One calf every 2 to 3 years; calves are generally 12 feet long at birth, weighing up to 2,000 pounds (1 ton)

them relatively easy to spot in the spring and early summer months, especially around **Sitka** and **Kodiak Island** and south of the **Kenai Peninsula,** where numerous whale-watching cruises depart from Seward into **Resurrection Bay.**

Orcas populate nearly all of Alaska's coastal regions. They're most commonly viewed in the **Inside Passage** and **Prince William Sound,** where they reside year-round. A jaunt on the Alaska Marine Highway is one option, but so is a kayaking or day-cruising trip out of **Whittier** to Prince William Sound.

When embarking on a whale-watching excursion, don't forget rain gear, a camera, and binoculars!

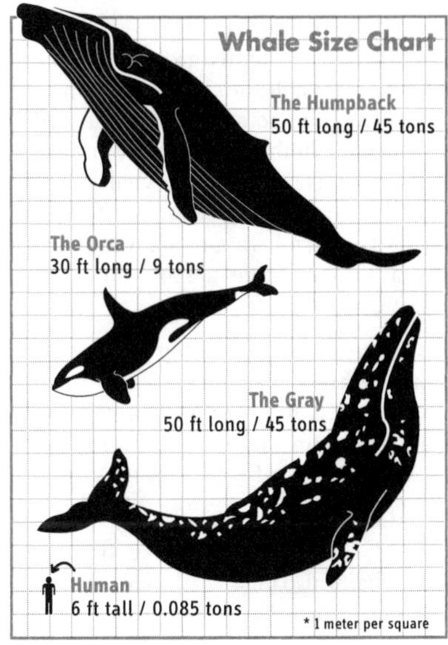

THE GRAY WHALE: Migrating Leviathan

Though the average lifespan of a gray whale is 50 years, one individual was reported to reach 77 years of age—a real old-timer.

While frequenting Alaska during the long days of summer, gray whales tend stay close to the coastline. They endure the longest migration of any mammal on earth—some travel 14,000 mi each way between Alaska's Bering Sea and their mating grounds in sunny Baja California.

Gray whales are bottom-feeders that stir up sediment on sea floor, then use their baleen—a comblike collection of long, stiff hairs inside their mouths—to filter out sediment and trap small crustaceans and tube worms.

Their predilection for near-shore regions, coupled with their easygoing demeanor—some "friendly" gray whales have even been known to approach small tour boats—cements their spot on the short list of Alaska's favorite cetacean celebrities. (Gray whales aren't always in such amicable spirits: whalers dubbed mother gray whales "devilfish" for the fierce manner in which they protected their young.)

QUICK FACTS:

Scientific name: *Eschrichtius robustus*

Length: Up to 50 feet

Weight: Up to 90,000 pounds (45 tons)

Coloring: Gray and white, usually splotched with lighter growths and barnacles

Life span: 50 years

Reproduction: One calf every 2 years; calves are generally 15 feet long at birth, weighing up to 1,500 pounds (3/4 ton)

An Age-Old Connection

Nearly every major native group in Alaska has relied on whales for some portion of its diet. The Inupiaq and Yup'ik counted on whales for blubber, oil, meat, and intestines to survive. Aleuts used whale bones to build their semisubterranean homes. Even the Tlingit, for whom food was perennially abundant, considered a beached whale a bounty.

Subsistence whaling lives on in Alaska: although gray-whale hunting was banned in 1996, the Eskimo Whaling Commission permits the state's native populations to harvest 50 bowhead whales every year.

Other Alaskan whale species:
Bowhead, northern right, minke, fin, and beluga whales also inhabit Alaskan waters.

BARNACLES These ragged squatters of the sea live on several species of whales, including humpbacks and gray whales. They're conspicuously absent from smaller marine mammals, such as Orcas, dolphins, and porpoises. The reason? Speed. Scientists theorize that barnacles are only able to colonize the slowest-swimming cetacean species, leaving the faster swimmers free from their unwanted drag.

THE ORCA: Conspicuous, Curious Cetacean

Why the name killer whale? Perhaps for this animal's skilled and fearsome hunting techniques, which are sometimes used on other, often larger, cetaceans.

Perhaps the most recognizable of all the region's marine mammals, Orcas (also called killer whales) are playful, inquisitive, and intelligent whales that reside in Alaskan waters year-round. Orcas travel in multigenerational family groups known as pods, which practice cooperative hunting techniques.

Orcas are smaller than grays and humpbacks, and their 17-month gestation period is the longest of any cetacean. They are identified by their white-and-black markings, as well as by the knifelike shape of their dorsal fins, which, in the case of mature males, can reach 6 feet in height.

Pods generally adhere to one of three common classifications: **residents**, which occupy inshore waters and feed primarily on fish; **transients**, which occupy larger ranges and hunt sea lions, squid, sharks, fish, and whales; and **offshores**, about which little is known.

QUICK FACTS:

Scientific name: *Orcinus orca*

Length: Up to 30 feet

Weight: Up to 18,000 pounds (9 tons)

Coloring: Smooth, shiny black skin with white eye patches and chin and white belly markings

Life span: 30 to 50 years

Reproduction: One calf every 3 to 5 years; calves are generally 6 feet long at birth, weighing up to 400 pounds (0.2 ton)

www.anchorageaudubon.org) has a bird-report recording and offers various trips, such as the Owl Prowl and Hawk Watch.

In **Juneau,** visit the Mendenhall Wetlands State Game Refuge, next to the airport, for ducks, geese, and swans (there are trails and interpretive signs). In **Fairbanks,** head for the Creamer's Field Migratory Waterfowl Refuge on College Road. Here, if you're lucky, you might see sandhill cranes in summer and spectacular shows of ducks and geese in spring.

Great crowds of bald eagles visit the Chilkat River, near **Haines** in Southeast Alaska, each November and December. In the summer, rafting on almost any Alaskan river brings the near certainty of sighting nesting shorebirds, arctic terns, and merganser mothers trailed by chicks. Approximately 200 species of birds have been sighted on the **Pribilof Islands,** but you will almost certainly need to be part of a guided tour to get there.

The folks at **Alaska Birding & Wildlife** (877/424–5637 www.alaskabirding.com) can take you to St. Paul Island to see the huge range of birds and get to know local Aleut culture and customs.

Alaska Discovery (907/780–6226 or 800/586–1911 www.akdiscovery.com) offers trips to Pack Creek, including a floatplane trip, sea-kayaking, and bear viewing.

With **Mariah Tours** (877/777–2805 www.alaskaheritagetours.com), the Kenai Fjords Nation Park comes to life on tailor-made birding and photography boat tours.

Ouzel Expeditions (800/825–8196 www.ouzel.com) offers seven-day birding float trips in Southwest Alaska and the Arctic National Wildlife Refuge. Trips are in remote fly-in locations; camping and floating quietly along rivers provides wonderful birding opportunities. Southwest birding trips begin in Anchorage; trips in Arctic National Wildlife Refuge begin in Fairbanks.

The Web site of the **University of Alaska Fairbanks** (www.uaf.edu/museum/bird/products/checklist.pdf) has a checklist of Alaska's 475 bird species.

★ The owners of **Wilderness Birding Adventures** (907/694–7442 www.wildernessbirding.com) are both experienced river runners and expert birders. Among their trips is a rafting, hiking, and birding expedition through one of the world's last great wilderness areas, the Arctic National Wildlife Refuge.

CARIBOU The migrations of caribou across Alaska's Arctic regions are wonderful to watch, but they are not always easy to time because of annual variations in weather and routes that the herds follow. The U.S. Fish and Wildlife Service and Alaska Department of Fish and Game will have the best guess as to where you should be and when. Or you can settle for seeing a few caribou in places such as Denali National Park & Preserve.

MARINE ANIMALS **■ TIP→ Skip ahead to the next section in this chapter for in-depth information about whale-watching cruises.**

At **Round Island,** outside Dillingham in the Southwest, bull walruses by the thousands haul out during the summer. Part of the Walrus Islands State Game Sanctuary, Round Island can be visited by permit only. For details, contact the **Alaska Department of Fish and Game** (☎ 907/842–2334 🌐 www.wildlife.alaska.gov/index.cfm?adfg=refuge.rnd_is). Access is by floatplane or, more commonly, by boat. Expect rain, winds, and the possibility of being weathered in. Rubber boots are essential, as are a four-season tent, high-quality rain gear, and plenty of food.

It's easier, but expensive (more than $1,000 for travel and tour) to visit the remote **Pribilof Islands,** where about 80% of the world's northern fur seals and 200 species of birds can be seen, but you may also encounter fog and Bering Sea storms. Tours to the Pribilofs leave from Anchorage. Contact the **Alaska Maritime National Wildlife Refuge** (☎ 907/235–6546 or 907/235–6961 🌐 www.r7.fws.gov/nwr/akmar/index.htm) for information about wildlife viewing.

WHALE-WATCHING CRUISES

Fodor's Choice ★ A close encounter with whales in their natural environment can be a thrilling experience. Hearing the resonant whoosh of a whale exhaling and witnessing such acrobatics as "spy-hopping" (a whale poking its head straight out of the water for a look around), breaching, and skimming, you can't help but feel amazed and humbled by their awesome presence.

It's possible to see migrating whales along much of Alaska's coast from March through September: from the Southeast region's Inside Passage to South Central's Prince William Sound, Kodiak Archipelago, and Kenai Fjords National Park, and then north through the Bering, Chukchi, and Beaufort seas in Arctic waters. The whales most commonly seen on whale-watching trips are Orcas (or killer whales) and humpbacks.

Whale-watching is not the average spectator sport. It's more like a seagoing game of hide-and-seek. Whales are unpredictable, so be prepared to wait and watch patiently, scanning the water for signs. Sometimes the whales can seem elusive; other times they might rub up against the boat. Also unpredictable are the weather and sea conditions. Bring along a jacket or fleece outer wear and rain gear to keep from getting wet and chilled, and consider using Dramamine or scopolamine patches if you're prone to seasickness.

Most cruises travel in or through waters that attract several species, although some focus on a particular type of whale. ■ **TIP→ Ask when the best time to take a specific trip is; the whale-sighting record is likely better during some months than others.** You have to weigh the pros and cons of traveling on small versus large boats. Make sure you know what kind of boat is used for the trip you are considering. A trip with 15 people is certain to be quite different from one with 150. Larger boats can handle stormy seas much better than smaller boats and offer much better indoor accommodations when the weather turns nasty. Smaller boats will appeal to those who want to steer clear of crowds and those who like to feel closer to the surrounding seascape. More flexible itineraries are another benefit of small boats.

Resources & Guides

Hop aboard the **Alaska Marine Highway** (☎ 800/642–0066 🌐 www.ferryalaska.com) and enjoy one of Alaska's greatest means of travel: its ferry system, which plies the waters of the Inside Passage and South Central all the way to the far reaches of the southwestern chain.

Fodor'sChoice ★ Part of the native-owned Alaska Heritage Tours, **Kenai Fjords Tours** (☎ 907/265–4501 or 877/777–2805 🌐 www.kenaifjords.com) will take you to explore Resurrection Bay and Kenai Fjords National Park. They range from three-hour natural-history tours to five-hour gray-whale-watching tours out of Seward.

Mariah Tours (☎ 907/777–2805 or 877/777–2805 🌐 www.alaskaheritagetours.com) offers small-boat trips out of Seward for summertime whale-watching and glacier tours in Kenai Fjords National Park. Besides orcas and humpback whales, you're likely to see bald eagles, sea otters, sea lions, seals, and birds.

Juneau-based **Orca Enterprises (with Captain Larry)** (☎ 907/789–6801 or 888/733–6722 🌐 www.orcaenterprises.com) offers whale-watching tours via jet boats designed for comfort and speed. The operator boasts a whale-sighting success rate of 99.9% between May 1 and October 15. Humpbacks and Orcas are most frequently seen.

Sailing out of Whittier into Prince William Sound since 1989, **Sound Eco Adventures** (☎ 888/471–2312 🌐 www.soundecoadventure.com) takes only six guests at a time aboard 30-foot boats. It's a convenient hour-long drive south of Anchorage; expect to see everything from harbor seals to humpbacks.

Step aboard the **M/V TAZ** (☎ 907/697–2726 or 888/698–2726 🌐 www.gustavus.com/taz/tours.html) and check out Glacier Bay, Icy Straits, and Point Adolphus for awesome views of humpback whales and many other marine mammals. All tours out of Gustavus include binoculars, snacks, and hot beverages. Half-day tours and custom charters accommodating up to 23 passengers are on offer.

Cruising in Alaska

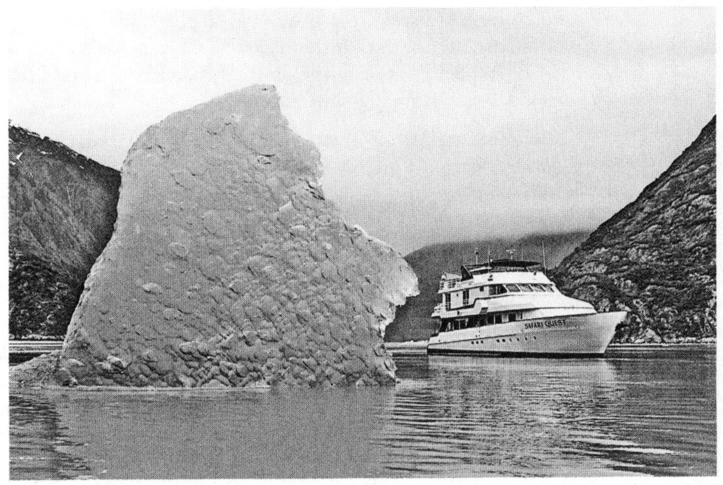

WORD OF MOUTH

"I just got back from an Inside Passage cruise. Bring layers. You will need a good rain/wind jacket and a long-sleeved sweater."

–IslandGrl

"If you decide to go on a cruise ship, consider spending the extra money for an outside cabin, preferably one with a deck."

–Orcas

www.fodors.com/forums

ALASKA, IT WOULD SEEM, was made for cruising. Alaska is one of cruising's showcase destinations, and there are a wide variety of options available. The traditional route to the state is by sea, through a 1,000-mi-long protected waterway known as the Inside Passage. From Vancouver, B. C., in the south to Skagway in the north, it winds around islands large and small, past glacier-carved fjords and hemlock-blanketed mountains. This great land is home to breaching whales, nesting eagles, spawning salmon, and calving glaciers. The towns here can be reached only by air or sea; there are no roads between them. Juneau, in fact, is the only water-locked state capital in the United States. Beyond the Inside Passage, the Gulf of Alaska leads to Prince William Sound—famous for its marine life and more fjords and glaciers—and Anchorage, Alaska's largest city.

Itineraries give passengers more choices than ever before—from traditional loop cruises of the Inside Passage, round-trips from Vancouver or Seattle, to one-way Inside Passage–Gulf of Alaska cruises. A number of smaller boats sail only in the Inside Passage and Prince William Sound, away from big-ship traffic.

For more detailed information on cruising in Alaska, check out *Fodor's Alaska Ports of Call 2007.*

CHOOSING YOUR CRUISE

Types of Ships

The type of ship you choose is the most important factor in your Alaska cruise vacation because it will determine how you see Alaska. Ocean liners sail farther from land and visit major ports of call such as Juneau, Skagway, and Ketchikan. Small ships spend much of their time hugging the coastline, looking for wildlife, waterfalls, and other natural and scenic attractions. For more independent types, there's no better way to see Alaska than aboard the ferries of the Alaska Marine Highway System, which allow you to travel with your car or RV and explore at your own pace.

Cruise Ships

Alaska's ocean-liner fleet represents the very best that today's cruise industry has to offer. Nearly all the ships were built within the last two decades and have atrium lobbies, state-of-the-art health spas, high-tech show lounges, elaborate dining rooms, and a variety of alternative restaurants. By night they come alive with Vegas-style revues, pulsating discos, and somewhat more sedate cabaret or comedy acts. Most of the latest liners have cabins with verandas—a great bonus in Alaska for watching the scenery go by from the privacy of your own stateroom. The newest cruise ships are lined with glass throughout their corridors and public rooms, so you're never far from the sea or a great view.

Small Ships

Unlike ocean liners, the smaller vessels cruising in Alaska are designed to reach into the most remote corners of the world. Shallow drafts

CLOSE UP

The Alaska Marine Highway System

IF YOU'RE LOOKING FOR REAL ALASKAN ADVENTURE, travel the ferries of the Alaska Marine Highway System. With 11 vessels serving 32 ports of call in Alaska as well as Bellingham, Washington, and Prince Rupert, British Columbia, Alaskan ferries are a scenic option for getting to and around Alaska. They're a great way to take in the landscape, maybe see a whale or two, and meet local people.

In addition to affordable fares, the ferry system also affords freedom of movement. Unlike cruise ships, which follow a set itinerary, ferries come and go frequently. You can get on and off whenever you wish. When planning your trip, ask about special onboard programming. Forest Service naturalists ride the larger ferries in summer, providing a running commentary on sights.

The ferries are less than luxurious but comfortable enough. Each has a glass-lined observation lounge and a gift shop, and all but the smallest ferries have a bar. Onboard cafeterias serve inexpensive meals. Most of the simple, serviceable cabins have private washrooms, and camping in the solarium is an option. Cabins fill up almost instantly for cruises in summer; booking in advance is essential if you're traveling with a vehicle.

Ferry travel is generally slow: maximum speed is 16.5 knots, compared with 21 knots or better for the typical large cruise ship. However, of the 11 vessels in the fleet, two fast ferries, the MV *Fairweather* and MV *Chenega*, motor at twice that speed.

A number of tour operators sell packages that include shipboard accommodations. One of the most established of these is **Knightly Tours** (☎ 206/938-8567 or 800/426-2123 🌐 www.knightlytours.com).

Contact: ☎ *907/465-3941 or 800/642-0066* 🌐 *www.ferryalaska.com.*

Fares & Schedules: Make reservations for ferry travel by calling the Alaska Marine Highway System. They'll mail you the tickets, or you can pick them up from the ferry office at your starting point. Call to request a copy of its printed schedule, or download it from the Web site. Online reservations are also available.

CUTTING COSTS

The **AlaskaPass** allows unlimited travel on bus, ferry, and rail lines in Alaska, along with bus and ferry travel in British Columbia, and the Yukon. Passes are available for 15 consecutive days of travel ($829), as well as for 8 days of travel in a 12-day period ($699) or 12 days of travel in a 21-day period ($849). There is a $75 booking fee. Most travelers book their entire itinerary in advance; if you don't have a car, there is usually room on ferries for those without prebookings.

Contact: ☎ *206/463-6550 or 800/248-7598* 🌐 *www.alaskapass.com.*

allow them to navigate up rivers, close to coastlines, and into shallow coves. Motorized rubber landing craft, known as Zodiacs, are usually kept on board, making it possible for passengers to go ashore almost anywhere. Alaska, not casinos or spa treatments, is the focus of these cruises. Lectures and talks—conducted daily by naturalists, Native Alaskans, and other experts in the Great Land's natural history and native cultures—are the norm. But in comparison with those on ocean liners, cabins on expedition ships can be quite small and are often less luxurious than cabins on large ships. Small ships usually have just one dining option, and entertainment is usually limited to lectures and videos, but passengers enjoy greater opportunities to see scenery and wildlife, and a better chance to get to know their fellow passengers.

Ferries

The state ferry system is known as the Alaska Marine Highway, because its vessels carry vehicles as well as passengers. Each ferry has a car deck that can accommodate every-size vehicle from the family car to a Winnebago. You can take your vehicle ashore, drive around, even live in it, and then transport it with you to the next port of call. From Skagway or Haines (the only Inside Passage towns connected to a road system), you can drive farther north to Fairbanks and Anchorage by way of the Alaska Highway. Each ferry also has a main, or "weather," deck to accommodate passengers, and onboard camping is allowed year-round.

Itineraries

You'll want to give some consideration to your ship's Alaskan itinerary when choosing your cruise. The length of the cruise will determine the variety and number of ports you visit, but so will the type of itinerary and the point of departure. **Loop cruises** start and end at the same point and usually explore ports close to one another; **one-way cruises** start at one point and end at another and range farther afield.

Cruise ships typically follow one of two itineraries: round-trip Inside Passage loops starting and finishing in Vancouver, B.C., or Seattle, and one-way Inside Passage–Gulf of Alaska cruises sailing between Vancouver or Seattle and Anchorage. Both itineraries are usually seven days, though some lines offer longer trips. A few lines also schedule one-way or round-trip sailings from San Francisco or Los Angeles. Small ships typically sail within Alaska, setting out from Juneau, Sitka, or other Alaskan ports.

Whether you sail through the Inside Passage or along it will depend on the size of your vessel. Smaller ships can navigate narrow channels, straits, and fjords. Larger vessels must sail farther from land, so don't expect to see much wildlife from the deck of a megaship.

Cruise Tours

Most cruise lines give you the option of an independent, hosted, or fully escorted land tour before or after your cruise. Independent tours allow maximum flexibility. You have a preplanned itinerary with confirmed hotel reservations and transportation arrangements, but you're free to follow your interests and whims in each town. A hosted tour is similar, but tour-company representatives are available along the route to help out should you need assistance. On fully escorted tours, you travel with a group, led by a tour director. Activities are preplanned (and typically prepaid), so you have a good idea of how much your trip will cost (not counting incidentals) before you depart. Most cruise-tour itineraries include a ride aboard the Alaska Railroad in a glass-dome railcar.

Independent travel by rental car or RV before or after the cruise segment is another popular option. Generally passengers will plan to begin or end their cruise in Anchorage, the most practical port city to use as a base for exploring the state. Almost any type of car or recreational vehicle, from a small, two-person RV to a large, luxurious motor home, can be rented.

Shore Excursions

Shore excursions arranged by the cruise line are a convenient way to see the sights, although you pay extra for this convenience. Before your cruise, you'll receive a booklet describing the shore excursions your cruise line offers. A few lines let you book excursions in advance; all sell them on board during the cruise. If you cancel your excursion, you may incur penalties, the amount varying with the number of days remaining until the tour. Because these trips are specialized, many have limited capacity and are sold on a first-come, first-served basis.

Among the many options available, some are "musts." At least once during your cruise, try flightseeing—it's the only way you'll grasp the grandeur of the land. Go to an evening salmon feast, where you can savor freshly caught fish cooked over an open fire. And experience an outdoor adventure—you don't have to be athletically inclined to raft down a river or paddle a sea kayak along the coastline.

When to Go

Cruise season runs from mid-May to late September; the most popular sailing dates are from late June through August. May and June are the driest months to cruise. Daytime temperatures along the cruise routes in May, June, and September are in the 50s and 60s. July and August averages are in the 60s and 70s, with occasional days in the 80s. Bargains can be found both early and late in the season. Cruising in the low seasons provides plenty of advantages besides discounted fares. Availability of ships and particular cabins is greater in the low and shoulder seasons, and the ports are almost completely free of tourists.

November is the best month for off-season ferry travel, after the stormy month of October and while

SEASONAL CHANGES

Keep in mind that the landcape along the Inside Passage changes dramatically over the course of the summer. You'll see snowcapped mountains and dramatic waterfalls that are made by the melting process cascading down the cliff faces in May and June, but by July and August, most of the snow and waterfalls will be gone.

it's still relatively warm on the Inside Passage (temperatures will average about 40°F). It's a good month for wildlife watching as well. Some animals show themselves in greater numbers during November. In particular, humpback whales are abundant off Sitka, and bald eagles congregate by the thousands near Haines.

Cruise Costs

Cruise costs can vary enormously. If you shop around and book early, you'll undoubtedly pay less. Your cruise fare typically includes accommodation and all onboard meals, snacks, and activities. It does not normally include airfare to the port city, shore excursions, tips, alcoholic drinks, or spa treatments. Only the most expensive Alaska cruises include airfare. Virtually all lines offer air add-ons, which may or may not be less expensive than the latest discounted fare from the airlines.

> **GO TO THE EXPERTS**
>
> Although most other kinds of travel are booked over the internet nowadays, for cruises, booking with a travel agent who specializes in cruises to Alaska is still your best bet. Agents have built strong relationships with the lines, and have a much better chance of getting you the cabin you want, and possibly even a free upgrade.

Shore excursions can be a substantial expense; the best in Alaska are not cheap. But if you skimp too much on your excursion budget, you may deprive yourself of an important part of the Alaska experience.

Tipping is another extra. At the end of the cruise, it's customary to tip your room steward, server, and the person who buses your table, though some lines include the tips in the fare. If tips are not included, expect to pay an average of $10 per day in tips. Each ship provides guidelines.

Single travelers should be aware that there are few single cabins on most ships; taking a double cabin for yourself can cost as much as twice the advertised per-person rates (which are based on two people sharing a room). Some cruise lines will find roommates of the same sex for singles so that each can travel at the regular per-person, double-occupancy rate.

BEFORE YOU GO

Once you've chosen your cruise and signed on to go, it's time to get ready. Preparations for a cruise may involve many distinct tasks, but none of them are difficult, especially if broken down into manageable steps. Most important, allow plenty of time to get ready so you don't get harried in the last couple of weeks.

Tickets & Vouchers

After you make the final payment to your travel agent, the cruise line will issue your cruise tickets and vouchers for airport–ship transfers. Depending on the airline, and whether you have purchased an air-sea package, you may receive your plane tickets or charter-flight vouchers at the

CLOSE UP

Health & Safety at Sea

FIRE SAFETY

The greatest danger facing cruise-ship passengers is fire. All cruise lines must meet international standards for fire safety, which require sprinkler systems, smoke detectors, and other safety features.

Once settled into your cabin, locate life vests and review posted emergency instructions. Make certain the ship's purser knows of any physical infirmities that may hamper a speedy exit from your cabin. If you're traveling with children, be sure that child-size life jackets are placed in your cabin. Within 24 hours of embarkation, you will be asked to attend a mandatory lifeboat drill. Only in the most extreme circumstances will you need to abandon ship—but it has happened.

HEALTH CARE

All large ships have an infirmary to deal with minor medical emergencies. For complicated medical conditions, the ship's medical team evacuates passengers to the nearest hospital ashore. You'll need supplementary insurance to cover these costs.

SEASICKNESS

Many first-time passengers are anxious about whether they'll be stricken by seasickness, but there is no way to tell until you actually sail. Modern vessels are equipped with stabilizers that eliminate much of the motion responsible for seasickness. On an Alaska cruise you will spend most of your time in very calm, sheltered waters, so, unless your cruise includes time in the open sea (say, between San Francisco and Vancouver), you may not even feel the ship's movement—particularly if your ship is a megaliner. You may feel slightly more movement on a small ship, but even on these ships, seasickness is not usually a problem as they keep, for the most part, to the shelter of the Inside Passage.

If you have a history of motion sickness, don't book an inside cabin. For the terminally seasick, it will begin to resemble a movable coffin in short order. If you do become seasick, you can use common drugs such as Dramamine and Bonine. Some people find anti-seasickness wristbands and the Transderm Scop "patch" helpful. You'll need a prescription from your physician for the patch and, while wearing it, be vigilant for possible side effects including blurred vision, dry mouth, and drowsiness.

NOROVIRUSES

Noroviruses are a group of related viruses that cause acute gastroenteritis in humans. Low-grade fever also occasionally occurs and vomiting is more common in children. Dehydration is the most common complication, especially among the young and elderly, and may require medical attention. Symptoms generally last 24 to 60 hours. To avoid illness, wash your hands thoroughly and often. The Centers for Disease Control (CDC) also advise the use of an alcohol-based hand sanitizer along with hand washing. If you become ill, the ship's doctor will probably quarantine you in your cabin.

same time; you may also receive vouchers for any shore excursions, although most cruise lines issue these aboard ship. Should your travel documents not arrive when promised, contact your travel agent or cruise line. If you book late, tickets may be delivered directly to the ship.

Passports & Visas

For Alaska cruises, whether they begin in the United States or in Canada, American and Canadian citizens require proof of citizenship. As of January 1, 2007, all American citizens will need to have a passport for all travel by air or sea to or from Canada. Permanent residents of the United States and Canada who are not citizens should also carry proof of permanent residence (their Green Card or Permanent Resident Card).

If you are a citizen of another country, you may be required to obtain visas in advance. Check with your travel agent or cruise line about specific requirements. If you do need a visa for your cruise, your travel agent should be able to help you obtain it, but there may be a charge for this service, in addition to the visa charge. Read your cruise documents carefully to see what documents you'll need for embarkation. You don't want to be turned away at the pier.

Immigration regulations require every passenger boarding a cruise ship from a U.S. port to provide additional personal data, such as your current mailing address and telephone number, to the cruise operator in advance of embarkation. Failure to provide this information required by the U.S. government may result in denial of boarding.

Disabilities & Accessibility

The latest cruise ships have been built with the needs of travelers with disabilities in mind, and many older ships have been modified to accommodate them. But several cruise lines operate older ships that have not been modified or do not have elevators: explorer-type vessels are not the easiest ships to navigate if you are in a wheelchair. The key areas to be concerned about are public rooms, outer decks, and, of course, your cabin.

If you need a specially equipped cabin, book as far in advance as possible and ask questions of your travel agent or a cruise-line representative. Specifically, ask how your cabin is configured and equipped. Is the entrance level or ramped? Are all doorways at least 30″ wide (wider if your wheelchair is not standard)? Are pathways to beds, closets, and bathrooms at least 36″ wide and unobstructed? In the bathroom, is there 42″ of clear space in front of the toilet and are there grab bars behind and on one side of it and in the bathtub and shower? Are elevators wide enough to accommodate wheelchairs?

The best cruise ship for passengers who use wheelchairs is one that ties up right at the dock at every port, at which time a ramp or even an elevator is always made available. Unfortunately, it's hard to ascertain this in advance, since a ship may tie up at the dock at one port on one voyage and, on the next, anchor in the harbor and have passengers transported to shore via tender. Ask your travel agent to find out which ships are capable of docking. If a tender is used, some ships will have crew members carry the wheelchair and passenger from the ship to the tender. Unfortunately, other ships will refuse to take wheelchairs on tenders, especially if the water is choppy.

What to Pack

Certain packing rules apply to all cruises. Always take along a sweater to counter cool evening ocean breezes or overactive air-conditioning. Rain gear is essential—many travelers who plan on indulging in some of the more active shore excursions pack a complete rain suit. Be prepared to dress in layers, since temperatures can vary considerably during the day. Make sure you take at least one pair of comfortable walking shoes for exploring port towns, and waterproof footwear will be useful as well. Ankle-high rubber boots are ideal for many shore trips.

Generally speaking, plan on one outfit for every two days of cruising, especially if your wardrobe contains many interchangeable pieces. Ships often have laundry facilities. Don't forget your toiletries and sundry items, but if you do, these are readily available in port shops or the ship's gift shop (though usually at a premium price). Cabin amenities typically include soap and often shampoo, conditioner, and other lotions and potions.

Outlets in cabin bathrooms are usually compatible with U.S.-purchased appliances. This may not be the case on older ships or those with European registries; call ahead if this is a concern for you. Most cabin bathrooms are equipped with low-voltage outlets for electric shavers, and many newer ships have built-in hair dryers.

Take an extra pair of eyeglasses or contact lenses in your carry-on luggage. If you use a prescription drug, pack enough to last the duration of the trip or have your doctor write a prescription using the drug's generic name, because brand names vary from country to country. Always carry medications in their original packaging to avoid problems with customs officials. Don't pack them in luggage that you plan to check, in case your bags go astray. Pack a list of the offices that supply refunds for lost or stolen traveler's checks. Make a copy of your passport and keep it separate from your actual passport. If you should lose your passport or it is stolen, having a copy of it can greatly facilitate replacement. Make copies, or write down the numbers, of your credit cards in case those should be lost or stolen.

Formal/Semiformal/Casual

Although no two cruises are quite the same, evening dress tends to fall into three categories.

Formal cruises celebrate the ceremony of cruising. Jackets and ties for men are the rule for dinner, tuxedos are not uncommon, and the dress code is observed faithfully throughout the evening.

Semiformal cruises are a bit more relaxed than their formal counterparts. Men wear jackets and ties most nights.

Casual cruises are the most popular. Shipboard dress and lifestyle are informal. Men wear sport shirts and slacks to dinner most nights and don jackets and ties only two or three evenings of a typical seven-day sailing.

In today's casual-Friday world, most cruise lines have reduced the focus on formal and semiformal dining and offer multiple dining options, including room service. However, it would be wise to ask the cruise line about its dining dress code so you know what to expect and what to pack.

ARRIVING & DEPARTING

If you have purchased an air-sea package, you will be met by a cruise-company representative when your plane lands at the port city and then shuttled directly to the ship in a bus or minivan. Some cruise lines arrange to transport luggage between airport and ship so passengers don't have to deal with baggage claim at the start of your cruise or with baggage check-in at the end. If you decide not to buy the air-sea package but still plan to fly, ask your travel agent if you can use the ship's transfer bus. Otherwise, you will have to take a taxi to the ship.

If you live close to the port of embarkation, bus transportation may be available. If you are part of a group that has booked a cruise together, this transportation may be part of your package. Another option for those who live close to their point of departure is to drive to the ship, an increasingly popular option. Major U.S. and Canadian cruise ports all have parking facilities.

Embarkation

Check-In

On arrival at the dock, you must check in before boarding your ship. An officer will collect or stamp your ticket, inspect or even retain your passport or other official identification, ask you to fill out a tourist card, check that you have the correct visas, and collect any unpaid port or departure tax.

Seating assignments for the dining room are often handed out at this time, too, although most cruise ships are now offering you the opportunity to dine when and with whom you like in any of several restaurants aboard. You may also register your credit card to open a shipboard account, or that may be done later at the purser's office.

PRE-BOARDING TIP

To expedite pre-boarding paperwork, some cruise lines have convenient forms on their Web sites. As long as you have your reservation number, you can provide the required immigration information, pre-reserve shore excursions, and even indicate any creature-comfort special requests. Be sure to print copies of any forms you fill out and bring them with you to the pier.

After this, you will be required to go through a security check and to pass your hand baggage through an X-ray inspection. These are the same machines in use at airports, so ask to have your photographic film inspected by hand.

Although it takes only 5 or 10 minutes per family to check in, lines are often long, so aim for off-peak hours. The worst time tends to be immediately after the ship begins boarding; the later it is, the less crowded.

For example, if boarding is from 2 to 4:30, lines are shorter after 3:30.

Boarding the Ship

Before you walk up the gangway, the ship's photographer will probably take your picture; there's no charge unless you buy the picture (usually $7 to $8). On board, stewards may serve welcome drinks in souvenir glasses—for which you're usually charged between $3 and $5.

You'll either be escorted to your cabin by a steward or, on a smaller ship, given your key—now usually a plastic card—by a ship's officer and directed to your cabin. Some elevators are unavailable to passengers during boarding, since they are used to transport luggage. You may arrive to find your luggage outside your cabin or just inside the door; if it hasn't arrived a half hour before sailing, contact the purser. If your luggage doesn't make it to the ship in time, the purser will have it flown to the next port.

> **FIRST THINGS FIRST**
>
> Do your plans for the cruise include booking shore excursions and indulging in spa treatments? The most popular tours sometimes sell out, and spas can be very busy during sea days, so if you haven't prebooked, your next stops should be the Shore Excursion Desk to book tours and the spa to make appointments.

Disembarkation

The last night of your cruise is full of business. On most ships you must place everything except your hand luggage outside your door, ready to be picked up by midnight or early in the morning. Color-coded tags, distributed to your cabin in a debarkation packet, should be placed on your luggage before the crew collects it. The color of your tag will determine when you leave the ship and help you retrieve your luggage on the pier.

Your shipboard bill is left in your room during the last day of a cruise or on the morning of your departure from the ship; to pay the bill (if you haven't already put it on your credit card) or to settle any questions, you must stand in line at the purser's office. Tips to the cabin steward and dining staff are distributed on the last night of the cruise or are automatically added to your onboard account. If you haven't already paid it by credit card or wish to dispute any charges on it, go to the purser immediately to settle or discuss your account. Some lines close down their computer files for the cruise by 9 AM or 10 AM to prepare for the next cruise, and may be unable to credit your account with any disputed charges, requiring you to contact your credit-card company or the cruise line later for a refund.

On the morning the cruise ends, in-room breakfast service may not be available because stewards are too busy, but you'll usually find breakfast being served in both the formal dining room and at the ship's buffet dining area. Most passengers clear out of their cabins as soon as possible, gather their hand luggage, and stake out a chair in one of the public lounges to await the ship's clearance through customs. Be patient—it takes a long time to unload and sort thousands of pieces of luggage.

Passengers are disembarked in groups according to color-coded luggage tags; those with the earliest flights get off first. If you have a tight connection, notify the purser before the last day, and he or she may be able to arrange faster pre-clearing and debarkation.

ON BOARD

Shipboard Accounts

Virtually all cruise ships operate as cashless societies. Passengers charge onboard purchases and settle their accounts at the end of the cruise with a credit card, traveler's checks, or cash. You can sign for wine at dinner, drinks at the bar, shore excursions, gifts in the shop—virtually any expense you may incur aboard ship. On some lines, an imprint from a major credit card is necessary to open an account. Otherwise, a cash deposit may be required and a positive balance maintained to keep the shipboard account open. Either way, you will want to open a line of credit soon after settling in, if an account was not opened for you at embarkation. This can easily be arranged by visiting the purser's office, in the central atrium or main lobby. On most ships, you can now view your account at any time on your in-cabin television. To make your stay aboard as seamless—and as cashless—as possible, many cruise lines now add dining-room gratuities at a set rate to your onboard account. Some lines offer access to personal records via Internet; you can alter automatic tips, for example, before your cruise begins.

MONEY MATTERS

Check the balance of your shipboard account before the end of your cruise. You'll avoid a long line at the purser's desk that last morning after the final bill arrives.

Tipping

For better or worse, tipping is an integral part of the cruise experience. Most companies pay their cruise staff nominal wages and expect tips to make up the difference between this nominal amount and a living wage. Most cruise lines have recommended tipping guidelines, and on many ships "voluntary" tipping for beverage service has been replaced with a mandatory 15% service charge, which is added to every bar bill. On the other hand, the most expensive luxury lines include tips in the cruise fare and may prohibit crew members from accepting additional gratuities. On many small adventure ships, a collection box is placed in the dining room or lounge on the last full day of the cruise, and passengers contribute anonymously.

Some large cruise lines now add dining-room tips of $10 to $12 per person per day directly to your bill. That sum is intended to cover all your dining-room service, other than the wine steward and the maître d' if he provides special service to you (although both those may also be included in the daily tip that is automatically added to your account); it may also include your room steward. Ask the purser if tips are being added to your bill and which personnel will receive them—waiter, busboy, and room steward are all expecting tips. You may adjust tips up or down.

Dining

2

Ocean liners serve food nearly around the clock. There may be as many as four breakfast options: early-morning coffee and pastries on deck, breakfast in bed through room service, buffet-style dining in the cafeteria, and a more formal breakfast in the dining room. There may also be several lunch choices, mid-afternoon hors d'oeuvres, teatime, and late-night buffets. You may eat whatever is on the menu, in any quantity, at any meal. Room service is traditionally, but not always, free.

Restaurants

Every large ship has at least one main restaurant and a casual, buffet alternative. Increasingly important are specialty restaurants. Meals in the primary and buffet restaurants are included in the cruise fare, as are round-the-clock room service, midday tea and snacks, and late-night buffets. Most mainstream cruise lines levy a surcharge for dining in alternative restaurants that may, or may not, also include a gratuity, although there generally is no additional charge on luxury cruise lines.

You may also find a pizzeria or a specialty coffee bar on your ship—increasingly popular favorites cropping up on ships old and new. Although pizza is complimentary, expect an additional charge for specialty coffees at the coffee bar and, quite likely, in the dining room as well. You will also likely be charged for any drinks during meals other than iced tea, regular coffee, tap water, and fruit juice; this includes soft drinks.

There is often a direct relationship between the cost of a cruise and the quality of its cuisine. The food is very sophisticated on some (mostly expensive) lines, but on most mainstream cruise lines, the food is the quality that you would find in any good hotel dining room—perfectly acceptable but certainly not great.

SMALL SHIPS Food on small ships is often less ubiquitous, but also very good. The food tends to be fresh and wholesome, but not elaborate, with a home-cooking, rather than restaurant-style presentation. There's usually just one dining room with set dining times, but drinks and snacks are generally available, such as during cocktail hour, or if the chef decides to whip up some freshly baked cookies. On very small ships, passengers eat together family-style at one table, though many meals are served as picnics on shore excursions.

Seatings

When it comes to your dining-table assignment, you should have options on four important points: early or late seating; smoking or no-smoking section (if smoking is allowed in the dining room); a table for two, four, six, or eight; and special dietary needs. When you receive your cruise documents, you'll usually receive a card asking for your dining preferences. Fill this out and return it to the cruise line, but remember that you will not get your seating assignment until you board the ship. Check it out immediately, and if your request wasn't met, see the maître d'—usually there is a time and place set up for changes in dining assignments.

On some ships, seating times are strictly observed. Ten to 15 minutes after the scheduled mealtime, the dining-room doors are closed, although this policy is increasingly rare. On other ships, passengers may enter the dining room at their leisure, but they must be out by the end of the seating. When a ship has just one seating, passengers may enter any time the kitchen is open.

Seating assignments often apply only to dinner. Most ships have open seating for breakfast or lunch, which means you may sit anywhere at any time the meal is served. Smaller or more luxurious ships offer open seating for all meals.

Several large cruise lines now offer several restaurant and dining options and have eliminated preassigned seating, so you can dine with whom you like at any table that's available and at any time the dining room is open.

Cuisine

Most ships serve food geared to the American palate, but there are also theme dinners featuring the cuisine of a particular country. Some European ships, especially smaller vessels, may offer a particular cuisine throughout the cruise—Scandinavian, German, Italian, or Greek, perhaps—depending on the ship's or the crew's nationality. The quality of cruise-ship cooking is generally good, but even a skilled chef is hard put to serve 500 or more extraordinary dinners per hour. Presentation is often spectacular, especially at gala midnight buffets.

There is often a direct relationship between the cost of a cruise and the quality of its cuisine. The food is very sophisticated on some (mostly expensive) lines, such as Crystal Cruises. In the more moderate price range, Celebrity Cruises has gained renown for the culinary stylings of French chef Michel Roux, who acts as a consultant to the line.

Special Diets

Cruise lines make every possible attempt to ensure dining satisfaction. If you have special dietary considerations—such as low-salt, kosher, or food allergies—be sure to indicate them well ahead of time and check to be certain your needs are known by your waiter once on board. In addition to the usual menu items, "spa," low-calorie, low-carbohydrate, or low-fat selections, as well as children's menus are usually available. Requests for dishes not featured on the menu can often be granted if you ask in advance.

Wine

Wine at meals costs extra on most ships; prices are usually comparable to those in shoreside restaurants and are charged to your shipboard account. A handful of luxury vessels include both wine and liquor. On some lines, you can also select the wines you might like for dinner before leaving home, and they will appear at your table and on your bill at the end of the cruise.

GOING ASHORE

Traveling by cruise ship presents an opportunity to visit many places in a short time. The flip side is that your stay in each port of call will be brief. For this reason cruise lines offer shore excursions, which maximize passengers' time. There are a number of advantages to shore excursions arranged by your ship: in some destinations, transportation may be unreliable, and a ship-packaged tour is the best way to see distant sights. Also, you don't have to worry about missing the ship. The disadvantage of a shore excursion is the cost—you pay more for the convenience of having the ship do the legwork for you. Of course, you can always book a tour independently, hire a taxi, or use foot power to explore on your own. Most of the towns have hiking trails easily accessible to port areas, and a stop at the local visitor center can help you plan a walking tour within your time limit. However, be sure to carry along rain gear and drinking water, even for the most leisurely stroll. The weather in Alaska is very fickle and subject to rapid changes.

> **GOING SOLO**
>
> Craving some alone time? If there's a port call that doesn't particularly interest you, you may choose to spend some time on the ship while almost everyone else is in town. Although the number of activities is somewhat curtailed, onboard programs don't cease entirely. There are still exercise classes, the spa and fitness center remain open, and games and movies are sometimes planned.

Many of the busier port cities tend to have several ships in port at a time, and the more popular shore trips can fill up quickly. If your heart is set on a particular experience, book it before your cruise or on board as soon as you can. Some excursions, such as flightseeing trips and the Skagway narrow-gauge rail trip, are in very high demand. Information on local tours is available at the visitor-information counter usually close to the pier in each port.

Ports of Call

Alaska cruise itineraries usually explore either the Inside Passage, or the Gulf of Alaska. Possible ports of call along the Inside Passage are: Haines, Juneau, Ketchikan, Metlakatla, Misty Fjords National Monument, Petersburg, Sitka, Skagway, and Wrangell. Ports of call on Gulf of Alaska cruises include: Anchorage, Cordova, Homer, Kodiak, Seward, Tracy Arm, and Valdez. Other ships sometimes sail to more out-of-the-way ports, such as Nome, or places on the way to Alaska from the lower 48, such as Prince Rupert, B.C., and Victoria, B.C. For more information about these ports, see the Southeast and South Central chapters of this book.

Arriving in Port

When your ship arrives in a port, it will either tie up alongside a dock or anchor out in a harbor. If the ship is docked, passengers walk down the gangway to go ashore. Docking makes it easy to go back and forth between the shore and the ship.

Tendering

If your ship anchors in the harbor, you will have to take a small boat—called a launch or tender—to get ashore. Tendering is a nuisance. Passengers wishing to disembark may be required to gather in a public room, get sequenced boarding passes, and wait until their numbers are called. The ride to shore may take as long as 20 minutes. If you don't like waiting, plan to go ashore an hour or so after the ship drops its anchor.

Because tenders can be difficult to board, passengers with mobility problems may not be able to visit certain ports. The larger ships are more likely to use tenders. It is usually possible to learn before booking a cruise whether the ship will dock or anchor at its ports of call.

Before anyone is allowed to walk down the gangway or board a tender, the ship must be cleared for landing. Immigration and customs officials board the vessel to examine passports and sort through red tape. It may be more than an hour before you're allowed ashore. You will be issued a boarding pass, which you'll need to get back on board.

Returning to the Ship

Cruise lines are strict about sailing times, which are posted at the gangway and elsewhere and announced in the daily schedule of activities. Be sure to be back on board at least a half hour before the announced sailing time or you may be stranded. If you are on a shore excursion that was sold by the cruise line, however, the captain will wait for your group before casting off. That is one reason many passengers prefer ship-packaged tours.

MISSING THE BOAT

If the ship sails without you, immediately contact the cruise line's port representative, whose phone number is often listed on the daily schedule of activities. You may be able to hitch a ride on a pilot boat, although that is unlikely. Passengers who miss the boat must pay their own way to the next port.

THE CRUISE FLEET

For each cruise line, we list only the ships (grouped by similar configurations) that regularly cruise in Alaska. When two or more ships are substantially similar, their names are given at the beginning of a review and separated by commas. Within each cruise line, ships are listed from largest to smallest.

Passenger-capacity figures are given on the basis of two people sharing a cabin (basis-2); however, many of the larger ships have 3- and 4-berth cabins, which can increase the total number of passengers tremendously when all berths are occupied. When total occupancy figures differ from basis-2 occupancy, we give them in parentheses.

Cruise Ships

Carnival Cruise Lines

Carnival Cruise Lines is the largest and most successful cruise line in the world, carrying more passengers than any other. Brash and sometimes rowdy, Carnival throws a great party. Activities and entertainment are nonstop, beginning just after sunrise and continuing well into the night. Under Carnival's "Total Choice Dining" plan, passengers are assigned seatings in the dining room, but pizza and room service are available at all hours and most ships have an alternative restaurant as well. ■ TIP→ **Carnival cruises are popular with young, single cruisers as well as with those older than 55. The line's offerings also appeal to parents cruising with their children.**

Gratuities of $10 per passenger, per day are automatically added to onboard accounts and are distributed to stewards and waitstaff. Passengers may adjust the amount based on the level of service experienced. A 15% gratuity is automatically added to bar and beverage tabs.

Carnival Cruise Lines, 3655 N.W. 87th Ave., Miami, FL 33178-2428 ☎ 305/599–2600, 800/438–6744, or 800/327–9501 www.carnival.com.

THE SHIP ***Carnival Spirit.*** The first of Carnival's Spirit-class ships entered service in 2001 with notable design improvements over previous lines. For example, all staterooms aboard these superliners are above ocean level, making for a more comfortable cruise. Cabins have ample drawer and closet space, and in-cabin TVs show first-run films. Other innovations include eye-popping, 11-story atriums, two-level promenades (partially glass enclosed to create a protected viewing perch), wide decks, shopping malls, and reservations-only supper clubs. Greater speed allows Spirit-class ships to visit destinations in a week that would take other ships 10 days or more. Most staterooms have ocean views, and of those, 80% have balconies. This is a great ship for kids, with a 2,400-square-foot enclosed play area, plus outdoor play areas, a video wall, and an arcade. The pool, open to all ages, has a retractable roof, so you can enjoy a swim even in Alaska. *1,062 cabins, 2,124 passengers (2,667 at full occupancy), 12 passenger decks Restaurant, café, dining room, ice-cream parlor, pizzeria, in-room safes, minibars, in-room VCRs, 4 pools (1 indoor), fitness classes, gym, hair salon, outdoor hot tubs, sauna, spa, steam room, 18 bars, casino, dance club, showroom, video game room, children's programs (ages 2–17), dry cleaning, laundry facilities, laundry service, no-smoking rooms, Internet; no kids under 4 months AE, D, MC, V.*

Celebrity Cruises

Celebrity Cruises has made a name for itself based on sleek ships and superior food. Celebrity has risen above typical mass-market cruise cuisine by hiring Chef Michel Roux as a consultant. All food is prepared from scratch, using only fresh produce and herbs, aged beef, and fresh fish—even the ice cream on board is homemade. Celebrity provides traditional assigned seating in the dining room, with a variety of casual and specialty dining options. In just a short time Celebrity has won the admiration of its passengers, and its competitors—who have copied its nouvelle cuisine, occasional adults-only cruises, and cigar clubs, and hired its personnel (a true compliment). ■ **TIP→ Celebrity attracts everyone from older couples to honeymooners.**

Tip your cabin steward/butlers $3.50 per day; chief housekeeper 50¢ per day; dining-room waiter $3.50 per day; assistant waiter $2 per day; and restaurant manager 75¢ per day, for a total of $10.25 per day. A 15% service charge is added to all beverage checks. Gratuities are typically handed out on the last night of the cruise, or they may be charged to your shipboard account.

Celebrity Cruises, 1050 Caribbean Way, Miami, FL 33132-2096 ☎ 305/539–6000 or 800/646–1456 🖷 800/437–5111 🌐 www.celebrity.com.

THE SHIPS ★ ***Infinity, Summit.*** Dramatic, exterior glass elevators, a glass-dome pool area, and a window-wrapped ship-top observation lounge keep the magnificence of Alaska well within the passenger's view. These are the newest and largest in Celebrity's fleet, and each stocks plenty of premium amenities, including a flower-filled conservatory, music library, Internet café with 18 workstations, golf simulator, brand-name boutiques, and an expansive spa with both a seawater thalassotherapy pool and a resistance swimming pool. Cabins are bright, spacious, and well appointed, and 80% have an ocean view (74% of those have private verandas). There is also in-cabin Internet access. With a staff member for every two passengers, service is especially attentive. *975 cabins, 1,950 passengers, 11 passenger decks Restaurant, café, dining room, food court, ice-cream parlor, pizzeria, in-room safes, minibars, in-room VCRs, 3 pools (1 indoor), fitness classes, gym, hair salon, hot tubs (indoor and outdoor), sauna, spa, steam room, 6 bars, casino, cinema, dance club, showroom, video game room, children's programs (ages 3–17), dry cleaning, laundry service, Internet room AE, D, DC, MC, V.*

WORD OF MOUTH

"We were just on *Infinity* and it was so fantastic . . . and Alaska is out of this world. Have a wonderful trip. Our weather was in the 70's so dress in layers."

–itsmlf

Mercury. With features such as a golf simulator, video walls, and interactive television systems in cabins, this ship is a high-tech pioneer, yet it is elegant and warm. Many large windows—including a dramatic two-story wall of glass in the dining room and wraparound windows in the Stratosphere Lounge, in the gym, and in the beauty salon—bathe the ship in natural light and afford excellent views of Alaska's natural beauty. Plus there are retractable glass sunroofs over the pools. The elaborate Elemis spas have enormous thalassotherapy pools and the latest in treatments. Standard cabins are intelligently appointed and apportioned, with few frills; space is well used, making for maximum elbow room in the bathrooms and good storage space in the closets. *935* *cabins, 1,870 passengers, 10 passenger decks* ♿ *Dining room, food court, ice-cream parlor, pizzeria, in-room safes, minibars, 4 pools (1 indoors), fitness classes, gym, hair salon, outdoor hot tubs, sauna, spa, steam room, 6 bars, casino, cinema, dance club, showroom, video game room, children's programs (ages 3–17), dry cleaning, laundry service, Internet room* ▭ *AE, D, DC, MC, V.*

Holland America Line

Founded in 1873, Holland America Line (HAL) is one of the oldest names in cruising. Steeped in the traditions of the transatlantic crossing, its cruises are classic, conservative affairs renowned for their grace and gentility. Service is taken seriously: the line maintains a school in Indonesia to train staff members, rather than hiring out of a union hall. The staff on the line's Alaska cruises includes a naturalist and a Native artist-in-residence. HAL passengers tend to be older and less active than those traveling on the ships of its parent line, Carnival, although the age difference is getting narrower. ■ TIP→ **As its ships attract a more youthful clientele, HAL has taken steps to shed its "old folks" image, such as offering trendier cuisine and a "Club Hal" children's program.**

Holland America's Alaska-bound ships have open seating for breakfast and lunch and four seatings for dinner. Most HAL ships also have specialty restaurants, and all provide 24-hour room service. HAL has a no-tips-required policy. For convenience, $10 per passenger, per day is automatically added to onboard accounts for stewards and waitstaff. Passengers may adjust the amount based on the level of service experienced. Tips for room service delivery are at passengers' discretion. A 15% gratuity is added to bar service tabs.

Holland America Line, 300 Elliott Ave. W, Seattle, WA 98119 ☎ *206/281–3535 or 877/932–4259* 🖷 *206/281–7110* 🌐 *www.hollandamerica.com.*

THE SHIPS **_Amsterdam._** Ships for the 21st century, these Vista-class vessels successfully integrate new youthful and family-friendly elements into Holland America Line's classic fleet. Multiple decks are termed "promenade," but the exterior teak promenade encircles public rooms, not cabins. As a result, there are numerous outside accommodations with views of the sea restricted by lifeboats on the Upper Promenade Deck. Comfortable and roomy, 85% of all Vista-class accommodations have an ocean view, and almost 80% of those also have the luxury of a private balcony furnished with chairs, loungers, and tables. Some suites have a whirlpool tub, powder room, and walk-in closet. All staterooms and suites are appointed flat-panel TVs and DVD players and some suites have a whirlpool tub, powder room, and walk-in closet. Flexible scheduling includes a selection of four dinner seatings in the two-deck formal restaurants, alternating between upper and lower levels at 5:45, 6:15, 8, and 8:30 PM. *680 cabins, 1,792 passengers, 9 passenger decks* ♿ *Specialty restaurant, dining room, buffet, Wi-Fi, in-cabin safes, in-cabin refrigerators, some minibars, in-cabin DVDs, 2 pools (1 indoor), 2 children's pools, Fitness classes, gym, hair salon, 2 hot tubs, sauna, spa, steam room, 6 bars, casino, cinema, dance club, library, showroom, video game room,* *children's programs (ages 3–17), dry cleaning, laundry facilities, laundry service, computer room* ▭ *AE, D, MC, V.*

WORD OF MOUTH

"I did the HAL trip to Alaska for my honeymoon a while ago, and my only advice is to remember that the guided trips of the small Alaskan towns really aren't necessary. You are in the US, without any language problems, and the size of the small towns really makes travelling around on foot absolutely reasonable."

–freiamaya

Noordam, Oosterdam, Zuiderdam. With the highest space-to-passenger ratio in the fleet, HAL's Vista-class ships—forward-looking both in design and spirit—launched in December 2002. Exterior panorama elevators, providing expansive sea views, link 10 passenger decks. All the HAL trademarks, including a covered promenade deck encircling the entire ship, two interior promenades, and white-gloved stewards, are here, as are such up-to-date touches as in-cabin Internet access, a golf simulator, extensive spa facilities, and an alternative Pacific Northwest restaurant. A retractable dome over the pool means you can enjoy a swim even in Alaska. These ships also offer a range of understated, spacious accommodation categories, 85% of which have ocean views, most with private verandas. *924 cabins, 1,848 passengers, 11 passenger decks* *Specialty restaurant, dining room, pizzeria, in-cabin safes, refrigerators, in-cabin DVDs, in-cabin data ports, Wi-Fi, 2 pools (1 indoors), fitness classes, gym, hair salon, 5 hot tubs, sauna, spa, steam room, 9 bars, casino, cinema, 2 dance clubs, library, showroom, video game room, children's programs (ages 3–17), dry cleaning, laundry service, children's pool, buffet, computer room* ▭ *AE, D, MC, V.*

Volendam, Zaandam. These ships are structurally similar to HAL's other vessels, with signature two-tier dining rooms and a retractable roof over the main pool, but they are newer, and their themed interior design inject elements of youthfulness. They are also slightly larger and have Internet cafés and practice-size tennis courts. Huge bouquets of fresh, fragrant flowers are everywhere (a Holland America trademark); and each ship has a teak promenade completely encircling the ship, which means there will always be room for you at the rail to watch the sunset. All standard outside cabins come with a bathtub, and all suites and minisuites have private verandas. The "Passport to Fitness" program encourages a healthy diet and exercise. In 2007, the *Zaandam* and *Volendam* will sail from Vancouver. *720 cabins, 1,440 passengers (1,848 at full occupancy), 10 passenger decks* *Specialty restaurant, dining room, in-cabin safes, refrigerators, in-cabin DVDs, Wi-Fi, 2 pools (1 indoors), fitness classes, gym, hair salon, 2 hot tubs, sauna, spa, steam room, 6 bars, casino, cinema, dance club, library, showroom, video game room, children's programs (ages 3–17), dry cleaning, laundry facilities, laundry service, children's pool, buffet, computer room* ▭ *AE, D, MC, V.*

Ryndam, Statendam. An abundance of glass, outdoor deck space, and a retractable roof over the main pool make these good ships for Alaska cruising. Great views can be found along the wraparound promenade. From bow to stern, these ships are full of lounges and restaurants—14 in all—some cozy, some grand, and most with expansive floor-to-ceiling windows. The Crow's Nest, redesigned on the Ryndam with hip banquettes and an underlighted bar, is a combined observation lounge and nightclub overlooking the bow; the view-blessed Explorations Café, a combined coffee bar, Internet café, library, and card room, is a popular hangout. A three-deck atrium and a two-tier dining room, replete with dual grand staircases framing an orchestra balcony, are among the welcoming public spaces. Staterooms are comfortable, with an understated elegance. In 2007, the *Ryndam,* and *Statendam* will cruise between Vancouver and Seward, via Glacier Bay or Hubbard Glacier. *633 cabins, 1,266 passengers (1,590 at full occupancy), 10 passenger decks Specialty restaurant, dining room, in-cabin safes, refrigerators, in-cabin DVDs, Wi-Fi, 2 pools (1 indoor), 2 children's pools, fitness classes, gym, hair salon, 2 hot tubs, sauna, spa, steam room, 9 bars, casino, cinema, dance club, library, showroom, video game room, children's programs (ages 3–18), dry cleaning, laundry facilities, laundry service, buffet, computer room AE, D, MC, V.*

Norwegian Cruise Line

In 1966, Norwegian Cruise Line (NCL) launched a new concept in cruising: regularly scheduled cruises on a single-class ship. No longer simply a means of transportation, the ship became a destination unto itself. NCL continues to innovate. It offers "Freestyle Cruising," which eliminates dinner table and time assignments and dress codes, and the widest choice of restaurants afloat. The line has even loosened the rules on disembarkation, which means passengers can relax in their cabins until it's time to leave the ship (instead of gathering in a lounge to wait for their numbers to be called). Most of NCL's Alaska fleet is based in Seattle rather than Vancouver, B.C., which can be a more convenient departure point for many U.S.-based passengers. ■ TIP→ **The line's passenger list usually includes seniors, families, and younger couples, mostly from the United States and Canada.**

NCL applies a service charge to passengers' shipboard accounts: $10 per passenger per day for those 13 and older, and $5 per day for children (ages 3–12). These automatic tips can be increased, decreased, or removed. A 15% gratuity is added to bar tabs and spa bills.

Norwegian Cruise Line, 7665 Corporate Center Dr., Miami, FL 33126 305/436–4000 or 800/327–7030 www.ncl.com.

THE SHIPS **Norwegian Pearl.** Norwegian Pearl is the next step up in the continuing evolution of "Freestyle" ship design-the interior location of some public rooms and restaurants has been tweaked, and Courtyard Villas, the latest category of deluxe accommodations, has been added. Ten dining rooms and ethnic restaurants with open seating and flexible hours offer continental and specialty dining. Two are complimentary; specialty restaurants, including NCL's signature Le Bistro, carry a cover charge and require reservations. Cherrywood cabinetry, tropical decor, refrigerator, Internet connection, bathrobes for use during the cruise, and a sitting area with sofa, chair, and table are typical standard features in all accommodations. Most bathrooms are compartmentalized with sink area, shower, and toilet separated by sliding glass doors. Family-friendly staterooms interconnect in most categories, enabling families of nearly any size to find suitable accommodations. Nearly every stateroom has a third or fourth berth and some even sleep as many as five and six. *1,233 cabins, 2,466 passengers, 12 passenger decks* *8 restaurants, 2 dining rooms, café, buffet, ice-cream parlor, pizzeria, in-cabin safes, refrigerators, Wi-Fi, 2 pools, children's pool, fitness classes, gym, hair salon, 6 hot tubs, sauna, spa, steam room, 9 bars, casino, cinema, dance clubs, showroom, video game room, children's programs (ages 2–17), dry cleaning, laundry facilities, laundry service, Internet room* *AE, D, DC, MC, V.*

Fodor'sChoice ★ ***Norwegian Star.*** Built specifically to accommodate Freestyle Cruising, this is one of NCL's largest and fastest ships. Offering more dining choices than any other ship in Alaska, *Star* has 10 different eateries, with everything from French, Italian, contemporary, and spa cuisine to tapas and sushi. The ship also has a 24-hour fitness center, a Balinese-theme spa, a golf driving range, and an indoor jet-current exercise pool. Garden Villas, the top-of-the-line staterooms, have private rooftop terraces. Standard cabins take their cue from high-end hotel rooms, with rich cherrywood, tea- and coffeemakers, and large bathrooms. Most staterooms can accommodate a third guest, and many cabins can be linked to create suites for larger groups. *1,120 cabins, 2,240 passengers, 11 passenger decks* *8 restaurants, 2 dining rooms, buffet, café, ice-cream parlor, pizzeria, in-cabin safes, refrigerators, Wi-Fi, 3 pools (1 indoors), fitness classes, gym, hair salon, 6 hot tubs, sauna, spa, steam room, 9 bars, casino, cinema, 2 dance clubs, showroom, video game room, children's programs (ages 2–17), dry cleaning, laundry service, computer room* *AE, D, DC, MC, V.*

Norwegian Sun. The *Sun* comes with all the bells and whistles, including a variety of dining options, specialty bars, and Internet access—both in a café and in cabins. The 24-hour health club has expansive ocean views, and the presence of the full-service Mandara Spa means you can turn your cruise into a spa vacation. Cabins are adequately laid out, with large circular windows and sitting areas, sufficient (but not generous) shelf and drawer space, and two lower beds that convert to a queen. *1,001 cabins, 2,002 passengers (2,400 at full occupancy), 10 passenger decks* *8 restaurants, 2 dining rooms, in-cabin safes, refrigerators, Wi-Fi, 2 pools, fitness classes, gym, hair salon, 4 hot tubs, sauna, spa, steam room, 13 bars, casino, cinema, dance club, showroom, video game room, children's programs (ages 2–17), dry cleaning, laundry facilities, Internet room* *AE, D, DC, MC, V.*

Princess Cruise Line

Princess was catapulted to stardom in 1977, when it became the star of *The Love Boat* television series, which introduced millions of viewers to the still-new concept of a seagoing vacation. The name and famous "seawitch" logo have remained synonymous with cruising ever since. Nearly everything about Princess is big, but the line doesn't sacrifice quality for quantity when it comes to building beautiful vessels. Service, especially in the dining rooms, is of a high standard. In short, Princess is refined without being pretentious. All Princess ships offer the line's innovative "Personal Choice Cruising" program, an individualized, unstructured style of cruising that gives passengers choice and flexibility in customizing their cruise experience, including a choice between traditional fixed seating in the dining room or open seating in any of the onboard restaurants. **■ TIP→ Princess passengers' average age is 45; you see a mix of younger and older couples on board.**

Princess suggests tipping $10 per person, per day. Gratuities are automatically added to accounts, which passengers can adjust at the purser's desk; 15% is added to bar bills.

Princess Cruises, 24844 Avenue Rockefeller, Santa Clarita, CA 91355-4999 ☎ 661/753–0000 or 800/774–6237 ⊕ www.princess.com.

THE SHIPS **Coral Princess, Island Princess.** While Princess includes *Coral Princess* and *Island Princess* in the Sun-class category, they're actually larger ships with a similar capacity, which results in more space per passenger. All the Personal Choice features attributed to the larger Grand-class ships were incorporated in this new ship design with a few unique additions, such as a demonstration kitchen and ceramics lab where ScholarShip @ Sea programs are presented. Each ship has one dining room with two traditional assigned dinner seatings and a second dining room for open-seating Personal Choice cruisers. Alternative dining options are the two specialty restaurants, Sabatini's and Bayou Café and Steakhouse, which both have a surcharge and require reservations. Stepped out in wedding-cake fashion, over 83% of oceanview staterooms include private balconies. Even the least expensive inside categories have plentiful storage and a small sitting area with chair and table. Cabins that sleep third and fourth passengers are numerous, but the best for families are interconnecting balcony staterooms on Aloha Deck (A624–A631 and A704–A722), which are adjacent to facilities dedicated to children and teens. *985 cabins, 1,970 passengers, 12 passenger decks 2 specialty restaurants, 2 dining rooms, buffet, ice-cream parlor, pizzeria, Wi-Fi, in-cabin safes, refrigerators, 3 pools (1 indoors), 2 children's pools, fitness classes, gym, hair salon, 5 hot tubs, sauna, spa, steam room, 7 bars, casino, 2 dance clubs, library, 2 showrooms, video game room, children's programs (ages 3–17), dry cleaning, laundry facilities, laundry service, computer room, no children under 6 months ▭ AE, D, MC, V.*

Diamond Princess, Sapphire Princess. These sister ships include all the features traditionally enjoyed on Princess's Grand-class vessels, but with a twist. They're larger than their Grand-class fleetmates, yet carry fewer passengers relative to their size. As a result, they have sleeker profiles, a higher ratio of space per person, and feel much roomier. Princess is all about choice, and *Diamond Princess* and *Sapphire Princess* offer expanded dining choices. In addition to a dining room with two traditional assigned dinner seatings, these ships have four additional dining rooms for open-seating Personal Choice cruisers. Each is smaller than those on other Princess Grand-class ships, but all offer the same menus with a few additional selections that reflect the "theme" of each dining room. Over 78% of oceanview staterooms include private balconies. Even the least expensive inside categories have ample storage and a small sitting area with chair and table. Typical stateroom features are personal safes, refrigerators, and bathrobes for use during the cruise. Cabins that sleep third and fourth passengers are numerous. The best for families are Family Suites with interconnecting balcony staterooms on Dolphin Deck. *1,337 cabins, 2,670 passengers, 13 passenger decks 2 specialty restaurants, 5 dining rooms, buffet, ice-cream parlor, pizzeria, Wi-Fi, in-cabin safes, refrigerators, 4 pools (1 indoors), 2 children's pools, fitness classes, gym, hair salon, 8 hot tubs, sauna, spa, steam room, 11 bars, casino, 2 dance clubs, library, 2 showrooms, video game room, children's programs (ages 3-17), dry cleaning, laundry facilities, laundry service, computer room; no children under 6 months AE, D, MC, V.*

Golden Princess. Second in Princess Cruises' lineup of Grand-class ships, *Golden Princess* boasts one of the most distinctive profiles at sea. The interior features soothing pastel hues with splashes of glamour in the sweeping staircases and marble-floored atriums, and the Skywalkers Disco appears futuristic hovering approximately 150 feet above the water line. Surprisingly intimate for such a large ship, human scale in public lounges is achieved by judicious placement of furniture as unobtrusive room dividers. Passengers have the choice between two traditional dinner seatings in an assigned dining room, open seating in the ships' other two formal dining rooms, or the extra-charge specialty restaurants. *1,300 cabins, 2,600 passengers, 13 passenger decks 2 specialty restaurants, 3 dining rooms, buffet, ice-cream parlor, pizzeria, Wi-Fi, in-cabin safes, refrigerators, 4 pools (1 indoors), children's pool, fitness classes, gym, hair salon, 9 hot tubs, sauna, spa, steam room, 9 bars, casino, 2 dance clubs, library, 2 showrooms, video game room, children's programs (ages 3-17), dry cleaning, laundry facilities, laundry service, computer room; no children under 6 months AE, D, MC, V.*

Pacific Princess. At 30,277 tons, *Pacific Princess* appears positively diminutive beside her megaship fleetmates, but provides a true alternative for passengers who prefer a clubby atmosphere on a smaller "boutique"-style ship, yet one that has big-ship features galore. *Pacific Princess* has cozy public spaces, a stunning observation lounge where the Alaska scenery is visible through floor-to-ceiling windows on three sides, and one of the loveliest libraries at sea. The only disappointment is the lack of a Personal Choice dining room. The lone formal dining room has two scheduled seatings with assigned tables for dinner, but there are other options. Sabatini's Italian Trattoria and Sterling Steakhouse specialty restaurants are reservations-required and extra-charge selections for dinner. The Lido buffet/bistro and complimentary room service are available 24-hours at no charge. Designed for longer cruises, all staterooms have ample closet and storage space, although bathrooms in lower categories are somewhat tight. In keeping with the rest of the fleet, 73% of all outside cabins and suites have a balcony and interiors are similar in size. Amenities in standard cabins are a bit spartan compared to other Princess ships, yet all have at least a small sitting area. *335 cabins, 670 passengers, 9 passenger decks 2 specialty restaurants, dining room, buffet, pizzeria, Wi-Fi, in-cabin safes, some refrigerators, pool, fitness classes, gym, hair salon, 2 hot tubs, spa,*

2

steam room, 8 bars, casino, dance club, library, showroom, children's programs (ages 3-17), dry cleaning, laundry facilities, laundry service, computer room; no children under 6 months ▭ *AE, D, MC, V.*

Sun Princess, Dawn Princess. Four-story atriums with circular marble floors, stained-glass domes, and magnificent floating staircases are ideal settings for relaxation, people-watching, and making a grand entrance. Each subtly decorated vessel has two main showrooms and several dining rooms and restaurants (some with extra charges), from large to intimate. More than 60% of outside cabins in these sister ships have private balconies. All standard cabins are decorated in light colors and have a queen-sized bed convertible to two doubles, and ample closet and bath space (with shower only). Several cabins on each ship are deemed fully accessible. A wraparound teak promenade lined with canopied steamer chairs provides a peaceful setting for reading, napping, or daydreaming, and a pool with a retractable glass roof allows for all-weather swimming. *975 cabins, 1,950 passengers, 10 passenger decks* *Restaurant, 2 dining rooms, ice-cream parlor, pizzeria, in-cabin safes, refrigerators, 4 pools, fitness classes, gym, hair salon, hot tubs, sauna, spa, 7 bars, casino, dance club, 2 showrooms, video game room, children's programs (ages 3–17), dry cleaning, laundry facilities, laundry service, computer room; no kids under 6 months* ▭ *AE, D, MC, V.*

Regent Seven Seas Cruises

The only luxury-class cruise line in Alaska, Regent Seven Seas Cruises is part of Carlson Hospitality Worldwide, one of the world's major hotel and travel companies. The cruise line was formed in December 1994 with the merger of the one-ship Diamond Cruises and Seven Seas Cruises lines. From these modest beginnings, RSSC has grown into a major luxury player in the cruise industry.

Regent Seven Seas Cruises manages to provide a high level of personal service and sense of intimacy on small to midsize ships, which have the stability of larger vessels. Onboard activities are oriented toward enrichment programs, socializing, and exploring the destinations on the itinerary. ■ TIP→ **Although passengers tend to be older and affluent, they are still active.** You'll always find open seating at dinner (which includes complimentary wine) and tips are included in the fare.

Regent Seven Seas Cruises, 600 Corporate Dr., Suite 410, Fort Lauderdale, FL 33334 ☎ *954/776–6123, 800/477–7500, or 800/285–1835* 🖷 *954/772–3763* 🌐 *www.rssc.com.*

> **WORD OF MOUTH**
>
> "Best cruise we ever went on was Alaskan cruise on the Mariner. Small ship, no waiting in lines, every cabin has a balcony and walk-in closet, outstanding service and food, friendly crew, and the most beautiful scenery we've ever seen."
>
> –newyorkgolfer41

THE SHIP
Fodor's Choice ★

Seven Seas Mariner. This all-suites, all-balcony ship, in service since 2003, is also one of Regent Seven Seas' largest, with the highest space-per-passenger ratio in the fleet. All cabins are outside suites ranging from 301 square feet to 2,002 square feet, including the verandas. Butler service is available to all but the least-expensive Deluxe Suite categories. The ship's dining rooms include Signatures, the only restaurant at sea staffed by chefs wearing the Blue Riband of Le Cordon Bleu of Paris, the famed culinary institute. Spa and salon services are provided by the high-end Carita of Paris and an outdoor pool remains open on Alaska voyages. *328 cabins, 700 passengers, 8 passenger decks 2 specialty restaurants, dining room, in-cabin safes, refrigerators, in-cabin DVDs, Wi-Fi, pool, fitness classes, gym, hair salon, 2 hot tubs, sauna, spa, steam room, 5 bars, casino, dance club, library, showroom, children's programs (ages 6–17), dry cleaning, laundry facilities, laundry service, buffet, computer room AE, D, MC, V.*

Royal Caribbean International

Imagine if the Mall of America were sent to sea. That's a fair approximation of what the megaships of Royal Caribbean Cruise Line (RCL) are all about. These mammoth vessels are indoor/outdoor wonders, with every conceivable activity in a resortlike atmosphere, including atrium lobbies, shopping arcades, large spas, and expansive sundecks. The main problem with these otherwise well-conceived vessels is that the line packs too many people aboard, making for an exasperating experience at embarkation, while tendering, and at disembarkation. Nevertheless, Royal Caribbean is one of the best-run and most popular cruise lines. **TIP→ Although the line competes directly with Carnival for passengers–active couples and singles in their thirties to fifties, as well as a large family contingent–there are distinct differences of ambience and energy.** Royal Caribbean is a bit more sophisticated and subdued than Carnival, even while delivering a good time on a grand scale.

Royal Caribbean suggests the following tips per passenger: dining-room waiter, $3.50 a day; stateroom attendant, $3.50 a day; assistant waiter, $2 a day; headwaiter, 75¢ a day. Gratuities for other service personnel are at your discretion. A 15% gratuity is automatically added to beverage and bar bills. All gratuities may be prepaid when you book, charged to your onboard account, or paid in cash at the end of the cruise.

Royal Caribbean International, Box 25511, 1050 Caribbean Way, Miami, FL 33132 305/539–6000 or 800/327–6700 800/722–5329 www.royalcaribbean.com.

THE SHIPS ★ **_Radiance of the Seas, Serenade of the Seas._** Royal Caribbean's Radiance-class ships aren't the largest in the fleet, but they offer great speed—allowing for longer itineraries to far-flung ports of call—and the line's highest percentage of outside cabins. They are also considered by many to be the fleet's most beautiful vessels, and include sea-facing elevators that offer panoramic ocean views while you move from deck to deck. The coffeehouse-bookstore is a novel touch. The solarium, filled with lush foliage and cascading waterfalls, has a retractable roof to convert it from an indoor pool to an outdoor pool. All cabins have two twin beds that can convert into a queen, a computer jack, a vanity table with an extendable working surface, and bedside reading lights. *1,050/1,055 cabins, 2,100/2,110 passengers (both 2,501 at full occupancy), 12 pas-*

senger decks ♁ *2 specialty restaurants, pizzeria, in-cabin safes, refrigerators, some in-cabin VCRs, in-cabin data ports, Wi-Fi, 2 pools (1 indoors), fitness classes, gym, hair salon, 3 hot tubs, sauna, spa, steam room, 11 bars, casino, cinema, dance club, library, showroom, video game room, children's programs (ages 3–17), dry cleaning, laundry service, children's pool, buffet, computer room* ▭ *AE, D, DC, MC, V.*

2

Vision of the Seas. Launched in 1998, *Vision of the Seas* is a few years older than Royal Caribbean's other Alaska-bound vessels, but still boasts such up-to-date amenities as a rock-climbing wall, a miniature golf course, and a broad menu of fitness classes, including yoga and Pilates. Large windows throughout and, on the uppermost deck, a viewing lounge with wraparound glass make the most of the passing scenery. The covered pool and indoor-outdoor deck area of the Solarium Spa are especially well suited to cruising in often rainy Alaska. Among the bright spacious cabins are connecting staterooms, cabins with private balconies, and family suites with separate bedrooms for parents and children. The main dining room has open seating at breakfast and lunch, and assigned seating at dinner. *999 cabins 1,998 passengers (2,435 at full occupancy), 11 passenger decks* ♁ *Dining room, in-cabin safes, some refrigerators, 2 pools (1 indoors), fitness classes, gym, hair salon, 2 indoor hot tubs, 4 outdoor hot tubs, sauna, spa, 6 bars, casino, dance club, library, showroom, video game room, children's programs (ages 3–17), dry cleaning, laundry service, buffet, computer room* ▭ *AE, D, DC, MC, V.*

Small Ships

American Safari Cruises

Unlike most yachts, which have to be chartered, American Safari's vessels sail on a regular schedule and sell tickets to individuals: there's no need to charter the whole boat, though that is an option. ■ TIP→ **With just 12 to 21 passengers and such decadent amenities as ocean-view hot tubs, American Safari's yachts are among the most comfortable small ships cruising Alaska.** The chefs serve a choice of creative dinner entrées, highlighting fresh local ingredients and plenty of seafood. Itineraries are usually flexible; there's no rush to move on if the group spots a pod of whales or a family of bears. All sailing is in daylight, with nights spent at anchor in secluded coves, and the yachts stop daily to let you kayak, hike, or beachcomb. An onboard naturalist gives informal lectures and guides you on shore expeditions. All three ships carry exercise equipment, kayaks, mountain bikes, Zodiac landing crafts, and insulated Mustang suits for Zodiac excursions. All shore excursions and alcoholic drinks are included in the fare.

Tips are discretionary, but 5%–10% of the fare is suggested. A lump sum is pooled among the crew at the end of the cruise.

American Safari Cruises, 19221 36th Ave. W, Suite 208, Lynnwood, WA 98036 ☎ *206/284–0300* *425/776–8889* *www.amsafari.com.*

THE SHIPS

★ ***Safari Quest.*** American Safari's largest vessel, this luxurious yacht has warm wood trim throughout. Four cabins have small balconies accessed by sliding glass doors, and a single cabin is available. There's plenty of outer deck space for taking in the views, and a reading lounge on the top deck is a pleasant hideaway. *11 cabins, 21 passengers, 4 passenger decks* *Dining room, in-room VCRs, outdoor hot tub, bar; no smoking.*

Safari Escape. Although *Escape* is one of Alaska's smallest cruise ships, it comes with all kinds of creature comforts usually associated with bigger ships, including exercise equipment, mountain bikes, and, in one cabin, a private sauna. Everyone dines together at one grand table; lunch might be a gourmet picnic on a secluded beach. Standard staterooms have queen or twin beds, and port lights rather than windows. The higher-end staterooms have a king-size bed and a window. All have rich fabrics and wood paneling. *6 cabins, 12 passengers, 3 passenger decks* *Dining room, in-room VCRs, outdoor hot tub, bar; no smoking.*

Safari Spirit. Completely remodeled in 2005 with cherry woodwork, the *Safari Spirit* is one of Alaska's most luxurious yachts. A forward-facing library with a 180-degree view, covered outside deck space, an on-deck hot tub, and even a sauna/steam bath are part of the pampering. Excellent meals are served at one grand table. The bright, cheerful cabins, all with plush bedding, jetted bathtubs, and heated bathroom floors, are among the roomiest in the American Safari fleet. *6 cabins, 12 passengers, 4 decks* *Dining room, in-cabin DVDs, in-cabin VCRs, gym, outdoor hot tub, sauna, bar; no smoking.*

American West Steamboat Company

In the 19th century, paddle wheelers were a key part of Alaska's coastal transport, taking adventurers and gold seekers north. In 2003 American West Steamboat Company launched the *Empress of the North,* the first overnight stern-wheeler to ply these waters in 100 years. A naturalist and historian gives lectures on local history and culture, and gold-rush follies, Russian-American dances, and Native American songs and dances bring the region's past to life. A shore excursion is included at each port of call, including a trip on the White Pass & Yukon Railroad. **■ TIP→ This novel small ship attracts primarily North American passengers, with an average age of about 55.**

As with most small ships, tips are pooled by the crew at the end of cruise. A tip of $12 to $14 per person per night is suggested.

American West Steamboat Company, 2101 4th Ave., Suite 1150, Seattle, WA 98121 *206/621–0913 or 800/434–1232* *206/340–0975* *www.americanweststeamboat.com.*

THE SHIP ***Empress of the North.*** Alaskan art and historical artifacts enrich the public areas, and the staterooms mimic Victorian opulence, with lush fabrics and rich colors. All cabins have big picture windows, and most have balconies. Lavish two-room suites, as well as single, triple, and wheelchair-accessible cabins are available. The chandelier-lighted dining room looks formal, but it is actually small-ship casual, with open seating and no need to dress up. Variety shows, ranging from golden oldies and big band to country and western, play nightly. *112 cabins, 235 passengers, 4 passenger decks* *Café, dining room, minibars, in-room DVDs, 3 bars, showroom; no smoking.*

2

Clipper Cruise Lines

Clipper Cruise Lines keeps the focus on fully experiencing each destination. A fleet of motorized Zodiacs is on hand to take passengers to isolated beaches, and on every voyage, onboard experts share their knowledge of the region's cultures, wildlife, history, and geography. Clipper chefs take pride in their healthful American cuisine. Each dish is made to order, and almost everything served is made from scratch on board. There's little formality on board these relaxed yacht-size cruisers. Casual attire is the norm, and sport coats and dresses don't usually appear until the captain's farewell party. ■ TIP→ **Passengers are typically active and well-traveled older adults.**

Tips are pooled together at the end of the cruise. Ten dollars per day per passenger is suggested.

Clipper Cruise Lines, 11969 Westline Industrial Dr., St. Louis, MO 63146-3220 ☎ 314/655–6700 or 800/325–0010 www.clippercruise.com.

THE SHIPS ★ ***Clipper Odyssey.*** The *Odyssey* brings elements of a luxury yacht experience to small-ship cruising in Alaska. A window-lined dining room and lounges keep the scenery in sight. Each cabin also has an ocean view, as well as a sitting area with a sofa and a bathroom with a shower and tub. Other amenities include a small pool, exercise equipment, a jogging track (18 laps to a mile), and a library. *64 cabins, 128 passengers, 5 passenger decks Dining room, in-room safes, refrigerators, pool, gym, hair salon, bar, laundry service; no smoking.*

Cruise West

A big player in small ships, Seattle-based Cruise West sends seven coastal cruisers to Alaska each summer. As with other smaller vessels, Alaskan wilderness, wildlife, and culture take precedence over shipboard diversions. An exploration leader, who is both naturalist and cruise coordinator, hosts evening lectures and joins passengers on many of the shore excursions—at least one of which is included at each port of call. Binoculars in every cabin, a library stocked with books of local interest, and crew members as keen to explore Alaska as the passengers all enhance the experience. A living room that feels like a lounge, wholesome meals with bread baked on board, open seating, and jeans are as formal as it gets. ■ TIP→ **The passengers, who inevitably get to know one another during the cruise, are typically active, well-traveled, over-fifties.** They come from all regions of the United States, as well as from Australia, Canada, and the United Kingdom.

Suggested tips are $12 per person per day; these are pooled for all the crew and staff at the end of the cruise.

Cruise West, 2301 5th Ave., Suite 401, Seattle, WA 98121 ☎ 206/441–8687 or 800/888–9378 www.cruisewest.com.

THE SHIPS Fodor'sChoice ★ ***Spirit of Yorktown.*** The *Spirit of Yorktown* looks more like a box yacht than a cruise ship. Its signature design is dominated by a large bridge and picture windows that ensure bright interior public spaces. In keeping with its small size, there are only two public rooms and deck space is limited. The glass-walled observation lounge does triple duty as the ship's bar, lecture room, and occasional movie "theater." A fleet of inflatable landing craft takes passengers ashore for independent exploration. Most cabins have a picture window, but a few have portholes; none have televisions. Toilets and showers are a combined unit (the toilet is inside the shower). Although the larger top-deck staterooms are quite spacious, there are only eight of them. For 2007, cabins will be refurbished in keeping with the ship's new owner, Cruise West. *69 cabins, 138 passengers, 4 passenger decks Dining room, in-room safes, bar; no room TVs, no smoking.*

> **WORD OF MOUTH**
>
> "On Cruise West, you spend most of the time either in the ship's lounge looking out the windows, or out on the decks. The focus is strictly on the natural beauty of Alaska, and you get amazing views of wildlife, because the ship can approach very close to the shoreline. We had whales and dolphins within 10 feet of the ship on multiple occasions, and we weren't viewing them from 100 feet up in the air, as on a standard cruise liner."
>
> –Moongoddess

Spirit of Oceanus. Cruise West's largest and only oceangoing vessel is also its most luxurious, with marble and polished wood in the dining room, lounges, library, and cabins. All staterooms are outside suites and 14 of them have teak-floor private balconies. Four of the five decks have outside viewing areas and there's an elevator on board. The ship, equipped with stabilizers for open ocean cruising, also carries a fleet of inflatable excursion craft for close-up visits to glaciers, waterfalls, and icebergs. Breakfast and lunch are served on deck when the weather permits. *59 cabins, 120 passengers, 5 decks Dining room, in-cabin safes, refrigerators, in-cabin VCRs, Wi-Fi, gym, outdoor hot tub, bar, laundry service; no smoking.*

Spirit of Endeavour. One of Cruise West's largest and fastest ships, the *Endeavour* provides ample deck space and a roomy lounge with large picture windows for superb views. Most of the cabins also have picture windows, and some have connecting doors, which make them convenient for families traveling together. As with Cruise West's other ships, itineraries are flexible: the captain can linger to let passengers watch a group of whales, and still make the next stop on time. *51 cabins, 102 passengers, 4 passenger decks Dining room, some refrigerators, in-cabin VCRs, Wi-Fi, bar; no smoking.*

Spirit of '98. With rounded stern and wheelhouse, old-fashioned smokestack, and Victorian decor, the *Spirit of '98* evokes a turn-of-the-20th-century steamer, although she is actually a modern ship, built in 1984. Mahogany trim inside and out, overstuffed chairs with plush floral upholstery, and an old-world bar in the grand salon add to the gold-rush-era motif. For private moments, you'll find plenty of nooks and crannies aboard the ship, including the cozy Soapy's Parlor bar at the stern. All cabins, including the two single cabins on board, have picture windows. The Owner's Suite has a living room and a whirlpool tub. Some of the cabins are wheelchair accessible and there's an elevator between the main and upper decks. *48 cabins, 96 passengers, 4 passenger decks* *Dining room, some refrigerators, in-cabin VCRs, Wi-Fi, bar; no smoking.*

Spirit of Discovery. Floor-to-ceiling windows in the main lounge provide stunning views aboard this snazzy cruiser. From here, passengers have direct access to a large outdoor viewing deck, one of two aboard. Every cabin has windows and two cabins are reserved for single travelers. *43 cabins, 84 passengers, 3 decks* *Dining room, some in-cabin VCRs, bar; no smoking.*

Spirit of Alaska. The sleek *Spirit of Alaska* carries a fleet of inflatable excursion craft for impromptu stops at isolated beaches and close-up looks at glaciers. She's also capable of bow landings, enabling passengers to go ashore at isolated spots without docks. Most cabins are small but cheerfully decorated. Toilets and showers are a combined unit (the toilet is inside the shower). Top-deck cabins have windows on two sides, so you can sample both port and starboard views. Solo travelers can book a lower-deck cabin with no single supplement. *39 cabins, 78 passengers, 4 passenger decks* *Dining room, some refrigerators, some in-cabin VCRs, bar; no TV in some cabins, no smoking.*

Spirit of Columbia. The *Columbia*'s interior is inspired by the national park lodges of the American West, with muted shades of evergreen, rust, and sand. Cabins range from windowless inside units (which solo travelers can book with no single supplement) to comfortable staterooms with chairs and picture windows. The Columbia Deluxe cabin stretches the width of the vessel; just under the bridge, its row of forward-facing windows gives a captain's-eye view of the ship's progress. Like the *Spirit of Alaska,* the *Columbia* can land at isolated spots without docks. *38 cabins, 78 passengers, 4 passenger decks* *Dining room, some refrigerators, some in-cabin VCRs, bar; no TV in some cabins, no smoking.*

Lindblad Expeditions

The ships of Lindblad Expeditions forgo port calls at larger, busier towns and instead spend time looking for wildlife, exploring out-of-the way inlets, and making Zodiac landings at isolated beaches. Each ship has a video-microphone, a hydrophone, and an underwater camera so passengers can listen to whale songs and watch live video of what's going on beneath the waves. In the evening, the ships' naturalists recap the day's sights and adventures over cocktails in the lounge. A video chronicler captures the whole cruise on tape. All shore excursions except flightseeing are included, and Lindblad charges one of the industry's lowest single supplements. ■ TIP→ **Lindblad attracts active, adventurous, well-traveled over-forties, with quite a few singles.** Some sailings are specially designed for families (fares are 25 percent off for kids under 21); other sailings focus on photography. Both itineraries—the 8-day Alaska Coastal Wilderness trip and the 12-day Alaska, British Columbia, and San Juan Islands cruise—offer an extension to Denali National Park.

Tips of $12 per person per day are suggested; these are pooled among the crew at journey's end.

Lindblad Expeditions, 96 Morton St., New York, NY 10014 212/ 765–7740 or 800/397–3348 www.expeditions.com.

THE SHIPS **_Sea Bird, Sea Lion._** These small, shallow-draft sister ships can tuck into nooks and crannies that bigger ships can't reach. An open-top sundeck, forward observation lounge, and viewing deck at the bow offer plenty of room to take in the scenery. These ships are comfortable, but public spaces and cabins are small. The ships are also equipped with bowcams (underwater cameras that monitor activity) and you can navigate the camera using a joystick to observe sealife. The ship's Internet kiosk provides e-mail access. Fitness equipment is set up on the bridge deck, and the LEX Wellness room offers massages, body treatments, and a morning stretching program on deck. A fleet of Zodiacs and kayaks can take you closer to the water. All staterooms are outside, and upper-category cabins have picture windows that open. *31 cabins, 62 passengers, 3 passenger decks Dining room, gym equipment, bar; no cabin TVs, no smoking.*

Southeast Alaska

3

INCLUDING KETCHIKAN, JUNEAU, HAINES, SITKA & SKAGWAY

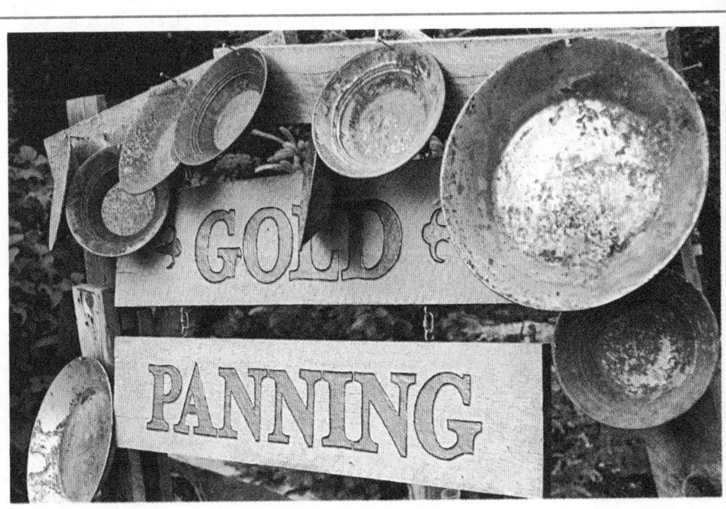

Exploring Skagway's preserved Gold-Rush riches is a fun way to learn about this region's colorful past.

WORD OF MOUTH

"Glacier Bay National Park is amazing. I took my son and we saw breaching humpbacks, a bear on the beach with cubs, puffins, eagles, sea otters, and sea lions."

–wolfie11

"We took the Alaska State ferry up the Inside Passage. We were lucky to see a couple of Orcas and also stopped to watch a glacier calve."

–dfrostnh

www.fodors.com/forums

WELCOME TO SOUTHEAST ALASKA

TOP REASONS TO GO

★ **Native art and culture:** Ancestral home of the Tlingit, Haida, and Tsimshian, the Southeast is dedicated to preserving native heritage. Native crafts include totem poles and masks.

★ **Rivers of ice:** Visitors relish the opportunity to place a crampon-clad foot on Southeast's accessible glaciers or to admire them from a flightseeing trip.

★ **Tongass National Forest:** America's largest national forest, the Tongass is home to old-growth forests, bears, eagles, Sitka black-tailed deer, wolves, and marine mammals.

★ **Taking the ferry:** The Alaska Marine Highway is the primary means of transportation here, providing scenic voyages to many communities. It's a low-cost, high-adventure alternative to cruise-ship travel.

★ **Fishing for nirvana:** Southeast is an angler's paradise. The region has healthy populations of salmon and halibut—as well as a wealth of charter boats and fishing lodges.

1 Ketchikan and Vicinty. The self-proclaimed Salmon Capital of the World, Ketchikan is a welcoming doorway to Southeast. The town retains its surly (but amiable) frontier spirit. Be sure to check out the area's charter-fishing opportunities and local art. Ketchikan is a jumping-off point for Misty Fiords National Monument and Metlakatla.

2 Wrangell & Petersburg. These towns provide access to the magnificent Stikine River. Wrangell, dependent on the dwindling timber trade, is learning to adapt to the cruise-ship industry; it's the primary hub for travel to bear-viewing at Anan Creek. Petersburg (a.k.a. "Little Norway") has a vibrant fishing community and stellar access to fishing and hiking.

3 Sitka. With its mixed history of Tlingit, Russian, and American rule, Sitka is home to a lively community, impressive architecture, an excellent park system (including Sitka National Historical Park), and outdoor activities galore. Sitka is a must-see for anyone traveling in Southeast.

4 Juneau & Vicinity. Cruise passengers flock by the hundreds of thousands to take in the state capital's historic charm, artsy community, and natural beauty, including world-famous Mendenhall Glacier. Juneau is also the access point for many surrounding attractions, including Admiralty Island National Monument, home to Southeast's largest population of brown bears.

5 Glacier Bay National Park & Preserve. Southeast's signature attraction, Glacier Bay is home to the continent's largest collection of tidewater glaciers, which make for incredible viewing. The park's remote, undeveloped location—Gustavus, the closest town, isn't really a town at all—ensures that travelers in search of quiet repose will not be disappointed.

6 Haines & Skagway. The northern outposts of the Inside Passage, these two towns seem to have it all. Haines, on stunning Chilkat Peninsula, is home to fishermen, helicopter-skiing guides, and eagle aficionados who flock to the nearby Chilkat Bald Eagle Preserve. Skagway has gorgeous scenery, an incredible railway, and rollicking Gold Rush history.

3

GETTING ORIENTED

As remote as it is, Southeast Alaska shares a few traits with heavily populated regions. It has skyscrapers (the towering peaks of the Coast Range), traffic jams (try to swim through a salmon creek in midsummer), and sprawl (the rain forests cover hundreds of thousands of acres). The area's settlements offer plenty of attractions, from Skagway's flashy Gold Rush delights to Glacier Bay's isolated fjords.

SOUTHEAST PLANNER

Getting There & Getting Around

Thanks to its unforgiving topography and countless waterways, Southeast Alaska is best explored by ship or by plane. Unless your destination is Haines, Skagway, or Hyder, all three of which are reachable by car, forget about driving to the towns of Southeast. Cars don't do much for travelers here, anyway, as roadways typically run just a few miles out from towns and villages, then they dead-end. Many people elect to transport their vehicles (and themselves) via the ferries of the Alaska Marine Highway system. Serious cyclists bring their bikes along.

Timing & Weather

The best time to visit is from May through September, when weather is mildest, rain is less frequent, daylight hours are longest, wildlife is most abundant, the fishing is best, and festivals and tourist-oriented activities are in full swing. Packing well is essential, though, as weather in the Southeast can vary wildly regardless of season. Summertime high temperatures hover around the low to mid 60s, with far warmer days interspersed throughout. Shoulder season temperatures are a bit cooler, but the region is often significantly less crowded during those months. Be sure to bring rain gear, layered clothing, sturdy footwear, a hat, and binoculars.

How Much Time?

Like all of Alaska's regions, the Southeast covers a vast area, and most of its communities, as well as its parks, national forest lands, and other wildlands, are accessible only by boat or plane. You should therefore allow yourself at least a week here. Plenty of adventures await ambitious independent travelers who plan ahead and ride state ferries.

If strolling through downtown shopping districts and museum-hopping is your idea of a perfect afternoon, consider boarding the Alaska Marine Highway at one of its main hubs (Juneau, for instance) for a journey to Haines, Skagway, Sitka, or Petersburg. Keep in mind that many of these trips are time-consuming (Juneau to Sitka can take 10 hours, for instance), and remember to evaluate how much you enjoy shipboard travel prior to booking.

If a wilderness experience in a remote location is more your idea of fun, consider booking a multiple-night stay at a remote fly-in lodge. The Southeast is peppered with such lodges, and they offer excellent opportunities for peaceful relaxation without the added stress of mid-vacation travel arrangements.

B&B Reservation Service

B&B's are exceedingly popular in the Inside Passage, and for good reason. Dozens of regional B&Bs are excellent alternatives to local hotels; they also provide the opportunity to meet fellow travelers, dig into a homemade breakfast (such as smoked salmon omelets or authentic sourdough pancakes), and learn about the area from local business owners.

Local Agents **Bed & Breakfast Association of Alaska Innside Passage Chapter** ☎ *907/789–8822* 🌐 *www.accommodations-alaska.com*

Cabins Galore

U.S. Forest Service Cabins are scattered throughout Tongass National Forest; these rustic sites offer a charming and cheap escape (up to $45/night per cabin). Most are fly-in units, accessible by floatplanes from virtually any community in the Southeast. They offer bunks for six to eight occupants, tables, stoves, and outdoor privies—but no electricity or running water. You provide your own sleeping bag, food, and cooking utensils. Bedside reading in most cabins includes a diary kept by visitors—add your own adventure. ☎ *907/586–8800, 877/444–6777 reservations* 🌐 *www.reserveusa.com*

About the Hotels & Restaurants

From scallops to king salmon, fresh seafood dominates menus in the Southeast. American standards such as burgers, steaks, chicken, and pizza can also be found. Juneau, Sitka, and Ketchikan all have a variety of ethnic eateries, along with notable gourmet restaurants.

Lodging choices along the Inside Passage range from remote Forest Service cabins to top-end hotels. In general, the latter is a pricey option, but rates drop substantially in the off-season (mid-September to mid-May).

Budget travelers will find hostels in many of the larger towns. Fine hotels are found in Ketchikan and Juneau, and luxurious fishing lodges attract anglers on Prince of Wales Island and other places in the Southeast.

What It Costs

	$$$$	$$$	$$	$	¢
Restaurants	over $25	$20–25	$15–20	$10–15	under $10
Hotels	over $225	$175–225	$125–175	$75–125	under $75

Restaurant prices are per person for a main course at dinner. Hotel prices are for two people in a standard double room in high season.

Flying Within Southeast

Southeast's dearth of roadways helps to make it one of the most pristine destinations in the country. And there's no better way to view the twisting channels, towering mountains, and gleaming glaciers than from one of the region's many small aircraft flights.

Flying between destinations in the Southeast–while significantly more expensive than traveling via ferry or marine shuttle–is an experience you won't soon forget. If your itinerary includes an extra day or two in the Southeast (particularly in Juneau), consider spending a day flying to and from a neighboring community. Round-trip tickets from Juneau to Skagway, for instance, start at $350, as compared to approximately $170 for a one-hour flightseeing trip in and around Juneau.

There are at least 4 services offering daily flights between the Southeast's larger towns–Juneau, Haines, Skagway, Ketchikan, Sitka, Petersburg, and Wrangell–as well as a bevy of helicopter flightseeing services that specialize in short, scenic flights. Tops among the fixed-wing carriers are **L.A.B. Flying Service** (☎ 907/789–9160 🌐 www.labflying.com) and **Wings of Alaska** (🌐 www.wingsofalaska.com), both of which offer connecting flights and scenic air tours of Southeast landmarks.

A host of floatplane services offer access to remote cabins. Check out **Southeast Aviation** (☎ 888/359-6478 🌐www.southeastaviation.com) for flight details.

Updated by Nick Horton

SOUTHEAST ALASKA STRETCHES BELOW THE STATE like the tail of a kite. It is a world of massive glaciers, steep-shouldered islands, cliff-rimmed fjords, and snowcapped peaks. Glacier Bay National Park and Preserve, one of the region's most prized attractions, is home to the largest concentration of coastal glaciers on Earth. Lush stands of spruce, hemlock, and cedar blanket thousands of islands. The region's myriad bays, coves, lakes of all sizes, and swift, icy rivers provide some of the continent's best fishing grounds—and scenery as majestic and unspoiled as any in North America. Many of Southeast Alaska's wildest and most pristine landscapes are within Tongass National Forest, which encompasses nearly 17 million acres—or almost three-quarters of the Panhandle's land.

It seems the Southeast lacks only one thing: pavement. The near-total lack of connecting roads between the area's communities presents obvious challenges to four-wheeled transport; this may be an advantage or a disadvantage, depending on your point of view. The isolation, combined with the wet weather, keeps people from moving in; without these elements Southeast Alaska would probably be as densely populated as Seattle. To help remedy the transportation question, Alaskans created the Alaska Marine Highway System, a well-run network of passenger and vehicle ferries, some of which have staterooms; observation decks; cafeterias; cocktail lounges; and heated, glass-enclosed solariums.

The Southeast's natural beauty and abundance of wildlife have made it one of the world's fastest-growing cruise destinations. About 20 big cruise ships ply the Inside Passage—once the traditional route to the Klondike goldfields and today the centerpiece of many Alaskan cruises—during the height of the summer. Regular air service to the Southeast is available from the Lower 48 states and other parts of Alaska.

Three groups of native peoples inhabit the Southeast coastal region: the Tlingit, Haida, and Tsimshian. These peoples, like their coastal neighbors in British Columbia, preserve a culture rich in totemic art forms, including carved poles, masks, baskets, and ceremonial objects. Many live among non-natives in modern towns and continue their cultural traditions.

Despite the region's growing tourist appeal, a pioneer spirit still dominates the towns of Southeast. Residents—some from other states, some who can trace their ancestors back to the gold-rush days, and some whose ancestors came over the Bering Land Bridge from Asia thousands of years ago—are an adventurous bunch. The rough-and-tumble spirit of the Southeast often

WET BUT WONDERFUL

The Southeast has its drawbacks. For one thing, it rains a lot. If you plan to spend a week or more here, be prepared to encounter showers during at least a few of those days. Die-hard Southeast residents simply throw on a slicker and rubber boots and shrug it off. Their attitude is philosophical: without the rain, there would be no forests; no lakes; no streams running with salmon and trout; and no healthy populations of brown and black bears, moose, deer, mountain goats, and wolves.

combines with a worldly sophistication: those who fish are also artists, Forest Service workers may run a bed-and-breakfast on the side, and homemakers may be native-dance performers.

Exploring Southeast Alaska

The Southeast Panhandle stretches some 500 mi from Yakutat at its northernmost point to Ketchikan and Metlakatla at its southern end. At its widest point, the region measures only 140 mi, and in the upper Panhandle just south of Yakutat, at 30 mi across, it's downright skinny by Alaskan standards. Most of the Panhandle consists of a sliver of mainland buffered on the west by islands and on the east by the imposing peaks of the Coast Mountains.

Those numerous coastal islands—more than 1,000 throughout the Inside Passage—collectively constitute the Alexander Archipelago. Most of them sport mountainous terrain replete with lush covers of timber, though large clear-cuts are also common. Most communities are on islands rather than on the mainland. The principal exceptions are Juneau, Haines, and Skagway, plus the hamlets of Gustavus and Hyder. Island outposts include Ketchikan, Wrangell, Petersburg, Sitka, and the villages of Craig, Pelican, Metlakatla, Kake, Angoon, and Hoonah. Bordering Alaska just east of the Panhandle lies the Canadian province of British Columbia.

TAKE THE STATE FERRY

The **Alaska Marine Highway System** operates stateroom-equipped vehicle and passenger ferries from Bellingham, Washington, and from Prince Rupert, British Columbia. Popular among budget-minded travelers and those seeking an alternative to cruise-ship travel, the Alaska Marine Highway allows you to construct an itinerary that is all your own. The vessels call at Ketchikan, Wrangell, Petersburg, Sitka, Juneau, Haines, and Skagway, and they connect with smaller vessels serving nearby communities. Some people take the ferry all the way to South Central and southwestern Alaska. ☎ *907/465-3941 or 800/642-0066* 🌐 *www.ferryalaska.com*

KETCHIKAN

Famous for its colorful totem poles, rainy skies, steep–as–San Francisco streets, and lush island setting, Ketchikan is a favorite stop for travelers. Some 13,000 people call the town home, and during the summer, cruise ships crowd the shoreline, floatplanes depart noisily for Misty Fiords National Monument, and salmon-laden commercial fishing boats motor through Tongass Narrows. In the last decade, Ketchikan's rowdy, blue-collar heritage of logging and fishing has been softened by the loss of many timber-industry jobs and the dramatic rise of cruise-ship tourism. With some effort, though, visitors can still glimpse the rugged frontier spirit that once permeated this hardscrabble cannery town.

Southeast Alaska
KEY
State Ferry
Haines Hwy.
Klondike Hwy.
Fraser
Glacier Bay National Park
see detail map, p.184
Haines
60 - 65
see detail map, p.189
Skagway
66 - 71
see detail map, p.195
58 Glacier Bay National Park & Preserve
Gustavus 59
TO YUKUTAT, ANCHORAGE
Lynn Canal
MENDENHALL GLACIER
Juneau
45 - 56
see detail map, p.165
COAST MOUNTAINS
BRITISH COLUMBIA
Pelican
Hoonah
Douglas
Chichagof Island
Tenakee Springs
Admiralty Island National Monument
Angoon
57 Admiralty Island
Sitka
35 - 44
see detail map, p.156
Tongass National Forest
Baranof
Frederick Sound
Baranof Island
Chatham Strait
Kuiu Island
Petersburg
30 - 34
see detail map, p.144
ALEXANDER ARCHIPELAGO
Gulf of Alaska
Stikine River
Wrangell
22 - 29
see detail map, p.138
Prince of Wales Island 21
Misty Fiords National Monument
18
Hyder 20
Stewart
Thorne Bay
Klawock
Craig
Hydaburg
Revillagigedo Island
Ketchikan
1 - 17
see detail map, p.123
Metlakatla 19
Annette Island
ALASKA
BRITISH COLUMBIA
0 50 miles
0 75 km
Alaska Marine Hwy.
TO BELLINGHAM, WA
Prince Rupert
Queen Charlotte Island

The town is situated at the foot of 3,000-foot Deer Mountain, near the southeast corner of Revillagigedo (locals shorten it to Revilla) Island. Prior to the arrival of white miners and fishermen in 1885, the Tlingit used the site, located at the mouth of Ketchikan Creek, as a summer fish camp. Gold discoveries just before the turn of the 20th century brought more immigrants, and valuable timber and commercial fishing resources spurred new industries. By the 1930s the town bragged it was the "salmon-canning capital of the world." You will still find some of the Southeast's best salmon fishing around here.

Exploring Ketchikan

This town is the first bite of Alaska that many travelers taste. Despite its imposing backdrop, hillside homes, and many staircases, Ketchikan is relatively easy to walk through. Downtown's favorite stops include the Spruce Mill Development shops and Creek Street. A bit farther away you'll find the Totem Heritage Center and Deer Mountain Hatchery. Out of town (but included on most bus tours) are two longtime favorites: Totem Bight State Historical Park and Saxman Native Village.

If you're traveling on the highway in either direction, you won't go far before you run out of road. The North Tongass Highway ends about 18 mi from downtown, at Settler's Cove Campground. The South Tongass Highway terminates at a power plant about 8 mi from town. Side roads soon end at campgrounds and at trailheads, viewing points, lakes, boat-launching ramps, and private property.

What to See

9 **City Park.** The Deer Mountain Hatchery and Eagle Center lead into this small park, which has picnic tables and paved paths and is bisected by Ketchikan Creek. ✉ *Park and Fair Sts.*

★ 12 **Creek Street.** Ketchikan's infamous red-light district once existed here. During Prohibition, Creek Street was home to numerous speakeasies, and, in the early 1900s, more than 30 houses of prostitution operated here. Today the small, colorful houses, built on stilts over the creek waters, have been restored as trendy shops. Sea-kayakers often paddle up the creek at high tide.

15 **Creek Street Footbridge.** Stand over Ketchikan Creek for good salmon viewing when the fish are running. During the summer, you can see impressive runs of coho, king, pink, and chum salmon, along with smaller numbers of steelhead and rainbow trout heading upstream to spawn. ■ TIP→ **Keep your eyes peeled for sea lions snacking on the incoming fish.**

8 **Deer Mountain Hatchery and Eagle Center.** Tens of thousands of king and coho (silver) salmon are raised at this unfussy hatchery on Ketchikan Creek. Midsummer visitors can view natural spawning in the creek by pink and chum salmon as well as workers collecting and fertilizing the salmon eggs for the hatchery. Tanks hold young salmon and those old enough to head out to the ocean; check out the video detailing the fascinating life cycle of salmon. Owned by the Ketchikan Indian Corporation, the hatchery has exhibits on traditional native fishing. Also here is a nesting pair of

CLOSE UP

Alaska's Salmon & the Aquaculture Debate

FIVE SPECIES OF WILD PACIFIC salmon are found in Alaskan waters. All are anadromous, and all five species have at least two common names, making them confusing to newcomers: pink (humpback) salmon, chum (dog) salmon, coho (silver) salmon, sockeye (red) salmon, and Chinook (king) salmon. The smallest of these five, the pink salmon, has an average weight of only about 3 or 4 pounds, while king salmon can often tip the scales at more than 25 pounds. King salmon is generally considered the most flavorful, but sockeye and coho are also very highly regarded. Pinks and chum salmon are the mainstay of canneries.

After spending a year or more in the ocean (the length of time varies among the species), Pacific salmon return to their native streams to spawn and die. The annual summertime return of adult salmon is a major event in Alaska, both for the animals (including bears) that depend upon this bounty, and also for thousands of commercial fishers and sport anglers who crowd local waters.

Alaska has long been famous for its seafood, and one of the first acts following statehood in 1959 was to protect fisheries from overharvesting. Today the stocks of salmon and other fish remain healthy, and careful management ensures that they will be there in the future. In the 1980s and 1990s, aquaculture, or fish-farming, grew into an enormous international business, particularly in Norway, Chile, the United Kingdom, and British Columbia. Leery of the consequences to wild salmon, Alaska has never allowed any salmon aquaculture.

Pen-raised fish are affordable, available year-round, and of a consistent quality, but controversy surrounds the practice of fish-farming. Many people believe it has a disastrous impact on the environment, citing such examples as disease; pollution from the waste of huge concentrations of fish; and fish farms harvesting non-native species, such as Atlantic salmon.

On the other side of the debate, there are those who believe that fish-farming is helping to protect the earth's valuable—and decreasing—populations of salmon. Proponents of fish farms point out that the practice also offers revenue and more jobs. Offshore fish-farming in the United States is a hugely incendiary topic of current debate; those supporting it believe that if the farms are placed in deep ocean pockets, the pollution from and medication given to the pen-raised fish will be scattered better by strong currents. Many environmentalists beg to differ, hoping to establish stringent guidelines before opening the ocean to fish-farming corporations.

One Alaskan bumper sticker says: "Friends don't let friends eat farmed salmon." Just across the border, in British Columbia, many people find employment as fish-farm workers. No matter which side you agree with in the aquaculture debate, be sure to enjoy a plate of delicious wild salmon during your visit to Alaska—with luck, it may even be a fish you've hooked yourself!

—Don Pitcher

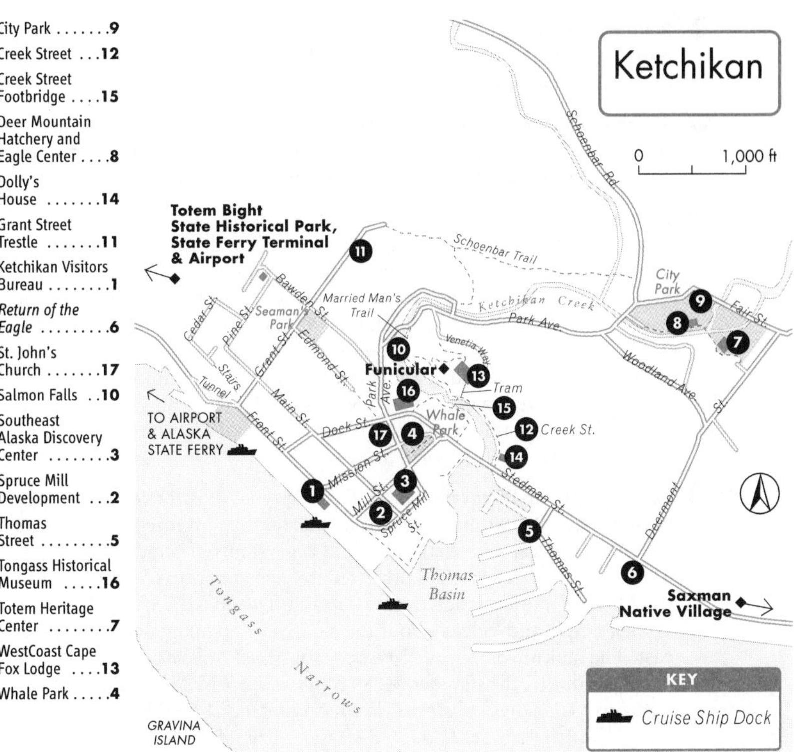

injured bald eagles. Although both are unable to fly, you may see them catching salmon that swim into their enclosure. ✉ *1158 Salmon Rd.* ☎ *907/225–6760 or 800/252–5158* 🌐 *www.kictribe.org/Hatchery/Hatchery.htm* 🎟 *$9* 🕓 *Early May–Sept., daily 8–4:30.*

14 **Dolly's House.** Formerly owned by the inimitable Dolly Arthur, this steep-roofed home once housed Creek Street's most famous brothel. The house has been preserved as a museum, complete with furnishings, beds, and a short history of the life and times of Ketchikan's best-known madam. ✉ *Creek St.* ☎ *907/225–6329* 🎟 *$5* 🕓 *Daily whenever cruise ships are in port (typically May to mid-Sept.), 8–4.*

11 **Grant Street Trestle.** At one time virtually all of Ketchikan's walkways and streets were made from wooden trestles, but now only one of these handsome wooden streets remains, constructed in 1908.

1 **Ketchikan Visitors Bureau.** This helpful visitor's bureau is located on Front Street, right next to the cruise-ship docks. ■ **TIP→ Half the space is occupied by day-tour, flightseeing, and boat-tour operators offering a range of nearby adventures.** ✉ *131 Front St.* ☎ *907/225–6166 or 800/770–3300* 🌐 *www.visit-ketchikan.com* 🕓 *May–Sept., daily 7–5 (until 6 PM when cruise ships are docked); Oct.–Apr., weekdays 8–5.*

6 ***Return of the Eagle.*** Twenty-one native students created this colorful mural on a wall of the Robertson Building on the Ketchikan campus of the University of Alaska–Southeast. ✉ *Stedman St.*

17 **St. John's Church.** Built in 1903, this church is the oldest remaining house of worship in Ketchikan. Its interior is formed from red cedar cut in the native-operated sawmill in nearby Saxman. ✉ *Bawden St.*

10 **Salmon Falls.** Get out your camera and set it for fast speed at the fish ladder, a series of pools arranged like steps that allow fish to travel upstream around a dam or falls. When the salmon start running from June onward, thousands of fish leap the falls (or take the easier fish-ladder route). They spawn in Ketchikan Creek's waters farther upstream. Many can also be seen in the creek's eddies, both above and below the falls. The falls, fish ladder, and a large carving of a jumping salmon are just off Park Avenue on Married Man's Trail. (The trail was once used by married men for discrete access to the red-light district on Creek Street.) ✉ *Married Man's Trail, off Park Ave.*

3 **Southeast Alaska Discovery Center.** This impressive visitor center features museum-quality exhibits—including one on the rain forest—that focus on the resources, native cultures, and ecosystems of Southeast Alaska. The U.S. Forest Service and other federal agencies provide information on Alaska's public lands, and a large gift shop sells natural-history books, maps, and videos about the sights in Ketchikan and the Southeast. The multimedia show "Mystical Southeast Alaska" is shown every half hour during the summer. ✉ *50 Main St.* ☎ *907/228–6220* 🌐 *www.fs.fed.us/r10/tongass/districts/discoverycenter* 🎫 *$5 May–Sept., free Oct.–Apr.* 🕒 *May–Sept., daily 8–5; Oct.–Apr., Tues.–Sat. 10–4:30.*

2 **Spruce Mill Development.** The Mill Street complex is modeled after 1920s-style cannery architecture. Spread over 6½ acres along the waterfront—much of it built out over the waters of Tongass Narrows—five buildings contain a mix of retail stores, souvenir shops, galleries, and restaurants. Cruise ships moor just a few steps away, filling the shops with tourists all summer long. ✉ *Mill and Front Sts.*

5 **Thomas Street.** From this street you can see Thomas Basin, the most accessible of Ketchikan's four harbors and home port to pleasure and commercial fishing boats. Old buildings, including the maroon-fronted Potlatch Bar, sit atop pilings, and you can walk out to the breakwater for a better view of busy Tongass Narrows.

16 **Tongass Historical Museum.** Native artifacts and pioneer relics revisit the mining and fishing eras at this homely museum in the same building as the library. Exhibits include a big, brilliantly polished lens from Tree Point Lighthouse and a well-presented collection of native tools and artwork. Other exhibits change periodically but always include Tlingit items. ✉ *629 Dock St.* ☎ *907/225–5600* 🎫 *$2* 🕒 *May–Sept., daily 8–5; Oct.–Apr., Wed.–Fri. 1–5, Sat. 10–4, Sun. 1–4.*

★ 7 **Totem Heritage Center.** Gathered from abandoned native villages, many of the authentic native totems in this rare collection are well over a century old—a rare age for cedar carvings, which are frequently lost to decay in the Southeast's exceedingly wet climate. The center also features guided tours and a video about the preservation efforts. Outside are several more poles carved in the three decades since this center opened. ✉ *Deermount St.* ☎ *907/225–5900* 🎟 *$5* ⏲ *May–Sept., daily 8–5; Oct.–Apr., weekdays 1–5.*

13 **WestCoast Cape Fox Lodge.** For the town's best harbor views and one of Southeast Alaska's most luxurious lobbies, walk to the top of steep Venetia Avenue or take the funicular ($2) up from Creek Street. ✉ *800 Venetia Way* ☎ *907/225–8001 or 800/225–8001* 🌐 *www.westcoasthotels.com.*

3

4 **Whale Park.** This park, across from St. John's Church, is the site of the **Chief Kyan Totem Pole,** now in its third incarnation. The original was carved in the 1890s, but over the decades it deteriorated and was replaced in the 1960s. The current replica was erected in 1993 and the 1960s version is now housed in the Totem Heritage Center.

Where to Stay & Eat

$$–$$$$ ✕ **Annabelle's Keg and Chowder House.** Nestled into the ground floor of historic Gilmore Hotel, this unpretentious Victorian-style restaurant serves a hearty array of seafood and pastas, including five kinds of chowder and steamer clams. Prime rib on Friday and Saturday evenings is a favorite, and an espresso bar and lounge with a jukebox add a friendly vibe. ✉ *326 Front St.* ☎ *907/225–6009* 🌐 *www.gilmorehotel.com* 💳 *AE, D, DC, MC, V.*

$$–$$$$ ✕ **Steamers.** Anchoring Ketchikan's Spruce Mill Mall, this lively, noisy, and spacious restaurant is popular with cruise passengers, and features an extensive menu of fresh seafood (including king crab and steamer clams), pasta, and steaks. Vegetarian choices are also available, and the servings are certain to fill you up. ■ TIP→ **The bar pours a whopping 125 draft beers, including a number of Alaskan brews, along with a substantial wine list.** Tall windows face Ketchikan's busy waterfront, where cruise ships and floatplanes vie for your attention. ✉ *76 Front St.* ☎ *907/225–1600* 💳 *AE, D, MC, V* ⏲ *Closed Oct.–Mar.*

¢–$$ ✕ **Ocean View Restaurant.** This locals' favorite eatery has burgers, steaks, pasta, pizzas, and seafood. They're all fine, but the main draw is authentic and very filling south-of-the-border dishes prepared under the direction of the Mexican-American owners. Service is fast and the atmosphere is pleasant. The restaurant is open until 11 PM nightly all year, and the TV always has Spanish-language sports. ✉ *1831 Tongass Ave.* ☎ *907/225–7566* 💳 *MC, V.*

$$$$ ✕🏨 **Salmon Falls Resort.** Perched along Clover Passage next to a beautiful waterfall, this resort is near the end of the road, 17 mi north of Ketchikan. Guests tend to appreciate the variety of deals, starting with a three-night package that includes two days of fishing, guide, cabin cruiser, and all meals for $1,350 per person. ■ TIP→ **The huge, octagonal restaurant is worth the half-hour drive from town, even for nonguests.** Specialties include steaks and Alaskan seafood, including blackened salmon or halibut. The restaurant is built of pine logs and, in the center, a 40-foot section of pipe manufactured to be part of the Alaska pipeline rises to

CLOSE UP

Ketchikan's Totem Pole Parks

There are 14 poles at Ketchikan's two most famous totem-pole parks. For the most part, they're 60-year-old replicas of older totem poles brought in from outlying villages as part of a federal works-cultural project during the late 1930s.

Totem Bight (✉ N. Tongass Hwy., 10 mi north of town ☎ 907/247-8574 🎫 Free ⏲ Dawn-dusk 🌐 www.alaskastateparks.org) has many totem poles and a hand-hewn native tribal house; it sits on a scenic spit of land facing the waters of Tongass Narrows. The clan house here is open daily in the summer. Most bus tours of Ketchikan include Totem Bight in their itinerary, but there is no public transportation to the site.

A 2½-mi paved walking path-bike trail parallels the road from Ketchikan to **Saxman Native Village** (✉ S. Tongass Hwy., 2 mi south of town ☎ 907/225-4846 🌐 www.capefoxtours.com), named for a missionary who helped native Alaskans settle here before 1900. A totem park dominates the center of Saxman, with poles moved here in the 1930s from abandoned village sites. The poles represent a wide range of human and animal-inspired figures, including bears, ravens, whales, and eagles.

Saxman's Beaver Clan tribal house is said to be the largest in the world. Carvers create totem poles and totemic art objects in the adjacent carver's shed (free and open whenever the carvers are working). You can get to the park on foot, by taxi, or by city bus, and you can visit the totem park on your own, but to visit the tribal house and theater you must take a tour. Tickets are sold at the gift shop across from the totems. Call ahead for tour schedules.

support the roof. Big windows overlook the waters of Clover Passage. ✉ *Mile 17, N. Tongass Hwy.* ☎ *907/225–2752, 800/247–9059 outside Alaska* 🌐 *www.salmonfallsresort.com* 🛏 *52 rooms* 🛎 *Restaurant, lounge, airport shuttle; no a/c, no room TVs* 💳 *AE, MC, V* ⏲ *Closed mid-Sept.–May.*

$$$ ✕🏨 **The Landing.** This Best Western property is named for the state ferry landing directly across the road. Featuring a recently completed addition (March 2006) that houses 33 new rooms, the Landing has clean, comfortable rooms decorated with Mission-style furniture, professional service, as well as a 25-spot underground parking garage. Although the hotel is situated over a mile from downtown, there's no need for a car; the free shuttle provides transport around town. The Landing Restaurant is almost always packed with families and a colorful breakfast clientele of locals and ferry passengers. Upstairs, Jeremiah's Fine Food and Spirits offers upscale dining in cozy digs and a relaxing no-smoking lounge built around a stone fireplace. ✉ *3434 Tongass Ave., 99901* ☎ *907/225–5166 or 800/428–8304* 🌐 *www.landinghotel.com* 🛏 *107 rooms* 🛎 *2 restaurants, microwaves, refrigerators, cable TV, Wi-Fi, exercise equipment, meeting rooms, airport shuttle, some pets allowed (fee); no a/c* 💳 *AE, D, DC, MC, V.*

★ $$$ **WestCoast Cape Fox Lodge.** Ketchikan's most distinctive property offers scenic views of the town and Thomas Basin from 135 feet above the village. The setting is cozy and luxurious, with a towering, log-framed lobby accented by Tlingit and Haida artwork, an interesting collection of museum-quality artifacts, and a roaring fire. The spacious rooms are attractively decorated with traditional tribal colors and watercolors of Alaskan birds. All rooms have views of either Tongass Narrows or Deer Mountain. The Heen Kahidi Dining Room serves seafood, pasta, chicken, and steaks. Be sure to reserve one of the window tables that overlook Ketchikan. *800 Venetia Way, 99901 907/225–8001, 866/225–8001 reservations www.westcoasthotels.com 70 rooms, 2 suites Restaurant, room service, cable TV with movies and video games, lounge, meeting room; no a/c AE, D, DC, MC, V.*

$$ **Gilmore Hotel.** Cramped between the large buildings along Front Street, the Gilmore is a boutique hotel with slightly-less-than-boutique prices. Thanks to its smallish dimensions, the 1930s-era lobby has a European feel. Rooms, though not large, blend old-fashioned comfort with modern furnishings. The lack of an elevator may be a problem for some travelers, but all the other amenities are here, including a courtesy van to shuttle you around town. A light breakfast is included each morning. Downstairs, Annabelle's Keg and Chowder House serves seafood, pasta, and prime rib. ⚠ **The Gilmore is situated right above one of the noisiest bars in town.** *326 Front St., 99901 907/225–9423 or 800/275–9423 www.gilmorehotel.com 38 rooms, 2 suites Restaurant, cable TV, bar, lounge, Wi-Fi, some pets allowed; no a/c AE, D, DC, MC, V CP.*

★ $–$$ **New York Hotel & Café.** Now more than a century old, this quaint little hotel has delightful rooms and one of the nicest eateries in Ketchikan. The menu includes breakfast and lunch, plus dinner six nights of the week that always includes steak and fresh seafood. On weekends in summertime, the café offers an outdoor crab-and-shrimp bar on a deck overlooking Thomas Basin. Hotel rooms are not large, but are comfortably furnished with antiques and queen beds. Three luxury suites along Creek Street are the real attraction here. Each of these includes a full kitchen, jetted tub, loft bedroom (with spiral staircase), and deck overlooking the water. *207 Stedman St., 99901 907/225–0246 or 866/225–0246 www.thenewyorkhotel.com 12 rooms Restaurant, some in-room hot tubs, some kitchens, cable TV, Wi-Fi; no a/c, no smoking AE, D, MC, V Restaurant closed mid-Sept. to May.*

$$–$$$ **The Narrows Inn.** Four miles from town and a mile north of the airport ferry terminal, the Narrows is a modern lodge where rustic wood trim and themed prints on the walls brighten the small rooms. Waterside rooms, including three spacious suites, have balconies overlooking Tongass Narrows—a good place to watch seals, otters, and eagles. The Inn offers complimentary shuttle service to the Ketchikan side of the airport ferry and to the Alaska Marine Highway Ferry Terminal just north of town. Don't feel like trekking into town for dinner? No worries: the Inn is also home to a delicious steak-and-seafood restaurant and Thornlow's Waterfront bar, which offers free binocular usage for patrons. *Box*

8296, 99901 ☎ 907/247–2600 or 888/686–2600 🌐 www.narrowsinn.com 44 rooms, 3 suites Restaurant, microwaves, refrigerators, cable TV, bar, Wi-Fi, airport shuttle; no a/c ▭ AE, D, MC, V.

$–$$$ **Cedars Lodge.** If you've come to cast your line, this is your spot: this small, fishing-focused lodge has motel-style accommodations on the street side and deluxe suites whose large windows face Tongass Narrows. The latter are great for a front-row view of the floatplanes, boats, and cruise ships that parade past all summer. All rooms have Jacuzzi baths, and suites also include full kitchens. Various fishing and lodging packages are available, including four nights' lodging and three days of meals and guided fishing for $1,839–$2,073 per person. Lodging-only rates apply if space is available. ✉ *1471 Tongass Ave., Box 8331, 99901* ☎ *907/225–1900 or 800/813–4363* 🌐 *www.cedarslodge.com* *8 rooms, 5 suites* *Restaurant, in-room hot tubs, some kitchens, cable TV; no a/c* ▭ *AE, D, DC, MC, V* *Closed Oct.–mid-May.*

$$ **Madame's Manor Bed & Breakfast.** This luxurious hillside B&B provides the full Victorian treatment, with three extravagantly decorated suites. You'll find rose wallpaper, queen-size canopy beds, antique furnishings, kitchenettes, dramatic harbor views, and exquisite private baths. The nicest suite includes a hot tub and solarium. Enjoy a gourmet breakfast of sourdough pancakes and seasonal fruit on the deck overlooking bustling Tongass Narrows. Two hillside apartments (Country Manor Vacation Rentals) are also available, starting for $110 a night plus $15 for extra guests. These are perfect for families. ✉ *324 Cedar St., 99901* ☎ *907/247–2774 or 877/531–8159 Ext. 2484* 🌐 *www.madamesmanor.com* *3 suites* *Cable TV; no a/c, no smoking* ▭ *MC, V* *BP.*

¢ **Ward Lake Campgrounds.** Two rain-forest campgrounds are located 8 mi north of Ketchikan; turn right onto Revilla Road and follow it to the exceptionally scenic Ward Lake area. Both are managed by the Forest Service, with sites reservable ($9 extra) through **Reserve USA** (☎ 518/885–3639 or 877/444–6777 🌐 www.reserveusa.com). Signal Creek Campground has 24 campsites adjacent to Ward Lake, a popular fishing, hiking, and picnicking area. Last Chance Campground is a mile farther up Revilla Road, and has 19 creek-side sites. Running water and restrooms (no showers) are provided. ☎ *907/225–2148* 🌐 *www.fs.fed.us/r10/tongass* *$10* ▭ *AE, D, MC, V.*

Nightlife

Bars

Ketchikan has quieted down in recent years as the economy shifted away from logging into tourism, but it remains something of a party town, especially when crews stumble off fishing boats with cash in hand. You won't have any trouble finding something going on at several downtown bars. **First City Saloon** (✉ 830 Water St. ☎ 907/225–1494) is the main dance spot, with live rock, blues, or jazz Tuesday through Saturday. The **Potlatch Bar** (✉ Thomas Basin ☎ 907/225–4855) delivers up music most weekends.

Shopping

Art Galleries

AlaskaMade Gallery (✉ 123 Stedman St. ☎ 907/225–5404 or 888/877–9706 🌐 www.alaskamade.com) is a small creek-side gallery with art, *ulus* (a curved Eskimo knife), cards, gifts, and even Alaskan-roasted coffees.

In business since 1972, **Scanlon Gallery** (✉ 318 Mission St. ☎ 907/247–4730 or 888/228–4730 🌐 www.scanlongallery.com) carries prints from a number of well-known Alaska artists, including Byron Birdsall, Rie Muñoz, John Fehringer, Barbara Lavallee, and Jon Van Zyle.

3

Design, art, and clothing, and collectibles converge in the stylish **Soho Coho Contemporary Art and Craft Gallery** (✉ 5 Creek St. ☎ 907/225–5954 or 800/888–4070 🌐 www.trollart.com), where you'll find an eclectic collection of art and T-shirts featuring the work of owner Ray Troll—best known for his wacky fish art—as well as that of other Southeast Alaskan artists.

Books

Upstairs from the Soho Coho Gallery, **Parnassus** (✉ 5 Creek St. ☎ 907/225–7690) is a book lover's bookstore, with creaking floors, cozy quarters, many Alaskan titles, and a knowledgeable staff.

Sports, the Outdoors & Guided Tours

Canopy Tours

Often associated with rain forests of the tropical sort, canopy tours are Ketchikan's fastest-growing outdoor activity. Featuring a series of zip lines, aerial boardwalks, and suspension bridges, canopy tours provide an up-close view of the coastal forests. Granted, you won't spend the whole tour admiring the foliage: at **Alaska Canopy Adventures** (🌐 www.alaskacanopyadventures.com)—a new course at the Alaska Rainforest Sanctuary, 16 mi south of town—the longest of the tour's eight zip lines stretches over 800 feet, and whisks you along some 130 feet off the ground. Book online or with your cruise line. Canopy tours are also offered through **Southeast Exposure** (☎ 907/225–8829 🌐 www.southeastexposure.com), a well-known kayaking outfit in the area.

Fishing

Sportfishing for salmon and trout is excellent in the Ketchikan area, in both saltwater and freshwater lakes and streams. As a result, a plethora of local boat owners offer charter and guide services. Contact the **Ketchikan Visitors Bureau** (☎ 907/225–6166 or 800/770–3300 🌐 www.visit-ketchikan.com) for information on guide services and locations.

SEAFOOD GALORE

For some of the Southeast's best canned, smoked, or frozen salmon and halibut, along with crab, and clams, try either of the two locations of **Salmon Etc.** ✉ *10 Creek St.* ☎ *907/225-6008 or 800/354-7256* ✉ *322 Mission St.* ☎ *907/225-6008* 🌐 *www.salmonetc.com*

Harbor & Air Tours

Owned by Goldbelt Native corporation, **Alaska Cruises** (☎ 907/225–6044 or 800/228–1905 🌐 www.mistyfjord.net) runs harbor tours of the Ketchikan waterfront during which you'll learn local history and get a sea-level view of this bustling town. The company also provides speedy catamaran excursions to Misty Fiords National Monument.

If you want to head out on a floatplane to see the environs, contact **Southeast Aviation** (☎ 907/225-2900 or 888/359-6478 🌐 www.southeastaviation.com). They offer tours of the glaciers and mountains of Misty Fiords National Monument.

Hiking

Get details on hiking opportunities around Ketchikan from the Southeast Alaska Discovery Center (⇨ What to See, *above*). If you're an avid hiker, the 3-mi trail from downtown to the 3,000-foot summit of **Deer Mountain** will repay your efforts with a spectacular panorama of the city below and the wilderness behind. The trail begins at the corner of Fair and Deermount streets, and passes through dense forests before emerging into the alpine. A shelter cabin near the summit provides a place to warm up.

Ward Lake Recreation Area, about 6 mi north of town, has hikes next to lakes and streams and beneath towering spruce and hemlock trees; it also has several covered picnic spots and a pleasant campground. An easy 1⅓-mi nature trail circles the lake, which is popular for steelhead and salmon fishing. **Ward Creek Trail** begins from the lake and follows the creek 2½ mi, with shoreside paths to creek-side platforms. The trail is hard-packed gravel, which is wide and gentle enough for wheelchairs. More ambitious hikers head up the 2-mi **Perseverance Trail**, a challenging set of steps and boardwalk that take hikers through the open muskeg (peat bog) to a small lake.

Local Interest

A native-owned company, **Cape Fox Tours** (☎ 907/225–4846 🌐 www.capefoxtours.com) leads tours of Saxman Native Village and the historic George Inlet Cannery. You can book most of these tours aboard the cruise ships or at the Ketchikan Visitors Bureau.

Scuba Diving

Alaska Diving Service (✉ 5194 Shoreline Dr. ☎ 907/225–3667) rents tanks and equipment and guides you to the best places to dive in these pristine waters. You'll see colorful fish, sea cucumbers, starfish, soft corals, and other creatures.

FOR THE LUMBERJACK IN YOU

The **Great Alaskan Lumberjack Show** is a 90-minute lumberjack contest providing a Disneyesque taste of old-time woodsman skills, including ax throwing, bucksawing, springboard chopping, logrolling duels, and a 50-foot tree climb. Shows take place in a covered, heated grandstand directly behind the Spruce Mill Development and go on rain or shine all summer. *✉ 50 Main St. ☎ 907/225-9050 or 888/320-9049 🌐 www.lumberjackshows.com 🎫 $31 ⏲ May–Sept., 3 times daily; hrs vary.*

Sea Kayaking

Popular with cruise-ship travelers, **Southeast Exposure** (☎ 907/225–8829 🌐 www.southeastexposure.com) offers waterfront paddles on Clover Pass. **Southeast Sea Kayaks** (☎ 907/225–1258 or 800/287–1607 🌐 www.kayakketchikan.com) leads kayak tours of Ketchikan's historic waterfront and offers kayak lessons and rentals. They specialize in guided multinight trips to Misty Fiords.

AROUND KETCHIKAN

Misty Fiords National Monument

⓲ *40 mi east of Ketchikan by air.*

Just east of Ketchikan, Misty Fiords National Monument is a wilderness of cliff-faced fjords (or fiords, if you follow the monument's spelling), mountains, and islands with an abundance of spectacular coastal scenery, wildlife, and recreation. Small boats enable close-up views of breathtaking vistas. Travel on these waters can be an almost mystical experience, with the greens of the forest reflected in the mirrorlike waters of the monument's many fjords. You may find yourself in the company of a whale, see a bear fishing for salmon along the shore, or even pull in your own salmon for an evening meal. ■ TIP→ **Note, however, that the name Misty refers to the weather you're likely to encounter in this especially rainy part of Alaska.**

Fodor's Choice ★ Most visitors to Misty Fiords arrive on day trips via floatplane from Ketchikan or on board a catamaran run by **Alaska Cruises** (☎ 907/225–6044 or 800/228–1905 🌐 www.mistyfjord.net). ✉ *3031 Tongass Ave., Ketchikan 99901* ☎ *907/225–2148* 🌐 *www.fs.fed.us/r10/tongass.*

Metlakatla

⓳ *12 mi south of Ketchikan.*

The village of Metlakatla—whose name translates roughly to "salt water passage"—is on Annette Island, just a dozen miles from busy Ketchikan but a world away culturally. A visit to this quiet community offers visitors a chance to learn about life in a small Inside Passage native community. Local taxis can take you to other sights around the island, including Yellow Hill and the old Air Force base.

In most Southeast native villages, the people are Tlingit or Haida in heritage. Metlakatla is the exception, as most folks are Tsimshian (*sim*-shee-ann). They moved to the island from British Columbia in 1887, led by William Duncan, an Anglican missionary from England. The town grew rapidly and soon contained dozens of buildings on a grid of streets, including a cannery, a sawmill, and a church that could seat 1,000 people. Congress declared Annette Island a federal Indian reservation in 1891, and it remains the only reservation in Alaska today. Father Duncan continued to control life in Metlakatla for decades, until the government finally stepped in shortly before his death in 1918.

During World War II the U.S. Army built a major air base 7 mi from Metlakatla that included observation towers for Japanese subs, airplane hangars, gun emplacements, and housing for 10,000 soldiers. After the war, it served as Ketchikan's airport for many years, but today the long runways are virtually abandoned save for a few private flights.

Metlakatla's religious heritage still shows today. The clapboard **William Duncan Memorial Church,** topped with two steeples, burned in 1948 but was rebuilt several years later. It is one of nine churches in tiny Metlakatla. **Father Duncan's Cottage** is maintained to appear exactly as it would have in 1891, and includes original furnishings, personal items, and a collection of turn-of-the-20th-century music boxes. ✉ *Corner of 4th Ave. and Church St.* ☎ *907/886–8687* 🌐 *www.metlakatlatours.com* 🎫 *$2* ⏲ *Weekdays 8:30–12:30 or when cruise ships are in port.*

Father Duncan worked hard to eliminate traditional Tsimshian beliefs and dances, but today the people of Metlakatla have resurrected their past; they perform old dances in traditional regalia. The best place to catch these performances is at the traditional **longhouse** (known as *Le Sha'as* in the Tsimshian dialect), which faces Metlakatla's boat harbor. Three totem poles stand on the back side of the building, and the front is covered with a Tsimshian design. Inside are displays of native crafts and a model of the fish traps that were once common throughout the Inside Passage. Native dance groups perform here on Wednesday and Friday in summer. Just next to the longhouse is an **Artists' Village** where booths display locally made arts and crafts. The village and longhouse open when groups and tours are present.

Two miles from town is a boardwalk path that leads up the 540-foot **Yellow Hill.** Distinctive yellow sandstone rocks and panoramic vistas make this a worthwhile detour on clear days.

Where to Stay & Eat

$ ✕🏨 **Metlakatla Inn and Restaurant.** This two-story building offers standard motel accommodations with private decks off the upstairs rooms. The restaurant has the usual American favorites such as burgers and steak, but the fresh halibut and shrimp are the real attractions. Breakfast is available only for hotel guests. ✉ *3rd Ave. and Lower Milton St., 99926* ☎ *907/886–3456* 🛏 *7 rooms, 2 apartments* 👍 *Restaurant, microwaves, refrigerators, cable TV, in-room VCRs; no a/c, no smoking* 💳 *AE, D, MC, V.*

$ 🏨 **Tuck'em Inn Bed & Breakfast.** This family-run lodging is located in two downtown houses. Rooms are functional, with down comforters, quilts, and access to a kitchen and sitting room. Ingredients for a make-it-yourself Continental breakfast are included. ✉ *Hillcrest and Western Aves., 99926* ☎ *907/886–6611* 🌐 *www.alaskanow.com/tuckem-inn* 🛏 *6 rooms* 👍 *Cable TV; no a/c, no smoking* 💳 *MC, V* 🍽 *CP.*

Sports, the Outdoors & Guided Tours

BOATING You can catch a ferry operated by the **Alaska Marine Highway System** (☎ 907/465–3941 or 800/642–0066 🌐 www.ferryalaska.com) to Metlakatla from Ketchikan.

FLOATPLANE **ProMech Air** (☎ 907/886–3845 or 800/860–3845 🌐 www.promechair.com) has scheduled floatplane flights between Ketchikan and Metlakatla.

LOCAL INTEREST Run by the Metlakatla community, **Metlakatla Tours** (☎ 907/886–4441 🌐 www.metlakatlatours.com) leads local tours that include visits to Duncan Cottage, the cannery, and the longhouse, along with a Tsimshian dance performance.

3

Hyder

⑳ *90 mi northeast of Ketchikan.*

The tiny town of Hyder sits at the head of narrow Portland Canal, a 70-mi-long fjord northeast of Ketchikan. The fjord marks the border between Canada and the United States, and Hyder sits just 2 mi from the larger town of Stewart, British Columbia. ■ **TIP→ It's also one of the few Southeast settlements that is accessible by road.** Highway 37A continues over spectacular Bear Pass from Stewart, connecting these towns with the rest of Canada.

HYDER TIPS

The town of Hyder is small and has only a handful of tourist-oriented businesses, a post office, and library. Nearby Stewart has more to offer, including a bank, museum, hotels, restaurants, and camping. You will need to check in at Canadian customs (open 24 hours) before crossing the border from Hyder into Stewart. Canadian money is primarily used in Hyder, but greenbacks are certainly accepted.

The 1898 discovery of gold and silver in the surrounding mountains brought a flood of miners to the Hyder area, and the town eventually became a major shipping port. Mining remained important for decades, but a devastating 1948 fire destroyed much of the town, which had been built on pilings over the water. A small amount of mining still takes place here, but the beauty of the area now attracts increasing numbers of tourists. Today, quiet Hyder calls itself "the friendliest ghost town in Alaska."

The **Stewart Historical Society Museum,** housed in the town's former fire hall, contains wildlife displays and exhibits on the region's mining history. ✉ *6th and Columbia Sts.* ☎ *250/636–2568* 🌐 *www.stewartmuseum.homestead.com* 🎫 *$2* ⏲ *May, June, and Sept., weekends 1–4; July and Aug., daily 1–4.*

NOW YOU KNOW

A small, empty stone storehouse stands along the road as you enter Hyder. Built in 1896, this is the oldest masonry building in Alaska.

Six miles north of Hyder on Salmon River Road is the **Fish Creek Wildlife Observation Site.** From late July to early September, a large run of salmon attracts black and brown bears here, which, in turn, attract more than a few photographers. The creek produces some of the largest chum salmon anywhere. Twenty-five miles east of Stewart on Highway 37A is the imposing **Bear Glacier.** The glacier sits across a small lake that is often crowded with icebergs. A dirt road from Hyder leads 17 mi to remote **Salmon Glacier,** one of few glaciers accessible by road in Southeast Alaska.

Getting "Hyderized" (which involves drinking and drinking-related silliness) is a term that you will hear upon arrival in the area. You can get Hyderized at **Glacier Inn** (✉ Main St. ☎ 250/636–9243), where the walls are papered with thousands of signed bills. The tradition supposedly began when prospectors would tack a dollar bill on the wall in case they were broke when they returned.

Where to Stay & Eat

$–$$$$ ✕ **Bitter Creek Cafe.** This bustling Stewart café serves a variety of cuisine, including gourmet steaks, pizzas, lasagna, burgers, seafood, and even Mexican dishes. It's all homemade, including the freshly baked breads. The quirky interior is adorned with a fun collection of antiques as well as a 1930 Pontiac. Relax on the outside deck on a summer afternoon. ✉ *5th Ave., Stewart* ☎ *250/636–2166* ▭ *AE, MC, V* ⊗ *Closed Oct.–Apr.*

¢–$ **Ripley Creek Inn.** Stewart's best lodging option covers three historic downtown buildings. All rooms are bright, with Mission-style furnishings; some also include sofa beds, decks, and glacier views. The main building also houses Toastworks Museum, a repository of antique toasters and other kitchen items. Fittingly enough, this is where Continental breakfasts are served for inn guests. *Box 625, Stewart* ☎ *250/636–2344* 🌐 *www.ripleycreekinn.homestead.com* *34 rooms* *Cable TV, sauna, some pets allowed; no a/c* ▭ *AE, DC, MC, V* *CP.*

Sports, the Outdoors & Guided Tours

AIR **Taquan Air** (☎ 907/225–8800, 800/770–8800, or 250/636–9150 🌐 www.taquanair.com) has year-round service between Ketchikan and Hyder every Monday and Thursday ($165 one way).

BUS **Seaport Limousine** (☎ 250/636–2622 🌐 www.seaportnorthwest.com) leads guided tours of the Hyder area, including Fish Creek and Salmon Glacier. (Don't expect any stretch Hummers here, though—Seaport uses buses for its tours.)

Prince of Wales Island

21 *15 mi northwest of Ketchikan.*

Prince of Wales Island stretches more than 130 mi from north to south, making it the largest island in Southeast Alaska. Only two American islands—Kodiak in Alaska and Hawaii in the Hawaiian chain—are larger. Prince of Wales (or "P.O.W." as locals call it) has a diversity of landforms, a plethora of wildlife, and exceptional sportfishing. The island has long been a major source of timber, both on Tongass National Forest lands and those owned by native corporations. While much of the native land has been cut over, environmental restrictions on public lands have greatly reduced logging activity. The island's economy is now supported by small-scale logging operations, tourism, and commercial fishing.

Approximately 7,000 people live on Prince of Wales Island, scattered in small villages and towns. A network of 1,500 mi of roads—nearly all built to access clear-cuts—crisscrosses the island, providing connections to even the smallest settlement. Paved roads now link Craig, Hollis, Thorne Bay, Hydaburg, and Coffman Cove. ■ TIP→ **The prevalence of roads, combined with ferry and air access from Ketchikan, makes it easy to explore this island, though few people choose to do so.**

The primary commercial center for Prince of Wales is **Craig,** on the island's western shore. This town of 1,500 retains a hard-edged aura fast disappearing in many Inside Passage towns, where tourism now holds sway. Although sightseeing attractions are slim, the town exudes a frontier spirit, and its small-boat harbors buzz with activity. *Prince of Wales Chamber of Commerce, Box 490, Klawock 99925 ☎ 907/755–2626 www.princeofwalescoc.org.*

The **Inter-Island Ferry Authority** (☎ 907/826–4848 or 866/308–4848 www.interislandferry.com) operates a daily vehicle and passenger ferry between Ketchikan and Prince of Wales Island. The ferry terminal is in the tiny settlement of Hollis, 31 mi from Craig on a paved road. Another IFA ferry connects Coffman Cove—located on the north end of Prince of Wales—with Wrangell and Petersburg. (Take note: This route, which was new in 2006, calls at South Mitkof Island, 25 mi of paved and gravel road from Petersburg proper.)

A half-dozen miles from Craig is the Tlingit village of **Klawock,** with a sawmill, cannery, hatchery, and the island's only airport. The town is best known for its striking 21 totem poles in **Totem Park.** Several of these colorful poles were moved here in the 1930s; others are more recent carvings. You can watch carvers restoring old totems at the carving shed, across the road from the grocery store. Klawock is also home to **Prince of Wales Hatchery** (☎ 907/755–2231 www.powhasalmon.org Tours June–Aug., Mon.–Sat. 1–5), one of the state's most effective hatcheries. It's open for free summertime tours, and it also has a small visitor center with an aquarium full of young coho salmon. Along the bay, you'll find **St. John's by the Sea Catholic Church,** with stained-glass windows picturing native Alaskans.

The Haida village of **Hydaburg,** approximately 40 mi south of Klawock (via chip-sealed road), lies along scenic Sukkwan Strait. A small collection of **totem poles** occupies the center of this Haida settlement, the only one in Alaska. Originally from British Columbia's Queen Charlotte Island, the Haida settled here around 1700.

A number of large natural caverns pockmark northern Prince of Wales Island. The best-known of these, **El Capitan Cave,** has one of the deepest pits in the United States and is open to the public. Paleontologists have found a wealth of black bear, brown bear, and other mammal fossils in the cave, including some that date back more than 12,000 years. The Forest Service leads free two-hour El Capitan tours several times a week in the summer. Reservations are required, and no children under age seven are permitted. Rubber boots and a light jacket are a good idea for spelunkers. ✉ *Mile 51 along North Prince of Wales Rd.* ☎ *907/828–3304 (Forest Service).*

Where to Stay & Eat

$$$$ ✕ **Shelter Cove Lodge.** Tall windows front the water at this modern restaurant and lodge along the South Boat Harbor in Craig. Fresh seafood tops the menu, along with steaks, delectable desserts, Alaskan beers, and nightly specials. Prime rib attracts the locals on Friday and Saturday nights. The lodge here runs all-inclusive fishing packages, starting at $1,750 per person for three days and four nights. Rooms are modern and each contains a queen and twin bed. Six of them face the harbor. ✉ *703 Hamilton Dr., Craig 99921* ☎ *907/826–2939 or 888/826–3474* 🌐 *www.sheltercovelodge.com* *10 rooms* *Microwaves, refrigerators, cable TV, boating, fishing; no a/c* *AE, MC, V* ⊗ *Restaurant closed Oct.–May.*

$$$$ **McFarland's Floatel.** You'll need a boat or floatplane to access this quiet resort 2 mi across the bay from the logging town of Thorne Bay on the eastern side of Prince of Wales. Each of the four beachfront log cabins sleeps up to six people and includes a loft, woodstove, full kitchen, and private bath. A 200-foot walkway leads to the floating main lodge, which was built in Ketchikan but floated by raft to its present location in 1981. The lodge now acts as dining room and gathering place for Floatel guests and visitors, who can feast on hearty home-cooked seafood dinners for $30 (reservations required). Co-owner Jeannie McFarland teaches basketry workshops and sells her pine-needle raffia baskets here. Charter-fishing trips are available, or you can rent a skiff and fishing gear and head out on your own. *Box 19149, Thorne Bay 99919* ☎ *907/828–3335 or 888/828–3335* 🌐 *www.mcfarlandsfloatel.com* *4 cabins* *Boating, fishing, car rental; no a/c, no room phones, no room TVs, no smoking* *MC, V.*

$$$$ **Waterfall Resort.** At this upscale fishing lodge, you sleep in Cape
Fodor's Choice ★
Cod–style cottages from the 1930s, eat bountiful meals with all the trimmings, and fish from custom-built 25-foot cabin cruisers under the care of a fishing guide. ■ **TIP→ You can also have the fish you catch processed, packaged, and shipped—there's no better Alaskan souvenir.** A three-night minimum stay with all meals, including floatplane fare from Ketchikan, comes to around $3,475 per person. *Box 6440, Ketchikan 99901* ☎ *907/225–9461 or 800/544–5125* 🌐 *www.waterfallresort.com* *10 lodge rooms, 4 suites, 26 cabins* *Restaurant, boating, fishing, meeting rooms; no a/c, no room phones, no room TVs, no kids under 10* *AE, D, MC, V* ⊗ *Closed Sept.–late May* *FAP.*

$–$$ **Inn of the Little Blue Heron.** With sweeping water views, comfortable-but-cozy rooms, and outdoor decks tailored for simultaneous coffee drinking and wildlife viewing, the Little Blue Heron is a favorite among regular visitors to Craig. Two locations in town cater to your desired luxury factor: the South Cove Boat Harbor outpost features four small but well-appointed rooms (two with water views), while the newer Bucareli Bay lodge offers up two spacious rooms with unimpeded bay views, queen-size Tempurpedic mattresses, and satellite TV. ✉ *406 9th St., Craig 99921* ☎ *907/826–3608* 🌐 *www.littleblueheroninn.com* *6 rooms, 1 suite* *Refrigerators, Wi-Fi, satellite TV; no a/c* *AE, MC, V.*

$ **Ruth Ann's Motel.** Victorian-style furnishings and details flavor this classy motel. The honeymoon suite includes a large hot tub and kitchenette.

Across the street, the popular Ruth Ann's Restaurant serves home-style food with seafood and steaks at dinner, and burgers, sandwiches, and fish-and-chips at lunch. Ask for a table in the back room, where picture windows face the harbor; a tiny bar at the front of the restaurant fills up most nights. ✉ *300 Water St., Craig 99921* ☎ *907/826–3378* *14 rooms, 1 suite* *Restaurant, some microwaves, refrigerators, cable TV; no a/c* *AE, D, DC, MC, V.*

3

WRANGELL

22–29 *87 mi north of Ketchikan.*

A small, unassuming timber and fishing community, Wrangell sits on the northern tip of Wrangell Island, near the mouth of the fast-flowing Stikine River—North America's largest un-dammed river. Like much of the Southeast, the town has suffered in recent years from a poor economy. Wrangell has flown three different national flags in its time. Russia established Redoubt St. Dionysius here in 1834. Five years later, Great Britain's Hudson's Bay Company leased the southern Alaska coastline, renaming the settlement Fort Stikine. It was rechristened Wrangell when the Americans took over in 1867; the name came from Baron Ferdinand Petrovich von Wrangel, governor of the Russian-American Company.

Exploring Wrangell

The rough-around-the-edges town of Wrangell is off the track of the larger cruise ships, so it does not suffer from tourist invasions to the degree that Ketchikan and Juneau do. Hence, it is nearly devoid of tourist-targeted shops that dominate so many other nearby downtown areas. The town is fairly compact, and most sights are within walking distance of the city dock or ferry terminal.

What To See

★ 24 **Chief Shakes Island.** This small island sits in the center of Wrangell's protected harbor, and is accessible by a footbridge from the bottom of Front Street. Seven totem poles surround a traditional-style tribal house, built in the 1930s as a replica of one that was home to many of the various Shakes and their peoples. ✉ *Off Shakes St.* ☎ *907/874–3747* *$2* *Daily when cruise ships are in port (ask at Wrangell Visitor Center) or by appointment.*

25 **Chief Shakes's grave site.** Buried here is Shakes V, who led the local Tlingit during the first half of the 19th century. A white picket fence surrounds the grave, and two killer-whale totem poles mark his resting spot overlooking the harbor. Find the grave on Case Avenue. ✉ *Case Ave.*

26 **Irene Ingle Public Library.** The library, behind the post office, has two ancient petroglyphs out front, and is home to a large collection of Alaskana books, computers with free Internet access, and a helpful staff. ✉ *124 2nd St.* ☎ *907/874–3535.*

23 **Kiksetti Totem Park.** You'll find a couple of recently carved totem poles at this pocket-size park of Alaska greenery. ✉ *Front St.*

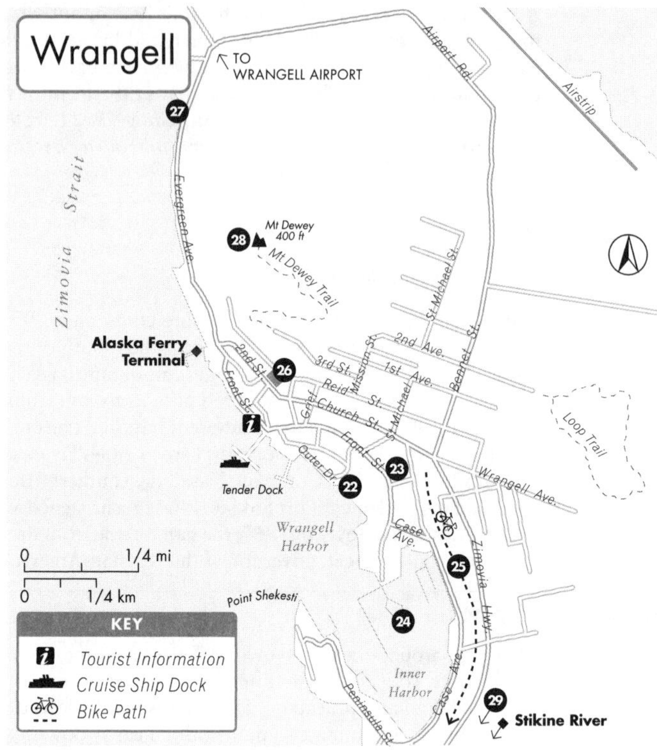

28 Mount Dewey. Despite the name, this landmark is more of a hill than a peak. Still, it's a steep 15-minute climb from town to the top through a second-growth forest. The trail begins from 3rd Street behind the high school, and a viewpoint on top provides an obscured vista of protected waterways and quirkily named islands, including Zarembo, Vank, and Woronkofski.

22 Nolan Museum and Civic Center. Wrangell's museum moved into spacious new quarters in 2004, a building that acts as a centerpiece for cultural life in Wrangell. Professionally produced exhibits provide a window on the region's rich history. Featured pieces include decorative posts from Chief Shakes's clan house, petroglyphs, century-old spruce-root and cedar-bark baskets, masks, gold-rush memorabilia, and a fascinating photo collection. If you're spending any time in town, don't pass this up. The building also houses a 200-seat movie theater/performance space and the **Wrangell Visitor Center** (☎ 907/874–3901 or 800/367–9745 ⊕ www.wrangellchamber.org). The latter is staffed when the museum is open and has details on local adventure options. ✉ *296 Outer Dr.* ☎ *907/874–3770* 🎫 *$5* ⏲ *May–Sept., Tues.–Sat. 10–5, and when ferry or cruise ships are in port; Oct.–Apr., Tues.–Sat. 1–5.*

A GOOD WALK

Bone up on local history and biology at the **Nolan Museum and Civic Center** which houses informative and surprisingly entertaining exhibits, a well-stocked gift shop, and a helpful visitor center. Farther along Front Street, check out **Kiksetti Totem Park** before turning onto Shakes Street to see the town's prized attraction, **Chief Shakes Island.** You will probably want to spend time here just soaking in the harbor view and examining the old totem poles. **Chief Shakes's grave site** is on the hill overlooking Wrangell Harbor. Get there from Chief Shakes Island by turning right on Case Avenue. From the grave site, head up Church Street to the **Irene Ingle Public Library,** one of the Southeast's better monuments. About ⅔ mi north of the ferry terminal along Evergreen Avenue, you'll find **Petroglyph Beach,** where ancient etchings are visible along the shore. Be prepared to leave the observation deck behind; most of the best petroglyphs are scattered across the rocky beach. For a woodsy hike, climb **Mount Dewey,** the hill right behind town. Farther afield (5 mi south of town) is the fun hike to **Rainbow Falls.**

TIMING TIPS→ It is a 1½-mi walk between Petroglyph Beach and Chief Shakes Island, so you should plan at least three hours to complete the walk and sightseeing around town.

27 **Petroglyph Beach.** Scattered among other rocks at this public beach are three dozen or more large stones bearing designs and pictures chiseled by unknown, ancient artists. No one knows why the rocks at this curious site were etched the way they were, or even exactly how old these etchings are. You can access the beach via a boardwalk, where you'll find signs describing the site along with carved replicas of the petroglyphs. When on the beach, be patient—the petroglyphs are somewhat difficult to spot. Because the original petroglyphs can be damaged by physical contact, the state discourages visitors from creating a rubbing off the rocks. But you are welcome to use the replicas to make a rubbing from rice paper and charcoal or crayons (available in local stores). ✉ *⅔ mi north of ferry terminal off Evergreen Ave.*

29 **Rainbow Falls.** The trail to this scenic waterfall starts across the road from Shoemaker Bay, 5 mi south of Wrangell. A ¾-mi trail climbs uphill through the rain forest, with long stretches of boardwalk steps, ending at an overlook just below the falls. Hikers with more stamina can continue another 3 mi and 1,500 vertical feet to Shoemaker Bay Overlook.

Where to Stay & Eat

$–$$$ ✕ **Zak's Cafe.** Despite its spartan, no-nonsense atmosphere, Zak's is a standout among Wrangell's limited dining choices, with good food and reasonable prices. Check out today's specials or try their steaks, chicken, seafood, and salads. At lunch, the menu includes burgers,

OFF THE BEATEN PATH & WORTH IT

Anan Creek Wildlife Observatory. About 30 mi southeast of Wrangell in the Tongass National Forest, Anan is one of Alaska's premier black- and brown-bear viewing areas. Each summer, from early July to mid-August, as many as 30 to 40 bears gather at this Southeast stream to feed on huge runs of pink salmon. On an average visit of about two hours you might spot two to four bears while strolling the 1/2-mi viewing boardwalk. Forest Service interpreters are on hand to answer questions. The site is accessible only by boat or floatplane. **Alaska Waters** (☎ 907/874-2378 or 800/347-4462 🌐 www.alaskawaters.com) is one of several local companies that offer day trips there. For additional details, contact the **Tongass National Forest Wrangell Ranger District** (☎ 907/874-2323 🌐 www.fs.fed.us/r10/tongass).

sandwiches, fish-and-chips, and wraps. ✉ *314 Front St.* ☎ *907/874–3355* 💳 *MC, V.*

$–$$$ **Harding's Old Sourdough Lodge.** This rambling lodge on the south side of the harbor began life as a construction camp, and traces of its rough-hewn origins remain today. The hallways are tight, but rooms are modestly furnished, and a private suite (handicap-accessible and large enough for six people) has a large bathroom with a heated floor and a hot tub. Hardy home-style meals ($16–20 for dinner), including fresh sourdough breads and fresh seafood, are also available for those not staying here (advance reservations required). Owner Bruce Harding, a longtime Wrangell resident, is an excellent source of local knowledge. ✉ *1104 Peninsula St., Box 1062, 99929* ☎ *907/874–3613 or 800/874–3613* 🌐 *www.akgetaway.com* *16 rooms* *Dining room, sauna, steam room, boating, Internet, meeting room, airport shuttle, some pets allowed; no a/c, no TV in some rooms, no smoking* 💳 *AE, D, DC, MC, V* *BP.*

★ **$$$$** **Rain Haven Lodge.** This one-room floating lodge is perfect for those in search of a peaceful retreat with up-close wildlife viewing. During the summer, the houseboat is anchored in a remote cove 30 mi south of Wrangell, with a canoe for access to nearby hiking trails and spectacular scenery. It's perfect for couples and small families, with a double bed and pull-out couch. The galley (stocked with staples) is equipped with a stove, sink, and cooler. There's a sunny atrium at the stern and a covered deck on the bow. Three-day stays cost $700, including transportation from Wrangell and a Stikine River jet-boat trip. Owner Marie Oboczky, a former Forest Service naturalist, leads local tours, and is very knowledgeable about the area. *Box 2074, 99929* ☎ *907/874–2549* 🌐 *www.rainwalkerexpeditions.com* *1 room* *Kitchen; no a/c, no room TVs, no smoking* 💳 *No credit cards.*

$$–$$$ **Stikine Inn.** After some down years, Wrangell's largest inn appears to be on the upswing; rooms have been updated, bathrooms have been remodeled, and the Garnet Room—the Stikine Inn's in-house restaurant—serves breakfast and lunch that may well be the best in town. Located on the waterfront in downtown Wrangell, the Inn is home to 33 rooms, half of which have excellent ocean views. One suite includes a kitchen; all rooms have new pillow-top beds. ✉ *107 Front St., 99929* ☎ *907/874–3901 or 800/367–9745* *33 rooms, 1 suite* *Cable TV, microwaves, Wi-Fi, some pets allowed; no a/c* *AE, MC, V.*

FOR STARTERS

Sourdough is a nickname for a longtime resident of Alaska. Prospectors who trekked here in search of gold often carried sourdough starter for pancakes and bread. To this day you'll find sourdough goods on just about every menu in the state.

$ **Grand View Bed & Breakfast.** Two miles from town—and perhaps within walking distance for avid pedestrians—this unassuming hillside home provides spectacular views across Zimovia Strait. Rooms, some with antiques and some decorated Alaskan style, have private baths and entrances, plus access to a large common area. Friendly owners John and Judy Baker have lived in Alaska for more than 50 years, and prepare delectable breakfasts, including freshly baked rolls. *Box 927, 99929* ☎ *907/874–3225* *www.grandviewbnb.com* *3 rooms* *Cable TV; no a/c* *No credit cards* *BP.*

$ **Rooney's Roost Bed & Breakfast.** This century-old home—easily

Fodor's Choice ★ Wrangell's most charming digs—is just a block from downtown. Decorated with a country theme that includes an amusing collection of rooster art, the Roost's cozy quarters are filled with the scent of freshly-baked cookies every afternoon. Friendly owners, a large-screen television, and a filling breakfast (featuring such heavenly fare as poached pears with raspberry sauce) add to its homey appeal. ✉ *206 McKinnon St., 99929* ☎ *907/874–2026* *www.rooneysroost.com* *5 rooms, 2 with bath* *Airport shuttle; no TV in some rooms* *MC, V* *BP.*

¢ **Shakes Slough Cabins.** If you're a hot-springs or hot-tub enthusiast, these Forest Service cabins on the Stikine River, accessible from Wrangell, are worth checking out. Shakes Slough Hot Springs are a short, 4-mi boat ride away from the cabins. Here you can soak in both an open-air hot tub and an enclosed version. These remote and very rustic cabins—which feature views of the Popof Glacier and Mt. Basargin—sleep six on plywood bunks, and feature basic facilities, including outhouses and woodstoves, but no water or electricity. Bring your own sleeping bag, food, and cooking utensils. Reservations are required for the cabins; request details from the Forest Service office in Wrangell or make reservations by calling **ReserveUSA** ☎ 877/444–6777). *Forest Service,* ✉ *525 Bennett St., Wrangell 99929* ☎ *907/874–2323* *www.reserveusa.com* *2 cabins* *Hot tub* *AE, D, MC, V.*

Shopping

A rocky ledge near the Stikine River is the source for **garnets** sold by local children for 25¢ to $10. The site was deeded to the Boy Scouts in 1962, so only children can collect these colorful but imperfect stones, the largest of which are an inch across. At several covered shelters near the city dock, you can buy locally crafted items or book an adventure. Local artist **Brenda Schwartz** (✉ 463 Shakes Ave. ☎ 907/874–3508 🌐 www.marineartist.com) has created a unique style that combines marine paintings with navigational charts. Find her studio at the base of Chief Shakes Island.

Sports, the Outdoors & Guided Tours

Air Charter

Sunrise Aviation (☎ 907/874–2319 or 800/874–2311 🌐 www.sunriseflights.com) is a charter-only air carrier that offers trips to the Anan Creek Wildlife Observatory, LeConte Glacier, or Forest Service cabins.

Bicycling

A newly completed waterfront trail connects Wrangell with Shoemaker Bay Recreation Area, 4½ mi south of town. The trail is mainly flat; more adventurous souls can brave the dozens of miles of logging roads that crisscross the island. Bicycle rentals are available from several suppliers including **Rain Walker Expeditions** (☎ 907/874–2549 🌐 www.rainwalkerexpeditions.com), which provides helmets and useful island maps.

Boating

Alaska Vistas (☎ 907/874–3006 or 866/874–3006 🌐 www.alaskavistas.com) has jet-boat trips to Anan Creek Wildlife Observatory that depart from Wrangell, plus a variety of guided sea-kayak adventures. **Breakaway Adventures** (☎ 907/874–2488 or 888/385–2488 🌐 www.breakawayadventures.com) leads day trips up the majestic Stikine River by jet boat, including a visit to Chief Shakes Glacier, along with time to take a dip at Chief Shakes Hot Springs. Mark Galla of **Alaska Peak Adventures** (☎ 907/874–2454 🌐 www.wedoalaska.com) guides wildlife trips, Stikine jet-boat tours, and boat trips to surrounding areas.

Fishing

Numerous companies schedule salmon- and trout-fishing excursions ranging in length from an afternoon to a week. Contact the **Wrangell Visitor Center** (☎ 907/874–2381 or 907/874–3699 🌐 www.wrangell.com) for information on guide services and locations.

Golf

Muskeg Meadows Golf Course (☎ 907/874–4653 🌐 www.wrangellalaskagolf.com), Southeast Alaska's first USGA regulation links, is a well-maintained, 2,950-yard 9-hole course with a driving range. Situated in a wooded area only ½ mi from town, the course is easily accessible, and golf clubs and pull carts can be rented on-site.

Outdoor Adventure & Natural History

Rain Walker Expeditions (☎ 907/874–2549 🌐 www.rainwalkerexpeditions.com) leads two-hour, half-day, and full-day guided natural-history, botany, wildlife, and bird-watching tours of wild places near Wrangell. The company also rents mountain bikes, canoes, and sea kayaks if you want to head out on your own.

PETERSBURG

 *22 mi north of Wrangell.*

Getting to Petersburg is an experience, whether you take the "high road" by air or the "low road" by sea. Alaska Airlines claims the shortest jet flight in the world, from takeoff at Wrangell to landing at Petersburg. The schedule calls for 20 minutes of flying, but it's usually more like 15. At sea level only ferries and smaller cruisers can squeak through Wrangell Narrows with the aid of more than 50 buoys and range markers along the 22-mi waterway, which takes almost four hours. But the inaccessibility of Petersburg is also part of its charm: in contrast to several other Southeast communities, you'll never be overwhelmed here by hordes of cruise passengers; only smaller ships can reach the town.

FISH & FLOWERS

At first sight Petersburg invokes the spirit of Norway: tidy white-painted homes and storefronts line the streets, bright-color swirls of leaf and flower designs (called rosemaling) decorate a few older homes, and row upon row of sturdy fishing vessels pack the harbor. No wonder—this prosperous fishing community was founded by Norwegian Peter Buschmann in 1897.

The Scandinavian heritage here is gradually being submerged by the larger American culture, but you may still occasionally hear Norwegian spoken, especially during the Little Norway Festival, held here each year on the weekend closest to May 17. If you're in town during the festival, be sure to partake in one of the fish feeds that highlight the Norwegian Independence Day celebration. You won't find better folk dancing and beer-batter halibut outside Norway.

One of the most pleasant things to do in Petersburg is to roam among the fishing vessels tied up at dockside in the town's expanding harbor. This is one of Alaska's busiest, most prosperous fishing communities, and the variety of seacraft is enormous. You'll see small trollers, big halibut vessels, and sleek pleasure craft. Wander, too, around the fish-processing structures (though be prepared for the pungent aroma). By watching shrimp, salmon, or halibut catches being brought ashore, you can get a real appreciation for this industry and the people who engage in it.

On clear days, Petersburg's scenery is second to none. Across Frederick Sound, the saw-like peaks of the Stikine Ice Cap scrape clouds from the sky, looking every bit as malevolent as their monikers suggest. (Some of the most wickedly-named summits include Devil's Thumb, Kate's Needle, and Witch's Tit.) **LeConte Glacier,** Petersburg's biggest draw, lies at the foot of the ice cap, about 25 mi east of town. Accessible only by water or air, the LeConte is the continent's southernmost tidewater glacier and one of its most active, often calving off so many icebergs that the tidewater bay at its face is carpeted shore to shore with floating bergs. Ferries and cruise ships pass it at a distance.

Clausen Memorial Museum 31
Eagle's Roost Park 34
Hammer Slough 33
Petersburg Visitor Information Center 30
Sons of Norway Hall 32

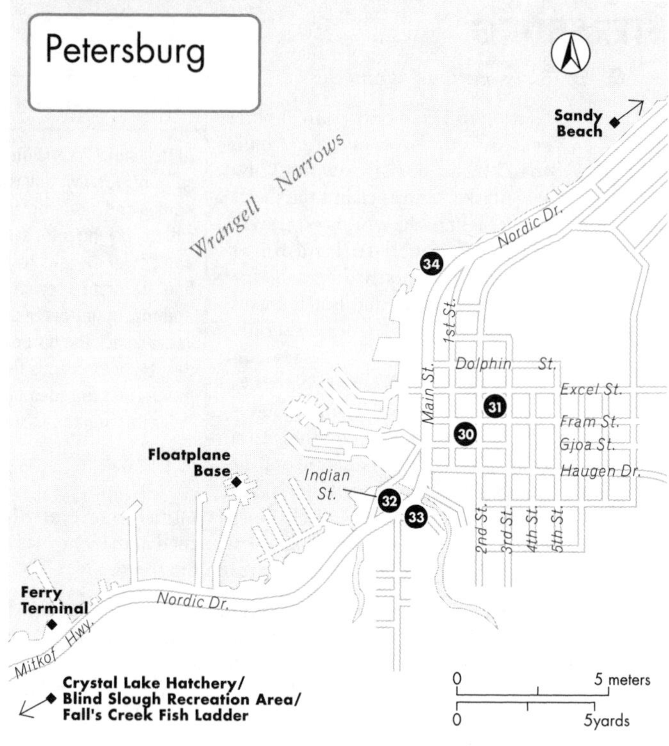

Exploring Petersburg

Although Petersburg is a pretty enough town to explore, here commercial fishing is more important than tourism. In other words, you'll find more hardware stores than jewel merchants. The main attractions are the town's Norwegian heritage, vibrant community, and its magnificent mountain-backed setting. The country around Petersburg provides a wide array of outdoor fun, from whale-watching and glacier-gazing to brown bear–viewing, hiking, and fishing.

What To See

31 **Clausen Memorial Museum.** The museum has exhibits exploring commercial fishing and the cannery industry, the era of fish traps, the social life of Petersburg, and Tlingit culture. Don't miss the 126½-pound king salmon—the largest ever caught commercially—as well as the Tlingit dugout canoe; the Cape Decision lighthouse station lens; and *Earth, Sea and Sky,* a 3-D wall mural outside. ✉ *203 Fram St.* ☎ *907/772–3598* 🌐 *www.clausenmuseum.alaska.net* 🎟 *$2* ⏲ *May–early Sept., Mon.–Sat. 10:30–4:30; mid-Sept.–Apr. by appointment.*

34 **Eagle's Roost Park.** Just north of the Petersburg Fisheries cannery, this small roadside park is a great place to spot eagles, especially at low tide.

On a clear day you will also discover dramatic views of the sharp-edged Coast Range, including the 9,077-foot summit of Devil's Thumb.

33 **Hammer Slough.** Houses on high stilts and the historic Sons of Norway Hall border this creek that floods with each high tide, creating a photogenic reflecting pool in the still waters.

30 **Petersburg Visitor Information Center.** This small office is a good source for local information, including details on tours, charters, and nearby Forest Service recreation opportunities. ✉ *1st and Fram Sts.* ☎ *907/772–4636* 🌐 *www.petersburg.org* ⏲ *May–Sept., Mon.–Sat. 9–5, Sun. noon–4; Oct.–Apr., weekdays 10–2.*

32 **Sons of Norway Hall.** The large, white barnlike structure that stands just south of the Hammer Slough is the headquarters of an organization devoted to keeping alive the traditions and culture of Norway. The window shutters are decorated with colorful Norwegian rosemaling designs. Outside sits a replica of a Viking ship that is a featured attraction in the annual Little Norway Festival each May. On the south side of the building is **Boyer Wikan Fisherman's Memorial,** where local fishermen lost at sea are honored with a bronze statue of a working fisherman. ✉ *Sing Lee Alley* ☎ *907/772–4575.*

OFF THE BEATEN PATH

FALLS CREEK FISH LADDER – Coho and pink salmon migrate upstream in late summer and early fall at this fish ladder south of town. Fish head up the ladder to get around a small falls. ✉ *Mile 10.8, Mitkof Hwy.*

BLIND SLOUGH RECREATION AREA (☎ 907/772–4772) – This recreation area includes a number of sites scattered along the Mitkof Highway 15–20 mi south of Petersburg. **Blind River Rapids Trail** is a wheelchair-accessible 1-mi boardwalk that leads to a three-sided shelter overlooking the river—one of the Southeast's most popular fishing spots—before looping back through the muskeg. Not far away is a bird-viewing area where several dozen trumpeter swans spend the winter. In the summer you're likely to see many ducks and other waterfowl here. At Mile 18, the state-run **Crystal Lake Hatchery** releases thousands of king and coho salmon each year. The kings return in June and July, the coho in August and September. Nearby is a popular picnic area. Four miles south of the hatchery is a Forest Service campground.

Where to Stay & Eat

$–$$$ ✕ **Northern Lights Restaurant.** Big windows face the harbor from this modest restaurant across from the Sons of Norway Hall. Family dining includes everything from simple spaghetti with meat sauce to cranberry-pecan chicken, rib steaks, and fresh-off-the-boat salmon and halibut. You can get an ice-cream cone to go. Boxed lunches are available if you're heading out to explore the country around Petersburg. The restaurant is open for breakfast, lunch, and dinner from 6 AM to 10 PM. ✉ *203 Sing Lee Alley* ☎ *907/772–2900* 💳 *D, DC, MC, V.*

$ ✕ **Papa Bear's Pizza.** Although it has a few tables, this oft-crowded pizza joint primarily specializes in take-out pizzas, pizza by the slice, wraps, and giant calzones. It also serves ice cream and espresso. Upstairs is a bar with pool tables. ✉ *1105 S. Nordic Dr., across from ferry terminal* ☎ *907/772–3727* ▭ *MC, V.*

¢ ✕ **Coastal Cold Storage.** This busy little shop in the heart of Petersburg serves daily lunch seafood specials, including fish chowders and halibut beer bits (a local favorite), along with grilled chicken wraps, steak sandwiches, and breakfast omelets and waffles. It's a great place to stop in for a quick bite en route to your next adventure; there isn't much seating in the shop's cramped interior. Live or cooked crab is available for takeout, and the shop can process your sport-caught fish. ✉ *306 N. Nordic Dr.* ☎ *907/772–4177* ▭ *AE, D, MC, V.*

$–$$$ **Scandia House.** This hotel on Petersburg's main street, a fixture since 1910, was rebuilt following a 1995 fire. You won't find much of the original charm, but what the Scandia lacks in quirky character it makes up for in humble hospitality. Rosemaling designs adorn the exterior. The interior is squeaky-clean, with contemporary oak furniture; some rooms have kitchenettes, king-size beds, or in-room hot tubs and harbor views. Homemade muffins and coffee warm the small but relaxing lobby in the morning. ✉ *110 Nordic Dr., Box 689, 99833* ☎ *907/772–4281 or 800/722–5006* 🌐 *www.scandiahousehotel.com* *30 rooms, 3 suites* *Some kitchenettes, cable TV, Internet, car rentals; no a/c* ▭ *AE, D, DC, MC, V* *CP.*

$ **Tides Inn.** The Tides, Petersburg's largest hotel, sits a block uphill from the town's main thoroughfare. Rooms have comfortable, but time-worn furnishings; some have kitchenettes. Rooms in the newer wing have views of the boat harbor. The coffee is always on in the small lobby, and in the morning there are complimentary juices, muffins, and pastries. ✉ *307 N. 1st St., Box 1048, 99833* ☎ *907/772–4288 or 800/665–8433* 🌐 *www.tidesinnalaska.com* *45 rooms* *Some kitchenettes, cable TV, Internet, some pets allowed, car rental; no a/c* ▭ *AE, D, DC, MC, V* *CP.*

$ **Water's Edge Bed & Breakfast.** Along the shore of Frederick Sound 1½ mi north of Petersburg, this family-run B&B offers either creek-side or waterside rooms. Seals, eagles, and whales are often seen just outside the door. A substantial Continental breakfast is served, and the library is stocked with books on Alaska and natural history. Take advantage of the owners' Kaleidoscope Cruises or borrow the bikes or canoe to explore on your own. Lodging-cruise packages are offered. ✉ *705 Sandy Beach Rd., Box 1201, 99833* ☎ *907/772–3736 or 800/868–4373* 🌐 *www.petersburglodgingandtours.com* *2 rooms* *Bicycles, library, airport and ferry shuttle; no a/c, no room phones, no room TVs, no smoking* ▭ *No credit cards* *CP.*

¢ **Alaska Island Hostel.** This friendly home hostel with no curfew offers separate male and female dorms, plus a family room. The second-floor kitchen and living room overlook the mountains and muskegs of Mitkof Island, and there's a big library of Alaskan books to thumb through in the evening. A guest phone and high-speed Internet access are available, along with luggage storage and a laundry. The owners provide ingredients for a self-serve breakfast, including freshly baked breads. Advance reservations are required; be sure to call, write, or e-mail in advance.

805 Gjoa St., Box 892, 99833 907/772–3632 www.alaskaislandhostel.com 3 dorm rooms Laundry facilities, Internet; no a/c, no kids under 6 MC, V CP.

Nightlife

The **Harbor Bar** (Nordic Dr. 907/772–4526), with ships' wheels, nautical pictures, and a mounted red snapper, is true to the town's seafaring spirit. Sample the brew and blastingly loud music at the smoky **Kito's Kave** (Sing Lee Alley 907/772–3207). The odd collection of wall hangings include a Mexican painting on black velvet, a mounted Alaska king salmon, and two stuffed sailfish from a tropical fishing expedition. Expect a rowdy crowd.

3

Shopping

Bookstore

Off an alley in a beautiful big white house that served as a boardinghouse to fishermen and schoolteachers, **Sing Lee Alley Books** stocks books on Alaska, best sellers, cards, and gifts. *11 Sing Lee Alley 907/772–4440.*

Seafood

At **Tonka Seafoods,** across the street from the Sons of Norway Hall, you can tour the small custom seafood plant and sample smoked or canned halibut and salmon. Be sure to taste the white king salmon—an especially flavorful type of Chinook that the locals swear by. Tonka will also ship. *Sing Lee Alley 907/772–3662 or 888/560–3662 Free Mon.–Sat. 8–5; tours at 1 PM (minimum 6 people).*

NORWEGIAN CRAFTS

The appropriately named **Cubby-Hole** sells items decorated by Norwegian-style rosemaling, including plates, trays, key chains, and other items. The museum gift shop also sells distinctive locally made crafts with Nordic designs. It's two blocks south of the Clausen museum. *14 Sing Lee Alley 907/772-2717.*

Sports, the Outdoors & Guided Tours

Stop by the **Petersburg Visitor Information Center** (1st and Fram Sts. 907/772–4636) for a complete listing of local tour companies.

Frederick Sound & LeConte Glacier Adventures

Featuring one of the world's only populations of bubble-net feeding humpback whales, Frederick Sound is a marquee whale-watching destination. **Kaleidoscope Cruises** (907/772–3736 or 800/868–4373 www.alaska.net/~bbsea) conducts whale-watching and glacier-ecology boat tours led by professional biologists and naturalists. **Viking Travel** (907/772–3818 or 800/327–2571 www.alaskaferry.com) books whale-watching, glacier, sea-kayaking, and other charters with local and regional operators.

Pacific Wing (✉ 1500 Haugen Dr. ☎ 907/772–9258 🌐 www.pacificwing.com) is an air-taxi operator that gets high marks from locals for its flightseeing tours over the Stikine River and LeConte Glacier.

The friendly folks at **Stick Dog Tours** (☎ 512/554-5677 🌐 www.stickdogalaska.com) can arrange both fixed-wing and helicopter flightseeing tours of the LeConte Glacier and Devil's Thumb, Stikine River jet-boat tours, and various kayaking adventures in the area.

Tongass Kayak Adventures (☎ 907/772–4600 🌐 www.tongasskayak.com) leads multiday sea-kayak trips to the Stikine River, LeConte Glacier, and elsewhere in the area. Their half-day trip up Petersburg Creek is especially popular.

Hiking

For an enjoyable loop hike from town, follow Dolphin Street uphill from the center of town. At the intersection with 5th Street, a boardwalk path leads 900 feet through forested wetlands to a baseball field, where a second boardwalk takes you to 12th Street and Haugen Drive. Turn left on Haugen and follow it past the airport to **Sandy Beach Park,** where low tide reveals a number of ancient petroglyphs. From here, you can return to town via Sandy Beach Rd., or hike the beach when the tide is out. Along the way is a covered **whale observatory** with binoculars to scan for humpback whales and Orcas. A pullout at Hungry Point provides views to the Coast Range and Frederick Sound. Across the road, the half-mile **Hungry Point Trail** takes you back to the baseball field, where you can return downtown on the nature boardwalk. Plan on an hour and a half for this interesting walk.

For something more strenuous, a 4-mi trail begins at the airport and climbs 1,600 feet in elevation to **Raven's Roost Cabin.** Along the way you take in a panorama that reaches from the ice-bound Coast Range to the protected waters and forested islands of the Inside Passage far below. The two-story Forest Service cabin is available for rent ($35 per night); contact ReserveUSA (☎ 518/885–3639 or 877/444–6777 🌐 www.reserveusa.com). Get details on these and other hikes from the Petersburg Visitor Information Center, or from the Forest Service office (✉ Nordic and Haugen Sts. ☎ 907/772–3871 🌐 www.fs.fed.us/r10/tongass).

SITKA

35–44 *110 mi west of Petersburg.*

Sitka was the home to the Kik.sádi clan of the Tlingit people for centuries prior to the 18th-century arrival of the Russians under the direction of territorial governor Alexander Baranof. The governor coveted the Sitka site for its beauty, mild climate, and economic potential; in the island's massive timber forests he saw raw materials for shipbuilding. Its location offered trading routes as far west as Asia and as far south as California and Hawaii. In 1799 Baranof built St. Michael Archangel—a wooden fort and trading post 6 mi north of the present town.

The Tlingits soon took exception to the ambitions of their new neighbors. Reluctant to pledge allegiance to the czar and provide free labor, they attacked the settlers and burned their buildings in 1802. Baranof, however, was away on Kodiak at the time. He returned in 1804 with a formidable force—including shipboard cannons—and attacked the Tlingits at their fort near Indian River, site of the present-day 105-acre Sitka National Historical Park, forcing them north to Chichagof Island.

By 1821 the Tlingits had returned to Sitka to trade with the Russians, who were happy to benefit from the tribe's hunting skills. Under Baranof and succeeding managers, the Russian-American Company and the town prospered, becoming known as the Paris of the Pacific. The community built a major shipbuilding and repair facility, sawmills, and forges and even initiated an ice industry, shipping blocks of ice from nearby Swan Lake to the booming San Francisco market.

> **WORD OF MOUTH: JUNEAU OR SITKA?**
>
> "Sitka has an incredible and interesting Russian heritage and is small enough that you can walk most places. It was my favorite Southeast Alaska town. One day in Sitka will allow you to see most everything." -MileKing

The town declined after its 1867 transfer from Russia to the United States but became prosperous again during World War II, when it served as a base for the U.S. effort to drive the Japanese from the Aleutian Islands. Today its most important industries are fishing, government, and tourism.

Exploring Sitka

It is hard not to like Sitka, with its eclectic blending of native Alaskan, Russian, and American history and its dramatic and beautiful, open-ocean setting. This is one of the best Inside Passage towns to explore on foot, with such sights as St. Michael's Cathedral, Sheldon Jackson Museum, Castle Hill, Sitka National Historical Park, and the Alaska Raptor Center topping the town's must-see list.

What to See

Alaska Raptor Center. The only full-service avian hospital in Alaska, the Raptor Center rehabilitates 100 to 200 birds each year. Situated just above the rushing waters of Indian Creek, the center is just a 20-minute walk from downtown. Well-versed guides provide an introduction to the rehabilitation center (including a short video) and guests are able to visit with one of these majestic birds. The Raptor Center's primary attraction is an enclosed 20,000-square-foot flight training center, built to replicate the rain forest, where injured eagles relearn survival skills, including flying and catching salmon. Visitors watch through one-way glass windows. A large deck out back faces an open-air enclosure for eagles and other raptors whose injuries prevent them from returning to the wild. Additional mews with hawks, owls, and other birds are along a rain-

A GOOD WALK

Most folks begin their tours of Sitka under the distinctive onion dome of **St. Michael's Cathedral,** right in town center. A block behind the cathedral along Harbor Drive is **Harrigan Centennial Hall,** a low-slung convention hall that houses the worthwhile Isabel Miller Museum and an information desk that opens when cruise ships are in port. A block east, along Lincoln Street, you'll find the **Russian Bishop's House,** one of the symbols of Russian rule. Continue out on Lincoln Street along the bustling boat harbor to Sheldon Jackson College, where the **Sheldon Jackson Museum** is packed with native cultural artifacts. Another ½ mi out along the gently-curving Metlakatla Street is the **Sitka National Historical Park,** where you can chat with native artisans as they craft carvings and silver jewelry. Behind the main building, a network of well-signed paths take you through the rain forest past more than a dozen totem poles and to the site of a Tlingit fort from the battle of 1804. A signed trail crosses the Indian River (watch for spawning salmon in late summer) and heads across busy Sawmill Creek Road to the **Alaska Raptor Center,** for an up-close look at bald eagles.

Return to town along Sawmill Creek Road. On your right, you'll see the white headstones of the small Sitka National Cemetery. Back downtown, you can browse the many shops or walk along Harbor Drive and take the path to the summit of **Castle Hill,** where Russia transferred Alaska to American hands—these are the best views in town. If you follow the path down the other side of the hill, check out the impressive **Sitka State Pioneers' Home,** with the statue of pioneer "Skagway Bill" Fonda. Across the street is **Totem Square,** with its tall totem pole and three ancient anchors. Adjacent to the Pioneers' Home is the **Sheet'ka Kwaan Naa Kahidi Community House** cultural center. Native dances take place here in the summer. End your walk at the haunting (not haunted) **Russian and Lutheran cemeteries,** which fill the dark woods along Marine Street a block from the blockhouse. The grave of Princess Maksoutoff, a member of the Russian royal family, is here.

TIMING TIPS→ Sitka has many attractions, and you can easily spend a full day exploring this culturally rich area. You can accomplish the walk in two to three hours if you do not spend much time at each stop. If you're especially hard-pressed for time, skip the loop to Sitka National Historical Park and the Alaska Raptor Center. You can pound the pavement around town in an hour or so.

forest path. The gift shop sells all sorts of eagle paraphernalia, the proceeds from which fund the center's programs. *1000 Raptor Way (off Sawmill Creek Rd.)* *907/747–8662 or 800/643–9425* *www.alaskaraptor.org* *$12* *Mid-May–Sept., Sun.–Fri. 8–4.*

Continued on page 156

MADE IN ALASKA

Intricate Aleut baskets, Athabascan birch-bark wonders, Inuit ivory carvings, and towering Tlingit totems are just some of the eye-opening crafts you'll encounter as you explore the 49th state. Alaska's native peoples—who live across 570,000 square miles of tundra, boreal forest, arctic plains, and coastal rain forest—are undeniably hardy, and their unique artistic traditions are just as resilient and enduring.

TIPS ON FINDING AN AUTHENTIC ITEM

1 The Federal Trade Commission has enacted strict regulations to combat the sale of falsely marketed goods; it's illegal for anything made by non-native Alaskans to be labeled as INDIAN, NATIVE AMERICAN, or ALASKA NATIVE.

2 Some authentic goods are marked by a silver hand symbol or are labeled as an AUTHENTIC NATIVE HANDICRAFT FROM ALASKA.

3 The Alaska State Council on the Arts, in Anchorage, is a great resource if you have additional questions or want to confirm a permit number. Call 907/269–6610 or 888/278–7424 in Alaska.

4 The MADE IN ALASKA label, often accompanied by an image of a polar bear with cub, simply denotes that the handicraft was made in the state.

5 Be sure to ask for written proof of authenticity with your purchase, as well as the artist's name. You can also request the artist's permit number, which may be available.

6 Materials should be legal. For example, only some feathers, such as ptarmigan and pheasant feathers, comply with the Migratory Bird Act. Only native artisans are permitted to carve new walrus ivory. The seller should be able to answer your questions about material and technique.

THE NATIVE PEOPLE OF ALASKA

There are many opportunities to see the making of traditional crafts in native environments, including the Southeast Alaska Indian Cultural Center in Sitka and Anchorage's Alaska Native Heritage Center.

After chatting with the artisans, pop into the gift shops to peruse the handmade items. Also check out prominent galleries and museum shops.

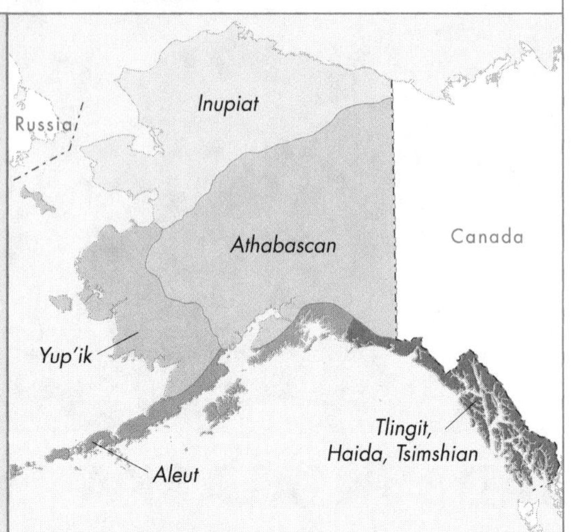

NORTHWEST COAST INDIANS: TLINGIT, HAIDA & TSIMSHIAN

Scattered throughout Southeast Alaska's rain forests, these highly social tribes traditionally benefited from the region's mild climate and abundant salmon, which afforded them a rare luxury: leisure time. They put this time to good use by cultivating highly detailed crafts, including ceremonial masks, elaborate woven robes, and, most famously, totem poles.

(left) A wagging tongue at the Juneau-Douglas City Museum
(right) A Tlingit totem reaches for the skies in Ketchikan

TOWERING TOTEM POLES

Throughout the Inside Passage's braided channels and forested islands, native peoples use the soft wood of the abundant cedar trees to carve totem poles, which illustrate history, pay reverence, commemorate a potlatch, or cast shame on a misbehaving person.

Every totem pole tells a story with a series of animal and human figures arranged vertically. Traditionally the totem poles of this area feature ravens, eagles, wolves, bears, frogs, the mythic thunderbird, and the likenesses of ancestors.

K'alyaan Totem Pole

Carved in 1999, the K'alyaan totem pole is a tribute to the Tlingits who lost their lives in the 1804 Battle of Sitka between invading Russians and Tlingit warriors. Tommy Joseph, a venerated Tlingit artist from Sitka, and an apprentice spent three months carving the pole from a 35-ft western red cedar. It now stands at the very site of the skirmish, in Sitka National Historical Park.

Raven: Atop the pole sits the striking raven, the emblem of one of the two moieties (large multi-clan groups) of Tlingit culture.

Woodworm: The woodworm—a Tlingit clan symbol—is wood-boring beetle that leaves a distinctive mark on timber.

Sockeye Salmon (above) and Dog/Chum Salmon (below): These two symbols signify the contributions of the Sockeye and Dog Salmon Clans to the 1804 battle. They also illustrate the symbolic connection to the tribe's traditional food sources.

Beaver: Sporting a fearsome pair of front teeth, this beaver symbol cradles a child in its arms, signifying the strength of Tlingit family bonds.

Frog: This animal represents the Kik.sádi Clan, which was very instrumental in organizing the Tlingit's revolt against the Russian trespassers. Here, the frog holds a raven helmet—a tribute to the Kik.sádi warrior who wore a similar headpiece into battle.

Tools and Materials

As do most modern carvers, Joseph used a steel adz to carve the cedar. Prior to European contact—and the accompanying introduction of metal tools—Tlingit artists carved with jade adzes. Totem poles are traditionally decorated with paint made from salmon-liver oil, charcoal, and iron and copper oxides.

ALEUT

The Aleut inhabit the Alaska Peninsula and the windswept Aleutian Islands. Historically they lived and died by the sea, surviving on a diet of seals, sea lions, whales, and walruses, which they hunted in the tumultuous waters of the Gulf of Alaska and the Bering Sea. Hunters pursued their prey in *baidarkas*, kayaklike boats made of seal intestine stretched over a driftwood frame.

WATERPROOF *KAMLEIKAS*

The Aleut prize seal intestine for its remarkable waterproof properties; they use it to create sturdy cloaks, shelter walls, and boat hulls. To make their famous cloaks, called *kamleikas*, intestine is washed, soaked in salt water, and arduously scraped clean. It is then stretched and dried before being stitched into hooded, waterproof pullovers.

FINE BASKETRY

Owing to the region's profusion of wild rye grass, Aleutian women are some of the planet's most skilled weavers, capable of creating baskets with more than 2,500 fibers per square inch. They also create hats, socks, mittens, and multipurpose mats. A long, sharpened thumbnail is their only tool.

ATHABASCANS

Inhabiting Alaska's rugged interior for 8,000 to 20,000 years, Athabascans followed a seasonally nomadic hunter-gatherer lifestyle, subsisting off of caribou, moose, bear, and snowshoe hare. They populate areas from the Brooks Range to Cook Inlet, a vast expanse that encompasses five significant rivers: the Tanana, the Kuskwin, the Copper, the Susitna, and the Yukon.

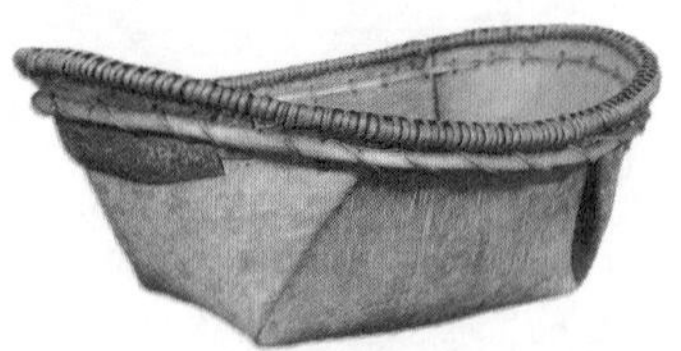

BIRCH BARK: WATERPROOF WONDER

Aside from annual salmon runs, the Athabascans had no access to marine mammals—or to the intestines that made for such effective boat hulls and garments. They turned to the region's birch, the bark of which was used to create canoes. Also common were birch-bark baskets and baby carriers.

FUNCTIONAL & ORNAMENTED PIECES

Much like that of the neighboring Eskimos, Athabascan craftwork traditionally served functional purposes. But tools, weapons, and clothing were often highly decorated with colorful embroidery and shells. Athabascans are especially well known for ornamenting their caribou-skin clothing with porcupine quills and animal hair—both of which were later replaced by imported western beads.

INUPIAT AND YUP'IK

Residing in Alaska's remote northern and northwestern regions, these groups are often collectively known as Eskimos or Inuit. They winter in coastal villages, relying on migrating marine mammals for sustenance, and spend summers at inland fish camps. Ongoing artistic traditions include ceremonial mask carving, ivory carving (not to be confused with scrimshaw), sewn skin garments, basket weaving, and soapstone carvings.

Thanks to the sheer volume of ivory art in Alaska's marketplace, you're bound to find a piece of ivory that fits your fancy—regardless of whether you prefer traditional ivory carvings, scrimshaw, or a piece that blends both artistic traditions.

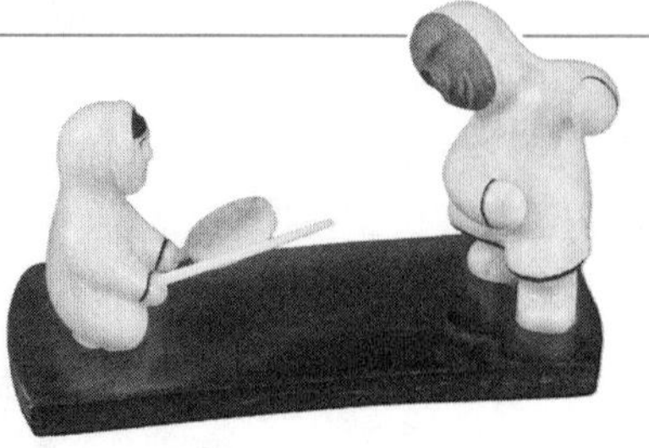

IVORY CARVING

While in Alaska, you'll likely see carved ivory pieces, scrimshaw, and some fake ivory carvings (generally plastic). Ivory carving has been an Eskimo art form for thousands of years. After harvesting ivory from migrating walrus herds in the Bering Sea, artisans age tusks for up to one year before shaping it with adzes and bow drills.

WHAT IS SCRIMSHAW?

The invention of scrimshaw is attributed to 18th-century American whalers who etched the surfaces of whale bone and scrap ivory. The etchings were filled with ink, bringing the designs into stark relief.

More recently the line between traditional Eskimo ivory carving and scrimshaw has become somewhat blurred, with many native artisans incorporating both techniques.

KEEP IN MIND

The Marine Mammal Protection Act states that only native peoples are allowed to harvest fresh walrus ivory, which is legal to buy after it's been carved by a native person. How can you tell if a piece is real and made by a native artisan? Real ivory is likely to be pricey; be suspect of anything too cheaply priced. It should also be hard (plastic will be softer) and cool to the touch. Keep an eye out for mastery of carving technique, and be sure to ask questions when you've found a piece you're interested in buying.

TIPS

Ivory carving is a highly specialized native craft that is closely regulated. As it is a by-product of subsistence hunting, all meat and skin from a walrus hunt is used.

Ivory from extinct mammoths and mastodons (usually found buried underground or washed up on beaches) is also legal to buy in Alaska; many native groups keep large stores of it, as well as antique walrus tusk, for craft purposes. Many of the older pieces have a caramelized color.

Alaska Raptor Center **40**
Castle Hill **41**
Harrigan Centennial Hall **36**
Russian and Lutheran cemeteries **44**
Russian Bishop's House **37**
St. Michael's Cathedral **35**
Sheldon Jackson Museum **38**
Sitka National Historical Park **39**
Sitka State Pioneers' Home **42**
Totem Square **43**

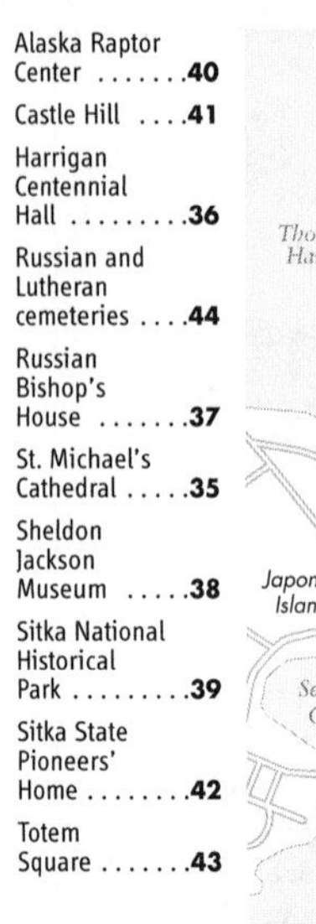

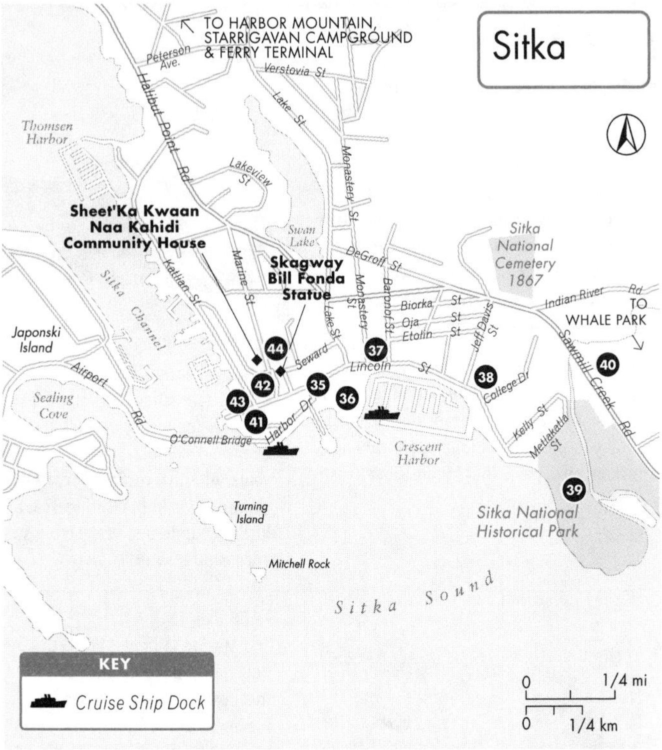

41 **Castle Hill.** On this hill Alaska was formally handed over to the United States on October 18, 1867, and the first 49-star U.S. flag was flown on January 3, 1959, signifying Alaska's statehood. To reach the hill, take the first right off Harbor Drive just before the O'Connell Bridge; then go into the **Baranof Castle Hill State Historic Site** entrance. A paved path takes you to the top, overlooking Crescent Harbor and downtown Sitka. On a clear day, look for the volcanic flanks of Mt. Edgecumbe on the horizon.

Harbor Mountain. During World War II the U.S. Army constructed a road to the 2,000-foot level of Harbor Mountain, providing the perfect vantage point to watch for invading Japanese subs or ships (none were seen). This road has been improved over the years, and those with vehicles can drive 5 mi to a spectacular summit viewpoint across Sitka Sound. A trail climbs uphill from the parking lot, and then follows the ridge 2½ mi to a Forest Service shelter. From there, ambitious hikers could continue downhill another 3½ mi to Sitka via the **Gavan Hill Trail.**

36 **Harrigan Centennial Hall.** A Tlingit war canoe sits in front of this brick building, which houses the **Isabel Miller Museum.** Check out its collection of Tlingit, Victorian-era, and Alaska purchase historical artifacts; there's an auditorium for New Archangel Dancers performances, which take place when cruise ships are in port. ✉ *Harbor Dr.* ☎ *907/747–6455 museum, 907/747–5940 Visitors Bureau* 🌐 *www.sitkahistory.org* 🎫 *Free* ⏲ *Museum May–Sept., daily 8–5; Oct.–Apr., Tues.–Sat. 10–4. Information desk May–Sept., daily 8–5.*

44 **Russian and Lutheran cemeteries.** Most of Sitka's Russian dignitaries are buried in these sites off Marine Street, which, thanks to their wooded locations, require a bit of exploring to locate. The most distinctive (and easily accessible) grave belongs to Princess Maksoutoff (died 1862), wife of the last Russian governor and one of the most illustrious members of the Russian royal family to be buried on Alaskan soil.

NEED ADVICE?

The Harrigan Centennial Hall has a volunteer-staffed information desk provided by the **Sitka Convention and Visitors Bureau** (✉ *303 Lincoln St.* ☎ *907/747-5940* 🌐 *www.sitka.org*), whose headquarters are a short walk away on Lincoln Street.

37 **Russian Bishop's House.** A registered historic landmark, this house facing the harbor was constructed by the Russian-American Company for Bishop Innocent Veniaminov in 1842. Inside the house, one of the few remaining Russian-built log structures in Alaska, are exhibits on the history of Russian America, including a room where a portion of the house's structure is peeled away to expose Russian building techniques. Park Service rangers lead guided tours of the second floor, which houses the residential quarters and a chapel. ✉ *501 Lincoln St.* ☎ *907/747–6281* 🌐 *www.nps.gov/sitk* 🎫 *$3* ⏲ *May–Sept., daily 9–5; Oct.–Apr. by appointment.*

★ 35 **St. Michael's Cathedral.** This cathedral, one of Southeast Alaska's best-known national landmarks, is treasured by visitors and locals alike—so treasured, in fact, that in 1966, as a fire engulfed the building, townspeople risked their lives and rushed inside to rescue the cathedral's precious Russian icons, religious objects, and vestments. Using original blueprints, an almost exact replica of onion-domed St. Michael's was built in 1976. Today you can see what could possibly be the largest collection of Russian icons in the United States, among them the much-prized *Our Lady of Sitka* (also known as the *Sitka Madonna*) and the *Christ Pantocrator* (*Christ the Judge*) on either side of the doors of the interior altar screen. Other objects include ornate Gospel books, chalices, crucifixes, much-used silver-gilt wedding crowns dating to 1866, and an altar cloth made by Princess Maksoutoff. ✉ *Lincoln St.* ☎ *907/747–8120* 🎫 *$2* ⏲ *May–Sept., 9–4 when large cruise ships are in port; Oct.–Apr., hrs vary.*

★ 38 **Sheldon Jackson Museum.** At **Sheldon Jackson College,** this octagonal museum, which dates from 1895, contains priceless Aleut and Eskimo items collected by Dr. Sheldon Jackson (1834–1909), who traveled the remote regions of Alaska as an educator and missionary. This state-run museum features artifacts from every native Alaskan culture; on display are carved masks, Chilkat blankets, dog sleds, kayaks, and even the impressive helmet worn by Chief Katlean during the 1804 battle against the Russians. ■ **TIP→ Native artisans are here all summer, creating baskets, carvings, or masks.** ✉ *104 College Dr.* ☎ *907/747–8981* 🌐 *www.museums.state.ak.us* 🎫 *$4 Mid-May–mid Sept., $3 mid-Sept.–mid-May* ⏲ *Mid-May–mid-Sept., daily 9–5; mid-Sept.–mid-May, Tues.–Sat. 10–4.*

39 Fodor's Choice ★ **Sitka National Historical Park.** The main building at this park houses a small museum with fascinating historical exhibits and photos of Tlingit native culture. Highlights include a brass peace hat given to the Sitka Kik.sádi by Russian traders in the 1830s and a Chilkat robe. Head to the theater to watch a video about Russian-Tlingit conflict in the 19th century. Also here is the **Southeast Alaska Indian Cultural Center,** where native artisans demonstrate silversmithing, weaving, wood carving, and basketry. Don't be afraid to strike up a conversation; the artisans are happy to talk about their work and Tlingit cultural traditions. At the far end of the building are seven totems (some more than a century old) that have been brought indoors to protect them from decay. Behind the center, a wide 1-mi path takes you through the forest and along the shore of Sitka Sound. Scattered along the way are some of the most skillfully carved native totem poles in Alaska. Keep going on the trail to see spawning salmon from the footbridge over Indian River. Park Service rangers lead themed walks in the summer, which focus on the Russian-Tlingit conflict, the area's natural history, and the park's totem poles. ✉ *106 Metlakatla St.* ☎ *907/747–6281, gift shop 907/747–8061* 🌐 *www.nps.gov/sitk* 🎫 *$3* ⏲ *Mid-May–Sept., daily 8–5; Oct.–mid-May, Mon.–Sat. 8–5.*

42 **Sitka State Pioneers' Home.** This large, red-roof structure has an imposing 14-foot statue in front, symbolizing Alaska's frontier sourdough spirit ("sourdough" generally refers to Alaska's American pioneers and prospectors); it was modeled by an authentic pioneer, William "Skagway Bill" Fonda. Adjacent to the Pioneers' Home is **Sheet'ka Kwaan Naa Kahidi Community House,** where you can watch native dance performances throughout the summer. ✉ *Lincoln and Katlian Sts.* ☎ *907/747–3213.*

43 **Totem Square.** On this grassy square directly across the street from the Pioneers' Home are three anchors discovered in local waters believed to be of 19th-century British origin. Look for the double-headed eagle of czarist Russia carved into the cedar of the totem pole in the park.

Whale Park. This small waterside park sits in the trees 4 mi east of Sitka out by Sawmill Creek Road. Boardwalk paths lead to five viewing platforms and steps take you down to the rocky shoreline. A gazebo next to the parking area contains signs describing the whales that visit Silver Bay, and you can listen to their sounds from recordings and an offshore hydrophone here. ■ **TIP→ Tune your radio to FM 88.1 anywhere in Sitka to hear a broadcast of humpback whale sounds picked up by the hydrophone.**

Where to Stay & Eat

$$–$$$$ ✕ **Channel Club.** Once you've surveyed the dozens of salads arrayed on the salad bar, you might not even make it to the steak and seafood for which this restaurant, festooned with fishnet, floats, and whalebone carvings, is known. While the prices might suggest a luxurious steak-house atmosphere, the Channel Club feels more dineresque than deluxe. Still,

the steaks are delicious, and a courtesy van provides door-to-door service if you're without transportation. ✉ *Mile 3.5, 2906 Halibut Point Rd.* ☎ *907/747–9916* 💳 *AE, DC, MC, V.*

$$–$$$$ **Ludvig's Bistro.** This convivial and remarkably creative eatery used to escape detection by most tourists (much to the pleasure of Sitkans). It's now packed at lunch and dinner with food lovers from all corners of the globe, so be prepared for a bit of a wait—but rest assured that Ludwig's is well worth it. The interior evokes an Italian bistro, with rich yellow walls and copper-topped tables. The menu changes often, and the blackboard lists the specials. Seafood (particularly king salmon and scallops) is a centerpiece, but you'll also find Caesar salads, vegetarian specials, prime rib, and one of the best wine lists in the state. From 3 to 5 each evening, the café serves Spanish-style tapas with house wine for $8–$10. Lunch includes fish-and-chips with locally caught rockfish; pita sandwiches; and housemade chowders. ✉ *256 Katlian Ave.* ☎ *907/966–3663* 💳 *AE, MC, V* ⊙ *Closed mid-Feb.–mid-Mar.*

Fodor'sChoice ★

$–$$$ **Little Tokyo.** Sitka is probably the last place you might expect to find Japanese food, but Little Tokyo delivers great rolls and *nigiri.* The atmosphere is nothing fancy, but this small restaurant does have a sushi bar where you can watch the chef preparing all the standards, plus Alaska rolls (with smoked salmon and cream cheese). Udon noodle soups are popular on rainy afternoons, and Bento box dinners—complete with sushi, pot stickers, miso soup, teriyaki chicken wings, and salad—are a bargain at $11. No alcohol is served. ✉ *315 Lincoln St.* ☎ *907/747–5699* 💳 *MC, V.*

$–$$ **Nugget Restaurant.** Travelers flying out from Sitka head here while hoping their jet will make it through the pea-soup fog outside. The setting is standard, and the menu encompasses burgers (15 kinds), sandwiches, tuna melts, salads, steaks, pasta, seafood, and Friday-night prime rib. There's a big breakfast menu, too, but the real attraction is their justly famous range of homemade pies, which are known throughout Southeast Alaska. Several types are available daily. **TIP→ Get a slice à la mode, or buy a whole pie to take home.** ✉ *Sitka Airport Terminal* ☎ *907/966–2480* 💳 *MC, V.*

$$$$ **Baranof Wilderness Lodge.** This cozy fishing lodge is nestled in Warm Springs Bay, 20 air mi from Sitka on the wild east side of Baranof Island. Guest cabins have pine paneling, private baths, and electricity from a small hydroelectric plant. Packages range from two-night stays ($1,185 per person) to seven-night fishing adventures ($4,350 per person). All include floatplane transport from Sitka, boats and guide service, lodging in cabins with private baths, plus gourmet food and wines served at communal meals. Special wildlife photography seminars, Elderhostel programs, and fly-fishing schools are offered throughout the summer. The lodge has two wood-fired hot tubs, and nearby is a natural hot springs that pours 110°F water into a series of pools overlooking a waterfall. Most of the surrounding land is within Tongass National Forest. *Box 2187, 99835* ☎ *907/738–3597 or 800/613–6551* 🌐 *www.flyfishalaska.com* *2 rooms, 6 cabins* *Hot tubs, Internet; no a/c* 💳 *No credit cards* ⊙ *Closed Oct.–Apr.* *FAP.*

$$–$$$$ **Westmark Sitka.** Sitka's nicest hotel has large rooms and a lobby dominated by a beautifully carved Tlingit screen. Many rooms overlook

Crescent Harbor; the best are the corner suites. Downstairs, the Raven Dining Room is open for three meals a day, with seafood (including beer-batter halibut), pasta, chicken, pork, and steak. Top dinner off with a slice of ultrarich Mississippi mud pie. Adjacent to the Raven, the Kadataan Lounge serves up a diverse menu of bar food. ✉ *330 Seward St., 99835* ☎ *907/747–6241, 800/544–0970 in U.S., 800/999–2570 in Canada* 🌐 *www.westmarkhotels.com* *97 rooms, 4 suites* *Restaurant, room service, cable TV, bar; no a/c* *AE, D, DC, MC, V.*

★ **$$** **Rockwell Lighthouse.** On an island ¾ mi from town, Burgess Bauder (a local veterinarian) rents out his 1,600-square-foot four-story lighthouse, which was hand-built in the 1980s with coastal woods and brass lights. The light at the top is built to Coast Guard specifications. The lighthouse can accommodate eight people in four rooms ($200 for four, plus $35 per person for extra guests)—you must rent the whole property. A curving staircase wraps up the inside of the lighthouse. The price includes transportation to and from the lighthouse; it's $35 per day extra for use of the hot tub, which most folks consider well worth the price. In summer, you can use a small motorboat to reach the island, but when it's stormy the owner runs a shuttle service. ■ **TIP→ Call up to a year ahead for midsummer reservations.** *Box 277, 99835* ☎ *907/747–3056* *Dining room, kitchen, hot tub; no a/c, no room TVs* *No credit cards.*

$$ **Shee Atiká Totem Square Inn.** Situated on Totem Square in downtown Sitka, this newly-remodeled inn is somewhat lacking in character; you'll find few eccentric or oddball touches in its design or decor. Still, it's one of the town's better-run outfits. The rooms are very clean and well furnished, and many offer views of the town and harbor. Thanks to its waterfront proximity, it's a popular choice for the fishing and corporate crowds. ✉ *201 Katlian St., 99835* ☎ *907/747–3693 or 866/300-1353* 🌐 *www.totemsquareinn.com* *67 rooms, 1 suite* *Cable TV, exercise room, business center, Internet; no a/c* *AE, D, DC, MC, V.*

$ **Alaska Swan Lake Bed & Breakfast.** This is one of the best B&Bs in town, with a lakeside setting, attractively appointed rooms with private baths, and friendly owners. Two downstairs rooms share a comfortable sitting room, while the two rooms upstairs adjoin a glassed-in porch. Private entrances provide access. Children have fun with the play equipment on the lawn that drops down to Swan Lake. The B&B is just six blocks from the center of town. ✉ *206½ Lakeview Dr., 99835* ☎ *907/747–5746* *4 rooms* *Cable TV; no a/c, no smoking or alcohol* *MC, V* *CP.*

$ **Sitka Hotel.** Right in downtown, this comfortable, old-fashioned hotel was built in 1939. The lobby and hallways emphasize a Victorian charm, with floral wallpaper and plush carpets. Some rooms feature contemporary furnishings, whereas others are small and not yet remodeled. A pub-style lounge (Victoria's Pourhouse) provides a comfy place to relax, and Victoria's Restaurant opens early—at 4:30 AM in summertime—to feed the charter-fishing crowd. ✉ *118 Lincoln St., 99835* ☎ *907/747–3288* 🌐 *www.sitkahotel.com* *55 rooms, 41 with bath* *Some refrigerators, cable TV, Wi-Fi, free parking; no a/c, no smoking* *AE, MC, V.*

¢ **White Sulphur Springs Cabin.** This Tongass National Forest public-use cabin is 65 mi northwest of Sitka. Like many other Forest Service cabins, this cabin sleeps four (bring your own sleeping bags) and has bunk beds, woodstove, table, and an outhouse. No mattresses, cooking utensils, or any services are provided, so you must bring all of your own supplies. The cabin, which faces the Pacific Ocean, boasts incredible views, and has a nearby hot-springs bathhouse, making this isolated retreat one of the Southeast's most prized cabins. Access is by boat (you'll need to walk in from a nearby cove) or helicopter. ☎ *907/747–6671 information, 877/444–6777 reservations* 🌐 *www.reserveusa.com* *1 cabin* ▭ *AE, D, MC, V.*

¢ **Starrigavan Campground.** Seven miles north of town, and just a mile from the ferry terminal, this popular Tongass National Forest campground has a mix of sites for car campers, backpackers, and RV travelers. All sites have tree cover, and facilities include tables, grills, potable water, and vault restrooms. Everything is fully ADA accessible, and group sites include a covered cooking shelter. Campsites are open year-round. ☎ *907/747–4216 information, 877/444–6777 reservations* 🌐 *www.reserveusa.com* ▭ *AE, D, MC, V.*

3

Nightlife & the Arts

Bars

As far as the locals are concerned, a spot in one of the green-and-white-vinyl booths at **Pioneer Bar** (✉ 212 Katlian St. ☎ 907/747–3456), across from the harbor, is a destination unto itself. It's vintage Alaska, with hundreds of pictures of local fishing boats, rough-hewn locals clad in Carhartts and Xtra-Tuff boots, occasional live music, pickup pool games, and a large brass bell that, when rung, signifies a round of drinks for everyone in the house.

Dance

★ The **New Archangel Dancers of Sitka** perform authentic Russian Cossack–type dances whenever cruise ships are in port. This all-female troupe tours extensively, with a mix of traditional dance styles. Tickets are $8, and are sold a half hour before performances. A **recorded message** (☎ 907/747–5516 🌐 www.newarchangeldancers.com) gives the schedule a week in advance. Performances take place in Harrigan Centennial Hall. **Sheet'ka Kwaan Naa Kahidi Dancers** (☎ 907/747–7290 or 888/270–8687 🌐 www.sitkatribal.com) perform Tlingit dances in full native regalia at the Sheet'ka Kwaan Naa Kahidi Community House on Katlian Street. The dance schedule is listed on the board at Harrigan Centennial Hall.

Festivals

Southeast Alaska's major chamber-music festival is the annual **Sitka Summer Music Festival** (☎ 907/747–6774 🌐 www.sitkamusicfestival.org), a three-week June celebration of concerts and special events that attracts musicians from as far away as Europe and Asia. All performances are held in Harrigan Centennial Hall. The **Sitka WhaleFest** (☎ 907/747–7964 🌐 www.sitkawhalefest.org) is held around town the first weekend of November, when the whales are plentiful (as many as 80) and tourists are not.

Shopping

Art Galleries

Fairweather Wearable Art & World Crafts (✉ 209 Lincoln St. ☎ 907/747–8677 🌐 www.fairweatherprints.com) sells shirts, dresses, and other clothing featuring hand-printed Alaskan designs. The shop also has two back rooms packed with works by local artisans. **Fishermen's Eye Fine Art Gallery** (✉ 239 Lincoln St. ☎ 907/747–5502 or 877/650–6080 🌐 www.fishermenseye.com) is a fine downtown gallery that prides itself on its vibrant collection of made-in-Sitka art. Housed within a Victorian-style 1895 home next to the Bishop's House, **Sitka Rose Gallery** (✉ 419 Lincoln St. ☎ 907/747–3030 or 888/236–1536 🌐 www.sitkarosegallery.com) is the town's most charming shop, and features two small galleries with Alaskan paintings, sculptures, native art, and jewelry.

Bookstore

Old Harbor Books (✉ 201 Lincoln St. ☎ 907/747–8808 🌐 litsite.alaska.edu/akbooksellers/oldharbor.html) has an impressive collection of Alaskan titles, along with a knowledgeable staff. Directly behind the bookstore is the cozy and ever-popular **Backdoor Café** (☎ 907/747–8856), with excellent espresso and fresh-baked pastries.

Gifts

Fresh Fish Company (✉ Katlian St. ☎ 907/747–5565, 888/747–5565 outside Alaska) sells fresh locally caught salmon, halibut, and shrimp. Located in the old pulp mill building 5 mi east of Sitka, **Theobroma Chocolate Company** (☎ 907/966–2345 or 888/985–2345 🌐 www.theobromachocolate.com) produces a range of rich treats, including chocolates shaped like halibut and salmon. Tours of this gourmet chocolate factory are available daily. **WinterSong Soap Company** (✉ 419 Lincoln St. ☎ 907/747–8949 or 888/819–8949 🌐 www.wintersongsoap.com) sells colorful and scented soaps handcrafted on the premises.

Sports, the Outdoors & Guided Tours

Bicycling

If it isn't raining, rent a high-quality mountain bike from **Yellow Jersey Cycle Shop** (✉ 329 Harbor Dr. ☎ 907/747–6317) and head out on the nearby dirt roads and trails. The staff—a helpful and jovial bunch—are more than happy to share their knowledge of Sitka's many mountain- and road-bike routes.

Boat & Kayak Tours

Alaska Travel Adventures (☎ 907/789–0052 or 800/478–0052 🌐 www.alaskaadventures.com) leads a three-hour kayaking tour in protected waters south of Sitka. The tour includes friendly guides, basic kayak instruction, and snacks at a remote cabin on the water.

Allen Marine Tours (☎ 907/747–8100 or 888/747–8101 🌐 www.allenmarinetours.com), one of the Southeast's largest and best-known tour operators, leads four different boat-based Sitka Sound tours throughout the summer. Their "Wildlife Quest" tours are a fine opportunity to view humpback whales, sea otters, puffins, and eagles in a spectacular setting. When seas are calm enough, they offer a tour to the bird sanctuary at **St. Lazaria Islands National Wildlife Refuge.** The company also offers challenging all-day Saturday trips that combine a boat ride with a guided 6-mi rain-forest hike across the northern end of Kruzof Island. Brown bears are sometimes seen on these hikes, and participants must be relatively fit.

Bus Tours & Historical Walks

Sitka Tours (☎ 907/747–8443) meets ferries and cruise ships and leads both bus tours and historical walks. In addition, it transports ferry passengers into Sitka, with the drivers sometimes providing colorful historical commentary. **Tribal Tours** (☎ 907/747–7290 or 888/270–8687 🌐 www.sitkatribal.com) emphasizes Sitka's rich native culture, with bus or walking tours and dance performances at the Tribal Community House.

Fishing

Sitka is a well-known commercial-fishing port, but the town is also home to an ever-growing fleet of charter boats. The Sitka Convention and Visitors Bureau Web site (🌐 www.sitka.org) has descriptions of and Web links to several dozen sportfishing operators. A good one is **Sitka's Secrets** (✉ 500 Lincoln St., B-9 ☎ 907/747–5089 🌐 www.sitkasecret.com), operated by naturalists who combine wildlife-viewing with fishing.

Four-Wheeled Fun

Alaska ATV Tours (☎ 907/966-2301 or 877/966–2301 🌐 www.alaskaatvtours.com) offers half-day tours of remote Kruzof Island aboard two-person Yamaha ATVs. Stops include Iris Meadows Estuary, a black-sand beach, and one of Kruzof's numerous salmon-laden creeks. The tour, which departs from Sitka, includes a scenic 30-minute boat transfer through the islands and channels of Sitka Sound.

Hiking & Bird-Watching

Seven miles north of Sitka, **Starrigavan Recreation Area** is a peaceful, end-of-the-road place to explore the rain forest. The state ferry terminal is less than a mile from Starrigavan, and a popular Forest Service campground is also here. Several easy trails lead hikers through the area, including the ¼-mi boardwalk **Estuary Life Trail.** It circles a small estuary and includes a bird-viewing shelter and access to a nearby artesian well. The **Forest and Muskeg Trail** winds through a spruce-hemlock forest and traverses a muskeg, with interpretive signs along the way. Across the road is the delightful 1¼-mi loop **Mosquito Cove Trail,** which skirts the rocky shoreline to Mosquito Cove before returning through thickly forested hills. Get a map of local trails from **Sitka Trail Works** (✉ 801 Halibut Point Rd. ☎ 907/747–7244).

Underwater Action

Sea Life Discovery Tours (☎ 907/966–2301 or 877/966–2301 🌐 www.sealifediscoverytours.com) operates the only semi-submersible tour vessel in Alaska. Large underwater windows provide views of kelp forests, fish, crab, sea urchins, anemones, and starfish, and an underwater camera zooms in for close-up views via the video monitor.

JUNEAU

45–56 *100 mi northeast of Sitka.*

Juneau, Alaska's capital and third-largest city, is on the North American mainland but can't be reached by road. The city owes its origins to two colorful sourdoughs (Alaskan pioneers)—Joe Juneau and Dick Harris—and to a Tlingit chief named Kowee, who led the two men to rich reserves of gold at Snow Slide Gulch, the drainage of Gold Creek around which the town was eventually built. That was in 1880, and shortly thereafter, a modest stampede resulted in the formation of a mining camp, which quickly grew to become the Alaska district government capital in 1906. The city may well have continued under its original appellation—Harrisburg, after Dick Harris—were it not for Joe Juneau's political jockeying at a miner's meeting in 1881.

For some 60 years after Juneau's founding, gold was the mainstay of the economy. In its heyday, the AJ (for Alaska Juneau) Gold Mine was the biggest low-grade ore mine in the world. It was not until World War II, when the government decided it needed Juneau's manpower for the war effort, that the AJ and other mines in the area ceased operations. After the war, mining failed to start up again, and government became the city's principal employer. Juneau's mines leave a rich legacy, though; the AJ Gold Mine alone produced more than $80 million in gold.

WORD OF MOUTH: JUNEAU OR SITKA?

"I think Juneau would be a better choice. The Alaska State Museum is fantastic–lots of Alaska history. The Mendenhall Glacier is accessible by hourly tour buses. There's more to do and see in Juneau than in Sitka. Yes, Juneau has more cruise ships but it does not distract from the experience." -jorr

Perhaps because of its colorful history, Juneau is full of contrasts. Its dramatic hillside location and historic downtown buildings provide a frontier feeling, but the city's cosmopolitan nature comes through in fine museums, noteworthy restaurants, and a literate and outdoorsy populace. Here you can enjoy the Mt. Roberts Tramway, plenty of densely forested wilderness areas, quiet bays for sea-kayaking, and even a famous drive-up glacier.

Exploring Juneau

Juneau is an obligatory stop on the Inside Passage cruise and ferry circuit. Hence, the town has an overabundance of visitors in midsummer. Downtown Juneau is compact enough so that most of its main attractions are within walking distance of one another. Note, however, that the city is very hilly, so your legs will get a real workout. Look for the 20 signs around downtown that detail Juneau's fascinating history. Along with the Alaska State Museum and Mt. Roberts Tramway, be sure to make time for a tour to Mendenhall Glacier and the Macaulay Salmon Hatchery.

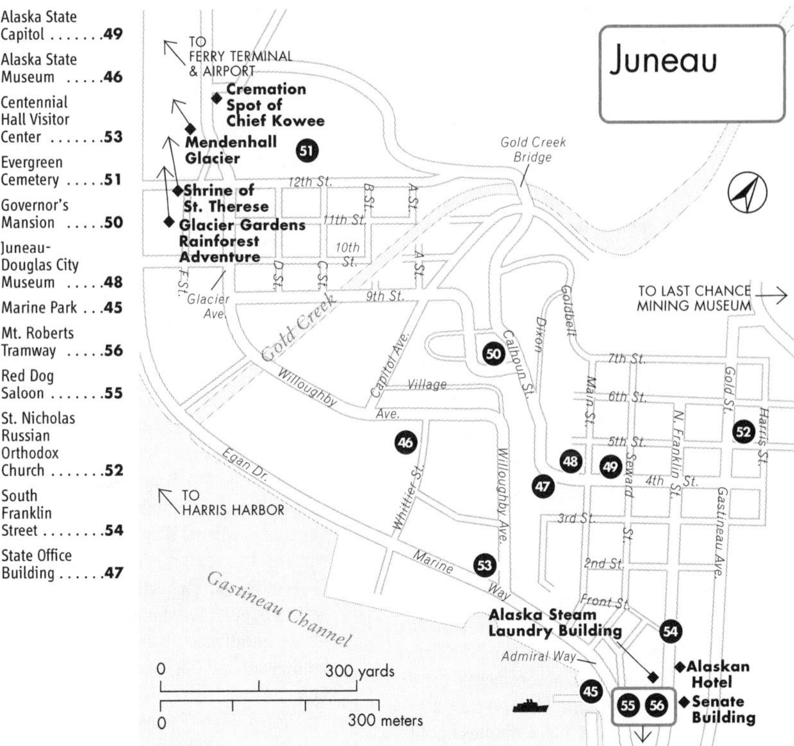

What to See

49 **Alaska State Capitol.** Built in 1930, this rather unassuming building houses the governor's office and hosts state legislature meetings in winter, placing it at the epicenter of Alaska's increasingly animated political discourse. Historic photos line the upstairs walls. Feel free to stroll right in; you can pick up a self-guided tour brochure as you enter. ✉ *Corner of Seward and 4th Sts.* ☎ *907/465–4648* ⏲ *Weekdays 8–5.*

★ 46 **Alaska State Museum.** This is one of Alaska's finest museums. Native-Alaskan buffs will enjoy examining the 38-foot walrus-hide *umiak* (an open, skin-covered Eskimo boat). Natural-history exhibits include preserved brown bears and a two-story-high eagle nesting tree. Russian-American and gold rush displays, and contemporary art complete the collection. **■ TIP→ Be sure to visit the cramped gift shop with its extraordinary selection of native art, including baskets, carvings, and masks.** ✉ *395 Whittier St.* ☎ *907/465–2901* 🌐 *www.museums.state.ak.us* *$5* ⏲ *Mid-May–mid-Sept., daily 8:30–5:30; mid-Sept.–mid-May, Tues.–Sat. 10–4.*

53 **Centennial Hall Visitor Center.** Here you can get complete details on Juneau sights and activities, plus walking-tour maps. You can also make ferry reservations and find out about hiking trails and other activities on nearby Tongass National Forest lands. ✉ *101 Egan Dr.* ☎ *907/586–*

A GOOD WALK

The most common starting spot is **Marine Park,** situated right along the cruise-ship dock. For an introduction to Alaska's human and natural history, head to the engaging **Alaska State Museum.** From here, circle back along Willoughby Avenue to the **State Office Building.** Catch the elevator to the eighth-floor atrium, which features an observation deck with vistas across Gastineau Channel. The snug but cheery **Juneau-Douglas City Museum,** a local treasure that's slightly off the beaten path, sits a short distance away at 4th and Calhoun streets. The looming, banklike building across the street is the **Alaska State Capitol,** which underwent a significant remodeling in 2006. For a far more attractive example of governmental architecture, visit the **Governor's Mansion,** a few minutes uphill on Calhoun Street. If you have the time and energy, you may want to continue along Calhoun, across the Gold Creek Bridge, and then down along 12th Street to the quiet **Evergreen Cemetery,** where town fathers Joe Juneau and Dick Harris are buried.

Back in downtown, the **St. Nicholas Russian Orthodox Church** is just a few blocks from the **Centennial Hall Visitor Center.** The historic buildings and busy shops of downtown Juneau, particularly those along **South Franklin Street,** make for easier walking. Check out the Alaskan Hotel, the Alaska Steam Laundry Building, and the Senate Building before dipping inside the terminally crowded **Red Dog Saloon** at the intersection of South Franklin Street and Admiral Way. Try a microbrew, then continue down the street to the **Mt. Roberts Tramway,** a popular way to reach alpine country for a hike overlooking Juneau and Gastineau Channel.

TIMING TIPS→ To cover downtown Juneau's many interesting sights, you should allow at least three or four hours for exploring. Add at least another hour if you're a museum fan, or if you plan to ride the Mt. Roberts Tramway.

2201 or 888/581–2201 www.traveljuneau.com May–Sept., weekdays 8:30–5, weekends 9–5; Oct.–Apr., weekdays 9–4.

51 **Evergreen Cemetery.** Many Juneau pioneers, including Joe Juneau and Dick Harris, are buried here. Juneau (1836–1899), a Canadian by birth, died in Dawson City, Yukon, but his body was returned to the city that bears his name. Harris (1833–1907), whose name can be found on downtown's Harris Street, died here. A meandering gravel path leads through the graveyard, and at the end of it is the monument commemorating the cremation spot of Chief Kowee.

50 **Governor's Mansion.** Completed in 1912, this stately colonial-style home overlooks downtown Juneau. With 14,400 square feet, six bedrooms, and 10 bathrooms, it's no miner's cabin. Out front is a totem pole that tells three tales: the history of man, the cause of ocean tides, and the

origin of Alaska's ubiquitous mosquitoes. Tours of the residence are, unfortunately, not permitted. ✉ *716 Calhoun Ave.*

48 **Juneau-Douglas City Museum.** Among the exhibits interpreting local mining and Tlingit history are old mining equipment, a reconstructed Tlingit fish trap, a three-dimensional model of the AJ Mine, historic photos, and pioneer artifacts, including a century-old store and kitchen. Youngsters will appreciate the hands-on room where they can try on clothes similar to ones worn by the miners or look at gold-rush stereoscopes. ✉ *114 4th St.* ☎ *907/586–3572* 🌐 *www.juneau.org/parksrec/museum* *$4* *Mid-May–Sept., weekdays 9–5, weekends 10–5; Oct.–mid-May, Tues.–Sat. noon–4.*

3

OFF THE BEATEN PATH

LAST CHANCE MINING MUSEUM – A 1½-mi hike or taxi ride behind town, this small museum is housed in the former compressor building of Juneau's historic AJ Gold Mine. The collection includes old mining tools, rail cars, minerals, and a 3-D map of the ore body. The surrounding country is steep and wooded, with trails leading in all directions, including one to the summit of Mt. Juneau. ✉ *1001 Basin Rd.* ☎ *907/586–5338* *$4* *Mid-May–mid-Sept., daily 9:30–12:30 and 3:30–6:30.*

45 **Marine Park.** On the dock where the cruise ships "tie up" is a little urban oasis with benches, shade trees, and shelter. It's a great place to enjoy an outdoor meal purchased from one of Juneau's many street vendors, and, on Friday evenings in summer, it features live performances by Juneau musicians. A visitor kiosk is staffed according to cruise-ship schedules.

★ 56 **Mt. Roberts Tramway.** One of Southeast Alaska's most popular tourist attractions, this tram whisks you from the cruise terminal 1,800 feet up the side of Mt. Roberts. After the six-minute ride, you can take in a film on the history and legends of the Tlingits, visit the nature center, go for an alpine walk on hiking trails (including the 5-mi round-trip hike to Mt. Roberts' 3,819-foot summit), purchase native crafts, meet an eagle from the Juneau Raptor Center, or chow down while enjoying mountain views. A local company leads guided wilderness hikes from the summit, and the bar serves locally brewed beers. ☎ *907/463–3412 or 888/461–8726* 🌐 *www.goldbelttours.com* *$22* *May–Sept., daily 9–9.*

55 **Red Dog Saloon.** The frontierish quarters of the Red Dog have housed an infamous Juneau watering hole since 1890. Every conceivable surface in this two-story bar is cluttered with life preservers, business cards, and memorabilia, including a pistol that reputedly belonged to Wyatt Earp, who failed to reclaim the piece after checking it in at the U.S. Marshall's office on June 27, 1900. When tourist season hits, a little atmospheric sawdust covers the floor as well. Bands pump out dance tunes when cruise ships are docked; the most notable (and bawdy) local performer is a legendary piano man named Phinneus Poon. ✉ *278 S. Franklin St.* ☎ *907/463–9954.*

52 **St. Nicholas Russian Orthodox Church.** This is the oldest Russian church in Southeast Alaska—but it was actually built in Siberia in 1894. (It was subsequently disassembled, shipped to Juneau, and reassembled by Tlin-

gits and Slavic immigrants.) The quaint, onion-domed white-and-blue church is used for services (sung in Slavonic, English, and Tlingit) on Saturdays and Sundays, and a small gift shop is adjacent. ✉ *326 5th St.* ☎ *907/845–2288* 🎫 *$2 requested donation* ⏲ *Tours mid-May–Sept., Mon.–Sat. 9–5.*

> **WORD OF MOUTH**
>
> "Juneau! With that gorgeous harbor and the way the mountains rise up behind town, it has to be the prettiest capital in the country. It's just big enough to have all the comforts of home, but just small enough to be charming and cozy."
>
> –Julie304

54 **South Franklin Street.** The buildings on South Franklin Street (and neighboring Front Street), among the oldest and most inviting structures in the city, house curio and crafts shops, snack shops, and two salmon shops. Many reflect the architecture of the 1920s and '30s. When the small **Alaskan Hotel** opened in 1913, Juneau was home to 30 saloons; the Alaskan gives today's visitors the most authentic glimpse of the town's whiskey-rich history. The barroom's massive, mirrored oak back bar is accented by Tiffany lights and panels. Topped by a wood-shingled turret, the 1901 **Alaska Steam Laundry Building** now houses a coffeehouse and other stores. The **Senate Building,** another of South Franklin's treasured landmarks, is across the street.

47 **State Office Building.** If you're in search of an ideal picnic spot, this government building, which sits above downtown on 4th Street, is your best bet. The building's sprawling eighth-floor patio, which faces Gastineau Channel and Douglas Island, is a popular lunch destination for state workers and assorted residents. On most Fridays at noon, concerts inside the four-story atrium feature a grand old theater pipe organ, a veteran of the silent-movie era. Also here is the historic old witch totem pole, the Alaska State Library, with a fine collection of historical photos, plus computers with public Internet access. If you're having trouble finding the building, just ask for directions to the "S.O.B."—the locals are fond of acronyms. ✉ *4th and Calhoun Sts.*

Where to Eat

$$$$ ✕ **Gold Creek Salmon Bake.** Trees, mountains, and the rushing water of Salmon Creek surround the comfortable, canopy-covered benches and tables at this authentic salmon bake. Fresh-caught salmon is cooked over an alder fire and served with a succulent sauce. For $32 there are all-you-can-eat salmon, pork spareribs, and chicken along with baked beans, rice pilaf, salad, corn bread, and blueberry cake. Wine and beer are extra. After dinner you can pan for gold in the stream, wander up the hill to explore the remains of the Wagner gold mine, or roast marshmallows over the fire. A round-trip bus ride from downtown is included. ✉ *1061 Salmon Lane Rd.* ☎ *907/789–0052 or 800/323–5757* 💳 *MC, V* ⏲ *Closed Oct.–Apr.*

$$$ ✕ **Thane Ore House Salmon Bake.** Four miles south of town is this all-you-can-eat-for-$22.95 restaurant with a waterside setting and indoor dining; it's one of the oldest and most authentic salmon bakes in the state. Your meal includes salmon, halibut, barbecued beef ribs, salad, baked beans, and bread, and an atmosphere devoid of haughty pretense. There are no linen tablecloths or string quartets here—just incredibly fresh seafood and a friendly staff. A free round-trip bus ride from downtown hotels is included. ✉ *4400 Thane Rd., 4 mi south of Juneau* ☎ *907/586–3442* ▭ *MC, V* ⊗ *Closed Oct.–Apr.*

$–$$$ ✕ **Hangar on the Wharf.** Crowded with both locals and travelers, the Hangar occupies the building where Alaska Airlines started business. Flight-themed puns dominate the menu (i.e. "Pre-flight Snacks" and the "Plane Caesar"), but the comfortably worn wood, stainless-steel accents, and vintage airplane photos create a casual dining experience that overcomes the kitsch. There are views of Gastineau Channel and Douglas Island from every seat. A wide selection of entrées, including locally caught halibut and salmon, filet mignon, great burgers, and daily specials makes this a Juneau hot spot. You'll also find two dozen draft beers available. On Friday and Saturday nights, jazz or rock bands take over the stage, and prime rib arrives on the menu. ✉ *2 Marine Way, Merchants Wharf Mall* ☎ *907/586–5018* ▭ *AE, D, MC, V.*

WORD OF MOUTH

"Our favorite local hangout is Hangar on the Wharf, with its huge selection of microbrews; it has the same owners as Twisted Fish. It's quieter and has a more varied menu and the best coconut shrimp I've had. It's fun to sit at the big windows and watch the harbor activity while you eat." -klondike

$–$$$ ✕ **Twisted Fish.** Juneau's liveliest downtown eatery serves up creative pan-Asian seafood and Alaskan classics. Housed in a log-frame waterfront building adjacent to Taku Smokeries and the base of the Mt. Roberts Tramway, Twisted's fish is as fresh as you'll find anywhere. Grab a seat on the deck for prime-time Gastineau Channel–gazing and a bowl of Captain Ron's chowder, a local favorite. Inside, you'll find a well-appointed dining room complete with a roaring river-rock hearth and flame-painted salmon, porpoises, marlin, and tuna decorating the walls. ✉ *550 S. Franklin St.* ☎ *907/463–5033* ▭ *AE, MC, V* ⊗ *Oct.–Apr.*

¢–$ ✕ **BaCar's.** This is the spot for hearty, inexpensive breakfasts and satisfying lunches. Fluffy omelets are $9 and come with home fries and a big side pancake. The blueberry pancakes are especially yummy. Lunches, including the halibut fish-and-chips, prime rib, and French dips, are simple and good. There are also a few interesting variations on diner standards, such as a salmon melt and (gulp) tempura Spam strips. ✉ *230 Seward St.* ☎ *907/463–4202* ▭ *AE, MC, V* ⊗ *No dinner.*

¢–$ ✕ **Douglas Cafe.** Many locals call this out-of-the-way café the best fast-food stop in the Juneau area, with 15 types of burgers available, including jalapeño burgers and Hawaiian burgers. Located in the heart of quiet Douglas, across the bridge and a couple of miles from downtown Juneau, this comfortable family eatery has Formica tables and a three-meals-a-day menu that includes omelets, blueberry pancakes, sandwiches, kids' favorites, and chicken adobo cooked by the Philippine-American chefs. It's a good choice for those seeking an alternative to downtown Juneau's occasionally nutty midsummer pace. ✉ *916 3rd St., Douglas* ☎ *907/364–3307* ▭ *MC, V.*

¢–$ ✕ **Wild Spice.** Modeled in the tradition of Mongolian-style eateries that have flourished of late, Wild Spice allows customers to assemble their own entrées from an assortment of meats, vegetables, rice, noodles, and 16 different sauces. Hand your concoction over to the chef and watch as he cooks it on an open, circular flat-top grill. Straightforward, quick, and (usually) delicious, this is a good mid-walk lunch or dinner stop. ✉ *140 Seward St.* ☎ *907/523–0444* ▭ *AE, MC, V.*

¢ ✕ **Heritage Coffee Company.** Juneau's favorite coffee shop, this is a downtown institution, with locally roasted coffees, fresh pastries, and all sorts of specialty drinks. ■ **TIP→ The window-front bar is especially popular for people-watching while you read the newspaper and sip a chai latte.** The same folks also operate three other coffee outposts, including the **Glacier Cafe** in Mendenhall Valley, which boasts a bigger menu that includes breakfast burritos and omelets, along with lunchtime paninis, wraps, soups, salads, and burgers, plus various vegetarian items. ✉ *174 S. Franklin St.* ☎ *907/586–1087* ▭ *No credit cards* ✉ *Mendenhall Mall Rd.* ☎ *907/789–0692* 🌐 *www.heritagecoffee.com* ▭ *MC, V* ⊗ *No dinner.*

¢ ✕ **Rainbow Foods.** Housed in a building that began life as an Assembly of God church, this crunchy natural foods market is a popular lunch-break spot for downtown workers. Organic produce, soy ice cream, vitamin supplements, and other items fill the shelves, but the real attraction is the weekday buffet, with various hot entrées, salads, soups, and deep-dish pizzas. Get there before 11 AM for the best choices. There are rotating ethnic menus every Thursday from 5 to 7. Espresso and freshly baked breads are available, along with a few inside tables. ✉ *224 4th St.* ☎ *907/586–6476* ▭ *MC, V.*

Where to Stay

$$–$$$ ✕🏨 **Goldbelt Hotel Juneau.** A high-rise by local standards, the seven-story Goldbelt is one of Juneau's better lodging places, with well-appointed (if somewhat overpriced) rooms that include amenities such as speaker phones, hair dryers, and irons. Waterside rooms on the upper level have views across Gastineau Channel, and some rooms have king-size beds. A Chilkat blanket and other artifacts are displayed in the lobby, and the adjacent Chinook's restaurant serves three meals a day. ✉ *51 W. Egan Dr., 99801* ☎ *907/586–6900 or 888/478–6909* 🌐 *www.goldbelt.com* *104 rooms, 1 suite* *Restaurant, room service, cable TV with movies, lounge, meeting room, airport shuttle; no a/c* ▭ *AE, D, DC, MC, V.*

$$ ✕🏨 **Frontier Suites Airport Hotel.** Near the airport in Mendenhall Valley, 9 mi from Juneau, this rambling hotel is a great option for families. All rooms have modern, functional furniture and full kitchens with a stove, refrigerator, microwave, dishes, silverware, and pans. Suites have separate bedrooms and living rooms (with sleeper sofas) and two televisions. Two bunk rooms include a mini-loft for older children. **Pasta Garden,** downstairs, serves American, Asian, Mexican, and Mediterranean fare three meals a day. ✉ *9400 Glacier Hwy., 99801* ☎ *907/790–6600 or 800/544–2250* 🌐 *www.frontiersuites.com* *72 rooms, 32 suites*

Restaurant, café, kitchens, microwaves, refrigerators, cable TV, bar; no a/c ▭ *AE, D, DC, MC, V.*

$$$$ Fodor'sChoice ★ **Pearson's Pond Luxury Inn and Adventure Spa.** On a small pond near Mendenhall Glacier, this large home may be Alaska's finest B&B. Owners Diane and Steven Pearson pull out all the stops for guests, with two outdoor hot tubs, an indoor fountain, gas fireplaces, whirlpool tubs with rain showers, Wi-Fi computer network, a big library of videotapes, four-poster beds, private balconies, and a well-stocked breakfast nook. Diane Pearson is an itinerary planner extraordinaire—her knowledge of local tours and activities is second to none—and she's even licensed to perform weddings (which are common at the B&B). Guests can paddle around the pond in a water bike, or borrow a fishing pole. There's yoga on the deck each morning, fine wine and cheese in the evening, and never a shortage of friendly conversation. The Pearsons also have two condos ($179) closer to town, which sleep four people each. ✉ *4541 Sawa Cir., 99801* ☎ *907/789–3772 or 888/658–6328* 🌐 *www.pearsonspond.com* *5 suites* *Cable TV, in-room VCRs, gym, massage, bicycles, Wi-Fi, meeting room, travel services; no a/c, no smoking* ▭ *AE, D, DC, MC, V* *BP.*

$$–$$$$ Fodor'sChoice ★ **Alaska's Capital Inn.** Gold-rush pioneer John Olds built this American foursquare home in 1906, and a major restoration in 2003 transformed it into Juneau's most elegant B&B. Rooms are furnished in ornate, handcrafted pieces, blending a nostalgic charm with such modern conveniences as an outdoor hot tub, in-room phones, TVs and VCRs, and high-speed Internet access. The Governor's Suite covers the entire fourth floor and includes a king-size sleigh bed, gas fireplace, a hot tub, and a 180-degree view of the downtown Juneau. Two small rooms on the bottom level have private entrances. Breakfast is practically a gift from the heavens, with a variety of Alaskan seafood dishes—including Dungeness Crab Eggs Benedict—highlighting the rotating menu. This B&B fills quickly for the summer season. ✉ *113 W. 5th St., 99801* ☎ *907/586–6507 or 888/588–6507* 🌐 *www.alaskacapitalinn.com* *4 rooms, 3 suites* *Cable TV, in-room VCRs, hot tub, Wi-Fi; no a/c, no kids under 12* ▭ *AE, D, MC, V* *BP.*

$$–$$$$ **Baranof Hotel.** The Baranof has long been Juneau's most prestigious address; it's as close to a big-city downtown boutique hotel as you're going to find in Southeast Alaska. Tasteful woods and period lamps in the dark art-deco lobby create an old-money atmosphere reminiscent of 1939, when the hotel first opened. Downstairs, breakfast and lunch are available in the Capitol Café and in the Gold Room with its embroidered chairs. Rooms on the front side have the best views, but street noise may keep you awake at the lower levels. The best are spacious corner suites on the upper floors, which overlook the busy harbor to the forested mountains of Douglas Island. Some of the other rooms are fairly small. ✉ *127 N. Franklin St., 99801* ☎ *907/586–2660 or 800/544–0970* 🌐 *www.westmarkhotels.com* *179 rooms, 17 suites* *Restaurant, coffee shop, some kitchenettes, cable TV, hair salon, lobby lounge, meeting room, travel services; no a/c* ▭ *AE, D, DC, MC, V.*

$–$$$ **Silverbow Inn.** Conveniently located in Juneau's historic downtown, the expanded Silverbow combines a downstairs bakery and café with a

11 rustic hotel rooms on the two upper levels. (Rumor has it that the ghost of Gus Messerschmitt—the bakery's original owner—still haunts the place. We weren't lucky enough to see him.) Four of the rooms are tiny, but all are tastefully furnished, and guests stroll downstairs each morning for a filling breakfast along with evening wine and cheese. Owned by former New Yorkers, the bakery is a gem: it crafts Alaska's only boiled bagels, and also serves deli sandwiches on homemade bread, salads, soups, and pastries. The back room is used for live jazz, films, and a dinner theater throughout the year. ✉ *120 2nd St.* ☎ *907/586–4146 or 800/586–4146* 🌐 *www.silverbowinn.com* *11 rooms* *Cable TV, Wi-Fi; no a/c* ▭ *AE, D, MC, V* 🍴 *CP.*

$$ **Aspen Hotel.** This corporate-style inn, within walking distance of the airport and 9 mi from downtown, is a popular choice with business travelers and families; what it lacks in charm and personality it makes up for in space and amenities. Rooms are large and clean, with in-room refrigerators, microwaves, and big TVs. This is also one of the few Juneau lodging options with an indoor pool, fitness center, hot tub, and hot breakfast. ✉ *1800 Shell Simmons Dr., 99801* ☎ *907/790–6435 or 866/483–7848* 🌐 *www.aspenhotelsak.com* *86 rooms, 8 suites* *Kitchenettes, microwaves, refrigerators, cable TV, indoor pool, exercise equipment, hot tub, Internet, business services, meeting rooms, airport shuttle; no a/c* ▭ *AE, D, MC, V* 🍴 *BP.*

$$ **Grandma's Feather Bed.** This humble Victorian-style hotel—the smallest property in the Best Western chain—is less than a mile from the airport in Mendenhall Valley. Cheerful colors brighten each of the spacious and homey rooms, which come with jetted bathtubs and, as the name would suggest, beds topped with voluminous feather comforters. Two of the rooms have gas fireplaces. Guests especially appreciate the big breakfast buffet that includes omelets, pancakes, and hot cereals. Dinners are also available Tuesday through Saturday. The hotel is not really set up for children. ✉ *2348 Mendenhall Loop Rd., 99801* ☎ *907/789–5566 or 888/781–5005* *14 rooms* *Restaurant, microwaves, refrigerators, cable TV, Internet, business services, airport shuttle; no a/c, no smoking* ▭ *AE, D, DC, MC, V* 🍴 *BP.*

WORD OF MOUTH

"In Juneau we always stay at Grandma's Feather Bed, closer to the airport than to the downtown area (Juneau is very spread out). The hotel is wonderfully appointed (all rooms have a Jacuzzi), plus breakfast buffet or breakfast cooked to order included in price."
–klondike

$–$$ **Glacier Trail Bed & Breakfast.** Owned by backcountry guides, this comfortable Victorian-style home is right on Mendenhall Lake across from Mendenhall Glacier. Guests can stay in two guest rooms with whirlpool baths or a private apartment with a full kitchen. Kayaks are available to explore Mendenhall Lake ($30 extra). ✉ *1081 Arctic Circle, 99801* ☎ *907/789–5646* *2 rooms, 1 apartment* *Some in-room hot tubs, boating; no a/c, no smoking* ▭ *MC, V* 🍴 *BP.*

$–$$ **The Prospector Hotel.** A short walk west of downtown and next door to the Alaska State Museum, this nicely appointed but visually unremarkable hotel is frequented by business travelers and legislators (during the winter legislative session). Rooms are spacious and have cherrywood furnishings, leather chairs, and ottomans. T. K. McGuire's dining room and lounge, which sits just off the lobby, serves prime rib, steaks, and seafood, along with Juneau's best Sunday brunch. ✉ *375 Whittier St., 99801* ☎ *907/586–3737, 800/331–2711 outside Alaska, 800/478–5866 in Alaska* 🌐 *www.prospectorhotel.com* *55 rooms, 7 suites* *Restaurant, kitchenettes, microwaves, refrigerators, cable TV, lobby lounge, meeting rooms, some pets allowed (fee); no a/c* 💳 *AE, D, DC, MC, V.*

$ **Driftwood Lodge.** This workaday downtown motel is one of Juneau's best values for the money, with a central location and well-maintained rooms, all of which include kitchenettes stocked with dishes, silverware, pots, and pans. The one- and two-bedroom units have twice the space of standard rooms, but cost just a few extra dollars. The shuttle to the airport and ferry is free. ✉ *435 Willoughby Ave., 99801* ☎ *907/586–2280 or 800/544–2239* 🌐 *www.driftwoodalaska.com* *31 rooms, 31 suites* *Kitchenettes, airport and ferry shuttle; no a/c* 💳 *AE, D, DC, MC, V.*

$ **Sentinel Island Lighthouse.** A few miles north of Juneau and adjacent to a rock where Steller's sea lions haul out, this operating lighthouse, complete with a 13-foot lantern that's visible from 17 mi away, provides a spectacular spot to watch whales and eagles. You have the entire cliff-bordered 6-acre island to roam around on. Simple accommodations include bunks in the lighthouse and in an adjacent building; you can also pitch a tent on a platform facing the water. Water and cooking facilities are provided for all accommodations. The lighthouse is managed by the Gastineau Channel Historical Society, and access is by charter boat, sea kayak, or helicopter. *Box 21264, 99802* ☎ *907/586–5338* *6 bunks in 2 buildings* *Kitchenettes* 💳 *No credit cards.*

★ ¢–$ **Alaskan Hotel.** This historic 1913 hotel in the heart of downtown Juneau sits over the popular bar of the same name; be prepared for noise Thursday through Saturday nights when bands are playing. The older but well-maintained guest rooms ramble across three floors and include pedestal sinks, old-fashioned radiators, and a smattering of antiques. The flocked wallpaper, red floral carpets, and Tiffany windows are reminiscent of the hotel's original gold rush–era opulence. The least-expensive rooms share a bath down the hall. ✉ *167 S. Franklin St., 99801* ☎ *907/586–1000 or 800/327–9347* *44 rooms, 22 with bath* *Bar; no a/c, no phones in some rooms, no TV in some rooms* 💳 *D, DC, MC, V.*

¢ Fodor'sChoice ★ **U.S. Forest Service Cabins.** Scattered throughout Tongass National Forest, these rustic cabins offer a charming and cheap escape. Most are fly-in units, accessible by floatplanes, with bunks for six to eight occupants, tables, stoves, and outdoor privies but no electricity or running water. You provide your own sleeping bag, food, and cooking utensils. ✉ *Juneau Ranger District, 8465 Old Dairy Rd., 99801* ☎ *907/586–8800, 877/444–6777 reservations* 🌐 *www.reserveusa.com* *150 cabins* 💳 *AE, D, MC, V.*

¢ **U.S. Forest Service Campgrounds.** Eight Forest Service–maintained campgrounds are scattered around Tongass National Forest and are accessible from the communities of Juneau, Sitka, Ketchikan, Petersburg, and Thorne Bay. All have pit toilets and sites for RVs and tents, but not all provide drinking water. Reservations are possible for some of these campgrounds, but space is generally available without a reservation. ✉ *Juneau Ranger District, 8465 Old Dairy Rd., 99801* ☎ *907/586–8800, 877/444–6777 reservations* 🌐 *www.reserveusa.com* 🎫 *$8* 💳 *D, MC, V.*

Nightlife & the Arts

Bars

The **Alaskan Hotel Bar** (✉ 167 S. Franklin St. ☎ 907/586–1000) is Juneau's most historically authentic watering hole, with flocked-velvet walls, antique chandeliers, and vintage Alaskan frontier-brothel decor. The atmosphere, however, is anything but dated, and the bar's live music and open mike night draw high-spirited crowds. When the ships are in, the music at **Red Dog Saloon** (✉ 278 S. Franklin St. ☎ 907/463–9954) is live and the crowd gets livelier. Past visitors to Juneau may recall **Imperial Saloon** (✉ 241 Front St. ☎ 907/586–1960) as one of the downtown dives, but a major remodeling transformed it into a favorite place to dance (live bands most weekends), drink, shoot pool, and meet singles. (The divey decor hasn't all disappeared, though, as the walls still feature mounted moose and bison heads. There's also an original pressed-tin ceiling.) Just down Front St. is the Southeast's number-one volume bar: the **Viking Lounge** (✉ 216 Front St. ☎ 907/586–2159) which is loved by cruise-ship workers and billiards enthusiasts for its rowdy vibe and seven pool tables.

If you're a beer fan, look for **Alaskan Brewing Company** (✉ 5429 Shaune Dr. ☎ 907/780–5866 🌐 www.alaskanbeer.com). These tasty brews, including Alaskan Amber, Pale Ale, Stout, and Smoked Porter, are brewed and bottled in Juneau. You can also visit the microbrewery (and sample the goods) May through September, Monday through Saturday 11 to 5, with 20-minute tours every half hour. Between October and April, tours take place Thursday through Saturday 11 to 4. ■ **TIP→ Keep in mind that this is no designer brewery—there is no upscale café/bar attached—but the gift shop sells classy T-shirts and beer paraphernalia.**

Music Festivals

The annual weeklong **Alaska Folk Festival** (📫 Box 21748, 99802 ☎ 907/463–3316 🌐 www.akfolkfest.org) is staged each April in Juneau, drawing singers, banjo masters, fiddlers, and even cloggers from all over the state, many of whom congregate at the Alaskan Hotel, the Festival's unofficial rallying point. During the last week of May, Juneau is the scene of **Juneau Jazz 'n Classics** (📫 Box 22152, 99802 ☎ 907/463–3378 🌐 www.jazzandclassics.org), which celebrates music from Bach to Brubeck.

Symphony

The **Juneau Symphony** (☎ 907/586–4676 🌐 www.juneausymphony.org) performs classical works October through April in the high-school auditorium.

Theater

Southeast Alaska's only professional theater company, the nationally renowned **Perseverance Theatre** (✉ 914 3rd St., Douglas ☎ 907/364–2421 🌐 www.perseverancetheatre.org), performs a wide range of classics and new productions, putting a distinctly Alaskan spin on every performance. Productions, which run throughout the year, range from statewide tours to radio shows to educational programming.

Shopping

Art Galleries

Annie Kaill's Gallery (✉ 244 Front St. ☎ 907/586–2880 🌐 www.annieandcojuneau.com) displays a mix of playful and whimsical original prints, pottery, jewelry, and other arts and crafts from Alaskan artists. The cooperatively run **Juneau Artists Gallery** (☎ 907/586–9891 🌐 www.juneauartistsgallery.com), on the first floor of the old Senate Building at 175 South Franklin Street, sells a nice mix of watercolors, jewelry, etchings, photographs, art glass, ceramics, Ukrainian-style decorated eggs, and pottery from more than 20 artists. Head through Heritage Coffee and climb the stairs for **Wm. Spear Designs** (✉ 174 S. Franklin St. ☎ 907/586–2209 🌐 www.wmspear.com), where this lawyer-turned-artist produces a fun and colorful collection of enameled pins and zipper pulls. Across from the tram, the **Raven's Journey** (✉ 439 S. Franklin St. ☎ 907/463–4686) specializes in high-quality native Alaskan masks, grass baskets, carvings, dolls, ivory and silver jewelry, and more.

A surprising exception to the cheesy-airport-gift-shop epidemic, Juneau's airport gift shop, **Hummingbird Hollow** (☎ 907/789–4672 🌐 www.hummingbirdhollow.net), is another fine place for authentic native art, including a diverse selection of jewelry, baskets, and Eskimo dolls.

Rie Muñoz, of the **Rie Muñoz Gallery** (✉ 2101 N. Jordan Ave. ☎ 907/789–7449 or 800/247–3151 🌐 www.riemunoz.com) in Mendenhall Valley, is one of Alaska's best-known artists. She's the creator of a stylized, simple, and colorful design technique that is much copied but rarely equaled. Other artists' work is also on sale at the Muñoz Gallery, including wood-block prints by nationally recognized artist Dale DeArmond. Various books illustrated by Rie Muñoz and written by Alaskan children's author Jean Rogers are for sale. In downtown Juneau, see Rie Muñoz's paintings and tapestries at **Decker Gallery** (✉ 233 S. Franklin St. ☎ 907/463–5536 or 800/463–5536).

Seafood

Taku Smokeries (✉ 550 S. Franklin St. ☎ 907/463–5033 or 800/582–5122 🌐 www.takusmokeries.com), at the south end of town near the cruise-ship docks and Mt. Roberts Tramway, processes nearly 6 million pounds of fish, mostly salmon, a year. ■ **TIP→ Their smoked sockeye fillets make excellent gifts.** You can view the smoking procedure through large windows and then purchase the packaged fish in the deli-style gift shop or have some shipped back home.

Side Trips from Juneau

Just a few miles outside of this ever-expanding city are some great day trips. The area's undisputed champion of visitor attractions is Mendenhall Glacier. Admiralty Island is also very popular—it has hikes through rain forest, excellent bear-viewing, and secluded sea-kayaking.

Native Culture Nearby

If you're interested in seeing how many native Alaskans of Southeast Alaska live today, you can fly or take one of the Alaska Marine Highway's ferries (☎ 907/465–3941 or 800/642–0066) to **Kake, Angoon,** or **Hoonah.** Hoonah's historic cannery building has been beautifully restored. Independent travelers won't find much organized touring in any of these communities, but you will find hotels (advance reservations strongly suggested), and guided fishing and natural-history trips can be arranged by asking around. In Kake, contact the **Keex' Kwaan Lodge** (☎ 907/785–3434 🌐 www.kakealaska.com). In Angoon, try the **Favorite Bay Sportfishing Lodge** (☎ 907/788–3344 or 866/788–3344 🌐 www.favoritebay.com). In Hoonah, **Icy Strait Lodge** (☎ 866/645–3636 🌐 www.icystraitlodge.com) provides very comfortable on-the-water accommodations.

Macaulay Salmon Hatchery

3 mi northwest of downtown Juneau.

Watch through an underwater window as salmon fight their way up a fish ladder, from mid-June to mid-October. Inside the busy hatchery, which produces almost 125 million young salmon annually, you will learn about the environmental considerations of commercial fishermen and the lives of salmon. A retail shop sells gifts and salmon products. Fishing poles are available for rent. ✉ *2697 Channel Dr.* ☎ *907/463–4810 or 877/463–2486* 🌐 *www.dipac.net* 🎫 *$3 including short tour* ⏲ *Mid-May–mid-Sept., weekdays 10–6, weekends 10–5; Oct.–Apr. by appointment.*

Glacier Gardens Rainforest Adventure

6½ mi northwest of Juneau.

Spread over 50 acres of rain forest, Glacier Gardens is a rain-forest wonderland replete with ponds, waterfalls, hiking paths, a large atrium, and gardens. The roots of fallen trees, turned upside down and buried in the ground, act as bowls to hold planters that overflow with begonias, fuchsias, and petunias. (Green thumbs are sure to delight in the well-executed landscaping.) Guided tours (in covered golf carts) lead you along the 4 mi of paved paths, and a 580-foot-high overlook provides dramatic views across Mendenhall Glacier. A café and gift shop are here, and the conservatory is a popular wedding spot. ■ **TIP→ The Juneau city bus, which departs from multiple locations in downtown Juneau (including 4th and Franklin), stops right in front of Glacier Gardens.** ✉ *7600 Glacier Hwy.* ☎ *907/790–3377* 🌐 *www.glaciergardens.com* 🎫 *$15 including guided tour* ⏲ *May–Sept., daily 9–6.*

> **FINDING THE RIGHT GUIDE**
>
> *See* the next section in this chapter ("Sports, the Outdoors & Guided Tours") for our favorite tour operators and guides who operate in and around Juneau.

Mendenhall Glacier

13 mi north of Juneau.

Fodor'sChoice ★

Juneau's famous drive-up glacier spans 12 mi and is fed by the massive Juneau Icefield. Like many other Alaskan glaciers, it is retreating up the valley, losing 100 feet a year as massive chunks of ice calve into the small lake separating Mendenhall from the **Mendenhall Visitor Center.** The center has highly interactive exhibits on the glacier, a theater and bookstore, educational exhibits, and panoramic views. It's a great place for children to learn the basics of glacier dynamics. Nature trails lead along Mendenhall Lake and into the mountains overlooking Mendenhall Glacier; the trails are marked by posts and paint stripes delineating the historical location of the glacier, providing a sharp reminder of the Mendenhall's hasty retreat. Look for spawning sockeye and coho salmon in Steep Creek, ½ mi south of the visitor center along the Moraine Ecology Trail. Several companies lead bus tours to the glacier. A glacier express bus leaves from the cruise-ship terminal and heads right out to Mendenhall Glacier; ask at the visitor information center there. ✉ *End of Glacier Spur Rd., off Mendenhall Loop Rd.* ☎ *907/789–0097* 🌐 *www.fs.fed.us/r10/tongass/districts/mendenhall* 🎟 *Visitor center $3 in summer, free in winter* ⏲ *May–Sept., daily 8–6:30; Oct.–Apr., Thurs.–Sun. 10–4.*

Shrine of St. Therese

23 mi northwest of downtown Juneau.

A self-guided pilgrimage to the shrine is well worth the 23-mi journey from downtown Juneau (a taxi costs at least $45 round-trip). Built in the 1930s, this beautiful stone church and its 14 stations of the cross are the only inhabitants of a serene tiny island that is accessible via a 400-foot-long pedestrian causeway. Sunday services are held at 1 PM from June through August. For those wishing to explore the area for more than a few hours, the Shrine offers a lodge and four rental cabins that run the gamut from rustic to resplendent. ✉ *5933 Lund St.* ☎ *907/780–6112* 🌐 *www.shrineofsainttherese.org* ⏲ *Daily.*

Admiralty Island

57 *10 mi south of Juneau.*

The island is famous for its lush rain forests and abundant wildlife, including one of the largest concentrations of brown bears anywhere on the planet. Tlingit inhabitants called it Kootznoowoo, meaning "fortress of the bears." Ninety-six miles long, with 678 mi of coastline, Admiralty—the second-largest island in Southeast Alaska—is home to an estimated 1,500 bears, almost one per square mile. The Forest Service's **Admiralty Island National Monument** has a system of public-use cabins, a canoe route that crosses the island via a chain of lakes and trails, the world's highest density of nesting bald eagles, large concentrations of humpback whales, and some of the region's best sea-kayaking and sportfishing. In short, it's a nature lover's Valhalla. ☎ *907/586–8790.*

Fodor's Choice ★ More than 90% of Admiralty Island is preserved within the Kootznoowoo Wilderness. Its chief attraction is **Pack Creek,** where you can watch brown bears feeding on salmon. One of Alaska's premier bear-viewing sites, Pack Creek is co-managed by the U.S. Forest Service and the Alaska Department of Fish and Game. Permits are required during the main viewing season, from June 1 through September 10, and only 24 people per day are allowed to visit Pack Creek from July 5 through August 25. If you're headed to Pack Creek without a guide or an experienced visitor, be sure to cover the basics of bear safety before your trip. ■ **TIP→ Reservations can be mailed to the Forest Service beginning February 20.** *907/586–8800 www.fs.fed.us/r10/tongass/districts/admiralty $50.*

WHERE TO STAY ★ $$$$ **Thayer Lake Lodge.** One of the Southeast's oldest lodges, Thayer Lake is on the sandy shores of a 9-mi lake within the Admiralty Island National Monument. Built in 1952 by Bob and Edith Nelson and now run by their grandkids, this wonderful rustic lodge with cabins houses up to 10 people (5 in each cabin). Borrow a canoe or motorboat for unsurpassed cutthroat and Dolly Varden trout fishing. Simple family-style meals are served. The lodge requires a minimum six-day, five-night stay, which includes all meals, bear-viewing excursions, fishing, other activities, and guides. You'll be deep in nature, without any neighbors for at least 25 mi around. *Box 8897, Ketchikan 99901 907/247–8897 2 cabins Dining room, kitchenettes, boating, fishing, hiking; no a/c, no room TVs MC, V Closed mid-Sept.–late May.*

Sports, the Outdoors & Guided Tours

Boating, Canoeing & Kayaking

Above & Beyond Alaska (907/364–2333 www.beyondak.com) guides overnight camping, Mendenhall Glacier, and kayaking trips in the Juneau area.

Adventure Bound (907/463—2509 or 800/228–3875 www.adventureboundalaska.com) offers all-day trips to Sawyer Glacier within Tracy Arm during the summer. Experienced kayakers can rent boats and equipment from ★ **Alaska Boat and Kayak Rental** (907/789–6886 www.juneaukayak.com) at the Auke Bay boat harbor 12 mi north of Juneau. The company also provides water-taxi services for kayakers looking to access remote paddling terrain. **Alaska Discovery** (800/586–1911 www.akdiscovery.com), a Juneau-based outfitter, leads 9- to 12-day trips down the Tatshenshini and Alsek. The trips begin in Canada and end in Glacier Bay. **Alaska Fjordlines** (907/766–3395 or 800/320–0146 www.alaskafjordlines.com) provides round-trips connecting Skagway and Haines with Juneau on a daily basis in the summer. The boat, a 65-foot high-speed catamaran, leaves Skagway at 8 AM, Haines at 9 AM, and reaches Juneau at 11:45 AM, where a bus transports visitors into town and then to Mendenhall Glacier, returning to the boat at 4:45 PM for the ride back to Haines.

WORD OF MOUTH

"The Adventure Bound folks served lunch and drinks—the staff was tops! They narrated at the right times and educated us when we were willing to stop hooting and hollering at Tracy Arm's massive, beautiful glaciers."
—OaktownTraveler

Alaska Travel Adventures (907/789–0052 or 800/478–0052 www.alaskaadventures.com) leads Mendenhall River floats and numerous other tours throughout the Juneau area. **Auk Nu Tours** (907/586–8687 or 800/820–2628 www.auknutours.com) has all-day catamaran tours to the beautiful glaciers of Tracy Arm Fjord. Juneau's highly successful ★ native corporation, **Goldbelt/Auk Ta Shaa Discovery** (☎ 907/586–8687 or 800/820–2628 🌐 www.goldbelttours.com) guides rafting trips down the Mendenhall River and operates sea-kayaking trips in the Juneau area, including a great Tracy Arm glacier day cruise.The **Juneau Steamboat Company** (☎ 907/723–0372 🌐 www.juneausteamboatco.com) offers scenic tours of Gastineau Channel aboard an authentic wood-fired steam launch, similar to those used around Juneau in the late 1800s and early 1900s. Tours come with entertaining narration that focuses on the historic mines of the area.

3

Climbing Gym

If it's pouring down rain—and in Juneau, it often is—head south of town to the **Rock Dump** (✉ 1310 Eastaugh Way ☎ 907/586–4982 🌐 www.rockdump.com), Alaska's largest indoor climbing facility. The Dump has climbing walls for all abilities from beginner to expert; day passes are $10.

Cross-Country Skiing

Find groomed cross-country ski trails near the Eaglecrest Ski Area and at Mendenhall Campground in the winter. You can rent skis and get advice about touring the trails and ridges around town from **Foggy Mountain Shop** (✉ 134 N. Franklin St. ☎ 907/586–6780 🌐 www.foggymountainshop.com). During the winter, the **Parks and Recreation Department** (☎ 907/586–5226, 907/586–0428 24-hr info 🌐 www.juneau.lib.ak.us/parksrec) sponsors a group ski and snowshoe outing each Wednesday and Saturday when there's sufficient snow.

Downhill Skiing

Southeast Alaska's only downhill ski area, **Eaglecrest** (☎ 907/790–2000, 907/586–5330 recorded ski information 🌐 www.juneau.org/eaglecrest), is located on Douglas Island, just 30 minutes from downtown Juneau. The resort typically offers late-November to mid-April skiing and snowboarding on 1,600 acres of well-groomed and off-piste terrain. Amenities include two double chairlifts, cross-country trails, a beginner's platter pull, ski school, ski-rental shop, cafeteria, and trilevel day lodge. Enjoy the northern lights while you night-ski from January through mid-March.

Fishing

Alaska Trophy Fishing (☎ 866/934–7466 🌐 www.alaskatrophyfishing.com) offers tailor-made fishing vacations and charters. Sportfishing is an exceedingly popular activity in the Juneau area, and many charter boats depart from local harbors. The **Juneau Convention and Visitors Bureau** (☎ 907/586–1737 or 888/581-2201 🌐 www.traveljuneau.com) Web site has a complete listing. Several companies lead whale-watching trips from Juneau. **Juneau Sportfishing & Sightseeing** (☎ 907/586–1887 🌐 www.juneausportfishing.com) has fishing trips aboard luxury boats.

Flightseeing

Several local companies operate helicopter flightseeing trips that take you to the spectacular glaciers flowing from Juneau Icefield. Most have booths along the downtown cruise-ship dock. All include a touchdown on a glacier, providing guests of almost all ages and abilities with a chance to romp on these rivers of ice. Some also lead trips that include a dogsled ride on the glacier, an increasingly popular tourist pastime. Note that though we recommend the best companies, even some of the most experienced pilots have been killed in helicopter accidents; always ask a carrier about their recent safety record before booking a trip. Flightseeing is quite controversial in Juneau, where locals are concerned about the almost constant din of helicopter activity throughout the summer.

> **A BREATHTAKING JOURNEY**
>
> **Taku Glacier Lodge** (☎ 907/586–6275 🌐 www.takuglacierlodge.com) is a remote, historic lodge south of Juneau along Taku Inlet. Hole-in-the-Wall Glacier is directly across the inlet from the lodge, and nature trails wind through the surrounding country, where black bears and bald eagles are frequently sighted. Floatplanes fly from Juneau on a scenic trip to the lodge, where you are served a delicious lunch or dinner and then flown back three hours later. No overnight stays are available.

Coastal Helicopters (☎ 907/789–5600 or 800/789–5610 🌐 www.coastalhelicopters.com) lands on several glaciers within the Juneau Icefield. Flying out of Douglas, **ERA Helicopters** (☎ 907/586–2030 or 800/843–1947 🌐 www.eraaviation.com) has a fully-narrated one-hour trip that includes landing on Norris Glacier. **NorthStar Trekking** (☎ 907/790–4530 🌐 www.glaciertrekking.com) has three levels of excellent glacier hikes, starting with a one-hour interpretive walk, up to a four-hour hike that includes the chance to practice basic climbing and rope techniques. No experience is necessary.

Temsco Helicopters (☎ 907/789–9501 or 877/789–9501 🌐 www.temscoair.com), the self-proclaimed pioneers of Alaskan glacier helicopter touring, offer glacier tours, dogsled adventures, and year-round flightseeing. **Ward Air** (☎ 907/789–9150 🌐 www.wardair.com) conducts flightseeing trips to Glacier Bay and the Juneau Icefield. **Wings of Alaska** (☎ 907/789–0790 🌐 www.wingsofalaska.com) leads flightseeing trips to many areas around Juneau.

Gold Panning

Gold panning is fun, especially for children, and Juneau is one of the Southeast's best-known gold-panning towns. Sometimes you actually uncover a few flecks of the precious metal in the bottom of your pan. You can buy a pan at almost any Alaska hardware or sporting-goods store. **Alaska Travel Adventures** (☎ 907/789–0052 or 800/478–0052 🌐 www.alaskaadventures.com) has gold-panning tours near the famous Alaska-Juneau Mine.

Golf

Juneau's par-three, 9-hole **Mendenhall Golf Course** (✉ 2101 Industrial Blvd. ☎ 907/789–1221) sports a modest layout but has views that any exclusive private course would die for. Club rentals are available.

Hiking

A private company, **Gastineau Guiding** (☎ 907/586–8231 🌐 www.stepintoalaska.com), leads a variety of hikes in the Juneau area. Especially popular are their walks from the top of the tram on Mt. Roberts, including an early-bird version that departs at 8 AM to avoid the crowds. The **Parks and Recreation Department** (☎ 907/586–5226, 907/586–0428 24-hr info 🌐 www.juneau.lib.ak.us/parksrec) in Juneau sponsors a group hike each Wednesday morning and on Saturday in summer. Hikers can contact the **U.S. Forest Service** (☎ 907/586–8790) for trail books and maps.

Mountain Biking

Drop by the Centennial Hall Visitor Center for details on local trails open to bikes. Nearby is **Driftwood Lodge** (✉ 435 Willoughby Ave. ☎ 907/586–2280 🌐 www.driftwoodalaska.com), which has basic mountain bikes for rent, along with trailers for toddlers.

Pack Creek Bear-Viewing

Alaska Discovery (✉ 5310 Glacier Hwy., Juneau ☎ 907/780–6226 or 800/586–1911 🌐 www.akdiscovery.com) leads single- and multiday trips to Pack Creek that include a floatplane trip, sea kayaking, and guided bear viewing.

Sightseeing & Glaciers

Former miners lead three-hour tours of the historic **AJ Gold Mine** (☎ 907/463–5017) south of Juneau. A gold-panning demonstration is included, and approximately 45 minutes of the tour take place inside the old tunnels that lace the mountains. Mine tours depart from downtown by bus. The **Juneau Convention and Visitors Bureau** (☎ 907/586–1737 or 888/581–2201 🌐 www.traveljuneau.com) has a list of other companies that provide tours to Mendenhall Glacier. **Juneau Trolley Car Company** (☎ 907/586–7433 🌐 www.juneautrolley.com) conducts narrated tours, stopping at a dozen or so of Juneau's historic and shopping attractions for $14. **Mighty Great Trips** (☎ 907/789–5460 🌐 www.mightygreattrips.com) leads guided bus tours that include a visit to Mendenhall Glacier.

Whale-Watching

AK Whale Watching (☎ 907/463–1066 or 888/432-6722 🌐 www.akwhalewatching.com) offers small-group excursions aboard a luxury yacht with an on-board naturalist.

Four Seasons Marine (☎ 907/790-6671 or 877/774–8687) combines whale-watching with an hour at Orca Point Lodge on Colt Island, where guests are served a grilled salmon lunch. The boat departs from Auke Bay with a free shuttle from Juneau. Several companies lead whale-watching trips from Juneau. **Juneau Sportfishing & Sightseeing** (☎ 907/586–1887 🌐 www.juneausportfishing.com) has been

WORD OF MOUTH

"Did we see whales or did we see whales with Captain Larry!! We saw group after group of whales. They were blowing, chasing, flipping, breaching. I was elated. I shot a roll and a half of film. The folks on my boat were great."
–OaklandTraveler

around for many years, and its boats carry a maximum of six passengers, providing a personalized trip.

★ **Orca Enterprises (with Captain Larry)** (☎ 907/789–6801 or 888/733–6722 🌐 www.orcaenterprises.com) offers whale-watching tours via jet boats designed for comfort and speed. The operator boasts a whale-sighting success rate of 99.9% between May 1 and Oct. 15.

GLACIER BAY NATIONAL PARK & PRESERVE

58 *60 mi northwest of Juneau.*

Fodor'sChoice ★

Near the northern end of the Inside Passage, Glacier Bay National Park and Preserve is one of the jewels of the entire national park system. Visiting Glacier Bay is like stepping back into the Little Ice Age—it's one of the few places in the world where you can approach such a variety of massive tidewater glaciers. With a noise that sounds like cannons firing, bergs the size of 10-story office buildings sometimes come crashing from the "snout" of a glacier, each cannon blast signifying another step in the glacier's steady retreat. The calving iceberg sends tons of water and spray skyward, propelling mini–tidal waves outward from the point of impact. **Johns Hopkins Glacier** calves so often and with such volume that large cruise ships can seldom come within 2 mi of its face.

Glacier Bay is a still-forming body of water fed by the runoff of the ice fields, glaciers, and mountains that surround it. In the mid-18th century, ice floes so covered the bay that Captain James Cook and then Captain George Vancouver sailed by and didn't even know it. At the time of Vancouver's sailing in 1794, the bay was still hidden behind and beneath a vast glacial wall of ice, which was more than 20 mi across and in places more than 4,000 feet in depth. It extended more than 100 mi north to its origins in the St. Elias Mountain Range, the world's tallest coastal mountains. Since then, due to warming weather and other factors not fully understood, the face of the glacial ice has melted and retreated with amazing speed, exposing 65 mi of fjords, islands, and inlets.

In 1879, about a century after Vancouver's sail-by, one of the earliest white visitors to what is now Glacier Bay National Park and Preserve came calling. The ever-curious naturalist John Muir, who would become one of the region's earliest proponents, was drawn by the flora and fauna that had followed in the wake of glacial withdrawals; he was also fascinated by the vast ice rivers that descended from the mountains to tidewater. Today the naturalist's namesake glacier, like others in the park, continues to retreat dramatically: The Muir Glacier's terminus is now scores of miles

FAIRWEATHER FOLLY

It was Vancouver who named the magnificent snow-clad **Mt. Fairweather,** which towers over the head of the bay. Legend has it that Vancouver named Fairweather on one of the Southeast's most beautiful blue days—and the mountain was not seen again during the following century. That's an exaggeration, to be sure, but overcast, rainy weather is certainly the norm here.

farther up the bay from the small cabin he built at its face during his time there.

Glacier Bay is a marvelous laboratory for naturalists of all persuasions. Glaciologists, of course, can have a field day. Animal lovers can hope to see the rare glacial "blue" bears of the area, a variation of the black bear, which is here along with the brown bear; whales feasting on krill; mountain goats in late spring and early summer; and seals on floating icebergs. Birders can look for the more than 200 species that have already been spotted in the park, and if you're lucky, you may witness two bald eagles engaging in aerobatics.

A remarkable panorama of plants unfolds from the head of the bay, which is just emerging from the ice, to the mouth, which has been ice-free for more than 200 years. In between, the primitive plants—algae, lichens, and mosses—that are the first to take hold of the bare, wet ground give way to more complex species: flowering plants such as the magenta dwarf fireweed and the creamy dryas, which in turn merge with willows, alders, and cottonwood. As the living plants mature and die, they enrich the soil and prepare it for new species to follow. The climax of the plant community is the lush spruce-and-hemlock rain forest, rich in life and blanketing the land around **Bartlett Cove.** ☎ *907/697–2230, boating info 907/697–2627* 🌐 *www.nps.gov/glba.*

Gustavus

59 *50 mi west of Juneau, 75 mi south of Skagway.*

For airborne visitors, Gustavus is the gateway to Glacier Bay National Park and Preserve. The long, paved jet airport, built as a refueling strip during World War II, is one of the best and longest in Southeast Alaska, all the more impressive because of its limited facilities at the field. Alaska Airlines, which serves Gustavus daily in the summer, has a large, rustic terminal at the site, and from a free telephone on the front porch of the terminal you can call any of the local hostelries for a courtesy pickup. Smaller, light-aircraft companies that serve the community out of Juneau also have on-site shelters. In addition a daily passenger ferry provides service between Juneau and Gustavus throughout the summer.

■ TIP→ **Before you get too excited about visiting this remote outpost, be forewarned: Gustavus has no downtown.** In fact, Gustavus is not really a town at all. The 150 or so year-round residents are most emphatic on this point; they regularly vote down incorporation. Instead, Gustavus is a scattering of homes, farmsteads, arts-and-crafts studios, fishing and guiding charters, and other tiny enterprises peopled by hospitable individualists. It is, in many ways, a contemporary example of the frontier spirit in Alaska.

Where to Stay & Eat

$$$$ **Bear Track Inn.** Built of handcrafted spruce logs, this inn sits on a 57-acre property facing Icy Strait. Soaring ceilings open up the lobby, where a central fireplace and moose-antler chandeliers invite relaxation. Spacious guest rooms are luxuriously furnished, and a full-service restau-

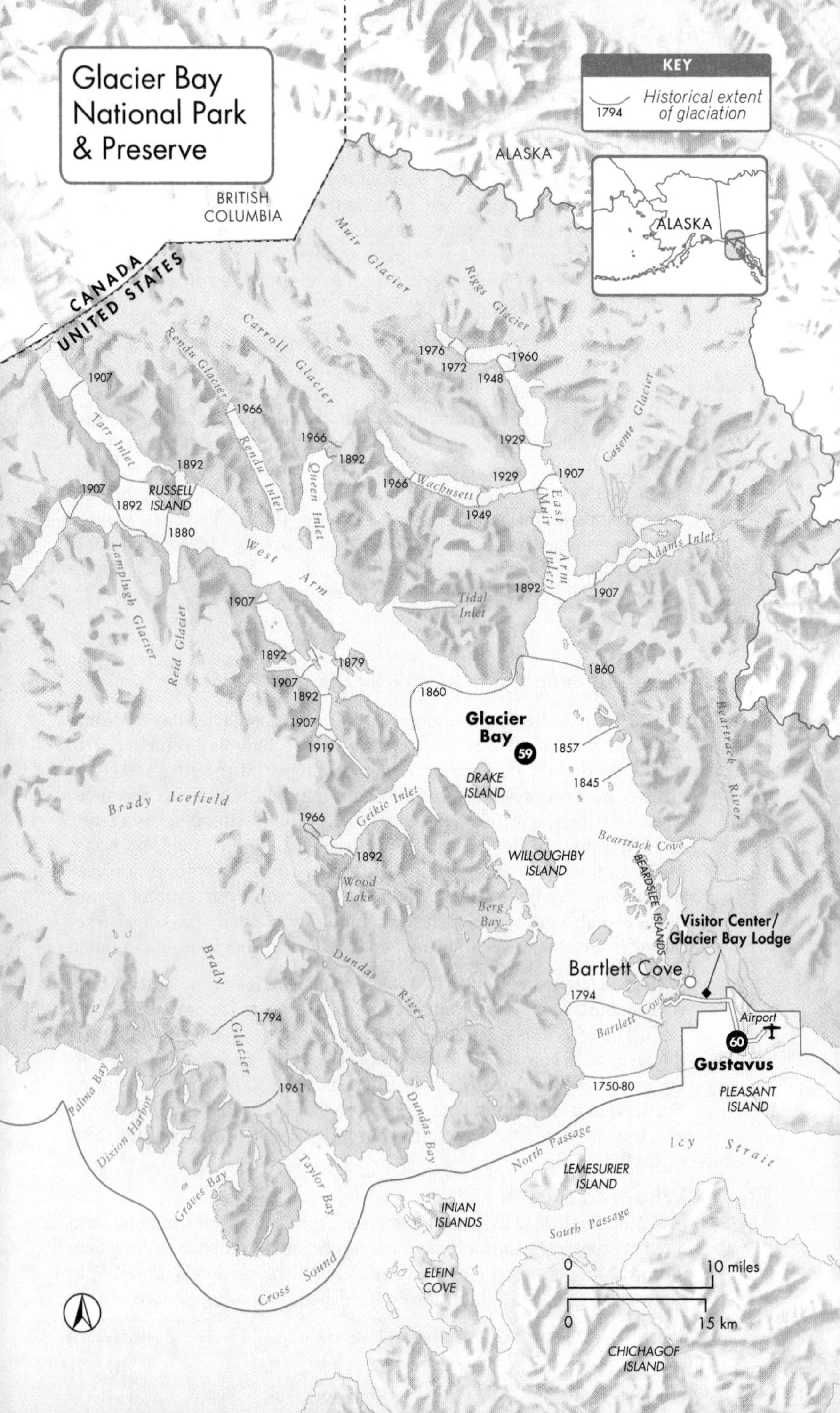

Glacier Bay National Park & Preserve
KEY
Historical extent of glaciation
1794
ALASKA
BRITISH COLUMBIA
CANADA
UNITED STATES
Muir Glacier
Riggs Glacier
Carroll Glacier
Rendu Glacier
Caseme Glacier
Tarr Inlet
RUSSELL ISLAND
Rendu Inlet
Queen Inlet
Wachusett
East Muir Arm Inlet
Adams Inlet
West Arm
Lamplugh Glacier
Reid Glacier
Tidal Inlet
Glacier Bay
59
DRAKE ISLAND
Beartrack River
Brady Icefield
Geikie Inlet
WILLOUGHBY ISLAND
Beartrack Cove
BEARDSLEE ISLANDS
Wood Lake
Berg Bay
Visitor Center/ Glacier Bay Lodge
Bartlett Cove
Brady Glacier
Dundas River
Airport
60
Gustavus
PLEASANT ISLAND
Palma Bay
Dixon Harbor
Dundas Bay
North Passage
Icy Strait
LEMESURIER ISLAND
Graves Bay
Taylor Bay
INIAN ISLANDS
South Passage
ELFIN COVE
Cross Sound
0
10 miles
0
15 km
CHICHAGOF ISLAND

THERE'S A WORLD GOING ON . . . UNDERGROUND

Glacier Bay's impressive landscape is the result of plate tectonics. The region sits directly above a chaotic intersection of fault lines—resulting in a 100-million-year-old crunchfest. While this movement can be credited for creating the region's stunning topography, it has also wreaked some havoc. On September 10, 1899, the area was rocked by a massive temblor registering 8.4 on the Richter scale. The quake, which had its epicenter in Yakutat Bay, rattled Glacier Bay so much that the entire bay was choked with icebergs. And on July 9, 1958, a tremendous earthquake—a 7.9 on the Richter scale—triggered a landslide of epic proportions in nearby Lituya Bay: 40 million cubic yards of rock tumbled into the bay, causing a tidal wave that reached 1,720 feet.

3

rant (open to the public for dinner) specializes in seafood but also serves steak, pork chops, and wild game. The Bear Track doesn't cater to the light-walleted set: room rates start at $465 per person per night; the price includes meals and air transport from Juneau. (There are better prices for multiple-night packages.) Also on offer are glacier tours. ✉ *255 Rink Creek Rd., 99826* ☎ *907/697–3017 or 888/697–2284* 🌐 *www.beartrackinn.com* *14 rooms* *Restaurant, boating, fishing, Internet, airport shuttle, some pets allowed; no a/c, no room phones, no room TVs, no smoking* 💳 *D, MC, V* ⏲ *Closed Oct.–Apr.* *FAP.*

$$$$ **Glacier Bay Lodge.** Within the national park, this lodge is constructed of massive timbers and blends well into the thick rain forest surrounding it on three sides. The modern yet rustic rooms are accessible by boardwalks. If it swims or crawls in the sea hereabouts, you'll find it on the menu in the rustic dining room, which is open to non-lodge guests as well. One favorite is the halibut baked *aleyeska,* a fillet baked in a rich sauce of sour cream, cheese, and onions. Activities include whale watching, kayaking, and naturalist-led hikes. The Lodge pushes package reservations, which include all meals, transfers, and a boat tour of Glacier Bay on your first day. ✉ *199 Bartlett Cove Rd., 99826* ☎ *907/264–4600 or 888/229–8687* 🌐 *www.visitglacierbay.com* *56 rooms* *Restaurant, boating, bicycles; no a/c, no room phones, no room TVs* 💳 *AE, D, DC, MC, V* ⏲ *Closed mid-Sept.–mid-May.*

$$$ Fodor'sChoice ★ **Gustavus Inn.** Built in 1928 and established as a hotel in 1965, this inn continues a tradition of gracious Alaska rural living. In the remodeled original homestead building, rooms are decorated in New England–farmhouse style. Here you can indulge in Glacier Bay sightseeing trips, fishing expeditions, bicycle rides, and berry picking in season. Hosts David and Jo Ann Lesh heap bountiful servings of seafood and fresh vegetables on the plates of overnight guests (all meals are included in the price) and others who reserve for family-style meals in the cozy dining room in advance. Dinnertime is 6:30 sharp. ✉ *Mile 1, Gustavus Rd., Box 60, 99826* ☎ *907/697–2254 or 800/649–5220* 🌐 *www.*

gustavusinn.com ⇨ *13 rooms, 11 with bath* ♁ *Restaurant, fishing, Internet, airport shuttle; no a/c, no room phones, no room TVs, no smoking* ▭ *AE, MC, V* ⏲ *Closed mid-Sept.–mid-May* 🍽 *FAP.*

★ $$$ **Glacier Bay Country Inn.** Bears and moose might peek into this rambling log structure with its marvelous cupolas, dormers, gables, and porches. Some cabins include antiques and open log-beam ceilings. Innkeepers Ponch and Sandi Marchbanks offer charter-fishing trips (extra charge) and a variety of sightseeing options. Meals and transfers to activities booked by the Inn are included in the room rate. Among the guests' favorite dishes here are steamed Dungeness crab, ale-marinated alder-grilled salmon, and crème brûlée. ⊠ *Halfway between airport and Bartlett Cove* ✉ *Box 5, 99826* ☎ *907/697–2288 or 800/628–0912* ⊕ *www.glacierbayalaska.com* ⇨ *5 rooms, 5 cabins* ♁ *Restaurant, boating, fishing, Internet; no a/c, no room phones, no room TVs, no smoking* ▭ *AE, D, MC, V* ⏲ *Closed mid-Sept.–mid-May* 🍽 *FAP.*

$–$$ **Annie Mae Lodge.** This quiet two-story lodge, one of the few Gustavus places open year-round, faces the Good River and is a five-minute walk from the beach. Seven guest rooms have doors that open to a wraparound veranda; one room is entirely wheelchair accessible. Lodging includes three meals a day plus ground transportation. Kayaking, flightseeing, and Glacier Bay cruises are arranged by the owner. ✉ *Box 55, 99826* ☎ *907/697–2346 or 800/478–2346* ⊕ *www.anniemae.com* ⇨ *11 rooms, 9 with bath* ♁ *Internet; no a/c, no room phones, no room TVs, no smoking* ▭ *AE, D, DC, MC, V* 🍽 *FAP.*

Sports, the Outdoors & Guided Tours

Glacier Bay is best experienced from the water, whether from the deck of a cruise ship, on a tour boat, or from the level of a sea kayak. National Park Service naturalists often come aboard to explain the great glaciers and to help spot bears, mountain goats, whales, porpoises, and birds.

BOATING & LOCAL INTEREST **Allen Marine** (☎ 888/289–0081 ⊕ www.allenmarine.com) provides daily passenger ferry service between Juneau and Gustavus in the summer. **Huna Totem Corporation/Aramark** (☎ 907/264–4600 or 888/229–8687 ⊕ www.visitglacierbay.com) provides daily summertime boat tours from the dock at Bartlett Cove, near Glacier Bay Lodge. These eight-hour trips into Glacier Bay have a Park Service naturalist and native guide aboard a high-speed 155-passenger catamaran. A light lunch is included. Campers and sea-kayakers heading up the bay ride the same boat.

FLIGHTSEEING **Air Excursions** (☎ 907/697–2375, 800/354–2479 in Alaska ⊕ www.airexcursions.com) operates Glacier Bay flightseeing tours from Gustavus, plus flights to Juneau several times a day in the summer.

HIKING Glacier Bay's steep and heavily-forested slopes aren't the most conducive to hiking, but there are several short hikes that begin at the Glacier Bay Lodge. Among the most popular is the **Forest Loop Trail,** a pleasant 1-mi jaunt that begins in a forest of spruce and hemlock and finishes on the beach. Also beginning at the lodge is the **Bartlett River Trail**—a 5-mi round-trip hike that borders an intertidal lagoon, culminating at the Bartlett River estuary. The **Bartlett Lake Trail,** a 6-mi walk that meanders through rain forest, ends at the quiet lakeshore.

3

SEA KAYAKING The most adventurous way to explore Glacier Bay is by paddling your own kayak through the bay's icy waters and inlets. But unless you're an expert, you're better off signing on with the guided tours. You can book a five- or eight-day guided expedition through **Alaska Discovery** (☎ 907/780–6226 or 800/586–1911 🌐 www.akdiscovery.com). Alaska Discovery provides safe, seaworthy kayaks and tents, gear, and food. Its guides are tough, knowledgeable Alaskans, and they've spent enough time in Glacier Bay's wild country to know what's safe and what's not. You can also take a guided one-day kayak trip from Bartlett Cove if you're just looking for a chance to explore the area. **Spirit Walker Expeditions** (☎ 907/697–2266 or 800/529–2537 🌐 www.seakayakalaska.com) leads 1- to 10-day sea-kayaking trips from Gustavus to various parts of Icy Strait (but not within Glacier Bay itself).

Kayak rentals for unescorted Glacier Bay exploring and camping can be arranged through **Glacier Bay Sea Kayaks** (✉ Bartlett Cove ☎ 907/697–2257 🌐 www.glacierbayseakayaks.com). Prior to going out, you will be given instructions on handling the craft plus camping and routing suggestions. **Sea Otter Kayak** (☎ 907/697–3007 in summer, 907/226–2338 in winter 🌐 www.he.net/~seaotter) rents kayaks, gives instructions on their use, and supplies the essentials.

HAINES

75 mi north of Gustavus and 80 mi northwest of Juneau.

Nestled on the collar of the Chilkat Peninsula, a narrow strip of land that divides the Chilkat and Chilkoot Inlets, Haines encompasses an area that has been occupied by Tlingit peoples for centuries. Missionary S. Hall Young and famed naturalist John Muir were intent on establishing a Presbyterian mission in the area, and with the blessing of local chiefs, they chose the site that later became Haines. It's hard to imagine a more beautiful setting—a heavily wooded peninsula with magnificent views of Portage Cove and the snowy Coast Range. Unlike most other towns in Southeast Alaska, Haines can be reached by the 152-mi Haines Highway, which connects at Haines Junction with the Alaska Highway. It's also accessible by the state ferry (907/465–3941 or 800/642–0066) and by scheduled plane service from Juneau. The Haines ferry terminal is 4½ mi northwest of downtown, and the airport is 4 mi west.

Haines is an interesting community: its history contains equal parts enterprising gold-rush boom town and regimented military outpost. The former is evidenced by Jack Dalton, who, in the 1890s, maintained a toll route from the settlement of Haines into the Yukon, charging $1 for foot passengers and

JUST BACK FROM ALASKA

"I fell in love with Haines. I went on a great bird-watching shore excursion where we saw lots of bald eagles and other amazing birds, as well as seals playing in a river. The town is very charming, with a long boardwalk, a great local coffee shop, and a good bakery."
–Felice Aarons, Fodor's Editor

$2.50 per horse. His Dalton Trail later provided access for miners during the 1897 gold rush to the Klondike.

The town's military roots are visible at Fort William Henry Seward, located at Portage Cove just south of town. For 17 years (1923–39) prior to World War II, the post, renamed Chilkoot Barracks in commemoration of the gold-rush route, was the only military base in the territory. The fort's buildings and grounds are now part of a National Historic Landmark.

Today, the Haines–Fort Seward community is recognized for the native dance and art center at Fort Seward, the Haines Public Library (which, in 2005, was named Best Small Library in the United States), as well as for the superb fishing, camping, and outdoor recreation to be found at Chilkoot Lake, Portage Cove, Mosquito Lake, and Chilkat State Park on the shores of Chilkat Inlet. Northwest of the city is the Alaska Chilkat Bald Eagle Preserve. Thousands of eagles come here each winter to feed on a late run of chum salmon, making it one of Alaska's premier bird-watching sites.

Exploring Haines

Though the downtown area feels as small as a postage stamp, Haines is a delightful place to explore on foot. Local weather is drier than in much of Southeast Alaska, and the town exudes a down-home friendliness. Perhaps this is because Haines sees fewer cruise ships, or maybe it's the grand landscape and ease of access to the mountains and sea. Whatever the cause, visitors should be prepared for a relative lack of knickknack shops and jewelry stores.

What to See

65 **Alaska Indian Arts.** Dedicated to the revival of Tlingit art, this nonprofit organization is housed in the former fort hospital, between the parade ground and the Chilkat Center for the Arts. You can watch Tlingits carving totem poles, metalsmiths working in silver, and other artists doing blanket weaving. ✉ *Fort Seward* ☎ *907/766–2160* 🌐 *www.alaskaindianarts.com* 🎟 *Free* ⏲ *Weekdays 9–5, and evenings when cruise ships are in port.*

62 **American Bald Eagle Foundation.** The main focuses here are bald eagles and associated fauna of the Chilkat Preserve, explored in lectures, displays, and videos. A taxidermy-heavy diorama also shows examples of local animals. The gift shop sells natural-history items. ✉ *2nd Ave. at Haines Hwy., Box 49* ☎ *907/766–3094* 🌐 *www.baldeagles.org* 🎟 *$3* ⏲ *May–Nov., daily 8–6 and whenever cruise ships are in port.*

★ 63 **Fort William H. Seward National Historic Landmark.** Circle the sloping parade ground of Alaska's first U.S. army post, where stately clapboard homes stand against a mountain backdrop. The Haines Convention and Visitors Bureau provides a walking-tour brochure of the fort.

60 **Haines Convention and Visitors Bureau.** At this helpful tourist office you can pick up hiking- and walking-tour brochures, learn about lodging and attractions, and check out menus from local restaurants. ✉ *2nd Ave.*

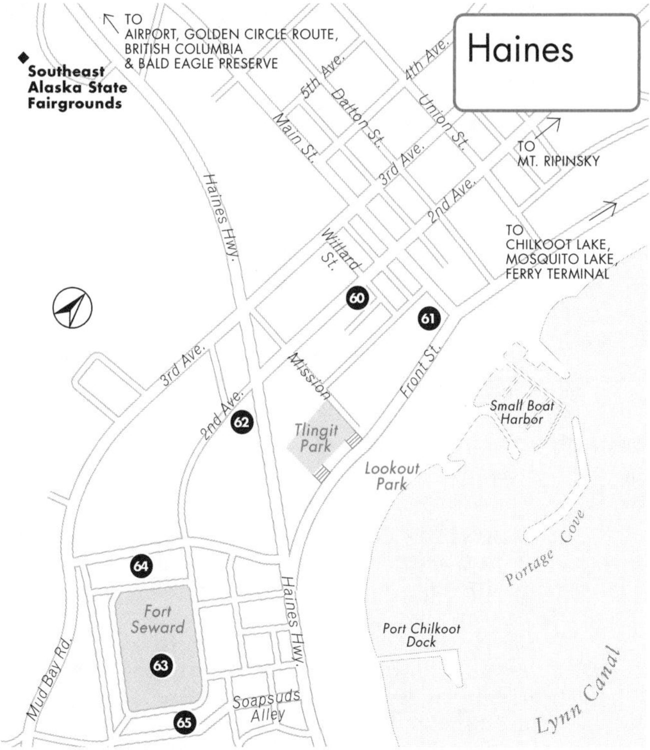

near Willard St., Box 530 ☎ 907/766–2234 or 800/458–3579 🌐 www.haines.ak.us ⏲ Mid-May–mid-Sept., weekdays 8–7, weekends 10–5; mid-Sept.–mid-May, weekdays 8–5 and when cruise ships are in port.

Haines Highway. This breathtaking highway, which starts at Mile 0 in Haines and continues 152 mi to Haines Junction, ranks among the continent's most beautiful roadways. You don't have to drive the entire length to experience its beauty, though, as worthwhile stops are located all along the route. At about Mile 6 there's a delightful picnic spot near the Chilkat River. At Mile 9.5 the view of Cathedral Peaks, part of the Chilkat Range, is magnificent. From Mile 19 to Mile 21 you can see the Alaska Chilkat Bald Eagle Preserve. At Mile 33 is a roadside restaurant called, aptly, **Mile 33 Roadhouse,** where you can refill your gas tank and coffee mug, grab a burger, and stock up on home-baked goods. The United States–Canada border lies at Mile 42; stop at Canadian customs and be sure to set your clock ahead one hour.

Fodor'sChoice ★

In winter, the **Alaska Chilkat Bald Eagle Preserve** (☎ 907/766–2292), on Mile 19–Mile 21 of the Haines Highway, harbors the largest concentration of bald eagles in the world. Thousands come to feast on the late run of salmon in the clear, ice-free waters of the Chilkat River, heated by underground warm springs. November and December are the best months for viewing.

64 **Hotel Halsingland.** In Fort Seward wander past the huge, gallant, white-columned former commanding officers' home, now a part of the hotel on Officers' Row.

61 **Sheldon Museum and Cultural Center.** Steve Sheldon began assembling native artifacts, Russian items, and gold-rush memorabilia, such as Jack Dalton's sawed-off shotgun, in the 1880s and started an exhibit of his finds in 1925. Today, the Alaskan family's personal collection anchors an impressive array of artifacts, including an 18th-century carved ceremonial hat from the Murrelet Clan, Chilkat blankets, and a model of a Tlingit tribal house. The impressive lens came from Eldred Rock Lighthouse, just south along Lynn Canal. *11 Main St.* *907/766–2366* *www.sheldonmuseum.org* *$3* *Mid-May–mid-Sept., weekdays 10–5, weekends 2–5; Winter hours, weekdays 1–4.*

OFF THE BEATEN PATH

CHILKAT STATE PARK – This park on the Chilkat Inlet has beautiful and accessible viewing of both the Davidson and Rainbow glaciers along with public campgrounds. *907/766–2292* *www.dnr.state.ak.us/parks.*

DALTON CITY – An 1890s gold-rush town was re-created as a set for the movie *White Fang* and moved to the **Southeast Alaska State Fairgrounds** (907/766–2476), less than a mile from downtown. The movie-set buildings now house local businesses, including the **Klondike Restaurant and Saloon,** with good Tex-Mex, an old-fashioned bar, a microbrewery, and live music on Friday night. The four-day-long **Southeast Alaska State Fair,** held the last week of July, is one of several official regional blowouts, and thanks to its homespun feel, it's a real winner. In addition to the usual collection of barnyard animals, the fair has live music, rides on a vintage 1920 Herschal-Spillman carousel, local culinary arts, native dances, totemic crafts, and fine art and photography. *907/766–2476* *www.seakfair.org* *$7.*

Where to Stay & Eat

$–$$$ **Bamboo Room.** Pop culture meets greasy spoon in this unassuming coffee shop with red-vinyl booths. The menu doesn't cater to light appetites—it includes sandwiches, burgers, fried chicken, chili, and halibut fish-and-chips, but the place really is at its best for an all-American breakfast (available until 3 PM). The adjacent bar has pool, darts, a big-screen TV, and a jukebox. *2nd Ave. near Main St.* *907/766–2800* *AE, D, DC, MC, V.*

¢–$ **Mountain Market.** Meet the locals over coffee (including espresso in all its variations) and a fresh-baked pastry at this busy corner natural-foods store and deli, Haines's de facto meeting hall and hitching post. Mountain Market is also great for lunchtime sandwiches, wraps, soups, and salads. Friday is pizza day, but get there early since it's often gone by dinnertime. *3rd Ave. and Haines Hwy.* *907/766–3340* *MC, V.*

$$$$ **Weeping Trout Sports Resort.** Enjoy wilderness with style at this small resort on Chilkat Lake—reachable only by boat or plane—where you can golf on a 9-hole course, fish, relax, and refresh and *not* be bothered by telephones (though the lodge has one for emergencies). All-inclusive package trips are available starting at $270 per person for one night and two days, and you stay in clean but simple cabins; showers are in the main lodge. Day trips are available for $135, including transport from Haines, a day of golf, and a meal. The restaurant is open to the public Saturday nights with a set four-course, family-style meal ($48 with transportation from Haines). *Box 129, 99827 907/766–2827 or 877/948–7688 4 cabins Restaurant, 9-hole golf course, fishing; no a/c, no room phones, no room TVs MC, V Closed Oct.–mid-May FAP.*

¢–$ **Fort Seward Lodge.** This lodge, restaurant, and saloon has, over time, served as the fort's PX, soda fountain, bowling alley, and gymnasium. The raw-wood decor and sparse interior bring the pioneering spirit of Alaska to life. The dining room even comes with a mechanical red-velvet swing left over from wilder times. All-you-can-eat Dungeness crab dinners are $23. Save room for the "ice screaming" pie. The lodge's rooms are clean but not at all fancy; the least expensive share a bath and lack televisions; two have well-equipped kitchenettes and ocean views. *39 Mud Bay Rd. 907/766–2009 or 800/478–7772 www.ftsewardlodge.com 10 rooms, 6 with bath Restaurant, some kitchenettes, cable TV, bar, airport shuttle; no a/c, no room phones, no smoking D, MC, V.*

¢–$ **Hotel Halsingland.** Fort Seward's commanding officers once lived in the big white Victorian building that today houses this gracious hotel. On the National Register of Historic Places, the hotel has original claw-foot bathtubs and nonworking fireplaces decorated with Belgian tiles. Rooms are charming and nicely maintained, but not large. A few inexpensive ones share a hall bath. The **Commander's Room Restaurant and Lounge** is one of the finest in the area, with a menu that includes locally caught crab and salmon, Caesar salads, filet mignon, and delicious desserts. *Fort Seward, Box 1649, 99827 907/766–2000 or 800/542–6363 www.hotelhalsingland.com 58 rooms, 52 with bath Restaurant, cable TV, bar, Internet, meeting rooms, some pets allowed; no a/c AE, D, DC, MC, V.*

$ **Captain's Choice Motel.** In the summer, overflowing flower boxes surround the perimeter of this contemporary motel in downtown Haines. While the accommodations are relatively plain, the staff is kind and helpful; you can even have meals delivered to your door courtesy of the Bamboo Room. The Motel's second floor opens onto a deck with tables and chairs, and most rooms have great views. A patio down below serves as a nightly meeting place where you can enjoy libations and conversation, and a Continental breakfast is available in the morning. The honeymoon suite has a hot tub. *108 2nd Ave. N, Box 392, 99827 907/766–3111 or 800/478–2345 www.capchoice.com 36 rooms, 4 suites Microwaves, refrigerators, cable TV, Wi-Fi, car rental, laundry, some pets allowed; no a/c AE, D, DC, MC, V CP.*

Nightlife & the Arts

The Arts

The **Chilkat Dancers' Storytelling Theater** (907/766–2540) performs at the Tribal House on the fort's parade grounds during the summer. This unique theatrical production includes elaborate carved masks and impressive costumes as dancers tell ancient Tlingit legends. Performances cost $12 and are held most weekdays at 4:30 PM. Call ahead for details.

The **Hammer Museum** (✉ 108 Main St. ☎ 907/766–2374 🌐 www.hammermuseum.org) is Haines at its most peculiar; check out this one-of-a-kind shrine to hammers on Main Street. The owner started his collection decades ago and founded the Hammer Museum—the world's first—in 2001. Among his impressive collection of 1,400 hammers are a Roman battle hammer and 6-foot-long farming hammers used to secure posts into the sides of barns.

Nightlife

Locals might rule the pool tables at **Fogcutter Bar** (✉ 122 Main St. ☎ 907/766–2555), but they always appreciate a little friendly competition. Like many bars in Southeast Alaska, the Fogcutter sells drink tokens that patrons often purchase for their friends; you'll often notice folks sitting at the bar with a small stack of these tokens next to their beverage. The Fogcutter's embossed metal tokens are among the Southeast's most ornate. Purchase one for a keepsake—or for later use. **Haines Brewing Company** (✉ 108 Whitefang Way ☎ 907/766–3823) is a microbrewery in the Dalton City buildings at the fairgrounds. Commercial fisherfolk gather nightly at **Harbor Bar** (✉ Front St. at the Harbor ☎ 907/766–2444), which dates from 1907. You might catch some live music here in summer. Inside one of the oldest buildings in town (it was once a brothel), the **Pioneer Bar** (✉ 2nd Ave. near Main St. ☎ 907/766–3443) has historical photographs on the walls, a large-screen television for sports, and occasional bands.

Shopping

Galleries & Gifts

A surprising number of artists live in the Haines area, and you will find their works in several local galleries. Tresham Gregg's **Sea Wolf Gallery** (✉ Fort Seward ☎ 907/766–2540 🌐 www.tresham.com) sells wood carvings, silver jewelry prints, and T-shirts with his native-inspired designs. Haines's most charming gallery, the **Wild Iris Gallery** (✉ Portage St. ☎ 907/766–2300) displays attractive jewelry, prints, and fashion wear created by owners Madeleine and Fred Shields. It's just up from the cruise-ship dock, and its gardens are to die for.

Birch Boy Products (☎ 907/766–5660 or 877/769–5660 🌐 www.birchboy.com) produces tart and tasty birch syrup; it's sold in local gift shops.

Sports, the Outdoors & Guided Tours

Bicycling

Sockeye Cycle Company (✉ 24 Portage St., Box 829 ☎ 907/766–2869 or 877/292–4154 🌐 www.cyclealaska.com) specializes in guided mountain tours in and around the backcountry of Haines, including the breathtaking 360-mi Golden Circle route that connects Haines and Skagway via the Yukon Territory. The outfit also rents, services, and sells bikes.

Boating & Fishing

Alaska Fjordlines (☎ 907/766–3395 or 800/320–0146 🌐 www.alaskafjordlines.com) operates a high-speed catamaran between Skagway, Haines, and Juneau throughout the summer, stopping along the way to watch sea lions and other marine mammals. **Chilkat Cruises** (☎ 907/766–2100 or 888/766–2103 🌐 www.chilkatcruises.com) provides a passenger catamaran ferry between Skagway and Haines, with special package rates for visitors who book a ride on Skagway's White Pass Summit Train. The service is offered up to three times a day in the summer, and the trip takes 35 minutes each way. A full-service kayak outfitter in Haines, **Deishu Expeditions** (☎ 907/766–2427 or 800/552–9257 🌐 www.seakayaks.com) leads guided trips for a day or a week. It also rents kayaks for do-it-yourselfers. The jet-boat tours offered by **River Adventures** (☎ 907/766–2050 or 800/478–9827) are a great way to experience the majestic Chilkat River Valley, just to the west and north of town.

For information on numerous sportfishing charter boats in Haines, contact the **Haines Convention and Visitors Bureau** (☎ 907/766–2234 or 800/458–3579 🌐 www.haines.ak.us).

Flightseeing

Housed a few doors up the street from the visitor center, **Mountain Flying Service** (☎ 907/766–3007 or 800/954–8747 🌐 www.flyglacierbay.com) leads flightseeing trips to nearby Glacier Bay National Park. **Wings of Alaska** (☎ 907/789–0790 🌐 www.wingsofalaska.com) has scheduled service to Juneau and Skagway. In addition to regional connections, **L.A.B. Flying Service** (☎ 907/766–2222) offers a variety of flightseeing options including Glacier Bay and the Skagway trail.

Hiking

Battery Point Trail is a fairly level path that hugs the shoreline for 2 mi, providing fine views across Lynn Canal. The trail begins a mile east of town, and a campsite can be found at Kelgaya Point near the end. For other hikes, pick up a copy of "Haines Is for Hikers" at the Haines Convention and Visitors Bureau. **Alaska Mountain Guides** (☎ 907/766–3396 or 800/766–3396), a guide service and climbing school, leads a variety of hiking and mountaineering trips from Haines, ranging from a half day to two weeks.

Nature & Ski Tours

Fodor's Choice ★ **Alaska Nature Tours** (☎ 907/766–2876 🌐 www.alaskanaturetours.net) conducts bird-watching and natural-history tours through the Alaska Chilkat Bald Eagle Preserve and leads hiking treks in summer and ski tours in winter.

SKAGWAY

66–71 *14 mi northeast of Haines.*

Located at the northern terminus of the Inside Passage, Skagway is only a one-hour ferry ride from Haines. By road, the distance is 359 mi, as you have to take the Haines Highway up to Haines Junction, Yukon, then take the Alaska Highway 100 mi south to Whitehorse, and then drive a final 100 mi south on the Klondike Highway to Skagway. North-country folk call this well-traveled sightseeing route the Golden Horse-shoe or Golden Circle tour, because it takes in a lot of gold-rush country in addition to spectacular lake, forest, and mountain scenery.

However you get to Skagway, you'll find the town an amazingly preserved artifact from North America's biggest, most storied gold rush. Most of the downtown district forms part of the Klondike Gold Rush National Historical Park, a unit of the national park system dedicated to commemorating and interpreting the frenzied stampede of 1897 that extended to Dawson City in Canada's Yukon.

Exploring Skagway

Skagway's compact, flat downtown makes it ideal to explore on foot. Nearly all the historic sights are within a few blocks of the cruise-ship and ferry dock, allowing visitors to meander through the town's attractions at whatever pace they choose. Whether you're disembarking from a cruise ship, a ferry, or a dusty automobile fresh from the Golden Circle, you'll quickly discover that tourism is the lifeblood of this town. Unless you're willing to hike into the backcountry on the Chilkoot Trail, you aren't likely to find a quiet Alaskan experience around Skagway.

What to See

★ 67 **Arctic Brotherhood Hall.** The Arctic Brotherhood was a fraternal organization of Alaskan and Yukon pioneers. Local members of the Brotherhood built the building's false front out of 20,000 pieces of driftwood and flotsam gathered from local beaches. The result: one of the most unique buildings in all of Alaska. The AB Hall now houses the **Skagway Convention and Visitors Bureau,** along with public restrooms. ✉ *Broadway, between 2nd and 3rd Aves., Box 1029* ☎ *907/983–2854, 888/762–1898 message only* 🌐 *www.skagway.org* ⏲ *May–Sept., daily 8–6; Oct.–Apr., weekdays 8–noon and 1–5.*

69 **Corrington's Museum of Alaskan History.** Inside a gift shop, this impressive (and free) scrimshaw museum highlights more than 40 exquisitely carved walrus tusks and other exhibits that detail Alaska's history. A bright flower garden decorates the exterior. ✉ *5th Ave. and Broadway* ☎ *907/983–2579* 🎫 *Free* ⏲ *Open when cruise ships are in port (mid-May–mid-Sept.).*

68 **Golden North Hotel.** Built during the 1898 gold rush, the Golden North Hotel was—until closing in 2002—Alaska's oldest hotel. Despite the closure, the building has been lov-

ALL THAT GLIMMERS

Old false-front stores, saloons, and brothels—built to separate gold-rush prospectors from their grubstakes going north or their gold pokes heading south—have been restored, repainted, and refurbished by the federal government and Skagway's citizens. Although the town feels a little like a Disney theme park in spots, the scene today is not appreciably different from what the prospectors saw in the days of 1898, except the street is now paved to make your exploring easier.

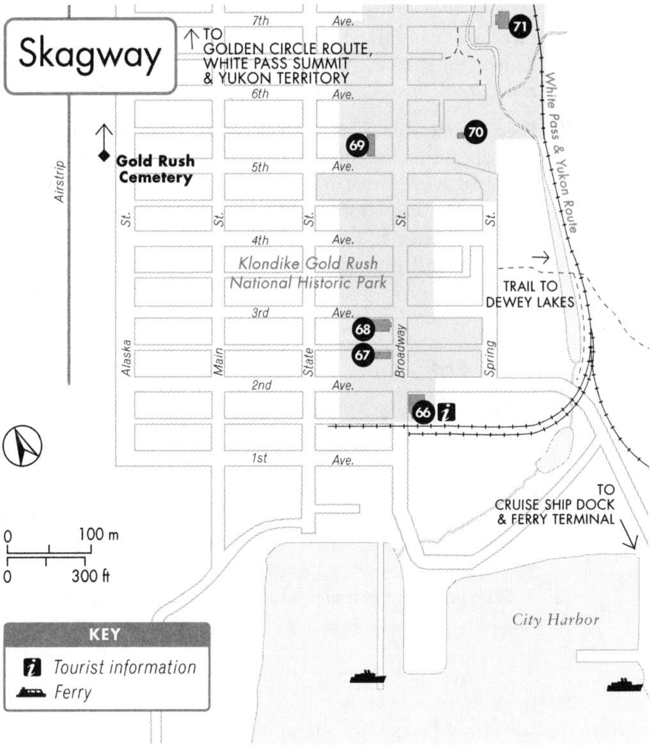

ingly maintained, and still retains its gold rush–era appearance; a golden dome tops the corner cupola. Today, the downstairs houses shops. ✉ *3rd Ave. and Broadway.*

★ 66 **Klondike Gold Rush National Historical Park.** Housed in the former White Pass & Yukon Route Depot, this wonderful museum contains exhibits, photos, and artifacts from the White Pass and Chilkoot trails. It's a must-see for anyone planning on taking a White Pass train ride, driving the nearby Klondike Highway, or hiking the Chilkoot Trail. Films, ranger talks, and walking tours are offered. Special free Robert Service poetry performances by Buckwheat Donahue—a beloved local character and head of the Chamber of Commerce—take place two evenings a week at the visitor center. ✉ *2nd Ave. at Broadway* ☎ *907/983–2921 or 907/983–9224* 🌐 *www.nps.gov/klgo* 🎫 *Free* 🕑 *May–Sept., daily 8–6; Oct.–Apr., weekdays 8–5.*

70 **Moore Cabin.** Built in 1887 by Captain William Moore and his son Ben Moore, the tiny cabin was the first structure built in Skagway. An early homesteader, Captain Moore prospered from the flood of miners, constructing a dock, warehouse, and sawmill to supply them, and selling land for other ventures. The cabin's interior walls are covered with turn-of-the-20th-century newspapers. Next door, the larger **Moore House**

(1897–98) contains interesting exhibits on the Moore family. Both structures are maintained by the Park Service, and the main house is open daily in the summer. ✉ *Off 5th Ave.* 🎟 *$2 suggested donation* ⏲ *Memorial Day–Labor Day, hrs vary.*

71 **Skagway Museum.** This nicely designed museum occupies the ground floor of the beautiful building that also houses Skagway City Hall. Inside, you'll find a 19th-century Tlingit canoe (one of the only two like it on the West Coast), historic photos, gold scales, a red-and-black sleigh, and other gold rush–era artifacts, along with a healthy collection of contemporary local art and post–gold rush history exhibits. ✉ *7th and Spring St.* ☎ *907/983–2420* 🎟 *$2* ⏲ *Mid-May–Sept., weekdays 9–5, weekends 1–4; Oct.–mid-May, hrs vary.*

Where to Stay & Eat

★ $–$$$$ ✕ **Stowaway Cafe.** Always crowded, this noisy little harborside café is just a few steps from the cruise-ship dock. Not surprisingly, seafood is the attraction—including prawns with Gorgonzola, seafood lasagna, and a hot scallop-and-bacon salad—but you also can choose tasty steaks, chicken, or smoked ribs. The café is open daily for lunch and dinner, and it serves to-go lunches from a walk-up window. ✉ *Congress Way* ☎ *907/983–3463* ✍ *Reservations essential* 💳 *AE, MC, V* ⏲ *Closed Oct.–Apr.*

$$ ✕ **Skagway Fish Company.** This small, seasonal eatery serves fresh seafood including salmon, oysters, clams, halibut, and prawns. Most popular are the halibut fish-and-chips, served with a side of homemade coleslaw. Tables overlooking the harbor surround the central bar. Baby back ribs, pork chops, and steaks, along with a New York–style cheesecake topped with strawberries, fill out the menu. ✉ *On waterfront* ☎ *907/983–3474* 💳 *MC, V* ⏲ *Closed Oct.–Apr.*

★ ¢–$$ ✕ **Haven Café.** One of the funkiest coffeehouses in Southeast, Haven Café is just a few blocks north of downtown. With gourmet coffee, a buzzworthy menu of focaccia sandwiches, pastries, and soups, Haven is a worthwhile stop for espresso fans in search of some true local flavor. The café's warm atmosphere—courtesy of hardwoods, big windows, comfy couches, and local art on display—has garnered a loyal following. Just take a look at the picture board in the back hallway for ample evidence. ✉ *9th Ave. and State St.* ☎ *907/983–3553* 💳 *MC, V.*

$–$$ ✕🏨 **Skagway Inn Bed & Breakfast.** Each room in this downtown Victorian inn (once a bordello) is named after a different gold-rush gal. The building, one of Skagway's oldest, was built in 1897 and has been lovingly restored. Rooms share a Victorian motif, with period antiques and cast-iron beds; some have mountain views. A big homemade breakfast is served downstairs each morning in Olivia's Restaurant, and the restaurant is open to everyone for light lunches and dinners of fresh Alaskan seafood. Outdoor seating is available next to the gardens. Chilkoot Trail hikers who spend two nights at the hotel get free transport to the trailhead, Coleman stove fuel, and storage of their gear while hiking. ✉ *655 Broadway, Box 500, 99840* ☎ *907/983–2289 or 888/752–4929* 🌐 *www.skagwayinn.com* 🛏 *10 rooms, 6 with private bath*

Continued on page 202

GOLD! GOLD! GOLD!

At the end of the 19th Century, scoundrels and starry-eyed gold seekers alike made their way from Alaska's Inside Passage to Canada's Yukon Territory, with high hopes for heavy returns.

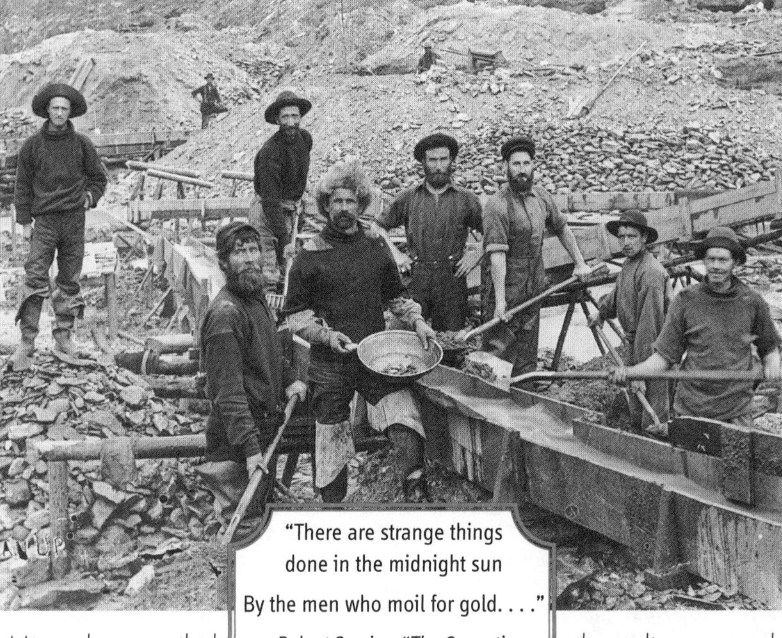

"There are strange things done in the midnight sun
By the men who moil for gold. . . ."

–Robert Service, "The Cremation of Sam McGee"

Miners have moiled for gold in the Yukon for many centuries, but the Klondike Gold Rush was a particularly strange and intense period of history. Within a decade, the towns of Skagway, Dyea, and Dawson City appeared out of nowhere, mushroomed to accommodate tens of thousands of people, and just about disappeared again. At the peak of the rush, Dawson City was the largest metropolis north of San Francisco. Although only a few people found enough gold even to pay for their trip, the rush left an indelible mark on the nation's imagination.

An 1898 photograph shows bearded miners using a gold pan and sluice as they search for riches.

A Great Stampede

Historians squabble over who first saw the glint of Yukon gold. All agree that it was a member of a family including "Skookum" Jim Mason (of the Tagish tribe), Kate and George Carmack, and Dawson Charlie, who were prospecting off the Klondike River in 1896. Over the following months, word spread and claims were quickly staked. When the first boatload of gold reached Seattle in July 1897, gold fever ignited with the *Seattle Post-Intelligencer's* headline: "GOLD! GOLD! GOLD! Sixty-Eight Rich Men On the Steamer Portland." Within six months, 100,000 people had arrived in Southeast Alaska, intent upon making their way to the untold riches.

Skagway had only a single cabin standing when the gold rush began. Three months after the first boat landed, 20,000 people swarmed its raucous hotels, saloons, gambling houses, and dance halls. By spring 1898, the town was labeled "little better than a hell on earth." When gold was discovered in Nome the next year and in Fairbanks in the early 1900s, Skagway's population dwindled to 700 souls.

(above) Rush hour on Broadway, Skagway, 1898.

A Gritty Reality

To reach the mining hub of Dawson City, prospectors had to choose between two risky routes from the Inside Passage. From Dyea, the Chilkoot Trail was steep and bitterly cold. The longer, bandit-ridden White Pass Trail from Skagway killed so many pack animals that it earned the nickname Dead Horse Trail. After the mountains, there were still over 500 mi to travel. For those who arrived, dreams were quickly washed away, as most promising claims had already been staked by the Klondike Kings. Many ended up working as labor. The disappointment was unbearable.

KLONDIKE KATE

The gold rush was profitable for clever entrepreneurs. Stragglers, outfitters, and outlaws took advantage of every opportunity to make a buck. Klondike Kate, a brothel keeper and dance-hall gal, had an elaborate song-and-dance routine that involved 200 yards of bright red chiffon.

TWO ENEMIES DIE IN A SKAGWAY SHOWDOWN

CON ARTIST "SOAPY" SMITH

Claim to Fame: Skagway's best-known gold-rush criminal, Soapy was the de facto leader of the town's loosely organized network of criminals and spies.

Cold-Hearted Snake: Euphemistically referred to as "colorful," he ruthlessly capitalized on the naïveté of prospectors.

Famous Scheme: Soapy charged homesick miners $5 to wire a message home in his counterfeit Telegraph Office (the wires ended in a tangled pile behind a shed).

Shot Through the Heart: In 1898, just days after he served as grand marshal of Skagway's 4th of July parade, Soapy barged in on a meeting set up by his rival, Frank Reid. There was a scuffle, and they shot each other.

Famous Last Words: When he saw Reid draw his gun, Soapy shouted, "My God, don't shoot!"

R.I.P.: Soapy's tombstone was continually stolen by vandals and souvenir seekers; today's grave marker is a simple wooden plank in Skagway's Gold Rush Cemetery.

GOOD GUY FRANK REID

Claim to Fame: Skagway surveyor and all-around good fellow, Frank Reid was known for defending the town against bad guys.

The Grid Man: A civil engineer, Reid helped to make Skagway's streets wide and gridlike.

Thorn in My Side: Reid set up a secret vigilante meeting to discuss one very thorny topic: Soapy Smith.

In Skagway's Honor: Reid killed Soapy during the shootout on the city docks, breaking up Soapy's gang and freeing the town from its grip.

Dyin' Tryin': Reid's heroics cost him his life—he died some days later from the injuries he sustained.

R.I.P.: The town built a substantial monument in Reid's memory in the Gold Rush Cemetery, which you can visit to this day; the inscription reads: HE GAVE HIS LIFE FOR THE HONOR OF SKAGWAY.

(above) Soapy Smith (front), so named for his first con, which involved selling "lucky soap," stands with five friends at his infamous saloon.

FOLLOWING THE GOLD TRAIL TODAY

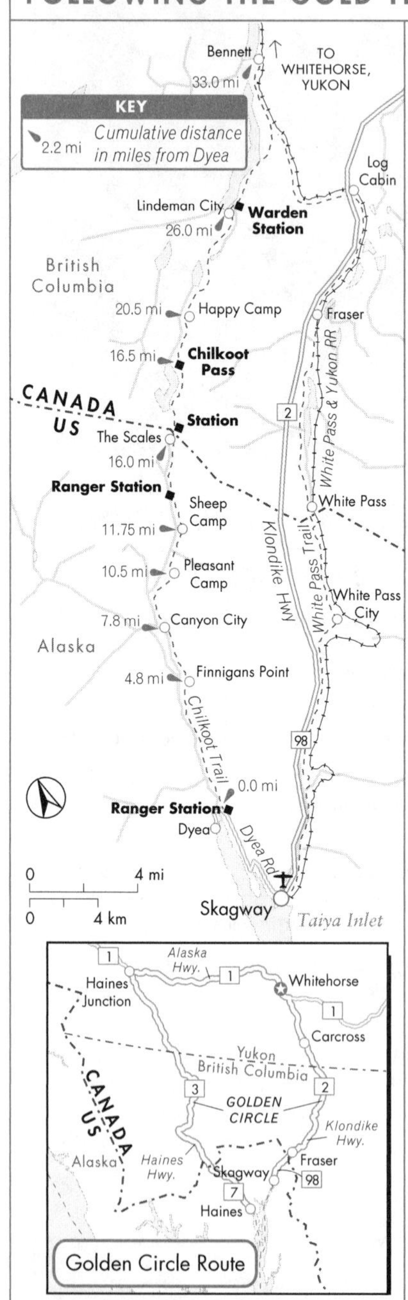

The Historic Chilkoot Trail

If you're an experienced backpacker, consider hiking the highly scenic Chilkoot Trail, the 33-mi route of the 1897–98 prospectors from Skagway into Canada. Most hikers will need four to five days. The trail is generally in good condition, with primitive campsites strategically located along the way. Expect steep slopes and wet weather, along with exhilarating vistas at the summit. Deep snow often covers the pass until late summer. The trail stretches from Dyea (just outside of Skagway) to Lake Bennett. The National Park Service maintains the American side of the pass as part of **Klondike Gold Rush National Historical Park;** the Canadian side is part of the **Chilkoot Trail National Historic Park.** A backcountry permit is required.

■ TIP→ To return to Skagway, hikers usually catch the White Pass & Yukon Route train from Lake Bennett. The fare is $80–$90 to Skagway; the train runs Saturday, Sunday, and Monday in the summer, departing at 1 PM.

For more details, including backcountry permits (C$55), contact the summer-only **Chilkoot Trail Center** ☎ 907/983–9234 ⊕ www.nps.gov/klgo. Or you can call Parks Canada ☎ 800/661–0486 ⊕ www.pc.gc.ca/chilkoot.

Golden Drives

The Golden Circle Route starts in Skagway on the Klondike Highway, then travels to Whitehorse. The route continues to Haines Junction, and then south to Haines. On the much longer Klondike Loop, you'll hop on the Klondike Highway, following the White Pass railway as it travels toward Whitehorse. The highway meets the Alaska Highway, ending at Dawson City on the banks of the Klondike River. From start to finish, it covers 435 mi. If you're taking the Klondike Highway north from Skagway,

(top left) Trekking the Chilkoot Trail (right) White Pass & Yukon Route (bottom left) A bridge on Chilkoot Trail

you must stop at Canadian customs, Mile 22. If you're traveling south to Skagway, check in at U.S. Customs, Mile 6.

White Pass & Yukon Route

You can travel the gold-rush route aboard the historic White Pass & Yukon Route (WP & YR) narrow-gauge railroad. The diesel locomotives tow vintage-style viewing cars up steep inclines, hugging the walls of precipitous cliffs with views of craggy peaks, forests, and plummeting waterfalls. It's open mid-May to late September only, and reservations are highly recommended.

■ **TIP→ Most of the commentary is during the first half of the trip and relates to sights out of the left side of the train, so sit on this side. A "seat exchange" at the summit allows all guests a canyonside view.**

Several options are available, including a fully narrated 3-hour round-trip excursion to White Pass summit (fare: $95). Sights along the way include Bridal Veil Falls, Inspiration Point, and Dead Horse Gulch. Through service to Whitehorse, Yukon (4 hours), is offered daily as well—in the form of a train trip to Fraser, where bus connections are possible on to Whitehorse (entire one-way fare to Whitehorse: $95). Also offered are the Chilkoot Trail hikers' service and a 4-hour roundtrip to Fraser Meadows on Sunday (fare: $125).

Call ahead or check online for details and schedules. ☎ 907/983–2217 or 800/343–7373 🌐 www.wpyr.com.

Restaurant, Internet, airport shuttle; no a/c, no room TVs, no smoking ▭ *AE, D, MC, V* ⊙ *Closed Oct.–Apr.* *BP.*

$–$$ **Mile Zero Bed & Breakfast.** In a quiet residential area a few blocks from downtown, this modern and comfortable B&B contains spacious and well-insulated guest rooms, all with private entrances, phones, and baths. Most have two queen beds and one room is entirely handicap-accessible. The owner, Tara Mallory, is a born-and-raised Alaskan who knows the Skagway area inside out. Local travel tips and hilarious anecdotes are commonplace in the communal dining and living rooms. A buffet-style breakfast is served each morning. Children are welcome, and those with laptops will appreciate the Wi-Fi throughout the B&B. ☒ *9th Ave. and Main St., 99840* ☎ *907/983–3045* ⊕ *www.mile-zero.com* *7 rooms* *Wi-Fi; no a/c, no smoking* ▭ *MC, V* *BP.*

$–$$ **The White House.** This B&B is about two blocks from downtown Skagway. Built in 1902 by Lee Guthrie, a gambler and owner of one of the town's most profitable gold-rush saloons, the white clapboard two-story house is furnished with original Skagway antiques and handmade quilts. The warm dining room and sitting room invite conversation while the light breakfasts are served, and children are welcome. ☒ *8th Ave. and Main St., Box 41, 99840* ☎ *907/983–9000* ⊕ *www.atthewhitehouse.com* *10 rooms* *Cable TV, Wi-Fi; no a/c, no smoking* ▭ *AE, D, MC, V* *CP.*

$ **Sgt. Preston's Lodge.** This lodge—which feels more like a motel—occupies the site of a former army barracks. Be aware that the Lodge has rooms of varying size—some are roomy and revamped, while others feel dated and cramped. All rooms are priced accordingly, though, and the lodge's downtown location and proximity to the cruise and ferry docks (a short walk to each) make it a good choice for budget-conscious travelers. The lodge also owns two apartment suites that are ideal for families or larger groups. ☒ *6th Ave. and State St., Box 538, 99840* ☎ *907/983-2521 or 866/983-2521* ⊕ *sgtprestons.eskagway.com* *38 rooms, 2 apartment suites* *Cable TV, Wi-Fi; no a/c* ▭ *AE, MC, V.*

Nightlife & the Arts

Bars

Imbibe with the locals at **Moe's Frontier Bar** (☒ Broadway between 4th and 5th Aves. ☎ 907/983–2238), a longtime fixture on the Skagway scene. At **Red Onion Saloon** (☒ Broadway at 2nd Ave. ☎ 907/983–2222), where upstairs was once a gold-rush brothel, you'll find a convivial crowd of Skagway locals and visitors. An impromptu jam with cruise-ship musicians gets under way almost every afternoon. Thursday night is when local musicians strut their stuff. The saloon closes up shop for winter.

Theater

★ Since 1927 locals have performed a show called ***The Days of '98 with Soapy Smith*** at Eagles Hall. You'll see cancan dancers (including Molly Fewclothes, Belle Davenport, and Squirrel Tooth Alice), learn a little local history, and watch desperado Soapy Smith being sent to his reward. If you stop in for the evening show, you can enjoy a few warm-up rounds of mock gambling with Soapy's money. Buckwheat Donahue's performances of Robert Service poetry start a half hour before each show

> **OUT & ABOUT**
>
> If you are up for a long walk, head 2 mi out of town along Alaska Street to the **Gold Rush Cemetery,** where you'll find the graves of combatants Soapy Smith and Frank Reid. The cemetery is also the trailhead for the short walk to Lower Reid Falls, an enjoyable jaunt through the valley's lush forest. (A city bus takes you most of the way to the cemetery for $2 each direction.) No tour of Skagway is complete without a train ride on the famed **White Pass & Yukon Route.** Trains depart from the corner of 2nd Street and Broadway several times a day in the summer.

3

time. ✉ *Broadway and 6th Ave.* ☎ *907/983–2545 May–mid-Sept., 808/328–9132 mid-Sept.–Apr.* 🌐 *www.alaskan.com/daysof98* 🎟 *$14* ⏲ *Mid-May–mid-Sept., daily at 10:30, 2:30, and 8.*

Shopping

Corrington's Alaskan Ivory (✉ 525 Broadway ☎ 907/983–2579) is the destination of choice for scrimshaw seekers; it has one the state's best collection of ivory art. In keeping with its theme-park atmosphere, Skagway is home to numerous gift shops. **Now & Then** (✉ 321 5th Ave. ☎ 907/983–2874) is a favorite spot among locals, and offers a wide selection of local arts and crafts. For those in search of locally produced silver jewelry and watercolor prints, the artist-owned **Skagway Artworks** (✉ 555C Broadway ☎ 907/983–3443 or 866/728–7830) can't be beat.

Sports, the Outdoors & Guided Tours

Biking

Alaska Bicycle Tours/Sockeye Cycle Company (☎ 907/766–2869 or 877/292–4154 🌐 www.cyclealaska.com), based in Haines, and, in summertime, in Skagway, specializes in guided bike tours in the area.

Boating

Alaska Fjordlines (☎ 907/766–3395 or 800/320–0146 🌐 www.alaskafjordlines.com) operates a high-speed catamaran connecting Skagway with Juneau throughout the summer, stopping along the way to watch sea lions and other marine mammals. The boat leaves at 8 AM, and gets to Juneau at 11:45 AM, where a bus transports visitors into town, returning to the boat at 4:45 PM for the ride back to Skagway, where the boat returns at 8:15 pm. **Chilkat Cruises** (☎ 907/766–2100 or 888/766–2103 🌐 www.chilkatcruises.com) provides a fast passenger catamaran ferry between Skagway and Haines, with service two to three times a day in the summer.

Local Interest By Bus

Skagway Street Car Co. (☎ 907/983–2908 🌐 www.skagwaystreetcar.com) revisits the gold-rush days in lovingly renovated, bright-yellow 1920s sightseeing buses. Costumed conductors lead these popular two-hour tours, but advance reservations are recommended for independent travelers, since most seats are sold aboard the cruise ships. Call a week ahead in peak season to reserve a space.

Outdoor Adventure

Alaska Excursions and Sled Dog Adventures (☎ 907/983–4444 ⊕ www.alaskasleddog.com) leads a 2½-hour wheeled (no snow) sled-dog tour on a dirt road that ends at historic Dyea. **Packer Expeditions** (☎ 907/983–2544 ⊕ www.packerexpeditions.com) guides day trips that include a helicopter flight from Skagway, a 5-mi hike to Laughton Glacier, and a train ride back to town. For an on-the-snow version, **Temsco Helicopters** (☎ 907/789–9501 or 877/789–9501 ⊕www.temscoair.com) will fly you to Denver Glacier for an hour of learning about mushing and riding on a dogsled.

SOUTHEAST ALASKA ESSENTIALS

Transportation

BY AIR

Alaska Airlines operates several flights daily from Seattle and other Pacific Coast and southwestern cities to Ketchikan, Wrangell, Petersburg, Sitka, Glacier Bay, and Juneau. The carrier also connects Juneau to the northern Alaskan cities of Yakutat, Cordova, Anchorage, Fairbanks, Nome, Kotzebue, and Prudhoe Bay. Several local airlines, including Wings of Alaska and L.A.B. Flying Service, can connect you from Juneau to several towns, including Haines and Skagway.

Every large community in Southeast Alaska, and many smaller ones, has air-taxi services that fly you from town to town and, if you're seeking backcountry adventures, into remote wilderness cabins. Local chambers of commerce can provide lists of bush-plane services.

Alaska Airlines ☎ 800/252-7522 ⊕ www.alaskaair.com **L.A.B. Flying Service** ☎ 907/766-2222 ⊕ www.labflying.com. **Wings of Alaska** ☎ 907/789-0790 ⊕ www.wingsofalaska.com.

BY BOAT & FERRY

From the south, the Alaska Marine Highway operates stateroom-equipped vehicle and passenger ferries from Bellingham, Washington, and from Prince Rupert, British Columbia. The Alaska Marine Highway allows you to construct an itinerary that is all your own; it's quite popular with budget-conscious, adventurous visitors. The vessels call at Ketchikan, Wrangell, Petersburg, Sitka, Juneau, Haines, and Skagway, and they connect with smaller vessels serving Bush communities; in all, 11 Southeast towns are served by state ferries. B.C. Ferries operates similar passenger and vehicle ferries from Vancouver Island, British Columbia, to Prince Rupert. From here, travelers can connect with the Alaska Marine Highway System. A separate ferry, operated by the Inter-Island Ferry Authority, runs between Ketchikan, Wrangell, Petersburg and Prince of Wales Island.

In the summer, staterooms on the ferries are always sold out before sailing time; reserve months in advance. If you are planning to take a car

on the ferry, early reservations for vehicle space are also highly recommended. This is particularly true for recreational vehicles.
Alaska Marine Highway ✉ 6858 Glacier Hwy., Juneau 99801 ☎ 907/465-3941 or 800/642-0066 📠 907/277-4829 🌐 www.ferryalaska.com. **B.C. Ferries** ✉ 1112 Fort St., Victoria, BC V8V 4V2 Canada ☎ 250/386-3431, 888/223-3779 in B.C. 🌐 www.bcferries.com. **Inter-Island Ferry Authority** 📫 Box 495, Craig 99921 ☎ 907/826-4848 or 866/308-4848 📠 907/826-2829 🌐 www.interislandferry.com.

Viking Travel ☎ 907/772-3818 or 800/327-2571 🌐 www.alaskaferry.com is a reservations service that can help you with your Alaska Marine Highway trip.

BY BUS

Alaska Direct Bus Lines has year-round service connecting Anchorage, Fairbanks, and Skagway. Though it's nearly a 29-hour ride, you can travel Greyhound Lines of Canada from Edmonton to Whitehorse (a $207 one-way fare; huge discounts for 7-day and 14-day advance purchase) and make a connection (nondaily) there with Alaska Direct buses to Skagway (a three-hour trip).
Alaska Direct Bus Lines 📫 Box 100501, Anchorage 99510 ☎ 907/277-6652, 800/770-6652, 403/668-4833 in Whitehorse, Canada. **Greyhound Lines of Canada** ☎ 604/482-8747 or 800/661-8747 🌐 www.greyhound.ca.

BY CAR

Only Skagway and Haines, in the northern Panhandle, and tiny Hyder, just across the border from Stewart, British Columbia, are accessible by conventional highway. Caution should always be exercised when driving these northern highways, as wildlife and weather are unpredictable hazards. Remember to bring your passport, too, as they greatly expedite border crossings between the United States and Canada.

To reach Skagway or Haines, take the Alaska Highway to the Canadian Yukon's Whitehorse or Haines Junction, respectively, and then drive the Klondike Highway or Haines Highway southwest to the Alaska Panhandle. You can reach Hyder on British Columbia's Cassiar Highway, which can be reached, in turn, from Highway 16 just north of Prince Rupert.

BY TRAIN

Southeast Alaska's only railroad, the White Pass & Yukon Route, operates between Skagway and Fraser, British Columbia. The tracks follow the historic path over the White Pass summit—a mountain-climbing, cliff-hanging route of 28 mi each way. Bus connections are available at Fraser to Whitehorse, Yukon. This route is far and away a tourist activity, though, and is rarely used for nonrecreational transportation.
White Pass & Yukon Route (WP & YR) ☎ 907/983-2217 or 800/343-7373 🌐 www.whitepassrailroad.com.

Contacts & Resources

BANKS

HAINES **First National Bank of Alaska** ✉ 123 Main St ☎ 907/766-6100 🌐 www.fnbalaska.com.

JUNEAU **Alaska Pacific Bank** ✉ 301 N. Franklin ☎ 907/586-1010 🌐 www.alaskapacificbank.com. **First Bank of Alaska** ✉ 1 Sealaska Plaza ☎ 907/586-8001 or 888/254-

8585 www.firstbankak.com. **First National Bank of Alaska** 238 Front St. 907/586–5400 www.fnbalaska.com. **Key Bank** 234 Seward St. 907/463–7222 www.key.com. **Wells Fargo** 123 Seward St. 907/586–3324 www.wellsfargo.com.

SMART TRAVEL TIPS

For invaluable tips about easy travel throughout Alaska, flip to the Smart Travel Tips section in the back of this book.

KETCHIKAN **Alaska Pacific Bank** 401 Mission St. 907/225-6146 www.alaskapacificbank.com. **First Bank of Alaska** 331 Dock St. 907/228–4474 www.firstbankak.com. **Wells Fargo** 306 Main St. 907/225–2184 www.wellsfargo.com.

PETERSBURG **First Bank of Alaska** 103 N Nordic Dr. 907/772-4277 or 888/539-8585 www.firstbankak.com. **Wells Fargo** 201 N Nordic Dr. 907/772–4277 or 888/539–8585 www.wellsfargo.com.

SITKA **Alaska Pacific Bank** 315 Lincoln St. 907/747-8688 www.alaskapacificbank.com. **First National Bank of Alaska** 318 Lincoln St. 907/747–7000 www.fnbalaska.com. **Wells Fargo** 300 Lincoln St. 907/747–3226 www.wellsfargo.com.

SKAGWAY **Wells Fargo** 6th and Broadway 907/983-2264 www.wellsfargo.com.

WRANGELL **First Bank of Alaska** 224 Brueger St. 907/874-3363 or 888/540-8585 www.firstbankak.com. **Wells Fargo** 115 Main St. 907/874–3341 www.wellsfargo.com.

EMERGENCIES

Emergency Services **Police, fire, ambulance** 911.

Hospitals **Bartlett Memorial Hospital** 3260 Hospital Dr., Juneau 907/586-2611 www.bartletthospital.org. **Haines Medical Clinic** Next to Convention and Visitors Bureau 907/766-6300. **Ketchikan General Hospital** 3100 Tongass Ave. 907/225-5171. **Petersburg Medical Center** 103 Fram St. 907/772-4291. **Sitka Community Hospital** 209 Moller Ave. 907/747-3241 www.sitkahospital.org. **Skagway Dahl Memorial Clinic** 310 11th Ave., between State St. and Broadway, Skagway 907/983-2255. **Wrangell General Hospital** 310 Bennett St. 907/874-7000 www.wrangellmedicalcenter.com.

JUNEAU Pharmacies **Juneau Drug Co.** 202 Front St. 907/586-1233. **Ron's Apothecary Shoppe** 9101 Mendenhall Mall Rd., about 10 mi north of downtown in Mendenhall Valley, next to Super Bear market 907/789-0458, 907/789-9522 after hours for prescription emergencies.

KETCHIKAN **Downtown Drugstore** 300 Front St. 907/225-3144. **Race Avenue Drugs** 2300 Tongass Ave., across from Plaza shopping mall 907/225-4151. After hours, call **Ketchikan General Hospital** 907/225-5171.

PETERSBURG **Rexall Drugs** 215 N. Nordic Dr. 907/772-3265. After hours, call **Petersburg Medical Center** 907/772-4291.

SITKA **Harry Race Pharmacy** 106 Lincoln St. 907/747-8006. **Sitka Community Hospital** 209 Moller Dr. 907/747-3241 after hours. **White's Pharmacy** 705 Halibut Point Rd. 907/747-8233.

WRANGELL **Stikine Drugs** ✉ 202 Front St. ☎ 907/874-3422. **Wrangell General Hospital** ✉ 310 Bennett St. ☎ 907/874-7000 after hours.

INTERNET, MAIL & SHIPPING

Internet cafés range, roughly, from free with a purchase to $6 per hour. FedEx, DHL and UPS all provide express package and document delivery services.

Internet Access **Seaport Cyber** ✉ 175 S. Franklin St., in the Senate Mall Bldg., Juneau ☎ 907/463-9875 🌐 www.seaportel.com. **Heritage Cafe** ✉ 174 S. Franklin St., Juneau ☎ 907/586-1087 🌐 www.heritagecoffee.com. **Hearthside Books** ✉ 8745 Glacier Hwy., in the Nugget Mall, Juneau ☎ 866/789-2750 🌐 http://www.hearthsidebooks.com. **Juneau Public Library** ✉ 292 Marine Way, Juneau ☎ 907/586-5249 🌐 http://www.ccl.lib.ak.us.

Mail & Shipping **U.S. Postal Service** ✉ 709 W. 9th St., Juneau ✉ 9491 Vintage Blvd. 🌐 www.usps.gov.

Overnight Services **DHL** ✉ Drop box: 8th floor lobby, State Office Building, 333 Willoughby Ave., Juneau ☎ 800/225-5345 🌐 www.dhl-usa.com/home/home.asp. **FedEx** ✉ 9203 Bonnett Way, Juneau ☎ 800/463-3339 🌐 www.fedex.com. **UPS** ✉ 1900 Renshaw Way, Juneau ☎ 800/742-5877 🌐 www.ups.com.

MEDIA

NEWSPAPER Juneau has one daily newspaper, two local television stations, and eight radio stations offering a wide range of music, news, and talk. The much-read *Juneau Empire* keeps tabs on state politics, business, sports, and local news for the greater capital region. *The Empire,* which recently celebrated its 75th anniversary, has a daily circulation of over 7,400, making it the third largest newspaper in the state.

RADIO Most of the local radio stations are owned by ABC Radio Networks, Alaska Broadcast Communications, or Alaska Juneau Communications. KJUD—channel 8 on the television dial—is the local ABC affiliate, while KTOO (channel 3) boasts a full schedule of public broadcasting.

On the AM-radio dial, KJNO 630 AM offers mostly conservative syndicated talk shows, while KINY 800 AM carries a mix of adult contemporary music and local news.

On the FM side, public radio can be found at KTOO 104.3 FM, while KTKU 105.1 FM features country, KFMG 100.7 FM and KSRJ 102.7 FM play contemporary pop and R&B, and KSUP 106.3 offers a mix of today's hard rock.

VISITOR INFORMATION

Hours of operation of the following visitor information centers are generally mid-May through August, daily 8 to 5, and additional hours when cruise ships are in port; September through mid-May, weekdays 8 to 5.

Alaska Department of Fish & Game 📫 Box 25526, Juneau 99802-5526 ☎ 907/465-4112, 907/465-4180 sportfishing seasons and regulations, 907/465-2376 license information 🌐 www.state.ak.us/adfg. **Alaska Division of Parks** ✉ 400 Willoughby Ave., Suite 400, Juneau 99801 ☎ 907/465-4563 🌐 www.alaskastateparks.org. **Haines Convention and Visitors Bureau** ✉ 2nd Ave. near Willard St. 📫 Box 530, Haines 99827

ALASKAPASS TIPS

The **AlaskaPass** allows unlimited travel on bus, ferry, and rail lines in Alaska, along with bus and ferry travel in British Columbia and the Yukon. Passes are available for 15 consecutive days of travel ($829), as well as for 8 days of travel in a 12-day period ($699) or 12 days of travel in a 21-day period ($849). There is a $75 booking fee. Most travelers book their entire itinerary in advance; if you don't have a car, there is usually room on ferries for those without prebookings. (☎ 206/463-6550 or 800/248-7598 🌐 www.alaskapass.com)

☎ 907/766-2234 or 800/458-3579 🌐 www.haines.ak.us. **Juneau Convention and Visitors Bureau** ✉ 1 Sealaska Plaza, Suite 305, Juneau ☎ 907/586-2201 or 888/581-2201 🌐 www.traveljuneau.com. **Ketchikan Visitors Bureau** ✉ 131 Front St., Ketchikan 99901 ☎ 907/225-6166 or 800/770-3300 🌐 www.visit-ketchikan.com. **Klondike Gold Rush National Historical Park** visitor center ✉ 2nd Ave. and Broadway 📫 Box 517, Skagway 99840 ☎ 907/983-2921 or 907/983-9224 🌐 www.nps.gov/klgo. **Petersburg Visitor Information Center** ✉ 1st and Fram Sts. 📫 Box 649, Petersburg 99833 ☎ 907/772-4636 🌐 www.petersburg.org. **Prince of Wales Chamber of Commerce** 📫 Box 497, Craig 99921 ☎ 907/826-3870 🌐 www.princeofwalescoc.org. **Sitka Convention and Visitors Bureau** ✉ 303 Lincoln St. 📫 Box 1226, Sitka 99835 ☎ 907/747-5940 🌐 www.sitka.org. **Skagway Convention and Visitors Bureau** 📫 Box 1029, Skagway 99840 ☎ 907/983-2854 or 888/762-1898 🌐 www.skagway.org. **Stewart-Hyder Chamber of Commerce** 📫 Box 306, Stewart, BC V0T 1W0 ☎ 250/636-9224 🌐 www.stewartbchyderak.homestead.com. **U.S. Forest Service** ✉ 648 Mission St., Ketchikan 99901 ☎ 907/225-3101 🌐 www.fs.fed.us/r10/tongass. **Wrangell Visitor Center** ✉ 107 Stikine Ave. 📫 Box 49, Wrangell 99929 ☎ 907/874-3901 or 800/367-9745 🌐 www.wrangellchamber.org.

Anchorage

4

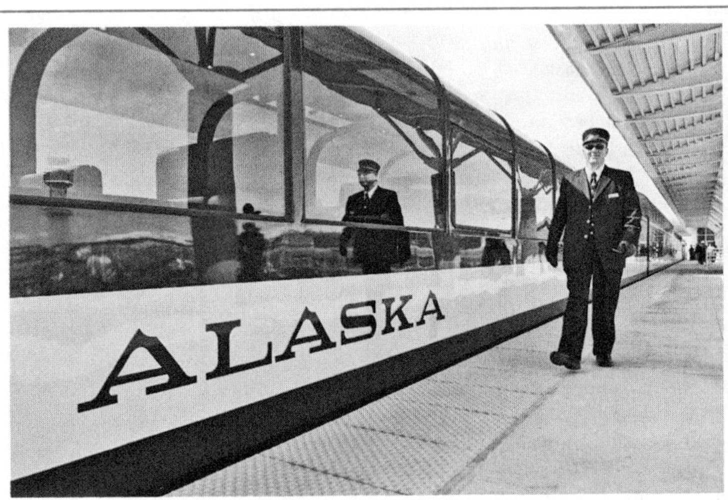

All aboard! You can hop on the Alaska Railroad and head south or north from Anchorage.

WORD OF MOUTH

"From Anchorage you can easily drive south to the Kenai Peninsula (a stunning drive), then from Seward take a day cruise and see some wildlife and glaciers."

–sluggo

"Alaska is a wonderful place for kids. It's all about scenery, mountains, animals, outdoors, hiking, walking, bird-watching, flowers, and blooming tundra."

–Wildflower

www.fodors.com/forums

WELCOME TO ANCHORAGE

TOP REASONS TO GO

★ **Hiking and biking:** Laced with paths leading to the Chugach Mountains and more than 120 mi of paved urban trails, Anchorage is a paradise for hikers and bicyclists.

★ **Winter celebrations:** In late February, locals celebrate Fur Rendezvous, Alaska's answer to Mardi Gras. Events include sled-dog races and parades—all leading up to the start of the Iditarod Trail Sled Dog Race in March.

★ **Shopping for mementos:** Shops sell everything from gold pans to mini totem poles. Native Alaskan handicrafts of all kinds are sold at downtown shops.

★ **Succulent seafood:** Dining out in Anchorage is a delight. Many restaurants offer dishes featuring local halibut, salmon, king-crab legs, scallops, and oysters.

★ **Tackling a salmon:** In Alaska's largest metropolis, anglers can cast for huge king salmon or feisty silvers while wading among reflections of skyscrapers. The spot to go to is Ship Creek.

1 Downtown. The city's cultural center, downtown has a festive atmosphere on summer afternoons, the streetlamps hung with flowers, the smell of grilled onions and hot dogs in the air along 4th Avenue. The streets are lined with art galleries and shops; the weekend markets promise good hunting for shoppers seeking souvenirs.

2 Midtown. Some 3 mi east of the airport, midtown is a newer neighborhood with an assortment of restaurants, shopping centers, and large hotels. The city's main library branch and a major movie theater complex are located a short walk from most hotels.

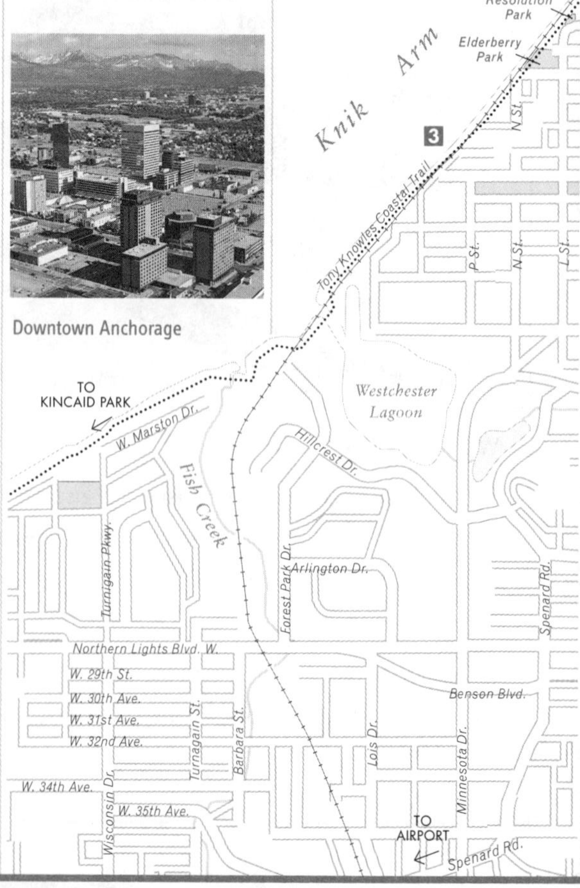

Downtown Anchorage

3 Tony Knowles Coastal Trail & Kincaid Park. An 11-mi ribbon of asphalt beginning downtown and stretching along the shoreline, the popular Tony Knowles Coastal Trail traverses tidal marshes, moose-inhabited greenbelts, and bluffs overlooking the inlet, Mt. Susitna, and the distant Alaska Range.

Anchorage Museum of History & Art

GETTING ORIENTED

Founded in 1915 as a railroad camp, Anchorage has grown into Alaska's largest city and main travel hub. It's connected to the state's road network by the Seward and Glenn highways and remains the headquarters for the Alaska Railroad, which runs from Seward to Fairbanks. It's bordered to the east by the Chugach foothills, to the west by Cook Inlet, to the south by Potter Marsh, and to the north by military bases.

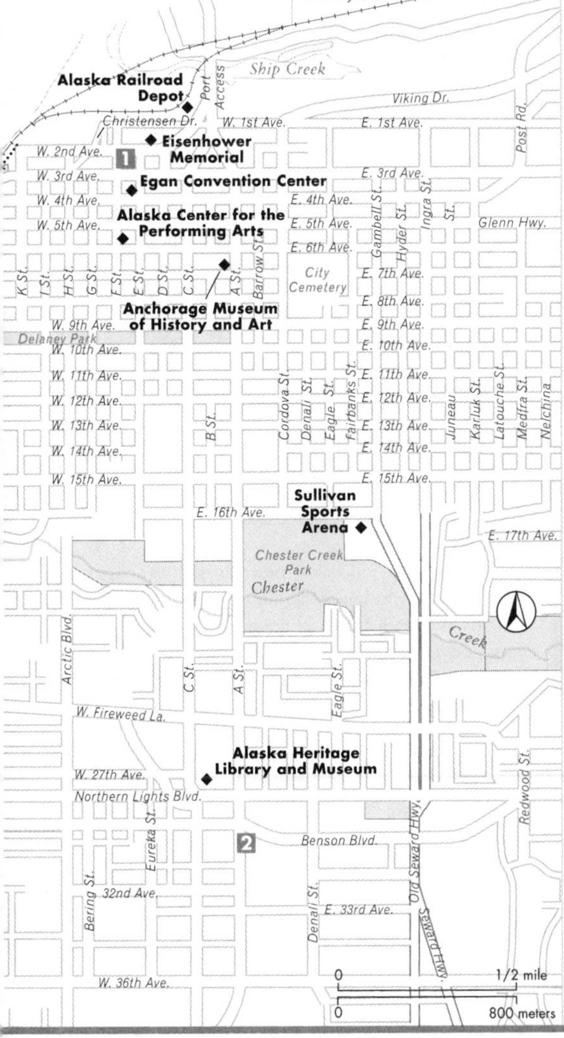

A native dancer in traditional moccasins

Alaska Railroad Depot
Ship Creek
Port Access
Viking Dr.
Christensen Dr.
W. 1st Ave.
E. 1st Ave.
Post Rd.
Eisenhower Memorial
1
W. 2nd Ave.
W. 3rd Ave.
Egan Convention Center
E. 3rd Ave.
W. 4th Ave.
E. 4th Ave.
Alaska Center for the Performing Arts
W. 5th Ave.
E. 5th Ave.
E. 6th Ave.
Glenn Hwy.
Gambell St.
Hyder St.
Ingra St.
St.
City Cemetery
E. 7th Ave.
K St.
I St.
H St.
G St.
F St.
E St.
D St.
C St.
A St.
Barrow St.
E. 8th Ave.
Anchorage Museum of History and Art
W. 9th Ave.
E. 9th Ave.
Delaney Park
W. 10th Ave.
E. 10th Ave.
W. 11th Ave.
E. 11th Ave.
W. 12th Ave.
E. 12th Ave.
W. 13th Ave.
E. 13th Ave.
W. 14th Ave.
E. 14th Ave.
W. 15th Ave.
E. 15th Ave.
B St.
Cordova St.
Denali St.
Eagle St.
Fairbanks St.
Juneau
Karluk St.
Latouche St.
Medfra St.
Nelchina
Sullivan Sports Arena
E. 16th Ave.
E. 17th Ave.
Chester Creek Park
Chester
Creek
Arctic Blvd.
C St.
A St.
Eagle St.
W. Fireweed La.
Alaska Heritage Library and Museum
W. 27th Ave.
Northern Lights Blvd.
Redwood St.
Eureka St.
2
Benson Blvd.
Old Seward Hwy.
Bering St.
32nd Ave.
Denali St.
E. 33rd Ave.
Seward Hwy.
W. 36th Ave.
0
1/2 mile
0
800 meters

ANCHORAGE PLANNER

Making the Most of Your Time

If You Have 1 Day. Above Cook Inlet and backed by the Chugach Mountains, Anchorage's distinctive setting is part of its allure. After breakfast at a downtown eatery, a walk along the Tony Knowles Coastal Trail provides views of the inlet, Mt. Susitna, and the Alaska Range. Afterward, check out some shops and galleries, historic sites, museums, and parks downtown. By car, visit the Alaska Aviation Heritage Museum and the Alaska Native Heritage Center.

If You Have 3 Days. Follow the one-day itinerary, then head down the Seward Highway for views of Potter Marsh and Turnagain Arm. Keep an eye out for Dall sheep along the cliffs and beluga whales in Turnagain Arm.

Continue farther down the highway to Alyeska Resort at Girdwood and ride the tram 2,300 feet up the mountain for lunch with a spectacular alpine view. Next, continue south to Portage Glacier and the Begich-Boggs Visitor Center for educational displays and lectures on area glaciers. Back in Anchorage on Day 3, take in a baseball game at Mulcahy Stadium or get a bird's-eye views of the city with a hike into the Chugach Mountains.

How's the Weather?

Located between the coast and several mountain ranges, Anchorage is a meteorologist's nightmare. Fickle weather patterns change less by the day than by the hour. Generally, fair-weather visitors should plan trips between the last week of May and mid-August.

Of the snow-free months, May is typically driest, August and September the wettest. July is the warmest month, with an average temperature of 58.4°F, and May the coolest at 46.6°F. But don't be fooled by statistics. Late-May temperatures can exceed 70°F, and "hot" July and August days sometimes break 80°F. Of course, rainy low-pressure systems from the Gulf of Alaska can skulk in at any time, bringing wet and cool weather.

So how to plan for such vagaries? Do as the locals do: come prepared to go with the flow. That means packing umbrellas and light rain jackets as well as tank tops and sunblock, and allowing for some flexibility with your planning.

Orientation

Anchorage is a pedestrian- and bike-friendly city. Downtown is easily explored on foot, and several businesses here rent bicycles. You'll need a car for serious shopping and stays in the city longer than a day or two, and for expeditions. National car-rental agencies work out of the airport, downtown, and along Spenard Road. Rates range from $50 to $65 per day for small sedans with unlimited mileage.

Several companies have bus tours of the Anchorage area; their brochures can be found at the Log Cabin Visitor Center downtown. For a one-hour overview, hop on a trolley with **Anchorage City Trolley Tours** (☎ 907/276–5603). **Gray Line of Alaska** (☎ 907/277–5581 or 800/312–5581 ⊕ www.graylineofalaska.com) has a city tour ($46) that lasts three hours.

Local Produce

Can you heft a 105-pound cabbage? Ever seen a 942-pound pumpkin? Produce gets big in South Central Alaska, as those two state records suggest. There are about 900 commercial vegetable farms in the state, reaping annual revenues of about $52 million. Growing seasons in South Central are short but intense, and vegetables soak up the long hours of summertime daylight to grow enormous. Still, seeing is believing, and each week between June and September, Anchorage hosts two open-air markets featuring such vegetables. Each Saturday between 9 AM and 2 PM, farmers from outlying areas set up shop in the Anchorage Daily News parking lot in East Anchorage. The Northway Mall Wednesday Market is open in East Anchorage Wednesdays between 11 AM and 5 PM. The biggest produce is saved for show in the annual Alaska State Fair in Palmer. At these markets, you'll meet Alaskan farmers with a little Valley soil under their fingernails, and stories of life on the Last Frontier under their belts.

About the Hotels & Restaurants

You can find anything from haute cuisine to burgers in Anchorage, but it's the city's ethnic diversity that lends vibrant flavor to the restaurant scene.

Girdwood, 40 mi south of downtown, has ski-resort amenities amid mountains. For a listing of hotels, contact the Anchorage Convention & Visitors Bureau. For campgrounds, contact the Alaska Public Lands Information Center. Reservations are a must for the major hotels. Smoking is not allowed in Anchorage restaurants.

What It Costs

	$$$$	$$$	$$	$	¢
Restaurants	over $25	$20–25	$15–20	$10–15	under $10
Hotels	over $250	$200–250	$150–200	$100–150	under $100

Restaurant prices are per person for a main course at dinner. Hotel prices are for two people in a standard double room in high season.

Airport Transfers

Ted Stevens Anchorage International Airport is 6 mi from downtown on International Airport Road. Taxis queue up at the lower level of the airport terminal outside the baggage-claim area; all are on a meter system, and you'll pay about $20, not including tip, for the ride downtown. Most of the larger hotels provide free airport shuttle services.

B&Bs

Anchorage B&Bs (✉ Box 242623, 99524 ☎ 907/272-5909 or 888/584-5147 🌐 www.anchorage-bnb.com) has a range of quaint to luxurious accommodations. Its Web site lists member B&Bs as well as contact information, locations, and prices.

B&Bs are spread throughout the city; whether you're looking for downtown or airport convenience or a mountainside view, a little shopping will take you to your Shangri-la.

4

Updated by Ken Marsh

BACKED BY THE CHUGACH RANGE TO THE EAST, and bordered by the tides of Cook Inlet and Turnagain Arm to the west and south, Anchorage is a vigorous, spirited, cosmopolitan city—by far Alaska's largest and most sophisticated. The relative affluence of this white-collar city—with a sprinkling of olive drab from nearby military bases—fosters fine restaurants and pricey shops, first-rate entertainment, and world-class sporting events. Flashy modern towers stab the skyline, and colorful flowers spill from hundreds of baskets on downtown lampposts. Traffic from the city's busy international airport, served by more than 15 international and domestic airlines, lends Anchorage more diversity than you might expect from a city with a population of roughly 261,000, nearly half the people in the state. You'll also discover some development you may not have come to Alaska to see—14 McDonald's, 2 Wal-Marts, a 16-plex movie theater, and dozens of espresso bars. Longtime Alaskans sometimes joke that the best thing about Anchorage is "you can see Alaska from there," but the city has not entirely lost touch with its frontier spirit. Sled-dog races are still among the most revered events held here; moose and occasionally even bears roam city bike trails, and spectacular wilderness is just a short drive away.

Incorporated in 1920, Anchorage is a young city. Nearly everything was built since the 1970s—an Anchorage home dating from the 1950s almost merits historic status. In addition to acting as the center for oil development in the state, Anchorage hustles its living as a government, banking, transportation, and communications hub. The median age of 32.4 years and an aggressive style make it—not the capital city of Juneau—the state's power center.

WELCOME!

In the last decade, Anchorage has become an increasingly important focus of travelers to Alaska. The central location, relatively mild climate, and excellent transportation system make it a natural place to begin or end a trip.

Anchorage is a melting pot. Its residents are primarily from elsewhere in America, though Alaska native peoples along with rapidly growing Asian and Hispanic populations add an important cultural dimension. The city's broad ethnic diversity is reflected in the school district where 95 languages were spoken by students in 2005.

The city got its start with the construction of the federally built Alaska Railroad, completed in 1917, and traces of its railroad heritage remain today. Once the tracks were laid, the town grew thanks to its pioneer forerunners, who actively sought growth by hook and—not infrequently—by crook. Anchorage officials used to delight in telling how they tricked a visiting member of Congress into dedicating a site for a not-yet-approved federal hospital.

Boom and bust periods followed major events: an influx of military bases during World War II; a massive buildup of Arctic missile-warning stations during the Cold War; reconstruction following the devastating Good Friday earthquake of 1964; and in the late 1960s the biggest jackpot of all—the discovery of oil at Prudhoe Bay and the construction of the trans-Alaska pipeline. Not surprisingly, Anchorage positioned itself as the perfect home for the trans-Alaska pipeline administrators and support industries, and it continues to attract a large share of the state's oil-tax dollars.

EXPLORING ANCHORAGE

Navigating downtown Anchorage's flower-lined streets is simple. The grid plan was laid out with military precision by the Army Corps of Engineers, and streets and avenues run exactly east–west and north–south, with numbers in the first direction and letters of the alphabet or Alaska place-names (Barrow, Cordova, Denali, etc.) in the other. The only aberration is the absence of a J Street—a concession, some say, to the city's early Swedish settlers, who had difficulty pronouncing the letter.

4

Outside of downtown, Anchorage is composed of widely scattered neighborhoods and large shopping malls clustered along busy thoroughfares. Fortunately, the city has a decent local bus system, and in the snow-free months a network of paved trails provides good avenues of in-city travel for bicyclists and walkers.

You'll find plenty to do year-round in Anchorage, though most visitors, particularly first-timers, might be happiest in June, July, or August, when the days are longer—up to 19 hours, 21 minutes during summer solstice—and the temperatures warmer. Locals embrace the extended daylight hours. Dog walkers, bikers, golfers, and softball players are out until it gets dark, which in late June can be nearly midnight. Spring arrives late and fall early to Anchorage. These are less desirable times to visit, because weather can be cool and rainy and some attractions might be closed, but you'll also encounter fewer travelers.

Downtown Anchorage

What to See

⑩ **Alaska Center for the Performing Arts.** The distinctive stone-and-glass building overlooks an expansive park filled with brilliant flowers all summer. Take a look inside for upcoming events, or just relax amid the blossoms on a sunny afternoon. You can watch IMAX films or slide shows about the northern lights. Hour-long tours are available. ✉ *621 W. 6th Ave., at G St., Downtown* ☎ *907/263–2900, 800/478–7328 tickets* 🌐 *www.alaskapac.org* 🎫 *Tours free* 🕑 *Daily 8–5. Tours Wed. at 1.*

★ ③ **Alaska Public Lands Information Center.** Stop here for information on all of Alaska's public lands, including national and state parks, national forests, and wildlife refuges. You can make reservations for a state ferry; watch nature videos; plan a hiking, sea-kayaking, bear-viewing, or fishing trip; find out about public-use cabins; learn about Alaska's plants and animals; or head to the theater for films highlighting different parts of the state. The bookstore sells maps and nature books. Guided walks to historic downtown sights depart daily. ✉ *605 W. 4th Ave., #105 at F St., Downtown* ☎ *907/271–2737* 🌐 *www.nps.gov/aplic* 🕑 *Memorial Day–Labor Day, daily 9–5; Labor Day–Memorial Day, weekdays 10–5.*

Downtown
Eisenhower Memorial
Saturday Market
Egan Convention Center
Central Bus Depot
Elderberry Park
W. 2nd Ave.
W. 3rd Ave.
W. 4th Ave.
W. 5th Ave.
W. 6th Ave.
W. 7th Ave.
W. 8th Ave.
L St.
K St.
I St.
H St.
G St.
F St.
E St.
D St.
C St.
B St.
A St.
0 1/8 mile
0 200 meters
0 1/2 mile
0 800 meters
KEY
Tony Knowles Coastal Trail
Rail Lines
Knik Arm
Cook Inlet
Westchester Lagoon
Delaney
P St.
N St.
L St.
W. Marston Dr.
Fish Creek
Hillcrest Dr.
Turnigain Pkwy.
Forest Park Dr.
Arlington Dr.
Spenard Rd.
TO EARTHQUAKE PARK, POINT WORONZOF
Northern Lights Blvd. W.
W. 29th St.
W. 30th Ave.
W. 31st Ave.
W. 32nd Ave.
Benson Blvd.
Turnagain St.
Barbara St.
Lois Dr.
Minnesota Dr.
W. 34th Ave.
W. 35th Ave.
McRae Dr.
Spenard Rd.
Aero Ave.
Wisconsin Dr.
W. 40th Ave.
Lois Dr.
Northwood Dr.
Lake Hood
44th Ave.
Spenard Beach
Lake Spenard
TO AIRPORT

Anchorage

Alaska Aviation Heritage Museum	**12**
Alaska Botanical Garden	**17**
Alaska Center for the Performing Arts	**10**
Alaska Heritage Library and Museum	**15**
Alaska Native Heritage Center	**16**
Alaska Public Lands Information Center	**3**
Alaska Railroad Depot	**4**
Alaska Zoo	**13**
Anchorage Museum of History and Art	**11**
Imaginarium	**9**
Log Cabin Visitor Information Center	**1**
Old City Hall	**2**
Oscar Anderson House Museum	**8**
Potter Marsh	**14**
Resolution Park	**7**
Ship Creek	**5**
Tony Knowles Coastal Trail	**6**

4 **Alaska Railroad Depot.** Totem poles and a locomotive built in 1907 are outside the station, the headquarters of the Alaska Railroad since 1915. A monument in front of the depot relates the history of the railroad, which brought an influx of people into the city during the early 1900s. During February's Fur Rendezvous festival, model-train buffs set up their displays here. ✉ *411 W. 1st Ave., Downtown* ☎ *907/265–2494* 🌐 *www.akrr.com* ⏲ *Daily, depending on train schedules.*

11 **Anchorage Museum of History and Art.** Fodor'sChoice ★ An impressive collection of historic and contemporary Alaskan art is exhibited along with dioramas and displays on Alaskan history and village life. You can join an informative 45-minute tour (given several times daily) or step into the theater to watch a film on Alaska. In July, the first-floor atrium is often the site of free daily presentations by local artists and authors. A café spills out into the atrium, serving delicious lunches from the Marx Brothers' Cafe, and the gift shop sells classy souvenirs. ✉ *121 W. 7th Ave., at C St., Downtown* ☎ *907/343–4326, 907/343–6173 recorded information* 🌐 *www.anchoragemuseum.org* 🎫 *$6.50* ⏲ *Mid-May–mid-Sept., Fri.–Wed. 9–6, Thurs. 9–9; mid-Sept.–mid-May, Wed.–Sat. 10–6, Sun. 1–5.*

9 **Imaginarium.** Children can stand inside a giant soap bubble at the bubble lab, visit a starfish in the intertidal marine exhibit, check out the creepy insects, learn about the northern lights, take a galaxy tour in the planetarium, or learn how planes fly at this experiential science museum. Other attractions include such "radical reptiles" as an iguana, an alligator, and even a 19-foot python. It's an educational fun house for children and adults alike. The upstairs gift shop features all sorts of unusual science toys. ✉ *737 W. 5th Ave., in Glacier BrewHouse Mall, Downtown* ☎ *907/276–3179* 🌐 *www.imaginarium.org* 🎫 *$5.50* ⏲ *Mon.–Sat. 10–6, Sun. noon–5.*

1 **Log Cabin Visitor Information Center.** A giant jade boulder stands outside this Bush-style log cabin, whose sod roof is festooned with huge hanging baskets of flowers. Anchorage calls itself the "Air Crossroads of the World" (it's a major stopping point for cargo jets en route to Asia), and a signpost out front marks the mileage to many international destinations. ■ **TIP→ After a stop in the visitor-center cabin, step out the back door to a more spacious visitor center stocked with brochures.** ✉ *4th Ave. and F St., Downtown* ☎ *907/274–3531* 🌐 *www.anchorage.net* ⏲ *June–Aug., daily 7:30–7; May and Sept., daily 8–6; Oct.–Apr., daily 9–4.*

2 **Old City Hall.** Offices of the Anchorage Convention and Visitors Bureau now occupy this 1936 building. A few exhibits and historic photos are right inside the lobby. Out front, take a look at the marble sculpture of William Seward, the secretary of state who engineered the purchase of Alaska from Russia. ✉ *524 W. 4th Ave., Downtown.*

8 **Oscar Anderson House Museum.** City butcher Oscar Anderson built Anchorage's first permanent frame house in 1915 at a time when most of Anchorage consisted of tents. A Swedish Christmas open house is held the first two weekends of December. Guided 45-minute tours are available whenever the museum is open. ✉ *420 M St., Downtown* ☎ *907/*

A GOOD WALK

Downtown Anchorage on a bright summer day is a feast for the senses. Baskets overflowing with petunias, marigolds, and lobelia hang from lampposts lining the streets, and the air smells of beefsteaks and salmon sizzling on restaurant grills. A pleasant two- or three-hour walk starts at 4th Avenue and F Street at the **Log Cabin Visitor Information Center** where volunteers stand by to answer questions and the walls are lined with racks of brochures. The **Old City Hall** is next door, fronted by a marble statue honoring William Seward. Many of Anchorage's original buildings, dating from 1920 when the city was incorporated, still stand along 4th Avenue. Catercorner from the Old City Hall is the **Alaska Public Lands Information Center,** where books, movies, and other information about Alaska's public lands are available.

A walk down F Street to 2nd Avenue takes you to the site of original town-site homes built by the Alaska Engineering Commission, which also built the Alaska Railroad in the early 1900s. Continue east along 2nd Avenue—toward the Chugach Mountains that form Anchorage's backdrop—to a set of stairs leading down to the **Alaska Railroad depot.** From here you will overlook **Ship Creek,** where salmon run from early June through August, attracting hundreds of anglers and curious visitors alike, all amid an unlikely setting of industrial dock facilities and adjacent skyscrapers.

Turning around and walking to the far west end of 2nd Avenue, you can step onto the **Tony Knowles Coastal Trail** which curls along between the city's edge and Cook Inlet, offering views of Mt. Susitna (locally called "Sleeping Lady" after a local Dena'ina Indian legend), Mt. McKinley, and the Alaska Range. Popular among walkers, runners, bicyclists, and inline skaters, the Coastal Trail passes by the **Oscar Anderson House Museum.** Set off the trail at the north end of Elderberry Park, the Oscar Anderson House was Anchorage's first permanent frame house, built in 1915 by city butcher Oscar Anderson. From Elderberry Park, head back up the 5th Avenue hill to the **Imaginarium,** an experiential science museum with a great gift shop.

Continue down 5th Avenue past the Egan Convention Center, whose lobby has several modern native Alaskan sculptures and a beaded curtain that evokes the northern lights. Across the street, next door to the **Alaska Center for the Performing Arts,** is a park (Town Square) packed with sculptures, fountains, and flowers in the summer. Walk on to A Street and 7th Avenue for the entrance to the **Anchorage Museum of History and Art,** which occupies the whole block between 6th and 7th avenues. The red metal sculpture out front is a favorite hide-and-seek site for children.

TIMING TIPS→ This walking tour should take two to three hours, or longer if you get caught up in shopping and museum-hopping. Volunteers from **Anchorage Historic Properties** (☎ 907/274-3600) lead historic walking tours on weekdays in the summer. These depart from Old City Hall at 524 West 4th Avenue and cost $5.

4

274–2336 $3 June–mid-Sept., Mon.–Sat. noon–5; mid-Sept.–May, by appointment.

7 **Resolution Park.** This tiny park has a cantilevered viewing platform dominated by a monument to Captain Cook (whose explorations in 1778 led to the naming of Cook Inlet and many other geographic features in Alaska). Mt. Susitna, known as the Sleeping Lady, is the prominent low mountain to the northwest. Mt. McKinley is often visible 125 mi away. *3rd Ave. at L St., Downtown.*

DID YOU KNOW?

Mt. McKinley is the nationally recognized name of the mountain, but most Alaskans call it by its original native name, Denali, which means "The High One." ***See*** **Chapter 6 for more details about this massive mountain.**

5 **Ship Creek.** The creek is dammed here, with a footbridge across the dam. You'll see a waterfall; salmon running upstream from June through August; anglers; and, above it all, the tall buildings of downtown. *Whitney Rd., Downtown.*

6 Fodor's Choice ★ **Tony Knowles Coastal Trail.** Strollers, runners, bikers, dog walkers, and in-line skaters cram this recreation trail on sunny summer evenings, particularly around Westchester Lagoon. In winter, cross-country skiers take to it by storm. The trail begins off 2nd Avenue, west of Christensen Drive, and curls along Cook Inlet for approximately 11 mi to Kincaid Park, beyond the airport. In summer, you might spot beluga whales offshore in Cook Inlet. Access points are on the waterfront at the ends of 2nd, 5th, and 9th avenues and at Westchester Lagoon.

Midtown & Beyond

What to See

12 **Alaska Aviation Heritage Museum.** The state's unique aviation history is presented here with 25 vintage aircraft—7 of which have been completely restored—a theater, an observation deck along **Lake Hood,** and a gift shop. Highlights include a historic Fairchild American Pilgrim and a Stearman C2B, the first plane to land on Mt. McKinley, back in the early 1930s. Volunteers are working to restore many of the planes and are eager to talk shop. *4721 Aircraft Dr., West Anchorage 907/248–5325 www.alaskaairmuseum.com $5 June–Sept., Wed.–Mon. 10–6; Oct.–May, Fri. and Sat. 10–4, Sun. noon–4.*

17 **Alaska Botanical Garden.** A pleasant 1-mi nature trail leads through the 110-acre garden, with some 480 varieties of plants. Other trails crisscross the grounds, which include perennial, rock, and herb gardens. An information kiosk is at the entrance. *4601 Campbell Airstrip Rd., off Tudor Rd. (park at Benny Benson School), East Anchorage 907/770–3692 www.alaskabg.org $5, $10 families Daily 9–9.*

★ 15 **Alaska Heritage Library and Museum.** Alaskan native artifacts are the main draw in the quiet, unassuming lobby of a large midtown bank. You'll also find paintings by Alaskan artists and a library of rare books. *Wells Fargo Bank, 301 W. Northern Lights Blvd., at C St., Midtown 907/265–2834 www.wellsfargohistory.com/museums Free*

Late May–early Sept., weekdays noon–5; early Sept.–late May, weekdays noon–4.

16 **Alaska Native Heritage Center.** On a 26-acre site facing the Chugach Mountains, this facility provides an introduction to Alaska's native peoples. The spacious Welcome House has interpretive displays, artifacts, photographs, demonstrations, performances, and films, along with a café and gift shop. Step outside for a stroll around the adjacent lake, where you will pass five village exhibits representing native cultural groups through traditional structures and exhibitions. **TIP→ The Heritage Center provides a free shuttle from the downtown Log Cabin Visitor Information Center several times a day in summer.** You can also hop a bus at the downtown transit center; Route 4 will take you to the Heritage Center front door. *8800 Heritage Center Dr. (Glenn Hwy. at Muldoon Rd.), East Anchorage 907/330–8000 or 800/315–6608 www.alaskanative.net $21, $9 Alaska residents Mid-May–Sept., daily 9–6; Oct.–mid-May, Sat. 10–5.*

Fodor's Choice ★

13 **Alaska Zoo.** Caribou, Dall sheep, reindeer, Siberian tigers, musk ox, seals, moose, and various Alaskan birds call this home—you'll even find the state's only elephant. The star attractions are Oreo, a brown bear, and Ahpun, a polar bear; the two were orphaned as cubs and grew up together at the zoo. During the summer, the zoo operates a shuttle from downtown ($10 round-trip). *4731 O'Malley Rd., South Anchorage, 2 mi east of New Seward Hwy. 907/346–3242 www.alaskazoo.org $9 May–Labor Day, daily 9–6; Labor Day–Apr., daily 10–4:30.*

OFF THE BEATEN PATH

EKLUTNA NATIVE VILLAGE – A small indigenous community in a tiny cluster of homes 26 mi north of Anchorage on the Glenn Highway is the oldest continually inhabited Athabascan Indian site in the area. At the village cemetery, note the hand-built Siberian-style prayer chapel, traditional Russian Orthodox crosses, and 80 colorful native spirit houses. Admission includes an informative 30-minute tour. A gift shop sells native crafts. *26339 Eklutna Village Rd. 907/688–6026 www.eklutna-nsn.gov/index.htm $10 Mid-May–mid-Sept., daily 8–6.*

14 **Potter Marsh.** Canada geese and other migratory birds, as well as the occasional moose or beaver, frequent this marsh about 10 mi south of downtown on the Seward Highway. An elevated boardwalk makes viewing easy. The **Potter Section House,**

GIRDWOOD

A ski resort, summer vacation spot, and home to an eclectic collection of locals, the town of Girdwood, 40 mi southeast of Anchorage near the head of Turnagain Arm, sits in the trees within a deep valley and is backdropped by tall mountains on three sides. The main attraction is the Mt. Alyeska Ski Resort, the largest ski area in Alaska. Besides enjoying the obvious winter attractions, you can hike up the mountain, rent a bike, or visit several restaurants (our favorite is Seven Glaciers) and gift shops open all year. Girdwood is wetter than Anchorage; it often rains (or snows) here while the sun shines 40 mi to the north. *www.girdwoodalaska.com.*

4

an old railroad service building just south of the marsh, operates as a state-park office. Out front is an old engine with a rotary snowplow that was used to clear avalanches. ✉ *Seward Hwy., South Anchorage* ☎ *907/345–5014* 🌐 *www.dnr.state.ak.us/parks* ⏲ *Weekdays 8–noon, 1–4:30.*

WHERE TO EAT

Downtown

American/Casual

$–$$$$ Fodor'sChoice ★ ✕ **Glacier BrewHouse.** The scent of hops permeates the air in the cavernous, wood-beam BrewHouse, where a dozen or so ales, stouts, lagers, and pilsners are brewed on the premises. Locals mingle with visitors in this always-busy heart-of-town restaurant where dinner selections range from thin-crust, 10-inch pizzas to seafood chowder and from whiskey barbecue pork ribs to jambalaya fettuccine. For dessert, don't miss the wood-oven roasted apple and currant bread pudding. You can watch the hardworking chefs in the open kitchen. The brewery sits behind a glass wall, and the same owners operate the equally popular Ristorante Orso, next door. ✉ *737 W. 5th Ave., Downtown* ☎ *907/274–2739* 🌐 *www.glacierbrewhouse.com* 💳 *AE, D, MC, V.*

$–$$$$ ✕ **Snow Goose Restaurant and Sleeping Lady Brewing Company.** Although you can dine indoors at this comfortable edge-of-downtown eatery, the real attraction in summer is alfresco dining on the back deck and on the rooftop. On clear days you can see Mt. McKinley on the northern horizon and the Chugach Mountains to the east. The menu emphasizes Alaskan fare (including Kachemak Bay seafood pasta), but also strays to buffalo burgers, fish-and-chips, and pork tenderloins marinated in the brewery's pale ale and Caribbean jerk seasoning. To sample the specialty beers, gather around oak tables in the upstairs bar for a brewed-on-the-premises ale, India Pale Ale, stout, barley wine, or porter. ✉ *717 W. 3rd Ave., Downtown* ☎ *907/277–7727* 🌐 *www.alaskabeers.com* 💳 *AE, D, DC, MC, V.*

$–$$ ✕ **F Street Station.** Space is at a premium in this minuscule downtown bar where the business crowd heads for a light meal. It isn't for kids, and the bar sometimes gets smoky, but the food is always delicious. The steak sandwich and cheeseburgers are good bets, but also check out the board for the day's seafood specials. A giant block of cheese occupies one corner of the bar, and the TVs are usually tuned to sports in this Cheers-type gathering place. ✉ *325 F St., Downtown* ☎ *907/272–5196* 💳 *AE, DC, MC, V.*

> **WORD OF MOUTH**
>
> "Excellent halibut sandwich–had to go back for a second one the next day."
>
> –Shawn

¢–$ ✕ **Downtown Deli.** A longtime favorite, this popular café is right across the street from the Log Cabin Visitor Information Center. Although you can choose from familiar sandwiches, like the French dip or the chicken teriyaki, this deli also has Alaskan favorites, like grilled halibut and reindeer stew. The dark, rich chicken soup comes with either noodles or homemade matzo balls, and breakfasts range from omelets and homemade granola to cheese blintzes. You can sit in one of the wooden booths for some privacy or out front at the sidewalk tables for some summertime people-watching. ☒ *525 W. 4th Ave., Downtown* ☎ *907/276–7116* ✍ *Reservations not accepted* ▭ *AE, D, DC, MC, V.*

¢ ✕ **Arctic Roadrunner.** Every year when locals vote for Anchorage's best burger joint, Arctic Roadrunner comes out on top. Forget McDonald's—these cheeseburgers are the real thing. Eat in or drive through and head to nearby Valley of the Moon Park for a sack lunch with the kids. Ultrathick milk shakes and crunchy onion rings are also on everybody's list of favorites. ☒ *2477 Arctic Blvd., Downtown* ☎ *907/279–7311* ▭ *No credit cards* ⏲ *Closed Sun.*

¢ ✕ **Sweet Basil Cafe.** Lunchtime sandwiches (hot or cold) on freshly baked sweet basil bread are a hit at this small and earthy juice bar accented by lavender walls and a big map of the planet. Fresh pastas, salads, wraps, fish tacos, smoothies, pastries, and light breakfasts fill out the menu, but the daily specials are often your best bet. ■ **TIP→ The juice bar is one of a handful in Anchorage, and the lattes may be the best downtown.** ☒ *335 E St., Downtown* ☎ *907/274–0070* ▭ *AE, D, MC, V* ⏲ *Closed weekends. No dinner.*

LOCALS WEIGH IN

"There is no comparison to any other 'local' burger joints and to even mention Arctic Roadrunner in the same sentence as McDonalds is a sin."

–Joanie Graham

"I am a local. For burgers, this place is decent, but I certainly wouldn't rate it the best burger in town. It does have a nice atmosphere if you're [visiting]."

–Sourdough

Contemporary

$$$$ ✕ **Crow's Nest Restaurant.** In the Hotel Captain Cook, American and French cuisine is the order of the day, along with the best view in Anchorage—the Chugach Mountains to the east, the Alaska Range to the north, and the sprawling city of Anchorage 20 stories below. Equally impressive are the 10,000-bottle wine cellar and hefty portions. The expert waitstaff presents a menu of seafood, along with game and other meats, served in an elegant setting with plenty of starched linen, brass, and teak. It's best known for a leisurely five-course set Chef's Tasting menu: $70 per person or $110 with wine pairings. ☒ *Hotel Captain Cook, 20th floor, 5th Ave. and K St., Downtown* ☎ *907/343–2217* ✍ *Reservations essential* ▭ *AE, D, DC, MC, V* ⏲ *Closed Sun. and Mon. in winter. No lunch.*

$$$$ Fodor'sChoice ★ ✕ **The Marx Bros. Cafe.** Inside a little frame house built in 1916, this nationally recognized 46-seat café opened in 1979 and is still going strong. Elegance is the operative term at this spot where the menu changes every week, and the wine list encompasses more than 400 international choices. For an appetizer, try the king crab–stuffed squash blossoms or fresh Kachemak Bay oysters. The outstanding made-at-your-table Caesar salad is a superb opener for the baked halibut with a macadamia crust served with coconut curry sauce and fresh mango chutney. ☒ *627*

Downtown
W. 2nd Ave.
Resolution Park
W. 3rd Ave.
Elderberry Park
W. 4th Ave.
W. 5th Ave.
W. 6th Ave.
L St.
K St.
I St.
H St.
G St.
F St.
E St.
D St.
W. 7th Ave.
W. 8th Ave.
0
1/8 mile
0
200 meters
0
1/2 mile
0
800 meters
SEE INSET
W. 9th Ave.
Delaney Park
W. 10th Ave.
W. 11th Ave.
W. 12th Ave.
W. 13th Ave.
W. 14th Ave.
W. 15th Ave.
N St.
P St.
KEY
Coastal Trail
Hotels
Rail Lines
Restaurants
Knik Arm
Cook Inlet
Westchester Lagoon
W. Marston Dr.
Hillcrest Dr.
Fish Creek
Turnigain Pkwy.
Arlington Dr.
Forest Park Dr.
Arctic Blvd.
W. Fireweed La.
Spenard Rd.
W. 27th Ave.
Northern Lights Blvd. W.
TO EARTHQUAKE PARK, POINT WORONZOF
W. 29th St.
W. 30th Ave.
W. 31st Ave.
W. 32nd Ave.
Benson Blvd.
Turnagain St.
Barbara St.
Lois Dr.
Minnesota Dr.
Bering St.
32nd Ave.
Eureka St.
W. 34th Ave.
W. 35th Ave.
W. 36th Ave.
McRae Dr.
Spenard Rd.
Aero Ave.
Wisconsin St.
W. 40th Ave.
Lois Dr.
Northwood Dr.
Tudor Rd.
Lake Hood
44th Ave.
Spenard Beach
TO AIRPORT
Lake Spenard

Where to Stay & Eat in Anchorage

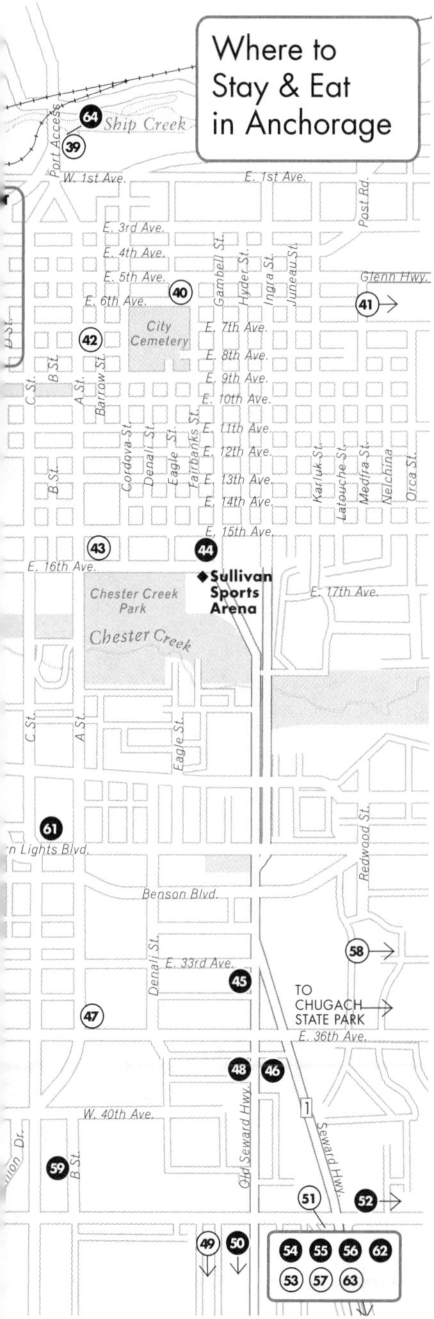

Restaurants ▼

- Arctic Roadrunner **13**
- The Bake Shop **56**
- Bombay Deluxe Restaurant **12**
- The Bridge **64**
- CampoBello Bistro **8**
- Charlie's Bakery & Dim Sum **61**
- Chiang Mai **46**
- Club Paris **37**
- Corsair Restaurant **65**
- Crow's Nest Restaurant . . **22**
- Double Musky Inn **54**
- Downtown Deli **35**
- F Street Station **31**
- Fu Du **52**
- Glacier BrewHouse **26**
- Gwennie's Old Alaskan Restaurant . . . **4**
- Jens' **9**
- Kincaid Grill **5**
- Kumagoro **34**
- The Marx Bros. Cafe **30**
- Mexico in Alaska **50**
- Middle Way Cafe & Coffee House **10**
- Moose's Tooth Pub & Pizzeria **45**
- New Sagaya's City Market **15, 48**
- Organic Oasis **11**
- Peter's Sushi Spot **59**
- Ristorante Orso **27**
- Sacks Café **28**
- Seven Glaciers **55**
- Simon & Seafort's Saloon & Grill **19**
- Snow City Cafe **21**
- Snow Goose Restaurant and Sleeping Lady Brewing Co. **29**
- Southside Bistro **62**
- Sweet Basil Cafe **36**
- Twin Dragon Mongolian Bar-B-Q **44**
- Villa Nova **60**

Hotels ▼

- Alyeska Prince Hotel **53**
- Anchorage Guesthouse **14**
- Anchorage Hilton **33**
- Anchorage Hotel **32**
- Anchorage Marriott Downtown **38**
- Anchorage Westmark Hotel **25**
- Aspen Hotel **42**
- Camai Bed & Breakfast **58**
- The Carriage House **63**
- Comfort Inn Ship Creek **39**
- Copper Whale Inn **20**
- Courtyard by Marriott **2**
- Dimond Center Hotel **49**
- 15 Chandeliers Bed & Breakfast **57**
- Hampton Inn **6**
- Hotel Captain Cook **23**
- Inlet Tower Hotel and Suites **16**
- Long House Alaskan Hotel **3**
- Mahogany Manor **43**
- Merrill Field Inn **41**
- Millennium Anchorage Hotel **1**
- Oscar Gill House **17**
- Parkwood Inn **51**
- Qupqugiaq Inn **7**
- Sheraton Anchorage **40**
- Sleeping Lady Bed & Breakfast **18**
- SpringHill Suites by Marriott **47**
- Voyager Hotel **24**

CLOSE UP

Uniquely Alaska

ALASKA HAS MORE THAN ITS SHARE of odd and unexpected attractions, including the handful of offbeat destinations described below. This is just a sampling; see elsewhere in this book for infamous bars (such as the Red Dog Saloon in Juneau and the Salty Dawg Saloon in Homer) and Alaskan thrills, including the world-famous 1,100-mile-long Iditarod Trail Sled Dog Race.

CHILKOOT CHARLIE'S, ANCHORAGE

Van Halen and Aerosmith have played concerts here, and *Playboy* named it the best bar in America in 2000: **Chilkoot Charlie's** (✉ 2435 Spenard Rd., Anchorage ☎ 907/272-1010), known as Koot's among locals, is not to be missed if you're in the mood for a uniquely Alaskan party. This rockin' and at times very crowded club in Anchorage has stages for rock, swing, DJs, and local Alaskan bands. Get a drink at one of the 11 bars, make your way past the three dance floors, and find a tree stump or an empty beer keg to sit on and enjoy the show.

HAMMERS IN HAINES

Alaska's most peculiar museum is owned by Dave Pahl, whose collection of more than 1,400 hammers is on display in the crowded little **Hammer Museum** (✉ 108 Main St., Haines ☎ 907/766-2374) in downtown Haines.

LAST TRAIN TO NOWHERE, NOME

Among Alaska's most interesting Bush settlements, Nome was founded following a major gold discovery in 1898, and is still home to summertime gold-dredging operations. During the gold rush, the Council City and Solomon River Railroad envisioned a rail system connecting Nome with the Lower 48—thousands of miles away. Construction only reached 35 mi before storms destroyed the tracks along the Bering Sea in 1907, and the project was abandoned. The company went under, but visitors still marvel at the engines and several railcars rusting away on the tundra south of Nome.

NORTH POLE, ALASKA

The world's tallest St. Nick (40 feet in all his wooden splendor) welcomes you to **Santa Claus House** (✉ 101 St. Nicholas Dr., North Pole ☎ 907/488-2200) in the town of North Pole just southeast of Fairbanks. Inside this large red-and-white store, kids can sit on Santa's lap any time of the year, while parents shop for all sorts of Christmas paraphernalia, from ornaments and musical CDs to certificates that grant you one square inch of land in the Santa Claus subdivision of North Pole. The town was started by Con Miller, who built a trading post here in the 1950s. He and his neighbors incorporated the new town as North Pole.

SURFING IN SOUTHEAST

The remote town of Yakutat lies along the Gulf of Alaska halfway between Juneau and Cordova. It isn't a major tourist destination, but it does have the state's longest beach, a 70-mi stretch that starts just outside town. It's never crowded, but local surfers and beach bums ride the swells that roll off the Gulf of Alaska throughout the year. There's even a surf shop, aptly named Icy Waves.

—Don Pitcher

W. 3rd Ave., Downtown ☎ *907/278–2133* 🌐 *www.marxcafe.com* ✍ *Reservations essential* ▭ *AE, DC, MC, V* ⏲ *Closed Sun. and Mon. No lunch.*

$$–$$$$ ✕ **The Bridge.** One of Anchorage's most distinctive restaurants, this establishment is built on a bridge spanning Ship Creek near downtown. The menu is as imaginative as the architecture, with an East-meets-West focus and vibrant choices such as citrus-marinated Alaska halibut with pan-seared lemongrass and jasmine-tea rice or Moroccan-spiced roast leg of lamb with couscous and vegetable stir-fry. ✉ *221 W. Ship Creek Dr., Downtown* ☎ *907/677–6771* 🌐 *www.thebridgesalmonbakeandgrill.com* ▭ *AE, DC, MC, V* ⏲ *Closed Sun.*

★ **$$–$$$$** ✕ **Sacks Café.** This bright and colorful restaurant serves light American cuisine such as homemade butternut squash ravioli; chicken and scallops over udon noodles; and free-range chicken stuffed with prosciutto, spinach, caramelized onion, and sharp cheddar cheese. Be sure to ask about the daily specials, particularly the fresh king salmon. Flowers adorn the tables, and singles congregate along a small bar, sampling wines from California, Australia, and France. The café is especially crowded during lunch, served from 11 to 2:30. The weekend brunch menu includes eggs Benedict, a Mexican scrambled egg dish called *migas,* and various salads and sandwiches. ✉ *328 G St., Downtown* ☎ *907/276–3546 or 907/274–4022* 🌐 *www.sackscafe.com* ✍ *Reservations essential* ▭ *AE, MC, V.*

$$–$$$$ ✕ **Simon & Seafort's Saloon & Grill.** Windows overlooking Cook Inlet vistas, along with the high ceilings and classy brass-and-wood interior have made this an Anchorage favorite since 1978. The diverse menu includes prime rib (aged 28 days), pasta, and sesame chicken salad, but the main attraction here is seafood: fish is blackened, grilled, fried, or prepared any other way you like it. Try the king crab legs or the grilled ahi tuna with ginger-and-mango salsa, and, for dessert, the Brandy Ice: vanilla ice cream whipped with brandy, Kahlúa, and crème de cacao. The bar is a great spot for microbrews and martinis; the best tables are adjacent to tall windows facing the water. ✉ *420 L St., Downtown* ☎ *907/274–3502* 🌐 *www.r-u-i.com/sim* ✍ *Reservations essential* ▭ *AE, DC, MC, V* ⏲ *No lunch weekends.*

Continental

$$$–$$$$ ✕ **Corsair Restaurant.** Founded in 1979, this fine dining establishment specializes in Continental and American cuisine with an emphasis on traditional French haute cuisine, and has earned an international reputation for its steak and seafood. More than 800 wine selections from its 10,000-bottle cellar have won the Corsair recognition from *Wine Spectator* magazine. ✉ *944 W. 5th Ave., Downtown* ☎ *907/278–4502* 🌐 *www.corsairrestaurant.com* ▭ *AE, D, DC, MC, V* ⏲ *Closed Sun.*

Eclectic

★ **¢–$** ✕ **New Sagaya's City Market.** Stop here for quick lunches and Kaladi Brothers espresso. The in-house bakery (L'Aroma) cranks out specialty breads and pastries of all types, and the international deli and grocery serves California-style pizzas, Chinese food, lasagna, rotisserie chicken, salads, and even stuffed cabbage. You can eat inside on the sheltered patio or grab an outside table on a summer afternoon. New Sagaya's has one of the best seafood counters in town and will even box and ship your fish. ✉ *900 W. 13th Ave., Downtown* ☎ *907/274–6173, 907/274–9797, or 800/764–1001* ✉ *3700 Old Seward Hwy., Midtown* ☎ *907/562–9797* 🌐 *www.newsagaya.com* ▭ *AE, D, DC, MC, V.*

¢–$ ✕ **Snow City Cafe.** At this unassuming café along "lawyer row" you'll find dependably good and reasonably priced breakfasts and lunches. Service is fast and the setting is a funky mix of mismatched chairs, Formica tables, and families and singles enjoying some of the best breakfasts in Anchorage. Breakfast is served all day, but arrive early on the weekend or be prepared to wait. Snow City's lunch menu consists of hot or cold sandwiches, fresh soups, and salads. The café closes at 4 most afternoons but stays open (with limited food service) until 11 on Wednesday night, when Irish musicians invade the space. ✉ *4th Ave. at L St., Downtown* ☎ *907/272–2489* 🌐 *www.snowcitycafe.com* ⏱ *No dinner* ▭ *AE, D, DC, MC, V.*

Italian

★ $$–$$$$ ✕ **Ristorante Orso.** One of Anchorage's culinary stars, Ristorante Orso ("bear" in Italian), evokes the earthiness of a Tuscan villa. Alaskan touches flavor rustic Mediterranean dishes that include traditional pastas, fresh seafood, wood-grilled meats, and locally famous desserts—most notably a delicious molten chocolate cake. Be sure to ask about the daily specials. If you can't get a table at dinner (reservations are advised), you can select from the same menu at the large, open bar. Upstairs you'll find a cozier, quieter space. ✉ *737 W. 5th Ave., at G St., Downtown* ☎ *907/222–3232* 🌐 *www.orsoalaska.com* ▭ *AE, D, MC, V* ⏱ *No lunch weekends.*

Japanese

$$–$$$$ ✕ **Kumagoro.** A favorite of the suit-and-tie lunch crowd, Kumagoro has traditional Japanese lunches and a take-out deli with such specialties as herring roe on kelp, and a sleek sushi bar (dinner only). The best items on the dinner menu are the sizzling salmon or beef teriyaki, both served with miso soup and a salad. With the shabu-shabu dinner ($39 for two people), you cook your own meats and vegetables in a stockpot of boiling broth. Inexpensive homemade ramen soups are also available. All entrée prices include a 10% gratuity. ✉ *533 W. 4th Ave., Downtown* ☎ *907/272–9905* ▭ *AE, D, DC, MC, V.*

Steak

$$$–$$$$ ✕ **Club Paris.** Alaska's oldest steak house has barely changed since opening in 1957, and many of the friendly staff members have been here since the 1980s. The restaurant has dark woods and an old-fashioned feel and serves tender, flavorful steaks of all kinds, including a 4-inch-thick filet mignon. If you have to wait for a table, have a martini at the bar and order the hors d'oeuvres platter ($26)—a sampler of top sirloin steak, cheese, and prawns that could be a meal for two. For dessert, try a tart key lime pie or triple-chocolate cheesecake. Dinner reservations are advised. ✉ *417 W. 5th Ave., Downtown* ☎ *907/277–6332* 🌐 *www.clubparisrestaurant.com* ▭ *AE, D, DC, MC, V* ⏱ *No lunch Sun.*

Greater Anchorage

American

¢–$$$$ ✕ **Gwennie's Old Alaskan Restaurant.** Historic Alaskan photos, stuffed animals, and memorabilia adorn this old family favorite, just south of city center toward the airport. Lunch and dinners are available—including an all-you-can-eat beef barbecue for $17—but the restaurant is best known for its old-fashioned breakfasts, available all day. Try the sourdough pancakes, reindeer sausage and eggs, or crab omelets. Start the morning the right way with Anchorage's best Bloody Mary. ✉ *4333 Spenard Rd., Midtown* ☎ *907/243–2090* ▭ *AE, D, DC, MC, V.*

WORD OF MOUTH

"Gwennie's has the best all-around meals in town. The fresh halibut steak and fried-in-beer-batter halibut & chips are fantastic!"
-Paul

¢–$ ✕ **The Bake Shop.** The atmosphere is vintage 1975 at this old-time Girdwood favorite where you order at the counter and wait for servers to bring your meal. Breakfasts are filling, with piles of sourdough pancakes, fluffy omelets, and homemade pastries. Skiers and snowboarders drop by for a fast lunch or dinner of homemade soups, sandwiches, or garden-fresh pizzas. Get a loaf of their hearty sourdough or rye bread to go. Dine out front in the summer, surrounded by hanging baskets filled with begonias, lobelias, and impatiens. ✉ *Alyeska Boardwalk, Girdwood* ☎ *907/783–2831* 🌐 *www.thebakeshop.com* ▭ *No credit cards.*

Cajun/Creole

$$–$$$$ ✕ **Double Musky Inn.** Anchorage residents say eating here is worth the one-hour drive south to Girdwood and the inevitable wait for dinner. It's very noisy, and the interior is completely covered with tacky art and Mardi Gras souvenirs of all types, but the windows frame views of huge Sitka spruce trees. The diverse menu mixes hearty Cajun-style meals with such favorites as garlic seafood pasta, rack of lamb, French pepper steak, and lobster kebabs. For dessert lovers, the biggest attraction here is the gooey, chocolate-rich Double Musky pie. The restaurant and lounge are both smoke-free. ✉ *Crow Creek Rd., Girdwood* ☎ *907/783–2822* 🌐 *www.doublemuskyinn.com* ✍ *Reservations not accepted* ▭ *D, DC, MC, V* ⏲ *Closed Mon. and Nov. No lunch.*

Chinese

¢–$ ✕ **Fu Du.** This is one of the oldest and best Chinese restaurants in Alaska. Although it's surrounded by fast-food spots and gas stations, when you step inside Fu Du, the flame-red Chinese wallpaper and lanterns, ultra-friendly staff, and Asian music take you to another continent. All the standards are available, including beef with oyster sauce, kung pao chicken, sweet-and-sour pork, and various vegetable entrées. Portions are enormous and always include soup, kimchee, rice, egg roll, and tea. Lunch specials are an even better deal, and free delivery is offered if you don't want to leave your hotel. ✉ *2600 E. Tudor Rd., Midtown* ☎ *907/561–6610* ▭ *AE, MC, V.*

¢–$ **Twin Dragon Mongolian Bar-B-Q.** If you haven't eaten Mongolian barbecue before, you're in for a treat. Choose your stir-fry ingredients and sauces, then watch as the chefs cook your meal with a flourish in the giant wok. The restaurant also has an impressive Chinese buffet with a multitude of choices; it's $8 for lunch or $12 for dinner. *612 E. 15th Ave., Midtown 907/276–7535 D, MC, V.*

¢ **Charlie's Bakery & Dim Sum.** Tucked away in a midtown strip mall, this little gem serves some of the finest authentic Chinese food in Anchorage—and at bargain prices. Atmosphere at this popular lunch spot is casual; get there early for dinner, since the doors close at 6:30 PM. But dishes like the vibrant Spicy Shrimp, loaded with vegetables, shrimp, and hot sauce, make this eatery worth a visit. *2729 C St., Midtown 907/677–7777 AE, D, MC, V Closed Sun.*

Contemporary

★ $$$$ **Seven Glaciers.** A 60-passenger aerial tram (free with dinner reservations, otherwise $16 round-trip) carries you to this refined yet relaxing mountainside Girdwood restaurant, perched at the 2,300-foot level on Mt. Alyeska. The comfortable dining room overlooks seven glaciers. Try the artfully presented smoked and grilled salmon or mesquite-grilled strip loin of buffalo. Appetizers—particularly the peppered crab cakes—are extraordinary. À la carte prices are high, but a four-course menu ($70 per person, including a matched wine) is available nightly in summer. Both tram and restaurant are wheelchair accessible. Dinner seatings are from 5:30 to 9:30 PM. *Alyeska Prince Hotel, 1000 Arlberg Rd., Girdwood 907/754–2237 www.alyeskaresort.com Reservations essential AE, D, MC, V Closed Sun.–Thurs. Nov.–May. No lunch.*

★ $$$–$$$$ **Kincaid Grill.** This out-of-the-way restaurant provides a respite after a summertime hike or wintertime ski in nearby Kincaid Park. Chef and owner Al Levinsohn worked his way up through some of Alaska's finest restaurants, and the experience shines with his diverse and creative menu. The upscale setting is lively, with old-time jazz spilling from the speakers, the buzz of conversations, and artistically presented meals. Low-backed metal stools line the wine bar, where you can sample a microbrew or vintages from around the globe. The menu changes every few weeks, but always includes filet mignon, grilled Hawaiian game fish, Alaskan salmon or halibut, and a rich seafood gumbo. *6700 Jewel Lake Rd., South Anchorage 907/243–0507 www.kincaidgrill.com Reservations essential AE, MC, V Closed Sun. and Mon. No lunch.*

★ $$–$$$$ **Jens'.** Despite its location in a midtown strip mall, Jens' is a classy and playful restaurant where the menu changes daily and everyone feels at home. Colorful paintings grace white walls, and friendly gray-haired waiters greet new arrivals. The dinner menu usually includes Alaskan salmon, halibut, and rockfish, along with such specialties as rack of lamb, tenderloin of veal, and an "almost world-famous" pepper steak. Head chef Jens Haagen Hansen's heritage reveals itself at lunch when the Danish specials appear. For a lighter evening meal, sample the appetizers in the wine bar, where Jens holds court. Reservations are highly recommended. *701 W. 36th Ave., at Arctic Blvd., Midtown 907/561–5367 www.jensrestaurant.com AE, D, DC, MC, V Closed Sun. and Jan. No lunch Sat., no dinner Mon.*

$$–$$$$ ✕ **Southside Bistro.** Established in 1995 in South Anchorage, this restaurant quickly became a local favorite for its Alaska seafood, veal, venison, and rack of lamb. A hardwood brick oven is used for flat breads and pizzas; cheesecakes, pastries and ice creams are decorated with hand-painted designs. The wine list includes more than 100 mostly American wines. ✉ *1320 Huffman Park Dr., South Anchorage* ☎ *907/348–0088* 🌐 *www.southsidebistro.com* 💳 *AE, D, MC, V* ⊗ *Closed Sun. and Mon.*

Indian

$–$$ ✕ **Bombay Deluxe Restaurant.** Anchorage's only Indian restaurant is a find for those searching for something more exotic. The eatery is housed in a collection of international shops at the Valhalla Center strip mall, flanked by a Korean restaurant on one side and an Asian market on the other. Indian music spills from the speakers, and the walls are decorated with Indian posters. Dinners include such spicy standards as lamb korma, chicken vindaloo, *palak paneer* (spinach and cheese), and 10 different types of Indian breads—from tandoori roti to garlic naan. The restaurant is especially popular for weekday lunch, when the big buffet ($10) provides a sampling of Indian favorites, including several vegetarian offerings. ✉ *555 W. Northern Lights Blvd., Midtown* ☎ *907/277–1200* 🌐 *www.bombaydeluxe.com* 💳 *AE, D, DC, MC, V.*

Italian

$$–$$$ ✕ **CampoBello Bistro.** Tucked into a midtown mall, CampoBello has surprisingly sophisticated Italian entrées and sinful desserts. Step inside for a romantic lunch or dinner surrounded by splashes of modern art on the walls and candles on the tables. Specialties include ample servings of seafood crepes, wild mushroom cannelloni, veal saltimbocca, homemade four-cheese ravioli, and shrimp and scallops Florentine. Service is attentive, and the wine list—particularly the Italian choices—is impressive. Dinner reservations are advised. ✉ *601 W. 36th Ave., Midtown* ☎ *907/563–2040* 💳 *DC, MC, V* ⊗ *Closed Sun. No lunch Sat.*

$–$$$ ✕ **Villa Nova.** Established in 1981, this restaurant is popular for its authentic Italian cuisine including veal, lamb, chicken, steak, and seafood entrées. Dim lighting, linen tablecloths, and fresh flowers create a romantic ambience (though dress is casual). The bar has domestic and imported liquors, wines, and beers. Make reservations for dinner. ✉ *5121 Arctic Blvd., Midtown* ☎ *907/561–1660* 💳 *AE, D, DC, MC, V* ⊗ *Closed Sun. and Mon.*

Japanese

$–$$$$ ✕ **Peter's Sushi Spot.** Anchorage's trendiest sushi restaurant serves customary Japanese fare along with a huge variety of traditional and creative "special" sushi rolls. Concoctions like the Alaska Roll with salmon, cooked shrimp, cream cheese, green onion, avocado, and asparagus, or the Kenai Roll, featuring crispy squid tempura, cream cheese, salmon, and radish sprouts in a sweet glaze are what make Peter's unique and popular. ✉ *4140 B St., Midtown* ☎ *907/276–5188* 💳 *AE, D, MC, V.*

Mexican

$$ ✕ **Mexico in Alaska.** Since 1972 the most authentic Mexican food in town, and maybe even in Alaska, has been served here. Owner Maria Elena Ball befriends everyone, particularly young children. Favorite dishes—

all are subtle and not greasy—include lime-marinated fried chicken, *chilaquiles* (tortilla casserole with mole sauce), and *entremesa de queso* (melted cheese, jalapeños, and onions with homemade tortillas). Weekday lunch buffets ($10) and Sunday dinner buffets ($12) are popular, and a vegetarian menu is available. The restaurant is several miles south of downtown, so you'll need to drive or catch the city bus. ✉ *7305 Old Seward Hwy., South Anchorage* ☎ *907/349–1528* 💳 *AE, D, MC, V* ⏲ *No lunch Sun.*

Pizza

★ $–$$$ ✕ **Moose's Tooth Pub & Pizzeria.** Always a top pick when local newspapers rate Anchorage pizzerias, Moose's Tooth is packed any night of the week. The reason is obvious at this down-home spot: creative pizzas and handcrafted beers from their own brewery. More than a dozen ales, ambers, porters, and stouts are the order of the day, and homemade root beers, cream sodas, and ginger ales are also available. You can match these brews with one of the 40 different pizzas with such varied toppings as roasted red peppers, jalapeños, cream cheese, halibut, and capers. Weekday lunches start at $5 for a slice of pizza and a salad. ✉ *3300 Old Seward Hwy., Midtown* ☎ *907/258–2537* 🌐 *www.moosestooth.net* 💳 *D, DC, MC, V.*

WORD OF MOUTH

"Who'd have thought I'd have to move to Alaska to find the BEST pizza! I am from New York, and I can honestly say that the best pizza I have ever had was at Moose's Tooth. It's a fun environment and an overall cool place to eat."

–Jennifer

Thai

★ ¢–$ ✕ **Chiang Mai.** Among the Thai restaurants scattered around Anchorage, this is one of the best, with authentic Thai cooking and quick and friendly service. You will find fare such as fresh rolls (a house specialty), pad thai (spicy cooked noodles with shrimp, chicken, and eggs), and *tom khar gai* (a flavorful soup of coconut milk, chicken, lemongrass, and ginger). Vegetarians have a number of choices, and unique Thai desserts are always on the menu board. The restaurant closes at 9 PM. ✉ *3637 Old Seward Hwy., Midtown* ☎ *907/563–8900* 💳 *AE, MC, V* ⏲ *Closed Sun.*

Vegetarian

¢–$$ ✕ **Organic Oasis.** Next to a yoga studio and just up the street from Chilkoot Charlie's, this popular café has a dark and airy interior accented by potted plants. Fresh-squeezed juices, smoothies, organic sandwiches, and tofu burgers dominate, but the menu spreads beyond to include buffalo burgers, chicken, fresh mussels, and other food for carnivores. There's live guitar music Tuesday through Saturday nights and free wireless Internet access anytime. Service can be slow at times. ✉ *2610 Spenard Rd., Midtown* ☎ *907/277–7882* 🌐 *www.alaska.net/~organicoasis* 💳 *AE, D, MC, V.*

¢ ✕ **Middle Way Cafe & Coffee House.** Vegetarian and nonvegetarian dishes are served at this cramped little lunchtime niche, including gussied-up grain-and-soy burgers, turkey cranberry sandwiches, avocado melts, vegan baked goods, and jumbo whole-grain tortillas wrapped around combinations of organic veggies, falafel, brown rice, and beans. You can get a fruit smoothie at the juice bar, choose from 35 different teas, or enjoy an espresso. Be sure to check out the daily specials. A kids' menu has smaller portions. The kitchen is closed on Sunday, but coffee, teas, juices and some baked goods such as cakes, cookies, and quiches are available. ✉ *1200 W. Northern Lights Blvd., Midtown* ☎ *907/272–6433* *Reservations not accepted* ▭ *AE, MC, V.*

WHERE TO STAY

Downtown

$$$$ **Anchorage Hilton.** Alaska's largest hotel is just a block from city center and fills with cruise-ship tourists all summer long. An inviting and ample lobby includes Alaskan touches—including a full-size mounted grizzly bear, and a gift shop with Alaskan native-made art and crafts—and is flanked by a café and a classy sports bar. The hotel's premier restaurant, **Top of the World,** occupies the 15th floor of the west tower. An outdoor deck provides the highest outdoor eating experience in town. Well-maintained rooms, decorated in a contemporary style with oak and maple furnishings, are in two towers, one of which is 22 floors. Request a corner north-facing suite on the upper levels for Mt. McKinley vistas. ✉ *500 W. 3rd Ave., Downtown, 99501* ☎ *907/272–7411 or 800/245–2527* *www.hilton.com* *572 rooms, 23 suites* *2 restaurants, cable TV with movies and video games, in-room broadband, indoor pool, health club, lounges, meeting rooms* ▭ *AE, D, DC, MC, V.*

$$$$ **Anchorage Marriott Downtown.** One of Anchorage's biggest lodgings, the brightly decorated Marriott appeals to business travelers, tourists, and corporate clients. The hotel's Cafe Promenade serves American cuisine with an Alaskan flair. All guest rooms have huge windows; views are breathtaking from the top floors. Well-designed furnishings include desks with two-line phones with voice mail. If you stay on one of the top three levels of this 20-story hotel, you have access to a concierge lounge and are served a light breakfast as well as evening hors d'oeuvres and desserts. ✉ *820 W. 7th Ave., Downtown, 99501* ☎ *907/279–8000 or 800/228–9290* *www.marriott.com* *392 rooms, 3 suites* *Restaurant, room service, some microwaves, cable TV with movies, in-room broadband, indoor pool, gym, hot tub, bar, shops, concierge, business services, meeting rooms* ▭ *AE, D, DC, MC, V.*

★ **$$$$** **Hotel Captain Cook.** This classy Anchorage hotel recalls Captain Cook's voyages to Alaska and the South Pacific, with dark teak paneling lining the interior and a nautical theme that continues into the

WORD OF MOUTH

"The Hotel Captain Cook was the best hotel in Alaska. The service was bar-none and the food was the best in Alaska. The staff was attentive, seemed to care, and was willing to help out in any situation. A bellman drove me to the airport for free in his own car when my cab didn't arrive." -Jon Goom recently remodeled guest rooms. All rooms have ceiling fans, and guests can use the full gym, business center, and other facilities, including three restaurants and a coffee bar. The hotel occupies an entire city block with three towers, the tallest of which is capped by the **Crow's Nest Restaurant.** The most luxurious accommodation is found on the 19th floor of Tower III—a sprawling, 1,600-square-foot two-bedroom suite, which costs a mere $1,500 per night. ✉ *4th Ave. and K St., Downtown, 99501* ☎ *907/276–6000 or 800/843–1950* 🌐 *www.captaincook.com* *451 rooms, 96 suites* *3 restaurants, room service, cable TV with movies and video games, pool, health club, hair salon, racquetball, shop, concierge, Internet, business services, meeting rooms; no a/c* ▭ *AE, D, DC, MC, V.*

$$$–$$$$ **Anchorage Westmark Hotel.** Each comfortable room in this 13-story hotel has a small private balcony and modern furnishings. Reserve a room or suite on the higher floors for the best mountain views. The downstairs restaurant, Solstice Bar & Grill, serves three meals a day, and several notable eateries are nearby, including Ristorante Orso and Glacier BrewHouse. (Do not confuse the Westmark Hotel with the reasonably priced but far more basic Westmark Inn.) ✉ *720 W. 5th Ave., Downtown, 99501* ☎ *907/276–7676 or 800/544–0970* 🌐 *www.westmarkhotels.com* *188 rooms, 12 suites* *Restaurant, coffee shop, room service, cable TV with movies, Internet, meeting room* ▭ *AE, D, DC, MC, V.*

$$$–$$$$ **Sheraton Anchorage.** A glass-canopy lobby with a jade-tile staircase, acres of cream-color marble, and guest rooms where you can pick up voice mail, iron a suit, and brew your own coffee make this 16-story hotel one of the city's best, despite its marginal neighborhood. Get a room high up on the north side to watch F-16s and other jets flying tight patterns over nearby Elmendorf Air Force Base. A downstairs restaurant (Ptarmigan Bar & Grill) serves three meals a day, and a 15th-floor restaurant (Josephine's) is open Sundays only, serving a brunch with a view all summer. ✉ *401 E. 6th Ave., Downtown, 99501* ☎ *907/276–8700 or 800/325–3535* 🌐 *www.sheraton.com* *375 rooms, 5 suites* *2 restaurants, room service, cable TV with movies and video games, health club, bar, Internet, meeting rooms* ▭ *AE, D, DC, MC, V.*

★ **$$$** **Anchorage Hotel.** The little Anchorage Hotel building has been around since 1916. Experienced travelers call it the only hotel in Anchorage with charm: the original sinks and tubs have been restored, and upstairs hallways are lined with old Anchorage photos. The rooms are nicely updated with dark cherrywood furnishings and stocked minibars. The small lobby, its fireplace crackling in chilly weather, has a quaint European feel, and the staff is adept at meeting your needs. Request a corner room if possible; rooms facing the street may have some traffic noise. The junior suites include comfortable sitting areas. ✉ *330 E St., Downtown, 99501* ☎ *907/272–4553 or 800/544–0988* 🌐 *www.historicanchoragehotel.com* *16 rooms, 10 junior suites* *Some kitchenettes, refrigerators, cable TV, Internet, meeting rooms; no a/c, no smoking* ▭ *AE, D, DC, MC, V* *CP.*

$$–$$$ **Comfort Inn Ship Creek.** Namesake Ship Creek gurgles past this popular family hotel, a short walk northeast of the Alaska Railroad depot. Rooms, which can be a bit noisy at times, come in a variety of configurations. A substantial Continental breakfast is served each morning, and the lobby features an enormous brown bear. The hotel stocks a limited number of fishing rods for those who want to try their luck catching salmon in Ship Creek, just a few steps away. ✉ *111 Ship Creek Ave., Downtown, 99501* ☎ *907/277–6887 or 800/424–6423* 🌐 *www.comfortinn.com* *88 rooms, 12 suites* *Some kitchens, microwaves, refrigerators, cable TV with movies and video games, pool, gym, hot tub, Internet, business services, some pets allowed (fee)* *AE, D, DC, MC, V* *CP.*

$$ **Aspen Hotel.** Part of a small Alaskan-owned chain, the Aspen opened in 2003 and is Anchorage's newest downtown hotel. Rooms are large and comfortably furnished with a single king or two queen beds, a writing table, 27-inch TV, DVD player, mini-refrigerator, and microwave. Two-room suites include a larger refrigerator, stovetop, and pull-out sofa; some also have in-room Jacuzzis. The hotel is just a block from the Anchorage Museum of History and Art and Delaney Park Strip, and has limited off-street parking plus a pool and Jacuzzi downstairs. ✉ *108 E. 8th Ave., Downtown, 99501* ☎ *907/868–1605 or 888/506-7848* 🌐 *www.aspenhotelsak.com* *75 rooms, 14 suites* *Refrigerators, cable TV with movies, in-room DVD, indoor pool, gym, hot tub, laundry service, Internet, business services, airport shuttle* *AE, D, DC, MC, V* *CP.*

$$ **Copper Whale Inn.** A view across Cook Inlet to Sleeping Lady and other mountains is a bonus at this small inn on the edge of downtown. Rooms furnished with cherrywood beds and a little backyard graced with a pleasant flower garden make it cozy. Great food is available just a few steps away at Simon & Seafort's or Snow City Cafe. Owner Tony Carter, a marine biologist, leads an excellent all-day wildlife ecotour for $75. ✉ *440 L St., Downtown, 99501* ☎ *907/258–7999* 🌐 *www.copperwhale.com* *15 rooms* *Dining room, Internet; no a/c, no room TVs, no smoking* *AE, D, DC, MC, V* *CP.*

★ **$$** **Inlet Tower Hotel and Suites.** Windows overlook either the Chugach Mountains, the Cook Inlet, or downtown Anchorage in the Inlet Tower. Built in 1952 in a residential area a few blocks south of downtown, this 14-story building was Alaska's first high-rise. A major remodeling in 2003 brought spacious rooms and suites, uniquely Alaskan wallpaper, high-end linens, large televisions, high-speed Internet lines (wireless Internet in the lobby), kitchenettes, and blackout curtains for summer mornings when the sun comes up at 3 AM. Downstairs, Mick's at the Inlet serves three meals a day, with a dinner menu that encompasses roasted duck, blackened wild salmon, elk ribs, and chicken cacciatore. ✉ *1200 L St., Downtown, 99501* ☎ *907/276–0110 or 800/544–0786* 🌐 *www.inlettower.com* *154 rooms, 26 suites* *Restaurant, some kitchens, microwaves, refrigerators, cable TV, laundry facilities, meeting room, business services, gym, Internet, airport shuttle, free parking; no a/c* *AE, D, DC, MC, V.*

$$ **SpringHill Suites by Marriott.** The city's main public library and a 16-plex movie theater are near this midtown Anchorage hotel. Spacious one-room suites have separate living and sleeping areas and either a king bed or two double beds with a pull-out sofa, plus two televisions. With no extra charge, up to five people can stay in these suites, and breakfast is included. ✉ *3401 A St., Downtown, 99503* ☎ *907/562–3247* *or 888/287–9400 ⊕ www.springhillsuites.com ⇨ 102 suites ♖ Microwaves, refrigerators, cable TV with movies, indoor pool, gym, hot tub, meeting rooms, airport shuttle ▭ AE, D, DC, MC, V ⚲ CP.*

$$ **Voyager Hotel.** Both business and leisure travelers stay here for the complete kitchens, sofa beds, coffeemakers, irons and ironing boards, quality linens, voice mail, and cable modems in the rooms. Decor, including furniture design and tapestries, is dated but rooms are very clean, tidy, and quiet. A downtown location places this modest, comfortable hotel close to a variety of fine dining establishments and shopping opportunities. ✉ *501 K St., Downtown, 99501* ☎ *907/277–9501 or 800/247–9070* ⊕ *www.voyagerhotel.com* ⇨ *40 rooms* ♖ *Kitchens, microwaves, refrigerators, cable TV, in-room data ports; no smoking* ▭ *AE, D, DC, MC, V* ⚲ *CP.*

$–$$ **Sleeping Lady Bed & Breakfast.** The Tony Knowles Coastal Trail is steps away from this attractive B&B. Unwind on the large back deck and take in the lengthy summer sunsets over Cook Inlet. Four spacious and private guest rooms are attractively furnished, with three facing the water. The largest contains high arched windows and a fireplace. Downtown restaurants and shopping are within easy walking distance. ✉ *545 M St., Downtown, 99501* ☎ *907/258–4455* ⊕ *www.anchsleepingladybnb.com* ⇨ *4 rooms* ♖ *Cable TV; no a/c, no smoking* ▭ *AE, MC, V* ⚲ *BP.*

$ **Oscar Gill House.** Gill originally built his home in the settlement of Knik (north of Anchorage) in 1913. Three years later, he floated it by boat to Anchorage, where he later served as the mayor for three terms and then Speaker of the Territorial House. The home has been transformed into a comfortable B&B in a quiet neighborhood along Delaney Park Strip, with downtown attractions a short walk away. Two rooms share a bath with a classic claw-foot tub, and the third contains a private bath and Jacuzzi tub. Little touches include down comforters, bicycles, and a delicious breakfast. ✉ *1344 W. 10th Ave., Downtown, 99501* ☎ *907/279–1344* ⊕ *www.oscargill.com* ⇨ *3 rooms* ♖ *Cable TV, Internet; no a/c, no smoking* ▭ *AE, MC, V* ⚲ *BP.*

Greater Anchorage

$$$$ Fodor'sChoice ★ **Alyeska Prince Hotel.** Lush forests surround this large and luxurious hotel at the base of Alyeska Ski Resort, in Girdwood, an hour south of Anchorage. Some rooms have views of the Chugach Mountains. Rooms are on the small side, but all have heated towel racks, ski-boot storage lockers, bathrobes, and slippers, plus phones in both the bathrooms and bedrooms. Guests relax in front of the big lobby fireplace, with tall windows facing the mountains. The large heated saltwater pool is a major attraction for families, and the hot tub is a hit after a day on the slopes. Dining choices include a family-style restaurant and a gourmet Japanese grill, Katsura Teppanyaki ($$$$). A spectacular aerial tram (free if you have dinner reservations) transports diners to the Seven Glaciers Restaurant at the 2,300-foot level on the mountain. ✉ *1000 Arlberg Rd., Box 249, Girdwood 99587* ☎ *907/754–1111 or 800/880–3880* ⊕ *www.alyeskaresort.com* ⇨ *296 rooms, 12 suites* ♖ *3 restaurants, room service, in-room safes, refrigerators, cable TV with movies, indoor pool, gym, hot tub, massage, sauna, cross-country skiing, downhill skiing, ice-*

skating, bar, shop, concierge, Internet, business services, meeting room, no-smoking rooms; no a/c ▭ *AE, D, DC, MC, V.*

$$$$ **Hampton Inn.** Midway between the airport and downtown, the Hampton has all the standard features, and a few that are better than average, such as designer furnishings, an indoor swimming pool, and a spa. All rooms have been recently renovated and have exceptionally comfortable, supportive mattresses. ✉ *4301 Credit Union Dr., Midtown, 99503* ☎ *907/550–7000 or 800/426–7866* 🌐 *www.stonebridgecompanies.com* *101 rooms* *Microwaves, refrigerators, cable TV with movies and video games, in-room data ports, indoor pool, exercise equipment, hot tub, spa, laundry service, Internet, business services, meeting room* ▭ *AE, D, DC, MC, V* *CP.*

★ **$$$$** **Millennium Anchorage Hotel.** Perched on the shore of Lake Spenard, the extensively renovated Millennium Anchorage Hotel is one of the city's best spots to watch planes come and go. The lobby resembles a hunting lodge with its stone fireplace, trophy heads, and mounted fish on every wall. The luxuriously appointed guest rooms continue the inviting Alaskan theme. Most have colorful native Alaskan–style bedding. All rooms have coffeemakers and hair dryers. The **Flying Machine Restaurant** is locally famous for its enormous Sunday brunch buffets ($29). ✉ *4800 Spenard Rd., Midtown, 99517* ☎ *907/243–2300 or 800/544–0553* 🌐 *www.millennium-hotels.com* *243 rooms, 5 suites* *Restaurant, room service, refrigerators, cable TV with movies and video games, gym, hot tub, sauna, steam room, lobby lounge, laundry service, Internet, business services, airport shuttle, some pets allowed* ▭ *AE, D, DC, MC, V.*

$$$–$$$$ **Dimond Center Hotel.** Owned by the Seldovia Native Association, this bright and modern hotel is popular with Alaskans from the Bush who appreciate nearby shopping (along with ice-skating and bowling) at Dimond Center Mall, Wal-Mart, Costco, and other big stores. The surprisingly plush facility has custom-designed furnishings and a huge lobby lighted by tall windows. Spacious high-ceilinged rooms include 36-inch TVs, relaxing soaking tubs, goose-down comforters on the queen or king beds, and Wi-Fi. Stuff yourself at the breakfast bar, which includes Belgian waffles, fresh fruit, yogurt, and pastries. Guests also receive a pass to an adjacent fitness center that includes two pools, Nautilus, steam rooms, hot tubs, and more. There's even a big freezer if you're bringing home fish from your trip. Check the Web site for frequent special rates. ✉ *700 E. Dimond Blvd., South Anchorage, 99515* ☎ *907/770–5000 or 866/770–5002* 🌐 *www.dimondcenterhotel.com* *108 rooms* *Microwaves, refrigerators, cable TV with movies, Wi-Fi, Internet, airport shuttle; no smoking* ▭ *AE, D, DC, MC, V* *CP.*

$$–$$$$ **The Carriage House.** This Girdwood bed-and-breakfast is conveniently located across from the Double Musky restaurant and close to Alyeska Resort's downhill ski slopes. Horse-drawn carriage tours are given of the spruce-studded, mountain-flanked resort area, about a 40-minute drive south of Anchorage. Rooms are accessed through a private entrance and patios; the rooms in the back have a view of Mt. Alyeska, and the purling of nearby California Creek can be heard through open windows on warm summer evenings. Passes are available to use a nearby pool and fit-

4

ness center. ✉ *Mile 0.2, Crow Creek Rd., Girdwood 99587* ☎ *907/783–9464 or 888/961–9464* 🌐 *www.thecarriagehousebandb.com* *4 rooms* *Cable TV, in-room broadband, kitchen* *AE, D, MC, V* *BP.*

$$$ **Mahogany Manor.** Escape from city life at this rambling B&B, hidden behind a tall fence along busy 15th Avenue and decorated with Alaska native art throughout. Unwind with the expansive decks, large picture windows, indoor waterfall, fireplaces, and big-screen television. An unusual 19-foot hot tub and jetted lap pool occupies a lower deck, with a solarium to hold in the heat. The spacious three-room suite is perfect for families and small groups. A hearty Continental breakfast is served anytime, and guests have access to a separate kitchen and a computer with high-speed Internet. ✉ *204 E. 15th Ave., Midtown, 99501* ☎ *907/278–1111 or 888/777–0346* 🌐 *www.mahoganymanor.com* *3 rooms, 1 suite* *Dining room, cable TV, pool, hot tub, Internet; no a/c, no smoking* *AE, D, MC, V* *CP.*

WORD OF MOUTH

"[Mahogany Manor] was warm, comfy, cozy, spotless and beautiful. Mary will make you feel like an old friend within 30 seconds . . . and you WILL be old friends by the time you leave."

–Steve Bennett

$$–$$$ **Courtyard by Marriott.** Business travelers pack this modern hotel near the airport. The restaurant serves breakfast and dinner and offers limited room service in the evening. Some rooms have a whirlpool bath and king-size bed; all have two phones, coffeemakers, and hair dryers. ✉ *4901 Spenard Rd., Midtown, 99517* ☎ *907/245–0322 or 800/314–0782* 🌐 *www.marriott.com* *148 rooms, 6 suites* *Restaurant, room service, some in-room hot tubs, cable TV with movies, pool, exercise equipment, hot tub, sauna, laundry service, meeting room, airport shuttle, no-smoking rooms* *AE, D, DC, MC, V.*

$$ **Long House Alaskan Hotel.** Just five minutes from the airport, this hotel consists of three log-covered two-story buildings. Rooms are large, modern, and comfortable, with two televisions in the suites (where no door separates the rooms). Anglers appreciate the big walk-in freezer to store their catch. ✉ *4335 Wisconsin St., Midtown, 99517* ☎ *907/243–2133 or 888/243–2133* 🌐 *www.longhousehotel.com* *54 rooms, 3 suites* *Microwaves, refrigerators, cable TV, airport shuttle; no a/c* *AE, D, DC, MC, V* *CP.*

$–$$ **15 Chandeliers Bed & Breakfast.** One of Alaska's premier B&Bs, 15 Chandeliers is a 7,000-square-foot mansion with a spacious front lawn and a big patio with floral gardens in the rear. Owners James and Audrey Schefers make guests comfortable in five theme rooms, all with private baths, antique furnishings, high ceilings and chandeliers, queen beds, phones, and televisions, plus access to the common areas. A filling breakfast is served buffet style. ✉ *14020 Sabine St., Hillside, 99511* ☎ *907/345–3032* 🌐 *www.15chandeliers.com* *5 rooms* *Cable TV; no a/c, no kids under 12, no smoking* *AE, MC, V* *BP.*

$ **Camai Bed & Breakfast.** Open since 1981, this elegant B&B is Anchorage's oldest. Two of the suites have private entries and plenty of space for families. All rooms have private baths and in-room TV and phones. Moose are frequent visitors to the yard, and the B&B is adjacent to Chester Creek Trail, a paved bike path that leads to downtown Anchorage. Breakfast is a high point, with such specials as French toast stuffed with peaches and cream or artichoke frittata. ✉ *3838 Westminster Way, East Anchorage 99508* ☎ *907/333–2219 or 800/659–8763* 🌐 *www.camaibnb.com* *3 suites* *Dining room, cable TV, in-room VCRs, Internet; no a/c, no smoking* *No credit cards* *BP.*

$ **Merrill Field Inn.** Reasonable prices and surprisingly large rooms make this well-maintained motel, 1 mi east of downtown and across from Anchorage's small-plane airfield, a favorite with families. A light breakfast is available in the lobby in the morning. ✉ *420 Sitka St., East Anchorage, 99501* ☎ *907/276–4547 or 800/898–4547* 🌐 *www.merrillfieldinn.com* *39 rooms, 1 suite* *Microwaves, refrigerators, cable TV, Internet, airport shuttle, some pets allowed (fee); no a/c* *AE, D, DC, MC, V* *CP.*

4

$ **Parkwood Inn.** Originally built as an apartment complex, this hotel provides reasonably priced family accommodations near the intersection of New Seward Highway and Tudor Road. Rooms are large and include full kitchens with dishes, a walk-in closet, and balcony. The two-bedroom suites can sleep six. ✉ *4455 Juneau St., South Anchorage, 99503* ☎ *907/563–3590 or 800/478–3590* 🌐 *www.parkwoodinn.net* *49 rooms, 2 suites* *Microwaves, refrigerators, cable TV with movies, Internet, airport shuttle, some pets allowed, no-smoking rooms; no a/c* *AE, D, DC, MC, V.*

¢ **Anchorage Guesthouse.** Popular with young outdoorsy travelers, this home hostel in a residential neighborhood near downtown has private rooms as well as dorm-style accommodations with bunks. All rooms share three bathrooms. You can rent bikes here, then head out for the Tony Knowles Coastal Trail, or store your gear in the garage before taking off for extended trips into the wilderness. The glassed-in sunroom has a computer to check your e-mail on while you sip coffee on a chilly morning. Make-it-yourself breakfasts of cereal, eggs, milk, bread, fruit, and more is included with price of room. Book well in advance for the busy summer season. ✉ *2001 Hillcrest Dr., Midtown, 99517* ☎ *907/274–0408* 🌐 *www.akhouse.com* *2 rooms, 1 dorm room, all with shared bath* *Kitchen, bicycles, library, laundry facilities, Internet; no a/c, no room phones, no room TVs, no smoking* *AE, MC, V* *CP.*

¢ **Qupqugiaq Inn.** A bland, boxy exterior disguises this cross between a motel and a hostel with an unpronounceable name. The interior architecture of "Q Inn" is distinctive, with curved walls and bright pine accents. This is a good option for budget travelers who can tolerate small quarters and the lack of in-room phones but appreciate clean and well-maintained facilities, including antique English beds. You have access to a communal kitchen and sitting room. A pleasant café is downstairs, and Europa Bakery is right across the street. ✉ *640 W. 36th Ave., Midtown, 99503* ☎ *907/563–5633* 🌐 *www.qupq.com* *26 rooms, 4 with shared bath* *Café, kitchens, Internet, meeting rooms; no a/c, no smoking* *AE, MC, V.*

NIGHTLIFE & THE ARTS

Nightlife

Anchorage does not shut down when it gets dark. Bars here—and throughout Alaska—open early (in the morning) and close as late as 3 AM on weekends. The listings in the *Anchorage Daily News* entertainment section, published on Friday, range from concerts and theater to movies and a roundup of nightspots featuring live music.

Bars & Nightclubs

Anchorage's favorite martini bar, **Bernie's Bungalow Lounge** (✉ 626 D St., Downtown ☎ 907/276–8808 🌐 www.berniesbungalowlounge.com) is a hip spot, with retro furnishings, splashy art, and a DJ most weekends. The cocktail to order here is a cosmopolitan.

Fodor'sChoice ★ **Chilkoot Charlie's** (✉ 2435 Spenard Rd., Midtown ☎ 907/272–1010 🌐 www.koots.com), a rambling timber building with sawdust floors, 11 bars (including one bar made of ice), three dance floors, loud music (rock or swing bands and DJs) nightly, and rowdy customers, is where young Alaskans go to get crazy. This legendary bar has all sorts of unusual nooks and crannies, including a room filled with Russian artifacts and serving the finest vodka drinks, plus a reconstructed version of Alaska's infamous Birdhouse Bar. "Koots" even made *Playboy*'s list as the number-one bar in America in 2000. If you haven't been to Koots, you haven't seen Anchorage nightlife at its wildest.

Lots of old-timers favor the dark bar of **Club Paris** (✉ 417 W. 5th Ave., Downtown ☎ 907/277–6332 🌐 www.clubparisrestaurant.com). Once the classiest place in downtown Anchorage, with its Paris mural and French streetlamps hanging behind the bar, it has lost the glamour but not the faithful clientele. There's mostly swing on the jukebox.

F Street Station (✉ 325 F St., Downtown ☎ 907/272–5196), a crowded little downtown bar, is a delightful spot for a perfectly prepared and reasonably priced lunch or dinner. Check the board for the day's specials, or just enjoy a beer and appetizers with the suit-and-tie crowd. A half-dozen small tables are available, or you can eat at the bar and chat with the chefs as they work.

Rumrunners (✉ 501 W. 4th Ave., Downtown ☎ 907/278–4493) is right across from Old City Hall in the center of town. A pub-grub menu brings the lunch crowd, but when evening comes the big dance floor gets packed as DJs spin the tunes. A trendy place for the dressy "in" crowd, the bar at **Simon & Seafort's Saloon & Grill** (✉ 420 L St., Downtown ☎ 907/274–3502 🌐 www.r-u-i.com/sim) has stunning views of Cook Inlet, a special single-malt Scotch menu, and a wide selection of imported beers.

Snow Goose Restaurant (✉ 717 W. 3rd Ave., Downtown ☎ 907/277–7727 🌐 www.alaskabeers.com) is a good place to unwind with a beer inside or on the airy outside deck overlooking Cook Inlet. There's excellent food, too.

GAY & LESBIAN BARS Anchorage's gay nightlife centers on a pair of bars, both of which attract a mixed crowd of straights, gays, and lesbians. **Mad Myrna's** (✉ 530 E. 5th Ave., Downtown ☎ 907/276–9762 🌐 www.alaska.net/~madmyrna) has karaoke on Wednesday, country dancing (with lessons) on Thursday, and drag shows every Friday. The **Raven** (✉ 708 E. 4th Ave., Downtown ☎ 907/276–9672) is a smoky neighborhood hangout where you'll meet regulars over a game of billiards or darts.

COFFEE INSTEAD? **Looking for one of the best cups of coffee in town? Kaladi Brothers Coffee has espresso, lattes, baked goods, and more (✉ *621 W. 6th Ave.* ☎ *907/277–1881*).**

Live Music

See the "Play" section in Friday editions of the *Anchorage Daily News* for complete listings of upcoming concerts and other musical performances, or get the same entertainment info online at 🌐 www.adn.com.

Blues Central/Chef's Inn (✉ 825 W. Northern Lights Blvd., Midtown ☎ 907/272–1341), a modest and smoky eatery, is also a blues mecca that stages bands seven nights a week. **Chilkoot Charlie's** (⇨ Bars & Nightclubs) is an exceptionally popular party place, with live music every night of the week. Fans of salsa, merengue, and other music crowd the dance floor at the downtown **Club Soraya** (✉ 333 W. 4th Ave., Downtown ☎ 907/276–0670). There are free Latin dance classes at 8 PM on Saturday, followed by live bands.

★ One of Anchorage's favorite singles bars, **Humpy's Great Alaskan Alehouse** (✉ 610 W. 6th Ave., Downtown ☎ 907/276–2337 🌐 www.humpys.com), serves up rock, blues, and folk five nights a week, including open mike on Mondays, along with dozens of microbrews (more than 40 beers are on tap) and surprisingly tasty pub grub. It's noisy, smoky, and always packed.

Latitude 61 (✉ 4848 Old Seward Hwy., Midtown ☎ 907/562–5701) has country music Wednesdays and poker tournaments Monday through Thursday; Friday and Saturday are dance nights. Downstairs, 16 an-

MUSIC ALFRESCO

On most summertime Fridays, open-air concerts are performed at noon on the stage in front of the **Old City Hall** (✉ 524 W. 4th Ave., Downtown). A range of performers play at the **Saturday Market** (✉ 3rd Ave. and E St., Downtown ☎ 907/272-5634 🌐 www.anchoragemarkets.com) every Saturday from late May to mid-September. The music includes everything from family bands (with daughter on violin and dad on guitar and vocals) to Peruvian pan-pipe musicians.

tique billiards tables attract pool sharks. Downtown's **Snow City Cafe** (✉ 4th Ave. at L St., Downtown ☎ 907/272–2489 🌐 www.snowcitycafe.com) has open mike sessions on Sunday evenings along with Irish music jam sessions on Wednesday evening.

The Arts

Anchorage often surprises visitors with its variety—and high quality—of cultural activities. In addition to top-name touring groups and performers, a sampling of local productions, including provocative theater, children's shows, improvisational troupes, Buddhist lectures, photography exhibits, poetry readings, and native Alaskan dance performances, is always going on around town. The Friday entertainment section of the *Anchorage Daily News* is packed with events and activities. Tickets for many cultural events can be purchased at any Carrs grocery store. **Carrs Tix** (☎ 907/263–2787 or 800/478–7328 🌐 www.tickets.com) has recorded information on cultural events of the week and the option to buy tickets by phone or from the Web site.

The **Alaska Center for the Performing Arts** (✉ 621 W. 6th Ave., Downtown ☎ 907/263–2787 or 907/263–2900 🌐 www.alaskapac.org) has three theaters and hosts local performing groups as well as traveling production companies that in the last few years have brought *Rent, Les Misérables,* and *Lord of the Dance* to the Anchorage stage. The lobby box office (Monday–Saturday, 10–6) sells tickets to the productions and is a good all-around source of cultural information. During the summer, you can watch IMAX movies at the Center for the Performing Arts, along with a special northern lights show.

Film

The popular **Bear Tooth Theatre Pub** (✉ 1230 W. 27th Ave., Midtown ☎ 907/276–4200 🌐 www.beartooththeatre.net) screens second-run and art films for only $3 and also serves tasty pizzas, sandwiches, burritos, salads, and beer while you watch.

Opera & Classical Music

The **Anchorage Opera** (☎ 907/279–2557 🌐 www.anchorageopera.org) produces three operas during its November through March season. The **Anchorage Symphony Orchestra** (☎ 907/274–8668 🌐 www.anchoragesymphony.org) performs classical concerts October through April. The box office of the Alaska Center for the Performing Arts sells tickets for both.

Theater

The **Alaska Center for the Performing Arts** stages major theater performances, and hosts the Anchorage Opera and the Anchorage Symphony Orchestra. **Cyrano's Off-Center Playhouse** (✉ 4th Ave. and D St., Downtown ☎ 907/274–2599 🌐 www.cyranos.org) mounts innovative productions in a cozy theater connected to a namesake café and bookstore. **Out North Contemporary Art House** (✉ 1325 Primrose St., just west of Bragaw Rd. off DeBarr Rd., East Anchorage ☎ 907/279–3800 🌐 www.outnorth.org), whose productions are thought-provoking and, at times, controversial, often earns critical acclaim from local reviewers. Student productions from the **University of Alaska Anchorage Theater** (✉ 3211 Providence Dr., East Anchorage ☎ 907/786–4849) are timely and well done. The theater is intimate, with seating on three sides.

SHOPPING

Stock up for your travels around Alaska in Anchorage, where prices are reasonable and there's no sales tax. It's a good choice for souvenirs as well; downtown gift shops sell trinkets and artwork. The Saturday and Sunday markets are packed with Alaskan-made products of all types, and you're likely to meet local artisans.

4

Malls & Department Stores

Anchorage's **5th Avenue Mall** occupies a city block at 5th Avenue and A Street and contains dozens of stores, including JCPenney, Banana Republic, and other popular chains, spread over several levels. The top level houses a food court. Just across 6th Avenue, and connected by a skywalk to the 5th Avenue Mall, is Alaska's only **Nordstrom.** The city's largest shopping mall, **Dimond Center,** is on the south end of town at Dimond Boulevard and Old Seward Highway. In addition to dozens of shops, Dimond Center has a movie theater. Nearby are several big-box discount stores, including Costco, Best Buy, and Wal-Mart.

Markets

Fodor'sChoice ★ During the summer, Anchorage's **Saturday and Sunday Markets** (☎ 907/272–5634 🌐 www.anchoragemarkets.com) are open in the parking lot at 3rd Avenue and E Street. Launched in 1992 as a Saturday-only affair, the Saturday Market has grown in popularity and now runs on Sundays as well. In 2005, more than 300 vendors offered Alaskan-made crafts, ethnic imports, and deliciously fattening food. The open-air markets run from mid-May to mid-September, Saturday and Sunday 10–6. A smaller market sells local produce and crafts July through August, on Wednesday from 11 to 5, at Northway Mall in East Anchorage.

Specialty Shops

Art

Anchorage's **First Friday** art openings have become a popular monthly event, with 15 or so galleries offering a chance to sample hors d'oeuvres while looking over the latest works by regional artists.

Alaska's oldest gallery, **Artique** (✉ 314 G St., Downtown ☎ 907/277–1663 🌐 www.artiqueltd.com), sells paintings, prints, and jewelry by prominent Alaskan artists. **Artic Rose Gallery** (✉ 420 L St., Downtown ☎ 907/279–3911) is in the same building as Simon and Seafort's restaurant. The **International Gallery of Contemporary Art** (✉ 427 D St., Downtown ☎ 907/279–1116 🌐 www.igcaalaska.org) is Anchorage's premier fine arts gallery, with changing exhibits monthly. **One People** (✉ 425 D St., Downtown ☎ 907/274–4063) offers the works of Alaskan artists and crafts workers, including an excellent selection of native pieces.

Continued on page 247

THE GLORIOUS AND RELENTLESS MIDNIGHT SUN

The side-lit afternoons seeping into late evening. The unforgettable sunsets streaking the sky with swaths of neon. The 9 PM golf tee offs and midnight baseball games. The black-out curtains and sleep masks. The bloodshot eyes. The madness of it all: Alaska's tilted life.

The light (and lack thereof) is one of Alaska's most dramatic characteristics. Long summer days goad visitors to sightsee well into the evening, while record-breaking vegetables (read: cabbages the size of coffee tables) grow in the fields. The feeble, or just plain absent, winter sun allows snow to recharge glaciers while the aurora borealis (a.k.a. the northern lights) dances above hibernating bears and humans alike.

Remember that the farther north you go in Alaska, the more pronounced the midnight sun will be. If you make it to Barrow, you'll experience nightless days in summer. Heading south means a less extreme case of the midnight sun, but often just as much revelry celebrating its presence. Summertime simply has a different feeling in Alaska—enjoy the local fairs and festivals, and the stunning mixture of persistent daylight, snow-capped mountains, and miles of vibrant wildland.

(above) A brave Midnight Sun runner (right) How does *your* garden grow?

THE MIDNIGHT SUN: HOW IT WORKS

The Earth spins on a slightly tilted axis as it rotates around the sun. The northern hemisphere is tilted toward the sun in summer and away from it in winter. So how does this explain Alaska's midnight sun? The globe's most northern areas, including much of Alaska, are tilted so far toward the sun in summer that there's continuous light.

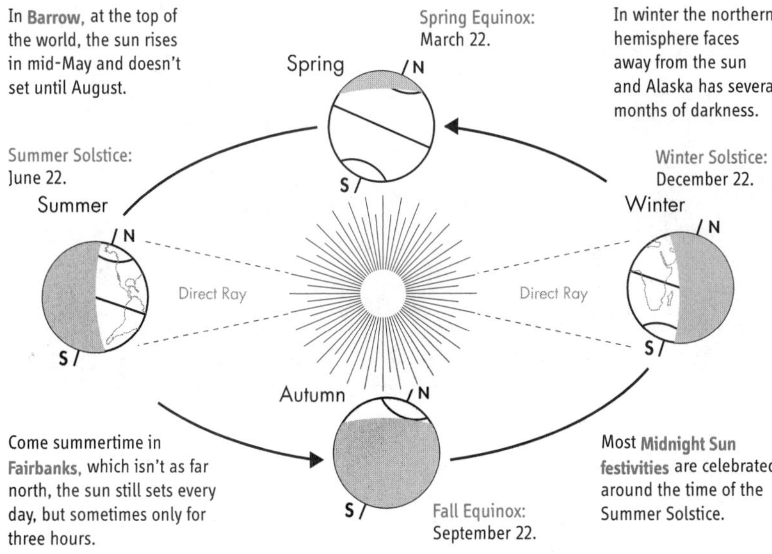

In **Barrow**, at the top of the world, the sun rises in mid-May and doesn't set until August.
Spring Equinox: March 22.
In winter the northern hemisphere faces away from the sun and Alaska has several months of darkness.
Spring
N
S
Summer Solstice: June 22.
Summer
N
S
Direct Ray
Winter Solstice: December 22.
Winter
N
S
Direct Ray
Autumn
N
S
Come summertime in **Fairbanks**, which isn't as far north, the sun still sets every day, but sometimes only for three hours.
Fall Equinox: September 22.
Most **Midnight Sun festivities** are celebrated around the time of the Summer Solstice.

TIPS FROM AN ALASKAN

Coping with the Midnight Sun

- Close your shades a few hours before bedtime. Bring a sleep mask or use the black-out curtains in your hotel room!
- Bring antihistamines to soothe the mosquito bites we *promise* you'll get—the added bonus is the drowsiness.
- You can always count sheep. Or count microbrews! Alaska has many to enjoy, including Silver Gulch, Sleeping Lady, Kodiak Brewery, and Moose's Tooth.
- If all else fails, go out and enjoy the eerie light. Many people find that they simply need less sleep in summer.

Surviving the Polar Winter

- Get what sunlight you can. Make sure you're up and at 'em whenever the sun is.
- Take your vitamins, especially vitamin D, and eat plenty of fruit.
- Some Alaskans go that extra step and visit tanning salons to boost their mood—and, of course, for a little color!
- Fool your body into thinking the sun is out: sip your morning coffee near a lamp (preferably full-spectrum).
- Did we mention Alaska's many excellent microbrews?

MIDNIGHT SUN REVELRY

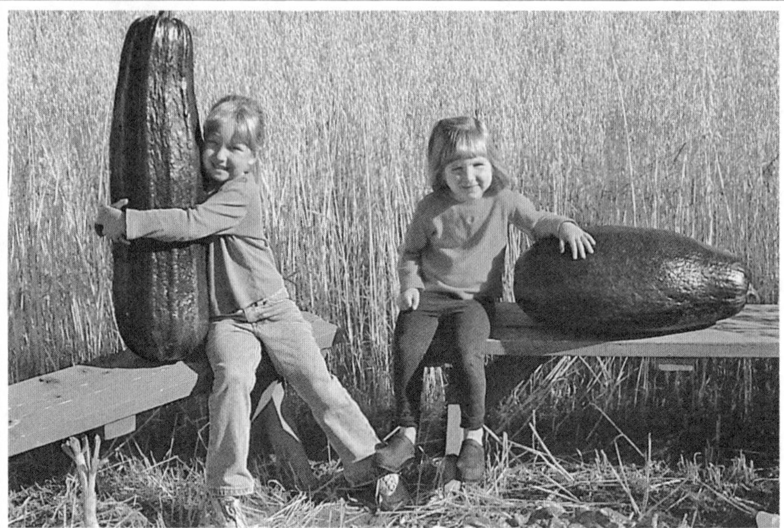

During the peak of the midnight sun season, June and early July, there's almost no end to the special activities and festivals celebrating the light. It's a good thing, too—you may have trouble falling asleep!

- Taking place the Saturday closest to the summer solstice, the **Mayor's Marathon and Half Marathon in Anchorage** attract runners from all over the country. (🌐 www.mayorsmarathon.com)

- The much less formal 10-km **Midnight Sun Run is held in Fairbanks** every June on the weekend closest to the summer solstice. The run starts at 10 PM. (🌐 fairbanks-alaska.com/midnight-sun-run.htm)

- The **midnight sun baseball game in Fairbanks** is the best-known midnight sun activity in Alaska. The Alaska Goldpanners are the stars of the Alaska League, comprised of college athletes from around the country. Every summer solstice, the Goldpanners host the "high noon at midnight" classic, a tradition since 1906. The first pitch is thrown at 10:30 PM, and the entire game is played without the use of artificial lights. (They haven't worked since they were struck by lightning years ago!) (🌐 www.goldpanners.com)

- If you'd rather steer clear of festivals and find a spot of your own, **drive out of Fairbanks** along Steese Highway or Chena Hot Springs Road for the unforgettable nighttime view.

- Almost every Alaskan town has a special event on or near the summer solstice, but one of the best is the **Nome Midnight Sun Festival,** which celebrates 22 hours of direct sunlight with parades, barbecues, and folk music. (🌐 www.nomealaska.org/vc)

- The **Alaska State Fair** runs for 12 days before Labor Day in the town of Palmer, 40 mi northeast of Anchorage. Check out the giant midnight sun–grown vegetables on display and colorful vending booths selling an array of goods from cookies to jewelry. (🌐 www.alaskastatefair.org)

Books & Music

Barnes & Noble Booksellers (✉ 200 E. Northern Lights Blvd., at A St., Midtown ☎ 907/279–7323 🌐 www.bn.com) is one of Anchorage's most popular bookstores. It also sells CDs and magazines, and has a Starbucks. The store stays open late, with literary events some nights. **Borders Books & Music** (✉ 1100 E. Dimond Blvd., west of Seward Hwy., South Anchorage ☎ 907/344–4099 🌐 www.borders.com) stocks a diverse selection of titles and has a café. **Cook Inlet Book Company** (✉ 415 W. 5th Ave., Downtown ☎ 907/258–4544 or 800/240–4148 🌐 www.cookinlet.com) has the largest collection of Alaskan titles in the state and a substantial newspaper and magazine section.

Metro Music & Book Store (✉ 530 E. Benson Blvd., Midtown ☎ 907/279–8622) carries a well-thought-out inventory of fiction and nonfiction, but the main draw is the impressive collection of CDs. You can listen to any of them before buying. Also here is Felix Cafe, serving crepes, espresso, and housemade yogurt. Easily the largest independent bookstore in Alaska, **Title Wave Books** (✉ 1360 W. Northern Lights Blvd., Midtown ☎ 907/278–9283 or 888/598–9283 🌐 www.wavebooks.com) fills a sprawling store next to REI. The shelves are filled with new and used titles, and the staff is very knowledgeable. Also here is **Kaladi Brothers Coffee Shop** with Wi-Fi access for Web surfers.

Gifts

Several downtown shops sell quality native Alaskan artwork, but the ★ best buys can be found in the gift shop at the **Alaska Native Medical Center** (✉ 4315 Diplomacy Dr., at Tudor and Bragaw Rds., East Anchorage ☎ 907/729–1122), which is open weekdays 10 to 2 and 11 to 2 on the first and third Saturday of the month. The gift shop at **Alaska Native Heritage Center** (✉ 8800 Heritage Center Dr. [Glenn Hwy. at Muldoon Rd.], East Anchorage ☎ 907/330–8000 or 800/315–6608 🌐 www.alaskanative.net) sells native crafts.

Laura Wright Alaskan Parkys sells distinctive Eskimo-style "parkys" (parkas) and will custom sew one for you. They're available at **Heritage Gifts** (✉ 333 W. 4th Ave., #227, at D St., Downtown ☎ 907/274–4215 🌐 www.alaskan.com/parkys). **Oomingmak** (✉ 6th Ave. and H St., Downtown ☎ 907/272–9225 or 888/360–9665 🌐 www.qiviut.com), a native-owned cooperative, sells items made of qiviut, the warm undercoat of the musk ox. Scarves, shawls, and tunics are knitted in traditional patterns.

★ Frozen seafood and smoked fish are available from **10th and M Seafoods** (✉ 1020 M St., Downtown ☎ 907/272–3474 or 800/770–2722 🌐 www.10thandmseafoods.com). **New Sagaya's City Market** (✉ 900 W. 13th Ave., Downtown ☎ 907/274–6173) sells an excellent selection of fresh seafood. If you don't want to carry the fish with you, the market will pack and ship it home. Get smoked reindeer meat and salmon products at **Alaska Sausage Company** (✉ 2914 Arctic Blvd., Midtown ☎ 907/562–3636 or 800/798–3636 🌐 www.alaskasausage.com).

Although furs may not be to everyone's taste or ethics, a number of Alaska fur companies have stores and factories in Anchorage. One of the city's largest and best-known furriers is **David Green Master Furrier** (✉ 130 W. 4th Ave., Downtown ☎ 907/277–9595). **Alaska Fur Exchange** (✉ 4417 Old Seward Hwy., Midtown ☎ 907/563–3877 🌐 www.alaskafurexchange.com) has a large midtown store that sells both furs and native artwork.

Jewelry

The **Kobuk Valley Jade Co.** (✉ Olympic Cir., Girdwood ☎ 907/783–2764), at the base of Mt. Alyeska, sells hand-polished jade pieces as well as native masks, baskets, and jewelry.

Sports & Outdoors Equipment

If you get to Alaska and discover you've left some critical camping or outdoor recreation gear behind, **REI** (✉ 122 W. Northern Lights Blvd., Midtown ☎ 907/272–4565) in Anchorage rents camping, skiing, and paddling equipment. They also give weekly seminars on season-specific outdoors subjects, and the salespeople are very knowledgeable about local conditions and activities, and the gear required to get you out and back safely.

SPORTS, THE OUTDOORS & GUIDED TOURS

Anchorage is an active city, with a blend of spectator and do-it-yourself fun. Wintertime brings hockey, dog mushing, and ski races, and the long summer days provide the chance to watch a semipro baseball game, bike the Coastal Trail, and still have time to watch the sun go down at midnight. **Sullivan Arena** (✉ 334 E. 16th Ave., Midtown ☎ 907/566–1596) is Anchorage's primary venue for large events, from ice hockey to boat shows. **Mulcahy Stadium** (✉ E. 16th Ave. at Cordova St., Midtown) is the center for semipro baseball in Anchorage.

Baseball

Two semiprofessional baseball teams, made up of college players, play at Mulcahy Stadium next to the Sullivan Arena. The games played here are intense—many players have gone on to star in the major leagues. The **Anchorage Bucs** (☎ 907/561–2827 🌐 www.anchoragebucs.com) have a dozen or so former players who went on to the majors, including standouts Wally Joyner, Jeff Kent, and Bobby Jones. The most famous player on the **Glacier Pilots** (☎ 907/274–3627 🌐 www.glacierpilots.com) was Mark McGwire, but many other pre–major leaguers have played for them over the years, including Dave Winfield, Randy Johnson, and Reggie Jackson.

Basketball

The University of Alaska Anchorage hosts the **Great Alaska Shootout** (🌐 www.shootout.net) at the Sullivan Arena over Thanksgiving weekend. In addition, the UAA Seawolves men's and women's basketball teams play on campus during the winter months.

Bicycling, Running & Walking

Anchorage has more than 120 mi of paved bicycle trails, and many streets have marked bike lanes. Although busy during the day, downtown

DOGSLED RACES & WINTER FUN

World-championship races are run in mid-February, with three consecutive 25-mi heats through downtown Anchorage, out into the foothills, and back. People line the route with cups of coffee in hand to cheer on their favorite mushers. The three-day races are part of the annual **Fur Rendezvous,** one of the largest winter festivals in the United States. Other attractions include a snow-sculpture competition, car races, Eskimo blanket toss (a holdover from earlier days when dozens of people would team up to grasp a round walrus hide blanket and launch a hunter high into the air, trampoline-style, in an effort to spot distant seals, walrus, and whales), dog weight-pulling contests (where canines of all breeds and sizes compete to see which can pull the most weight piled on a sled), a carnival, and even snowshoe softball. Fur Rondy events take place from late February to the start of the Iditarod in early March. The **Fur Rondy office** (✉ 400 D St., No. 200, Downtown, 99501 ☎ 907/274-1270 🌐 www.furrondy.net) has a guide to the festival's events.

In March, mushers and their dogs compete in the 1,100-mi **Iditarod Trail Sled Dog Race** (☎ 907/376-5155, 800/545-6874 Iditarod Trail Headquarters 🌐 www.iditarod.com). The race commemorates the delivery of serum to Nome by dog mushers during the diphtheria epidemic of 1925. The serum run was the inspiration for the animated family film *Balto*. Dog teams leave downtown Anchorage and wind through the Alaska Range, across the Interior, out to the Bering Sea coast, and on to Nome. Depending on weather and trail conditions, winners can complete the race in nine days (⇨ Alaska's Well-Worn Trail box).

4

streets are uncrowded and safe for cyclists in the evening. ■ **TIP→ Pick up a guide to local trails at the Alaska Public Lands Information Center** (✉ 4th Ave. and F St., Downtown ☎ 907/271–2737 🌐 www.nps.gov/aplic) or at area bookstores.

At the far west end of Raspberry Road in South Anchorage, the 40 mi of trails at **Kincaid Park** (☎ 907/343–6397 🌐 www.muni.org/parks/parkdistrictsw.cfm) wind through 1,400 acres of mixed spruce and birch forest. Mountain bikers will find easy-to-moderate riding along with some challenging hills. Parking lots are open 6 AM to 11 PM daily. The Kincaid Outdoor Center—locally called Kincaid Chalet—is available for a fee for social functions such as weddings, receptions, and meetings.

The **Tony Knowles Coastal Trail** (🌐 www.trailsofanchorage.com) and other bike trails in Anchorage are used by runners, cyclists, in-line skaters, and walkers. It begins downtown off 2nd Avenue and is also easily accessible from Westchester Lagoon near the west end of 15th Avenue. The trail runs from the lagoon 2 mi to Earthquake Park and then continues an additional 7 mi to Kincaid Park, where a series of unpaved trails provides for more adventurous biking and hiking.

A number of popular running events are held annually in Anchorage, including the **Alaska Run for Women** (🌐 www.akrfw.org) in early June, which raises money for the fight against breast cancer. The late-April **Heart Run** is a fund-raiser for the American Heart Association's work to prevent heart disease. It's been taking place for more than 25 years. Alaska's biggest and most famous running event is the **Mayor's Midnight Sun Marathon** (🌐 www.mayorsmarathon.com), held on summer solstice in late June.

Downtown Bicycle Rental (✉ 333 W. 4th Ave., Downtown ☎ 907/279–5293 🌐 www.alaska-bike-rentals.com) rents mountain bikes and provides trail recommendations. The **Arctic Bicycle Club** (☎ 907/566–0177 🌐 www.arcticbike.org) organizes races and tours.

Bird-Watching

Popular bird-watching places include the Tony Knowles Coastal Trail, which provides access to Westchester Lagoon and nearby tide flats, along with Potter Marsh on the south end of Anchorage. The local chapter of the **Anchorage Audubon Society** (☎ 907/276–7034 🌐 www.anchorageaudubon.org) refers you to local birders who will advise you on the best bird-watching spots. You can also sign up for bird-watching classes and field trips. The society's **bird hot line** (☎ 907/338–2473) tracks the latest sightings in town. Naturalists Lisa Moorehead and Bob Dittrick of **Wilderness Birding Adventures** (☎ 907/694–7442 🌐 www.wildernessbirding.com) guide backcountry birding trips to remote parts of Alaska.

Canoeing & Kayaking

Local lakes and lagoons, such as Westchester Lagoon, Goose Lake, and Jewel Lake, have favorable conditions for canoeing and kayaking. More adventurous paddlers should head to Whittier or Seward for sea kayaking. Rent sea kayaks from **Kayak and Custom Adventures Worldwide** (✉ 328 3rd Ave., Seward ☎ 907/224–3960 or 800/288–3134 🌐 www.kayakak.com), which also leads day trips in the Seward area. Better known as REI, **Recreational Equipment Inc.** (✉ 1200 W. Northern Lights Blvd., Midtown ☎ 907/272–4565 🌐 www.rei.com) sells and rents all sorts of outdoor gear, including canoes and sea kayaks.

Fishing

Nearly 30 local lakes are stocked with trout. ■ **TIP→ You must have a valid Alaska sportfishing license to fish in the state. Fishing licenses may be purchased at any Fred Meyer or Carrs grocery or local sporting goods store.** Rainbow trout, arctic char, landlocked salmon, and northern pike are among the species found in waters like Jewel Lake in South Anchorage and Mirror and Fire lakes near Eagle River. Coho salmon return to Ship Creek (downtown) in August, and king salmon are caught between late May and early July. Campbell Creek and Bird Creek just south of town are also good spots for coho—locally called silver—salmon. Contact the **Alaska Department of Fish and Game** (☎ 907/267–2218 🌐 www.state.ak.us/adfg) for licensing information. For maps showing locations and public access to Anchorage-area lakes, visit www.sf.adfg.state.ak.us and click on Region II, then Lake Maps.

Golf

Anchorage is Alaska's golfing capital, with several public courses. They won't compare to offerings in Phoenix or San Diego, but courses are open until 10 PM on long summer days.

Anchorage Golf Course (✉ O'Malley Rd., South Anchorage ☎ 907/522–3363) has 18 holes. Golf carts and clubs are available for rent. The city-run **Russian Jack Springs Park** (✉ 5200 DeBarr Rd., South Anchorage ☎ 907/343–6992) is generally open May through September. It has 9 holes and clubs for rent. **Tanglewood Lakes Golf Club** (✉ 11701 Brayton Dr., South Anchorage ☎ 907/345–4600) is a 9-hole course in South Anchorage.

Hockey

Hockey is in the blood of any true Alaskan, and kids as young as four years crowd local ice rinks in hopes of becoming the next Scott Gomez (who still lives in Anchorage when he's not playing for the New Jersey Devils).

The East Coast Hockey League's **Alaska Aces** (☎ 907/258–2237 🌐 www.alaskaaces.com) play minor-league professional hockey in the Sullivan Arena. The **University of Alaska Anchorage** (☎ 907/786–1293 🌐 www.goseawolves.com) has a Division I NCAA hockey team that draws several thousand loyal fans to home games at the Sullivan Arena.

Ice-Skating

Ice-skating is a favorite wintertime activity in Anchorage, with several indoor ice arenas, outdoor hockey rinks, and local ponds opening when temperatures drop.

Ben Boeke Ice Arena (✉ 334 E. 16th Ave., Midtown ☎ 907/274–5715 🌐 www.benboeke.com) is a city-run indoor ice arena with open skating and skate rentals year-round. The **Dimond Ice Chalet** (✉ 800 E. Dimond Blvd., South Anchorage ☎ 907/344–1212 🌐 www.dimondcenter.com) has an indoor ice rink at Dimond Mall that is open to the public daily, with lessons and skate rentals. In winter, **Westchester Lagoon,** 1 mi south of downtown, is a favorite outdoor family (and competitive) skating area, with smooth ice and piles of firewood next to the warming barrels.

Racquet Sports & Fitness Club

The park strip at 9th Avenue and C Street has several tennis courts. On the south side of Anchorage, the **Dimond Athletic Club** (✉ 800 E. Dimond Blvd., at Old Seward, South Anchorage ☎ 907/344–7788) has a lap pool, Nautilus equipment, free weights, saunas, hot tubs, steam rooms, and racquetball courts, plus various exercise classes. You can buy a daily guest pass for $15.

Rafting

Based in Girdwood, **Class V Whitewater** (📭 Box 591, Girdwood 99587 ☎ 907/783–2004 🌐 www.alaskanrafting.com) leads scenic floats on the Twenty Mile and Portage rivers, along with white-water trips on the Talkeetna and Sixmile rivers. Alaska's oldest adventure and wilderness guiding company (in business since 1975), **Nova** (📭 Box 1129, Chickaloon 99674 ☎ 907/745–5753 or 800/746–5753 🌐 www.novalaska.com), provides both scenic and white-water wilderness rafting trips statewide.

Skiing

Cross-country skiing is extremely popular in Anchorage. Locals ski on trails in town at Kincaid Park or Hillside and farther away at Girdwood Valley, Turnagain Pass, and Chugach State Park. Downhill skiing is convenient to downtown. A number of cross-country ski events are held annually in Anchorage. The **Alaska Ski for Women** (🌐 www.alaskaskiforwomen.org), held on Super Bowl Sunday in early February, is the biggest women's ski race in North America, attracting more than 1,500 skiers. The **Nordic Skiing Association of Anchorage** (🌐 www.anchoragenordicski.com) sponsors many other ski races and events throughout the winter, from wooden ski classics to the highly competitive Besh Cup series. Biggest of all is the **Tour of Anchorage** (🌐 www.tourofanchorage.com), a grueling 50-km marathon in early March.

★ **Alyeska Ski Resort** (☎ 907/754–1111, 800/880–3880, 907/754–7669 recorded information and snow conditions, 907/753–2275 for ticket office 🌐 www.alyeskaresort.com), at Girdwood, 40 mi south of the city, is Alaska's premier destination resort, where snowfall averages 782 inches annually. Owned by a large Japanese corporation, Alyeska features a day lodge, hotel, restaurants, six chairlifts, a tram, a vertical drop of 2,500 feet, and runs for all abilities. Lift tickets cost $48 for adults; $21 for night skiing. The tram ($16) is open during the summer, providing access to the Seven Glaciers restaurant and hiking trails. **Alyeska Accommodations** (☎ 907/783–2000 or 888/783–2001 🌐 www.alyeskaaccommodations.com) can set you up in a privately owned cabin or condo. **Alpenglow at Arctic Valley** (✉ Mile 7, Arctic Valley Rd., off Glenn Hwy., just past Muldoon Exit ☎ 907/428–1208 🌐 www.skialpenglow.com) is a small ski area just north of Anchorage. On the eastern edge of town, **Hilltop Ski Area** (✉ Abbott Rd. near Hillside Dr., East Anchorage ☎ 907/346–1446 🌐 www.hilltopskiarea.org) is a favorite ski area with families.

On 1,400 acres of rolling, timbered hills and bordered on the west by Cook Inlet, **Kincaid Park** (✉ Main entrance at far west end of Raspberry Rd., Southwest Anchorage ☎ 907/343–6397 🌐 www.muni.org/parks/parkdistrictsw.cfm) is a scenic treasure with maintained trails groomed for diagonal and skate-skiing that are perfect for cross-country skiing. National cross-country skiing events (including U.S. Olympic team qualifying events and national masters championships) are held each winter along the 60 km of interwoven trails—including 20 km that are lighted for night skiing. The park is open year-round:

WORD OF MOUTH

"I spent a week in Anchorage and it wasn't long enough! I enjoyed biking along the Tony Knowles Coastal Trail and hiking north of Anchorage. The beer-battered fried halibut at the Anchorage Saturday Market was fantastic."

–Postal

CLOSE UP

Alaska's Well-Worn Trail

SINCE 1973 MUSHERS AND THEIR SLED-DOG TEAMS have raced more than 1,000 mi across Alaska in a marathon vision quest unlike any other: the Iditarod Trail Sled Dog Race, the longest sled-dog race in the world. After a ceremonial start in downtown Anchorage on the first Saturday in March, dog teams wind through Alaska, battling almost every imaginable winter challenge. Ten days later, the "Last Great Race" ends with spectacular fanfare in Nome, on the Bering Sea coast.

The Iditarod's origins can be traced to two events: an early 1900s long-distance race called the All-Alaska Sweepstakes and the delivery of a lifesaving serum to Nome by dog mushers during a diphtheria outbreak in 1925. Fascinated with the trail's history, Alaskan sled-dog enthusiasts Dorothy Page and Joe Redington Sr. staged the first race in 1967 to celebrate the role of mushing in Alaska's history. Only 50 mi long and with a purse of $25,000–no small amount at that time–it attracted the best of Alaska's competitive mushers. Enthusiasm waned in 1969, however, when the available winnings fell to $1,000. Instead of giving up, Redington enlarged it.

In 1973, after three years without a race, he organized a 1,000-mi race from Anchorage to Nome, with a then-outrageous purse of $50,000. Critics scoffed, but 34 racers entered. First place went to a little-known musher named Dick Wilmarth, who finished in 20 days. Redington then billed the Iditarod as a 1,049-mi race to symbolize Alaska, the 49th state (still the official distance, even though the race really covers 1,100 mi).

The race actually begins in Wasilla, home of the Iditarod headquarters, a 50-mile drive north of Anchorage. The first few hundred miles take mushers and dogs through wooded lowlands and hills, including a stretch known as Moose Alley. Teams then cross the Alaska Range. Then they enter Interior Alaska, with Athabascan villages and gold-rush ghost towns, including Iditarod. Next, the trail follows the frozen Yukon River, then cuts over to the Bering Sea coast for the final 270-mi "sprint" to Nome. It was here, in 1985, that Libby Riddles drove her team into a blinding blizzard, en route to a victory that made her the first woman to win the race. After that, Susan Butcher won the race four times, but the all-time record holder is Rick Swenson, with five victories. The fastest time was recorded in 2002, when Swiss-born musher Martin Buser finished in just under nine days.

Iditarod mushers and dogs may have to endure extreme cold, deep snow, gale-force winds, whiteouts, river overflow, and moose attacks, not to mention fraying tempers. The race has sparked criticism from animal-rights supporters, and Iditarod policy continues to enforce humane care and treatment of dogs.

More than three decades after its establishment, the Iditarod race purse tops $600,000, with more than $70,000 to the champion. International journalists report from the trail, and entrants have come from more than a dozen countries. Though racers such as Swenson, Dee Dee Jonrowe, Martin Buser, and Jeff King draw the most media attention, all mushers–and dogs–who reach Nome are appropriately treated like champions after surviving their 1,049-mi run across Alaska's wilderness.

for skiing in winter; and for mountain biking, hiking, and other outdoor activities in summer. The Raspberry Road parking lot is open 6 AM–11 PM daily; lots inside the park are open 10 AM to 10 PM daily.

The locally owned **Alaska Mountaineering and Hiking** (✉ 2633 Spenard Rd., Midtown ☎ 907/272–1811 🌐 www.alaskamountaineering.com) outdoors shop has a highly experienced staff and plenty of cross-country skis for sale or rent. Ski sales and rentals are available from **Recreational Equipment Inc.** (REI; ✉ 1200 W. Northern Lights Blvd., Midtown ☎ 907/272–4565 🌐 www.rei.com).

Water Sports

★ **H2Oasis Water Park** (✉ 1520 O'Malley Rd., South Anchorage ☎ 907/522–4420 or 888/426–2747 🌐 www.h2oasiswaterpark.com) is Alaska's first—and only—water park. Housed within a medieval castle–shaped structure, this large indoor facility opened in 2003. Attractions include a pool that generates 3-foot bodysurfing waves, a 475-foot-long water-powered roller coaster, a 350-foot open flume slide, plus a pirate ship with water cannons and slides. A children's lagoon and lazy river, a splash pool, and two hot tubs are some of the calmer soaks. All told, the park has pools filled with more than 350,000 gallons of water. H2Oasis is open daily year-round and costs $20 for a day ($15 for kids).

The large pool and high ceilings at the **University of Alaska Anchorage** (✉ 2801 Spirit Way, off Providence Dr., East Anchorage ☎ 907/786–1231 🌐 www.uaa.alaska.edu) are geared toward fitness swimmers. Your $5 admission to the UAA pool also provides access to the ice rink, weight room, saunas, racquetball courts, and gym. For something simple, head to the **West High School Pool** (✉ 2508 Blueberry Rd., Midtown ☎ 907/343–4506), where a spiral waterslide is available, along with diving boards and lap lanes.

ANCHORAGE ESSENTIALS

Transportation

BY AIR

Ted Stevens Anchorage International Airport is 6 mi from downtown Anchorage on International Airport Road. It is served by Alaska, American, Continental, Delta, Northwest, and United airlines, along with a number of international carriers. Several carriers, including ERA and PenAir, connect Anchorage with smaller Alaskan communities. Floatplane operators and helicopters serve the area from Lake Hood, which is adjacent to and part of Anchorage International Airport. There are also a number of smaller air taxis and air-charter operations at Merrill Field, 2 mi east of downtown on 5th Avenue.

A major redevelopment project at Ted Stevens Anchorage International Airport has brought a new air terminal and Alaska Railroad station with direct service to downtown.

Ted Stevens Anchorage International Airport ☎ 907/266–2529 🌐 www.anchorageairport.com.

AIRPORT TRANSFERS Taxis queue up at the lower level of the airport terminal outside the baggage-claim area. Alaska Cab, Borealis Shuttle, Checker Cab, and Yellow Cab (⇨ Taxis), as well as Anchorage Taxi Cab, all operate here; you'll get whichever cab is next in line. All are on a meter system, and you'll pay about $17, not including tip, for the ride to downtown hotels.

BY BOAT & FERRY

Cruise ships sailing the Gulf of Alaska and the Alaska Marine ferries call in Seward, two hours by train or bus south of Anchorage. The South Central route of the Alaska Marine Highway connects Kodiak, Port Lions, Homer, Seldovia, Seward, Valdez, Cordova, and Whittier.

Alaska Marine Highway System ✉ 605 W. 4th Ave., inside Alaska Public Lands Information Center, Downtown ☎ 907/272-4482 or 800/642-0066 📠 907/277-4829 🌐 www.ferryalaska.com.

4

BY BUS

The municipal People Mover covers the whole Anchorage Bowl. Get schedules and information from the central bus depot at 6th Avenue and G Street. The one-way fare is $1.75 for rides outside the downtown area; rides within downtown are free.

People Mover ☎ 907/343-6543 🌐 www.peoplemover.org.

BY CAR & RV

The Glenn Highway enters Anchorage from the north and becomes 5th Avenue near Merrill Field; this route will lead you directly into downtown. Gambell Street leads out of town to the south, becoming New Seward Highway at about 20th Avenue. South of town, it becomes the Seward Highway.

If, like many visitors to Alaska, you bring your RV or rent one on arrival, you should note that parking an RV downtown on weekdays is challenging. The big parking lot on 3rd Avenue between C and E streets is a good place to park and walk. Parking usually is not a problem in other parts of town, and most of the big discount stores allow free parking in their lots.

BY TAXI

Prices for taxis are $2 to $3 for pickup, plus an additional $2.50 for each mile. Most people in Anchorage telephone for a cab; it is not common to hail one. Allow 20 minutes for arrival of the cab during morning and evening rush hours. Alaska Cab has taxis with wheelchair lifts. Borealis Shuttle has lower rates if you are willing to share the ride.

Alaska Cab ☎ 907/563-5353. **Borealis Shuttle** ☎ 907/276-3600. **Checker Cab** ☎ 907/276-1234. **Yellow Cab** ☎ 907/272-2422.

BY TRAIN

The Alaska Railroad runs between Anchorage and Fairbanks via Denali National Park and Preserve daily, mid-May through September, and also south between Anchorage and Seward during the same period. Year-round passenger service is available from Anchorage north to Talkeetna. Call for schedule and fare information.

Alaska Railroad ☎ 907/265-2494 or 800/544-0552 📠 907/265-2323 🌐 www.akrr.com.

Contacts & Resources

BANKS

Alaska USA Federal Credit Union ✉ 500 W. 36th Ave., Suite 100, Midtown ☎ 907/563-4567 🌐 www.alaskausa.org. **Credit Union 1** ✉ 3500 Eide St., Midtown ☎ 907/339-9485 🌐 www.cu1.org. **First National Bank Alaska** ✉ 101 E. 36th Ave., Midtown ☎ 907/777-4362 🌐 www.fnbalaska.com. **Northrim Bank** ✉ 3111 C St., Midtown ☎ 907/562-0062 🌐 www.northrim.com. **Wells Fargo Bank NA** ✉ 7731 E. Northern Lights Blvd., East Anchorage ☎ 907/331-2008 🌐 www.wellsfargo.com.

EMERGENCIES

Doctors & Dentists **Physician-referral service** ☎ 888/254-7884 Alaska Regional Hospital, 907/261-4900 Providence Alaska Medical Center.

Emergency Services **Police, fire, and ambulance** ☎ 911. **Poison Control Center** ☎ 800/222-1222.

Hospitals **Alaska Regional Hospital** ✉ 2801 DeBarr Rd., East Anchorage ☎ 907/276-1131 🌐 www.alaskaregional.com. **First Care** ✉ 3710 Woodland Dr., East Anchorage ☎ 907/248-1122 ✉ 1301 Huffman Rd., South Anchorage ☎ 907/345-1199. **Providence Alaska Medical Center** ✉ 3200 Providence Dr., East Anchorage ☎ 907/562-2211 🌐 www.providence.org.

24-hour Pharmacy **Carrs** ✉ 1650 W. Northern Lights Blvd., at Minnesota Dr., Midtown ☎ 907/297-0560.

INTERNET, MAIL & SHIPPING

Dark Horse Coffee has two terminals with high-speed Internet service for $2 for 15 minutes or $6 for 30 minutes and a specialty drink of your choice. Complimentary wireless is offered with purchases. Popular local coffee house Kaladi Brothers has six Anchorage locations with wireless access for $4 a day.

Internet Access **Dark Horse Coffee** ✉ 646 F St., Downtown ☎ 907/279-0647 🌐 www.darkhorsecoffee.com. **Kaladi Brothers** ✉ 6921 Brayton Dr., Downtown ☎ 907/344-6510 ✉ Titlewave Books, 1360 W Northern Lights Blvd., Midtown ✉ 6th and G Sts., Downtown ✉ 6901 E. Tudor Rd., East Anchorage ✉ 12350 Industry Way, off Huffman Rd., South Anchorage ✉ 9900 Old Seward Hwy., South Anchorage 🌐 www.kaladi.com.

Mail & Shipping **FedEx** ✉ 549 W. International Airport Rd. ☎ 800/463-3339 🌐 www.fedex.com.

TOURS

FLIGHTSEEING Any air-taxi company (check the Anchorage Yellow Pages) can arrange for a flightseeing trip over Anchorage and environs. The fee will be determined by the length of time you are airborne and the size of the plane. Tours of about an hour and a half generally cost around $200 per person. Three-hour flights over Mt. McKinley, including a landing on a remote backcountry lake, run about $250 per person.

ERA Helicopters offers a 50-minute trip over Anchorage and the Chugach Mountains as well as a two-hour glacier expedition that includes a landing on the ice. ERA Classic Airlines offers travelers a nostalgic air cruise aboard elegantly restored DC-3s from the 1940s. These 90-minute flights vary in destination, depending upon the weather, flying over Mt. McKinley or the mountains of South Central Alaska. Ketchum Air Service on Lake Hood has a number of flightseeing tours, including one to Mt. McKinley, as well as fly-in service to remote lake cabins for hunting and fishing, and houseboat rentals. Also at Lake Hood, Rust's Flying Service flies ski-planes over Mt. McKinley that include a landing on Ruth Glacier—a spectacular alpine amphitheater high on the mountain.

SMART TRAVEL TIPS

For invaluable tips about easy travel throughout Alaska, flip to the Smart Travel Tips section in the back of this book.

ERA Classic Airlines ☎ 907/266-8394 or 800/866-8394. **ERA Helicopters** ☎ 907/266-8351 or 800/843-1947 🌐 www.eraaviation.com. **Regal Air** ☎ 907/243-8535 🌐 www.regal-air.com. **Rust's Flying Service** ☎ 907/243-1595 or 800/544-2299 🌐 www.flyrusts.com.

WILDLIFE VIEWING

Kenai Fjords Tours has day packages to Kenai Fjords National Park April through November.

Kenai Fjords Tours ✉ 509 W. 4th Ave., Downtown ☎ 907/276-6249 or 800/468-8068 🌐 www.kenaifjords.com.

VISITOR INFORMATION

The Alaska Public Lands Information Center has natural and cultural resource exhibits, fish and wildlife information, trip-planning assistance, films and videos, book and map sales, recreation and visitor information, and interpretive programs.

Alaska Public Lands Information Center ✉ 4th Ave. and F St., Downtown ☎ 907/271-2737 🖷 907/271-2744 🌐 www.nps.gov/aplic. **Anchorage Convention and Visitors Bureau** (ACVB) ✉ 524 W. 4th Ave., Downtown, 99501-2212 ☎ 907/276-4118, 800/478-1255 to order visitor guides 🖷 907/278-5559 🌐 www.anchorage.net. **Daily events** ☎ 907/276-3200. **Log Cabin Visitor Information Center** ✉ 4th Ave. and F St., Downtown ☎ 907/274-3531 🌐 www.anchorage.net.

South Central Alaska

INCLUDING PRINCE WILLIAM SOUND, HOMER & THE KENAI PENINSULA

Hiking, exploring, or paddling in this region is easy and unforgettable.

WORD OF MOUTH

"We loved the Kenai Peninsula. We drove from Seward to Homer and saw wildlife, had some wonderful hikes and picnics, went clamming, visited art galleries and museums, and ate great food."

–lcuy

"Exit Glacier is wonderful. It's a 1½-mile hike to get up close and personal with a spectacular glacier. Early June is a wonderful time to go."

–tcapp

www.fodors.com/forums

WELCOME TO SOUTH CENTRAL

A dancer displays a native costume

TOP REASONS TO GO

★ **To catch a fish:** Fishing opportunities here are too numerous to list. You can fish for saltwater species such as halibut and salmon from charter boats out of Homer or Seward, or fish the rivers with a guide.

★ **Best on a budget:** Travel within South Central is relatively cheap when compared to other parts of the state.

★ **Take a hike:** You can experience wilderness without rubbing elbows with crowds; chances of spotting wildlife increase exponentially with your distance from the road system.

★ **The people:** South Central residents are friendly and helpful. Locals are used to dealing with lots of curious visitors.

★ **Bear watching:** During summer, brown bears congregate along the salmon streams of the Alaska Peninsula, a short hop across Cook Inlet. Air-taxi services offer guided bear-watching and flightseeing trips.

1 Prince William Sound. A short drive south of Anchorage is Prince William Sound. While Anchorage receives about 15 inches of precipitation per year, Whittier gets more than 10 times as much. Anchorage is home to over 260,000 citizens. The combined population of Valdez, Cordova, and Whittier is around 7,000.

Beluga whale

2 Kenai Peninsula. A look at Friday-afternoon traffic pouring out of Anchorage in the summer onto the single road south to the Kenai is all the evidence you need that the peninsula's nick-name "Anchorage's playground" is accurate. The Kenai has world-class recreation options that include fishing, hiking, canoeing, and whale-watching.

GETTING ORIENTED

South Central is the population and commercial center of Alaska, and its attractions are largely road accessible. The region includes the Kenai Peninsula south of Anchorage, Prince William Sound and Wrangell–St. Elias National Park to the east, and the Interior gateway town of Talkeetna to the north. Geographic features include four mountain ranges, three national parks, the country's second-largest national forest, Cook Inlet, and more glaciers, rivers, and lakes than you could visit in a lifetime.

5

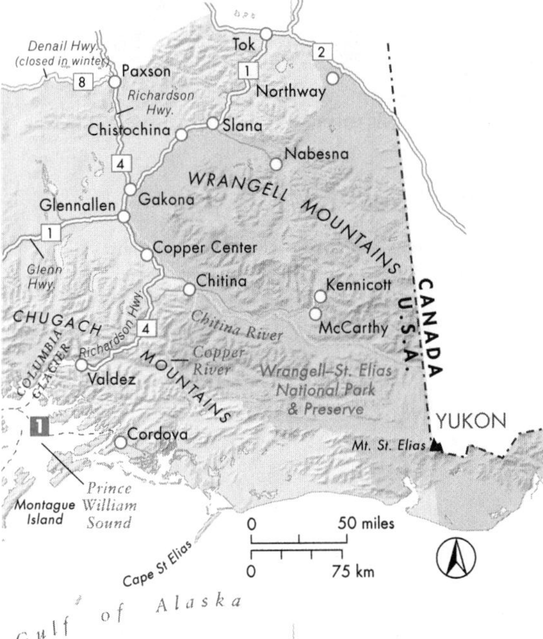

A Russian Orthodox Church in Kenai

3 Homer. Literally the end of the road, Homer is an interesting blend of commercial fishermen, artists, bohemians, and tourists. Kachemak Bay is stunning, with mountain and ocean views, plus hiking, fishing, and sea kayaking. Be sure to try the excellent restaurants and sip a local beer.

4 Mat-Su Valley and Beyond. Just north of Anchorage, the Matanuska-Susitna Valley is a diverse mixture of bedroom communities, agricultural concerns, and recreation options; it's the gateway to the Interior. Several spectacular mountain ranges converge here: the Chugach, the Talkeetna, and the Alaska, with rivers and streams stocked with trophy-class salmon and trout every summer.

SOUTH CENTRAL PLANNER

How's the Weather?

Summer is peak season here, with the major population influx coinciding with the end of the school year and the beginning of the salmon runs. The long daylight hours make it easy to burn the candle at both ends. Some of this can be avoided by using the shoulder seasons, but spring and fall can be a bit iffy. If you're choosing between one or the other, choose fall. Autumn starts early here with the tundra plants and the deciduous trees beginning to show color in mid-August. The animals are pretty active getting ready for winter, there are still plenty of fish to catch, and most of the visitor services stay open well into September. If you venture outdoors, be prepared for any weather. Rain and wind can kick up seemingly out of nowhere, and temperatures can vary from 40 degrees to the 70s on a summer day.

Pack Right

Carry a daypack with an extra layer (or two) of clothing including rain gear, water, and snacks as a bare minimum. Everyone should have his or her own pair of binoculars, even if it's just an inexpensive set. There are few things more frustrating than having the wildlife sighting of a lifetime with everyone grabbing for the same set of field glasses.

How Much Time?

We like to recommend no less than two weeks, three being a much better option. That'll give you time to hit the hot spots: see Kenai Fjords and/or Prince William Sound, Denali, the Kenai, and points in between without turning the trip into a test of endurance. It goes without saying that even just five days here can be sublime.

Travel Times from Anchorage

DESTINATION	TIME
Chugach State Park	20 mins–1 hr by car, depending on section of park
Cordova	1 hr to Whittier by car, then 3 hrs by ferry
Denali State Park	3 hrs by car
Glennallen	4 hrs by car
Homer	4–5 hrs by car
Kenai/Soldotna	2–3 hrs by car
Lake Clark	1–2 hrs by air taxi
Portage Glacier	50 mins by car
Seward	2 hrs by car
Wrangell–St. Elias	6–8 hrs by car

Doing It All vs. Doing It Right

One of the biggest problems faced by Alaska visitors is being overwhelmed by the size of the place and the range of choices involved. The temptation is to cram everything the state has to offer into a two-week trip, and it just can't be done. If you succumb to this type of schedule, you'll find yourself frantically rushing from attraction to attraction and wind up seeing a blur of visions as they pass by your windshield.

Don't see it all through glass. Take some hikes, catch some fish, watch some birds, see some whales. If you're prepared to rough it a bit, all the better. Bring, borrow, or rent some camping gear and look into the public-use cabins scattered across the state. Or, just do an overnight in a tent—the opportunities for getting an hour or two away from a trailhead and bedding down for the night with no remnants of civilization other than what you carry on your back are too numerous to enumerate. You'll acquire a new understanding of Alaska's allure, and have experienced a part of the state that too few visitors ever enjoy.

About the Hotels & Restaurants

Informal is the best way to describe the hospitality industry in Alaska. So don't worry that you still have your hiking clothes on when you go out to eat—chances are you won't be the only one in the place so attired. From mid-September through May, your dining and lodging options once you leave Anchorage decline, sometimes dramatically. For many hotels and restaurants, staying open through the long, dark winter just doesn't make economic sense. Any time you're traveling the road system, carry a copy of *The Milepost* (🌐 www.themilepost.com), which covers the roads mile by mile.

What It Costs

	$$$$	$$$	$$	$	¢
Restaurants	over $25	$20–25	$15–20	$10–15	under $10
Hotels	over $225	$175–$225	$125–$175	$75–$125	under $75

Restaurant prices are per person for a main course at dinner. Hotel prices are for two people in a standard double room in high season.

Making the Most of Your Time

If You Have 3 Days. Head for the Kenai Fjords National Park. Take the Seward Highway along Turnagain Arm. Stop for lunch at the Bake Shop in Girdwood, then head down to Portage Glacier. Continue south to Seward, visit the SeaLife Center or Exit Glacier. Day 2 is reserved for a Kenai Fjords tour, the longer the better. Back in time for dinner, spend another night, then head up to Cooper Landing for a half-day rafting or fishing trip on the Kenai River. Spend the night in Cooper Landing, or head to Hope.

If You Have 5 Days. Follow the three-day trip above, then head back through Anchorage. Head for Talkeetna and a flightseeing tour of Denali State Park. Spring for a glacier landing—it's worth it. Spend the night, then head back south, taking the Fishhook-Willow Pass road turnoff at Mile 71.2 over Hatcher Pass. On the way down, stop at the Independence Mine near Palmer, then Hatcher Pass Lodge for lunch. Continue to Glenn Highway for a stop at the Musk Ox Farm or the Iditarod Headquarters in Wasilla on your way back to Anchorage.

If You Have 7 Days. Follow the above trip. From the Glenn Highway, turn left toward Valdez. Stop for a short hike at Thompson Pass. In Valdez, take a rafting or kayaking trip. Spend the night, then catch the ferry to Whittier, passing local landmarks like the Valdez Narrows, Columbia Glacier, and the infamous Bligh Reef where the Exxon Valdez came to grief in 1989. From Whittier, go through the tunnel to Seward Highway and head back to Anchorage.

Updated by Tom Reale

ANCHORAGE MAY DOMINATE THE REGION IN SIZE, recognition, and political clout, but don't let that mislead you into thinking Anchorage *is* South Central Alaska. The city functions as the gateway to some of Alaska's most spectacular parks and wilderness areas, most of which are accessible by floatplane, the Alaska Railroad, or car, and is a modern, urban environment amid historic ports, wilderness outposts, and fishing towns.

The city lies near the convergence of two of Alaska's most magnificent mountain systems. To the east of the city and sweeping on to the southwest are the Chugach Mountains, a young, active, and impressively rugged range notable for its high coastal relief. Near-mile-high valley walls and peaks rise almost directly from the sea. Across Cook Inlet to the southwest march the high volcanic peaks of the Alaska Range, part of the Pacific Ocean's great Ring of Fire, but snowcapped nonetheless. Farther north in the Alaska Range, and visible from Anchorage on clear days, shimmers Mt. McKinley, with Mt. Foraker at its shoulder—the towering granite giants of the North American continent. Also visible from town are the Talkeetna Range, to the northeast, and the Kenai Range, just across Turnagain Arm and forming the spine of Anchorage's playground, the Kenai Peninsula.

WORD OF MOUTH

"The best thing about Alaska is the no-billboard law on the highways, which results in stunning scenery. We had ten days of driving and not once did anyone even think to turn the radio on–that says a lot for how Alaska can really make a change in you." -Miss_Maple

South Central is bordered on the south and west by the port towns on the Gulf of Alaska, Prince William Sound, and Cook Inlet—Cordova, Valdez, Whittier, Seward, Seldovia, Kodiak, Homer, and Kenai—with their harbors, ferries, glaciers, and ocean life. Unlike the towns and cities of Interior Alaska, where the common theme of gold-rush history links most of the communities, South Central towns and cities have very different personalities. Kodiak, for example, is a busy commercial-fishing port, whereas Homer is a funky tourist town and artists' colony on beautiful Kachemak Bay. Then come those mountains, curled like an arm embracing the region. Talkeetna, the northern edge of the region, is where mountaineers gather to launch their assaults on towering Mt. McKinley. On the eastern border, the defunct copper mine outside McCarthy lies at the foot of the Wrangell Mountains.

Nature lovers can rejoice at the meeting of these mountain ranges, for they bring together a wide sampling of Alaska's flora and fauna. Dall sheep and mountain goats dance their way around the heights of the Chugach and Kenai mountains. Tree species mingle here, too, including three different varieties of spruce—Sitka, black, and white. You'll see larch, birch, cottonwood, and aspen turn golden in the crisp days of late summer and early autumn. South Central is also Alaska's farm country. In the Matanuska-Susitna Valley, under an ever-present summertime sun, 75-pound cabbages are common.

Exploring South Central

South Central Alaska can be broken down into three general subregions—the towns and bays of Prince William Sound, communities south of Anchorage on the Kenai Peninsula, and communities north of Anchorage in the Matanuska-Susitna (Mat-Su) Valley and beyond. The region is ideal for exploring by boat, train, car, RV, or plane. All but a couple of the coastal communities are on the road system. For the most part, roads have two lanes and are paved. Traffic, especially on the Kenai Peninsula, can be frustrating on summer weekends, so give yourself plenty of time; better yet, try to travel midweek. Be especially wary of impatient drivers passing in inappropriate places—this is a perpetual problem on Alaska's rudimentary road system. Long summer days give you plenty of daylight for exploring.

PRINCE WILLIAM SOUND

The sound covers some 15,000 square mi—15 times the size of San Francisco Bay. It receives an average of 150 inches of rain a year and is home to more than 150 glaciers, 20 of them reaching tidewater. Along its shoreline are quiet bays, trickling waterfalls, and hidden coves perfect for camping. In addition to hosting brown and black bears, gray wolves, and Sitka blacktail deer, the sound thrives with a variety of birds and all manner of marine life, including salmon, halibut, humpback and killer whales, sea otters, sea lions, and porpoises. Bald eagles often soar overhead or perch in tall trees. The sound was heavily damaged by the *Exxon Valdez* oil spill in 1989. The oil has sunk into the beaches below the surface and is sometimes uncovered after storms and high tides. What lasting effect this lurking oil will have on the area is still being studied and remains the topic of much debate.

Unless you have access to a boat and are competent in its use in challenging conditions, the sound is best explored by charter boat or guided excursion out of Whittier, Cordova, or Valdez. Even though the waters are mostly protected, open stretches are common, and the always fickle Alaska weather can fool even experienced boaters. From the road system, Whittier and Valdez are your best bets for finding charter outfits to explore the sound.

Chugach State Park

❶ *Bordering Anchorage to the east.*

Chugach State Park is Alaska's most accessible wilderness. Nearly half a million acres in size, the park rises from the coast to more than 8,000 feet, with mountains bearing such colorful names as Williwaw Peak, Temptation Peak, Mt. Magnificent, and Mt. Rumble. The park has nearly 30 trails—from 2 mi to 30 mi long—totaling more than 150 mi, suitable for shorter hikes, weeklong backpacking, and mountain biking. Easy-to-follow cross-country routes extend from one park entrance to another, allowing multiday excursions and a variety of loop trips. This is not your typical urban park—it's real wilderness, home to Dall sheep, mountain

South Central Alaska
ALASKA
Denali National Park and Preserve
Denali (Mt. McKinley)
Denali State Park 21
Petersville
Trapper Creek
Talkeetna 20
Independence Mine State Historical Park
Hatcher Pass Rd.
Willow
Wasilla 19
Palmer 18
Sutton
Glenn Hwy.
Matanuska R.
Eagle River
Anchorage
Chugach State Park 1
Hope 7
Girdwood
Portage
Whittier 4
Portage Glacier 3
Cooper Landing 10
Seward 8
Kenai Fjords National Park 9
Resurrection Bay
Montague Island
Kenai National Wildlife Refuge 11
Kenai & Soldotna 12
Sterling
Seward Hwy.
Sterling Hwy.
Clam Gulch
Ninilchik
Anchor Point
KENAI PENINSULA
Homer 13
Kachemak Bay
Tutka Bay
Halibut Cove
Seldovia 15
Kachemak Bay State Park & State Wilderness Park 14
Cook Inlet
Lake Clark National Park & Preserve 17
Nondalton
Newhalen
Iliamna Lake
Dillingham
Naknek
King Salmon
Bristol Bay
Edegik
Katmai National Park
Becharof Lake
Shelikof Strait
Shuyak Is.
Shuyak Island State Park
Afognak Island
Chugach National Forest
Port Lions
Kodiak
Kodiak Island 16
Kodiak National Wildlife Refuge
ALASKA RANGE
Parks Hwy.
ALASKA RR
Cantwell
Denali Hwy. (closed in winter)
Paxson
Richardson Hwy.
Chistochina
Slana
Tok
Northway
Beaver Creek
Nabesna
Gakona
Glennallen 22
Copper Center
Chitina
WRANGELL MOUNTAINS
Kennicott
McCarthy
Chitina River
Copper River
CHUGACH MOUNTAINS
COLUMBIA GLACIER
Richardson Hwy
Valdez 5
Chugach National Forest 2
Cordova 6
Prince William Sound
Wrangell–St. Elias National Park & Preserve 23
Mt. Logan
Mt. St. Elias
CANADA
U.S.A.
YUKON
Burwash Landing
Alaska Hwy.
Yakutat
Cape St Elias
Gulf of Alaska
0
100 miles
0
150 km
KEY
Ferry Lines
Rail Lines

goats, brown bears, and several packs of wolves who reside on the edge of Anchorage. Many of the trails were blazed by early miners who usually sought the easiest passes. There are also some comfortable roadside campgrounds for people traveling by car or bicycle. Trailheads are scattered around the park's perimeter from Eklutna Lake, 30 mi north of Anchorage, to the trailhead for the Crow Pass Trail near Girdwood, 37 mi to the south. Some of the more popular trailheads charge a daily parking fee of $5. The Eagle River Nature Center or the park headquarters near Potter Marsh 12 mi south of town has park information.

JUST BACK FROM ALASKA

"Anchorage's backyard is huge, vibrant, and accessible Chugach State Park. On my first trip to Alaska, as our plane descended toward the city, we had midnight-sun-infused views of the mountains. Magnificent."
–Heidi Johansen, Fodor's Editor

5

The views from high perches in this park are heady. You can look down on the city of Anchorage, observe the great tides in Cook Inlet, gaze north toward Mt. McKinley, or delineate the grand procession of snowy peaks across the inlet, marching down the Alaska Peninsula, including Mt. Spurr, Mt. Redoubt, and Mt. Iliamna, all active volcanoes. The most frequently climbed alpine perch in Alaska is **Flattop Mountain,** on Chugach Park's western edge, ascended by hikers of all abilities. The trailhead is at the Glen Alps parking lot on the hillside above town. Even though you might see hikers heading up the trail in everything from full-on climbing gear to flip-flops, be advised that a trek to the peak can be challenging. Wear sturdy hiking footwear and attire, carry water and a snack, and prepare for sudden weather changes. Every year people are rescued from this trail because they underestimated its potential for calamity, so be prepared and don't become a statistic. ✉ *Headquarters, Mile 115, Seward Hwy.* 📫 *HC 52, Box 8999, Indian 99540* ☎ *907/345–5014* 🌐 *www.dnr.state.ak.us/parks/units/chugach* 🎫 *$5 parking.*

Eagle River Road leads 12 mi into the mountains from the bedroom community of Eagle River. The **Eagle River Nature Center,** at the end of Eagle River Road, has wildlife displays, telescopes for wildlife spotting, hiking trails, and volunteers to answer questions, lead hikes, and host naturalist programs throughout the year. A cabin that sleeps eight, and a pair of yurts (insulated tents) that sleep four and six are available for rental. Cost is $65 per night, and a hike in of about 1½ mi is required. Amenities include woodstoves, firewood, and outdoor latrines. ✉ *Eagle River Rd.* ☎ *907/694–2108* 🌐 *www.ernc.org* 🎫 *$5 parking* ⏲ *May and Sept., Tues.–Sun. 10–5; June–Aug., Sun.–Thurs. 10–5, Fri. and Sat. 10–7; Oct.–Apr., Fri.–Sun. 10–5.*

Camping

⛺ **Alaska State Park Campgrounds.** You'll find three road-accessible campgrounds in Chugach Park: at Eklutna Lake, Bird Creek, and Eagle River. All are within a short drive from Anchorage. The sites are available on a first-come, first-served basis. The Eklutna Lake site has a ranger station, and Eagle River has running water and a dump station. Fishing is best at Bird Creek during the annual silver salmon run in July and August, and there are several hiking trails of varying degrees of difficulty at Eklutna. *Pit toilets, drinking water, fire grates, picnic tables* *135 sites* *Alaska State Parks, HC 52, Box 8999, Indian 99540* *907/345–5014* *www.dnr.state.ak.us/parks/units/chugach/facility.htm* *$10 for Bird Creek and Eklutna, $15 for Eagle River* *No credit cards* *Closed roughly Oct.–Apr.*

Sports, the Outdoors & Guided Tours

Main trailheads in the park are at the top of O'Malley, Huffman, and DeArmoun roads; south of Anchorage at Potter Valley, McHugh Creek, and Bird Ridge on the Seward Highway; and to the north of town at Arctic Valley Road (6 mi out) and Eagle River Road (13 mi out). The **Little Rodak Trail** is less than 1 mi long and has a viewing platform that overlooks the Eagle River valley. **Albert Loop Trail** behind the nature center has markers that coordinate with a self-guided hike along its 3-mi route; pick up a brochure at the Eagle River Nature Center.

CLIMB IT

Every summer solstice (falling near June 21–22), locals climb to the top of Flattop Mountain to celebrate the longest day of the year.

HIKING Several trailheads along the edge of Anchorage lead into the park and its 3,000- to 5,000-foot-tall peaks. The park's most popular day climb is **Flattop Mountain,** which towers 3,500 feet above sea level. It's reached via the Glen Alps Trail Head off Upper Huffman Road on Anchorage's Hillside. A 1-mi trail climbs 1,300 feet from the Glen Alps parking area to the top. On a bright summer day you'll encounter plenty of company. Bring along a daypack with plenty of water and energy bars, a rainproof jacket, and wear good hiking boots.

MOUNTAIN BIKING Mountain biking has become very popular in the park, and most, but not all, trails are open to bikes; check the signs and symbols at the trailheads if in doubt. The Powerline Pass trail from the Glen Alps parking lot is wide and well-maintained for bikes. If your lungs and legs are up to it, you can pedal all the way to the pass for a spectacular view. Along the way the observant visitor can almost always spot moose and Dall sheep, and the lucky few will see brown and black bears, and maybe even a wolf or two. **Sunshine Sports** (1231 W. Northern Lights Blvd. 907/272–6444) rents mountain bikes.

Chugach National Forest

❷ *40 mi east of Anchorage.*

Sprawling east of Chugach State Park, Chugach National Forest encompasses nearly 6 million acres to embrace a major part of the Kenai Peninsula as well as parts of Prince William Sound. It's the second-largest national forest in the United States, exceeded in size only by the Tongass in Southeast Alaska.

Recreational opportunities here include hiking, camping, backpacking, fishing, boating, mountain biking, horseback riding, hunting, rock climbing, flightseeing, and, in the winter, snowshoeing, cross-country skiing, ice climbing, snowmobiling, and dog mushing. Hiking trails offer easy access into the heart of the forest. You can go for a short walk in the woods, pack a lunch and go for a hike looking for birds and wildlife, or embark on a multiday backpacking excursion. You can also take the opportunity to fish a backcountry lake or just indulge yourself in a part of Alaska that's seldom seen by visitors. At all but the most popular trailheads, a five-minute stroll down a wooded trail leads you to the sights, smells, and tranquillity of backcountry Alaska.

The Seward Highway between Anchorage and Seward has a number of trail access points. (Check the highway for mile markers, with the distance measured from Seward.) At Mile 63.7 south of Turnagain Pass is the turnoff to the Johnson Pass Trail, a relatively flat trail to walk. Seven miles farther south, take the Hope Highway 18 mi to its end and find the Porcupine Campground. From there, the Gull Rock Trail follows the shore of Turnagain Arm for 5 mi, offering scenic views across the Arm and the chance to spot beluga whales as they forage for salmon. Farther south from the Hope cutoff on the Seward Highway at Mile 23.1, the Ptarmigan Creek trail starts at the campground and climbs into the mountains, ending next to a placid lake surrounded by snowy peaks.

Chugach National Forest is the second-largest national forest in the United States, exceeded in size only by the Tongass in Southeast Alaska.

⚠ **Be prepared to be self-sufficient when entering Chugach Forest. Trailheads typically offer nothing more than a place to park and perhaps an outhouse. Running water, trail maps, and other amenities that you may have come to expect when visiting national forests in the Lower 48 are not available here.** Also, be "bear aware" whenever you travel in bear country—and all of Alaska is bear country (⇨ *Welcome to Bear Country,* Chapter 7). Be aware of your surroundings, and make noise when traveling, especially in areas of reduced visibility. Bears will most likely make themselves scarce as long as they've got some advance warning of your arrival.

For information on recreational opportunities in the forest, call **forest headquarters** (☎ 907/743–9500 Anchorage) or the **Alaska Public Lands Information Center** (☎ 907/271–2737 🌐 www.nps.gov/aplic).

Where to Stay

¢ **U.S. Forest Service Cabins.** Along trails, near wilderness alpine lakes, in coastal forests, and on saltwater beaches, these rustic cabins offer retreats for the solo hiker or a group of friends. Some cabins are built of logs, and some are A-frames. Most have tables, chairs, wood-burning stoves, and bunks but no electricity, running water, or bedding. Many require a fly-in or boat ride, although some can be reached by car and then on foot. If you're suitably equipped and sufficiently adventurous, these cabins are Alaska's best bargain for getting away from town and enjoying backcountry wilderness while still having a roof over your head.

877/444–6777 reservations www.reserveusa.com 41 cabins D, MC, V.

CAMPING **U.S. Forest Service Campgrounds.** The Forest Service maintains 18 campgrounds, 14 of them road-accessible, within Chugach National Forest. The campgrounds do not have hookups for RVs. The Russian River Campground has a three-day limit during salmon-fishing season in June and July. Most have sites suitable for RVs as well as tents. Reservations (for a fee) are accepted at only five campgrounds—Cooper Creek South, Ptarmigan Creek, Russian River, Trail River, and Williwaw. *Pit toilets, picnic tables, fire grates, drinking water 414 tent and RV sites 877/444–6777 www.reserveusa.com $35–$45 (depending on site size) D, MC, V.*

Sports, the Outdoors & Guided Tours

★ **Resurrection Pass Trail,** a 38-mi-long backpacking trail through the Chugach National Forest, draws hikers and backpackers from around the world for its colorful wildflowers in spring and summer and the chance to spot wildlife. Moose, caribou, Dall sheep, mountain goats, black and brown bears, wolves, coyotes, and lynx all traverse the forest. Carry binoculars for the best wildlife-viewing opportunities. Scan your surroundings frequently for movement or anything that doesn't look like a rock, a bush, or a tree.

The northern end of the trail starts south of the town of Hope, following an old mining trail through the Kenai Mountains to its end near the town of Cooper Landing. Side trails lead to trailheads along the Seward Highway at Summit Creek and Devil's Pass Creek. The well-maintained trail offers easy access to open country above the tree line. Besides U.S. Forest Service cabins, the Forest Service has provided several "official" campsites along the trail where you'll find a cleared patch of ground and a fire ring; however, you're free to pitch your tent wherever you like.

Portage Glacier

❸ *54 mi southeast of Anchorage.*

Portage Glacier is one of Alaska's most frequently visited tourist destinations. A 6-mi side road off the Seward Highway leads to the **Begich-Boggs Visitor Center** (907/783–2326 www.fs.fed.us/r10/chugach/chugach_pages/bbvc), on the shore of Portage Lake and named after two U.S. congressmen who disappeared on a small-plane journey out of Anchorage in 1972. The center is staffed by Forest Service personnel, who can help plan your trip and explain the natural history of the area. A film on glaciers is shown hourly, and icebergs sometimes drift down to the center from Portage Glacier.

The glacier has receded from view in recent years, as have most of the glaciers in Alaska. If you want to see the glacier close-up, the Gray Line ★ tour on the ***Ptarmigan*** is the way to go. The view of Portage Lake and the surrounding peaks and hanging glaciers (the ones high up that terminate at the tops of cliffs), is spectacular, especially on a sunny day when the icy blue hues of the glaciers shine through.

The mountains surrounding Portage Glacier are covered with smaller glaciers. A 1-mi hike west brings you to the **Byron Glacier** overlook. The glacier is notable for its accessibility—it's one of the few places where you can hike onto a glacier from the road system. In summer, naturalists lead free weekly treks in search of microscopic ice worms.

Several hiking trails are accessible from the Seward Highway, including the Old Johnson Trail and the path up Bird Ridge. Both offer spectacular views of **Turnagain Arm,** where explorer Captain Cook searched for the Northwest Passage. Local lore has it that the Arm is so named because Cook entered it repeatedly, only to be forced to turn back by the huge tide. The tide is so powerful it sometimes rushes up the arm as a tidal bore—a wall of water that goes up an inlet. During the summer months, beluga whales are frequent visitors to the Arm as they patrol the muddy waters in search of salmon and hooligan, a variety of smelt. The whales travel in pods of adult and juvenile animals, the adults distinguishable by their bright white color. They're smaller than other whales that frequent Alaska's coastal waters, reaching only 15 feet in length and weighing up to a ton. When the tide is high and the surface of the water is calm, belugas are often spotted from the highway, frequently causing traffic jams as tourists and residents alike pull off the road for a chance to view the whales as they travel up and down the shoreline. Also, keep an eye out for black bears in all the Portage side valleys in the summer.

5

Alaska Wildlife Conservation Center is a 144-acre drive-through wildlife center just before the Portage Glacier turnoff. Moose, bison, elk, caribou, Sitka black-tailed deer, musk ox, great horned owls, a brown bear, and a bald eagle, many of them orphaned in the wild, now live in the park. There are also snack and gift shops. ✉ *Mile 79, Seward Hwy.* ☎ *907/783–2025* 🌐 *www.alaskawildlife.org* *$7.50* *May–Sept., daily 8–8; Oct.–Apr., daily 10–dusk.*

Little remains of the community of **Portage** as a result of the 1964 earthquake. The ghost forest of dead spruce in the area was created when the land subsided by 6 to 10 feet after the quake, and salt water penetrated inland from Turnagain Arm, killing the trees. A tumbledown building or two still stand along the highway, and there's a café at the turnoff to Portage Glacier.

EN ROUTE

On your way to Portage, look for **Indian Valley Meats** (✉ Huot Circle, 23 mi south of Anchorage on Seward Hwy. at Mile 103.9 ☎ 907/653–7511 🌐 www.indianvalleymeats.com), where workers sell the smoked salmon and musk ox, reindeer, and buffalo sausage made on the premises. They'll also smoke, can, and package the fish you've caught and arrange for shipping anywhere in the world.

Sports, the Outdoors & Guided Tours

NOVA (✉ Mile 76.2, Glenn Hwy. ☎ 800/746–5753 🌐 www.novalaska.com) has been guiding residents and visitors since 1975. The company conducts river rafting, glacier hiking, fishing, and backcountry combo trips from its office in tiny Chickaloon between Palmer and Glennallen.

BOATING **Gray Line of Alaska** (☎ 907/277–5581 or 800/544–2206 🌐 www.graylinealaska.com) leads summer boat tours (from mid-May to mid-September) along the face of Portage Glacier aboard the 200-passenger *Ptarmigan* for $29.

ROCK & ICE CLIMBING For information about rock- and ice-climbing activities, check with the folks at the **Alaska Rock Gym** (✉ 4840 Fairbanks St., Anchorage ☎ 907/562–7265 🌐 www.alaskarockgym.com). Local climbers have set routes along the Seward Highway south of town that are close to Anchorage.

Whittier

❹ *60 mi south of Anchorage.*

Whittier serves as an access point for those who want to visit Prince William Sound, and as a cruise-ship port. In years past, the only way to get to the town was by boat or through a pair of railroad tunnels through the surrounding mountains. Things have changed quite a bit in the last few years, however, and now the tunnel into town is a combination rail and highway road. Travel hours are restricted, so it's not always possible to just breeze into and back out of Whittier. Tolls through the tunnel are $12 for passenger vehicles and $20 to $35 for RVs and trailers; waits of up to an hour are possible, and summer hours are from 6 AM until 11 PM. (For current tunnel info and schedules, check www.tunnel.alaska.gov.) Along with the return of cruise ships to the port after a long respite, the town is looking forward to increased visitor traffic. There's a small-boat harbor; a cruise-ship terminal and dock; a ferry terminal for trips to Valdez, Seward, and Cordova; fishing and sightseeing charter companies; and sea-kayak rentals and tours. A few restaurants and shops surround the harbor, but lodging facilities are limited.

The most charitable description of the town is that it's unlovely. The dominant structure in town and home to almost all of the local inhabitants is a large World War II–era apartment building known as Begich Towers. Due to its recent paint job it no longer resembles a structure from the Russian gulag, but the rest of the buildings in town are a hodgepodge of hastily erected and largely unplanned businesses, many surrounding a single parking lot. Weather is also a bit of a problem here. The annual precipitation in nearby Anchorage is a mere 16 inches per year, but once you pass through the tunnel to the sound, that figure jumps more than tenfold to 200 inches.

However, the view looking away from Whittier on a clear day is jaw-droppingly gorgeous. The surrounding mountain peaks cradle alpine glaciers, and when the summer weather melts off the huge winter snow load, you can catch glimpses of the brilliant blue ice underneath. Sheer cliffs drop into Passage Canal and provide nesting places for flocks of black-legged kittiwakes, sea otters and harbor

WORD OF MOUTH

"Whittier is a great place to access Prince William Sound. Great fishing, glaciers, and whales. But staying in the town may be a little boring." –alaskalocal seals cavort in the small-boat harbor, and salmon return to spawn in nearby streams. A short boat ride out into the sound reveals tidewater glaciers, and an alert wildlife watcher can catch sight of mountain goats clinging to the mountainsides and black bears patrolling the beaches and hillsides in their constant search for food. Waterborne traffic includes commercial fishing boats, charter boats, cruise ships, tugboats, and the Alaska state ferry. It can be an amazingly memorable place.

Where to Stay & Eat

¢–$$$$ ✕ **Varly's Swiftwater Seafood.** Place your order at the window and then grab a seat at the counter and wait for your food. There's outdoor seating that overlooks the small-boat harbor. Menu items include homemade chowders, hand-battered seafood, peel-and-eat shrimp, burgers, and chicken. A smoked prime rib dinner is served on Friday and Saturday nights. ✉ *Harbor Loop* ☎ *907/472–2550* ▭ *MC, V* ⊗ *Closed mid–Sept.–mid-May.*

5

$ ✕ **Tunnel's End Café.** The café is primarily a breakfast and lunch joint, but owner and waitress Jo Anne also serves up a diner-style dinner, with meat loaf, seafood, burgers, and sandwiches. Breakfast and lunch items take up a couple of pages of the menu, with breakfast burritos, omelets, and pancakes, and lunches consisting of Philly cheesesteaks, burgers, hot dogs, and deli sandwiches. A cute little dining room has American farmhouse–style furnishings and a fireplace, and you can receive takeout and espresso from the order window. ✉ *12 Harbor Loop Dr.* ☎ *907/472–3000* ▭ *MC, V.*

$–$$$$ **June's Whittier Condo Suites.** June's rents out 10 condominiums in the Begich Towers building, half with bay views, half with mountain views. There's a large variety of room sizes and types—some that can accommodate large groups. June's also operates Bread-n-Butter Charters, which can arrange fishing or sightseeing tours and even overnight trips into the sound. ✉ *Begich Towers, Kenai St.* 📫 *Box 715, 99693* ☎ *888/472–2396* 🌐 *www.breadnbuttercharters.com* *10 rooms* *Kitchens, microwaves, refrigerators, cable TV, in-room VCRs, no-smoking rooms; no a/c* ▭ *AE, MC, V* *CP.*

WORD OF MOUTH

"We took a private charter out of Whittier (strange little community). It was arranged through www.breadnbuttercharters.com. It was magnificent day: the Captain prepared a delicious onboard lunch while my children kayaked and explored the glaciers–absolutely amazing." -visormom

$ **Soundview Getaway.** When the Begich Towers building was used by the military during the war, the Bachelor Officer's Quarters were home to soldiers stationed in Whittier. Today these rooms have been refurbished as B&B condos with full kitchens and full baths. The larger rooms sleep four, and two smaller rooms can be joined as a suite sleeping up to six. ✉ *Begich Towers, Kenai St., Whittier* 📫 *5800 E. 142nd Ave., Anchorage 99516* ☎ *800/515–2358, 907/472–2358, or 907/440–9114* 🌐 *www.soundviewalaska.com* *5 rooms* *Microwaves, cable TV, in-room VCRs; no a/c, no smoking* ▭ *AE, MC, V* *CP.*

Sports, the Outdoors & Guided Tours

BOATING & WILDLIFE VIEWING

Alaska Sea Kayakers (☎ 877/472–2534 or 907/440–4155 🌐 www.alaskaseakayakers.com) can supply sea kayaks and gear for exploring Prince William Sound and also conducts guided day trips, multiday tours, instruction, and boat-assisted and boat live-aboard kayaking trips. The company practices a leave-no-trace camping ethos, and is very conscientious about avoiding bear problems by using preventive measures. Trips are May through September 15.

The small fleet of boats at **Honey Charters** (☎ 907/472–2493 🌐 www.honeycharters.com) is available for charter, sightseeing, and sea-kayak drop-offs. Groups of up to 30 people can join trips through Prince William Sound; you can also get transport to Cordova and Valdez. Standard sightseeing trips run from three to six hours, and custom tours are available on request.

Major Marine Tours (☎ 800/764–7300 or 907/274–7300 🌐 www.majormarine.com) runs a five-hour cruise from Whittier that visits two tidewater glaciers. The waters of Prince William Sound are well protected and relatively calm, making this a good option if you're inclined toward queasiness. Seals, sea lions, and sea otters are frequently sighted, and several species of whales and porpoises inhabit the area as well. Seabirds, waterfowl, and bald eagles are always present, and the chance to get close to the enormous walls of ice of the glaciers is not to be missed. The cruise is $99 per person, and runs from mid-May to mid-September. You can opt for an onboard meal for $15.

From Whittier, tours with **Prince William Sound Cruises and Tours** (✉ Pier 1, Whittier ☎ 800/992–1297 or 907/472–2410 🌐 www.princewilliamsound.com) travel through the sheltered bays, fjords, and canals of Prince William Sound. You can view glaciers, seabirds, and wildlife such as seals, sea lions, sea otters, whales, bears, and mountain goats. The company can arrange transportation from Anchorage to Whittier by bus or rail, or you can drive to Whittier in your own vehicle. Prices vary according to length of trip and travel options; cruises take place mid-May through mid-September.

Retired marine biologist Gerry Sanger runs a number of tours in his six-passenger, 30-foot boat with **Sound Eco Adventures** (☎ 888/471–2312 or 907/472–2312 🌐 www.soundecoadventure.com) from March through mid-November. He'll take you whale-watching, glacier-viewing, or on a general wildlife-viewing trip for anywhere from 5 to 10 hours. He can also transport sea-kayakers, cabin renters, and anyone else needing a charter boat out of Whittier. Group discounts are available, and longer trips include lunch and a beach stop.

Phillips' Cruises and Tours has been running the **26 Glacier Cruise** (☎ 800/544–0529 or 907/276–8023 🌐 www.26glaciers.com) through Prince William Sound for many years. The high-speed catamaran covers 135 mi of territory in 4½ hours, leaving Whittier and visiting Port Wells, Barry Arm, and College and Harriman fjords. The boat is a very stable platform, and even visitors who might be prone to seasickness can take this cruise with no ill effects. The heated cabin has large windows, upholstered booths, and wide aisles. There's a snack bar and a saloon on board, and wildlife encounters are commonplace. You can drive to Whittier and catch the boat at the dock, or you can arrange with the company to travel from Anchorage by rail or bus. The trip is $139 per person; tours are given May through September.

Valdez

5 *6 hrs northeast of Whittier by water, 304 mi east of Anchorage.*

Valdez (pronounced val-*deez*) is the largest of the Prince William Sound communities. This year-round ice-free port was originally the entry point for people and goods going to the Interior during the gold rush. Today that flow has been reversed, with Valdez Harbor being the southern terminus of the trans-Alaska pipeline, which carries crude oil from Prudhoe Bay and surrounding oil fields nearly 800 mi to the north. This region, with its dependence on commercial fishing, is still feeling the aftereffects of the massive oil spill in 1989. Much of Valdez looks modern because the business area was relocated and rebuilt after its destruction by the 1964 Good Friday earthquake. Even though the town is younger than the rest of developed Alaska, it's gradually acquiring a lived-in look.

If you're driving to Valdez, the route into and out of town is a stunning trip through the Thompson Pass area of the Chugach Range. Due to their proximity to coastal weather systems, these peaks and glaciers offer some of the best venues for extreme skiing and snowboarding in North America. In summer, you'll have the unique opportunity to drive to roadside glaciers and trailheads above the tree line.

Many Alaskan communities have summer fishing derbies, but Valdez may hold the record for the number of such contests, stretching from late May into September for halibut and various runs of salmon. If you go fishing, by all means enter the appropriate derby. Every summer the newspapers run sob stories about tourists who landed possible prizewinners but couldn't share in the glory because they hadn't forked over the five bucks to officially enter the contest. The **Valdez Silver Salmon Derby** is held the entire month of August. Fishing charters abound in this area of Prince William Sound, and for good reason: these fertile waters provide some of the best saltwater sportfishing in all of Alaska.

A pleasant attraction on a rainy day, if you ever tire of gazing at the 5,000-foot mountain peaks surrounding Valdez, is the **Valdez Museum.** It explores the lives, livelihoods, and events significant to Valdez and surrounding regions. Exhibits include a restored 1880s Gleason & Baily hand-pump fire engine, a 1907 Ahrens steam fire engine, a 19th-century saloon, information on the local native peoples, and an exhibit on the 1989 oil spill. Every summer the museum hosts an exhibit of quilts and fiber arts made by local and regional artisans. At a separate site, a 35-by-40-foot model of

> **WORD OF MOUTH**
>
> "We would definitely drive the Richardson Highway to Valdez again. It's a beautiful drive with incredible scenery." –chelsea

Historical Old Town Valdez (✉ 436 Hazlet Ave.) depicts the original town, which was devastated by the 1964 earthquake. There's also an operating seismograph and an exhibit on local seismic activity. A Valdez History Exhibits Pass includes admission to both the museum and the annex. ✉ *217 Egan Dr.* ☎ *907/835–2764* 🌐 *www.valdezmuseum.org* *$5* *June–Aug., daily 9–6; Sept.–May, weekdays 1–5, Sat. noon–4.*

NEED A BREAK?

If you need a shot of caffeine or Internet to keep you going (and keep you connected to "the Outside"), the espresso shop Bad Ass Coffee (✉ 201 North Harbor Dr. ☎ 907/835–2560) is just the ticket.

★ A visit to **Columbia Glacier,** which flows from the surrounding Chugach Mountains, certainly should be on the agenda. Its deep aquamarine face is 5 mi across, and it calves icebergs with resounding cannonades. This glacier is one of the largest and most readily accessible of Alaska's coastal glaciers. The state ferry travels past the face of the glacier, and scheduled tours of the glaciers and the rest of the sound are available by boat and aircraft from Valdez and Whittier.

Where to Stay & Eat

If you roll into town without reservations, especially if it's after hours, stop at the **Valdez Visitor's Center** (✉ 200 Chenega St. ☎ 907/835–2984) on the corner of Fairbanks. They post vacancies in bed-and-breakfasts on the window when they close for the day, and there's a pay phone there so you can start making calls.

$$–$$$$ ✕ **Alaska's Bistro.** The view of the small-boat harbor is complemented inside by the nautical theme and color scheme. Local art adorns the walls, and the two-tier dining room guarantees a view for all. The house specialty is paella for two (or more); fresh local seafood dominates the menu. There's also a large selection of appetizers, salads, and poultry, pork, steaks, and pizza. The wine cellar includes more than 250 selections. ✉ *100 Fidalgo Dr.* ☎ *907/835–5688* *AE, MC, V.*

$–$$$ ✕ **Mike's Palace.** On the harbor, this convivial restaurant with Italian-diner decor is a local favorite. The pizza is terrific, but the menu also includes veal, beer-batter halibut, steaks, and Greek gyros. ✉ *201 N. Harbor Dr.* ☎ *907/835–2365* *MC, V.*

¢–$ ✕ **Alaska Halibut House.** At this very casual place you can order at the counter, sit at the Formica-covered tables, and check out the photos of local fishing boats. The battered halibut is excellent—light and not a bit greasy. There are other items on the menu, including homemade clam chowder, but if you're eating at the Halibut House, why try anything else? ✉ *208 Meals Ave.* ☎ *907/835–2788* *MC, V.*

$$$$ **Prince William Sound Lodge.** This fly-in lodge on a remote shore of northeastern Prince William Sound offers opportunities for a wide range of vacation activities, including hiking, bird-watching, wildlife-viewing, exploring nearby Alaska native villages, and the chance for some of the best silver salmon fishing in the state. You can also go halibut fishing, take seaplane rides, or join boat trips on a converted commercial fishing boat. Gourmet meals add to the list of attractions. One of the local bears just might amble past during your stay. Lodging price does not include the $150 (round-trip) per person floatplane flight to the lodge.

✉, *Ellamar* ✉ *3900 Clay Products Dr., Anchorage 99517* ☎ *907/248–0909 or 907/440–0909* 🌐 *www.princewilliamsound.us* *5 rooms* *Dining room, beach, boating, fishing; no a/c, no room phones, no room TVs, no smoking* 💳 *No credit cards* ⏲ *Closed late Sept.–mid-May* *FAP.*

$$ **Aspen Hotel Valdez.** The Aspen hotels are part of a small, local chain with hotels in Anchorage, Fairbanks, Juneau, and Soldotna, all with modern and up-to-date facilities. The owners pride themselves on hiring service-oriented and compassionate personnel. The hotel is within easy walking distance of shops, restaurants, and the small-boat harbor, the center of summertime activity. The business center and pool are especially noteworthy in small-town Alaska. ✉ *100 Meals Ave., 99686* ☎ *907/835–4445* 🌐 *www.aspenhotelsak.com/valdez.htm* *102 rooms* *Microwaves, refrigerators, cable TV, in-room VCRs, in-room data ports, pool, gym, hot tub, spa, laundry facilities, Wi-Fi, business services, meeting room, no-smoking rooms; no a/c* 💳 *AE, D, DC, MC, V* *CP.*

5

$$ **Best Western Valdez Harbor Inn.** Near the small-boat harbor, this hotel has an inlet from the sound complete with sea otters, seals, and waterfowl right outside the lobby windows, and visible from some of the rooms. The standard Best Western rooms have Alaska artwork. ✉ *100 Harbor Dr., Box 468, 99686* ☎ *907/835–3434 or 888/222–3440* 🌐 *www.bestwestern.com* *88 rooms* *Restaurant, room service, microwaves, refrigerators, cable TV, in-room data ports, exercise equipment, spa, laundry facilities, Wi-Fi, meeting room, some pets allowed, no-smoking rooms* 💳 *AE, D, DC, MC, V.*

$$ **Thompson Pass Mountain Chalet.** This rustic cabin in sub-alpine forest sits just off the trans-Alaska pipeline and within minutes of skiing and hiking at Thompson Pass. Open year-round, the chalet has a small kitchen and facilities for four, and the owners can direct you to the local hiking and ski trails, or for an additional fee, guide you on backcountry excursions. Ski season runs from mid-October to mid-May most years. Be advised that the narrow spiral staircase to the sleeping loft demands a bit of agility, but the view from the upstairs window is worth the trip. ✉ *Mile 19, Richardson Hwy., 99686* ☎ *907/835–4817* 🌐 *www.alaska.net/~chalet* *1 cabin* *Kitchen, Wi-Fi, cross-country skiing; no a/c, no room TVs, no smoking* 💳 *No credit cards* *CP.*

CAMPING **Bayside RV Park.** This full-service RV park with a few tent site areas has a panoramic view of the mountains and wide, crushed-stone parking spots. The folks here can help you book fishing and sightseeing trips with local charter outfits. *Flush toilets, full hookups, dump station, drinking water, guest laundry, showers, picnic tables, electricity, public telephone* *110 RV/tent sites* ✉ *230 E. Egan Dr., 99686* ☎ *888/835–4425 or 907/835-4425* 🌐 *www.baysiderv.com* *$18–$31 (depending on hookup capabilities)* 💳 *MC, V* ⏲ *May–Sept. 10.*

Sports, the Outdoors & Guided Tours

ADVENTURE If you want a taste of backcountry snowmobiling action, **Alaska Snow Safaris** (✉ 6543 Brayton Dr., Anchorage ☎ 907/868–7669 or 888/414–7669 🌐 www.snowmobile-alaska.com) has an enormous winter playground available near Valdez. From mid-February to the end of April, they'll take you into the wilderness on your machine or theirs to explore mile after mile of untouched, ungroomed snow. The trips are best enjoyed by intermediate- to advanced-level riders, but trips can be tailored to suit any level of expertise.

Anadyr Adventures (☎ 907/835–2814 or 800/865–2925 🌐 www.anadyradventures.com) offers sea-kayak trips into Prince William Sound. Guides will escort you on day trips, multiday camping trips, "mother ship" adventures based in a remote anchorage, or lodge-based trips for the ultimate combination of adventure by day and comfort by night. If you're already an experienced kayaker, they'll outfit you and you can travel on your own. Also available are guided hiking and glacier trips, ice caving at Valdez Glacier, and soft-adventure charter-boat trips in the sound. Anadyr can arrange water-taxi service to transport you to or from anyplace in the sound.

Whether you're looking for a full-on winter backcountry heli-ski excursion or a half-day walk on a glacier, **H2O Guides** (✉ 100 N. Harbor Dr. ☎ 907/835–8418 🌐 www.h2oguides.com) can hook you up. For most visitors, their day trips to Worthington Glacier State Park will suffice. They can set up any level of icy adventure you desire, from a half-day walk on the glacier to a full-day or multiday ice-climbing trip. Their office is in the lobby of the Best Western hotel, and they can also arrange fishing, flightseeing, and multiday, multisport trips as well.

BOATING & WILDLIFE VIEWING

Valdez-based **Columbia Glacier Wildlife Cruises/*Lu-Lu Belle*** (☎ 907/835–5141 or 800/411–0090 🌐 www.lulubelletours.com) leads small-group whale-watching, wildlife-viewing, and Columbia Glacier cruises.

Keystone Raft & Kayak Adventures (☎ 907/835–2606 or 800/328–8460 🌐 www.alaskawhitewater.com) provides all gear for guided half-day and full-day raft and kayak tours on rivers rated up to Class V in the Valdez and Copper River valley areas from mid-May to mid-September. They can also arrange longer expeditions for up to 10 days.

Stan Stephens Glacier & Wildlife Cruises (☎ 907/835–4731 or 866/867–1297 🌐 www.stanstephenscruises.com), based in Valdez, leads Prince William Sound glacier and wildlife-viewing cruises to Columbia and Meares glaciers from mid-May through mid-September. Their trips include narration on local commercial fishing operations as well as commentary on the Alyeska Pipeline terminal and history of defunct gold mines. The company is Alaskan owned and bills itself as "the local experts since 1971."

FLIGHTSEEING

Alpine Aviation Adventures (☎ 907/835–4304, 800/478–4304 in Alaska), based in Valdez, gives aerial tours of Columbia Glacier, Prince William Sound, and the Wrangell Mountains.

Cordova

❻ *6 hrs southeast of Valdez by water, 150 mi east of Anchorage by air.*

A small town with the spectacular backdrop of snowy Mt. Eccles, Cordova is the gateway to the Copper River Delta—one of the great birding areas of North America. Perched on Orca Inlet in eastern Prince

William Sound, Cordova began life early in the 20th century as the port city for the Copper River and Northwestern Railway, which was built to serve the Kennicott copper mines 191 mi away in the Wrangell Mountains. Since the mines and the railroad shut down in 1938, Cordova's economy has depended heavily on fishing. Attempts to develop a road along the abandoned railroad line connecting to the state highway system were dashed by the 1964 earthquake, so Cordova remains isolated. Access to the community is limited to airplane or ferry.

The **Cordova Museum** emphasizes native artifacts as well as pioneer, mining, and fishing history. Displays tell of early explorers to the area, native culture, the Copper River and Northwestern Railway/Kennicott Mine era, and the growth of the commercial fishing industry. Afternoon video programs and an informative brochure outline a self-guided walking tour of the town's historic buildings. Monthly evening programs and art exhibits are sponsored by the Historical Society. The gift shop sells masks, pottery, and children's and local history books. ✉ *622 1st St.* ☎ *907/424–6665* 🌐 *www.cordovamuseum.org* 🎫 *$1* 🕒 *Memorial Day–Labor Day, Mon.–Sat. 10–6, Sun. 2–4; Labor Day–Memorial Day, Tues.–Fri. 10–5, Sat. 2–5.*

5

Drive out of town along the Copper River Highway and visit the **Copper River Delta.** This 700,000-acre wetland is one of North America's most spectacular vistas. The two-lane highway crosses marshes, forests, streams, lakes, and ponds that are home to countless shorebirds, waterfowl, and other bird species. Numerous terrestrial mammals including moose, wolves, lynx, mink, and beavers live here as well, and the Copper River salmon runs are world famous. When the red and king salmon hit the river in the spring, there's a frantic rush to net the tasty fish and rush them off to waiting markets and restaurants all over the country.

FOR BIRDERS

At Mile 17 there's a turn-off to Alaganik Slough. This 5-mi road leads to a wheelchair-accessible boardwalk as well as covered viewing shelters, restrooms, and picnic areas. A dedicated bird-watcher can spend hours poking along the waterways and peering into the vegetation, seeking out rare and interesting avian species at every turn.

The **Million Dollar Bridge,** at Mile 48, was a railroad project completed in 1910 for the Copper River and Northwestern Railway to carry copper ore to market from the mines at Kennicott. Soon after construction was completed, the nearby Childs and Miles glaciers threatened to overrun the railroad and bridge. Although the glaciers stopped short of the railroad, the copper market collapsed in 1938, making the route economically obsolete. The far span of the bridge was toppled by the Good Friday earthquake in 1964 and has not been rebuilt. There's still occasional talk about restoring the bridge and punching a road through from Cordova to connect with the road system, but the money required has not been forthcoming.

From the end of the road you can view the **Childs Glacier.** Although there is no visitor center, a covered viewing area next to the bridge enables you to watch the face of the glacier and read the informational plaques while you wait for a huge chunk of ice to topple into the river. The waves produced by falling ice frequently wash migrating salmon onto the riverbank, and the local brown bears have been known to patrol the river's edge looking for an easy meal, so keep your eyes wide open.

Where to Stay & Eat

$–$$$ ✕ **Powder House Bar & Restaurant.** On clear summer evenings you can relax on the deck overlooking Eyak Lake at this roadside bar and enjoy whatever the cook's in the mood to fix: homemade soups, sandwiches, sushi, and seasonal seafood are all possibilities. If you're lucky or skillful in your fishing endeavors, the kitchen staff will cook your catch. On Friday and Saturday, shrimp and steak are added to the menu. ⊠ *Mile 2.1, Copper River Hwy.* ☎ *907/424–3529* ▭ *AE, D, MC, V.*

¢–$$ ✕ **Ambrosia.** Pastas, hamburgers, and steaks are served behind the storefront, but it's the hearty pizzas that have earned this place its reputation among locals. ⊠ *410 1st St.* ☎ *907/424–7175* ▭ *AE, MC, V.*

¢ ✕ **Killer Whale Café.** Have a breakfast of espresso and baked goods or an omelet at this café. For lunch you can choose from a deli menu of soups, salads, and sandwiches, followed by a fresh, homemade dessert. On the back balcony, tables overlook the harbor. ⊠ *507 1st St.* ☎ *907/424–7733* ▭ *MC, V* ⊗ *Closed Sun.*

$ ✕🏨 **Cordova Lighthouse Inn.** If you've ever dreamed of living in a bakery, here's your chance. This four-room inn is home to an artisan bakery and restaurant (¢–$$$) where everything is made from scratch. The restaurant serves breakfast and lunch only, along with a very creative and extensive menu of wood-fired pizzas. Two of the rooms have mountain views, but if at all possible, get one of the two with harbor views for the full Alaskan fishing-village ambience. ⊠ *112 Nicholoff Way, Box 1495, 99574* ☎ *907/424–7080* 🌐 *www.cordovalighthouseinn.com* *6 rooms* *Restaurant, cable TV, in-room data ports; no a/c, no room phones, no smoking* ▭ *MC, V.*

$–$$ ✕🏨 **Reluctant Fisherman Inn.** At this waterfront hotel and restaurant you can watch the commercial-fishing fleet and other maritime traffic sail by. Comfortable, nautical-theme rooms overlook the harbor, and native art and artifacts decorate the public spaces. The restaurant (¢–$$$$) serves local seafood, including a king salmon chili, as well as pastas and espresso. A new large, south-facing deck for alfresco dining overlooks the harbor. ⊠ *407 Railroad Ave., 99574* ☎ *907/424–3272 or 800/770–3272* *reluctantfishermaninn@ak.net* *41 rooms* *Restaurant, cable TV, in-room data ports, Wi-Fi, bar, laundry facilities, meeting rooms, airport shuttle; no a/c* ▭ *AE, MC, V.*

$–$$ 🏨 **Cordova Rose Lodge.** A truly unique lodge, the Cordova Rose sits on a barge on the Prince William Sound breakwater. There's a working lighthouse on the site, used by boats transiting the channel. The accommodations range from cabins to semiprivate to private rooms, and families and groups are especially welcomed. A large, hot breakfast is the order of the day, and dinner can be arranged if enough guests request it. Vacation packages including hiking, fishing, bird-watching, and wildlife viewing are also available. ⊠ *1315 Whitshed, Box 1494, 99574* ☎ *907/424–7673* 🌐 *www.cordovarose.com* *11 rooms, 2 cabins* *Dining* *room, kitchens, sauna, Internet, airport shuttle; no a/c, no phones in some rooms, no TV in some rooms, no smoking* ▭ *MC, V* 🍽 *BP.*

$ **Orca Adventure Lodge.** The list of activities at the lodge goes on and on: fishing, kayaking, river rafting, hiking, bear-viewing, flightseeing. There's also the opportunity to fly out to one of Orca's remote wilderness camps for fishing or just relaxing. The lodge is a converted cannery on the Cordova waterfront and it oozes old Alaska charm. ✉ *301 Orca Rd.* *Box 2105, 99574* ☎ *907/424–7249 or 866/424–6722* 🌐 *www.orcaadventurelodge.com* *23 rooms, 4 suites* *Restaurant, airport shuttle; no a/c, no room phones, no room TVs, no smoking* ▭ *AE, MC, V* ⏲ *Restaurant closed Oct.–May.*

¢–$ **Northern Nights Inn B&B.** Commanding a dramatic view of Orca Inlet just a couple of blocks above downtown Cordova, this bed-and-breakfast has rooms furnished with turn-of-the-20th-century antiques. If owner Becky Chapek doesn't have room for you, she'll serve as a valuable source of information on other B&Bs in town. She operates bus tours around town and to the Million Dollar Bridge, and she can transport you to and from the airport as well. She also operates Chinook Auto Rentals at the airport. ✉ *500 3rd St., Box 1564, 99574* ☎ *907/424–5356* 🌐 *www.northernnightsinn.com* *3 rooms, 1 suite* *Some kitchens, some microwaves, cable TV, some in-room VCRs, laundry facilities, car rental; no a/c* ▭ *AE, D, MC, V.*

5

¢ **U.S. Forest Service Cabins.** The Cordova Ranger District of the Chugach National Forest maintains a series of 18 backcountry cabins for rent. These cabins are very basic: four walls, roof, floor, wooden bunks, usually a woodstove, table, benches, counter space for preparing meals, and a pit toilet out back. There's no bedding, cooking utensils, electricity, or running water. Bring everything you need to be self-sufficient for your stay. Most of the cabins are accessible only by boat or floatplane, although the McKinley Trail cabin is accessible by motor vehicle on the Copper River Highway. Two others can be reached by hiking from the road. A map of the district and the cabin locations is available at www.fs.fed.us/r10/chugach/cordova/pages/cabins/cabmap.html. Rentals are arranged through a Forest Service concessionaire, ReserveUSA. Check the Web site for directions to each cabin. *18 cabins* ☎ *877/444–6777* 🌐 *www.reserveusa.com* ▭ *AE, D, MC, V.*

Shopping

Orca Book & Sound Co. (✉ 507 1st St. ☎ 907/424–5305) is much more than a bookstore. In addition to books, it sells music, art supplies, children's toys, and locally produced art. The walls often double as a gallery for local works or traveling exhibits, and the store specializes in old, rare, out-of-print, and first-edition books, especially Alaskana. ■ **TIP→ In the back is an espresso/smoothie bar; the upstairs area has wireless Internet access for a small fee. It's closed Sunday.**

Sports, the Outdoors & Guided Tours

Spring migration to the **Copper River Delta** provides some of the finest avian spectacles in the world. Species include the western sandpiper, American dipper, orange-crowned warbler, and short-billed dowitcher. Trumpeter swans and dusky Canada geese can also be seen. The **Copper River**

Delta Shorebird Festival (☎ 907/424–7260 🌐 www.cordovachamber.com), held the first week of May, includes five days of workshops and guided field trips. As many as 5 million birds, mostly western sandpipers and dunlins, descend on the Copper River Delta, feeding and resting on their long migration to their northern nesting grounds. This migration respite is critical for these birds, and the food they gather from the rich mudflats of the delta keeps them alive and healthy.

Alaskan Wilderness Outfitting Co. (☎ 907/424–5552 🌐 www.alaskawilderness.com) operates an air-taxi service out of Cordova and arranges fresh- and saltwater fly-out fishing experiences, from drop-offs to guided tours with lodge accommodations. They also offer floating cabins in Prince William Sound and a full-service lodge for silver salmon on the Tsiu River.

Cordova Air Service (☎ 907/424–3289, 800/424–7608 in Alaska) leads aerial tours of Prince William Sound on planes with wheels or floats.

Cordova Coastal Outfitters (☎ 800/357–5145 🌐 www.cordovacoastal.com) conducts half- and full-day sea-kayak tours. They rent kayaks, canoes, bikes, small motorboats, and camping and fishing gear, and can arrange custom tours to fit your desired level of activity. They also run half- and full-day wildlife/natural history tours on their 32-foot commercial fishing boat, observing local wildlife and the fishing fleet at work. If you rent a kayak or bring your own, they'll provide pick-up and drop-off service anywhere on the road system.

KENAI PENINSULA

The Kenai Peninsula, thrusting into the Gulf of Alaska south of Anchorage, is South Central's playground, offering salmon and halibut fishing, spectacular scenery, and wildlife viewing. Commercial fishing is important to the area's economy; five species of Pacific salmon run up the aqua-color Kenai River every summer. Campgrounds and trailheads for backwoods hiking are strung along the roads. Along the way, you can explore three major federal holdings on the peninsula—the western end of the sprawling Chugach National Forest, Kenai National Wildlife Refuge, and Kenai Fjords National Park.

Hope

7 *39 mi west of Portage, 87 mi south of Anchorage.*

The little gold-mining community of Hope is 87 mi south of Anchorage by road but just across Turnagain Arm. To visit, however, you must drive all the way around, as no ferry service exists. It's at the end of a 16-mi-long spur road, so it's not on the way to anywhere—you really have to go there on purpose. However, your reward is a quiet little community, accessible but not overrun with tourists, where the pace of life slows just a little. Hope was founded by miners in 1896 but now consists mainly of retirement homes for former Anchorage residents. The old log cabins and weathered frame buildings in the town center are favorite photography subjects. You'll find lots of gold-panning, fishing, and hiking opportunities here, and the northern trailhead for the 38-mi-long Resurrection Pass Trail is nearby. Contact the U.S. Forest Service for information on campgrounds, cabin rentals, and hikes in this area.

Where to Stay & Eat

¢–$$$ ✕ **Summit Lake Lodge.** One of the Kenai Peninsula's most popular roadside restaurants, the lodge has been satisfying the appetites of residents and visitors for more than 50 years. The building is made of local, hand-hewn spruce timbers, and the dining room has expansive windows to take in the view of Summit Lake and the mountains. Main courses include fresh seafood, pasta, and a nice selection of steaks. Desserts are worth stopping for even if you've already had dinner. ✉ *Mile 45.5, Seward Hwy., Moose Pass* ☎ *907/244–2031* 🌐 *www.summitlakelodge.com* ▭ *MC, V* ⊗ *Closed Oct.–mid-Apr.*

¢–$$ ✕ **Tito's Discovery Cafe.** When the "Original Tito's" restaurant burned down, uninsured, in 1999, the owner was faced with financial ruin. But this tiny community got together and put Tito back on his feet and rebuilt the restaurant. Today Tito's serves basic American roadhouse food, along with seafood pasta, the ubiquitous halibut, and fresh-baked pies. ✉ *Mile 16.5, Hope Hwy.* ☎ *907/782–3274* ▭ *MC, V.*

Hope is not on the way to anywhere—you really have to go there for a purpose. However, your reward is a quiet little community, accessible but not overrun with tourists.

$ ✕ **Bowman's Bear Creek Lodge.** Of the five cabins here, four are around a pond and one is down by the creek. Each is carpeted and has both a woodstove and an electric heater. Interior walls are chinked logs, beds are covered with colorful quilts, and the lighting fixtures are modeled after gold rush–era styles. The cabins vary in size, the largest sleeping up to six. A central bathhouse has hot showers and toilets. The lodge café ($–$$) serves breakfast, lunch, and dinner, with nightly dinner and pasta specials, local seafood, and smoked-salmon chowder every day (the specialty of the house). ■ TIP→ **Bowman's runs guided fishing and rafting trips, rents mountain bikes, and sets up a nightly campfire around the pond.** ✉ *Mile 15.9, Hope Hwy.* *Box 4, Hope 99605* ☎ *907/782–3141* 🌐 *www.bowmansbearcreeklodge.com* *5 cabins with shared bath* *Café, some pets allowed; no a/c, no room phones, no room TVs, no smoking* ▭ *MC, V.*

¢ ✕ **Seaview Cafe & Bar.** This rustic little establishment is situated where Resurrection Creek flows into Turnagain Arm. It has a café (¢–$) with outdoor seating, a bar, a campground and RV park ($5/night) on the property, and two cabins to rent. The rooms are very basic, but you've got a great view of the Arm and the Chugach Mountains, you can pan for gold or fish for trout and salmon in the creek, or you can just relax in the unhurried atmosphere of small-town Alaska. ✉ *Main St., Box 110, 99605* ☎ *907/782–3300* 🌐 *http://home.gci.net/~hopeak* *50 tent sites, 16 RV sites with hookups, 2 cabins* *Restaurant, some kitchens, fishing, bar; no a/c, no room phones, no room TVs* ▭ *MC, V* ⊗ *Closed mid-Sept.–mid-May.*

5

CAMPING **Coeur d'Alene Campground.** If you really want to get away from the civilized camping spots you'll find elsewhere, this place is for you. It sits high above the Resurrection Creek valley, quite literally in mountain-goat country. It's a great place for spotting goats on the nearby peaks, and numerous black bears frequent the area as well. The road up is a twisty 6-mi drive over areas not recommended for RVs or trailers. There's no water at the site, but the views of the Kenai Mountains are world-class. No reservations are taken for the site, and there's no charge for camping. From Hope take the Resurrection Creek road for 1⁶⁄₁₀ mi to the Palmer Creek Road, and head up the mountain. The road is frequently closed due to avalanches until mid- to late May. *Pit toilets, fire pits, picnic tables* *6 tent sites* *No phone* *Free* *Closed Oct.–Apr.*

Porcupine Campground. The highway dead-ends into this campground. You're right on the shore of Turnagain Arm, with access to the Gull Rock Trail along the shoreline. The trail is relatively flat as it traces the shore for 5 mi. Occasionally you can spot beluga whales as they prowl for salmon up and down the coast. Under no circumstances should you venture onto the mudflats at low tide—it's very dangerous out there, and chances for rescue if you're stranded are nil. Be careful! Some of the campsites overlook the Arm, but you'll have to be quick or lucky to snag one of these. *Pit toilets, drinking water, fire pits, picnic tables* *24 RV/tent sites* *Mile 17.8, Hope Hwy.* *No phone* *$10* *No credit cards* *Mid-May–mid-Sept.*

Seward

8 *74 mi south of Hope, 127 mi south of Anchorage.*

Fodor'sChoice ★ Seward, at the head of Resurrection Bay, was founded in 1903 when survey crews arrived at this ice-free port to begin planning for a railroad to the Interior. Since then the town has relied heavily on tourism and commercial fishing, and its harbor is important for loading coal bound for Asia. One of the peninsula's major communities, it lies at the south end of the Seward Highway, which connects with Anchorage and is the southern terminus of the Alaska Railroad. Seward also is the launching point for excursions into Kenai Fjords National Park, where you can spy calving glaciers, sea lions, whales, and otters.

Seward, like Valdez, was badly damaged by the 1964 earthquake. A movie illustrating the upheaval caused by the disaster is shown from Memorial Day until Labor Day, Monday through Saturday at 2 PM in the **Seward Community Library.** Russian icons and paintings by prominent Alaskan artists are on exhibit. *5th Ave. and Adams St.* *907/224–4082* *Movie $3* *Weekdays 10–9, Sat. 10–7.*

The **Seward Museum** displays photographs of the quake's damage, model rooms and artifacts from the early pioneers, and historical and

WORD OF MOUTH

"I would definitely take a cruise out of Seward, but even in June make sure to bring a jacket, a pair of gloves, and money for cocoa or coffee aboard the ship. You will love the cruise!" –tcapp current information on the Seward area. ✉ *336 3rd Ave., at Jefferson St.* ☎ *907/224–3902* *$3* ⏲ *Mid-May–Sept., daily 9–5; Oct.–mid-May, weekends noon–4. Hrs may vary seasonally; call for recorded information.*

The first mile of the historic original **Iditarod Trail** runs along the beach and makes for a nice, easy stroll, as does the city's printed walking tour—available at the visitor's bureau, the converted railcar at the corner of 3rd Avenue and Jefferson Street, or the Seward Chamber of Commerce Visitor Center at Mile 2 on the Seward Highway. For a different view of the town, drive out **Nash Road,** around Resurrection Bay, and see Seward as it appears nestled at the base of the surrounding mountains. If you drive south from the SeaLife Center for about 15 minutes, you'll reach **Miller's Landing,** a great place for camping, walking, kayaking, or a day trip.

WORD OF MOUTH

"On my last day in Seward, I went fishing (and caught another big salmon). Then we went to the Alaska SeaLife Center, which was really nice. We stopped at Exit Glacier, and it was fabulous and worth the time. We did the three easy trails: overlook, glacier, and nature walk. This is as close to a glacier as you'll come, don't miss it. We really enjoyed it." -birder

Fodor'sChoice ★ The **Alaska SeaLife Center** is a world-class research and visitor facility complete with massive cold-water tanks and outdoor viewing decks. The center performs cold-water research on fish, seabirds, and marine mammals, including harbor seals and sea lions. It also rehabilitates injured marine wildlife and provides educational experiences for the general public and school groups. The center was partially funded with reparations money from the *Exxon Valdez* oil spill. Films, hands-on activities, a gift shop, and behind-the-scenes tours ($12 and up) complete the offerings. ✉ *301 Railway Ave.* ☎ *907/224–6300 or 800/224–2525* 🌐 *www.alaskasealife.org* *$14* ⏲ *Apr. 15–Sept. 15 daily, 8–7; Sept. 16–Apr. 14, daily 10–5.*

★ A short walk from the parking lot along a paved path will bring you face to face with **Exit Glacier** (⇨ Kenai Fjords National Park), just outside Seward. Look for the marked turnoff at Mile 3.7 as you enter town or ask locals for directions. There's a small walk-in campground here, a ranger station, and access to the glacier. This mass of ice caps the Kenai Mountains, covering more than 1,100 square mi, and it oozes more than 40 glaciers from its edges and down the mountainsides. From Mile 3.7 you can also access **Harding Icefield.** The hike to the ice field from the parking lot is a 9-mi round-trip that gains 3,000 feet in elevation, so it's not for the timid or out of shape. But if you're game and feeling up to the task, the hike and views are, literally, breathtaking. Local wildlife of note includes mountain goats and bears both black and brown, so keep a sharp eye out for them. Once you reach the ice, don't travel across. Glacier ice is notoriously deceptive—the surface can look solid and unbroken, while underneath a thin crust of snow, crevasses lie in wait for the unwary.

Where to Stay & Eat

\$\$–\$\$\$\$ ✕ **Harbor Dinner Club.** Don't let the name deter you—it's not a private club. The dining room is broken up into small sections, and lots of green plants contribute to the intimate feel. Alaskan artwork, mostly with a nautical theme, adorns the walls. The large menu, complete with multipage wine list, features local seafood, fresh whenever possible (it's frozen during the off-season), as well as steaks. ✉ *220 5th Ave.* ☎ *907/224–3012* ▭ *AE, D, DC, MC, V.*

\$–\$\$\$\$ ✕ **Chinooks Waterfront Restaurant.** On the waterfront in the small-boat harbor, Chinooks has a dazzling selection of fresh seafood items, an extensive wine list, and a great view from the upstairs window seats. The theme is marine, with fish photos and carvings, antique fishing tackle, and mounted fish on the walls. Pasta dishes and a few beef specialties round out the menu. ✉ *1404 4th Ave.* ☎ *907/224–2207* ⊗ *Closed mid-Sept.–May.*

¢–\$\$\$\$ ✕ **Christo's Palace.** Serving a menu of Greek, Italian, Mexican, and seafood meals, this ornately furnished downtown restaurant is a surprisingly elegant hidden treasure. The nondescript facade belies the high, beamed ceilings, dark-wood accents, ornate chandeliers, and large, gorgeous mahogany bar reputed to have been built in the mid-1800s and imported from San Francisco. There's an extensive wine list to complement the menu, a decent selection of wines by the glass, and salads for those looking for lighter fare. For those less concerned with counting calories, meal portions are very generous, desserts are tempting, and there is a small selection of after-dinner cognacs. ✉ *133 4th Ave.* ☎ *907/224–5255* ▭ *MC, V.*

★ **\$\$–\$\$\$** ✕ **Ray's Waterfront.** True to its name, this dining spot has views of the bay and a small-boat harbor. Sea otters and sea lions have occasionally been known to swim right past the large picture windows. Seafood is the specialty here; the seafood chowder is a must-try. The walls are lined with stuffed and mounted fish so you can point to the kind you'd like to eat. ✉ *Small-boat harbor* ☎ *907/224–5606* ▭ *AE, D, MC, V* ⊗ *Closed Nov.–mid-Mar.*

¢ ✕ **Railway Cantina.** This little hole-in-the-wall near the small-boat harbor is a local favorite. A wide selection of burritos, quesadillas, and tacos incorporates local seafood and is supplemented by an array of hot sauces, many contributed by customers who bring back exotic items from their travels. Feel free to add to the collection. ✉ *1401 4th Ave.* ☎ *907/224–8226* ▭ *MC, V.*

\$ ✕🏨 **Salmon Bake Cabins.** Hidden from the main flow of tourist traffic along Exit Glacier Road, the Salmon Bake Restaurant (¢–\$\$\$) is a local favorite. The rough-hewn decor of the restaurant and the cabins fits in well with the forest environment. There's outdoor seating in the summer, dinner specials featuring local seafood, and Alaskan beers served in mason jars. The cabins have room for two to four adults. Each room has a microwave and refrigerator, and there's freezer storage available if you get lucky on your fishing trip. ✉ *Mile 0.5, Exit Glacier Rd., Box 3151, 99664* ☎ *907/224–4752 cabin rentals, 907/224–2204 restaurant* 🌐 *www.sewardalaskacabins.com* ⇆ *4 cabins* 👍 *Restaurant, microwaves, refrigerators, cable TV, some pets allowed; no a/c, no room phones, no smoking* ▭ *MC, V* ⊗ *Closed Sept. 11–Apr.*

$$$$ **Kenai Fjords Wilderness Lodge.** An hour's boat ride from Seward, this wilderness lodge sits within a quiet, forest-lined cove on Fox Island in Resurrection Bay. Built of local wood with natural finish on interior walls, each cabin has two beds, private baths with shower, propane stoves, and expansive views of the bay and mountains. Lodging rates include meals, boat transportation to the island, and a cruise of Kenai Fjords National Park. Meals are served family style in the main lodge. Hiking trails make it possible to explore the island. Guided kayak trips and coastal wildlife tours can also be arranged. *Fox Island 1304 4th Ave., 99664 907/224–8068 or 800/478–8068 www.kenaifjords.com 8 cabins Dining room, hiking, travel services; no a/c, no room phones, no room TVs, no smoking AE, D, MC, V Closed Sept.–May FAP.*

¢–$$$$ **Miller's Landing.** This one-stop-shopping choice for lodging and services offers cabins, B&Bs, campsites for tents and RVs, water-taxi service to remote sites, sea-kayak and boat and motor rentals, and a booking service for fishing trips, dogsled rides, hiking expeditions, sailing tours, and wildlife cruises. The range of available lodgings runs the gamut from one-room cabins with no running water and a woodstove for heat, to a full-service cottage with full kitchen, TV, and VCR that sleeps 12. The campground has wooded sites and full hookups for motor homes, laundry, showers, Internet and Wi-Fi, bait, ice, and fishing-tackle sales and rental. To reach Miller's, take the road to Lowell Point from the SeaLife Center and follow the shoreline for 3½ mi until you hit its parking lot on the beach. *Lowell Point Rd., Box 81, 99664 907/224–5739 or 866/541–5739 www.millerslandingak.com 7 cabins, 29 tent sites, 29 RV sites with hookups, 13 B&B rooms, 10 cottages D, MC, V.*

$$$ **Hotel Seward.** Decorated in resplendent gold-rush style, this downtown hotel is convenient to restaurants, shopping, and the Alaska SeaLife Center. In each of its rooms you'll find a king- or queen-sized pillow-top bed, and a phone in the bathroom as well as the bedroom; some rooms have bay views. The hotel is close to the ferry. *221 5th Ave., Box 670, 99664 907/224–2378 or 800/655–8785 www.hotelsewardalaska.com 38 rooms Refrigerators, cable TV, in-room data ports, outdoor hot tub, no-smoking rooms; no a/c AE, D, DC, MC, V.*

$$$ **Seward Windsong Lodge.** In a forested setting near the banks of the Resurrection River, the Seward Windsong has rooms decorated in warm plaids, pine furniture, and Alaskan prints. The lodge is just down the road from Exit Glacier. A full-service restaurant is on the premises. *Mile 0.5, Exit Glacier Rd., about 2 mi north of Seward 2525 C St., Anchorage 99503 907/265–4501 or 888/959–9590 www.sewardwindsong.com 98 rooms, 10 suites Restaurant, cable TV, in-room VCRs, in-room data ports, bar, shop, meeting rooms, travel services; no a/c, no smoking AE, D, MC, V.*

$$ **Breeze Inn.** A mile or so from downtown and across the street from the small-boat harbor, this modern hotel is convenient—very convenient if you're planning an early-morning fishing or sightseeing trip. Shops and restaurants are all within easy strolling distance. The rooms are bright and airy, with custom-made wooden furnishings and Alaskan wildlife photos on the walls. Some rooms in the annex building overlook the harbor. ✉ *1306 Seward Hwy.* ⓑ *Box 2147, 99664* ☎ *907/224–5237 or 888/224–5237* 🌐 *www.breezeinn.com* *100 rooms* *Restaurant, coffee shop, refrigerators, cable TV, lounge, shop, Wi-Fi, laundry, meeting rooms, some pets allowed, no-smoking rooms; no a/c in some rooms* 💳 *AE, D, MC, V.*

$$ **Hotel Edgewater.** The rooms at Seward's newest and snazziest hotel overlook Resurrection Bay, and on days of bluebird weather, the panorama of mountains, glaciers, and the bay is breathtaking. Continental breakfast is served in the lobby, a three-story atrium complete with a small waterfall, lots of plants, plus plush seating. A side room has a fireplace and a selection of work by local artists. Rooms are decorated with warm colors, artwork, and wooden crown moldings that complement the cabinetwork. The downtown location is convenient to the SeaLife Center, restaurants, and shops. ✉ *200 5th Ave., 99664* ☎ *888/793–6800 or 907/224–2700* 🌐 *www.hoteledgewater.com* *76 rooms* *Coffee shop, some microwaves, some refrigerators, cable TV, in-room VCRs, in-room data ports, hot tub, sauna, shop, laundry service, concierge, Wi-Fi, meeting room, airstrip, airport shuttle, travel services, no-smoking rooms* 💳 *AE, D, MC, V* *CP.*

JUST BACK FROM ALASKA

"The Edgewater is lovely, but be sure to book a room with views of the bay. Check out the indoor hot tub!"

–Heidi Johansen, Fodor's editor

$$ **Spruce Moose B&B.** You get maximum privacy in a spectacular setting with views of the Kenai Mountains and Trail Lake at the Spruce Moose. Two fully equipped chalets sleep up to eight people each. A breakfast of fresh baked goods is delivered to your door every morning, and if your fishing trips are successful, there's a gas grill available. You can bask in the hot tub while your salmon sizzles on the grill. ⓑ *Box 7, Moose Pass, 99631* ☎ *907/288–3667* 🌐 *http://seward.net/sprucemoose* *2 chalets* *Kitchens, microwaves, refrigerators, cable TV, outdoor hot tub, laundry facilities; no a/c, no smoking* 💳 *AE, D, MC, V* *CP.*

$$ Fodor'sChoice ★ **Teddy's Inn the Woods.** Set back from the road in a forest of spruce trees in parklike surroundings, this B&B has room for up to six in an outbuilding. The furnishings are impeccable, with lots of natural-wood accents, comfortable seating, local artwork, and flower arrangements. Two cubbyhole bunks are especially child friendly, and the two decks are prime sun-lounging spots. The breakfast of fresh homemade pastries just might be complemented by freshly smoked salmon. ✉ *Mile 23, Seward Hwy., Moose Pass* ⓑ *29792 Seward Hwy., 99664* ☎ *907/288–3126* 🌐 *www.seward.net/teddys* *1 room* 💳 *MC, V* *BP.*

$–$$ **Van Gilder Hotel.** Built in 1916 and listed on the National Register of Historic Places, the Van Gilder is an elegant building steeped in local history. Photos of Seward from the early 20th century adorn the walls, beds are brass or carved wood, and the common rooms foster a cozy, B&B feel. This is definitely not a mass-market, chain hotel, and the staff gives tours of the property, pointing out interesting historical information. There's a common kitchen area for guests' use, a sitting room with books of local interest, and a player piano in the lobby. ✉ *308 Adams St., 99664* ☎ *907/224–3079 or 800/204–6835* 🌐 *www.vangilderhotel.com* *20 rooms, 4 suites* *Kitchen, cable TV; no a/c, no smoking* *AE, D, DC, MC, V.*

★ $ **Alaska's Treehouse B&B.** Enjoy spectacular views of the Chugach Mountains from the solarium and from the hot tub on the tiered deck at this quiet, rustic retreat. The house has vaulted cedar ceilings and skylights, and the suite has a skylight, too. The hand-built wood-fired sauna is perfect for relaxing in after a hike or ski along nearby trails. Breakfast includes sourdough pancakes with homemade wild-berry sauces. A two-bedroom suite sleeps five comfortably, and occupants of the three-person room can also rent the adjoining Loft Room for the kids. ✉ *½ mi off Seward Hwy., at Mile 7* *Box 861, 99664* ☎ *907/224–3867* 🌐 *www.virtualcities.com/ak/treehouse.htm* *2 suites* *Dining room, cable TV, outdoor hot tub, sauna; no a/c* *No credit cards* *BP.*

CAMPING **Waterfront Park.** The city of Seward operates Waterfront Park, a sprawling facility that occupies some of the town's premier real estate. Campsites are all first-come, first served except for "caravans" of 10 units or more. The payoff is camping on the shore of Resurrection Bay with an unparalleled view of the waterfront and the mountains across the way. Fishing boats, cruise ships, ferries, pleasure craft, and work boats parade past the park day and night; seals, sea lions, and sea otters cruise past; seabirds, waterfowl, and bald eagles glide overhead; and the fishing from the beach is very good during the silver salmon run that peaks in July. Expect crowds and a limited selection of sites on holiday and salmon derby weekends and anytime the fishing is especially hot. *Pit toilets, full hookups, drinking water, fire pits, picnic tables* *500 spaces, 99 with hookups* ✉ *Ballaine Blvd.* *City of Seward, SPRD/Parks & Campgrounds, Box 167, 99664-0167* ☎ *907/224–4055* 🌐 *www.cityofseward.net* *$8 tent, $12 RV, $25 with hook-ups* *No credit cards.*

Nightlife

The **New Seward Saloon** (✉ 209 5th Ave. ☎ 907/224–3095) is the best bet for Seward nightlife. They've got a carved-wood bar, a great bar menu of oysters, seafood, appetizers, and soups, and a large beer selection. You can check your e-mail here or play a game of pool. Weekends during the summer they have a DJ and outdoor seating (with heaters—this is Alaska, after all).

Shopping

Bardarson Studio (✉ Across from small-boat harbor ☎ 907/224–5448 or 800/354–0141 🌐 www.bardarsonstudio.com), selling everything from prints and watercolors to sculpture and beaded earrings, is a browser's dream. There's a kiddie cave for children and a video-viewing area with Alaska programs for nonshoppers. Owner Dot Bardarson is a talented watercolorist and her paintings are prized by local collectors. At **I.R.B.I. Custom Alaska Knives** (✉ Mile 20, Seward Hwy. ☎ 907/288–3616) father-and-son craftsmen Irvin and Virgil Campbell handcraft beautiful, functional knives and *ulus* (Alaska native "women's knives"), with local and exotic antler ivory and horn for handles. The

Ranting Raven (✉ 224 4th Ave. ☎ 907/224–2228) is a combination gift shop, bakery, and lunch spot, adorned with raven murals on the side of the building. You can indulge in fresh-baked goods, espresso drinks, and daily lunch specials such as quiche, focaccia, and homemade soups while perusing the packed shelves of Russian handicrafts and artwork, native crafts, and jewelry.

Sports, the Outdoors & Guided Tours

TIP→ For more information about Kenai Fjords, flip ahead to the next section.

ADVENTURE & WILDLIFE VIEWING **Alaska Wildland Adventures** (☎ 907/783–2928 or 800/334–8730 🌐 www.alaskawildland.com), in Cooper Landing, operates a tidy, pleasant resort and outdoor adventure center on the Kenai River at Mile 50.1 of the Sterling Highway. It arranges a large variety of adventure travel packages all over the state, from 2-day fishing trips and 12-day exploration safaris to small-ship cruising trips, bear-viewing adventures, and trips to backcountry lodges in several locations.

BOATING **Kenai Fjords Tours** (☎ 907/276–6249, 800/478–8068, 907/224–8068 in Seward 🌐 www.kenaifjords.com) is the oldest and largest company running tours through the park. From March through November, it leads 3- to 10-hour cruises, which include lunch. Transportation and overnight options are also available. **Mariah Tours** (☎ 907/224–8068 or 800/270–1238 🌐 www.kenaifjords.com) operates smaller boats through the park and into the Chiswell Islands, with a maximum of 16 passengers per boat mid-May through mid-September. This is a great option for birders or groups.

Major Marine Tours (☎ 907/274–7300 or 800/764–7300 🌐 www.majormarine.com) conducts half-day and full-day cruises of Resurrection Bay and Kenai Fjords National Park. Park cruises are narrated by a national park ranger, and meals of salmon and prime rib are an option. They can also arrange transportation between Anchorage and Seward.

Renown Charters and Tours (☎ 907/272–1961 or 800/655–3806 🌐 www.renowncharters.com) operates its custom-built catamaran daily from March through October. Summer cruises include a three-hour whale-watching tour and a six-hour Kenai Fjords trip, featuring narration by a national park ranger. Transportation packages from Anchorage are available.

DEEP-SEA FISHING **Fish House** (✉ Small-boat harbor ☎ 907/224–3674 or 800/257–7760 🌐 www.thefishhouse.net) is Seward's oldest booking agency for deep-sea fishing.

HIKING The **Caines Head Trail** allows easy, flat hiking along the coast, but a large portion of the hike is over tidal mud flats, so care must be taken to time the hike correctly—with tides here running in the 10- to 20-foot range, bad planning isn't just a case of getting your feet wet. The state parks Web site advises that the trail only be hiked when there's a "plus 4-foot tide or greater" in the summer. The trail is 4½ mi, starting from Lowell Point, and two cabins are available for rent at Derby Cove and Callisto Canyon. Check 🌐 www.dnr.state.ak.us/parks/cabins for detailed cabin info.

The **Lost Lake/Primrose Trail** is a 15-mi end-to-end loop through spruce forests and up into the high alpine area. The Lost Lake trailhead is near Mile 5 of the Seward Highway, and the other end is at the Primrose campground at Mile 17. The trails are steep and usually snow-covered through late June, but the views along the Lost Lake valley are worth the climb. Above tree line you're in mountain-goat country—look for white, blocky figures perched on the precarious cliffs. The lake is a prime spot for rainbow trout fishing. As usual, be bear-aware. The Dale Clemens cabin, at Mile 4.5 from the Lost Lake trailhead, has propane heat and a stunning view of Resurrection Bay. For info, check 🌐 www.fs.fed.us/r10/chugach/cabin_web_page.

For a comprehensive listing of all the trails, cabins, and campgrounds in the Seward Ranger District of Chugach National Forest, go to 🌐 www.fs.fed.us/r10/chugach/seward/rec/index.htm.

RUNNING The footrace best known among Alaskans is Seward's annual **Mt. Marathon Race,** run on July 4 since 1915. Its tenure in the United States is second only to the Boston Marathon. It doesn't take the winners very long—44 minutes or so—but the route is straight up the mountain (3,022 feet) and back down to the center of town. The field is limited, past participants have priority, and early registration is required—applications go out February 1. For more information, contact the **Seward Chamber of Commerce** (✉ Box 749, Seward 99664 ☎ 907/224–8051 🌐 www.sewardak.org).

Kenai Fjords presents a rare opportunity for an up-close view of blue tidewater glaciers as well as some remarkable ocean wildlife, including humpbacks and orcas.

Kenai Fjords National Park

★ ❾ *125 mi south of Anchorage.*

Photogenic Seward is the gateway to the 670,000-acre Kenai Fjords National Park. This is spectacular coastal parkland incised with sheer, dark slate cliffs rising from the sea, ribboned with white waterfalls, and tufted with deep-green spruce. Kenai Fjords presents a rare opportunity for an up-close view of blue tidewater glaciers as well as some remarkable ocean wildlife, but access is quite limited unless you charter a boat or airplane, or arrange for a tour with one of the local companies. If you take a day trip on a tour boat out of Seward, you can be pretty sure of seeing sea otters, crowds of Steller's sea lions lazing on the rocky shelves along the shore, a porpoise or two, bald eagles soaring overhead, and tens of thousands of seabirds. Humpback whales and orcas are also sighted occasionally, and mountain goats frequent the seaside cliffs. Tours range in length from 4 hours to 10 hours. The park's coastal fjords are also a favorite of sea-kayakers, who can camp or stay in public-use cabins reserved through headquarters.

Before venturing out into the far reaches of the park, you should gather as much data as possible from the locals concerning the weather, tides, and dangerous beaches. Once you leave Seward, you're a long way from help, and it's not uncommon for unwary kayakers to fall victim to the harsh conditions. Backcountry travelers should also be aware that some

Continued on page 296

DID YOU KNOW?

The blue glow of a glacier is caused by the light-absorbing properties of glacial ice. Ice readily absorbs long-wavelength frequencies of light (associated with the color red) but reflects short-wavelength frequencies, which, you guessed it, are blue.

ALASKA'S GLACIERS

NOTORIOUS LANDSCAPE ARCHITECTS

(opposite) Facing the Taku Glacier challenge outside of Juneau (top) River of ice

Glaciers—those massive, blue-hued tongues of ice that issue forth from Alaska's mountain ranges—perfectly embody the harsh climate, unforgiving terrain, and haunting beauty that make this state one of the world's wildest places. Alaska is home to roughly 100,000 glaciers, which cover almost 5% of the state's land.

Frozen Giants

A glacier occurs where annual snowfall exceeds annual snowmelt. Snow accumulates over thousands of years, forming massive sheets of compacted ice. (Southeast Alaska's **Taku Glacier,** popular with flightseeing devotees, is one of Earth's meatiest: some sections measure over 4,500 feet thick.) Under the pressure of its own weight, the glacier succumbs to gravity and begins to flow downhill. This movement results in sprawling masses of rippled ice (Alaska's **Bering Glacier,** at 127 miles, is North America's longest). When glaciers reach the tidewaters of the coast, icebergs calve, or break off from the glacier's face, plunging dramatically into the sea.

THE RAPIDLY RETREATING GLACIERS IN KENAI FJORDS NATIONAL PARK

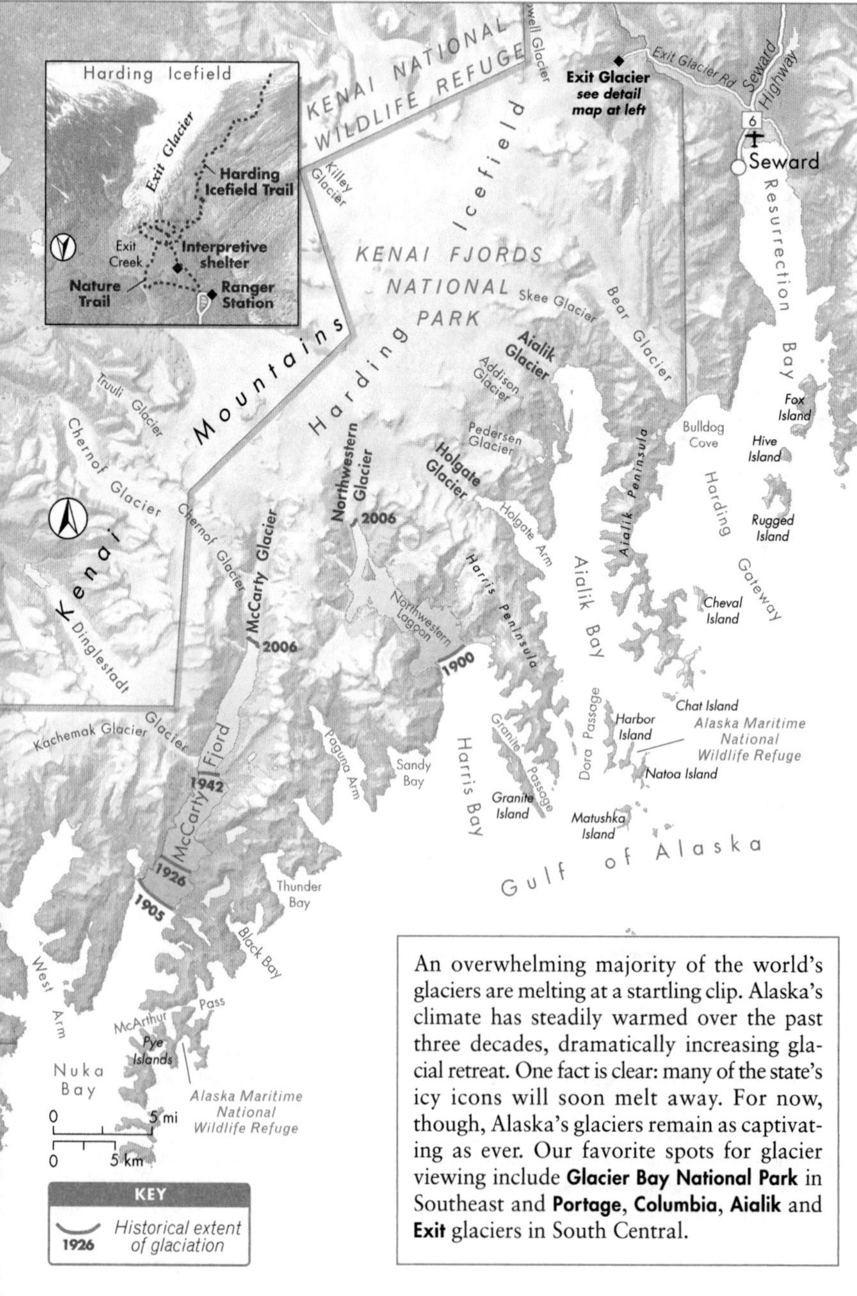

An overwhelming majority of the world's glaciers are melting at a startling clip. Alaska's climate has steadily warmed over the past three decades, dramatically increasing glacial retreat. One fact is clear: many of the state's icy icons will soon melt away. For now, though, Alaska's glaciers remain as captivating as ever. Our favorite spots for glacier viewing include **Glacier Bay National Park** in Southeast and **Portage, Columbia, Aialik** and **Exit** glaciers in South Central.

Icy Blue Hikes & Thunderous Boating Excursions

Glaciers enchant us with their size and astonishing power to shape the landscape. But let's face it: nothing rivals the sheer excitement of watching a bus-size block of ice burst from a glacier's face, creating an unholy thunderclap that resounds across an isolated Alaskan bay.

Most frequently undertaken with a seasoned guide, **glacier trekking** is becoming increasingly popular. Many guides transport visitors to and from glaciers (in some cases by helicopter or small plane), and provide ski excursions, dogsled tours, or guided hikes on the glacier's surface. Striding through the surreal landscape of a glacier, ice crunching underfoot, can be an otherworldly experience. Whether you're whooping it up on a dogsled tour, learning the fundamentals of glacier travel, or simply poking about on a massive field of ice, you're sure to gain an acute appreciation for the massive scale of the state's natural environment.

You can also experience glaciers **via boat,** such as the Alaska Marine Highway, a cruise ship, a small chartered boat, or even your own bobbing kayak. Our favorite out of Seward is the ride with Kenai Fjords Tours. Don't be discouraged by rainy weather. Glaciers often appear even bluer on overcast days. When piloting your own vessel, be sure to keep your distance from the glacier's face.

■ TIP→ **For more information about viewing Alaska's glaciers,** *see* **Chapter 1: Sports & Wilderness Adventures.**

Taking in the sights at Mendenhall Glacier

DID YOU KNOW?

What do glaciers and cows have in common? They both *calve*. While bovine calving refers to actual calf-birth, the word is also used to describe a tidewater glacier's stunning habit of rupturing icebergs from its terminus. When glacier ice meets the sea, steady tidal movement and warmer temperatures cause these frequent, booming deposits.

GLACIER-VIEWING TIPS

- The most important rule of thumb is never to venture onto a glacier without proper training or the help of a guide.
- Not surprisingly, glaciers have a cooling effect on their surroundings, so wear layers and bring gloves and rain gear.
- Glaciers can powerfully reflect sunlight, even on cloudy days. Sunscreen, sunglasses, and a brimmed hat are essential.
- Warm, thick-soled waterproof footwear is a must.
- Don't forget to bring a camera and binoculars (preferably waterproof).

of the park's coastline has been claimed by local native organizations and is now private property. Check with park headquarters to avoid trespassing on native property.

One of the park's chief attractions is **Exit Glacier,** which can be reached only by the one road that passes into Kenai Fjords. Trails inside the park lead to an overlook of the vast **Harding Icefield.** *Box 1727, Seward 99664 907/224–7500 www.nps.gov/kefj.*

Where to Stay

¢ **National Park Service Cabins.** The Kenai Fjords National Park manages four cabins, including three along the coast, favored by sea kayakers and for summer use only. Accessible only by boat or floatplane, they must be reserved in advance. The cabins cost $50 per night: three have a three-night limit, and the North Arm cabin can be reserved for up to nine nights, since it's considerably farther out than the others. The park's lone winter cabin is at Exit Glacier and is a stopping place for many skiers, mushers, and snow machiners (the local name for snowmobilers). Cabins have wooden bunks, heating stoves, and tables. There's no electricity, running water, indoor plumbing, or bedding. *1212 4th Ave. Box 1727, Seward 99664 907/224–7500 to reserve winter cabin, 907/271–2737 in Anchorage for summer rentals www.nps.gov/kefj/trip_planning/Backcountry/PUC/PUC.htm 4 cabins MC, V.*

Sports, the Outdoors & Guided Tours

BOATING **Major Marine Tours** (907/274–7300 or 800/764–7300 www.majormarine.com) runs ranger-led boat tours through the park, with both half- and full-day excursions available.

COMBO TOURS **Kenai Coastal Tours** (907/277–2131 or 800/478–8068) leads day trips into Kenai Fjords National Park. It also conducts combination train–cruise–motor-coach trips from Anchorage.

Cooper Landing

10 *100 mi south of Anchorage.*

Centrally located on the Kenai Peninsula, Cooper Landing is within striking distance of some of Alaska's most popular fishing locations. The **Russian River** flows into the **Kenai River** here, and spectacular fishing opportunities abound. Solid lines of traffic head south from Anchorage every summer weekend, and the confluence of the two rivers can get very crowded with enthusiastic anglers, to the point where the pursuit of salmon is often referred to as "combat fishing." However, a short walk upstream will separate you from the crowds and afford a chance to enjoy this gorgeous little river.

Don't let the presence of dozens if not hundreds of fellow anglers lull you into a sense of complacency: in recent years the amount of brown bear activity at the Russian has increased noticeably. This needn't deter you from visiting and enjoying yourself, though. Be aware of the posted signs warning of recent bear sightings, observe the local "rules of the road" about fishing and disposing of carcasses, and keep your senses tuned. If you're lucky, you'll enjoy one of the hundreds of innocuous bear/human encounters that occur every year on the river, and come away with a fresh respect for our ursine friends.

WORD OF MOUTH

"Wow. What a beautiful area Cooper Landing is. The river is just amazing. As we floated down the Upper Kenai, we saw too many bald eagles to count and a black bear eating dinner on a riverbank. It was a very relaxing, peaceful way to see the river and the wildlife." -Sid

The Russian River supports two runs of red (sockeye) salmon every summer, and it's known as the most popular fishery in the state. The Kenai River is famous for its runs of king, red, and silver (coho) salmon, as well as the resident populations of large rainbow trout and Dolly Varden char. Several guide services operate out of Cooper Landing, and the travel services at Gwin's Lodge and the Kenai Princess can recommend competent and trustworthy fishing guides. A number of nearby freshwater lakes, accessible only by hiking trail, also provide excellent fishing for rainbow trout and Dolly Varden.

5

Cooper Landing serves as a trailhead for the 38-mi-long Resurrection Pass Trail, which connects to the village of Hope, and the Russian Lakes/Resurrection River trails, which run south to Exit Glacier near Seward. The town's central location also affords easy access to saltwater recreation in Seward and Homer.

Where to Stay & Eat

¢–$ ✕ **Sunrise Inn.** On the shore of Kenai Lake, this restaurant serves breakfast, lunch, and dinner, dishing up homemade soups, chowders, and salsas. The eclectic and very reasonably priced menu includes wraps and vegetarian items. Fish feature prominently in what the owners describe as a "backwoods bistro" environment. There's even a spotting scope in the parking lot for spying on the Dall sheep and mountain goats in the surrounding peaks. The bar hosts live music on Saturday come summertime. ✉ *Mile 45, Sterling Hwy.* ☎ *907/595–1222* ▭ *D, MC, V.*

$–$$$ ✕🏨 **Gwin's Lodge.** Gwin's is surely the epicenter of much of the activity on the peninsula. This roadside establishment is a one-stop shop for visitors and locals alike, providing food, lodging, shopping, and fishing tackle around the clock in the summer. The lodge is the fishing headquarters of prospective anglers during the annual salmon runs on the nearby Russian and Kenai rivers. Cabins vary in configuration from standard log cabin with beds and private baths to deluxe chalets with lofts, vaulted ceilings, and full kitchens. The restaurant ($–$$) serves a full menu of fresh fish when available, sandwiches, steaks, and hearty breakfasts. ■ **TIP→ The travel agency can book fishing, hiking, rafting, and other adventure travel anywhere on the peninsula.** ✉ *Mile 52, Sterling Hwy., 99572* ☎ *907/595–1266* 🌐 *www.gwinslodge.com* *13 rooms* *Restaurant, bar, shop, travel services, Wi-Fi, no-smoking rooms; no a/c, no room phones, no room TVs* ▭ *D, MC, V* *Restaurant closed Oct.–Mar.*

★ **$$$$** 🏨 **Great Alaska Adventure Lodge.** Midway between Seward and Homer, this lodge lives up to its name. Activities include natural history, soft-adventure options, and a remote bear-viewing camp. If you're here to fish, you've come to the right place: the guides are top-notch, and seven world records have been set along the camp's riverbanks. They offer 2- to 10-day trips with any-day arrivals and free Anchorage pick up. Rates include lodging, meals, and most activities, and the basic fishing package—two days and one night, all expenses covered, including a fishing guide—runs $995 per person. Rooms, which are in the main lodge or in riverside cabins, have fireplaces, artwork, and comfortable seating. Some of the cabins are two-story, complete with spiral staircases. ✉ *Mile 82.5, 33881 Sterling Hwy., Sterling 99672* 📭 *Box 2670, Poulsbo, WA 98370* ☎ *907/262–4515, 800/544–2261, 360/697–6454 in winter* 🌐 *www.greatalaska.com* *25 rooms* *Dining room, boating, fishing, hiking, airport shuttle; no a/c, no room phones, no room TVs* 💳 *AE, MC, V* ⏲ *Closed Oct.–mid-May* 🍴 *FAP.*

$$$$ **Kenai Princess Wilderness Lodge.** "Elegantly rustic" might best describe this sprawling complex approximately 45 mi from Seward, on a bluff overlooking the Kenai River. Paths lead from the main lodge to charming bungalows, each containing four spacious units. Buildings higher on the bluff house eight units. Each has a king or two double beds, a wood-burning fireplace, a comfortable sitting area, and a porch. Vaulted ceilings of natural-finish wood complement the Alaskan art prints on the walls. Staff can arrange for fishing, flightseeing, horseback riding, and river rafting. There's also a nature trail. The Eagle's Crest Restaurant serves a variety of Alaska fare, including seafood, and the Rafter's Lounge offers a good menu of bar food and local beers that can be enjoyed from the spacious deck overlooking the river. ✉ *Mile 47.7, Sterling Hwy.* 📭 *Box 676, Cooper Landing 99572* ☎ *907/595–1425 or 800/426–0500* 🌐 *www.princessalaskalodges.com* *86 rooms* *Restaurant, cable TV, exercise equipment, outdoor hot tubs, bar, shop, travel services; no a/c* 💳 *AE, DC, MC, V* ⏲ *Closed Oct.–May.*

Fodor's Choice ★

$–$$$$ **Ingram's Base Camp.** Cabins come in three variations—regular, deluxe, and riverfront, all with private baths, heat, and kitchens. Ingram's serves as an overnight base for fishing, sightseeing, or bear-viewing anywhere on the peninsula. You can arrange for a remote guided or unguided fishing trip, a backpacking drop-off, or for air transportation to one of the Forest Service cabins in the area. They also offer guided drift-boat fishing from the camp, and fly-in trips for bear-watching, and can transport you and your mountain bikes to a remote mountain trail for an exhilarating ride back to civilization. ✉ *Mile 48.1, Sterling Hwy., Box 748, 99572* ☎ *907/595–1213 or 866/595–1213* 🌐 *www.ingramsbasecamp.com* *10 cabins* *Picnic area, BBQs, fishing; no a/c, no room phones, no room TVs, no smoking* 💳 *MC, V.*

$$ **The Inn at Tern Lake.** The owners of the Spruce Moose B&B in nearby Moose Pass completed their dream house and B&B here in June 2003. The house sits in a valley of spruce trees between the jagged peaks of the Kenai mountain range. The location is within a short drive of Seward and Cooper Landing, providing easy access to the myriad recreational opportunities of those communities. Or you can stay at the inn and walk (or in the winter, cross-country ski) through the woods to the shore of Tern Lake, soak in the hot tub, practice your tennis or putting, or just scan the mountainsides for Dall sheep, mountain goats, or bears. As many as seven black bears at a time have been spotted during the evening bear watch. The rooms and common areas are decorated with antiques and Alaskan artifacts, and the Hetricks will help you book any other adventures. There's also a barbecue, and a sitting area with TV and fireplace. ✉ *Mile 36, Seward Hwy.* 📫 *Box 7, Moose Pass 99631* ☎ *907/288–3667* 🌐 *www.ternlakeinn.com* *4 rooms* *Kitchen, microwave, refrigerator, cable TV, in-room data ports, putting green, tennis court, gym, outdoor hot tub, cross-country skiing, Internet, business services, airstrip; no a/c, no smoking* 💳 *AE, D, MC, V* 🍽 *CP.*

$$ **Kenai River Sportfishing Lodge.** This lodge is actually a collection of buildings on the bank of the Kenai River. Guests stay in clean, comfortable, newly renovated cabins with private baths. Meals are served family style in the log-cabin dining room. Fishing expeditions ranging from two to five days can be arranged, in addition to transportation to and from Anchorage. The lodge can also arrange Kenai Fjords sightseeing trips and Alaska Railroad travel options, half- and full-day rafting trips on the Kenai River, as well as trips to its Kenai Backcountry Lodge downstream on Skilak Lake. ✉ *Mile 50.1, Sterling Hwy.* 📫 *Box 389, Girdwood 99587* ☎ *907/783–2928 or 800/478–4100* 🌐 *www.alaskasportfish.com* *8 cabins* *Dining room, sauna; no a/c, no room phones, no room TVs, no smoking* 💳 *D, MC, V* ⏲ *Closed Oct.–mid-May* 🍽 *CP.*

5

Kenai National Wildlife Refuge

11 *95 mi northwest of Kenai Fjords National Park, 150 mi southwest of Anchorage.*

The U.S. Fish and Wildlife Service administers nearly 2 million acres on the Kenai Peninsula in one of its prime wildlife refuges. The **Kenai National Wildlife Refuge** takes in a portion of the Harding Icefield as well as two large and scenic lakes, Skilak and Tustumena. The refuge is not only the finest moose habitat in the region, but its waterways are great for canoeing and kayaking. The refuge maintains two **visitor centers.** The main one, open all year, is in Soldotna on Ski Hill Road. Turn south on Funny River Road just west of the Kenai River bridge and follow the signs. The center has wildlife dioramas, free films and information, and a bookstore and gift shop. There's also a seasonal visitor center at Mile 57.8 of the Sterling Highway, open from Memorial Day to Labor Day.

Access to the refuge's interior regions is limited. The Sterling Highway skirts the edges, and the Funny River Road from Soldotna takes you into a small section of the refuge's nonwilderness area. The Skilak Lake Loop intersects the highway at mileposts 58 and 75 and provides the best way for car-bound visitors to reach camping, fishing, and hiking opportunities.

Wildlife is plentiful by Alaska standards. That doesn't mean you're going to find herds of animals standing around looking photogenic. To consistently spot wild animals, you have to make an active effort to see them. Learn to scan every opening in the woods, every meadow you come across, every cliff and mountainside you see when you're hiking or even riding in the car. Every member of your party should carry binoculars at all times. Once something interesting shows up, having to share field glasses can provoke even the most even-tempered soul.

There are caribou here, but they seldom appear near the road. Dall sheep and mountain goats live on the peaks near Cooper Landing, and black and brown bears, wolves, coyotes, lynx, beavers, and lots of birds abide here as well. Mornings and evenings are the prime hours for spotting game, but don't be lulled into complacency during midday.

The refuge also contains a canoe trail system through the **Swan Lake** and **Swanson River** areas. Covering over 140 mi on 100 lakes and the Swanson River, this route is an underused portion of the refuge that escapes the notice of most visitors and residents alike. This series of lakes linked by overland portages offers fantastic access to the remote backcountry, well away from what passes for civilization in the sub-Arctic. No motorized access is allowed, and no floatplanes may land on the lakes either, an almost unheard-of situation in Alaska. ■ **TIP→ You must paddle into the refuge; access is generally by canoe.** The fishing improves exponentially with distance from the road system, and opportunities for undisturbed wildlife-viewing are nearly unlimited. Road access to the canoe trailheads is off the Swanson River Road at Mile 83.4 of the Sterling Highway.

KEEP AN EYE OUT!

Moose are the most commonly seen large animal on the refuge—it was originally named the Kenai National Moose Range for that very reason.

Other than canoeing, the only other way to get into the far reaches of the refuge is by airplane. Floatplane services in Soldotna, where the refuge is headquartered (⇨ *below*), can fly you into the backcountry, and the Fish and Wildlife Service maintains two shelter cabins on a first-come, first-served basis, and 11 others by reservation. The refuge office maintains lists of transporters, air taxis, canoe rentals, and big-game guides that are permitted to operate on refuge lands.

Where to Stay

$$$$ **Kenai Backcountry Lodge.** A trip to the Kenai Backcountry Lodge involves much more than driving up to the door and booking a room—in fact, that's not even an option. Access is by boat across Skilak Lake to reach the lodge. There you can stay in a traditional Alaskan tent cabin or a log cabin, taking all your meals, included in the price, at the main lodge. Hot water and showers are available at the shared bathhouse, and the company stresses a low-impact, environmentally friendly facility—the company has been nationally recognized for its ecotourism ethos. Trip cost also includes all guided activities, such as hiking, kayaking, motorboat tours, and wildlife-viewing. Local wildlife is plentiful and includes moose, caribou, wolves, bears, eagles, and spawning salmon—chances are you'll see more animals than people during your stay (two-night minimum). *Box 389, Girdwood 99587* ☎ *800/334–8730 or 907/783–2928* *www.alaskawildland.com/kenaibackcountrylodge.htm* *2 log* *cabins, 6 tent cabins* ♿ *Dining room, lake, boating, fishing, hiking, airport shuttle; no a/c, no room phones, no room TVs, no smoking* 💳 *D, MC, V* ⏲ *Closed Sept.–May* 🍴 *FAP.*

CAMPING ⛺ **Kenai National Wildlife Refuge Campgrounds.** The U.S. Fish and Wildlife Service maintains 14 road-accessible campgrounds in the Kenai Refuge. They do not have hookups. Only two of the campgrounds (Hidden Lake and Upper Skilak Lake) charge fees for camping. All but three campgrounds have drinking water; all have nearby hiking trails and fishing. The maximum length of stay is 14 consecutive days, with a few exceptions—the Russian River Ferry site limit is three days, and the Hidden Lake and Upper Skilak limit is seven days. ♿ *Flush toilets, picnic tables, fire pits, some drinking water* *130 sites (110 suitable for RVs)* 📫 *Kenai National Wildlife Refuge, Box 2139, Soldotna 99669-2139* ☎ *907/262–7021* 🌐 *http://kenai.fws.gov* ✍ *Reservations not accepted* *$6–$10* 💳 *No credit cards.*

⛺ **USFWS Cabins.** These cabins are in remote areas of the refuge accessible only by air or boat. The reservation system is a bit more cumbersome than the one in use by the Forest Service and it involves mailing, faxing, or phoning your information to the refuge office in Soldotna. But if you're willing to overcome these hurdles, you'll find tranquility and true wilderness, and won't have to worry about your tent springing a leak. *11 cabins* 📫 *Kenai National Wildlife Refuge, attn: Cabin Reservation, Box 2139, Soldotna 99669* ☎ *907/262–7021 or 877/285–5628* 📠 *907/262–3599* 🌐 *http://kenai.fws.gov/VisitorsEducators/cabin/reserve.htm* *$35–$45* 💳 *D, MC, V.*

Sports, the Outdoors & Guided Tours

CANOEING If you have the time and inclination, the best way to experience the refuge's backcountry is by canoe. The **Swan Lake Canoe System** and the **Swanson River Canoe System** are accessed from the road system at the turnoff at Mile 83.4 of the Sterling Highway. These systems link a large number of lakes with two rivers in the wilderness area. There are several loop trips that enable visitors to fish, hike, and camp away from the road system and motorized boat traffic. Fishing for trout, salmon, and Dolly Varden is excellent, and the series of lakes and portages offer access to more than 100 mi of waterways. Canoe rentals are available in Sterling and Soldotna. The **Kenai National Wildlife Refuge Visitor Center** (✉ 43655 Kalifornsky Beach Rd., Soldotna ☎ 907/262–7021 🌐 http://kenai.fws.gov) has a list of canoeing outfitters.

HIKING Hiking trails branch off from the Sterling Highway and the Skilak Lake Loop. Degree of difficulty ranges from easy half-mile walks to strenuous climbs to mountain lakes. These trails are all "primitive" when compared with what you may be used to in the Lower 48. There's usually a sign and parking lot at the trailhead, and not much else in the way of amenities. Be prepared with topographic maps, water, food, insect repellent, and bear awareness before you set out. You won't find toilets, water fountains, or signposts. ■ **TIP→ Once you leave the parking lot, you're on your own, and you're responsible for your party's safety.** Brown and black bears are numerous on the Kenai Peninsula, and if you have any questions about how best to avoid them, consult with refuge staff, the

Alaska Department of Fish and Game, or any of the bear behavior books available nearly everywhere in South Central Alaska. Check out *Welcome to Bear Country,* in Chapter 7.

Kenai & Soldotna

12 *116 mi northwest of Seward, 148 mi southwest of Anchorage.*

The towns of Kenai and Soldotna are often mentioned almost interchangeably due to their physical proximity. Soldotna, with its strategic location on the peninsula's northwest coast, takes its name from a nearby stream; it's a corruption of the Russian word for "soldier," although some say the name came from a Native American word meaning "stream fork." Today this city of 3,900 residents is the commercial and sportfishing hub of the Kenai Peninsula. Along with its sister city, Kenai, whose onion-dome Holy Assumption Russian Orthodox Church highlights the city's old town, it is home to Cook Inlet oil-field workers and their families. Soldotna's commercial center stretches along the Sterling Highway, making this a stopping point for those traveling up and down the peninsula. The town of Kenai lies near the end of the road that branches off the Sterling Highway in Soldotna. Near Kenai is Captain Cook State Recreation Area, one of the least-visited state parks on the road system. This portion of the peninsula is level and forested, with numerous lakes and streams pocking and crisscrossing the area. Trumpeter swans return here in the spring, and sightings of moose are common.

In addition to fishing, clam digging is also popular at **Clam Gulch,** 24 mi south of Soldotna on the Sterling Highway. This is a favorite of local children, who love any excuse to dig in the muddy, sloppy goo. Ask locals on the beach how to find the giant razor clams (recognized by their dimples in the sand). You also need to ask for advice on how to clean the clams. Cleaning is pretty labor intensive, and it's easy to get into a clam-digging frenzy when the conditions are favorable, only to regret your efforts when cleaning time arrives. The clam digging is best when tides are minus 4 or 5 feet. ■ **TIP→ A sportfishing license, available at grocery, sporting-goods, and drug stores, is required.**

Where to Stay & Eat

★ **$–$$$** ✕ **The Duck Inn.** The variety of items on the menu—pizzas, burgers, chicken, steaks, and seafood—guarantees something for everyone. Portions are generous and the pricing is reasonable. Locally caught halibut is a specialty, prepared in enough different ways to stave off feelings of halibut overload. Muted lighting, soft background music, hanging plants, and lots of artwork featuring ducks create an enjoyable dining experience. ✉ *43187 Kalifornsky Beach Rd., Soldotna* ☎ *907/262–1849* ▭ *AE, D, MC, V.*

¢–$ ✕ **Suzie's Cafe.** This roadside café is a cut above most roadside cafés in Alaska. There's a deck for outside dining, the interior has antiques, and fresh flowers adorn the tables. Food is homemade and portions are very generous. Main courses include burgers, seafood, pot roast, real mashed potatoes with a choice of gravies, and homemade soups and desserts. The coffee is excellent, another rarity on the road system. ✉ *Mile 82.7, Sterling Hwy., Sterling* ☎ *907/260–5751* ▭ *MC, V.*

¢–$ **Sal's Klondike Diner.** A true diner-type atmosphere, Sal's is open 24 hours and the menu tends toward breakfast and lunch items rather than dinner main courses. Portions are very generous; there's even a sign on the wall that says, "If you're still hungry, tell us." Burgers, sandwiches, fish-and-chips, halibut, salmon, and some steaks are available, and they bake their own bread and pies every day. You can buy loaves of sourdough, white, or wheat bread. The decor is busy, to say the least, and it's a favorite spot for locals as well as visitors. *44619 Sterling Hwy., Soldotna 907/262–2220 AE, D, MC, V.*

$$ **Timber Wolf Lodge & The Cabin Restaurant.** The lodge sits on the bank of the Kenai River and has a small fleet of fishing boats and guides. Four species of salmon run up the Kenai from May through September, and if that's not enough for you, the lodge also has a floatplane and access to remote fishing spots on the far side of Cook Inlet. They also offer bear-viewing trips, sightseeing, and rafting adventures. Patios overlook the river, and three barbecue grills are available for fortunate fishermen. The restaurant ($$–$$$$) is an intimate, elegant room (eight tables) with a fireplace, soft background music, table linens, fresh flowers, and candles. The varied menu of beef, fish, lamb, and local seafood is exquisitely prepared and presented. *44485 Sterling Hwy., Soldotna 99669 907/260–5752 or 888/352–3888 www.timberwolflodgeak.com 9 rooms Restaurant, picnic area, kitchens, microwaves, refrigerators, cable TV, dock, fishing, billiards, Ping-Pong, travel services; no a/c, no smoking AE, D, DC, MC, V.*

$$ **Aspen Hotel Soldotna.** You'll find Aspen Hotels in five Alaska cities; the Soldotna facility opened in spring of 2002. It sits on a bluff overlooking the Kenai River, a world-famous fishing destination drawing hopeful anglers from all over the world. Rooms that face away from the street overlook the river, and during the very popular salmon runs, you'll have a front-row seat to the fishing action. The contemporary decor is open and airy, with bright wood accents throughout. *326 Binkley Cir., Soldotna 99669 907/260–7736 or 888/308–7848 www.aspenhotelsak.com 63 rooms Microwaves, refrigerators, cable TV, in-room DVD, in-room data ports, pool, exercise equipment, spa, laundry facilities, Internet, business services, meeting room; no a/c AE, D, DC, MC, V CP.*

$–$$ **Best Western King Salmon Motel.** This member of the reliable Best Western franchise has large, airy rooms, including some with kitchenettes. If you're traveling by RV, you can take advantage of the park with full hookups, available for $20 per night. *35546-A Kenai Spur Hwy., Soldotna 99669 907/262–5857 or 888/262–5857 www.bestwestern.com 49 rooms Restaurant, some kitchenettes, some microwaves, cable TV, in-room data ports, laundry facilities, meeting room AE, D, DC, MC, V.*

Sports, the Outdoors & Guided Tours

FISHING Anglers from around the world come for the salmon-choked streams and rivers, most notably the **Kenai River** and its companion, the **Russian River.** The Kenai River is home to the largest king salmon in the world. In 1985 a local resident, Les Anderson, caught a 97-pound, 4-ounce fish.

That record still stands, but knowledgeable fisheries professionals figure it's only a matter of time before someone with sportfishing gear catches a 100-pounder. There are two runs of kings up the Kenai every summer. The first run starts in mid-May and tapers off in early July, and the second run is from early July until the season closure on July 31. Generally speaking, the first run has more fish, but they tend to be a bit smaller than second-run fish. Smaller, of course, has a whole different meaning when it comes to these fish. Fifty- and sixty-pounders are unremarkable here, and 40-pound fish are routinely tossed back as being "too small." The limit is one king kept per day, five per season, no more than two of which can be from the Kenai. The river also supports two runs of red (sockeye) salmon every year, as well as runs of silver (coho) and pink (humpback) salmon. Rainbow trout of near mythic proportions inhabit the river, as do Dolly Varden char. Fishing pressure is heavy, so don't expect a wilderness experience, especially in the lower river near Soldotna.

Farther up the river, between Kenai Lake in Cooper Landing and Skilak Lake, motorboats are banned, so a more idyllic experience can be had. Scores of guide services ply the river, and if you're inexperienced at the game, hiring a guide for a half-day or full-day trip can more than pay for itself. Fishing techniques are quite specialized and unlike anything you're likely to be used to in the Lower 48. Deep-sea fishing for salmon and halibut out of **Deep Creek** is challenging Homer's position as the preeminent fishing destination on the southern Kenai Peninsula. This fishery is unusual in that tractors launch boats off the beach and into the Cook Inlet surf. The local campground and RV lot is packed on summer weekends.

The Kenai River is home to the largest king salmon in the world. In 1985 a local resident, Les Anderson, caught a 97-pound, 4-ounce fish. That record still stands.

Area phone books list some 300 fishing charters and guides, all of whom stay busy during the hectic summer fishing season. **Hi Lo Charters** (☎ 907/283–9691 or 800/757–9333 ⊕ www.hilofishing.com) runs salmon-fishing trips on the world-famous Kenai River. The **Sports Den** (☎ 907/262–7491 ⊕ www.alaskasportsden.com) arranges fishing trips on the river, on the saltwater, or to a remote fly-in location for salmon, trout, or halibut.

For fly-fishing for trout and salmon, **Alaska Troutfitters** (☎ 907/595–1212 ⊕ www.aktroutfitters.com) in Cooper Landing will accommodate every level of fisherperson, from rank amateur to seasoned veteran. The company conducts a school covering everything from casting technique to fishing entomology, and can arrange package deals with instruction, fishing, transportation, and accommodations.

HOMER

13 *77 mi south of Soldotna, 226 mi south of Anchorage.*

At the southern end of the Sterling Highway lies the city of Homer, at the base of a narrow spit that juts 4 mi into beautiful Kachemak Bay. Glaciers and snowcapped mountains form a dramatic backdrop across the bay.

Founded just before the turn of the 20th century as a gold-prospecting camp, this community was later used as a coal-mining headquarters. (Chunks of coal are still common along local beaches; they wash into the bay from nearby slopes where the coal seams are exposed.) Today the town of Homer is an eclectic community filled with tacky tourist paraphernalia, commercial-fishing facilities—including boats, canneries, and repair yards—and a thriving group of local artists, sculptors, actors, and writers. Much of the commercial fishing centers on halibut, and the popular Homer Jackpot Halibut Derby is often won by enormous fish weighing more than 300 pounds. The local architecture includes everything from dwellings that are little more than assemblages of driftwood, flotsam, and jetsam to featureless steel commercial buildings and magnificent homes on the hillside overlooking the surrounding bay, mountains, forests, and glaciers. In addition to highway and air access, Homer also has regular ferry service to Seldovia and Kodiak Island.

A DISTRACTING VIEW

First-timers be warned: As you turn the final corner and crest the hill above town, if the weather is clear and sunny, the view can be extremely distracting—try not to run off the road when the panorama unfolds in front of you.

5

Exploring Homer

What to See

Start your visit with a stop at the Homer Chamber of Commerce's **Visitor Information Center,** where racks are filled with brochures from local businesses and attractions. ✉ *Homer Bypass at Main St.* ☎ *907/235–7740* 🌐 *www.homeralaska.org* ⏲ *Memorial Day–Labor Day, weekdays 9–7, weekends 10–6; early Sept.–late May, weekdays 9–5.*

Fodor's Choice ★ Protruding into Kachemak Bay, the **Homer Spit** provides a sandy focal point for visitors and locals. A paved path stretches most of the 4 mi and is great for biking or walking. A commercial-fishing-boat harbor at the end of the path has restaurants, hotels, charter fishing businesses, sea-kayaking outfitters, art galleries, and on-the-beach camping spots. Fly a kite, walk the beaches, drop a line in the Fishing Hole, or just wander through the shops looking for something interesting; this is one of Alaska's favorite summertime destinations.

Fodor's Choice ★ The **Pratt Museum** has a saltwater aquarium; an exhibit on the 1989 Prince William Sound oil spill; a wildflower garden; a gift shop; and pioneer, Russian, and Alaska native displays. You can spy on wildlife with a robotic video camera set up on a seabird rookery. There's also a refurbished homestead cabin and outdoor summer exhibits along the trail out back. ✉ *Bartlett St., off Pioneer Ave.* ☎ *907/235–8635* 🌐 *www.prattmuseum.org* 🎟 *$6* ⏲ *Mid-May–mid-Sept., daily 10–6; mid-Sept.–mid-May, Tues.–Sun. noon–5.*

★ **Islands and Ocean Center** provides a wonderful introduction to the **Alaska Maritime National Wildlife Refuge.** The refuge covers some 3.5 million acres spread across some 2,500 Alaskan islands, from Prince of Wales

Island in the south to Barrow in the north. Opened in 2003, this 37,000-square-foot facility with towering windows facing Kachemak Bay is a must-see for anyone interested in wild places. A film takes visitors along on a voyage of the Fish and Wildlife Service's research ship, the MV *Tiglax*. Interactive exhibits detail the birds and marine mammals of the refuge (the largest seabird refuge in America), and one room even re-creates the noisy sounds and pungent smells of a bird rookery. During the summer, guided bird-watching treks and beach walks are offered. *95 Sterling Hwy. 907/235–6961 www.islandsandocean.org Free Memorial Day–Labor Day, daily 9–6; Labor Day–Memorial Day, hours vary (call or check Web site).*

HOMER FESTIVALS

Early-summer visitors to Homer join thousands of migrating shorebirds for the **Kachemak Bay Shorebird Festival** on the first weekend of May. Experts offer bird-watching trips and photography demonstrations, and a simultaneous **Wooden Boat Festival** provides a fun chance to meet some of Alaska's finest boatbuilders. Various kid events add to the fun. In late July the **KBBI Concerts on the Lawn** (907/235–7721 www.kbbi.org) brings a weekend of folk and rock music to Karen Hornaday Park.

Kachemak Bay abounds in wildlife, including a large population of puffins and eagles. Tour operators take you past bird rookeries or across the bay to gravel beaches for clam digging. Most fishing charters include an opportunity to view whales, seals, porpoises, and birds close up. At the end of the day, walk along the docks on Homer Spit and watch commercial-fishing boats and charter boats unload their catch.

Directly across from the end of the Homer Spit is **Halibut Cove** (907/235–7847 or 800/478–7847), a small community of people who make their living on the bay or by selling handicrafts. Spend a relaxing afternoon or evening meandering along the boardwalk and visiting galleries. The cove itself is lovely, especially during salmon runs, when fish leap and splash in the clear water. You'll find several lodges on this side of the bay, on pristine coves away from summer crowds. The *Danny J* ferries people across from Homer Spit, with a stop at the rookery at Gull Island and two or three hours to walk around Halibut Cove, for $47 apiece. The ferry makes two trips daily: the first leaves Homer at noon and returns at 5 PM, and the second leaves at 5 PM and returns at 10 PM. **Central Charters** handles all bookings. (*See* "Sports, the Outdoors & Guided Tours" later in this chapter.)

The town of **Seldovia** is another off-the-road-system settlement on the south side of Kachemak Bay. For many years this was the primary fishing town on the bay, but today the focus is on tourism. The town was heavily damaged in the 1964 earthquake, but a few stretches of old boardwalk still exist and houses stand on stilts along Seldovia Slough. Access is via the Alaska Marine Highway ferry (twice weekly from Homer), aboard a water taxi ($35–$45), or by air from Homer ($50). Seldovia has several restaurants (Mad Fish Restaurant is particularly notable) and lodging places, plus a small museum and a hilltop Russian Orthodox church. The area abounds with hiking, mountain-biking, and sea-kayaking options.

Across Kachemak Bay from the Homer Spit lies one of the largest coastal parks in America, the 400,000-acre **Kachemak Bay State Park** (☏ 907/235–7024 ⊕ www.alaskastateparks.org). Flip ahead to the next section in this chapter for more information about this park. The park encompasses a line of snowcapped mountains and several large glaciers; the prominent one visible from the Spit is called Grewingk Glacier. One of the most popular trails leads 2 mi, ending at the lake in front of Grewingk Glacier. Several state park cabins can be rented for $50–$65 a night, and a number of luxurious private lodges occupy remote coves. Park access is primarily by water taxi from the Spit; contact **Mako's Water Taxi** (☏ 907/235–9055 ⊕ www.makoswatertaxi.com).

Where to Stay & Eat

$$–$$$$ Fodor'sChoice ★ ✕ **Homestead Restaurant.** This former log roadhouse 8 mi from town is a favorite of locals who appreciate artfully presented food served amid contemporary art. The Homestead specializes in seasonal fish and shellfish prepared with garlic, citrus fruits, or spicy ethnic sauces, as well as steak, rack of lamb, and prime rib. Epic views of the bay, mountains, and hanging glaciers are yours for the looking. Homestead has an extensive wine list and locally brewed beer on tap. ✉ *Mile 8.2, East End Rd.* ☏ *907/235–8723* ▭ *AE, MC, V* ⊗ *Closed Jan.–Mar.*

★ **$–$$$$** ✕ **Café Cups.** It's hard to miss this place as you drive down Pioneer Avenue—look for the huge namesake cups on the building's facade. A longtime Homer favorite, this café serves lunches and dinners that make the most of the locally abundant seafood, complemented by a terrific wine list. The menu includes a mix of fare, from Reubens to a better-than-it-sounds "twisted fettuccine" that blends seafood, raspberries, and chipotle in an Alfredo cream sauce. ■ TIP→ **Locals know to ignore the menu and just ask to hear the day's specials;** there's always a big variety of meats and fresh seafood dishes that never fail to please. Vegetarian options are also offered, and singles enjoy dining at the wine bar. ✉ *162 W. Pioneer Ave.* ☏ *907/235–8330* ▭ *MC, V* ⊗ *Closed Sun.*

$–$$$ Fodor'sChoice ★ ✕ **Saltry Restaurant.** On a hill overlooking Halibut Cove, this is a wonderful place to soak up a summer afternoon. Local seafood, naturally, is the main attraction, prepared in everything from curries and pastas to sushi. For libations, you can choose from a wide selection of imported beers. The restaurant is small, and although the tables aren't exactly crowded together, it's definitely intimate. When weather permits, get a table on the deck. Dinner seatings are at 6 and 7:30; before or after dinner you can stroll around the boardwalks at Halibut Cove and visit the art galleries or just relax on the dock. Sea otters often play just offshore. Reservations are essential for the ferry ($25 round-trip), which leaves Homer Spit at 5 PM. A noon ferry ($47) will take you to the Saltry for lunch (¢–$), stopping along the way for wildlife viewing. ✉ *Halibut Cove* ☏ *907/235–7847, 800/478–7847 Central Charters* ✍ *Reservations essential* ▭ *D, MC, V* ⊗ *Closed Labor Day–Memorial Day.*

★ $$ ✕ **Fat Olives Restaurant.** Pumpkin-colored walls, light streaming through tall front windows, and a playful collection of Italian posters add to the appeal of this fine Tuscany-inspired bistro. The atmosphere is noisy and fun, and the menu encompasses enticing appetizers, salads, sandwiches, calzones, and pizzas throughout the day, along with oven-roasted chicken, fresh seafood, pork loin, and other fare in the evening. If you're in a hurry, just get a giant slice of the thin-crust pizza to go for $3. You can order meals at the bar, and there's always something decadent for dessert. Fat Olives is just off the Homer Bypass near the Chamber of Commerce office. ✉ *276 Olson La.* ☎ *907/235–8488* ▭ *D, MC, V* ⊙ *Closed Feb.*

★ ¢ ✕ **Fritz Creek Store.** Directly across the road from Homestead Restaurant is this old-fashioned country store, gas station, liquor store, post office, video-rental shop, and deli. The last of these is the main reason for a visit, and the food is amazingly good, from the hot and fattening turkey sandwiches to freshly baked breads and pastries, pizza by the slice, veggie burritos, tamales, and ribs to go. Pull up a chair at a table crafted from an old cable spool and join the back-to-the-land crowd as they drink espresso, talk Alaskan politics, and pet the cats. ✉ *Mile 8.2, East End Rd.* ☎ *907/235–6521* ▭ *AE, D, MC, V.*

¢ ✕ **Two Sisters Bakery.** This very popular café has an ideal location just a short walk from both Bishops Beach and the Islands and Ocean Center. In addition to fresh breads and pastries, Two Sisters specializes in deliciously healthful lunches, such as vegetarian focaccia sandwiches, homemade soups (including a ginger-carrot-almond soup), quiche, and salads. Sit on the wraparound porch on a summer afternoon, or take your espresso and pastry down to the beach to watch the waves roll in. Upstairs are three comfortable guest rooms ($), all with private baths. Your latte and Danish pastry breakfast is served in the café. ✉ *233 E. Bunnell Ave.* ☎ *907/235–2280* 🌐 *www.twosistersbakery.net* ▭ *MC, V.*

$$ ✕🏨 **Land's End Resort.** This sprawling blue-and-white complex at the end of Homer Spit has wide-open views of the bay. Most of the rooms face the bay; some have nautical decor, and others are more floral. Some are perfect for a couple; the five rooms with lofts are big enough for a family. Its restaurant ($$–$$$$) specializes in seafood, including salmon, halibut, scallops, and oysters; burgers and steak are also served. ■ **TIP→ Call ahead to reserve a window table with views of Kachemak Bay and the Kenai Mountains.** During the winter, chefs craft a special once-a-month "Uncorked" theme dinner with paired wines for $60 per person. ✉ *4786 Homer Spit Rd., 99603* ☎ *907/235–0400 or 800/478–0400* 🌐 *www.lands-end-resort.com* *96 rooms* *Restaurant, cable TV, pool, hot tub, spa, bar, meeting rooms, travel services; no a/c* ▭ *AE, D, DC, MC, V.*

$$$$ 🏨 **Land's End Lodges.** Adjacent to the Land's End Resort, this group of fully furnished luxury condos sits at the end of the Homer Spit, with decks and windows fronting on Kachemak Bay. Commercial and charter fishing boats, Alaska Marine Highway ferries, and pleasure boats parade past your front door day and night, against a stunning view of snowcapped mountains, spruce forest, and glaciers. Most units sleep six comfortably, some have four bedrooms, and with a mere additional $10

per-person charge per night above two people, these places can be surprisingly economical for a small group. ✉ *4786 Homer Spit Rd., 99603* ☎ *907/235–0400 or 800/478–0400* 🌐 *www.landsendlodges.com* *13 condos* *Kitchens, microwaves, refrigerators, cable TV, laundry facilities; no a/c* *AE, D, DC, MC, V.*

$$$$ **Tutka Bay Wilderness Lodge.** On a small cove 9 mi from the Homer Spit, this luxurious small resort is adjacent to Kachemak Bay State Park. The deluxe modern cabins have private baths and comfortable beds. Other facilities include a cozy main lodge, sauna, hot tub, and three hearty meals a day. Hikers can head into the park from the lodge for day trips, watch eagles and otters just offshore, or pay extra for guided sea-kayaking, charter fishing trips, and other activities. Access is by water taxi ($70 extra) from Homer. *Box 960, 99603* ☎ *907/235–3905 or 800/606–3909* 🌐 *www.tutkabaylodge.com* *4 cabins, 2 suites* *Hot tub, sauna; no a/c* *MC, V* *FAP.*

$$$ **Alaskan Suites.** These modern log cabins offer million-dollar views from a hilltop on the west side of Homer. Each contains two queen beds and a kitchenette, plus a barbecue grill on the deck. Guests can soak in a large hot tub with a backdrop of Kachemak Bay, snowcapped mountains, glaciers, and three volcanoes. ✉ *3255 Sterling Hwy., 99603* ☎ *907/235–1972 or 888/239–1972* 🌐 *www.alaskansuites.com* *5 cabins, 1 cottage* *Kitchenettes, cable TV, in-room DVD, hot tub, some pets allowed; no a/c, no smoking* *AE, D, MC, V.*

¢–$$ **Driftwood Inn.** Unparalleled in its variety of accommodation choices, the Driftwood has standard hotel-type bedrooms; a "ship's quarters," with cedar walls and a pull-down bed; and a family-friendly "deluxe room," with queen-sized beds, dining-room table, microwave, refrigerator, full private bath, and private outside entrance. Downstairs is a comfortable sitting room with fireplace, TV, books, and videos. A small eating area has serve-yourself coffee, tea, pastries, and cereal. There's a suite with a queen-sized bed and a twin in a private room with full bath, a full kitchen, dining room, and small living room and private outside entrance. The Lodge, which sleeps up to 12, has large spacious rooms overlooking Kachemak Bay with private bathrooms and king-sized beds; the Cottage—which sleeps up to eight and overlooks the bay—consists of two bedrooms, a loft, and a full and half bath. A microwave, refrigerator, barbecue, and fish-cooking and -cleaning area are also available. You have full access to the inn's facilities if you stay at the on-site campground and full-hookup RV park. ✉ *135 W. Bunnell St., 99603* ☎ *907/235–8019 or 800/478–8019* 🌐 *www.thedriftwoodinn.com* *20 rooms, 11 with bath; lodge; cottage* *Dining room, cable TV, Wi-Fi, laundry facilities, some pets allowed; no a/c, no phones in some rooms, no smoking* *D, MC, V.*

$ **Old Town Bed & Breakfast.** Housed in a restored trading post, the Old Town B&B is on the second floor, above the Bunnell Street Art Gallery and Panarelli's Deli. Rooms are elegantly appointed with period furnishings and fixtures, and the second-story setting provides sweeping views of the bay and mountains. The art gallery hosts occasional evening music, poetry, or arts programs, and breakfast is served in the parlor upstairs. ✉ *106 W. Bunnell St., 99603* ☎ *907/235–7558* 🌐 *www.*

5

oldtownbedandbreakfast.com ⇨ *3 rooms, 1 with bath* ☝ *No a/c, no room phones, no room TVs, no smoking* ▭ *MC, V* 🍽 *BP.*

Camping

⛺ **Homer Spit Campground.** Homer's 4-mi-long Spit is popular not just as a jumping-off point for fishing, kayaking, and other adventures, but also because it provides great camping with a view. Find a spot on the sand between the other tents and RVs and pay your fee at the city's camping office. The beach is often windy, and it's not far from the road, but it's hard to beat the spectacular setting. A few campsites are open year-round. Two private RV parks on the Spit provide amenities such as showers, water and sewer hookups, and laundry. ☝ *Flush toilets, partial hook-ups, dump station, drinking water, guest laundry, showers, grills, picnic tables, electricity, public telephone, ocean* ⇨ *122 RV sites, 25 tent sites* ✉ *4535 Homer Spit Rd.* ☎ *907/235–8206* 💵 *$25, $35 with hook-ups* ▭ *MC, V.*

Nightlife

Dance to lively bands on weekends at **Alice's Champagne Palace** (✉ 195 E. Pioneer Ave. ☎ 907/235–7650). The bar attracts nationally known ★ singer-songwriters on a regular basis. The Spit's infamous **Salty Dawg Saloon** (☎ 907/235–6718) is a tumbledown lighthouse of sorts, sure to be frequented by a carousing fisherman or two, along with half the tourists in town. The ceilings are low and the pool table is usually busy, woodchips cover the floors, and the Dawg's walls are covered with business cards, signed dollar bills, and bras. The members of **Pier One Theater** (☎ 907/235–7333 🌐 www.pieronetheatre.org) perform plays on weekends throughout the summer. Find them in the old barn-like building on the Spit.

Shopping

Art & Gifts

A variety of art by the town's residents can be found in the galleries on and around Pioneer Avenue. The **Bunnell Street Gallery** (✉ Main St. and Bunnell Ave. ☎ 907/235–2662 🌐 www.bunnellstreetgallery.org) displays innovative contemporary art primarily produced in Alaska. The gallery, which occupies the first floor of a historic trading post, also hosts workshops, lectures, musical performances, and other community events. The gift shop at the **Pratt Museum** (✉ Bartlett St., off Pioneer Ave. ☎ 907/235–8635) stocks natural-history books, locally crafted or inspired jewelry, note cards, and gifts for children. **Ptarmigan Arts** (✉ 471 E. Pioneer Ave. ☎ 907/235–5345) is one of just three cooperative galleries in Alaska, with photographs, paintings, pottery, jewelry, woodworking, and other pieces by local artisans.

Clothing

Nomar (✉ 104 E. Pioneer Ave. ☎ 907/235–8363 or 800/478–8364 🌐 www.nomaralaska.com) creates Polarfleece garments and other rugged Alaskan outerwear, plus duffel bags, purses, raingear, and children's clothing. The company also manufactures equipment and clothing for commercial fishermen, so you know their gear will hold up to years of use. You'll find a good choice of outdoor supplies and home accessories next door at **Main Street Mercantile** (✉ 102 E. Pioneer Ave., Suite A ☎ 907/235–9102), housed in a 1936 building.

Foodstuffs

Alaska Wild Berry Products (✉ 528 E. Pioneer Ave. ☎ 907/235–8858 🌐 www.alaskawildberryproducts.com) sells chocolate-covered candies, jams, jellies, sauces, and syrups made from wild berries handpicked on the Kenai Peninsula, as well as Alaskan-theme gifts and clothing. Drop by for free samples of the chocolates. **Two Sisters Bakery** (✉ 235 E. Bunnell Ave. ☎ 907/235–2280) serves fresh bread baked on the premises as well as coffee, muffins, soup, and pizza. **Fritz Creek Store** (✉ Mile 8.2, East End Rd. ☎ 907/235–6521) sells fresh, homemade food in an old log building. Homer is famous for its halibut, salmon, and Kachemak Bay oysters. For fresh fish, head to **Coal Point Trading Company** (☎ 907/235–3877 or 800/325–3877 🌐 www.welovefish.com) on the Spit. In addition to selling salmon and halibut, Coal Point will package and ship fish that you caught.

5

Sports, the Outdoors & Guided Tours

Boating & Fishing

Homer is both a major commercial fishing port (especially for halibut) and a very popular destination for sport anglers in search of giant halibut or feisty king and silver salmon. Near the end of the Spit, Homer's famous **Fishing Hole** is a small bight that is stocked with king and silver salmon smolt (baby fish) by the Alaska Department of Fish and Game. The salmon then head out to sea, returning several years later to the Fishing Hole, where they are easy targets for wall-to-wall bankside anglers throughout the summer. The Fishing Hole isn't anything like casting for salmon along a remote Kodiak Island stream, but your chances are good and you don't need to drop $800 for a flight into the wilderness. Fishing licenses and rental poles are available from fishing supply stores on the Spit.

Quite a few companies offer charter fishing in the summer, for around $175 per person per day (including bait and tackle). **Central Charters** (✉ 4241 Homer Spit Rd., 99603 ☎ 907/235–7847 or 800/478–7847 🌐 www.centralcharter.com) arranges fishing and ferry trips to Halibut Cove, around Kachemak Bay, and across to Seldovia.

Homer Ocean Charters (☎ 907/235–6212 or 800/426–6212 🌐 www.homerocean.com) on the Spit sets up fishing and sightseeing trips, as well as sea kayaking and water-taxi services and remote cabin rentals. Some of their most popu-

> **BEAR-WATCHING**
>
> Homer is a favorite departure point to view Alaska's famous brown bears in coastal Katmai National Park. **Emerald Air Service** (☎ 907/235–6993 🌐 www.emeraldairservice.com) is one of several companies offering all-day trips for around $525 per person. **Hallo Bay Wilderness** (☎ 907/235–2237 🌐 www.hallobay.com) is popular for day trips, but the comfortable camp is primarily used by visitors on guided multinight bear-viewing trips.

lar cruises go to the **Rookery Restaurant** at Otter Cove Resort. The narrated lunch cruise leaves at noon ($55), and dinner trips to the restaurant leave at 4:30 and 7; the ferry trip is $20, and dinner main courses run $18–$24. Also try **Inlet Charters** (☎ 907/235–6126 or 800/770–6126 🌐 www.halibutcharters.com) for fishing charters, water-taxi services, and wildlife cruises.

Anyone heading out on a halibut charter is advised to buy a $10 ticket for the **Homer Jackpot Halibut Derby** (☎ 907/235–7740 🌐 www.homerhalibutderby.com); first prize for the largest halibut is more than $40,000.

Sea Kayaking

Several local companies offer guided sea-kayaking trips to protected coves within Kachemak Bay State Park and nearby islands. **True North Kayak Adventures** (☎ 907/235–0708 🌐 www.truenorthkayak.com) has a range of such adventures, including a six-hour paddle to Elephant Rock for $120 and an all-day boat and kayak trip to Yukon Island for $135 (both trips include round-trip water taxi to the island base camp, guide, all kayak equipment and bakery lunch). For something more unique, book an overnight trip to Kasitsna Bay through **Across the Bay Tent & Breakfast** (☎ 907/235–3633 🌐 www.tentandbreakfastalaska.com). Facilities are basic, but guests can take kayak tours, rent a mountain bike, or just hang out on the shore.

Kachemak Bay State Park & State Wilderness Park

14 *10 mi southeast of Homer.*

Kachemak Bay State Park & State Wilderness Park, accessible by boat or bush plane, protects more than 350,000 acres of coast, mountains, glaciers, forests, and wildlife on the lower Kenai Peninsula. Recreational opportunities include boating, sea-kayaking, fishing, hiking, and beachcombing. Facilities are minimal but include 20 primitive campsites, five public-use cabins, and a system of trails accessible from Kachemak Bay.

Kenai State Parks Office, Box 1247, Soldotna 99669 ☎ 907/262–5581 or 907/235–7024 🌐 www.dnr.state.ak.us/parks/units/kbay/kbay.htm.

Where to Stay

★ $$$$ **Kachemak Bay Wilderness Lodge.** Across Kachemak Bay from Homer, this luxurious lodge provides wildlife-viewing opportunities and panoramic mountain and bay vistas in an intimate setting for up to 12 guests. The main log building has a piano and a big stone fireplace to warm you after a day of hiking, fishing, kayaking, or touring in one of the lodge's five guided boats (some of the guided fly-out trips may cost extra). Scattered throughout the woods, the rustic cabins, all with electricity, full baths, and decks, are decorated with antiques, original artworks, and homemade quilts. Cabin layouts differ slightly; some are suited for couples, some for groups or families. Dinners spotlight seafood—clams, mussels, and fish—caught in the bay. The price ($2,800) is per person for a five-day, four-night all-inclusive package, and there's no single-supplement charge. *Box 956, Homer 99603 ☎ 907/235–8910 🌐 www.alaskawildernesslodge.com 4 cabins, 1 room in lodge*

Dining room, hot tub, sauna, boating, fishing, hiking; no room phones, no room TVs, no smoking *No credit cards* *Closed Oct.–Apr.* *FAP.*

¢ **Alaska State Parks Cabins.** Three public-use cabins are within Kachemak Bay's Halibut Cove Lagoon area, another is near Tutka Bay Lagoon, and a fifth is at China Poot Lake. All but the lakeside cabin are accessible by boat; China Poot can be reached only on foot from the boat landing on the beach or by floatplane to the lake. The spartan cabin furnishings consist of wooden bunks and sleeping platforms, table, and chairs but no running water or electricity. Four of the five cabins sleep up to six people (the other, the Overlook cabin at Halibut Cove, sleeps eight), and all must be reserved up to six months in advance. *Alaska State Parks Information Center, 550 W. 7th Ave., Suite 1260, Anchorage 99501-3557* *907/269–8400* *www.dnr.state.ak.us/parks/cabins/kenai.htm* *5 cabins* *No credit cards.*

CAMPING

¢ **Alaska State Parks Campsites.** Twenty primitive, free campsites with pit toilets and fire rings are scattered along the shores of Kachemak Bay across from Homer and are accessible by boat (water taxis operate here daily in summer). The sites are available on a first-come, first-served basis, and camping is allowed nearly everywhere in the park, not restricted to developed sites. *Some pit toilets, some fire pits, some picnic tables* *6 campgrounds with 20 tent sites* *Alaska State Parks, Kenai Area Office, Box 1247, Soldotna 99669* *907/235–7024 or 907/262–5581* *www.dnr.state.ak.us/parks/units/kbay/kbay.htm* *Free* *Reservations not accepted.*

Seldovia

15 *16 mi south of Homer.*

Seldovia, isolated across the bay from Homer, retains the charm of an earlier Alaska. The town's Russian bloodline shows in its onion-dome church and its name, meaning "herring bay." Those who fish use plenty of herring for bait, catching record-size salmon, halibut, and king or Dungeness crab. You'll find excellent fishing whether you drop your line into the deep waters of Kachemak Bay or cast into the surf for silver salmon on the shore of Outside Beach, near town. Stroll through town and along the slough, where frame houses rest on pilings.

Where to Stay

$$–$$$ **Across the Bay Tent & Breakfast Adventure Co.** A step up the comfort ladder from camping, this beachfront compound is reachable via water taxi from Homer. You stay in sturdy canvas-wall tents with carpeted floors and twin beds, and a large common room has hardwood floors and a piano. Prices vary depending on whether you do your own cooking or eat meals prepared by the staff. A propane stove and grill, as well as pots, pans, and picnic tables, are provided. Otherwise, host-prepared meals are hearty and served family style. A beach is great for walking and beachcombing; escorted kayak trips and mountain bikes are available for an extra charge. *Mile 8, Jakalof Bay Rd., 8 mi east of Seldovia* *Box 112054, Anchorage 99511* *907/235–3633 in summer, 907/345–2571 in winter* *www.tentandbreakfastalaska.com* *5*

tents ♿ *Dining room, sauna, beach, bicycles; no a/c, no room phones, no room TVs* ▭ *MC, V* ⊙ *Closed early Sept.–late May.*

$–$$ **Seldovia Boardwalk Hotel.** This hotel with a fabulous view of the harbor has immaculate modern rooms, half of which face the water. The rooms are bright, with white walls and ceilings, lots of plants, and locally produced artwork and Alaskana. A large, sunlit parlor downstairs has a woodstove and coffee service. The proprietors can also arrange charter-fishing or sea-kayaking trips. Package trips are available, including a two-hour nature cruise on the MV *Discovery*, overnight stay in the hotel, and return on a 30-minute flightseeing tour over glaciers. One night, two night, or two nights plus all-day kayaking tour packages are also an option. You can also rent bikes and fishing tackle here. ✉ *Main St.* *Box 72, 99663* ☎ *907/234–7816 or 800/238–7862* 🌐 *www.alaskaone.com/boardwalkhotel* *14 rooms* *Travel services; no room TVs, no smoking* ▭ *MC, V* *BP.*

Kodiak Island

16 *248 mi southwest of Anchorage by air.*

Alaska's largest island is accessible only by air from Anchorage and by ferry from Homer and Seward. Russian explorers discovered the island in 1763, and Kodiak served as Alaska's first capital until 1804, when the government was moved to Sitka. Situated as it is in the northwestern Gulf of Alaska, Kodiak has been subjected to several natural disasters. In 1912 a volcanic eruption on the nearby Alaska Peninsula covered the town site in knee-deep drifts of ash and pumice. A tidal wave resulting from the 1964 earthquake destroyed the island's large fishing fleet and smashed Kodiak's low-lying downtown area.

Today commercial fishing is king in Kodiak. Despite its small population—about 15,000 people scattered among the several islands in the Kodiak group—the city is among the busiest fishing ports in the United States. The harbor is also an important supply point for small communities on the Aleutian Islands and the Alaska Peninsula.

Visitors to the island tend to follow one of two agendas: either immediately fly out to a remote lodge for fishing, kayaking, or bear-viewing; or stay in town and access whatever pursuits they can reach from the limited road system. If the former is too pricey an option, consider combining the two: driving the road system to see what can be seen inexpensively, then adding a fly-out or charter-boat excursion to a remote lodge or wilderness access point.

LOCAL BREW

The **Kodiak Island Brewing Co.** (✉ 338 Shelikof Ave. ☎ 907/486-2537 🌐 www.kodiakbrewery.com) sells fresh-brewed beer in a variety of styles and sizes of containers, from 20-ounce bottles up to full kegs, so you can stock up for your wilderness expedition without suffering from beer withdrawal. Brewer Ben Millstein will also give you a tour of the facility on request. It's open from noon to 7 daily in summer and noon to 6 Monday through Saturday in winter.

Your first stop in exploring the island should be the **Kodiak Island Convention & Visitors Bureau** (✉ 100 Marine Way ☎ 907/486–4782 🌐 www.kodiak.org). Here you can pick up brochures, pamphlets, and lists of all the visitor services on Kodiak and the surrounding islands, and get help with planning your adventures. If you want to strike out and hike the local trails, there's a *Hiking and Birding Guide* published by the Kodiak Audubon Society that's very informative.

Floatplane and boat charters are available from Kodiak to numerous remote attractions not served by roads. Chief among these areas is the 1.6-million-acre **Kodiak National Wildlife Refuge,** lying partly on Kodiak Island and partly on Afognak Island to the north, where spotting the enormous Kodiak brown bears is the main goal of a trip. Seeing the Kodiak brown bears, which weigh a pound at birth but up to 1,500 pounds when fully grown, is worth the trip to this rugged country. The bears are spotted easily in July and August, feeding along salmon-spawning streams. Chartered flightseeing trips are available to the area, and exaggerated tales of encounters with these impressive beasts are frequently heard. ✉ *1390 Buskin River Rd.* ☎ *907/487–2600* 🌐 *www.r7.fws.gov/nwr/kodiak.*

5

As part of America's North Pacific defense in World War II, Kodiak was the site of an important naval station, now occupied by the Coast Guard fleet that patrols the surrounding fishing grounds. Part of the old military installation has been incorporated into **Fort Abercrombie State Historical Park,** 3½ mi north of Kodiak on Rezanof Drive. Self-guided tours take you past concrete bunkers and gun emplacements. There's a spectacular scenic overlook, great for bird- and whale-watching, and there are 13 campsites suitable for tents or RVs (no hookups), with pit toilets, drinking water, fire grates, and picnic tables. ✉ *Mile 3.7 Rezanof Dr.* 📫 *Alaska State Parks, Kodiak District Office, 1400 Abercrombie Dr., 99615* ☎ *907/486–6339* 🌐 *www.dnr.state.ak.us/parks/units/kodiak* 🎫 *Park free, campsites $10* 💳 *No credit cards.*

The **Baranov Museum** presents artifacts from the area's Russian past. On the National Register of Historic Places, the building was built in 1808 by Alexander Baranov to warehouse precious sea-otter pelts. W. J. Erskine made it his home in 1911. On display are samovars, Russian Easter eggs, native baskets, and other relics from the early native Koniags and the later Russian settlers. A collection of 40 albums of archival photography portrays various aspects of the island's history. ✉ *101 Marine Way* ☎ *907/486–5920* 🌐 *www.baranov.us* 🎫 *$3* 🕐 *May–Sept., Mon–Sat. 10–4, Sun. noon–4; Oct.–Apr., Tues–Sat. 10–3.*

The ornate **Holy Resurrection Russian Orthodox Church** is a visual feast, both inside and out. The cross-shape building is topped by two onion-shape blue domes, and the interior contains brass candlestands, distinctive chandeliers, and numerous icons representing Orthodox saints. Three different churches have stood on this site since 1794. Built in 1945, the present structure is on the National Register of Historic Places. ✉ *Mission and Kashevaroff Rds.* ☎ *907/486–3854 (parish priest)* 🎫 *Donations accepted* 🕐 *By appointment.*

★ The **Alutiiq Museum and Archaeological Repository** is home to one of the largest collections of Eskimo materials in the world, and contains archaeological and ethnographic items dating back 7,500 years. The museum displays only a fraction of its more than 100,000 artifacts, including harpoons, masks, dolls, stone tools, seal-gut parkas, grass baskets, and pottery fragments. The museum store sells native arts and educational materials. ✉ *215 Mission Rd., Suite 101* ☎ *907/486–7004* 🌐 *www.alutiiqmuseum.com* *$3 donation requested* ⏲ *Memorial Day–Labor Day, weekdays 9–5, Sat. 10–5, Sun. by appointment; Labor Day–Memorial Day, Wed.–Fri. 9–5, Sat. 10:30–4:30.*

Where to Stay & Eat

$–$$$$ ✕ **Henry's Great Alaskan Restaurant.** Henry's is a big, boisterous, friendly place at the mall near the small-boat harbor. The menu is equally big, ranging from fresh local seafood and barbecue to pastas and even some Cajun dishes. Dinner specials, a long list of appetizers, salads, rack of lamb, and a tasty dessert list round out the choices. ✉ *512 Marine Way* ☎ *907/486–8844* ▭ *AE, MC, V.*

$–$$$ ✕ **Old Powerhouse Restaurant.** This converted powerhouse facility allows a close-up view of Near Island and the channel connecting the boat harbors with the Gulf of Alaska. Enjoy fresh sushi and sashimi made with local seafood while watching the procession of fishing boats gliding past on their way to catch or deliver your next meal. Keep your eyes peeled for sea otters, seals, sea lions, and eagles, too. The menu also features tempura, *yakisoba* (fried noodles), and rice specials; there's live music on occasion. ✉ *516 E. Marine Way* ☎ *907/481–1088* ▭ *MC, V.*

¢–$ ✕ **Mill Bay Coffee & Pastries.** Serving soups, sandwiches, and fabulous pastries, this charming little shop is well worth the trip. The coffee is fresh roasted on-site every other day. Inside, elegant antique furnishings are complemented by local artwork and handicrafts. ✉ *3833 Rezanof Dr. E* ☎ *907/486–4411* 🌐 *www.millbaycoffee.com* ▭ *MC, V* ⏲ *No dinner.*

★ **$$** ✕ **Kodiak Buskin River Inn.** This modern lodge is a five-minute walk from the main terminal at the airport, about 4½ mi from downtown. Dark woods and bedspreads offset the light-colored walls in the large, well-kept rooms. You can fish for salmon in the river out back. The Eagle's Nest ($$–$$$$) serves local seafood, including king crab, scallops, and a chilled seafood sampler. It also serves Cajun prawns, tempura vegetables, pasta, and steaks. The atmosphere is semiformal (in Alaska that means hip waders would be a bit out of place), with candlelike lamps on each table. ✉ *1395 Airport Way, 99615* ☎ *907/487–2700 or 800/544–2202* ✉ *BuskinRiverLodge@gci.net* *50 rooms* *Restaurant, cable TV, some in-room data ports, fishing, bar, Internet, meeting room, airport shuttle, some pets allowed (fee), no-smoking rooms; no a/c* ▭ *AE, D, DC, MC, V.*

WORD OF MOUTH

"There is no way to predict what kind of weather you will have; it's so variable from place to place. South Central is huge, and at any given time the weather may change. Dress in layers and be prepared for wet, cold weather. Don't forget warm gloves."

–dwooddon

$$ **Best Western Kodiak Inn.** Rooms here have soothing floral decor, and some overlook the harbor. However, the harbor-view rooms are on the street, so if a quiet room is a priority, take one in the back. The Chartroom Restaurant has harbor views and serves local seafood and American fare, including steak and pasta. ✉ *236 W. Rezanof Dr., 99615* ☎ *907/486–5712 or 888/563–4254* 🌐 *www.kodiakinn.com* *81 rooms* *Restaurant, microwaves, refrigerators, cable TV, in-room data ports, hot tub, bar, some pets allowed (fee); no a/c* *AE, D, DC, MC, V.*

$ **Kodiak B&B.** Kodiak's first B&B commands a view of the St. Paul harbor and the waterways beyond. It's a short walk downtown and easily accessible to most of the town's businesses. Owner Mary Monroe is a gracious and knowledgeable host and can help you make the most of your Kodiak stay with plenty of helpful local information. The guest rooms share a bath and common sitting area, and bookshelves contain loads of local history. Internet available. ✉ *308 Cope St., 99615* ☎ *907/486–5367* *2 rooms share 1 bath* *Cable TV, in-room data ports;no smoking* *Closed Dec. and Jan.* *BP.*

5

Sports, the Outdoors & Guided Tours

Kodiak Island Charters (☎ 907/486–5380 or 800/575–5380 🌐 www.ptialaska.net/~urascal) operates boat tours for fishing, hunting, and sightseeing aboard the 43-foot *U-Rascal*. They'll take you on a combined halibut and salmon trip, with sightseeing and whale-watching thrown in as well.

MAT-SU VALLEY & BEYOND

Giant homegrown vegetables and the headquarters of the best-known dogsled race in the world are among the most prominent attractions of the Matanuska-Susitna (Mat-Su) Valley. The valley, lying an hour north of Anchorage by road, draws its name from its two largest rivers, the Matanuska and the Susitna, and is bisected by the Parks and Glenn highways. Major cities are Wasilla on the Parks Highway and Palmer on the Glenn Highway. To the east, the Glenn Highway connects to the Richardson Highway by way of several high mountain passes sandwiched between the Chugach Mountains to the south and the Talkeetnas to the north. ■ **TIP→ At Mile 103 of the Glenn Highway, the massive Matanuska Glacier comes almost to the road.**

Lake Clark National Park & Preserve

17 *100 mi west of Anchorage by air.*

When the weather is good, an idyllic choice beyond the Mat-Su Valley is the 3.4-million-acre Lake Clark National Park & Preserve, on the Alaska Peninsula and a short flight from Anchorage or Kenai and Soldotna. There's no road access to the park, so all visits are via small plane. The parklands stretch from the coast to the heights of two grand volcanoes: **Mt. Iliamna** and **Mt. Redoubt,** both topping out above 10,000 feet. The country in between holds glaciers, waterfalls, and turquoise-tinted lakes. The 50-mi-long **Lake Clark,** filled by runoff waters from the mountains that surround it, is an important spawning ground for thousands of red (sockeye) salmon.

The river running is superb in this park. You can make your way through dark forests of spruce and balsam poplars or you can hike over the high, easy-to-travel tundra. The animal life is profuse: look for bears, moose, Dall sheep, wolves, wolverines, foxes, beavers, and minks on land; seals, sea otters, and white (or beluga) whales offshore. Wildflowers embroider the meadows and tundra in spring, and wild roses bloom in the shadows of the forests. Plan your trip to Lake Clark for the end of June or early July, when the insects may be less plentiful. Or consider late August or early September, when the tundra glows with fall colors. *Administrative Headquarters: 4230 University Dr., Suite 311, Anchorage 99508 907/271–3751 Park visitor center: 1 Park Pl., Port Alsworth 907/781–2218 www.nps.gov/lacl.*

Where to Stay

$$$$ **Farm Lodge.** Near park headquarters in Port Alsworth, the farm was built as a homestead back in the 1940s and has been a lodge since 1977. Five modern duplexes house as many as 40 guests in private rooms that have either bunk or double beds. A large, manicured, and fenced lawn with flower and vegetable gardens surrounds the main lodge, where home-cooked meals including fresh vegetables, salmon, wild game, and domestic meats are served. The lodge also provides flight services and guided trips. *Box 1, Port Alsworth 99653 907/781–2208 or 888/440–2281 www.lakeclarkair.com/farm_lodge.html 10 rooms Dining room, some microwaves, fishing, meeting room, travel services; no a/c, no room TVs, no smoking AE, D, MC, V FAP.*

Palmer

18 *40 mi northeast of Anchorage.*

In 1935 the federal government relocated about 200 farm families from the Depression-ridden Midwest to the Mat-Su Valley, and some elements of these early farms remain around Palmer. The valley has developed into the state's major agricultural region. Good growing conditions of rich soil combined with long hours of summer sunlight result in some huge vegetables—such as 100-pound cabbages.

On a sunny day the town of Palmer looks like a Swiss calendar photo, with its old barns and log houses silhouetted against craggy Pioneer Peak. On nearby farms (on the Bodenburg Loop off the old Palmer Highway) you can pay to pick your

SEPTEMBER'S STATE FAIR

Giant vegetables (such as a record cabbage in excess of 105 pounds and a 300-plus-pound summer squash that took four people to carry) are main attractions at Palmer's **Alaska State Fair** (Mile 40.2, Glenn Hwy. 907/745-4827 or 800/850-3247 www.alaskastatefair.org). You can shop for Alaskan-made gifts and crafts, and whoop it up with midway rides, livestock and 4-H shows, bake-offs, home-preserved produce contests, food, and live music. The fair runs 12 days, ending on Labor Day (it will be held August 23-September 3 in 2007). Admission is $10.

own raspberries and other fruits and vegetables. At **Pyrah's Pioneer Peak Farm** (✉ Mile 2.8, Bodenburg Loop ☎ 907/745–4511), which cultivates 35 kinds of fruits and vegetables and begins harvesting in mid-June, the peak picking time occurs around mid-July.

Forty-some animals roam at the **Musk Ox Farm,** which conducts 30-minute guided tours from May to September. There's a hands-on museum and a gift shop featuring hand-knitted items made from the cashmere-like underfur (qiviut) combed from the musk ox. The scarves and caps and more are made by Oomingmak, an Alaskan native collective. ✉ *Mile 50.1, Glenn Hwy.* ☎ *907/745–4151* 🌐 *www.muskoxfarm.org* 🎫 *$9* ⏲ *May–Sept., daily 10–6; Oct.–Apr., by appointment.*

Gold mining was an early mainstay of the Mat-Su Valley's economy.
★ You can tour the long-dormant **Independence Mine** on the Hatcher Pass Road, a loop that in summer connects the Parks Highway just north of Willow to the Glenn Highway near Palmer. The road to Independence Mine from the Palmer side was paved in the summer of 2003. The remainder of the roadway to Willow is gravel. In the 1940s as many as 200 workers were employed by the mine. Today it is a 271-acre state park and a cross-country ski area in winter. Only the wooden buildings remain; one of them, the red-roof manager's house, is now used as a visitor center. Guided tours are given on weekdays at 1:30 and 3:30 PM. ✉ *Independence Mine State Historical Park, 19 mi from Glenn Hwy. on Hatcher Pass Rd.* ☎ *907/745–3975* 🌐 *www.dnr.state.ak.us/parks/units/indmine.htm* 🎫 *$5 per vehicle, $3 tours* ⏲ *Visitor center early June–Labor Day, daily 11–7; grounds year-round.*

5

Where to Stay & Eat

$ **Colony Inn.** All guest rooms in this lovingly restored historic building are tastefully decorated with antiques and quilts. The building was used as a women's dormitory during the farm colonization of the 1930s. The small café ($–$$) serves light breakfasts, lunches, and Friday- and Saturday-night dinners. Be sure to try one of the homemade pies; the recipes have won blue ribbons at the Alaska State Fair. Inn reservations and check-in are handled at the Valley Hotel at 606 S. Alaska Street. ✉ *325 E. Elmwood Ave., 99645* ☎ *907/745–3330, 800/478–7666 in Alaska* *12 rooms* *Restaurant, cable TV, in-room data ports; no smoking* 💳 *AE, D, MC, V.*

$–$$ **Hatcher Pass Lodge.** This lodge has spectacular views and can serve as base camp for hiking, berry picking, and—in fall and winter—skiing. Most rooms and cabins have queen-size beds. Three dormer-style rooms provide cozy accommodations for one or two guests. The cabins, some with lofts, are carpeted and have large picture windows with views of Hatcher Pass Valley. The cabins' half baths have chemical toilets and water coolers; showers are in the lodge. The restaurant's Continental menu includes fondues, halibut, and pizzas. The bar serves cappuccinos and hot buttered rum for chilly nights. ✉ *Mile 17, Hatcher Pass Rd., Box 763, 99645* ☎ *907/745–5897 or 907/745–1200* 🌐 *www.hatcherpasslodge.com* *3 rooms, 9 cabins with shared showers* *Restaurant, sauna, bar, some pets allowed (fee); no a/c, no room phones, no room TVs, no smoking* 💳 *AE, D, MC, V.*

$ **Valley Hotel.** Built in 1948, this three-story budget hotel was remodeled in 2003. Small, well-kept rooms have quilts and carpets. The hotel is close to shopping, the library, and the local tourist information center. The restaurant—which serves all homemade desserts—is the only 24-hour operation in the area. ✉ *606 S. Alaska St., 99645* ☎ *907/745–3330, 800/478–7666 in Alaska* *43 rooms* *Restaurant, cable TV, in-room data ports, bar, no-smoking rooms; no a/c* *AE, D, MC, V.*

Wasilla

19 *42 mi north of Anchorage, 10 mi west of Palmer.*

Wasilla is one of the valley's original pioneer communities, and over time has served as a supply center for farmers, gold miners, and mushers. Today, fast-food restaurants and strip malls line the Parks Highway. Rolling hills and more scenic vistas can be found by wandering the area's back roads.

> **MUSH!**
>
> Wasilla is the headquarters and official starting point for the **Iditarod Trail Sled Dog Race,** run each March from here to Nome, more than 1,000 mi to the northwest. A ceremonial start is held on Anchorage's 4th Avenue the first Saturday in March, then continues from Wasilla the following day.

The **Museum of Alaska Transportation and Industry,** on a 20-acre site, exhibits some of the machines that helped develop Alaska, from dogsleds to jet aircraft, and everything in between. The Don Sheldon Building houses aviation artifacts as well as antique autos and photographic displays. A snowmachine (Alaskan for snowmobile) exhibit also is on display. ✉ *From Parks Hwy., turn south onto Neuser Rd. at Mile 47, follow road ¾ mi to end* ☎ *907/376–1211* *www.museumofalaska.org* *$8* *May–Sept., Tues.–Sun. 10–5.*

The **Iditarod Trail Headquarters** displays dogsleds, mushers' clothing, and trail gear, and you can catch video highlights of past races. The gift shop sells Iditarod items. Take dogsled rides in winter; during the summer, dogsled rides on wheels are available for $5. ✉ *Mile 2.2, Knik Rd.* ☎ *907/376–5155* *www.iditarod.com* *Free* *Memorial Day–mid-Sept., daily 8–7; mid-Sept.–Memorial Day, weekdays 8–5.*

Where to Stay & Eat

$–$$$ ✕ **Evangelo's Trattoria.** The food is good and the servings are ample at this spacious local favorite on the Parks Highway. Try the garlic-sautéed shrimp in a white-wine butter sauce or a mammoth calzone. The pizzas are loaded with goodies, and a salad bar provides a fresh selection. ✉ *301 Parks Hwy.* ☎ *907/376–1212* *AE, MC, V.*

$–$$ ✕ **Cadillac Café.** Hearty fare fills the menu at this diner-style café, including homemade pies; big, hand-pressed burgers; exotic pizzas turned out of a stone, wood-fired oven; and Southwestern-style Mexican food. The decor is described by the owner as "Alaska minimalist," but the booths are plush and comfortable, and hand-rubbed wood is much in evidence. Breakfast is served only on weekends. ✉ *Mile 49, Parks Hwy., at Pittman St.* ☎ *907/357–5533* *AE, D, MC, V.*

$$ **Best Western Lake Lucille Inn.** This well-maintained resort on Lake Lucille provides easy access to several recreational activities, including boating in summer and ice-skating and snowmobiling in winter. Half of the inn's bright and cheery rooms have private balconies overlooking the lake. Room decor includes art prints and quilts. *1300 W. Lake Lucille Dr., 99654, Mile 43.5 on the Parks Hwy. 907/373–1776 or 800/528–1234 www.bestwestern.com/lakelucilleinn 50 rooms, 4 suites Restaurant, cable TV, in-room data ports, health club, boating, lobby lounge, meeting room, some pets allowed; no a/c AE, D, DC, MC, V.*

★ **$–$$** **Pioneer Ridge Bed and Breakfast Inn.** Each of the spacious, log-partitioned rooms in this converted barn is decorated according to a theme. The Denali Room has posters of the mountain, snowshoes, crampons, and other climbing gear. A dogsled and other race paraphernalia mark the Iditarod Room. A rooftop common room has a spectacular 360-degree panorama of the mountains and river valleys. *2221 Yukon Cir., HC31, Box 5083K, 99654 907/376–7472 or 800/478–7472 www.pioneerridge.com 1 suite, 1 cabin, 4 rooms with private baths, 1 room with separate, unshared bath Exercise equipment, sauna, Wi-Fi; no a/c, no room TVs AE, D, MC, V BP.*

5

Talkeetna

20 *56 mi north of Wasilla, 112 mi north of Anchorage.*

Talkeetna lies at the end of a spur road near Mile 99 of the Parks Highway. Mountaineers congregate here to begin their assaults on Mt. McKinley in Denali National Park. The Denali mountain rangers have their climbing headquarters here, as do most glacier pilots who fly climbing parties to the mountain. A carved pole at the town cemetery honors deceased mountaineers. The **Talkeetna Historical Society Museum,** across from the Fairview Inn, explores the history of Mt. McKinley climbs. The museum has a scale model of Mt. McKinley and features information on the history of climbing attempts on the continent's highest peak. A Talkeetna walking-tour map points out sites of historical interest. *1st Alley and D St. 907/733–2487 www.talkeetnahistory.org $3 May 15–Sept. 15, daily 10–6.*

Where to Stay & Eat

$ **Swiss-Alaska Inn.** Family-run since 1976, this rustic-style property is well known among those who come to fish in the Talkeetna, Susitna, and Chulitna rivers. Floral decor embellishes the bright rooms. Menu selections at the restaurant (¢–$$) include halibut, salmon, buffalo burgers, and the owner's secret-recipe Swiss-style French toast. *East Talkeetna, by boat launch, Box 565, 99676 907/733–2424 www.swissalaska.com 20 rooms Restaurant, in-room VCRs, Internet; no a/c, no room phones, no room TVs, no smoking AE, D, MC, V.*

★ **¢–$** **Talkeetna Roadhouse.** This circa-1917 log roadhouse has a common sitting area and rooms in a variety of sizes, including a bunk room with four beds ($21). Rooms are very basic: bed, table, window, period. Sizable breakfasts are the order of the day at the restaurant (¢), along with soup, sandwiches, desserts, and pies, all made from scratch. It's a popular place with locals and with climbers who use Talkeetna's air taxis to reach Mt. McKinley. In the winter, the café is open only on weekends and evenings. ✉ *Main St., Box 604, 99676* ☎ *907/733–1351* 🌐 *www.talkeetnaroadhouse.com* *8 rooms share 4 baths* *Restaurant, Internet room, some pets allowed; no a/c, no room phones, no room TVs, no smoking* 💳 *MC, V.*

★ $$$$ **Talkeetna Alaskan Lodge.** This luxury hotel has excellent views of Mt. McKinley as well as access to nature trails. Rooms are modern, in the style of an Alaskan lodge, and mountainside room upgrades are available. The Great Room has comfortable seating, a 45-foot river-rock fireplace in the center of the room, and an espresso bar. The tour desk can arrange flightseeing, river trips, or any other Alaska adventure you can imagine. ✉ *Mile 12.5, Talkeetna Spur Rd.* *2525 C St., Suite 405, Anchorage 99503* ☎ *907/265–4501 or 888/959–9590* 🌐 *www.talkeetnalodge.com* *201 rooms, 3 suites* *Restaurant, some microwaves, cable TV, in-room data ports, hiking, bar, meeting room, travel services; no a/c, no smoking* 💳 *AE, D, MC, V.*

SMALL-TOWN FLAVOR

Talkeetna is a must-visit if you're driving between Anchorage and Denali or Fairbanks. A true small town, Talkeetna has a genuine **Roadhouse** (with delicious home-made berry pies), quirky locals, and a pebbly shore along the Susitna with fantastic views of Mt. McKinley on a clear day. If you do come through town, be sure to check out the **West Rib Restaurant** (907/733-3354), which is in the back of historic **Nagley's Store** on Main St. (a mini-museum of sorts). Grab a seat out back and wash down the delicious chili, burgers, and fries with a local micro-brew!

¢ **Fairview Inn.** Built in 1923, the Fairview is listed on the National Register of Historic Places. It oozes local color, from the bear rug nailed to the ceiling over the bar to photographs of local characters and former owners on the wall. You're likely to meet members of Mt. McKinley climbing expeditions during the early-summer climbing season. You'll also hear lots of good, local music, but be forewarned: you'll hear it even if you don't want to, so if a good night's sleep is important, check first to see if the band will be playing. The inn is open year-round, but food is served only from Memorial Day to Labor Day in the outdoor beer garden. ✉ *101 Main St., Box 1109, 99676* ☎ *907/733–2423* 🌐 *www.denali-fairview.com* *5 rooms with shared baths* *Restaurant, bar; no a/c, no room phones, no room TVs* 💳 *AE, MC, V.*

Sports, the Outdoors & Guided Tours

BOATING, FLOATING & FISHING

Denali Floats (☎ 907/733–2384 or 800/651–5221) leads scenic raft trips on the Susitna River, complete with shore lunch and occasional musical accompaniment, and can arrange wilderness expeditions to suit your schedule. **Mahay's Riverboat Service** (☎ 907/733–2223 or 800/736–2210 🌐 www.mahaysriverboat.com) conducts guided jet-boat tours, scenic cruises, and fishing on the Susitna and Talkeetna rivers.

Tri-River Charters (Box 312, 99676 ☎ 907/733–2400 🌐 www.tririvercharters.com) operates fishing trips out of Talkeetna and on the nearby Deshka River, and can provide all the necessary tackle and gear.

CLOSE UP

A Privileged Communion

BETWEEN 1903 AND 1912, eight expeditions walked the slopes of 20,320-foot Mt. McKinley. But none had reached the absolute top of North America's highest peak. Among those who failed were some of North America's premier explorers and climbers. Thus the stage was set for Hudson Stuck, a self-described American amateur mountaineer.

Stuck came to Alaska in 1904, drawn not by mountains but by a missionary calling. As the Episcopal Church's archdeacon for the Yukon River region, he visited native villages year-round. His passion for climbing was unexpectedly rekindled in 1906, when he saw from afar the "glorious, broad, massive uplift" of McKinley, the "father of mountains." Five years after that wondrous view, Stuck pledged to reach McKinley's summit—or at least try. For his climbing party he picked three Alaskans experienced in snow and ice travel, though not in mountaineering: Harry Karstens, a well-known explorer and backcountry guide who would later become the first superintendent of Mt. McKinley National Park; Robert Tatum, Stuck's missionary assistant; and Walter Harper, part native, who served as Stuck's interpreter.

Assisted by two sled-dog teams, the group began its expedition on St. Patrick's Day, 1913, at Nenana, a village 90 mi northeast of McKinley. A month later, they began their actual ascent of the great peak's northern side, via the Muldrow Glacier. The glacier's surface proved to be a maze of crevasses, some of them wide chasms with no apparent bottom. Carefully working their way up-glacier, the climbers established a camp at 11,500 feet. From there they had to ascend a steep and jumbled ridgeline. Moving slowly, the team chopped a staircase up several miles—and 3,000 vertical feet—of rock, snow, and ice. Their progress was delayed several times by high winds, heavy snow, and near-zero visibility.

By May 30 the climbers had reached the top of the ridge (later named in Karstens's honor) and moved into a high glacial basin. Despite temperatures ranging from subzero to 21°F, they kept warm at night by sleeping on sheep and caribou skins and covering themselves with down quilts, camel's-hair blankets, and a wolf robe.

On June 6 the team established its high camp at 18,000 feet. The following morning was bright, cloudless, and windy. Three of the climbers suffered headaches and stomach pains, but given the clear weather everyone agreed to make an attempt. They left camp at 5 AM and by 1:30 PM stood within a few yards of McKinley's summit. Harper, who had been leading all day, was the first to reach the top, soon followed by the others. After catching their breath, the teammates shook hands, said a prayer of thanks, made some scientific measurements, and reveled in their magnificent surroundings. In his classic book *The Ascent of Denali*, Hudson Stuck later reflected, "There was no pride of conquest, no trace of that exultation of victory some enjoy upon the first ascent of a lofty peak, no gloating over good fortune that had hoisted us a few hundred feet higher than others who had struggled and been discomfited. Rather, was the feeling that a privileged communion with the high places of the earth had been granted."

For information about flightseeing out of Talkeetna, turn to p. 378.

Denali State Park

21 *34 mi north of Talkeetna, 132 mi north of Anchorage.*

Overshadowed by the larger and more charismatic Denali National Park & Preserve in the Interior, "Little Denali" offers excellent access (it's bisected by the Parks Highway), beautiful views of Mt. McKinley, scenic campgrounds, and prime wilderness hiking and backpacking opportunities within a few miles of the road system. Between the Talkeetna Mountains and the Alaska Range, Denali State Park combines wooded lowlands and forested foothills topped by alpine tundra. ✉ *From Parks Hwy. Milepost 131.7 to Mile 169.2* ✆ *Alaska State Parks, Mat-Su Area Office, HC 32, Box 6706, Wasilla 99687* ☎ *907/745–3975.*

The park's chief attraction, other than McKinley views, is the 35-mi-long **Curry-Kesugi Ridge,** which forms a rugged spine through the heart of the park that is ideal backpacking terrain. The initial climb to get to the ridge is strenuous, but once you get up high, it's mostly gentle up-and-down terrain until you head back down to the road. The trail runs from the Troublesome Creek trailhead at Mile 137.3 to the Little Coal Creek trailhead at Mile 163.9. The Byers Lake campground at Mile 147 has a trailhead for a spur trail that intersects the Kesugi Ridge trail, offering an alternative to hiking the entire 35 mi of the main trail. Views of Mt. McKinley and the Alaska Range from the ridge trail are stunning. ■ **TIP→ Be advised that this is a very bear-intensive area, especially the Troublesome Creek area in late summer when the salmon runs are in full force.**

Another destination favored by backcountry travelers is the **Peters Hills,** accessible from Petersville Road in Trapper Creek. Denali State Park borders the hills, and primitive trails and campgrounds are used year-round. It's especially popular with snowmobilers in the winter and mountain-bikers in summer.

Where to Stay

$$$ **McKinley Princess Wilderness Lodge.** When the sky is clear and Mt. McKinley is visible, this lodge has excellent views of North America's highest peak, especially from the lobby, with its large stone fireplace. On private land inside Denali State Park, this hillside lodge is surrounded by forest and overlooks the Chulitna River. You stay in bungalow-style guest rooms with separate sitting rooms. The tour desk can arrange horseback rides, river-rafting trips, naturalist walks, flightseeing excursions, fishing trips, mountain-bike rentals, and alpine hikes. ✉ *Mile 133, Parks Hwy., Trapper Creek 99683* ☎ *907/733–2900 or 800/426–0500* 🌐 *www.princessalaskalodges.com* *238 rooms, 4 suites* *Restaurant, café, some in-room hot tubs, cable TV, gym, hik-*

ing, shop, meeting rooms, travel services; no a/c ▭ *AE, D, DC, MC, V* ⊙ *Closed mid-Sept.–mid-May.*

¢ **Alaska State Parks Cabins.** Two public-use cabins are in Denali State Park, along the shores of Byers Lake. One cabin is on a gravel road, 1 mi from the highway, and the other is accessible by canoe or by a ½-mi walk-in trail. Both are equipped with bunks to sleep six, wood-burning stove, table, and benches, but they have no running water (they have pit toilets) or electricity. *Alaska State Parks Information Center, 550 W. 7th Ave., Suite 1260, Anchorage 99501-3557* ✣ *Mile 43.5 on the Parks Hwy.* ☎ *907/269–8400* 🌐 *www.dnr.state.ak.us/parks/cabins/matsu.cfm* *2 cabins* ▭ *No credit cards.*

CAMPING **Alaska State Parks Campgrounds.** Three roadside campgrounds are within Denali State Park—Byers Lake, Lower Troublesome Creek, and Denali Viewpoint North. All are easily accessible from the Parks Highway. The Byers Lake campground also has a boat launch, canoe and kayak rentals, and nearby hiking trails. Sites are available on a first-come, first-served basis. Sites do not have hookups. *Pit toilets, drinking water, fire pits, picnic tables* *123 tent/RV sites* *Alaska State Parks, HC 32, Box 6706, Wasilla 99654* ☎ *907/745–3975* 🌐 *www.dnr.state.ak.us/parks/units/denali2.htm* *$10* ▭ *No credit cards* *Reservations not accepted* ⊙ *Closed Oct.–May.*

5

Glennallen

22 *187 mi northeast of Anchorage.*

This community of 900 residents is the gateway to Wrangell–St. Elias National Park and Preserve. It's 124 mi from Glennallen to McCarthy, the last 58 mi on unpaved gravel. This town is also the service center for the Copper River basin and is a fly-in base for several wilderness outfitters.

Where to Stay & Eat

¢–$$ ✕ **Caribou Restaurant.** This convivial place serves such typical roadside fare as burgers, hot sandwiches, meat loaf, pancakes, and charbroiled steak. Sweet rolls, pies, and other treats are baked fresh daily. If you haven't managed to spy any of the local wildlife on your trip, just check out the walls here for numerous taxidermied examples. ✉ *Mile 186.5, Glenn Hwy.* ☎ *907/822–4222* ▭ *AE, D, MC, V.*

$$ **Caribou Hotel.** Rooms decorated in mauve and sea green fill this modern hotel. ■ **TIP→ Unless you're on a strict budget, ask for a room in the main building and not in the trailer-like annex out front,** where rooms are spartan and share a bath. There are also a pair of rustic cabins available for those who want to get a taste of living in "Bush Alaska." Several rooms in the main building have hot tubs. The owners operate a nearby B&B and a property with three two-bedroom apartments and a one-bedroom apartment. ✉ *Mile 186.5, Glenn Hwy.* *Box 329, 99588* ☎ *907/822–3302 or 800/478–3302* 🌐 *www.cariboubotel.com* *83 rooms, 63 with bath; 3 suites, 2 cabins* *Some in-room hot tubs, some kitchens, some microwaves, some refrigerators, cable TV, in-room data ports, meeting room, some pets allowed; no a/c* ▭ *AE, D, DC, MC, V.*

Wrangell–St. Elias National Park & Preserve

23 *77 mi southeast of Glennallen, 264 mi east of Anchorage.*

In a land of many grand and spectacularly beautiful mountains, those in the 9.2-million-acre Wrangell–St. Elias National Park and Preserve have been singled out by many Alaskans as the finest of them all. This extraordinarily compact cluster of immense peaks toward the southeastern part of Alaska belongs to four different mountain ranges.

Mile 106.8, Richardson Hwy. Box 439, Copper Center 99573 907/822–5234 www.nps.gov/wrst.

Covering an area some 100 mi by 70 mi, the **Wrangells** tower above the 2,500-foot-high Copper River Plateau, and the peaks of Mts. Jarvis, Drum, Blackburn, Sanford, and Wrangell rise 15,000 feet to 16,000 feet from sea level. The white-iced spire of **Mt. St. Elias,** in the St. Elias Range, reaches more than 18,000 feet. It's the fourth-tallest mountain on the North American continent and the crown of the planet's highest coastal range.

The park's coastal mountains are frequently wreathed in snow-filled clouds, their massive height making a giant wall that contains the great storms brewed in the Gulf of Alaska. As a consequence, they bear some of the continent's largest ice fields, with more than 100 glaciers radiating from them. One of these, the **Malaspina Glacier,** is 1,500 square mi—larger than the state of Rhode Island. This tidewater glacier has an incredible pattern of black-and-white stripes made by the other glaciers that coalesced to form it. ■ **TIP→ Look for Malaspina Glacier on the coast north of Yakutat if you fly between Juneau and Anchorage.**

Rising through many life zones, the Wrangell–St. Elias Park and Preserve is largely undeveloped wilderness parkland on a grand scale. The area is perfect mountain-biking and hiking terrain, and the rivers invite rafting for those with expedition experience. The mountains attract climbers from around the world; most of them fly in from Glennallen ★ or Yakutat. The nearby abandoned **Kennicott Mine** is one of the park's main visitor attractions. Limited services are available in the end-of-the-road town of **McCarthy.** Facilities include guest lodges, a B&B, and a restaurant. There's no gas station or post office.

The park is accessible from Alaska's highway system, via one of two gravel roads. The unpaved **Nabesna Road** leaves the Glenn Highway–Tok Cutoff at the village of Slana and takes you 45 mi into the park's northern foothills. The better-known route is the **McCarthy Road,** which stretches 60 mi as it follows an old railroad bed from Chitina to the Kennicott River. At the end of the road you must park and cross the river via a footbridge.

★ **$$$$** **Ultima Thule Outfitters.** This remote fly-in-only lodge on the Chitina River in Wrangell–St. Elias National Park and Preserve provides a wonderful chance to experience an "air-safari adventure." The cost is $1,000 per person per day, with a four-day minimum. Included in your stay are breathtaking flightseeing, rafting, climbing, hiking, fishing, mushing, and skiing excursions, among others. Any adventure you can dream up, the

WARNING 

Before setting out on the McCarthy Road, make sure both you and your car are prepared. Your car should be equipped with a working jack and a properly inflated spare tire, or else potholes, old railroad ties, and occasional railroad spikes may leave you stranded.

Claus family will make it happen. Three generations of the family make their home here, and their knowledge of the area is unsurpassed. At the age of 18, daughter Ellie was the youngest person to ever finish the Iditarod Trail Sled Dog Race as a rookie in 2004. The family-style meals include local foods such as fish, game, and vegetables from the garden as well as homemade bread, pies, and cakes. Oak floors, wallpaper, wood-burning stoves, and brass beds provide the comforts of home, Bavarian-style. *Summer: Box 109, Chitina 99566 Winter: Box 770361, Eagle River 99577 907/688–1200 www.ultimathulelodge.com 6 cabins Dining room, sauna, boating, fishing, hiking, cross-country skiing, Internet; no a/c, no room phones, no room TVs, no smoking No credit cards FAP.*

★ **$$$–$$$$** **Kennicott Glacier Lodge.** Artifacts and photos of the era when mining was the main order of business in the ghost town of Kennicott adorn the small rooms in this modern wood lodge. Rooms have cold-water sinks and shared bathroom and shower facilities. The South Wing rooms have private bathrooms. Fresh-baked goods are favorites at the buffet breakfast. Sit-down lunches are served, or you can request a sack lunch to take with you. Dinner is a "wilderness gourmet" spread served family style. Afterward, you can relax in the spacious living room or on the front porch. The front desk can arrange glacier trekking, flightseeing, rafting, and alpine hiking for additional fees, and an evening tour of Kennicott is included in the room rate. A vacation package that includes room and all meals is available. The lodge provides a shuttle from the end of the road in McCarthy. *5 mi from McCarthy Box 103940, Anchorage 99510 907/258–2350 or 800/582–5128 www.kennicottlodge.com 35 rooms, 10 with bath Dining room, hiking, meeting room; no a/c, no room phones, no room TVs, no smoking AE, D, MC, V Closed mid-Sept.–mid-May.*

$$$ **Copper River Princess Wilderness Lodge.** At the gateway to the park, this lodge has views of the Wrangell–St. Elias mountain range and the Copper and Klutina rivers. A wall of windows two stories high provides dramatic views of towering peaks and the Copper River. Dark-wood accents and Alaska wildlife and scenery prints, conveying the ambience of a well-appointed hunting lodge, adorn each room. *Brenwick Craig Rd., Mile 102, Richardson Hwy., Copper Center 99573 907/822–4000, 800/426–0500 reservations www.princesslodges.com 85 rooms Restaurant, coffee shop, cable TV, bar, shop, meeting room, airport shuttle; no smoking AE, DC, MC, V Closed mid-Sept.–mid-May.*

CAMPING **Alaska State Parks Campgrounds.** The state maintains 23 road-accessible campgrounds in the Matanuska-Susitna–Copper River region. Most can accommodate RVs up to 35 feet long, though electrical hookups are not available. The allowed length of stay varies from 4 to 15 days. Most campgrounds have nearby hiking trails. *Flush toilets, some drinking water, some fire pits, some picnic tables* *23 campgrounds* *Alaska State Parks, Mat-Su Area Office, HC 32, Box 6706, Wasilla 99654* *907/745–3975* *Reservations not accepted* *$5–$12* *No credit cards* *Closed Oct.–May.*

Sports, the Outdoors & Guided Tours

ADVENTURE TOURS **St. Elias Alpine Guides** (888/933–5427 or 907/554–4445 www.steliasguides.com) gives introductory mountaineering lessons, leads excursions ranging from half-day glacier walks to monthlong backpacking trips, and is the only company contracted by the Park Service to conduct guided tours of historic Kennicott buildings. Daylong raft trips leave from Kennicott. This service, founded by Bob Jacobs, has been in business more than 25 years and will continue to operate under experienced mountaineer Wayne Marrs, with Bob working as a guide.

SOUTH CENTRAL ALASKA ESSENTIALS

Transportation

Anchorage is the central hub of the region, connected by rail and road to Seward and Whittier. Valdez can be reached by a rather indirect but interesting driving route (the Glenn Highway to the Richardson Highway) out of Anchorage. The Seward and Sterling highways connect to most of the places you'll want to see on the Kenai Peninsula, including the small towns of Hope, Soldotna, and Homer. South Central's other "highway," the ferry-driven Alaska Marine Highway, connects with Kodiak, Whittier, Seward, Valdez, Dutch Harbor, Homer, Seldovia, and Cordova via the gulf. Air taxis are also a viable means of transportation around South Central.

BY AIR

Anchorage is served by major national and international airlines and well-stocked with smaller carriers and local air-taxi operators. Alaska Airlines has in-state jet service from Anchorage to Cordova and Kodiak; and ERA Aviation flies turbo-prop planes to Homer, Kenai, Valdez, Cordova, and Kodiak. For flights to the Alaska Peninsula, the Aleutians, and western Alaska Bush villages, call PenAir. Frontier Flying Service flies to Fairbanks, Deadhorse, Barrow, and several western Alaska Bush villages.

Alaska Airlines 800/252–7522 www.alaskaair.com. **ERA Aviation** 907/243–3300 or 800/866–8394 www.flyera.com. **Frontier Flying Service** 907/474–0014, 800/478–6779 in Alaska www.frontierflying.com. **PenAir** 907/243–2323 or 800/448–4226 www.penair.com.

BY BOAT & FERRY

Ferries are a great way to explore the South Central coast, with its glaciers, mountains, fjords, and sea mammals. The ferries between Valdez and Whittier run by way of Columbia Glacier in summer, where it is not unusual to witness giant fragments of ice calving from the face of the glacier into Prince William Sound.

The Alaska Marine Highway, the state-run ferry operator, has scheduled service to Valdez, Cordova, Whittier, Seward, Homer, and Seldovia on the mainland; to Kodiak and Port Lions on Kodiak Island; and to the port of Dutch Harbor in the Aleutian Islands. The same agency runs the ferries that operate in Southeast Alaska, but the two systems connect only on once-a-month sailings. The system operates on two schedules; summer (May–September) sailings are considerably more frequent than fall and winter service. Check your schedules carefully: ferries do not stop at all ports every day. ■ TIP→ **Reservations are required on all routes; they should be made as far in advance as possible, particularly for summer trips.**

Alaska Marine Highway ✉ 6858 Glacier Hwy., Juneau 99801 ☎ 907/465-3941 or 800/642-0066 🌐 www.ferryalaska.com.

BY BUS

Year-round service runs between Fairbanks and Anchorage by way of Denali National Park and also down to Homer, at the very tip of the Kenai Peninsula. Alaska Direct Bus Lines provides service between Anchorage and Fairbanks and also to Whitehorse and Skagway. The Park Connection has regularly scheduled shuttle service between Seward, Anchorage, and Denali National Park mid-May to mid-September. Seward Bus Line serves Anchorage, Portage, and Seward. A subsidiary offers service between Anchorage and Homer.

Alaska Direct Bus Lines ☎ 907/277-6652 or 800/770-6652. **Park Connection** ☎ 800/208-0200, 907/224-7116 for Seward same-day bookings, 907/683-1240 for Denali same-day bookings. **Seward Bus Line** ☎ 907/563-0800 or 907/224-3608.

BY CAR

Keep in mind that all but a few miles of the road system consist of two-lane highways, not all of which are paved. Two highway routes offer a choice for travel by car between Fairbanks and Anchorage. Heading north from Anchorage, the Parks Highway (turn left off Glenn Highway near Palmer) passes through Wasilla, up the Susitna River drainage area and through a low pass in the Alaska Range, then down into the Tanana Valley and Fairbanks. This route passes the entrance to Denali National Park and roughly parallels the Alaska Railroad. A longer route (436 mi) follows the Glenn Highway to the Richardson Highway, then heads north to Fairbanks through the Copper River valley. This route makes possible a side trip to Valdez, and it's the most direct connection to the Alaska Highway, joining it at Tok.

You can also link the two routes by using the Denali Highway, which, despite its name, doesn't run through Denali National Park. Rather, it connects the Richardson Highway with the Parks Highway between the towns of Paxson and Cantwell. You can make a huge figure eight by using the Denali, but be advised that this 135-mi-long road isn't paved except for relatively short sections at either end, and services are limited. Don't start the trip without a full tank of gas and at least one real spare tire, just to be on the safe side.

Chinook Auto Rentals ✉ Cordova Airport ☎ 877/424-5279. **State Department of Transportation** ☎ 907/835-4242 in Anchorage for hotline reports on highways during snow season.

BY TRAIN

The Alaska Railroad Corporation operates the Alaska Railroad, which is said to be the last railroad in North America that still makes flag stops to accommodate the homesteaders, hikers, fishing parties, and other travelers who get on and off in remote places. The 470-mi main line runs up Alaska's rail belt between Seward and Fairbanks via Anchorage. There's daily service between Anchorage and Fairbanks in summer, and in winter there's one round-trip per week (Anchorage to Fairbanks on Saturday, Fairbanks to Anchorage on Sunday). Service to Seward from Anchorage runs mid-May to September 1 only. Adults are allowed two pieces of luggage to a maximum of 50 pounds. There's a $20 charge for bicycles; camping equipment is allowed on a space-available basis.

For information on the luxury-class Ultradome service between Anchorage and Fairbanks, contact Princess Tours about its *Midnight Sun Express*. Westours/Gray Line of Alaska operates the *McKinley Explorer* on Alaska Railroad trains as well.

Alaska Railroad ☎ 907/265-2494 or 800/544-0552 🌐 www.akrr.com. **Princess Tours** ☎ 206/728-4202 or 800/835-8907. **Westours/Gray Line of Alaska** ☎ 907/277-5581 or 800/478-6388.

Contacts & Resources

BANKS

Alaska USA Federal Credit Union ✉ 2685 Mill Bay Rd., Kodiak ☎ 486-0900. **First National Bank Alaska** ✉ 3655 Heath St., Homer ☎ 907/235-5800 ✉ 218 Center Ave., Kodiak ☎ 907/486-7900 ✉ 303 W. Evergreen, Palmer ☎ 907/746-8900 ✉ 303 4th Ave., Seward ☎ 907/224-4200 ✉ 44501 Sterling Hwy., Soldotna ☎ 907/260-6000 ✉ 101 Egan St., Valdez ☎ 907/834-4800. **Keybank Alaska** ✉ 1150 S. Colony Way., Palmer ☎ 907/745-6100. **Wells Fargo Bank** ✉ 515 Main St., Cordova ☎ 907/424-3258 ✉ Mile 187, Glenn Hwy., Glennallen ☎ 907/822-3214 ✉ 88 Sterling Hwy., Homer ☎ 907/235-8151 ✉ 202 W. Marine Way, Kodiak ☎ 907/486-3126 ✉ 2645 Mill Bay Rd., Kodiak ☎ 907/486-6900 ✉ 705 S. Bailey St., Palmer ☎ 907/745-2161 ✉ 908 3rd Ave., Seward ☎ 907/224-5283 ✉ 44552 Sterling Hwy., Soldotna ☎ 907/262-4435 ✉ 337 Egan St., Valdez ☎ 907/835-4745.

EMERGENCIES

Emergency Services **Police, ambulance, emergency** ☎ 911. **Alaska State Troopers** ☎ 907/269-5722 in Anchorage, 907/822-3263 in Glennallen, 907/235-8239 in Homer, 907/486-4121 in Kodiak, 907/745-2131 in Palmer, 907/224-3346 in Seward, 907/262-4052 in Soldotna, 907/835-4359 in Valdez.

Hospitals **Central Peninsula General Hospital** ✉ 250 Hospital Pl., Soldotna ☎ 907/262-4404. **Community Hospital** ✉ 911 Meals Ave., Valdez ☎ 907/835-2249. **Cordova Medical Center** ✉ 602 Chase Ave., Cordova ☎ 907/424-8000. **Crossroads Medical Center** ✉ Mile 187.5, Glenn Hwy., Glennallen ☎ 907/822-3203. **Mat-Su Regional Medical Center** ✉ 2500 S. Woodworth Loop, Palmer ☎ 907/861-6000. **Providence Kodiak Island Medical Center** ✉ 1915 E. Rezanof Dr., Kodiak ☎ 907/486-3281. **Providence Seward Medical Center** ✉ 417 1st Ave., Seward ☎ 907/224-5205. **Seldovia Medical Clinic** ✉ 252 Seldovia St., Seldovia ☎ 907/234-7825. **South Peninsula Hospital** ✉ 4300 Bartlett St., Homer ☎ 907/235-8101.

MEDIA

RADIO Once you get away from Anchorage, your radio options are severely limited. Most small towns have a National Public Radio station or a repeater that broadcasts the Anchorage station. Occasionally you'll find a local station transmitting canned programs from the Lower 48. Of the stations you can find, odds are that the format will be either NPR, country, or religious. If you need more variety than that, stock up on CDs before you head out of town.

NEWSPAPERS Here the media news is a bit more characteristic of normal small-town life. Many towns have weekly papers, or a regional publication. They offer a glimpse into what rural Alaska life is really like, with school athletic news, logs of calls to the police department, letters to the editor, etc. They're all well worth picking up at the grocery store or gas station.

Weekly newspapers are the *Cordova Times* (www.alaskanewspapers.com/cordovatimes.asp); *The Homer News* (www.homernews.com); *The Seward Phoenix Log* (www.alaskanewspapers.com/sewardphoenix.asp); and *The Peninsula Clarion* (www.peninsulaclarion.com), serving Kenai and Soldotna. Other newspapers are *The Kodiak Daily Mirror* (www.kodiakdailymirror.com); *The Mat-Su Valley Frontiersman* (www.frontiersman.com), published Tuesday, Friday, and Sunday; and *The Valdez Star* (www.valdezstar.net).

5

TOURS

BOATING & GLACIERS Tour Operators **Alaskan Wilderness Sailing & Kayaking** Box 1313, Valdez 99686 ☎ 907/835–5175. **Columbia Glacier Wildlife Cruises/*Lu-Lu Belle*** ☎ 907/835–5141 or 800/411–0090 ☎ 800/411–0090 off-season. **Homer Ocean Charters** ☎ 907/235–6212 or 800/426–6212. **Kenai Coastal Tours** ☎ 907/277–2131 or 800/770–9119. **Kenai Fjords Tours** ☎ 907/224–8068 in Seward, 907/276–6249, 800/478–8068. **Keystone Raft & Kayak Adventures, Inc.** ☎ 907/835–2606 or 800/328–8460. **Kodiak Island Charters** ☎ 907/486–5380 or 800/575–5380. **Mariah Tours** ☎ 907/224–8623 or 800/270–1238. **Prince William Sound Cruises and Tours** ☎ 907/835–4731 or 800/992–1297. **26 Glacier Cruise** ✉ Phillips' Cruises & Tours, 519 W. 4th Ave., Suite 100, Anchorage 99510 ☎ 800/544–0529 or 907/276–8023 ⊕ www.26glaciers.com.

FISHING Tour Operators **Central Charters** ✉ 4241 Homer Spit Rd., Homer 99603 ☎ 907/235-7847 or 800/478-7847. **Fish House** ✉ Small-boat harbor, Seward ☎ 907/224-3674 or 800/257-7760. ***U-Rascal*** ☎ 907/486-5380.

FLIGHTSEEING Tour Operators **Alpine Aviation Adventures** ✉ Valdez ☎ 907/835-4304, 800/478-4304 in Alaska. **Cordova Air Service** ☎ 907/424-3289, 800/424-7608 in Alaska. **Prince William Sound Adventures** ☎ 907/424-3350.

GENERAL INTEREST Alaska Heritage Tours offers booking for lodges, day cruises, and custom packages from Anchorage to Talkeetna, Denali, Prince William Sound, and Kenai Fjords National Park.

Tour Operators **Alaska Heritage Tours** ☎ 907/265-4500 or 877/258-6877 ⊕ www.alaskaheritagetours.com. **Alaska Wildland Adventures** ☎ 907/783-2928 or 800/334-8730. **Gray Line of Alaska** ☎ 206/281-3535 or 800/544-2206.

HIKING Information on locations and difficulty of trails is available at the Alaska Public Lands Information Center at 4th and F streets in Anchorage. Another good resource is *55 Ways to the Wilderness in South Central Alaska*, published by the Mountaineers and available at most local bookstores. Check with the salespeople at the REI store on Northern Lights Boulevard in Anchorage, and for hard-core mountaineering types, stop by Alaska Mountaineering and Hiking on Spenard Road. REI also has maps and local travel books and info.

VISITOR INFORMATION

Alaska Public Lands Information Center ⊠ 605 W. 4th Ave., Anchorage 99501 ☎ 907/271-2737 🌐 www.nps.gov/aplic. **Bureau of Land Management** 📫 Box 147, Glennallen 99588 ☎ 907/822-3217 🌐 www.glennallen.ak.blm.gov. **Cordova Chamber of Commerce** 📫 Box 99, Cordova 99574 ☎ 907/424-7260 🌐 www.cordovachamber.com. **Homer Chamber of Commerce** ⊠ 135 Sterling Hwy. 📫 Box 541, Homer 99603 ☎ 907/235-5300 🌐 www.homeralaska.org. **Kenai Peninsula Visitor Information Center** ⊠ 44790 Sterling Hwy., Soldotna 99669 ☎ 907/262-1337. **Kodiak Island Convention and Visitors Bureau** ⊠ 100 Marine Way, Kodiak 99615 ☎ 907/486-4782 🌐 www.kodiak.org/cvb.html. **Palmer Chamber of Commerce** 📫 Box 45, Palmer 99645 ☎ 907/745-2880 🌐 www.palmerchamber.org. **Seward Visitors Bureau** ⊠ Mile 2, Seward Hwy. 📫 Box 749, Seward 99664 ☎ 907/224-8051 🌐 www.sewardak.org. **U.S. Fish and Wildlife Service** ⊠ Alaska Regional Office, 1011 E. Tudor Rd., Anchorage 99503 ☎ 907/786-3487 🌐 http://alaska.fws.gov. **U.S. Forest Service** ⊠ 3301 C St., Room 300, Anchorage 99503 ☎ 907/271-2500 🌐 www.fs.fed.us/r10/chugach. **Valdez Convention and Visitors Bureau** ⊠ 200 Chenega St. 📫 Box 1603, Valdez 99686 ☎ 907/835-2984 🌐 www.valdezalaska.org. **Wasilla Chamber of Commerce** ⊠ 1830 E. Parks Hwy., A-116, Wasilla 99654 ☎ 907/376-1299 🌐 www.wasillachamber.org.

The Interior and Denali National Park & Preserve

WITH FAIRBANKS & THE YUKON

The "Big 5" inhabit Denali: wolves, Dall sheep, bears, moose, and caribou (pictured).

6

WORD OF MOUTH

"Backcountry hiking is wonderful in Denali. With the tundra, there's little need for bushwhacking."

–repete

"Dawson City is a stunning, eye-opening glimpse of history, and the Yukon River is grand to behold."

–John

www.fodors.com/forums

WELCOME TO THE INTERIOR

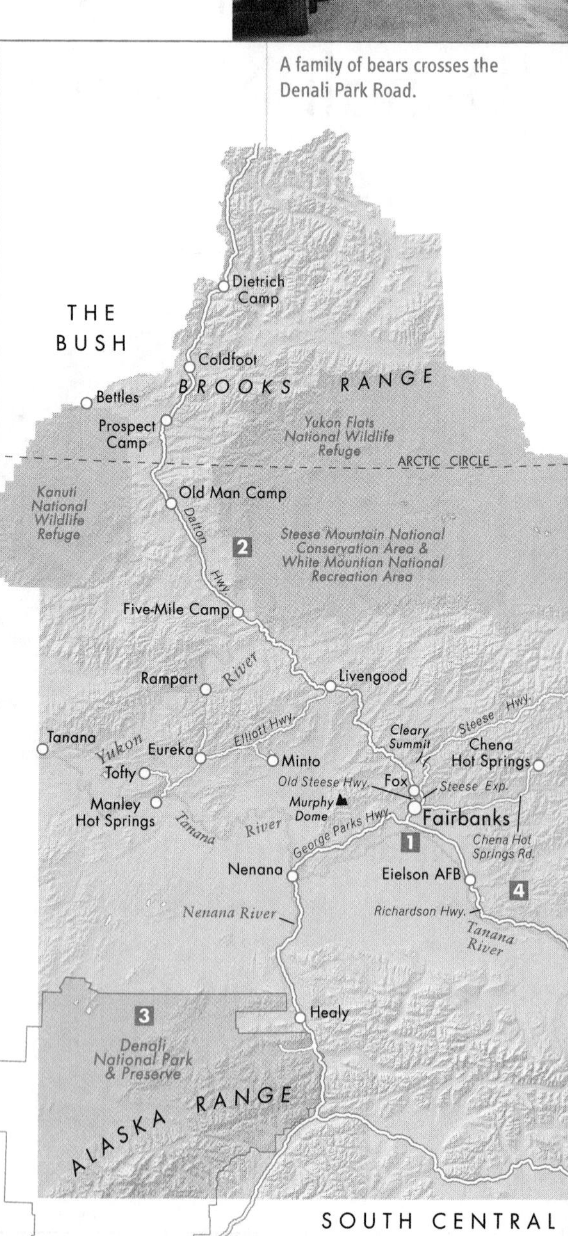

A family of bears crosses the Denali Park Road.

TOP REASONS TO GO

★ **Denali National Park & Preserve:** Denali is breathtaking and unforgettable. Larger than the state of Massachusetts, the park captures the spirit and beauty of Alaska.

★ **Gold Rush heritage:** The frontier spirit of the richest gold rush in Alaska remains alive in Fairbanks, which prides itself on being "Alaska's Golden Heart."

★ **Stern-wheeler cruises:** The riverboat *Discovery* is an authentic stern-wheeler that offers visitors a glimpse into the history of Alaska through a cruise on the Chena and Tanana rivers.

★ **Gateway to the Arctic:** Fairbanks is a hub for connections via ground or air to the vast expanse of northern Alaska—land of the midnight sun and the northern lights. Magnificent mountains, glaciers, river valleys, and abundant wildlife lie beyond.

★ **Dog mushing:** Alaska is to dog mushing what Kentucky is to horse racing, and the Interior is the prime mushing spot in the state.

1 Fairbanks. This is the home to the main campus of the University of Alaska and is a point along the oil pipeline. It's a rough-edged town, but one that has a symphony, Alaska's largest library, and a vibrant arts scene.

2 Around Fairbanks. The Alaska wilderness is right outside the city, with miles of wilderness waiting to be explored. Hiking, canoeing, dog-mushing, and fishing are part of daily life.

3 Denali National Park & Preserve. A 6-million-acre wonderland of wildlife, forest, tundra, rushing rivers, and, of course, Mt. McKinley—which we like to call The High One.

4 Richardson Highway. Alaska's first highway remains a striking scenic corridor for travelers, connecting Valdez with the heart of Alaska. The road offers a trip through Alaska history, from the gold rush to the 21st century.

5 Fortymile Country. Eastern Interior yielded some of the first gold discoveries in Alaska. Mining operations can be seen along the Taylor Highway, a narrow road that connects the Alaska Highway to Eagle on the Yukon River.

6 Yukon Territory. The attraction here is Dawson City, the Canadian boomtown that hit its peak during the Klondike Gold Rush, which brought thousands north to the goldfields on both sides of the border.

GETTING ORIENTED

Interior Alaska is the central part of the state, a vast and broad plateau bordered by the Alaska Range to the south and the Brooks Range to the north. The Yukon River and its many tributaries, including the Tanana River, are dominant features of the landscape. There are few roads and numerous isolated villages reached only by aircraft. Fairbanks is the major town in the Interior and serves as the transportation hub for northern and central Alaska.

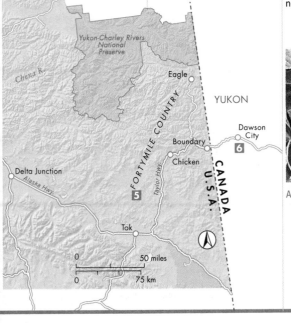

Autumn tundra

INTERIOR PLANNER

Making the Most of Your Time

If You Have 3 Days. Spend a day in Fairbanks, taking in the trans-Alaska pipeline, University of Alaska Museum, and the Riverboat Discovery tour. End your day at Pioneer Park so that you can have dinner at the Alaska Salmon Bake. The next day head to Denali National Park & Preserve and do some hiking or take a white-water rafting trip down the nearby Nenana River. Spend the night in the park area. Call ahead for room or campsite reservations; it's very crowded in the summer. The third day get up early to take a shuttle bus (again, reserve!), and spend the third day exploring the national park. Stay in Fairbanks the last night; catch dinner and a show at the Ester Gold Camp.

If You Have 5 Days. Follow the three-day itinerary; spend the fourth day in Fairbanks, taking the tour of El Dorado Gold Mine, where you can pan for gold, and visiting the Fairbanks Ice Museum. That afternoon head out on the scenic Chena Hot Springs Road for a relaxing soak at Chena Hot Springs Resort. Spend the night at the resort or head back to town and consider stopping for dinner at Two Rivers Lodge.

Tour Options

Adventure **Go North Alaska Adventure Travel Center** (☎ 907/479–7272 or 866/236–7272 🌐 www.gonorthalaska.com). **Northern Alaska Tour Company** (☎ 907/474–8600 🌐 www.northernalaska.com). **Trans Arctic Circle Treks** (☎ 907/479–5451 or 800/336–8735 🌐 www.arctictreks.com).

Climbing **Alaska Mountaineering School** (☎ 907/733–1016 🌐 www.climbalaska.org). **Mountain Trip** (☎ 907/345–6499 🌐 www.mountaintrip.com).

Sea & Land Tours **Denali Park Resorts** (☎ 907/276–7234 or 800/276–7234). **Gray Line of Alaska** (☎ 800/478–6388 🌐 www.graylinealaska.com). **Northern Alaska Tour Company** (☎ 907/474–8600). **Princess Tours** (☎ 907/479–9660 or 800/426–0442). **Trans Arctic Circle Treks** (☎ 907/479–5451). **Westours** (☎ 907/456–7741 or 800/478–6388).

River Trips **Greatland River Tours** (✉ 1020 Hoselton Rd., Fairbanks ☎ 907/452–8687 or 866/452–8687 🌐 www.greatlandrivertours.com). **Riverboat *Discovery*** (✉ Alaska Riverways, Dale Rd. Landing, near Fairbanks International Airport, Fairbanks ☎ 907/479–6673 or 866/479–6673 🌐 www.riverboatdiscovery.com).

Custom Sightseeing **Alpenglow Alaska/Yukon Tours** (☎ 907/479–2277 or 800/770-7275 🌐 www.akalpenglow.com).

Fishing **Wilderness Enterprises** (☎ 907/488–7517 🌐 www.wildernessenterprises.com).

Nature **NatureAlaska Tours** (☎ 907/488–3746 🌐 www.naturealaska.com).

Getting Around

Fairbanks is a sprawling city, with a layout that isn't ideal for pedestrians. There is public transportation, but service is limited. Hotels run shuttle buses to and from the airport, and you can get around by taxi. If you plan to spend more than a couple of days in the city, rent a car.

Alaska's Wild Rivers

A canoe or raft trip on a remote river can be exhilarating, but the logistics can be a nightmare. Only the most resourceful and independent travelers should consider this without expert help. There are many options available through outfitters in the Fairbanks area, from week-long forays hundreds of miles off the road system to four-hour cruises. If white water is more your style, numerous companies operate on the Nenana River outside Denali National Park. Be prepared for a wild ride. You'll need the dry suit provided.

About the Hotels & Restaurants

Even though the salmon streams and saltwater are hundreds of miles away, most restaurants fly in salmon and halibut regularly. Meat-and-potatoes main courses and the occasional pasta dish fill out the menus, but the majority of restaurants offer palatable choices for vegetarians. Most restaurants stay open late during the summer, and attire is definitely casual—leave the jacket and tie in your luggage.

Ultraluxurious hotels are absent in the Interior, but you can find a range of bed-and-breakfasts, rustic-chic lodges, and national chains, the best of which will please even the most discriminating travelers. Reservations for summer dates at the more popular hotels and at campsites near Denali need to be made months in advance, but comfortable choices can usually be found at the last minute if need be.

WHAT IT COSTS

	$$$$	$$$	$$	$	¢
Restaurants	over $25	$20–$25	$15–$20	$10–$15	under $10
Hotels	over $225	$175–$225	$125–$175	$75–$125	under $75

Restaurant prices are per person for a main course at dinner. Hotel prices are for two people in a standard double room in high season.

Timing

The months of the midnight sun, especially June and July, bring sunny or partly cloudy days, sometimes punctuated by afternoon cloudbursts. In the winter it gets so cold (–30°F or below) that a glass of boiling water flung out a window will reach the ground as particles of ice.

Tourism is big business in Alaska, but many of the attractions shut down in mid-September. Consider a trip in May to avoid the rush, but be forewarned—it's been known to snow in Fairbanks in spring. Late August brings fall colors, ripening berries, active wildlife, and the start of northern-lights season. Winter sports enthusiasts should come in March, when the dark days of winter are over, snow blankets the ground, and there's lots of radiant sun.

From Fairbanks to:

TRAVEL BY CAR	(HRS:MINS)
Anchorage	7:00
Dawson City	14:00
Denali	2:00
Seward	9:30
Skagway	15:00
Whitehorse	12:00

From Fairbanks to:

TRAVEL BY AIR	(HRS:MINS)
Anchorage	1:00
Barrow	1:30
Juneau	3:15
Nome	2:00
Prudhoe Bay	1:30
Seattle	4:30

Updated by
Dermot Cole

THE IMAGE OF 1900 ALASKA, with its heady gold rushes set to the harsh pitches of countless honky-tonk saloons and the clanging of pans, has its roots in the Interior. Gold fever struck in Circle and Eagle in the 1890s, spread into Canada's Yukon Territory in the big Klondike Gold Rush of 1898, then came back to Alaska's Interior when Fairbanks hit pay dirt in 1903. The broad, swift Yukon River was the rush's main highway. Flowing almost 2,300 mi from Canada to the Bering Sea, just below the Arctic Circle, it carried prospectors across the border in search of instant fortune.

Although Fairbanks has grown up into a small city, many towns and communities in the Interior seem little changed. While soaking in the water of the Chena Hot Springs Resort, you can almost hear the whispers of gold seekers exaggerating their finds and claims, ever alert for the newest strike. When early missionaries set up schools in the Bush, the nomadic native Alaskan peoples were herded to these regional centers for schooling and "salvation," but Interior Alaska is still flecked with native villages. Fort Yukon, on the Arctic Circle, is the largest Athabascan village in the state.

Alaska's current gold rush—the pipeline carrying black gold from the oil fields in Prudhoe Bay south to the port of Valdez—snakes its way through the Interior. The pipeline itself is something of an enigma: it's a symbol of commercial interests against the environment yet also a monumental construction that hugs the land like a giant necklace. The Richardson Highway, which started as a gold stampeders' trail, parallels the trans-Alaska pipeline on its route south of Fairbanks. Actual gold glitters anew in the Interior. Fairbanks, the site of the largest gold production in Alaska in pre–World War II days, is home to the Fort Knox Gold Mine, which has about doubled Alaska's gold production. The mine started up in 1996.

The Alaska Range—the "great wall" dividing the Interior from the South Central region—rises more than 20,000 feet. Its grandest member, Mt. McKinley, at 20,320 feet above sea level, it is the highest peak in North America. This tumultuous landscape was formed by the head-on collision of two tectonic plates. Between them, in the Denali fault system, lies the largest crack in the Earth's crust on the North American continent. This barrier between South Central and the Interior Plateau gathers colder weather and bears a fine glacial system because of its high altitude. These ice-capped mountains resemble the way a large part of the continent looked during the Ice Age. Flying in a small plane over the black-striped glaciers of the Alaska Range can be a dazzling experience.

HOW THE GARDENS GROW

Interior Alaska gets an extra-large helping of sunlight between May and August. The growing season is short in days, but every day counts for more because the sun is rarely out of sight. The long daylight hours help create vivid colors in flowers that must be seen to be believed. They also allow vegetables to grow to gargantuan dimensions. Cabbages that top 50 pounds and zucchini with the diameter of telephone poles are quite common.

Exploring the Interior

Interior Alaska is neatly sandwiched between two monumental mountain ranges: the Brooks Range to the north and the Alaska Range to the south. Many of the region's residents define their area by a limited network of four two-lane highways.

The George Parks Highway runs south to Denali National Park & Preserve and on to Anchorage, the state's largest city, 360 mi away on the coast. The Richardson Highway extends to the southeast to Delta Junction before turning south to Valdez, which is 368 mi from Fairbanks.

There are two major roads to the north. The Dalton Highway follows the trans-Alaska pipeline to its origins at Prudhoe Bay on Alaska's North Slope. The Steese Highway ends at the Yukon River and the town of Circle.

Beyond the highways there are many native villages reached by small airplanes that make daily connections out of Fairbanks, which is the regional hub and the thriving commercial center of the Interior.

FAIRBANKS

Native Alaskans have lived and traveled through Interior Alaska for thousands of years, but it wasn't until the early 1900s that a permanent settlement took shape along the banks of the Chena River. In one sense, Fairbanks was an accident waiting to happen. In 1901, E. T. Barnette, a merchant traveling upstream, was forced to get off the boat with all of his trading goods at a wooded spot along the Chena River because the water was too low to pass. He was left for a year, awaiting passage farther east. His luck improved when an Italian prospector discovered gold 12 mi north of Barnette's settlement the next summer. The resulting gold rush created customers for Barnette's stockpile of goods and led to the birth of the city.

GOLDEN DAYS

The gold strike by Felix Pedro in 1902 is commemorated annually in late July with the celebration of Golden Days, an occasion marked by a parade and several days of gold rush-inspired activities.

At first glance Fairbanks appears to be dominated by a sprawling conglomeration of strip malls, chain stores, and other evidence of suburbia (or, as a local writer once put it, "su-brrr-bia"). But look beyond the obvious in the biggest town in Interior Alaska and you'll discover why thousands insist that this is the best place to live in Alaska. Many of the old homes and commercial buildings trace their history to the early days of the city, especially in the downtown area, with its narrow, winding streets following the contours of the Chena River. And if there are more chain stores with each year, they are far outnumbered by the beautiful hillsides and river valleys just waiting to be explored.

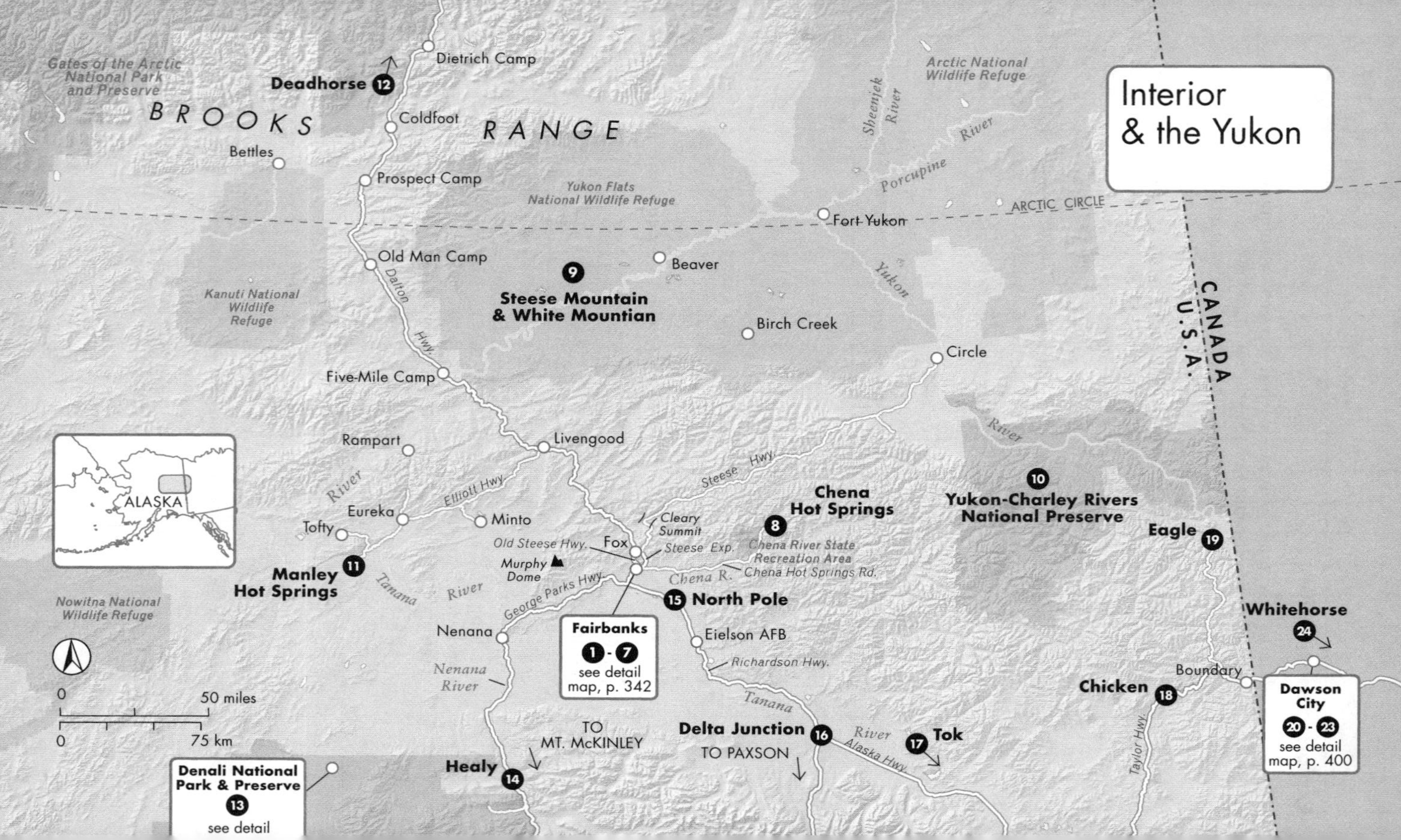

Interior & the Yukon
BROOKS RANGE
Gates of the Arctic National Park and Preserve
Deadhorse 12
Dietrich Camp
Coldfoot
Bettles
Prospect Camp
Yukon Flats National Wildlife Refuge
Arctic National Wildlife Refuge
Sheenjek River
Porcupine River
ARCTIC CIRCLE
Fort Yukon
Old Man Camp
Dalton Hwy.
9 Steese Mountain & White Mountian
Beaver
Yukon
Birch Creek
Kanuti National Wildlife Refuge
Circle
Five-Mile Camp
CANADA
U.S.A.
River
Rampart
Livengood
ALASKA
Steese Hwy.
10 Yukon-Charley Rivers National Preserve
River
Elliott Hwy
Eureka
Minto
Tofty
Chena Hot Springs 8
Cleary Summit
Eagle 19
Old Steese Hwy.
Fox
Steese Exp.
Chena River State Recreation Area
Murphy Dome
Chena R.
Chena Hot Springs Rd.
Manley Hot Springs 11
Tanana
River
George Parks Hwy.
15 North Pole
Nowitna National Wildlife Refuge
Whitehorse 24
Nenana
Fairbanks 1 - 7 see detail map, p. 342
Eielson AFB
Richardson Hwy.
Nenana River
Boundary
Chicken 18
Dawson City 20 - 23 see detail map, p. 400
0 50 miles
0 75 km
Tanana
TO MT. McKINLEY
Delta Junction 16
TO PAXSON
River
Alaska Hwy.
17 Tok
Taylor Hwy.
Healy 14
Denali National Park & Preserve 13 see detail

SIGHTSEEING TOURS

Gray Line of Alaska (☎ 800/478-6388 🌐 www.graylinealaska.com) runs several scenic and informative trips through the Fairbanks area, including a four-hour Discover the Gold sightseeing tour of the city that features the *Gold Dredge Number 8* and a lunch of miner's stew for $60.

Princess Tours (☎ 800/426-0442 🌐 www.princesslodges.com) has city bus tours.

Exploring Fairbanks

The city's nickname, the Golden Heart, reflects Fairbanks's gold-rush history and its geographical location: it's the gateway to the Far North—the Arctic and the Bering Coast—and to Canada's Yukon Territory. The city lies between the rugged Alaska and Brooks mountain ranges and serves as the Interior's hub. The Parks and Richardson highways end in Fairbanks, and several Bush commuter air services base their operations here.

6

As you walk the streets of Fairbanks today, it takes a good deal of imagination to envision the rough-and-tumble gold mining camp that first took shape along the Chena River in the early 1900s. There are a few neighborhoods in the oldest parts of town where weathered log cabins are the dominant architectural influence. The rest is a Western hodgepodge that reflects a desire to build whatever one wants, wherever one wants, a trait that has long been a community standard.

There are continuing attempts to preserve parts of the Gold–Rush past, most notably in the 44-acre Pioneer Park, where dozens of cabins and many other relics were moved out of the path of progress. Fairbanks has long been a town were people have been impatient to tear down the old and build anew, without much thought for what others might think.

There are some fine examples of old buildings remaining here and there in the city. For details on all local attractions, historical and otherwise, stop by the Fairbanks Convention and Visitors Bureau visitor center in the log cabin on First Avenue, next to the Cushman Street Bridge. Downtown Fairbanks began to deteriorate in the 1970s, before and after the boom associated with the building of the trans-Alaska pipeline. But the downward spiral ended and most of downtown has been rebuilt.

We recommend a trip to the campus of the University of Alaska Fairbanks, where the new University of Alaska Museum of the North is housed in a striking landmark building that evokes images of glaciers and mountains. A walking tour that lasts about 90 minutes begins at the visitor center and provides a good overview of local history.

What to See

5 **Alaska Range Overlook.** The entire north side of the Alaska Range is visible at this overlook, a favorite spot for time-lapse photography of the midwinter sun just peeking over the southern horizon on a low arc. The

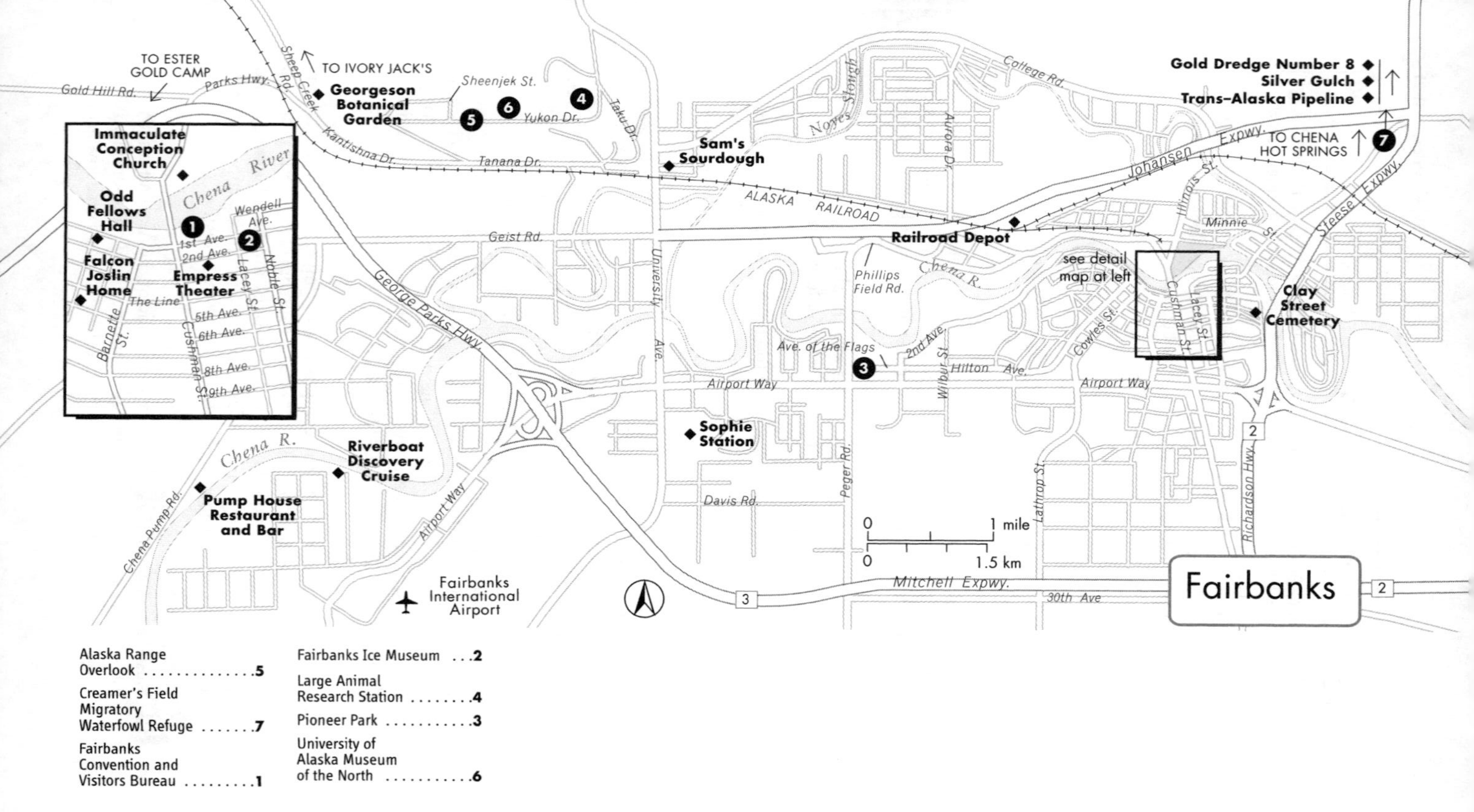

Fairbanks
Gold Dredge Number 8
Silver Gulch
Trans-Alaska Pipeline
TO CHENA HOT SPRINGS
TO ESTER GOLD CAMP
TO IVORY JACK'S
Georgeson Botanical Garden
Sam's Sourdough
Railroad Depot
see detail map at left
Clay Street Cemetery
Sophie Station
Riverboat Discovery Cruise
Pump House Restaurant and Bar
Fairbanks International Airport
Immaculate Conception Church
Odd Fellows Hall
Falcon Joslin Home
Empress Theater
Chena River
Chena R.
ALASKA RAILROAD
Gold Hill Rd.
Parks Hwy.
Sheep Creek Rd.
Kantishna Dr.
Sheenjek St.
Yukon Dr.
Taku Dr.
Tanana Dr.
College Rd.
Noyes Slough
Aurora Dr.
Johansen Expwy.
Steese Expwy.
Illinois St.
Minnie St.
Geist Rd.
University Ave.
George Parks Hwy.
Phillips Field Rd.
Ave. of the Flags
2nd Ave.
Wilbur St.
Hilton Ave.
Airport Way
Cowles St.
Cushman St.
Lacey St.
Richardson Hwy.
Peger Rd.
Davis Rd.
Lathrop St.
Mitchell Expwy.
30th Ave
Chena Pump Rd.
Wendell Ave.
1st Ave.
2nd Ave.
Noble St.
The Line
5th Ave.
6th Ave.
8th Ave.
9th Ave.
Barnette St.
0 1 mile
0 1.5 km
Alaska Range Overlook .5
Creamer's Field Migratory Waterfowl Refuge .7
Fairbanks Convention and Visitors Bureau .1
Fairbanks Ice Museum .2
Large Animal Research Station .4
Pioneer Park .3
University of Alaska Museum of the North .6

three major peaks, called the Three Sisters because of their similar appearance, are nearly always distinguishable on a clear day. From your left are **Mt. Hayes,** 13,832 feet; **Mt. Hess,** 11,940 feet; and **Mt. Deborah,** 12,339 feet. Much farther to the right, toward the southwest, hulks **Mt. McKinley,** the highest peak in North America. On some seemingly clear days it's not visible at all. At other times the base is easy to see but the peak is lost in cloud cover. ✉ *West Ridge, University of Alaska Fairbanks campus, Yukon Dr.; look for parking area just east of University of Alaska Museum.*

❼ **Creamer's Field Migratory Waterfowl Refuge.** Thousands of migrating ducks, geese, and cranes can be seen stopping here in the spring as they head north to nesting grounds, and in late summer, as they head south before the cold hits. This is also a great place to view songbirds and moose. Three nature trails lead through fields, forest, and wetlands. The barns and buildings of **Creamer's Dairy** are also still standing here. Now on the National Register of Historic Places, Creamer's Dairy was the farthest-north dairy in North America from 1910 to 1966. The farmhouse is now a nature and visitor center. ✉ *1300 College Rd., Lemeta* ☎ *907/459–7307 or 907/459–7301* 🌐 *www.creamersfield.org.*

JUST BACK FROM ALASKA

"When I asked my guide how to pronounce the name of the state bird (it's the Willow Ptarmigan; pronounced TAR-mi-gan), he coolly replied: 'It's pronounced mos-KEE-to.' It's true: those little rascals are fierce. Bring plenty of bug dope with DEET! Creamer's is just one place you'll be happy you remembered it."

–Heidi Johansen, Fodor's editor

❶ **Fairbanks Convention and Visitors Bureau.** At this visitor center on the river at the Cushman Street Bridge you can pick up a map for a self-guided 1½-hour walking tour through the historic downtown area. ✉ *550 1st Ave., Downtown* ☎ *907/456–5774, 800/327–5774 recording* 🌐 *www.explorefairbanks.com.*

★ ❷ **Fairbanks Ice Museum.** You'd think that the last thing that Fairbanksans would want to hang onto through the too-brief summer would be a reminder of the brutal winters. However, the folks at the Ice Museum do just that every year. Sculptors work behind glass in large freezers where they create intricate sculptures from ice. About 25 are usually on display. Billed as "the coolest show in town," the Ice Showcase, a large glass-wall display, is kept at 20°F. The chilly environment allows ice sculptors to demonstrate their skills and sculptures throughout the summer. "Freeze Frame" is a large-screen film demonstrating the techniques of ice sculpture. The museum is in the historic Lacey Street Theater, on the corner of 2nd Avenue and Lacey Street. ✉ *500 2nd Ave., Downtown* ☎ *907/451–8222* 🌐 *www.icemuseum.com* 🎫 *$11* 🕓 *June–Sept., daily 10–9.*

★ **Georgeson Botanical Garden of the Agricultural and Forestry Experiment Station Farm.** When most people think of Alaska vegetation they tend to conjure up images of flat, treeless tundra, so the amazing variety of

CLOSE UP

Just Outside Fairbanks: Gold Rush History & Liquid Gold

GOLD DREDGE NUMBER 8. Imagine a giant gold dredge making its own waterway as it chews through the gold pay dirt, crawling along at a snail's pace and processing tons of rock and gravel. Built by Bethlehem Shipbuilders in 1928, the dredge was operated by the Fairbanks Exploration Company until its retirement in 1959. The five-deck ship is more than 250 feet long and took millions of dollars' worth of gold out of the Goldstream and Engineer creeks north of Fairbanks. *Gold Dredge Number 8* has been declared a National Historic District by the National Park Service, one of the few privately owned districts in the nation. This mining vessel came to rest at Mile 9, Old Steese Highway. The price of admission entitles you to the necessary tools, some gold-panning instructions, and a chance to find "colors" at the sluice or to seek gold independently in old tailings from the mining days. A sit-down, family-style, all-you-can-eat, miner's beef stew is served from 11 AM to 3 PM for an additional $9.75. The dredge (and the miner's stew) is a featured stop on Holland America's tours operated by Gray Line of Alaska. ✉ *1755 Old Steese Hwy. N, Fairbanks 99712* ☎ *907/457-6058* 🌐 *www.golddredgeno8.com* 🎫 *$25* ⏲ *Mid-May–mid-Sept., daily 9:30–3:30.*

TRANS-ALASKA PIPELINE. Just north of Fairbanks you can see and touch the famous trans-Alaska pipeline. This 48-inch diameter pipe travels 800 mi from the oil fields on the north slope of the Brooks Range over three mountain ranges and more than 800 rivers and streams to the terminal in Valdez. There the crude oil is pumped onto tanker ships and transported to oil refineries in the Lower 48 states. Since the pipeline began operations in 1977, more than 15 billion barrels of North Slope crude have been pumped. Currently the pipe is carrying about 900,000 42-gallon barrels of oil per day. The parking lot is right off the Steese Highway and has a sign loaded with information. Informative guides staff a small visitor center, and there's a gift shop with pipeline-company memorabilia. ✉ *Mile 8.4 Steese Hwy.* ☎ *907/456-9391* 🎫 *Free* ⏲ *Visitor center mid-May–Sept., daily 8–5.*

SILVER GULCH BREWING AND BOTTLING CO. You'll find some unique souvenirs and an interesting collection of Fairbanks citizens at North America's northernmost brewery. Brewing a variety of styles since 1998, Silver Gulch is probably best known for its pilsner. Fairbanks and Anchorage are the major markets, but a few spots on the Kenai carry Silver Gulch as well. Stop by for free tours and beer tastings every Friday evening from 5 to 7 PM or by appointment. The brewery is in the Fox Roadhouse building (around to the right and through the side door) 10 mi north of Fairbanks on the Old Steese Highway. ✉ *2195 Old Steese Hwy., Fox* ☎ *907/452-2739* 🌐 *www.silvergulch.com* 🎫 *Free* ⏲ *Fri. 5–7 PM or by appointment only.*

native and cultivated flowers on exhibit here are often unexpected. This is where researchers at the University of Alaska Fairbanks study Interior Alaska's unique, short, but intense midnight-sun growing season. The results are spectacular. There are about 3,000 annuals and 300 types of perennials on the grounds. The nonstop daylight helps bring out rich and vibrant colors that must be seen in person. The best times are from mid-June to late August. ✉ *117 West Tanana Dr., west end of campus, 4 mi west of downtown* ☎ *907/474–6921* 🎫 *$2* ⏲ *May–Sept., daily 8–8. Tours Fri. at 2.*

Golden Heart Plaza. This riverside park is the hub of downtown celebrations, including free concerts in the park on Friday evenings in summer. The plaza is dominated by the towering statue of the "Unknown First Family," encircled by plaques containing the names of 4,500 local families who contributed to the building of the plaza, a symbol of the rebirth of downtown Fairbanks.

★ 👶 ❹ **Large Animal Research Station.** Out on the fringes of the University of Alaska campus is a 134-acre home to about 40 musk oxen, 15 caribou, and 40 domestic reindeer. Resident and visiting scientists study these large ungulates to better understand their physiologies and the ways that they adapt to arctic conditions. The station also serves as a valuable outreach program. Most people have little chance to see these animals in their natural habitats, especially the musk oxen. Once nearly eradicated from Alaska, these shaggy, prehistoric-looking beasts are marvels of adaptive physiques and behaviors. They are also being studied for potential commercial uses: qiviut, the soft, delicate musk-ox underfur, is combed out (without harming the animals) and made into scarves, hats, and gloves by Alaska native women. It has the feel of cashmere and is remarkably warm. The station has limited amounts of unprocessed wool for sale at about $280 a pound. On tours you get great information about the research and the animals and visit the pens for close-up looks at the animals and their young. ✉ *Yankovich Rd. off Ballaine Rd., behind University of Alaska Fairbanks* ☎ *907/474–7207 tour information* 🌐 *www.uaf.edu/lars* 🎫 *Tours $10* ⏲ *Memorial Day–Labor Day by tour only; tours daily at 1:30 and 3:30.*

★ 👶 ❸ **Pioneer Park.** The 44-acre park, formerly known as Alaskaland, is along the Chena River near downtown Fairbanks and has several museums, an art gallery, theater, civic center, native village, large children's playground, miniature-golf course, antique merry-go-round, and restaurants. The park also has a re-created gold-rush town with historic buildings saved from urban renewal, log-cabin gift shops, and **Mining Valley,** an outdoor museum of mining artifacts surrounding an indoor-outdoor Alaska salmon-bake restaurant. The 227-foot stern-wheeler ***Nenana*** is the second-largest wooden vessel in existence and a national historic landmark. A diorama inside the stern-wheeler details the course the riverboat took on the Yukon and Tanana rivers around the turn of the 20th century. The **Crooked Creek and Whiskey Island Railroad,** a small-gauge train, circles the park. The newest addition to the park is a museum housing the first railroad locomotive in Fairbanks, which has been restored to its 1905 condition and is run on special occasions. ■ **TIP→ No-frills RV camp-**

TOURING THE OLD TOWN

Points of interest on the Convention & Visitors Bureau's self-guided walking tour include **Golden Heart Park,** home of the *Unknown First Family* statue; the **Clay Street Cemetery,** with its marked and unmarked graves of early pioneers; the **Empress Theater,** the first concrete structure in Interior Alaska; the stately **Falcon Joslin Home,** the oldest frame house in Fairbanks still at its original location; the **Line,** home of the red-light district until the mid-1950s; **Odd Fellows Hall,** a bathhouse for gold miners until the pipes froze in the winter of 1910–11; and the historic **Immaculate Conception Church,** which was raised off its foundation in 1911 and rolled across the frozen Chena River on logs pulled by horses.

ing is available for $10 a night in the west end of the large parking lot on Airport Way. ✉ *Airport Way and Peger Rd.* ☎ *907/459–1087* 🌐 *http://co.fairbanks.ak.us/ParksandRecreation* 🎫 *Free* ⏲ *Park 24 hours. Museum and shops Memorial Day–Labor Day, daily 11–9.*

6 Fodor's Choice ★ **University of Alaska Museum of the North.** A stuffed grizzly bear—8 feet, 9 inches tall—guards the entrance to the Gallery of Alaska, divided into five Alaska regions: Southeast, Interior, South Central, Southwest, and the Western Arctic Coast. The collection includes the state's largest display of gold, Alaska native art and artifacts, and Blue Babe, a mummified steppe bison that lived 36,000 years ago during the Pleistocene. Babe was preserved in permafrost (permanently frozen ground), complete with claw marks indicating attack by an American lion. The bison's remains were found by gold miners in 1979. The museum has several "please touch" items, including the molars of a mammoth and a mastodon, a gray-whale skull, and a 5,495-pound copper nugget. A multiyear effort to expand the museum concluded in 2006 with the opening of a striking new addition that has become a Fairbanks architectural landmark. The new space includes an art gallery and a two-story viewing window looking out on the Alaska Range and the Tanana Valley. ✉ *University of Alaska Fairbanks, 907 Yukon Dr.* ☎ *907/474–7505* 🌐 *www.uaf.edu/museum* 🎫 *$10* ⏲ *Mid-May–mid-Sept., daily 9–7; mid-Sept.–mid-May, weekdays 9–5, weekends noon–5.*

Where to Stay & Eat

★ **$$$$** ✕ **Alaska Salmon Bake.** Mouthwatering salmon cooked over an open fire with a special lemon and brown-sugar sauce is a favorite at this indoor-outdoor restaurant in Pioneer Park's Mining Valley. Halibut, cod, prime rib, a salad bar, and homemade blueberry cake are also available at the nightly all-you-can-eat dinner. ✉ *Airport Way and Peger Rd., Pioneer Park* ☎ *907/452–7274 or 800/354–7274* 🌐 *akvisit.com/salmon.html* 💳 *MC, V* ⏲ *No lunch mid-May–mid-Sept.*

★ **$$$–$$$$** ✕ **Pike's Landing.** Enjoy lunch on a huge outside deck (it seats 420) overlooking the Chena River, or dine inside in the elegant dining room of an extended log cabin. The meals run in price up to $40 for steak and lobster and rank with the best in the Interior. For a dinner in the $10 range, relax in the sports bar and catch a view of the river. The palate-pleasing Sunday brunch delivers tempting dishes and an irresistible dessert table. ✉ *4438 Airport Way, near airport* ☎ *907/479–7113* 💳 *AE, D, DC, MC, V.*

$$$–$$$$ ✕ **Turtle Club.** Don't go to this windowless and nondescript dining room expecting great variety on the menu. Do go if you are hungry for prime rib, lobster, or king crab and have a big appetite. There's a good salad bar, the service is prompt, and every order comes with homemade bread. The "Turtle Cut" serving of prime rib, advertised as a "medium portion," weighs a pound. Many of the patrons make this a regular stop. It's worth the effort to drive the 10 mi north of Fairbanks. ✉ *Mile 10, Old Steese Hwy., Fox* ☎ *907/457–3883* 💳 *AE, D, MC, V.*

$$–$$$$ ✕ **Geraldo's.** The sign outside is more than likely to contain a plug for the virtues of garlic. Rightly so, for no one in Fairbanks puts fresh chopped garlic to better use than Geraldo's, which has gourmet pizza, along with seafood, pasta, and veal dishes. There is a painting of Don Corleone on the wall and the likes of Frank Sinatra and Dean Martin provide the background music for this friendly place, which is cozy and likely to be crowded. ✉ *701 College Rd., Lemeta* ☎ *907/452–2299* 💳 *AE, D, DC, MC, V.*

6

★ $$–$$$$ ✕ **Pump House Restaurant.** Alongside the Chena River this mining pump–station-turned-restaurant turns out several variations of salmon and halibut main courses. Alaskan reindeer stew and seafood chowder are house specialties. The furnishings and floor are rich, polished wood, and an Alaskan grizzly bear in a glass case is on sentry next to the hostess station. Wednesday night is karaoke night in the bar. ✉ *Mile 2, Chena Pump Rd.* ☎ *907/479–8452* 💳 *AE, D, MC, V* ⏲ *No lunch mid-Sept.–June 1.*

$–$$$$ ✕ **Lavelle's.** With offerings ranging from rack of lamb and lobster cakes to halibut and New York steaks, this impressive Fairbanks restaurant has won a loyal local following. Lavelle's features an extensive 3,000-bottle wine cellar and holds regular wine tastings and other events that give the restaurant a sophisticated atmosphere far removed from the frontier image cultivated elsewhere in Fairbanks. This is one of the few places where Fairbanksans dress for dinner. ✉ *SpringHill Suites hotel, 575 1st Ave., Downtown* ☎ *907/450–0555* 💳 *AE, D, DC, MC, V.*

¢–$$$$ ✕ **Ivory Jack's.** Jack "Ivory" O'Brien used to deal in Alaskan ivory and whalebone out of this small restaurant tucked into the gold-rich hills of the Goldstream Valley on the outskirts of Fairbanks. Crab-stuffed mushrooms are a specialty of this large, open, and airy bar-restaurant. You can choose from more than 15 appetizers as well as burgers, pizza, and entrées such as halibut Dijon and Alaskan king crab. You'll catch some live local music on some weekends; the cover charge depends on the band. ✉ *2581 Goldstream Rd., Goldstream* ☎ *907/455–6666* 💳 *AE, D, DC, MC, V.*

★ $–$$$ ✕ **The Cookie Jar.** Tucked away in a nondescript neighborhood on a street not found on most Fairbanks maps, this gorgeous little restaurant is well worth tracking down. The open, airy space predictably features lots of cookie jars, along with plants and artwork to complete the picture. Spanning breakfast, lunch, and dinner, the huge menu includes scads of homemade items, an extensive kids' menu, and vegetarian selections. Entrées range from steak and shrimp to coq au vin. For dessert, try the homemade tortes or a variety of cookies to match anything your grandma ever baked. Weekend breakfasts are especially popular, so allow extra time. Take Danby Street off the Johansen Expressway, and the restaurant is behind Aurora Motors. ✉ *1006 Cadillac Ct., Aurora* ☎ *907/479–8319* 💳 *AE, D, MC, V.*

★ $–$$$ ✕ **Gambardella's Pasta Bella.** Locals crowd the family-run Italian restaurant known simply as Gambardella's, which has earned a reputation as one of the best restaurants in town. The menu includes salads, pasta, pizza, vegetarian entrées, and submarine sandwiches on homemade bread. Its specialties, however, are lasagna, which the *Seattle Times* described as "the mother of all lasagnas"; the seafood *fra diavolo*; and the tiramisu. The two-story restaurant has outdoor seating on a balcony and at street level. ✉ *706 2nd Ave., Downtown* ☎ *907/456–3417* 💳 *AE, MC, V* ⊗ *No lunch Sun.*

WORD OF MOUTH

"Gambardella's has the best Italian food in Alaska." -elg

★ ¢–$$ ✕ **Sam's Sourdough Cafe.** Although Sam's serves meals all day, Fairbanksans know it as the best breakfast place in town. Sourdough recipes are a kind of minor religion in Alaska, and Sam's serves an extensive menu of sourdough specialties, including hotcakes and French toast, as well as standard meat-and-eggs items, all at very reasonable prices. On weekends get here early or be prepared for a wait. The address is Cameron Street, but it's really fronted on University, just over the railroad tracks. ✉ *3702 Cameron St., College* ☎ *907/479–0523* 💳 *MC, V.*

¢–$ ✕ **Cafe Alex.** Part dinner destination, part wine bar, Alex has an eclectic menu that includes dependable salmon and halibut preparations, as well as tapas. Private side rooms off the main dining area are available for groups or romantic dinners. Bright colors help create a welcoming atmosphere. It's a point of pride with owner Alex Mayberry to feature live music every weekend. ✉ *310 1 Ave., Downtown* ☎ *907/452–2539* 💳 *MC, V.*

★ $$$–$$$$ 🏨 **Pike's Waterfront Lodge.** Log columns and beams support the high-ceiling lobby of this hotel and conference center on the banks of the Chena River. The grounds are strewn with more than 20,000 flowering plants, and a ½-mi river walk borders the property. There are several warm and cozy common areas, including a piano room and a fireplace lounge, and during the summer an ice-cream parlor operates on the premises. Rooms with a river view are worth the extra $10 per night. If you're looking for real Alaskan ambience, try one of the 28 rustic log cabins. ✉ *1850 Hoselton Rd., near airport, 99709* ☎ *877/774–2400 or 907/456–4500* 🌐 *www.pikeslodge.com* *180 rooms, 28 2-bedroom cabins* *Restaurant, cable TV with movies and video games, in-room data ports, gym, sauna, spa, steam room, bar, concierge, Wi-Fi, business services, meeting rooms, airport shuttle, no-smoking rooms* 💳 *AE, D, MC, V.*

$$$ 🏨 **Cranberry Ridge B&B.** The proprietors, Mike and Floss Caskey, a fifth-generation Alaskan family, designed and built this small B&B with

one two-bedroom apartment, north of Fairbanks off Farmers Loop Road. The contemporary house's position affords magnificent views of the Alaska Range. Mike Caskey leads custom Arctic Circle and Mt. McKinley flightseeing tours in his Cessna 185 for up to three passengers. ✉ *705 Cranberry Ridge Dr., Farmers Loop, 99712* ☎ *907/457–4424 or 888/326–4424* 🌐 *www.alaskaflyingtours.com* *1 apartment* *Cable TV, in-room data ports; no a/c, no smoking* *D, DC, MC, V* *CP.*

★ $$$ **Fairbanks Princess Riverside Lodge.** An expansive wooden deck facing a scenic section of the Chena River draws a crowd at this luxury lodge in summer. Gold, russet, green, and burgundy accents warm the rustic decor. You can stop by the tour desk to book additional excursions around Fairbanks. The Edgewater Restaurant welcomes diners in suits and dresses or duct-tape-patched Carhartt's work clothes, and there's a daily breakfast buffet during the high season. The lodge is just off the road to Fairbanks International Airport. ✉ *4477 Pikes Landing Rd., near airport, 99709* ☎ *907/455–4477 or 800/426–0500* 🌐 *www.princesslodges.com/fairbanks_lodge.cfm* *326 rooms* *2 restaurants, cable TV, in-room data ports, health club, bar, shop, laundry facilities, business services, meeting rooms, airport shuttle, travel services, no-smoking rooms* *AE, D, DC, MC, V.*

6

$$$ **River's Edge Resort.** If you want the privacy of a cottage, a bit of elbow room, and all the amenities of a luxury hotel, you can find it along the banks of the Chena River at the River's Edge Resort. The individual cottages all have patios or garden spaces, many fronting the river and surrounded by beautifully landscaped grounds. On summer evenings many people choose to sit outside and watch canoes, rafts, and powerboats passing by. Chena's Restaurant serves breakfast, lunch, and dinner at the lodge, which has a banquet hall, meeting rooms, and executive suites. ✉ *4140 Boat St., University West, 99709* ☎ *907/474–0286 or 800/770–3343* 🌐 *www.riversedge.net* *94 cottage* *Restaurant, cable TV, Wi-Fi, meeting rooms, RV park, airport shuttle* *AE, D, MC, V* *Closed mid-Sept.–mid-May.*

$$$ **Sophie Station Hotel.** Its quiet location and helpful staff make this spacious hotel near the airport one of Fairbanks' best. It has comfy furniture, rich upholstery, and Alaskan artwork throughout. Rooms are suites with kitchens that include a full-size range and refrigerator. You can try a buffalo burger at Zach's, the hotel restaurant, which serves breakfast, lunch, and dinner. ✉ *1717 University Ave., near airport, 99709* ☎ *907/479–3650 or 800/528–4916* 🌐 *www.fountainheadhotels.com* *148 suites* *Restaurant, kitchens, microwaves, refrigerators, cable TV, bar, Internet, meeting room, airport shuttle* *AE, D, DC, MC, V.*

$$$ **SpringHill Suites by Marriott.** At the center of what was once the heart of the commercial district, the SpringHill Suites is a welcome symbol of the rehabilitation of downtown Fairbanks. The hotel features 140 comfortable suites, each with a microwave, refrigerator, living room furniture, and well-lighted work areas. The Continental breakfast by the fireplace next to the lobby is a cut above standard fare. Ask for a room facing the river, the scenic side of the hotel. ✉ *575 1st Ave., Downtown,*

99701 ☎ 907/451–6552 🌐 www.marriott.com 140 suites Cable TV, refrigerators, microwaves, meeting rooms, in-room broadband, Wi-Fi, airport shuttle, pool, exercise room AE, D, DC, MC, V CP.

$$$ **A Taste of Alaska Lodge.** The strong point of the Eberhardt family's lodge is that it is just 20 minutes from Fairbanks, yet far enough away to convey a feeling that you are out in the woods on a wilderness retreat. On 280 acres of fields and forested woodlands, the lodge has great view of the Alaska Range mountains to the south. In winter you can clearly see the northern lights. Stay in the remote cabins, a two-story log home, or the main lodge. Try gold panning at the on-site gold mine. The rooms are decorated with collectibles, and the resort owners strive to create the friendly atmosphere of an old-time roadhouse—and succeed. Breakfast is served at 8 AM sharp. ✉ *551 Eberhardt Rd., Two Rivers 99712* ☎ *907/488–7855* 🌐 *www.atasteofalaska.com 8 rooms in lodge, 2 cabins Cable TV, Wi-Fi, hot tub, exercise room AE, D, MC, V BP.*

$$$ **Westmark Fairbanks Hotel and Conference Center.** Built on a courtyard on a quiet street, this full-service and recently expanded and renovated complex is within easy walking distance of downtown. All of the rose-and-burgundy rooms have a writing desk; some have a StairMaster or stationary bike. A conference center and personal voice mail make it a good choice for business travelers. The Red Lantern Steak & Spirits restaurant serves steaks and seafood, and the Northern Latitudes room offers a buffet. ✉ *813 Noble St., Downtown, 99701* ☎ *907/456–7722 or 800/544–0970* 🌐 *www.westmarkhotels.com 400 rooms Restaurant, cable TV with movies, in-room data ports, exercise equipment, bar, shop, laundry service, Internet, meeting room, airport and railroad shuttle, no-smoking floor AE, D, DC, MC, V.*

$$ **Bridgewater Hotel.** In the heart of downtown Fairbanks, overlooking the Chena River, this elegant hotel has gone through a number of incarnations and is now a thoroughly modern, European-style hotel convenient to shops and restaurants. Rooms have floral accents, and the ambience is a far cry from the sameness and sterility of too many chain motels. ✉ *723 1st Ave., Downtown, 99701* ☎ *907/452–6661 or 800/528–4916* 🌐 *www.fountainheadhotels.com/bridgewater/bridgewater.htm 94 rooms Café, cable TV, in-room data ports, dry cleaning, airport shuttle; no smoking AE, D, DC, MC, V Closed mid-Sept.–mid-May CP.*

$$ **Comfort Inn–Chena River.** Its location on a wooded bank of the Chena River directly across the water from Pioneer Park makes this hotel a popular choice. Rooms are done in green and dark wood and punctuated with artwork. ✉ *1908 Chena Landings Loop, Railroad Industrial Area, 99701* ☎ *907/479–8080 or 800/228–5150* 🌐 *www.choicehotels.com 74 rooms Some microwaves, some refrigerators, cable TV with movies and video games, in-room data ports, indoor pool, hot tub, airport shuttle, some pets allowed, no-smoking rooms AE, D, DC, MC, V CP.*

$$ **Wedgewood Resort.** Both wild and cultivated flowers adorn the landscaped grounds of the Wedgewood Resort, which borders on Creamer's Field Migratory Waterfowl Refuge. Headquartered on the very resort is the Alaska Bird Observatory, a local nonprofit that researches and promotes the conservation of Alaska's birds. You'll also find a replica of a miner's cabin, a bush plane, courtyards, and gazebos. All rooms are suites, decorated with local artwork that's available for purchase. The Bear Lodge hotel—also part of the resort—has 157 large rooms available in summer. Shuttles make the run to downtown Fairbanks and local shopping spots. *212 Wedgewood Dr., Lemeta, 99701 800/528–4916 or 907/456–3642 www.fountainheadhotels.com 297 suites 2 restaurants, kitchens, microwaves, refrigerators, cable TV, in-room data ports, shops, dry cleaning, business services, meeting rooms, airport shuttle AE, D, DC, MC, V EP.*

FodorsChoice ★

$ **Crestmont Manor B&B.** Handmade quilts and furnishings and antique fixtures accent this elegant colonial-style B&B. The rooms provide privacy, and comfort is a top priority of the house. You can relax on the deck while contemplating the sweeping view of the Chena River valley and the Alaska Range. Breakfast, with quiche, fresh pastries, juice, and coffee, is a pleasant affair. *510 Crestmont Dr., 99709 907/456–3831 www.mosquitonet.com/~crestmnt 5 rooms Laundry service, business services; no a/c, no smoking AE, MC, V BP.*

6

Nightlife & the Arts

Fairbanks supports a year-round arts program that rivals that of many larger communities. In summer you will find that the lack of a true "night"—thanks to the midnight sun—doesn't seem to hinder nightlife at all. Check the "Kaleidoscope" section in the Thursday *Fairbanks Daily News–Miner* for current nightspots, plays, concerts, and art shows.

The Arts

FESTIVALS **Golden Days** (www.fairbankschamber.org) is the annual celebration of Fairbanks' Gold Rush past. Several days of events are capped by a big parade through the city in late July. **Tanana Valley State Fair** (1800 College Rd., Aurora 907/452–3750 www.tananavalleyfair.org) is Interior Alaska's largest annual gathering. It fills a week in early August with attractions such as giant vegetables and the handiwork of local artisans.

Every July Fairbanks hosts the **World Eskimo-Indian Olympics** (www.weio.org), when northern peoples from Alaska and Canada gather to compete in traditional athletic games and dances. The **World Ice Art Championships** (www.icealaska.com) in March draws ice artists from around the world for an international ice-sculpting competition. The annual **Winter Carnival** (www.fairbankswintercarnival.com), held in mid-March, hosts dog-mushing and skijoring competitions, basketball tournaments, a crafts fair, fur auctions, and various winter events in Fairbanks and in outlying areas.

Nightlife

CABARET THEATER For an evening of varied and high-quality entertainment head to **Ester Gold Camp** (⊠ Ester ☎ 907/479–2500 or 800/676–6925 ⊕ www.akvisit.com), a former gold-mining town about 5 mi west of Fairbanks on the Parks Highway. Its 11 historical structures date to the early 1900s and include the rustic Malemute Saloon, which is open daily from 4 PM to midnight. The camp, which is on the National Register of Historic Places, comes alive at night with a show in the saloon ($18) featuring gold rush–era songs, stories, and Robert Service poetry; a beautiful northern-lights photography show ($8) in the Firehouse Theatre; and a dinner buffet ($28) of crab, chicken, and reindeer stew in yet another building. Plan your evening to catch dinner and all the shows. The camp has a hotel with semiprivate bathrooms, RV parking, a gift shop, and evening bus service to and from Fairbanks. The camp is open late May to early September.

The *Golden Heart Revue* ($18), at the **Palace Theatre and Saloon** (⊠ Pioneer Park, Airport Way and Peger Rd. ☎ 907/456–5960 or 800/354–7274 ⊕ www.akvisit.com) is a musical-comedy show about the founding and building of Fairbanks. It begins at 8:15 nightly.

SALOONS ★ The **Blue Loon** (⊠ Parks Hwy., Mile 353.5 ☎ 907/457–5666), between Ester and Fairbanks, presents year-round rock and roll and folk music, concerts, DJ events, and dance events. Microbrews complement its menu of gourmet pizza, plus sandwiches and salads. There are a volleyball court, a campfire area, RV parking, and movies every evening at 5:30 and 8. The **Howling Dog Saloon** (⊠ 2160 Old Steese Hwy. ☎ 907/456–4695) has live music, bar food, a beer, wine, and liquor menu, and huge gobs of atmosphere. The clientele is a mix of college students, airline pilots, tourists, miners, and bikers. Out back there are a volleyball court, horseshoe pit, and 10 rustic cabins for rent.

★ Don't be alarmed by the exterior appearance of the **Midnight Mine** (⊠ 308 Wendell St. ☎ 907/456–5348), within walking distance of downtown. It's a friendly, *Cheers*-like neighborhood bar with darts, Foosball, pool, and a big-screen TV. Sam the dog is likely to greet you as you come in—be sure to ask to see her trick. It'll cost you a buck, but it's well worth it. The **Palace Theatre and Saloon** (⇨ *above*) at Pioneer Park is one of the livelier summer spots. The **Senator's Saloon** (⊠ Mile 2.0, Chena Pump Rd. ☎ 907/479–8452) at the Pump House Restaurant is the place to hear

ALL THAT JAZZ

Alaska's premier cultural gathering, the **Fairbanks Summer Arts Festival** (☎ 907/474–8869 ⊕ www.fsaf.org) takes place over two weeks in late July and early August. It grew from a small jazz festival to a major University of Alaska–affiliated event attracting students and instructors worldwide. The festival presents music, dance, theater, opera, storytelling, creative writing, healing arts, visual arts, and ice-skating instruction. Hundreds of people plan their summers around the festival.

easy-listening music alongside the Chena River on a warm summer evening.

SQUARE DANCING The square-dancing clubs in Fairbanks, North Pole, Delta Junction, and Tok are all affiliated with the **Northern Lights Council of Dancers** (☎ 907/452–5699 ⊕ www.fairnet.org/Agencies/DanceAlaska/PHPBB/portal.php) and hold frequent dances.

Shopping

Crafts

Known for handwoven rugs, the **Alaska Rag Company** (✉ 603 Lacey St., Downtown ☎ 907/451–4401 ⊕ www.alaskaragco.com) carries the work of many local artists.The **Arctic Travelers Gift Shop** (✉ 201 Cushman St., Downtown ☎ 907/456–7080) has a wide selection of Athabascan beadwork. **The Artworks** (✉ 3677 College Rd., No. 3, College ☎ 907/479–2563) is known for high-quality fine art and crafts.

Beads and Things (✉ 537 2nd Ave., Downtown ☎ 907/456–2323) sells native handicrafts from around the state. The **Great Alaskan Bowl Company** (✉ 4630 Old Airport Rd. ☎ 907/474–9663 ⊕ www.woodbowl.com) sells lathe-turned bowls made out of Alaskan birch.

If Only (✉ 215 Cushman St., Downtown ☎ 907/456–6659) carries a wide range of unique Alaska items. **New Horizons Gallery** (✉ 519 1st Ave., Downtown ☎ 907/456–2063 ⊕ www.newhorizonsgallery.com) is one of Alaska's largest art galleries. **A Weaver's Yarn** (✉ 1810 Alaska Way, College ☎ 907/374–1995) has musk-ox qiviut to spin.

Jewelry

In her small, eponymous shop **Judie Gumm Designs** (✉ 3600 Main St., Ester ☎ 907/479–4568 ⊕ www.judiegumm.com), Ms. Gumm fashions stunning silver and gold designs best described as sculptural interpretations of northern images. Moderately priced and easy to pack, her jewelry makes a nice memento of your trip north. Ester is 6 mi south of Fairbanks off the George Parks Highway—follow the signs.

Larson's Fine Jewelers (✉ 405 Noble St., Downtown ☎ 907/456–4141) has been making Alaskan gold-nugget jewelry and other contemporary designs for six decades. **Taylor's Gold-N-Stones** (✉ 3578-N Airport Way, University Avenue ☎ 907/456–8369 or 800/306–3589) uses gemstones mined in Alaska and creates unique gold designs.

Outerwear & Outdoor Gear

Apocalypse Design (✉ 201 Minnie St. ☎ 907/451–7555 or 866/451–7555 ⊕ www.akgear.com) makes its own specialized cold-weather clothing for dog-mushers and other winter adventurers. Travelers from colder sections of the Lower 48 will appreciate the double-layer fleece mittens, among other items.

Sports, the Outdoors & Guided Tours

Adventure Tours

Northern Alaska Tour Company (☎ 907/474–8600 or 800/474–1986 ⊕ www.northernalaska.com) leads year-round half- and full-day excur-

COME WINTER . . .

The temperature gets down to 40 below zero every winter in Fairbanks, but school is never cancelled, no matter how cold it gets. In recent years, in fact, the only times schools have closed were when some rare winter warm spells created icy conditions on the roads that made it too hazardous for bus travel. One measure of the hardy attitude encouraged in young Alaskans toward the weather is that outdoor recess takes place in Fairbanks down to 20 below zero. The weather is a great unifying factor among Fairbanks residents.

Winter is the great equalizer. It freezes the pipes of university professors as well as laborers. After a night of 40 below, it's common to see cars bumping along as if the tires were flat. The tires freeze so that they are flat on the bottom and it takes a quarter mile or so before they return to round in frigid weather. Every car has an electric plug hanging out front between the headlights because every car has to be plugged in during the winter to keep running. In this environment, the sense of community is strong.

sions to the Arctic Circle and the Yukon River and two- and three-day fly-drive tours to Prudhoe Bay, Barrow, and the Brooks Range. They also have aurora-watching trips in the winter.

Baseball

Scores of baseball players, including Tom Seaver, Dave Winfield, and Jason Giambi, have passed through Fairbanks on their way to the major ★ leagues. The Interior city is home to the **Alaska Goldpanners** (☎ 907/451–0095 🌐 www.goldpanners.com), a member of the Alaska Baseball League, a string of amateur baseball organizations throughout the state. Players are recruited from college teams nationwide, and the summer season (mid-June–early August) generates top-caliber competition. Home games are played at Growden Field, along Lower 2nd Avenue at Wilbur Street, not far from Pioneer Park. The baseball park hosts the **Midnight Sun Baseball Game,** a Fairbanks tradition in which the Goldpanners play baseball at midnight of the summer solstice without benefit of artificial lights. This is thrilling (and possibly chilly) to watch on a clear, sunny night when the daylight never ends.

Bicycling

Bicyclists in Fairbanks use the paved paths from the University of Alaska campus around Farmers Loop to the Steese Highway. Another path follows Geist and Chena Pump roads into downtown Fairbanks. A shorter, less strenuous route is the bike path between downtown and Pioneer Park along the south side of the Chena River. Maps showing all the bike paths are available at the **Fairbanks Convention and Visitors Bureau** (⇨ Exploring Fairbanks). Mountain bikers can test their skills during the summer on the ski trails of the University of Alaska Fairbanks and the Birch Hill Recreation Area or on many of the trails and dirt roads around Fairbanks. Stop by the **Alaska Public Lands Information Center** (✉ 250 Cushman St. ☎ 907/456–0527) for mountain-biking information.

Boating

For relaxing boating in or near Fairbanks, use Chena River access points at Nordale Road east of the city, the Cushman and Wendell Street bridges near downtown, Pioneer Park above the Peger River Bridge, the state campground, and the University Avenue Bridge.

The Tanana River, with a current that is fast and often shallow, is ideally suited for riverboats. On this river and others in the Yukon River drainage, Alaskans use long, wide, flat-bottom boats powered by one or two large outboard engines. The boats include a lift to raise the engine a few inches, allowing passage through the shallows, and some of the engines come equipped with a jet unit instead of a propeller to allow more bottom clearance. Arrangements for riverboat charters can be made in almost any river community. Ask at the **Fairbanks Convention and Visitors Bureau** (⇨ Exploring Fairbanks).

Alaska Outdoor Rentals & Guides (✉ Pioneer Park Boat Dock, along Chena River next to Peger Rd. ☎ 907/490–4444 🌐 www.2paddle1.com) has canoe and kayak rentals and guided tours (⇨ *below*). ■ **TIP→ The company also rents bicycles.**

6

Test the Waters Adventure Sports (✉ 1511 Richardson Hwy. ☎ 907/457–2453 🌐 www.testthewaters.com) rents canoes, kayaks, inflatable boats and other outdoor gear.

CRUISING & CANOEING TOURS Fodor'sChoice ★

Alaska Outdoor Rentals & Guides (⇨ *above*) organizes canoeing and kayaking tours for groups of up to 50 on Class 1 waters of the lower Chena River. The only real challenge for canoeists on the lower river is watching out for power boats. **Greatland River Tours** (✉ 1020 Hoselton Rd., University Avenue ☎ 907/452–8687 or 866/452–8687 🌐 www.greatlandrivertours.com) provides nightly dinner cruises on the Chena River aboard the stern-wheeler *Tanana Chief*, a replica of the riverboats that once plied Interior rivers. The dinner cruise costs $49.95 and boards at 6:30 PM.

Fodor'sChoice ★

The excitement and color of the city's riverboat history and the Interior's cultural heritage are relived each summer aboard the **Riverboat *Discovery*** (✉ 1975 Discovery Dr. ☎ 907/479–6673 or 866/479–6673 🌐 www.riverboatdiscovery.com), a 3½-hour narrated trip by stern-wheeler along the Chena and Tanana rivers to a rustic native village on the Tanana River. The cruise provides a glimpse of the lifestyle of the dog-mushers, subsistence fishermen, traders, and native Alaskans who populate the Yukon River drainage. Sights along the way include operating fish wheels, a Bush airfield, floatplanes, a smokehouse and cache, log cabins, and Iditarod champion Susan Butcher's dog kennels. The late Captain Jim Binkley and his wife, Mary, began giving tours more than 50 years ago. Today their children and grandchildren carry on the tradition. The Binkley family, with four generations of river pilots, has run the great rivers of the north for more than 100 years. Cruises are $46.95 and run twice daily (at 8:45 and 2) mid-May to mid-September.

Curling

Hundreds of Fairbanksans participate each year in curling, a game in which people with brooms play a giant version of shuffleboard on ice.

PANNING FOR GOLD

The gold information center for Interior Alaska, **Alaskan Prospectors** (✉ 504 College Rd., Lemeta ☎ 907/452-7398 🌐 www.mosquitonet.com/~lmadonna) is the oldest mining and prospecting supply store in the state. Stop here for your gold pans and books or videos, or to check out the rocks and minerals museum. The employees have valuable advice for the neophyte gold bug.

El Dorado Gold Mine (✉ Mile 3, Elliott Hwy. ☎ 907/479-6673 or 866/479-6673 🌐 www.eldoradogoldmine.com) conducts two-hour tours ($29.95) of a seasonal mining operation that include a ride on a narrow-gauge railroad. Experienced miners Dexter Clark and his wife "Yukon Yonda" demonstrate modern and historical mining techniques and help you pan for gold. **FE Chatanika Gold Camp** (✉ Mile 27.5 Steese Hwy. ☎ 907/389-2414 🌐 www.fegoldcamp.com) provides a water trough for panners at an authentic gold camp.

Curlers have an almost fanatical devotion to their sport, and they're eager to explain its finer points to the uninitiated. This ancient Scottish game was brought to Alaska and the Yukon during the Klondike Gold Rush. The **Fairbanks Curling Club** (✉ 1962 2nd Ave. ☎ 907/452–2875 🌐 www.curlfairbanks.org) hosts an annual international *bonspiel* (match) on the first weekend of April. The club season runs from early October through the middle of April.

Dog Mushing

From November to March, a constant string of sled-dog races is held throughout the region, culminating in the **North American Open Sled-Dog Championship,** which attracts international competition to Fairbanks. Throughout Alaska, sprint races, freight hauling, and long-distance endurance runs are held in late February and March, during the Alaska season when longer days afford enjoyment of the remaining winter snow. Men and women often compete in the same classes in the major races. For children, various racing classes are based on age, starting with the one-dog category for the youngest.

In Fairbanks many of the sprint races are organized by the **Alaska Dog Mushers Association** (☎ 907/457–6874 🌐 www.sleddog.org), one of the oldest organizations of its kind in Alaska, and held at its Jeff Studdert Sled Dog Racegrounds at Mile 4, Farmers Loop. The **Yukon Quest International Sled-Dog Race** (☎ 907/452–7954 🌐 www.yukonquest.org) is an endurance race held in February that covers more than 1,000 mi between Fairbanks and Whitehorse, Yukon Territory, via Dawson and the Yukon River. You can get more details from the visitor center in either city or by calling the Yukon Quest office in Fairbanks.

★ If you want to experience dog mushing for yourself, **Sun Dog Express Dog Sled Tours** (☎ 907/479–6983 🌐 www.mosquitonet.com/~sleddog), with more than 20 years' mushing experience, offers summer and winter tours and demonstrations. When there is no snow, the dogs pull a wheeled cart.

Fishing

Although a few fish can be caught right in town from the Chena River, avid fishermen can find outstanding angling by hopping a plane or riverboat. Fishing trips include air charters to **Lake Minchumina** (an hour's flight from Fairbanks), known for good pike fishing and a rare view of the north sides of Mt. McKinley and Mt. Foraker. Another charter trip by riverboat or floatplane will take you pike fishing in the **Minto Flats,** west of Fairbanks off the Tanana River, where the mouth of the Chatanika River spreads through miles of marsh and sloughs.

Salmon run up the **Tanana River** most of the summer, but they're not usually caught on hook-and-line gear. Residents take them from the river with gill nets and fish wheels, using special commercial and subsistence permits. Check the "Outdoors" section in the Friday *Fairbanks Daily News–Miner* for weekly updates on fishing in the Interior. ■ **TIP→ You can purchase fishing licenses (good for one day or longer; $20 and up) at many sporting-goods stores and online at www.admin.adfg.state.ak.us/license.**

6

Arctic Grayling Guide Service (☎ 907/479–0479 🌐 www.wildernessfishing.com) offers guided and unguided fishing trips via jet boat to a popular fishing spot 60 mi south of Fairbanks. Fish for grayling and salmon. Cabins are available.

Golf

Chena Bend (☎ 907/353–6223), a well-maintained Army course open to civilians, is an 18-hole spread on nearby Ft. Wainwright. The 9-hole course at the **Fairbanks Golf and Country Club** (☎ 907/479–6555) straddles Farmers Loop just north of the university. The 18-hole course at the **North Star Golf Club** (✉ 330 Golf Club Dr. ☎ 907/457–4653, 907/455–8362 in winter) is on the Old Steese Highway, 7/10 mi past Chena Hot Springs Road. It is the northernmost course in the United States and perhaps the only one where you are encouraged to mark your scorecard with a tally of the wildlife you see.

FORGET SLEEP

For summertime Midnight Golf at the Fairbanks Golf and Country Club, a 3 AM tee time is considered normal.

Hiking

Creamer's Field Migratory Waterfowl Refuge (⇨ Exploring Fairbanks) has three nature trails within its 1,800 acres on the edge of Fairbanks. The longest trail is 2 mi, and one is wheelchair accessible.

Hockey

At the University of Alaska Fairbanks, the **Nanooks** (☎ 907/474–6868) play NCAA Division I hockey.

Riverboat Racing

Another summer highlight is riverboat racing sanctioned by the **Fairbanks Outboard Association** (☎ 907/459–2023 🌐 www.yukon800.com). These

CLOSE UP

Celestial Rays of Light: Aurora Borealis

THE LIGHT SHOW OFTEN BEGINS simply, as a pale yellow-green luminous band that arches across Alaska's night sky. Sometimes the band will quickly fade and disappear. Other nights, however, it may begin to waver, flicker, and pulsate. Or the quiescent band may suddenly explode and fill the sky with curtains of celestial light that ripple wildly above the northern landscape. Growing more intense, these dancing lights take on other colors: pink, red, blue, or purple. At times they appear to be heavenly flames, leaping across the sky. Or perhaps they're exploding fireworks or cannon fire.

The Fairbanks area is one of the best places in the world to see what is known to scientists as the aurora borealis and commonly called the northern lights. Here they may appear more than 200 nights per year; they're much less common in Anchorage, partly because of urban glare.

As you watch these dazzling lights spreading from horizon to horizon, it is easy to imagine why many northern cultures, including Alaska's native peoples, have created myths to explain auroral displays. What start out as patches, arcs, or bands can be magically transformed into vaporous, humanlike figures. Some of Alaska's native groups have traditionally believed the lights to be spirits of their ancestors. According to one belief, the spirits are celebrating with dance and drumming; another says they're playing games. Yet another tradition says the lights are torches, carried by spirits who lead the souls of recently deceased people to life in the "afterworld."

During Alaska's gold-rush era some non-native stampeders supposed the aurora to be reflections of ore deposits. Even renowned wilderness explorer John Muir allowed the northern lights to spark his imagination. Once while traveling through Southeast Alaska in 1890, Muir stayed up all night to watch a gigantic, glowing auroral bridge and bands of "restless electric auroral fairies" who danced to music "too fine for mortal ears."

Scientists have a more technical explanation for these heavenly apparitions. The aurora borealis is an atmospheric phenomenon that's tied to explosive events on the sun's surface, known as solar flares. Those flares produce a stream of charged particles, the "solar wind," which shoots off into space. When such a wind intersects Earth's magnetic field, most of the particles are deflected; some, however, are sent into the upper atmosphere, where they collide with gas molecules such as nitrogen and oxygen. The resulting reactions produce glowing colors. The aurora is most commonly a pale yellowish green, but its borders are sometimes tinged with pink, purple, or blue. Especially rare is the all-red aurora, which appears when charged solar particles collide with oxygen molecules from 50 to 200 mi above the earth's surface.

■ TIP→ **Alaska's long hours of daylight hide the aurora in summer, so the best viewing is from September through March.** Scientists at the University of Alaska Geophysical Institute give a daily forecast from late fall to spring of when the lights will be the most intense at www.gi.alaska.edu/cgi-bin/predict.cgi and in the *Fairbanks Daily News-Miner*.

WHERE AND HOW TO SEE THE NORTHERN LIGHTS

The **Aurora Borealis Lodge** (✉ Mile 20.5, Steese Hwy., Cleary Summit ☎ 907/389-2812 🌐 www.auroracabin.com) has late-night tours to a log lodge on Cleary Summit, with big picture windows to see the sky. The $75 tour includes hot drinks and transportation from Fairbanks.

About 60 mi northeast of Fairbanks, the **Chena Hot Springs Resort** (✉ End of Chena Hot Springs Rd., Chena Hot Springs ☎ 907/451-8104) has a glassed-in and heated hut set up on a hillside for gazing at the northern lights.

Ski resort **Mount Aurora Fairbanks Creek Lodge** (✉ Mile 20.5, Steese Hwy., Cleary Summit ☎ 907/389-2000 🌐 http://home.att.net/~Mt.Aurora/index.htm) has prime aurora-viewing conditions about 20 mi north of Fairbanks in an old mining bunkhouse, reconfigured with modern facilities.

Visitors fill the two warm mountaintop lodges at **Mount Aurora Skiland** (✉ Mile 20.5, Steese Hwy., Cleary Summit ☎ 907/389-2314 🌐 www.skiland.org) after 10 PM on winter nights, waiting for the lights. Images from an aurora Web cam are shown on a large-screen TV. Admission is $25 and includes hot drinks.

Northern Alaska Tour Company (☎ 907/474-8600 or 800/474-1986 🌐 www.northernalaska.com) has a variety of single or multiday winter aurora tours going north to the Arctic Circle and the Brooks Range.

6

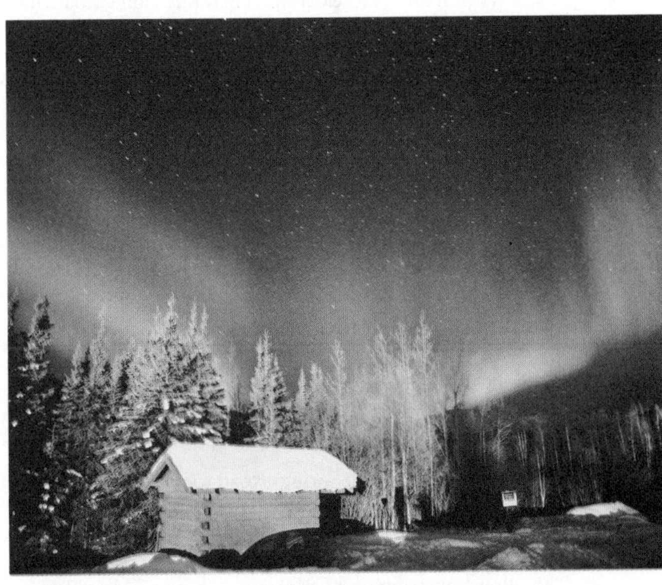

specially built 24-foot racing boats are powered by 50-horsepower engines and reach speeds of 75 mph. Weekend races throughout the summer and fall begin and end either at the Pump House Restaurant or at Pike's Landing, just off Airport Way near Fairbanks International Airport. The season's big event in late June is the **Yukon 800 Marathon,** a two-day, 800-mi race between Fairbanks and Galena by way of the Chena, Tanana, and Yukon rivers. The **Roland Lord Memorial Race,** from Fairbanks to Nenana and back, is held in early August, and the **Tanana 440** is held in late July.

Skiing

CROSS-COUNTRY The Interior has some of the best weather and terrain in the nation for cross-country skiing, especially during the late fall and early spring. Among the developed trails in the Fairbanks area, the ones at the **Birch Hill Recreation Area,** on the city's north side, and the **University of Alaska Fairbanks** are lighted to extend their use into the winter nights. Cross-country ski racing is a staple at several courses on winter weekends. The season stretches from October to late March or early April. Other developed trails can be found at **Chena Hot Springs Resort, White Mountains National Recreation Area,** the **Chena Lakes Recreation Area,** and the **Two Rivers Recreation Area.** For more information check with the **Alaska Public Lands Information Center** (☎ 907/456–0527).

DOWNHILL **Mt. Aurora/Skiland** (☎ 907/389–2314), on the Steese Highway about 20 mi from Fairbanks at Cleary Summit, has a chairlift, 20-plus runs ranked intermediate to expert, and a 1,100-foot vertical drop. There's lodging in an old gold-camp bunkhouse, dog-mushing, snowmobile rides, and aurora-viewing. It's open weekends from December to mid-April. **Moose Mountain** (☎ 907/479–4732, 907/459–8132 for ski report 🌐 www.shredthemoose.com), off Murphy Dome Road, has 42 runs from two summits for all skiing levels, all accessed by a bus lift system; it's open November through April, Friday through Sunday, plus school and government holidays. **Birch Hill** (☎ 907/353–7053), in Ft. Wainwright, has a chairlift and beginner and intermediate runs; it's open November through April, Thursday through Sunday.

AROUND FAIRBANKS

When you drive out of Fairbanks you quickly enter territory where people are few and far between. Away from the highways there are hundreds or thousands of square miles with few signs of human habitation.

The three roads heading north of Fairbanks are like pieces of string stretched out on a gym floor, making long slivers of the Alaska wilderness accessible. Each road has its unique characteristics and story to tell. ■ **TIP→ Road conditions can be rough, and if you break down, help may be a long way off, so be sure to check your fuel and your spare tire before you go.**

Follow the Chena Hot Springs Road to its end and you'll encounter natural hot springs that are among the best in the state. The Steese Highway connects to historic goldfields in Central and Circle, while the Elliott Highway leads north and connects to the Dalton Highway, built to allow construction of the trans-Alaska pipeline that runs along it.

All three roads present great opportunities for hiking, skiing, camping, fishing, canoeing, and other outdoor activities.

Chena Hot Springs

8 *62 mi northeast of Fairbanks.*

The 57-mi paved Chena Hot Springs Road, which starts 5 mi outside Fairbanks, leads to Chena Hot Springs, a favorite playground of many Fairbanks residents. Several attractions lie along the road, including Chena River State Recreation Area and Chena Hot Springs Resort. If you're heading to the resort, there are ample opportunities along the way to prolong your trip with hiking, fishing, camping, and canoeing. ■ **TIP→ The chances of spotting the occasional moose along the way are excellent if you keep a sharp eye on the roadside.**

From Mile 26 to Mile 51, the road passes through the **Chena River State Recreation Area,** a diverse facility of nearly 400 square mi. You can also stop for a picnic, take a hike for an hour or an extended backpacking trip, fish for the beautiful yet gullible arctic grayling, or rent a rustic back-country cabin and savor a truly wild Alaska adventure. Grayling fishing in the Chena River is catch-and-release, single-hook artificial lure only. There are several stocked lakes along the road affording catch-and-keep fishing for rainbow trout, which are well suited to the frying pan.

6

Where to Stay & Eat

★ $–$$$$ ✕ **Two Rivers Lodge.** Fairbanksans are known to make the 40-mi round-trip for the delicious dinners here, including hand-cut, aged filet mignon; prime rib; and frequent crab specials and other Alaskan seafood dishes. Don't be discouraged by the outward appearance of the building. Rustic logs belie the elegance of the menu. For a study in contrasts, Alaskan style, stop in the Trapline Lounge first for a predinner refreshment. ✉ *Mile 16, Chena Hot Springs Rd.* ☎ *907/488–6815* 🌐 *www.tworiverslodge.com* 💳 *AE, D, MC, V* ⊗ *No lunch.*

WORD OF MOUTH

"The best meal we had during our trip in Alaska was in the Two Rivers Lodge. It took about a half hour to drive there from Fairbanks on a bad road but it was [worth it.] The place was charming with great service and you could take a walk outside among many flowers."

–Gina

$$$ Fodor'sChoice ★ 🏨 **Chena Hot Springs Resort.** Fairbanksans come in droves to this resort to soak in the hot-springs-warmed hot tubs and natural-water rock lake or indoor, chlorinated swimming pool. Summer activities include gold-panning, flightseeing, and mountain-biking. In winter you can go snow-mobiling, dogsledding, and Snow-Cat touring. ATV tours are given year-round. The Aurorarium is a large, glassed-in room for viewing the northern lights in the winter, and there's a snow-coach ride to a hilltop yurt offering a 360-degree panorama. The latest addition is a year-round Ice Museum with an ice bar, four ice bedrooms and a multitude of ice carvings. Tours are $15. There are also sports-equipment rentals, camping sites, and a yurt ($65/night). ✉ *Mile 57, Chena Hot Springs*

Rd. ✆ *Box 58740, Fairbanks 99711* ☎ *907/451–8104 or 800/478–4681* 🌐 *www.chenahotsprings.com* ⇨ *80 rooms* ♨ *Restaurant, cable TV, massage, fishing, mountain bikes, horseback riding, cross-country skiing, sleigh rides, snowmobiling, bar, laundry facilities, some in-room data ports, meeting room, some pets allowed (fee); no phones in some rooms* ▭ *AE, D, DC, MC, V.*

CAMPING **Department of Natural Resources Cabins.** Used by those with extensive backcountry experience, these cabins have woodstoves, bunks, and tools for cutting wood. You have to supply everything else—food, bedding, water, cooking utensils. This is basic, Alaskan shelter, but it can't be beat for leaving the "real" world behind. Hiking distance in from the road varies from a few hundred yards (one site) up to 8 mi, and the nightly fee ranges from $25 for the Colorado and Angel Creek cabins to $50 per night for the larger North Fork and Chena River cabins. Wildlife in the area includes moose, porcupines, lynx, fox, pine marten, wolves, coyotes, and black and, occasionally, grizzly bears. Facilities vary with each cabin; potable water is available near some. *Pit toilets, firewood* ⇨ *5 cabins* ✉ *Miles 32 to 50, Chena Hot Springs Rd., Chena River State Recreation Area* ☎ *907/451–2705* 🖷 *907/451–2706* 🌐 *www.dnr.state.ak.us* *Reservations essential* ▭ *MC, V* *$25–$50.*

Red Squirrel Campground. If you want to combine easy fishing access with your camping, the Red Squirrel at Mile Marker 42.8 has a pond stocked with grayling. *Pit toilets, drinking water, bear boxes, fire pits, picnic tables, swimming (pond)* ⇨ *12 RV and tent sites* ✉ *Mile 42.8, Chena Hot Springs Rd.* *$10* *Reservations not accepted* ▭ *No credit cards.*

Rosehip Campground. At Mile 27 you'll find these campgrounds are very basic but have the essentials for family camping. There's a nature trail nearby, but access to the river is limited. *Pit toilets, drinking water, bear boxes, fire pits, picnic tables* ⇨ *37 sites* ✉ *Mile 27, Chena Hot Springs Rd.* *$10* *Reservations not accepted* ▭ *No credit cards.*

Tors Trail Campground. Campers at Mile 39.5 have easy access to the Granite Tors Trail, a 15-mi loop into the high country. *Pit toilets, drinking water, bear boxes, fire pits, picnic tables* ⇨ *24 sites* ✉ *Mile 39.5, Chena Hot Springs Rd.* *$10* *Reservations not accepted* ▭ *No credit cards.*

Sports, the Outdoors & Guided Tours

DOGSLEDDING **Chena Dog Sled Adventures** (✉ Mile 24, Chena Hot Springs Rd., Two Rivers ☎ 907/488–5845 🌐 www.ptialaska.net/~sleddogs) provides winter visitors a chance to drive a dog team or ride in a sled. Ice fishing and snowshoeing are also available. Summer visits and rides (on a sled with wheels) are available as well.

HIKING **The Granite Tors Trail,** a 15-mi loop, can be done in a day and offers a view of the upper Chena Valley and an opportunity to see these dramatic "tors" (fingers of rock protruding through grassy meadow) which are reminiscent of the *moai* monuments of Easter Island. The trail is steep and not to be taken lightly, but the views at the top are worthwhile. Although the Interior landscapes lack the impressive mountain views of other parts of the state, the enormous expanse of rolling hills and seemingly endless tracts of forest are every bit as awe-inspiring. However, since there are no mountains here to collect snow and contribute to the water table, water sources along the way are unreliable. ■ **TIP→ Be sure to bring a couple of liters of water per person, plus mosquito repellent.** Hiking uphill on a hot summer day requires it. Also, weather is quite fickle here, and a bright, sunny morning can easily turn into an overcast, rainy, and windy afternoon. Be prepared with adequate clothing, including rain gear, no matter how promising the skies look in the morning. A shorter hike is the 3½-mi Angel Rocks Trail, near the eastern boundary of the area.

PADDLING The **Chena River State Recreation Area** has numerous well-marked river-access points (the Chena Hot Springs Road parallels the Chena River, and canoeists use several put-in points along the way). The lower sections of the river area are placid, but the area above the third bridge, at Mile 44.1, can be hazardous for inexperienced boaters.

Wilderness Enterprises (☎ 907/488–7517 🌐 www.wildernessenterprises.com) has canoe rentals as well as guided fishing and float trips on the Chena and Gulkana rivers. Half-day, full-day, and multiday trips are available.

Steese Highway

From Fairbanks: 128 mi northeast to Central, 162 mi to Circle.

The Steese Highway follows the Chatanika River and several other creeks along the southern part of the White Mountains. It eventually climbs into weatherworn alpine mountains, peaking at Eagle Summit (3,624 feet), about 100 mi from Fairbanks, and drops back down into forested creek beds en route to Central. At Central you can drive the 30-plus mi on a winding gravel road to Circle, a small town on the Yukon River. The highway is paved to Mile 44 and usually in good shape. A possible exception is during winter, when Eagle Summit is sometimes closed due to drifting snow.

Where to Stay

¢–$ **F. E. Chatanika Gold Camp.** Miners working the dredges for the Fairbanks Exploration Co. in the early 1900s bunked at this 48-acre site. The grounds are on the National Register of Historic Places, and Alaska's largest coal cookstove still operates in the dining room. The spartan rooms in the hotel, with bargain prices, share eight bathrooms. The place still has the feel of an old mining bunkhouse. Additionally, there are two four-room log cabins that share four complete baths. The area is a wonderland for local winter-sports enthusiasts, summertime hikers, and aurora viewers. ✉ *Mile 27.9, 5550 Steese Hwy., Fairbanks 99712* ☎ *907/389–2414* 🌐 *www.fegoldcamp.com* *26 rooms with shared bath, 2 cabins with shared*

WORD OF MOUTH

"A great place to consider watching [the northern lights] is on the Steese, up and over the hill just past the Chena Hot Springs exit. For your best options, take responsibility for the viewing yourself and consult the Geophysical site of the Alaska U at Fairbanks for their daily predictions. That is what I do and it pays off." –BudgetQueen

CLOSE UP

Native Alaska by Bush Plane

From Fairbanks, you can easily catch a ride on regularly scheduled mail planes to small, predominantly native villages along the Yukon River or to Eskimo settlements on the Arctic coast. All of the smaller air services operate the mail runs on varying schedules. If you want to visit a particular village, or just have the desire to see a bit of native Alaska village life, contact any one of the services.

Frontier Flying Service (☎ 907/450-7200, 800/478-6779 in Alaska 🌐 www.frontierflying.com) has an extensive roster of scheduled flights to many of the Bush villages in northwest Alaska, the Interior, and the North Slope of the Brooks Range.

Larry's Flying Service (☎ 907/474-9169 🌐 www.larrysflying.com) has scheduled flights to more than a dozen Bush villages as well as charter service and flightseeing tours. **Tanana Air Service** (☎ 907/474-0301) flies freight and passengers to almost 30 villages along the Yukon and in the Interior and western Alaska. **Warbelow's Air Ventures** (☎ 907/474-0518 or 800/478-0812 🌐 www.warbelows.com) serves more than 25 villages. **Wright Air Service** (☎ 907/474-0502, 800/478-0502 in Alaska 🌐 www.wrightair.net) flies from its Fairbanks base to Interior and Brooks Range villages.

bath ♿ *Restaurant, bar, meeting room; no a/c, no room phones, no room TVs* ▭ *AE, MC, V.*

¢ **Chatanika Lodge.** Rocket scientists from the nearby Poker Flat Research Range gather at this cedar lodge, as do mushers (guests can take dogsled rides), snowmobilers, and local families. The eclecticism of the clientele is matched by that of the furnishings: diamond willow lamps and a variety of wild-animal trophy heads and skins, including bear, lynx, and wolf. Most of the 20,000 Christmas lights at the lodge stay up year-round and add to the rustic atmosphere favored by owners Ron and Shirley Franklin. The rooms generally have a double and single bed, sink, and TV. The bathrooms and showers are down the hall. ✉ *Mile 28.5, 5760 Steese Hwy., Fairbanks 99712* ☎ *907/389–2164* *10 rooms with shared bath* ♿ *Restaurant, cable TV, snowmobiling, bar, some pets allowed; no a/c, no room phones* ▭ *MC, V.*

Sports & the Outdoors

Tour companies aren't common in the area. Outdoor activities are generally do-it-yourself.

PADDLING The **Chatanika River,** a choice spot for canoeists and kayakers, has a wilderness feel to it yet it's still fairly close to Fairbanks. The most northerly **access point** is at Cripple Creek campground, near Mile 60 of the Steese Highway. Other commonly used access points are at Long Creek (Mile 45, Steese Highway); at the state campground, where the Chatanika River crosses the Steese Highway at Mile 39; and at the state's Whitefish Campground, where the river crosses the Elliott Highway at Mile 11. The stream flows into the Minto Flats below this point, and river access is more difficult.

Water in the Chatanika River may or may not be clear, depending on mining activities along its upper tributaries. In times of very low water, the upper Chatanika River is shallow and difficult to navigate. ⚠ **Avoid the river in times of high water,** especially after heavy rains, because of the danger of sweepers, floating debris, and hidden gravel bars. Contact the **Alaska Public Lands Information Center** (☎ 907/456–0527) to find out the status of the river.

Steese Mountain & White Mountain

9 *30 mi north of Fairbanks.*

For those who want to immerse themselves in nature for several days at a time, the **Steese National Conservation Area and the White Mountains National Recreation Area** (☎ 907/474–2200 Bureau of Land Management) have opportunities for backcountry hiking and paddling. Both preserves are accessible by car. The White Mountains Recreation Area has limited camping facilities from June to November; reservations are not accepted. The BLM also has three campsites on the Taylor Highway between Tok and Eagle at Miles 48.5, 82, and 160.

6

In the Steese National Conservation Area you can take a four- to five-day float trip on the lively, clear-water **Birch Creek,** a challenge with its several rapids and sweepers along its 126 mi. Moose, caribou, and birds are easily spotted. Access is at Mile 94 of the Steese Highway. This stream winds its way north through the historic mining country of the Circle District. The take-out point is at the Steese Highway Bridge, 15 mi from Circle. From there Birch Creek meanders on to the Yukon River well below the town. Fairbanks outfitters Test the Waters and Alaska Outdoor Rentals and Guides (⇨ Boating, *above*) arrange these trips.

Rising out of the White Mountains National Recreation Area, **Beaver Creek** makes its easy way north. If you have enough time, it's possible to run its entire 268-mi length to the Yukon (if you make a shorter run, you will have to go out by small plane). A lot of people make this trip in five or six days. Contact Test the Waters and Alaska Outdoor Rentals and Guides (⇨ Boating, *above*) to schedule a trip.

Where to Stay

¢ **BLM Public-Use Cabins.** The BLM manages 12 public-use cabins in the White Mountains National Recreation Area, with 300 mi of interconnecting trails. Designed primarily for winter use by dog-mushers, snow-machiners (snowmobilers), and cross-country skiers, cabins provide shelter for summer backpackers, although summer access is limited by mountainous and boggy terrain. The cabins have bunk beds, woodstoves, tables, pit toilets, and chairs. Permits are required and available up to 30 days in advance. ✉ *BLM Headquarters, 1150 University Ave., Fairbanks 99709* ☎ *907/474–2251 or 800/437–7021* *11 cabins* *MC, V.*

CAMPING **BLM Campgrounds.** The BLM manages three road-accessible campgrounds in the Steese Highway area, off the road between Mile 57 to Mile 60, and another along the Dalton Highway at Mile 180. The Cripple Creek Campground at Mile 60 Steese is the best for RVs, with a dozen sites and a half-dozen places for tents. The campgrounds are available on a first-come, first-served basis. In addition, you'll find several undeveloped campsites along the Dalton—old gravel pits with no facilities, available free of charge. *Latrines, fire pits, picnic tables, running water* *4 campsites* *907/474–2251 or 800/437–7021* *$6* *Reservations not accepted* *No credit cards.*

Sports & the Outdoors

HIKING The BLM maintains the moderately difficult 18-mi **Summit Trail,** from the Elliott Highway, near Wickersham Dome, north into the White Mountains National Recreation Area. This hiking trail can be done as a day hike or overnight backpacking trip. It quickly rises into alpine country with 360-degree vistas that include lots of wildland, the trans-Alaska pipeline, and a pipeline pump station. You can see many wildflowers in early summer. Look for the parking lot at Mile 28.

Yukon–Charley Rivers National Preserve

10 *20 mi north of Eagle, 100 mi east of Fairbanks.*

The 126-mi stretch of the Yukon River running between the small towns of Eagle and Circle—former gold-rush metropolises—is protected in the 2.5-million-acre **Yukon–Charley Rivers National Preserve.** In the pristine Charley River watershed, a crystalline white-water stream flows out of the Yukon-Tanana uplands, allowing for excellent river running for expert rafters.

In great contrast to the Charley River, the Yukon River is an inexorably powerful stream, dark with mud and glacial silt. The only bridge built across it in Alaska holds the trans-Alaska pipeline, north of Fairbanks. The river surges deep, and to travel on it in a small boat is a humbling and magnificent experience. You can drive from Fairbanks to Eagle (via the Taylor Highway off the Alaska Highway) and to Circle (via the Steese Highway) and from either of these arrange for a ground-transportation shuttle back to your starting city at the end of your Yukon River trip. Weeklong float trips down the river from Eagle to Circle, 150 mi away, are possible. For information contact the **National Park Service** (907/547–2233) in Eagle. **TIP→ Note that no developed campgrounds or other visitor facilities exist within the preserve itself,** though low-impact backcountry camping is permitted. *National Park Service, 201 1st Ave., Doyon Bldg., Fairbanks 99701* *907/457–5752* *www.nps.gov/yuch/index.htm.*

Sports, the Outdoors & Guided Tours

HIKING The **Alaska Public Lands Information Center** (907/456–0527) has detailed information about the trails in the Yukon–Charley Rivers National Preserve.

The BLM maintains the **Pinnell Mountain National Recreation Trail,** connecting Twelve-Mile Summit and Eagle Summit on the Steese Highway. This 27-mi-long trail passes through alpine meadows and along mountain ridges, all above the tree line. It has two emergency shelters. No dependable water supply is available in the immediate vicinity. Most hikers spend three days making the trip.

The **Circle-Fairbanks Historic Trail** stretches 58 mi from the vicinity of Cleary Summit to Twelve-Mile Summit. This route, which is not for novices, follows the old summer trail used by gold miners; in winter they generally used the frozen Chatanika River to make this journey. The trail has been roughly marked and cleared, but there are no facilities and water is scarce along much of it. Most of the trail is on state land, but it does cross valid mining claims, which must be respected. Although you'll find rock cairns and mileposts while hiking, no well-defined tread exists, so it's easy to become disoriented. ■ TIP→ **The State Department of Natural Resources strongly recommends that backpackers on this trail equip themselves with the following USGS topographical maps: Livengood (A-1), Circle (A-6), Circle (A-5), and Circle (B-4).**

RAFTING Rafting trips on the Charley River are for experts only. With access via a small plane, you can put in a raft at the headwaters of the river and travel 88 mi down this exhilarating, bouncing waterway. Contact the National Parks Service (⇨ *above*). The river here is too rough for kayaks and open canoes.

WINTER SPORTS Once past Mile 20 of the Steese Highway you enter a countryside that seems to have changed little in 100 years, even though you're only an hour from downtown Fairbanks. Mountains loom in the distance, and in winter, a solid snowpack of 4 to 5 feet makes the area great for snowshoeing, backcountry skiing, and riding snowmachines.

LOCAL LINGO

Alaskans refer to snowmobiles as snowmachines; calling them snowmobiles automatically brands you as someone from "Outside."

Snow-RV (✉ 5760 Old Steese Hwy., off Steese Hwy. at Mile 28.5, at Chatanika Lodge ☎ 907/389–7669) rents Arctic Cat snowmobiles. Rentals are available by the hour or for several days. Guided rides are required for those from out of state. They'll supply the guides.

For wilderness tours by snowmachine to prime backcountry destinations, contact **Alaska Snowmachine Adventures** (☎ 907/488–1330 🌐 www.alaskasnowmachineadventures.com). They have half-day, full-day, or nighttime rides, all with guides.

Elliott Highway

From Fairbanks: 28 mi north to Wickersham Dome, north 73 mi to Dalton Hwy. junction, 152 mi northwest to Manley.

The Elliott Highway, which starts in Fox, takes you to the Tanana River
11 and the small community of **Manley Hot Springs.** A colorful, close-knit "end-of-the-road" place, this town originally was a trading center for placer miners who worked the nearby creeks. Residents maintain a small public campground, across from Manley Roadhouse. Northern pike are caught in the nearby slough, and a dirt road leads to the Tanana

River with its summer runs of salmon. The Manley Hot Springs Resort has closed, but the hot springs are only a short walk from the campground. The highway is paved for 28 mi outside Fairbanks.

Where to Stay

¢–$ **Manley Roadhouse.** Built in 1903 in the midst of the gold rush into the Interior, this roadhouse is among the oldest in Alaska. Today it caters to a diverse crowd of vacationers, miners, and road maintenance crews. Not only is the roadhouse known for the food and the rooms, which occupy the original roadhouse and several cabins, but the bar earns bragging rights for its 250 brands of liquor and 20 varieties of beer. The restaurant serves breakfast, lunch, and dinner. ✉ *Mile 152, Elliott Hwy., Box 1, Manley Hot Springs 99756* ☎ *907/672–3161* *13 rooms, 6 with bath; 3 cabins* *Restaurant, bar, some pets allowed; no a/c, no room phones, no TV in some rooms* *AE, MC, V.*

Sports & the Outdoors

HIKING The BLM maintains the 22-mi **Summit Trail** from the Elliott Highway, near Wickersham Dome, north into the White Mountain National Recreation Area. Water is scarce on the trail, so be sure to carry plenty with you.

Dalton Highway

From Fairbanks: 140 mi north to the Yukon River, 199 mi to the Arctic Circle, 259 mi to Coldfoot, 329 mi to Atigun Pass, 499 mi to Deadhorse.

The Dalton Highway is a road of "onlys." It's the only road that goes to the Beaufort Sea, it's the only Alaskan road to cross the Arctic Circle, and it has the state's only bridge across the Yukon River. The 414-mi gravel road starts 84 mi from Fairbanks on the Elliott Highway and runs northwest of Fairbanks to the North Slope oil fields at Prudhoe Bay. It was built in 1974 and 1975 to open a truck route necessary to build the facilities at Prudhoe and the northern half of the trans-Alaska pipeline.

Unless you're an experienced outdoorsperson, areas off the Dalton Highway are best explored on a guided adventure tour. Services and comforts are few and far between, and the only lodging options are down-at-the-heels motels or wilderness camping. At **Coldfoot,** 250 mi north of Fairbanks, a first-rate **visitors center** (☎ 907/678–5209) provides information on backcountry conditions. A picnic area and a large, colorful sign mark the spot where the road crosses the Arctic Circle. ⚠ **There are no services between Coldfoot and Prudhoe Bay, a distance of nearly 250 mi.**

12 Today the Dalton Highway is still used to carry oil-field supplies and is open all the way to **Deadhorse,** just shy of the Arctic coast. This town exists mainly to service the oil fields of Prudhoe Bay. **Oil-field tours** (☎ 877/659–2368) and shuttles to the Arctic Ocean leave daily from the two hotels in Deadhorse: the Arctic Caribou Inn and the Prudhoe Bay Hotel. The tours ($37) include a video presentation of the oil field and a tour of the grounds with a stop at the Arctic Ocean, providing a good sense of how industrialization has come to Alaska's North Slope. A minimum 24-hour advance reservation is required to go on the tour. For security

WHEN DRIVING THE DALTON HIGHWAY

- Slow down and move to the side of the road for trucks
- Leave your headlights on at all times
- Yield on one-lane bridges
- Pull to the side of the road when stopping for pictures
- Carry at least one spare tire
- Consider bringing extra gas
- Consider purchasing a citizens band radio

Note: Car-rental companies have different policies on whether they allow customers to take vehicles on this rugged highway, so check that out in advance.

reasons, when making reservations you will need a valid government ID number for everyone in your group (driver's license, state ID, passport, Social Security card, etc.). Children are required to be with their legal guardian and need only provide their date of birth.

Where to Stay

$$ **Coldfoot Camp.** Fuel, tire repairs, and towing are available here in Coldfoot. Basic and clean rooms are built from surplus pipeline-worker housing. The 24-hour restaurant serves generous portions of truck-stop fare. Although the place looks more than a little offbeat, bear in mind that it's the only facility of any sort within 100 mi or more, so you may have to adjust your standards accordingly. Adventure-travel options include flightseeing, river-rafting, and mountain-bike rentals in the summer and aurora safaris and dog-mushing trips and school in the winter. The complex has a post office and 20 RV spaces ($30) with hookups—they're nothing fancy. ⊠ *Mile 175, Dalton Hwy., Coldfoot* ☎ *866/474–3400* 🌐 *www.coldfootcamp.com* *81 rooms, 52 with bath* *Restaurant, shop; no room phones, no room TVs* *MC, V.*

$ **Yukon Ventures Alaska.** You'll find a motel, a tire-repair shop, and gasoline, diesel fuel, and propane on this property on the Yukon River. The motel is basic and clean, built from surplus pipeline-worker housing. None of the rooms has a private bath, but two (one for men, one for women) have showers. The restaurant serves large portions of diner fare. ⊠ *Mile 56, Dalton Hwy.* ☎ *907/655–9001* *40 rooms share 3 baths* *Restaurant; no a/c, no room TVs* *MC, V.*

Sports, the Outdoors & Guided Tours

FISHING Although this is not a prime fishing area, fish, mostly grayling, populate the streams along the Dalton. You'll do better if you are willing to hike more than ¼ mi from the road, where fishing pressure is the heaviest. Lakes along the road have grayling, and some have lake trout and arctic char. The Alaska Department of Fish and Game (⇨ Interior Essentials, *below*) puts out a pamphlet titled "Sport Fishing Along the Dalton Highway," which is also available at the Alaska Public Lands Information Center.

Marina Air Fly-In Fishing (⊠ 1195 Shypoke Dr., Fairbanks ☎ 907/479–5684 🌐 www.akpikefishing.com) has fly-in trips to remote lakes for northern pike, rainbow trout, grayling and silver salmon. Overnight packages with a cabin are $180.

LOCAL ADVENTURE TOURS

Alaskan Arctic Turtle Tours (☎ 907/457–1798 or 888/456–1798 🌐 www.wildalaska.info) specializes in Dalton Highway–area trips, with tours in 15-passenger vans. Destinations include Arctic Circle, Yukon River, Brooks Range, and Prudhoe Bay on the Arctic Coast.

Northern Alaska Tour Company (☎ 907/474-8600 or 800/474-1986) is the most well-established tour company for the Dalton Highway. It has numerous tours to the Arctic Circle and beyond, some with fly/drive options that operate year-round. **Princess Tours** (☎ 907/479–9660 or 800/426–0442 🌐 www.princessalaskalodges.com) runs tour buses on the Dalton from Fairbanks all the way to Prudhoe Bay, with a variety of services, including an overnight at Coldfoot, a tour of the oil field, and air service from Prudhoe Bay back to Fairbanks or Anchorage. Tours operate once a week from June through August.

DENALI NATIONAL PARK & PRESERVE

13 Fodor'sChoice ★

11 mi south of Healy, 120 mi south of Fairbanks, 240 mi north of Anchorage.

The most accessible of Alaska's national parks and one of only three connected to the state's highway system, 6-million-acre Denali National Park & Preserve is one of North America's finest and easiest places to see wildlife in its natural environment. Nowhere in the world is there more spectacular background scenery to these wildlife riches, with 20,320-foot Mt. McKinley looming above forested valleys, tundra-topped hills, and the glacier-covered peaks of the Alaska Range.

McKinley, commonly known by its Athabascan name, *Denali,* meaning "the high one," is North America's tallest mountain. Unfortunately for visitors with little time to spend in the area, McKinley is wreathed in clouds an average of two days of every three during the summer. However, if you plan ahead and venture far enough into the park, you'll have a better chance of seeing the mountain in all its glacier-capped magnificence. Although most Denali visitors are content to contemplate Mt. McKinley from afar, more than 1,000 adventurers climb the mountain's slopes each summer.

You need not climb Mt. McKinley to appreciate the park; in fact, most people who visit Denali will never come closer than 35 mi of the mountain's snowy, glacier-covered base. The park is both a hiker's and wildlife-watcher's paradise. The 92-mi Denali Park Road (the one road in the park) is unpaved after the first 15 mi; while private-vehicle access is limited, in summer you can

WELCOME TO DENALI

You are about the enter one of the country's most pristine, wildlife-rich parks. Explorers across the globe dream of visiting this vast wilderness. Comprised of healthy forests, great tundra expanses, the continent's tallest mountain, and a huge roster of resident wildlife, Denali is teeming with adventure and possibility.

travel into the heart of Denali on shuttle buses. Those bus rides present the best opportunity to see grizzly bears, wolves, caribou, moose, Dall sheep, and many other critters, from soaring golden eagles to the chattering ground squirrels that scurry along the road. If you love biking, you can take on the park road with sturdy tires. It's also possible to gain an eagle-eye view of this mountainous landscape on flightseeing tours. The bulk of the parkland, however, is accessible only on foot in summer or by dog team or cross-country skis in winter.

For all the challenges of access and planning, those who explore Denali are certain to reap many rewards: wilderness solitude, a sense of discovery, wildlife encounters, and a greater appreciation of the landscape's immensity and the rigors of the sub-arctic climate.

Exploring Denali

You can have one of North America's premier hiking and wilderness experiences in Denali with the proper planning: know your goals, consult park staff before setting out, carry proper clothing, food, and water, and don't try to cover too much ground in too short a time. Most of Denali is "trail-less wilderness," so you have to make your own way across the landscape. Distances in the wide-open tundra can be deceiving; what looks like a 2-mi walk may in fact be 6 mi. Also deceiving is the tundra; though it looks like a smooth carpet from a distance, it may have bogs and thickets of willow. With 6 million acres of sub-arctic wilderness, Denali National Park & Preserve has too much area for even the most dedicated vacationer to explore. It's wise to consider some main questions before you plan your trip: Do you want to strike out on your own as a backcountry traveler, or do you want to stay at a lodge nearby and enjoy Denali as a day hiker and from the relative ease of a tour or shuttle bus?

Park Basics

Admission to Denali is $10 per person and $20 per family. The **Wilderness Access Center,** near the park's entrance (at Mile 237.3 of the George Parks Highway), is where reservations for roadside camping and bus trips into the park are handled. A smaller building nearby is the **Backcountry Information Center,** for those visitors who want to travel and stay overnight in the wilderness. The Backcountry Information Center has backcountry permits and hiking information, including current data on animal sightings, river-crossing conditions, weather, and closed areas. ■ TIP→ **Permits are required for overnight backpacking trips, but you won't need one for day hiking.** Other than the restricted areas, recognizable by signs posted prominently next to the road, the park is yours to roam. A new building, the **Murie Science & Learning Center,** is now the place to get general information about the park and learn more

> **WORDS OF WISDOM**
>
> Keep in mind that, as one park lover put it, "this ain't no zoo." You might hit an off day and have few viewings—enjoy the surroundings anyway. Of course, under no circumstances should you feed the animals (a mew gull or ground squirrel may very well try to share your lunch).

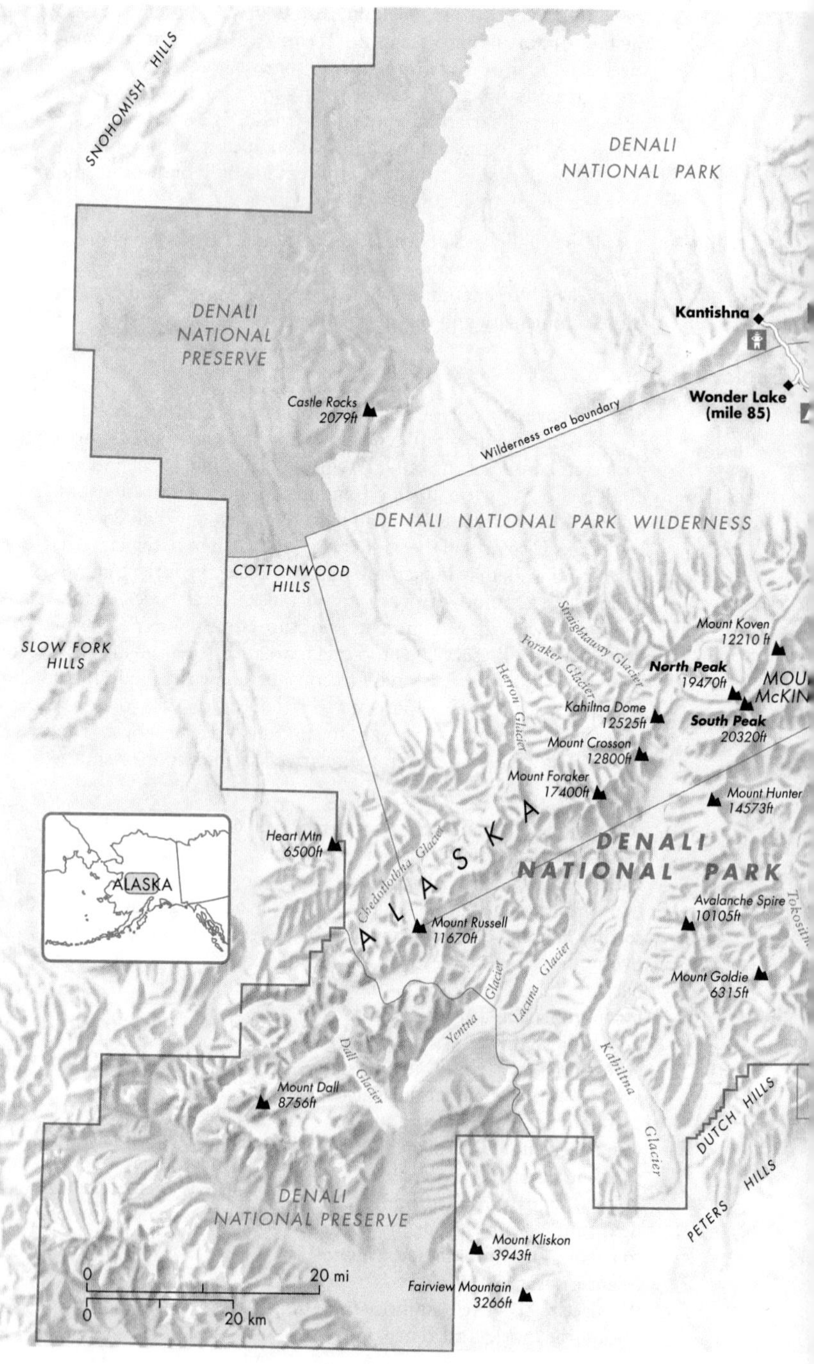
SNOHOMISH HILLS
DENALI NATIONAL PARK
DENALI NATIONAL PRESERVE
Kantishna
Wonder Lake (mile 85)
Castle Rocks 2079ft
Wilderness area boundary
DENALI NATIONAL PARK WILDERNESS
COTTONWOOD HILLS
SLOW FORK HILLS
Straightaway Glacier
Foraker Glacier
Herron Glacier
Mount Koven 12210 ft
North Peak 19470ft
South Peak 20320ft
Kahiltna Dome 12525ft
Mount Crosson 12800ft
Mount Foraker 17400ft
Mount Hunter 14573ft
ALASKA
DENALI NATIONAL PARK
Heart Mtn 6500ft
Chedotlothna Glacier
Mount Russell 11670ft
Avalanche Spire 10105ft
Mount Goldie 6315ft
Glacier
Lacuna Glacier
Yentna
Dall Glacier
Kahiltna Glacier
Mount Dall 8756ft
DUTCH HILLS
PETERS HILLS
DENALI NATIONAL PRESERVE
Mount Kliskon 3943ft
Fairview Mountain 3266ft
0 20 mi
0 20 km

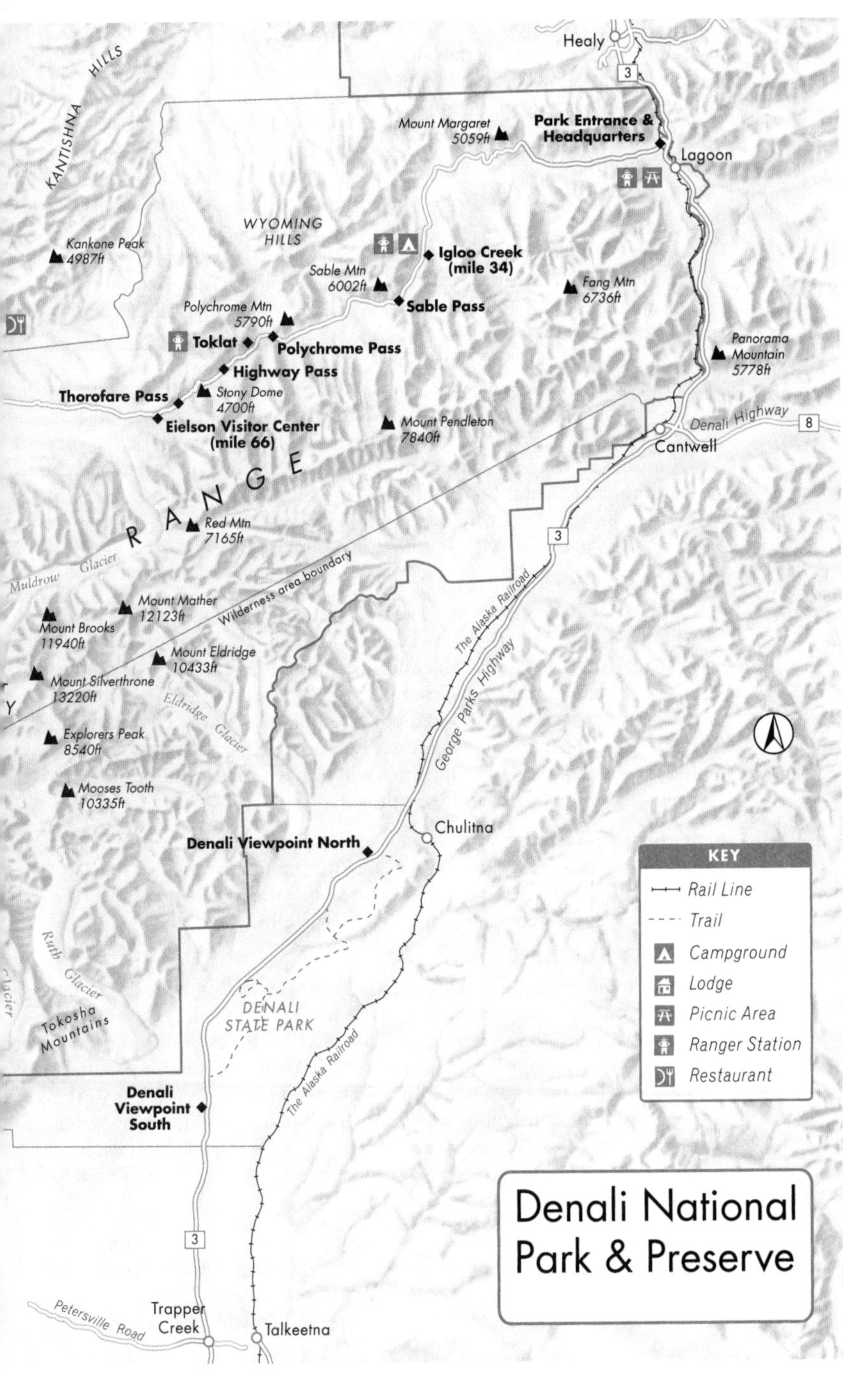
Healy
3
Park Entrance &
Headquarters
Lagoon
Mount Margaret
5059ft
KANTISHNA HILLS
WYOMING HILLS
Kankone Peak
4987ft
Igloo Creek
(mile 34)
Sable Mtn
6002ft
Sable Pass
Fang Mtn
6736ft
Polychrome Mtn
5790ft
Toklat
Polychrome Pass
Highway Pass
Panorama
Mountain
5778ft
Thorofare Pass
Stony Dome
4700ft
Eielson Visitor Center
(mile 66)
Mount Pendleton
7840ft
Denali Highway
8
Cantwell
RANGE
Red Mtn
7165ft
3
Muldrow Glacier
Wilderness area boundary
Mount Mather
12123ft
Mount Brooks
11940ft
Mount Eldridge
10433ft
Mount Silverthrone
13220ft
Eldridge Glacier
Explorers Peak
8540ft
Mooses Tooth
10335ft
The Alaska Railroad
George Parks Highway
Chulitna
Denali Viewpoint North
KEY
Rail Line
Trail
Campground
Lodge
Picnic Area
Ranger Station
Restaurant
Ruth Glacier
Tokosha Mountains
DENALI STATE PARK
The Alaska Railroad
Denali
Viewpoint
South
3
Petersville Road
Trapper
Creek
Talkeetna
Denali National
Park & Preserve

about Denali's interpretive programs. You can also visit the bookstore and natural-history exhibits here. ✉ *Box 9, Denali National Park 99755* ☎ *907/683–2294* 🌐 *www.nps.gov/dena.*

AT THE ENTRANCE

Denali's entrance area and road corridor (from the highway to Savage River) has plenty of adventure and learning. Besides the visitor and Murie centers, there are sled-dog demonstrations, interpretive walks, and the only maintained trails within the park. Keep an eye out for wildlife, especially moose.

Roads & Transportation

You can reach the park by bus or by car along the George Parks Highway. On its route between Anchorage and Fairbanks, the Alaska Railroad (www.akrr.com) makes a stop at Denali. Only one road penetrates Denali's expansive wilderness: the 92-mi Denali Park Road, which winds from the park entrance to Wonder Lake and Kantishna, the historic mining community in the heart of the park. The first 15 mi of the road are paved and open to all vehicles, but beyond the checkpoint at Savage River only tour and shuttle buses and vehicles with permits are allowed to travel. Bicycles are currently allowed on the park road, which is suitable only for mountain bikes.

Beyond Savage

Private vehicle traffic is restricted past the Savage River checkpoint at Mile 15. Campers with permits for the Teklanika campground can drive into and back out from their campsites at Mile 29, but they cannot tour the park road in their vehicles. Except for a few professional photographers with special permits and permit holders from the community of Kantishna, the only other vehicles are tour buses, shuttle buses, camper buses (offering transport for people with reservations for campsites), and those driven by Park Service employees.

If you decide to venture past the gatekeepers at Savage, and you won't be camping, you have two choices: either sign up for one of the sightseeing bus tours offered by a park concessionaire or ride the shuttle bus. The differences between the two are significant.

Tour & Shuttle Buses

Traveling in a bus down Denali Park Road is a journey filled with natural wonders and mystery. Starting at the developed and semi-tamed entrance area, you'll be transported into a wild landscape. From the bus, you'll have the opportunity to see Denali's wildlife in natural settings; the animals have become habituated to the road and vehicles, so they go about their daily routine with little bother. You also have the opportunity to view wildlife in the grand context of Denali's wilderness landscape, which in places seems to stretch forever, with no sign of humans beyond the narrow road corridor.

Passing through all of Denali's major ecosystems—taiga forest, wet tundra, dry alpine tundra—the road crosses large, braided rivers that pour out of the Alaska Range; it skirts the edges of brightly colored volcanic cliffs; and it's dwarfed by the surrounding wildlands, all the while

Continued on page 379

THE HIGH ONE

In the heart of mainland Alaska, within 6-million-acre Denali National Park & Preserve, the continent's most majestic peak rises into the heavens. Officially known as **Mount McKinley,** this 20,320-foot massif of ice, snow, and rock is most commonly referred to by its native name of Denali, or "the High One." Some simply call it "The Mountain." One thing is certain: It's a giant among giants, and the most dominant feature in a land of extremes and superlatives.

Those who have walked McKinley's slopes know it to be a wild, desolate place. As the highest peak in North America, McKinley is a target of mountaineers who aspire to ascend the "seven summits"—the tallest mountains on each continent. A foreboding and mysterious place, it was terra incognita—unclimbed and unknown to most people—as recently as the late 1890s. Among Athabascan tribes, however, the mountain was a revered landmark; many generations regarded it as a holy place and a point of reference.

NAMING TERRA INCOGNITA

Linguists have identified at least eight native Alaskan names for the mountain, including Deenaalee, Doleyka, Traleika, and Dghelay Ka'a. The essence of all the names is "the High One" or "Big Mountain." The first recorded sighting of Mt. McKinley by a foreign explorer was in 1794, when Captain George Vancouver spotted it in the distance. More than a century later, after a summer of gold-seeking, Ivy Leaguer William Dickey reported his experiences in the *New York Sun.* His most significant news was of a massive peak, which he dubbed "Mt. McKinley," after Republican William McKinley of Ohio. Mountaineer Hudson Stuck, who led the first mountaineering team to McKinley's summit, was just one in a long line of Alaskans to protest this name. In Stuck's view, the moniker was an affront to both the mountain and Alaska's native people. For these very reasons, a vast majority of Alaskans call the continent's highest peak by its original name.

Mount McKinley Facts & Figures

■ The mountain's vertical rise is the highest in the world. This means that at 18,000 feet over the lowlands (which are some 2,000 feet above sea level), McKinley's vertical rise is even greater than Mt. Everest, at 29,035-feet (which sits 12,000 feet above the Tibetan plateau, some 17,000 feet above sea).

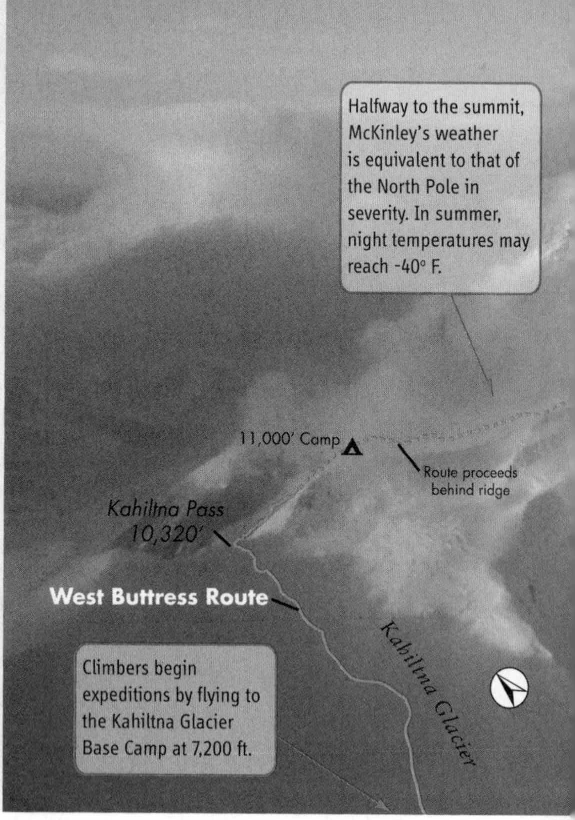

Halfway to the summit, McKinley's weather is equivalent to that of the North Pole in severity. In summer, night temperatures may reach -40° F.

11,000' Camp

Route proceeds behind ridge

Kahiltna Pass 10,320'

West Buttress Route

Kahiltna Glacier

Climbers begin expeditions by flying to the Kahiltna Glacier Base Camp at 7,200 ft.

THE WEST BUTTRESS ROUTE

■ The safest route to the summit is the West Buttress. Eighty to 90% of climbers attempting to ascend the peak take this route, with only about half reaching the top.

■ More than 30 people—including some world-class mountaineers—have been killed on the West Buttress.

■ From base camp to high camp, climbers must trek some 16 miles and 10,000 vertical feet—a trip that takes two to three weeks.

■ The most technically challenging stretch is the ascent to 18,200-foot Denali

■ In addition to coping with severe weather, climbers face avalanches, open crevasses, hypothermia, frostbite, and high-altitude illnesses. Nearly 100 people have died on the mountain and hundreds more have been seriously injured.

■ McKinley's awesome height and its subarctic location make it one of the coldest mountains on Earth, if not the coldest.

■ Primarily made of granite, McKinley undergoes continual shifting and uplift thanks to plate tectonics (the Pacific plate pushing against the North American Plate); it grows about 1 mm per year.

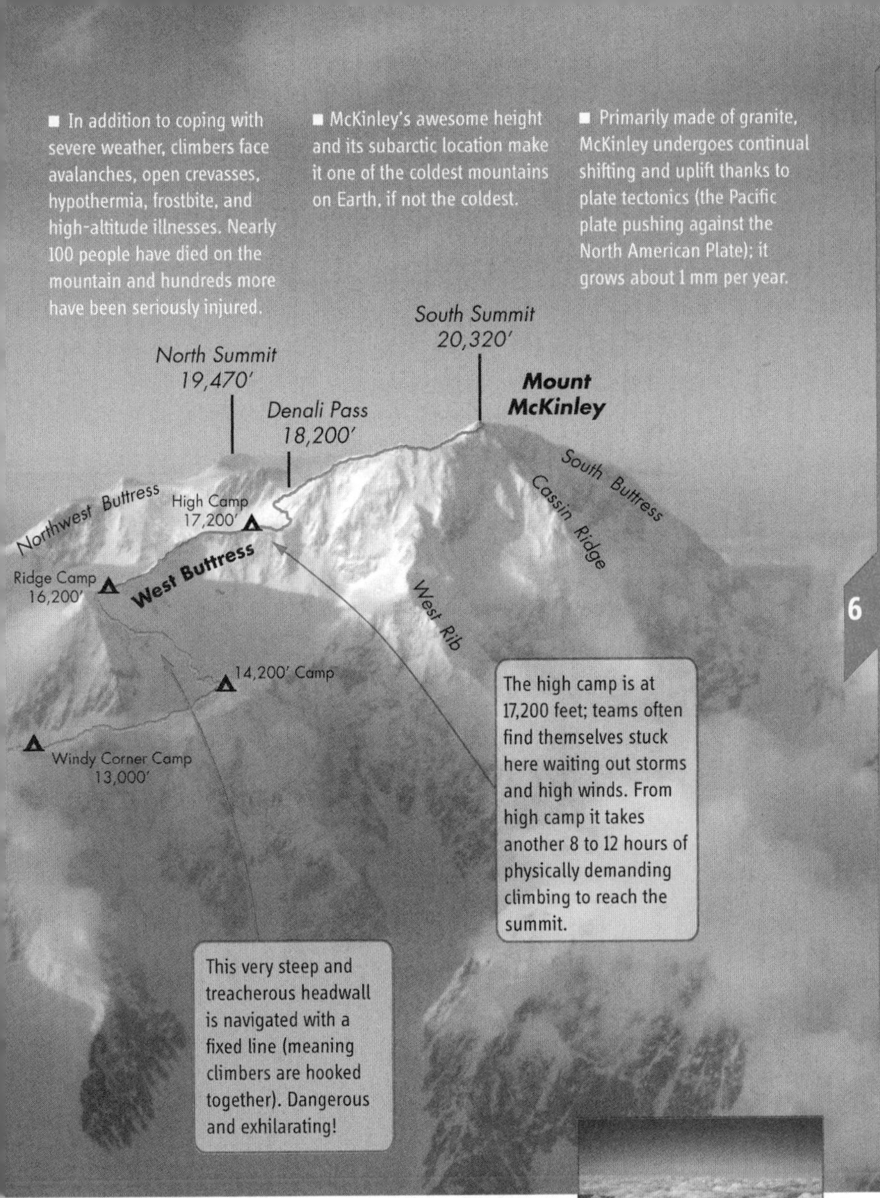

South Summit
20,320′

North Summit
19,470′

Denali Pass
18,200′

Mount McKinley

South Buttress

Cassin Ridge

Northwest Buttress

High Camp
17,200′

West Buttress

Ridge Camp
16,200′

West Rib

14,200′ Camp

Windy Corner Camp
13,000′

The high camp is at 17,200 feet; teams often find themselves stuck here waiting out storms and high winds. From high camp it takes another 8 to 12 hours of physically demanding climbing to reach the summit.

This very steep and treacherous headwall is navigated with a fixed line (meaning climbers are hooked together). Dangerous and exhilarating!

Pass; climbers must cross a steep snow-covered slope then a shallow bowl called the Football Field.

■ Then, still roped together, climbers ascend an 800-foot snow-and-ice wall to reach the "top of the continent" itself.

Fearless climbers facing the icy challenge at 16,400 feet on the West Buttress Route.

EARLY MILESTONES

Climbing Mt. McKinley in the early 1900s

- In **1903**, two different expeditions made the first attempts to climb Mt. McKinley. The highest point reached? 11,000 feet. Over the next decade, other expeditions would try, and fail, to reach the top.
- Finally, in **1913**, a team led by Hudson Stuck reached the summit. The first person to the top was Walter Harper, a native Alaskan.
- After the Stuck party's success in **1913**, no attempts were made to climb the mountain until **1932**. That year, for the first time, a pilot landed a small plane on one of the mountain's massive glaciers. Another first: a party climbed both the 20,320-foot South Peak and 19,470-foot North Peak. More tragically, the first deaths occurred on the mountain.
- Alaskans Dave Johnston, Art Davidson, and Ray Genet completed the first winter ascent of McKinley in February **1967**. Japanese climber Naomi Uemura completed the first solo ascent of McKinley in **1970**.

A FLIGHT TO REMEMBER

Talkeetna is the home of the popular Denali Flyers. Pilots take you on a variety of air tours into the Alaska Range in small, ski-equipped planes. Flights usually include a passage through the Ruth Glacier's Great Gorge, which is bordered by breathtaking granite spires. Leaving the gorge, you'll enter immense glacial basins of the Don Sheldon Amphitheater (named in honor of the first Denali Flyer). Most trips also include flights past McKinley's southern flanks and show glimpses of its climbing routes. Longer tours circle the mountain, passing among the perennially ice-capped upper slopes, sawtoothed ridges, and vertical rock faces. Flights generally range from 30 minutes to 3 hours and cost \$150 to \$300 per person.

HUDSON AIR SERVICE has a fleet of four airplanes. In 2006, they celebrated their 60th anniversary in business. A 1-hour flight costs \$150 per person. The McKinley Grand Tour is 90 minutes and costs \$210 per person. A glacier landing adds 30 minutes to your flight and costs an additional \$65.

☎ *907/733-2321 or 800/478-2321*
🌐 *www.hudsonair.com*

K2 AVIATION specializes in flightseeing and glacier landings in the Alaska Range. Prices range from \$155 (for a 1-hour flightsee) to \$300 (for a 90-minute flightsee with a glacier landing).

☎ *907/733-2291 or 800/764-2291*
🌐 *www.flyk2.com*

TALKEETNA AIR TAXI conducts a breathtaking exploration flight close to massive Mt. McKinley, as well as glacier landings. The McKinley Base Camp Tour (\$190) shows you where climbers set off; the Summit McKinley Tour (\$240) climbs to over 20,000 ft.

☎ *907/733-2218 or 800/533-2219*
🌐 *www.talkeetnaair.com*

presenting startling views of the ice-crowned High One (at least when the weather cooperates), which in places is within 35 mi of the road.

Though visitors who have the time, experience, and know-how to spend days or even weeks in the backcountry will gain a more intimate connection with this place, the buses that travel into the heart of Denali will present a good idea of the park's spirit—and, for most, a lifetime of memories.

Be advised that the bus trips in and back out take quite a bit of time. The road is not paved past the Savage River checkpoint, and the maximum speed limit is 35 mph. Add in rest stops, wildlife sightings, and slowing down to let other buses pass on the narrow road, and you've got the makings of a fairly long day if you want to see the park's interior. The round-trip journey to Fish Creek is roughly eight hours, and the extended trip to Wonder Lake is a good 11-hour day. Seeing the best part of the park demands a full-day commitment, but it's well worth the effort, no matter what the weather's doing. The best views of Mt. McKinley are between Stony Hill and Wonder Lake, miles 62 and 85, respectively.

Tour buses (☎ 800/622–7275, 907/276–7234 in Alaska or outside the U.S.) offer a comfortable introduction to the park. Reservations for all bus trips and campsite stays are accepted beginning in late February. Advance reservations are required for the tour buses but not the park shuttles. Many large tour groups reserve well in advance, so be sure to call ahead. Rides through the park include a five-hour Natural History Tour and a Tundra Wilderness Tour, which lasts from six to eight hours depending on season and weather. These trips are fully narrated and led by naturalists, and include a snack or box lunch and hot drinks. Although the Natural History Tour lasts five hours, it only goes 17 mi into the park (2 mi beyond the private-vehicle turnaround). This tour actually is more of a cultural history tour, emphasizing Denali's human and natural history. Those wishing to see wildlife or gain the best views of Denali should not take the Natural History Tour. ■ **TIP→ The Tundra Wilderness Tour is a great way to go if you're a first-time visitor wanting a fun and thorough introduction to the park.** Prices range from $60.30 to $90.75 for adults, including the $10 park admission fee. Another important consideration: these trips don't allow you to leave the bus and travel independently through the park.

The park's **shuttle buses** (☎ 800/622–7275 or 907/272–7275) don't include a formal interpretive program or food and drink. ■ **TIP→ They're less expensive, and, it's important to note, you can get off the bus and take a hike or just stop and sightsee, and catch another bus along the road.** Most of the drivers are well versed in the park's features and will point out plant, animal, and geologic sights as the bus progresses through the park. The shuttles are

RESERVING A SPOT

It's a very good idea to reserve tickets for buses ahead of time; call the numbers provided here or log on to www.reservedenali.com.

much more free-form than the tour buses, with all of the passengers enlisted to help watch for wildlife and to call out when animals are spotted. The shuttles will stop to watch wildlife, but there is a schedule to keep, so stopping time is somewhat limited. But if a bear, a wolf, or another large animal is observed, the drivers make certain that passengers have plenty of time to watch and take photos. Shuttle bus round-trip fares are $19 to the Toklat River stop at Mile 53; $24.25 to Fish Creek at Mile 63; and $33.25 to Wonder Lake at Mile 85.

If you decide to get off the shuttle bus and head across the tundra, just tell the driver ahead of time where you'd like to get out. Some areas are closed to all hiking, so before you decide where to go, check with the rangers at the visitor center. Some areas are closed permanently, such as the Sable Pass area, which is heavily traveled by bears, including sows with cubs; others close as conditions warrant. There may be a sensitive den site that's vulnerable to disturbance, or a kill site (an area where bears or wolves are feeding off a carcass) that's off-limits for safety reasons.

When it's time to catch a ride back to your point of origin, just stand next to the road and wait; it's seldom more than 15 minutes or so between buses, and if there's room on board, the driver will stop. However, during the mid- and late-summer peak season, an hour or more may pass as you wait, because many buses are full. If your party is large and the park is especially busy, you may have to split up into smaller groups or singles to catch a lift.

When to Go

Late May through early September is the prime visiting time for Denali—the area is loosed from winter's icy grip and the animals are awake, active, and cruising for food and companionship. In early summer trails may be muddy and all the trees won't be fully leafed out, but young animals may be more readily visible. Most of the park lies above the tree line and gets 16 to 20 hours of daylight at this time of year—which means you'll have plenty of time to enjoy the expansive view of unspoiled landscape and catch a few glimpses of Alaskan wildlife in the open spaces.

Late spring and early autumn provide opportunities to see the area when visitor traffic is lessened, but be advised that the onset of winter and the appearance of spring are far different from those in the Lower 48 and even from the seasonal changes in Anchorage. One advantage to going early or late is that before Memorial Day and sometime after Labor Day, visitors are allowed to drive their own vehicles as far as Teklanika, for as long as the weather permits.

The park is open all winter, although services are curtailed and the road into the park is blocked by snow beyond park headquarters at Mile 3.1. Intrepid travelers can visit the park on dog sleds, snowshoes, or cross-country skis and get a glimpse of Denali that's seldom enjoyed by outsiders.

Weather conditions can change in a hurry in Alaska, going from bluebird weather to duck or even penguin weather in a short time. Snow squalls may occur at any time of year, particularly in the hills and mountains.

WHAT TO PACK

Even if you're not planning on taking a long hike, you should carry durable rain gear, preferably made of a breathable material. Good, sturdy, broken-in hiking boots, a hat, and warm gloves are a must. In the Far North, cotton is not your friend–once it gets wet, it stays wet for too long, drawing warmth away from your body. Think layers. If you'll be hiking, use polypropylene long underwear followed by layers of wool or fleece. There's little or no shelter available, so pack accordingly. Remember to bring insect repellent, binoculars, and a camera. Carry plenty of water and snack food; water in the park isn't considered safe to drink, and once you pass the park entrance, there's no food available unless you want to compete with the bears for roots and berries.

Making the Most of the Scenery

If you get an early start on a morning bus, you will get far enough into the park to increase your wildlife-viewing opportunities, and maybe catch a glimpse of Mt. McKinley. The animals are generally most active early in the morning and in the evening, but as with all rules, this one is occasionally broken and a grizzly or caribou may show up along the road at midday.

On the way to the Savage River checkpoint, there are chances of spotting plenty of wildlife: moose, black bears, and red foxes frequent the spruce forest areas near the road. From the parking lot at Savage River, get out your binoculars and glass the ridges to the west of the river for Dall sheep, usually visible as white specks on or near the skyline. Once you get above tree line, scan the open tundra for caribou and grizzlies.

Primrose Ridge, not far beyond the Savage River bridge, is favored by Dall sheep, especially in spring and early summer. Dall sheep are also commonly seen in the Igloo and Cathedral Mountains (between Mile 34 and Mile 37) and Polychrome Pass area (Mile 43.5). Moose are best seen in the forested entrance area and along the stretch of road from Eielson to Wonder Lake (Miles 66 to 85). Grizzlies, like gold nuggets, are where you find them, but alpine areas from Sable Pass (Mile 38) to Eielson (Mile 66) are especially worth noting. Caribou are true nomads, almost always on the move, but they tend to congregate along the Eielson–Wonder Lake stretch of road in August and September. Wolves are seen as often as Denali's other large mammals, but they may happen to pass near the road anywhere from the entrance area to Kantishna, as several different packs inhabit the park.

■ TIP→ **The farther into the park you venture and the longer you stay, the better your chances of seeing the park's charismatic megafauna.** Getting an early start or making your way deep in the park doesn't guarantee that you'll see wildlife; the whereabouts of Denali's animals is almost always impossible to predict. Still, the possibility is always present, so stay alert.

Fauna & Flora

Nearly every wild creature that walks or flies in South Central and Interior Alaska inhabits the park. Thirty-eight species of mammals reside here, from wolves and bears to little brown bats and pygmy shrews that weigh a fraction of an ounce. The park also has a surprisingly large avian population in summer; some 160 species have been identified. Most of the birds migrate in fall, leaving only two dozen year-round resident species, including ravens, boreal chickadees, and hawk owls. Some of the summer birds travel thousands of miles to nest and breed in sub-arctic valleys, hills, and ponds. The northern wheatear comes here from southern Asia, warblers fly here from Central and South America, and the arctic tern annually travels 24,000 mi while seasonally commuting between Denali and Antarctica.

The most sought-after species among visitors are the large mammals: grizzlies, wolves, Dall sheep, moose, and caribou. All inhabit the forest or tundra landscape that surrounds Denali Park Road. You can expect to see Dall sheep finding their way across high meadows, grizzlies and caribou frequenting stream bottoms and tundra, moose in the forested areas both near the park entrance and deep in the park, and the occasional wolf or fox that may dart across the road.

Vegetation in the park consists largely of taiga and tundra. Taiga is coniferous forest that exists in moist areas below a tree line of 2,000 feet and consists mainly of white and black spruce trees. These trees have very shallow root systems due to the layer of permafrost that lies just under the surface of the land, and they are subject to the vagaries of wind and land movements. A turnoff and informational sign on the road near the park entrance points out an area of "drunken forest," where the uppermost layer of soil has shifted on the permafrost, moving the black spruce trees around and leaving them in a disheveled state that suggests some sort of arboreal inebriation. Ground cover in the taiga forest includes such shrubs as dwarf birch, blueberry, and willows. From the road the taiga looks open, with wide views and very few trees, but the dense bushes may make it difficult

WORD OF MOUTH

"We saw Dall sheep, grizzlies, caribou, brown bears, lynx, and a lot more from the shuttle bus in late May. It's a great way to experience the park without hiking in yourself." –shorebrau

"I recommend the shuttle buses. Why would you pay triple the cost for less distance? I am always on the first bus out–just my preference. I also make the drive to Savage River while there, and have always seen something. Last trip I watched three bears for close to an hour on the wash-out before Savage River. Binoculars are necessary. There are no restrooms on any of the Denali Park buses. Bathroom breaks are about every 1.5 hours." –BudgetQueen for inexperienced travelers. One good way to get around the thick brush is to follow broad creek bottoms that are often dry in summer.

The rest of the land mass that isn't permanently covered by ice and snow is overlaid by tundra, which consists of a variety of plant types including lichens, berries, bright wildflowers, and woody plants—all in miniature. This complex carpet of low-lying vegetation generates brilliant color, especially in August. Higher alpine tundra areas are often dry and therefore enable easy hiking; tundra at lower elevations may be very wet and spongy. After a while you may learn to evaluate tundra "walkability" from a distance, distinguishing by color and texture which areas are like a springy carpet and delightful to walk on and which are too moist for comfort and can turn an enjoyable hike into a boot-sucking slog.

Geology & Terrain

The most prominent geological feature of the park is the Alaska Range, a 600-mi-long crescent of summits that separates South Central Alaska from the Interior. Many of these peaks soar high above the surrounding lowlands, but the truly towering ones are Mt. Hunter (14,573 feet), Mt. Foraker (17,400 feet), and Mt. McKinley (20,320 feet). Glaciers are abundant along the entire Alaska Range.

Another, smaller group of mountains is located north of Denali's park road: the Outer Range, a mix of volcanics and heavily metamorphosed sediments. Though not as breathtaking as the Alaska Range, the Outer Range is popular with hikers and backpackers, because its summits and ridges are not as technically difficult to reach.

Several of Denali's most spectacular landforms are deep in the park, but are still visible from the park's lone road. The multicolored volcanic rocks at Cathedral Mountain and Polychrome Pass remind many travelers of the vivid hues of the American Southwest. The braided channels of glacially fed streams such as the Teklanika, Toklat, and McKinley rivers serve as "highway routes" for both animals and hikers. The debris- and tundra-covered ice of the Muldrow Glacier, one of the largest glaciers to flow out of Denali National Park's high mountains, is visible from Eielson Visitor Center, at Mile 66 of the park road. (One of the few visitor facilities between the entrance area and Wonder Lake, Eielson is primarily an interpretive center. Undergoing extensive renovations, it is scheduled to re-open in summer 2007 or 2008.) Wonder Lake, a dark and narrow "kettle pond" that's a remnant from Alaska's Ice Ages, lies near the end of the park road (Mile 85), just a few miles from the former gold-boom camp of Kantishna.

Hiking Terrain & Backcountry Travel

Maintained trails are nonexistent in the park interior beyond the entrance area, but the open tundra on the Alaska Range's northern side is very conducive to cross-country travel, with a few caveats. For starters, not all tundra is created equal. There's wet tundra and dry tundra, and your ability to make good time across the landscape depends on which type you're dealing with.

Dry tundra, composed mostly of ankle-high woody vegetation, makes for fairly easy walking. Notable side benefits are the tiny but beautiful and hardy wildflowers that somehow survive the long, harsh subarctic winters. They range from the sky-blue forget-me-nots and yellow Arctic poppies to blue harebells and white mountain avens. The wet stuff is more problematic; it's usually composed of tussocks, which are knobby growths of grassy vegetation surrounded by water and mud. Hiking wet tundra can be slow and inconvenient at best, or it can be a nightmare, depending on conditions. Stepping between the tussocks demands careful foot placement, and trying to walk on top of them is a fool's errand. They look firm and stable until you try walking on them, which is when they collapse and dump you off. After a while you can identify tundra types from a distance, but it takes some practice.

Another deceptive aspect of tundra hiking is the distortion of distance—that hill over there is a lot farther away than it looks. With no trees to help judge perspective, it's difficult to gauge distances and heights. Hiking times tend to expand considerably over terrain that looks like it's no more challenging than walking across a carpet, so be conservative when making plans.

At lower elevations, the wet tundra is often intermixed with thickets of willow and alder, which means you may have to do some bushwhacking. If you find game trails through thick brush, be advised that these trails were pioneered by bears, moose, and caribou. Whenever you're in an area of restricted visibility, make plenty of noise to announce your presence, and allow the resident creatures to move away ahead of you.

A big draw for more experienced hikers and backpackers are the foothills and ridges accessible from the park road. As long as you don't go deep into the Alaska Range, it's possible to reach some summits and high ridges without technical climbing expertise. Stamina and physical fitness are required, however. Once up high, visitors often find easy walking and views that show the landscape's sweep from river-rich lowlands and tundra benches and foothills to ice-capped mountains that culminate in the High One.

Nature Trails & Short Walks

While both day hiking and backpacking can be supreme in Denali's trailless backcountry, there are options for those who prefer to stay on marked and groomed pathways. The park's entrance area has a system of more than a half-dozen forest and tundra trails. These range from easy to challenging and are therefore suitable for all ages and hiking abilities. Some, like the **Taiga Loop Trail** and **Morino Loop Trail,** are less than 1½ mi; others, like the **Rock Creek Trail** and **Triple Lakes Trail,** are several miles round-trip, with an altitude gain of several hundred feet. Along these paths you may see beavers working on their lodges in Horseshoe Lake; red squirrels chattering in trees; red foxes hunting for rodents; sheep grazing on tundra; golden eagles soaring above high alpine ridges; and moose feeding on willow, one of their favorite foods. You should be cautious around moose and enjoy them from a distance;

weighing 1,000 pounds or more, they can cause severe injuries despite their harmless appearance. ■ **TIP→ If you encounter a moose at close range acting aggressively, run from it immediately to leave its personal space. Just the opposite is true for Denali's grizzlies. Never run from a bear.** You may trigger its predatory chase instincts and encourage the bear to respond to you as prey. A little caution and a large dose of common sense will assure you a safe trip in the park. A summary of bear-safety tips is available at the Denali visitor center. For more information, flip to *Welcome to Bear Country* in Chapter 7 of this book.

The only relatively long, marked trail for hiking in the park, **Mt. Healy Overlook Trail,** is accessible from the entrance area; it gains 1,700 feet in 2½ mi and takes about 4 hours round-trip, with outstanding views of the Nenana River below and the Alaska Range, including the upper slopes of Mt. McKinley. It's also a great starting point for backcountry hiking.

A LITTLE HELP FROM YOUR FRIENDS

Those with little backcountry hiking experience may choose to go on a guided "discovery" walk with one of Denali's rangers. Rangers will talk about the area's plants, animals, and geological features. Before heading into the wilderness, even on a short hike, check in at the Backcountry Information Center. Rangers can give you advice and general suggestions. Because this is bear country, the Park Service provides backpackers with bearproof food containers. Use of these containers is mandatory if you're staying overnight in the backcountry. You can plan your itinerary with rangers and use the shuttle bus for transportation.

6

Where to Stay & Eat

Healy

14 *11 mi north of Denali National Park, 109 mi south of Fairbanks, 251 mi north of Anchorage.*

Each summer overflow crowds from Denali National Park & Preserve stream into this small community of 500 people on the George Parks Highway, north of the park entrance. In addition to great year-round lodging and the magnificent views, Healy is home to the Usibelli Coal Mine, the largest mine of its kind in the state and Alaska's only commercially viable coal-mining operation.

From the **Stampede Trail,** you can enter Denali by snowmobile, dogsled, cross-country skis, or mountain bike. This wide, well-traveled path begins where Stampede Road ends and leads to the former gold-rush boomtown of Kantishna, 90 mi inside the park. Take the George Parks Highway 2 mi north of Healy to Mile 251.1, where Stampede Road intersects the highway. Eight miles west on Stampede Road is a parking lot and the start of the Stampede Trail.

¢–$$ ✕ **Totem Inn.** Travelers from the George Parks Highway, Healy, and Denali come here for standard American food at reasonable prices. Pizzas, steaks, sandwiches, and a Sunday lunch buffet are served year-round.

The kitchen is open daily 7 AM–10 PM. ✉ *Mile 248.7, George Parks Hwy.* ☎ *907/683–2420* ▭ *D, MC, V.*

$$ **Earthsong Lodge.** Above the tree line at the edge of Denali National Park, Earthsong yields views of open tundra backed by peaks of the Alaska Range. Each hand-built cabin has a decor theme (Denali, Sled Dog, Mountaineering) and private bath, a rarity in such small cabins in remote settings. ■ TIP→ **In winter, Earthsong Lodge is one of two concessionaires permitted to lead multiday dog-mushing tours into Denali.** The restaurant, **Henry's Coffeehouse**, named after a beloved sled dog, serves a surprisingly varied menu of pizza and pasta, Middle Eastern fare including vegetarian entrées, sandwiches, subs, and baked goods along with espresso drinks. Slide shows of Denali are a nightly treat, and tours of the sled-dog kennel are offered as well. ✉ *Box 89, Healy 99743* ☎ *907/683–2863* ⊕ *www.earthsonglodge.com* *11 cabins* *Restaurant, fans, Internet; no a/c, no room phones, no room TVs, no smoking* ▭ *MC, V* *EP.*

$$ **Denali Dome Home.** A 7,200-square-foot modified geodesic dome houses this all-year B&B. One room has a sauna and two rooms have jetted tubs. A common room has a TV, fireplace, and Alaska-related books and videos. Sit by the fireplace to take in spectacular views of nearby mountains through the tall windows. There's an extensive videotape and DVD collection at your disposal as well as high-speed Internet access. ✉ *137 Healy Spur Rd., Box 262, 99743* ☎ *907/683–1239 or 800/683–1239* ⊕ *www.denalidomehome.com* *7 rooms* *In-room hot tubs, in-room VCRs, Internet room; no a/c, no smoking* ▭ *AE, D, MC, V* *BP.*

$$ **Motel Nord Haven.** Five wooded acres protect this motel from the road, providing a secluded feeling that other lodgings along the George Parks Highway lack. There's wood trim throughout, and rooms have one or two queen-size beds. Rooms with two queen beds can accommodate up to five people at no additional charge. For a minimal charge, box lunches can be prepared to carry along on your explorations. No breakfast is served in the winter. ✉ *Mile 249.5, George Parks Hwy.* *Box 458, Healy 99743* ☎ *907/683–4500 or 800/683–4501* ⊕ *www.motelnordhaven.com* *28 rooms* *Some kitchenettes, cable TV, meeting room; no smoking, no a/c* ▭ *AE, D, MC, V* *CP.*

TENT & RV CAMPING ¢ **McKinley RV Park and Campground.** A variety of RV sites, from "basic" to those with full electricity, water, and sewer, as well as two-person tent sites are available at this campground, about 11 mi north of the park entrance. A dump station, public showers, laundry facilities, deli, espresso bar, ice, and gasoline, diesel, and propane are also available. ✉ *Mile 248.5, Parks Hwy., Healy 99743* ☎ *907/683–2379 or 800/478–2562* ⊕ *www.mtaonline.net/~rvcampak* *$16–$27.*

Within Denali

If you can afford the price tag, it's worth it to book your stay at a wilderness lodge within Denali. Camp Denali/North Face Lodge and the Denali Backcountry Lodge are in Kantishna, a private inholding at the end of the park road, in the heart of the wilderness. If you are traveling on foot with gear on your back, there are a handful of campground options within Denali—and there are the miles of pristine backcountry, as well. Just don't forget your backcountry permit!

WILDERNESS LODGES

★ $$$$ **Camp Denali and North Face Lodge.** Camp Denali and North Face are in the heart of the park near the end of the park road, and both properties have views of "the Mountain." At Camp Denali, guests stay in one of 17 cozy and comfortable cabins, located on a hillside that faces the Alaska Range. Cabins include a small wood-burning stove, wall-mounted propane lights, Alaskan artwork, and quilts crafted by members of the staff. Guests share bathing facilities, though each cabin also has its own outhouse. North Face Lodge is a north country–style inn built in on a tundra meadow. It has 15 rooms, each with private bath. The knowledgeable naturalist guides on staff offer outings during the three-, four- or seven-night stays. Each property has its own kitchen and dining room. Evening programs focus on the natural and cultural history of Alaska and the park. Lodging costs include round-trip transport from the park entrance on custom buses, all meals, guided activities, and use of canoes, mountain bikes, and fishing gear. The rate is based on a three-night minimum stay at $1,275 per person. *Box 67, Denali Park 99755 907/683–2290 www.campdenali.com 17 cabins (Camp Denali), 15 rooms (North Face Lodge) Dining room, boating, fishing, mountain bikes, hiking; no a/c, no room phones, no room TVs No credit cards Mid-Sept.–early June FAP.*

$$$$ Fodor'sChoice ★ **Denali Backcountry Lodge.** These cabins in the community of Kantishna at the end of the park road have private baths and individual climate controls, a rarity in such remote parts. Meals and before-dinner social hour occur in the main lodge building, which has a sitting area and small library in addition to kitchen and dining room. There is also a day lodge for day-trippers who travel to Kantishna, where they have a meal and rest break before returning to the park's entrance. Activities for overnight guests include naturalist programs; hiking; fishing; gold-panning; mountain-biking; and, for an extra fee, flightseeing when weather permits. Family-style meals emphasizing Alaskan fare are included in the room rate. Access to the lodge by private bus along the park road is the same system used by Camp Denali, and it takes a good part of a day to travel either way; the bus driver typically presents natural-history information. Staying for at least two nights is necessary if you want to participate in any activities. As at Camp Denali, DBL brings in writers, photographers, naturalists, and historians, to give talks and slide shows to its guests. *410 Denali St., Anchorage 99501 907/376–1992 or 877/233–6254 www.denalilodge.com 30 cabins Restaurant, fishing, mountain bikes, hiking, bar; no a/c, no room phones, no room TVs, no smoking MC, V Closed mid-Sept.–early June FAP.*

TENT & RV CAMPING

If you want to camp in the park, either in a tent or an RV, six campgrounds are available with varying levels of access and facilities. Two of the campgrounds—Riley Creek (near the park entrance) and Savage River (Mile 15)—have spaces that accommodate tents, RVs, and campers; visitors can drive to their sites without special permits to travel the park road. Visitors with RVs or campers can also drive to the Teklanika campsite (Mile 29), but they must first obtain park-road travel permits; in recent years no tent camping has been allowed at Teklanika, but visitors should check with park staff for updates. Sanctuary River (Mile 22), Igloo

6

Creek (Mile 34), and Wonder Lake (Mile 85) have tent spaces only. Access to these three camping areas is by shuttle bus only. The bus service runs special camper buses with extra storage space for campers with gear.

Visitors to the Sanctuary and Igloo Creek campsites should come very prepared: Sanctuary has no drinking water, and the water at Igloo must be taken from a stream and treated. All sites have flush or chemical toilets and food lockers for proper storage of food. Individual sites are all beyond sight of the park road, though within easy walking distance.

Fees for individual sites range from $9 to $19 per night. ■ **TIP→ Campsites can be reserved in advance in several ways:** online, through the Denali National Park Web site (www.reservedenali.com); by faxing a reservation form (form available at www.nps.gov/dena; fax to 907/264–4684); by mailing in the reservation form; or by calling the reservation service, 800/622–7275 or 907/272–7275. Reservations can also be made in person at the park. It's best to visit Denali's Web site before making reservations, both to see the reservation form and to learn if any changes in the reservation system have been made.

If you're camping overnight in Denali's wilderness, you must obtain a special permit (free of charge) from rangers at the Backcountry Information Center. This must be done in person, at the park; no advance reservations are possible. Only those with previous backcountry travel experience should try this option. You must also choose an area to camp in. Denali's backcountry is divided into 43 units, and only a limited number of campers are allowed each night in most units. The most desirable units are near the middle of the park, in areas with open tundra and wide-open vistas. These fill up faster than the low-lying areas, many of which are moist and have high mosquito populations. The best strategy for securing good backpacking areas is to arrive a couple of days early, stay at one of the facilities near the park entrance (or at the Riley Creek Campground), and check in at the backcountry desk early each morning until you can get the unit you want. It is also wise to check the park's Web site in advance (www.nps.gov/dena) and read up on such topics as bear and wildlife safety, clean camping, river crossings, and proper food storage; when you're at the park, talk with the rangers and tap into their local knowledge.

¢ **National Park Service Campgrounds.** Six campgrounds are inside the park: three are open to private vehicles for tent and RV camping, three are reached by shuttle bus only and are restricted to tent camping. All have toilet facilities, most have drinking water, and a couple have nearby hiking trails. All are open from late May or early June to mid-September, depending on snow conditions, and one (Riley Creek, near the park entrance) is open year-round. There is a onetime $10 park entrance fee, in addition to the nightly rate. You can apply for a site in person at the visitor center, but it's wise to reserve in advance. *Denali National Park Headquarters, Box 9, Denali Park 99755 ☎ 907/683–2294 information, 907/272–7275 or 800/622–7275 reservations ⊕ www.nps.gov/dena $9–$19 AE, D, MC, V All but Riley Creek (no visitor facilities) closed mid-Sept.–late May.*

Along the George Parks Highway

Hotels, motels, RV parks, B&Bs, campgrounds, and some restaurants are clustered along the highway near the park entrance, which is at Mile 237.3. You can judge distance from the park by mileage markers.

$–$$$$ ✕ **The Perch.** The bay windows of this fine-dining restaurant atop a forested hillside give the restaurant an appealing spaciousness and present a panoramic view of the surrounding Alaska Range foothills. The Perch serves breakfast, lunch, and dinner, offering home-baked breads and desserts along with steak and seafood; the Panorama Pizza Pub also serves soup and sandwiches. If you're looking for a quiet, quality sit-down meal away from the crowds of Glitter Gulch, this restaurant about 13 mi south of the park entrance is the place to check out. Cabin rentals are available year-round (summer rates are $125 with a private bath, $85 shared, with breakfast included; call for winter rates). ✉ *Mile 224, George Parks Hwy.* ☎ *907/683–2523 or 888/322–2523* 🌐 *www.denaliperchresort.com/9.html* ▭ *D, MC, V.*

¢–$$$ ✕ **Lynx Creek Pizza.** Though it's not much to look at from the highway, this restaurant (with attached bar) is a favorite with park staff and seasonal workers. Locals head here for pizza, sandwiches, salads, ice cream, and some Mexican entrées. You order at the front and grab a seat at picnic-table benches. It's 1 mi north of the park entrance. ✉ *Mile 238.5, George Parks Hwy.* ☎ *907/683–2547* ▭ *AE, D, DC, MC, V* ⊙ *Closed mid–Sept.–mid-May.*

¢–$$ ✕ **McKinley/Denali Salmon Bake.** Fresh salmon tops the menu at this rustic building, which looks as if it might blow away in a stiff wind, but in fact is one of the oldest buildings in the development strip north of the park entrance known locally as Glitter Gulch. Steaks, burgers, and chicken are also available, and breakfast, lunch, and dinner are served. It's 1 mi north of the park entrance; shuttle service is provided to area hotels. ✉ *Mile 238.5, Parks Hwy.* ☎ *907/683–2733 in summer* ▭ *AE, D, DC, MC, V* ⊙ *Closed Oct.–Apr.*

$$$ ✕🏨 **Denali Princess Wilderness Lodge.** This "wilderness" lodge is located along the Parks Highway, in the Glitter Gulch community a mile north of the park entrance. Unlike the lodges at Kantishna, in the heart of the park, this one features rooms with TVs and telephones in case you want to catch up with the outside world. There is also a high-ceiling two-story main lodge with tour desk, sitting areas, gift shop, café, and dining room. Views from this hotel take in the Nenana River, and rich forest colors in rooms mimic the surroundings. Complimentary shuttle service is provided to the park and railroad station. The large **Summit Dining Room** offers an estimable view and fine dining, and a dinner theater combines a meal with a musical comedy that recounts the first ascent of Mt. McKinley. Burgers and more casual fare are available at the **Summit Bistro**, which can also supply picnic lunches. ✉ *Mile 238.5, George Parks Hwy., 1 mi north of park entrance* 📫 *Box 110, Denali Park 99755* ☎ *907/683–2282, 800/426–0500 reservations* 🌐 *www.princesslodges.com/denali_lodge.cfm* 🛏 *353 rooms* 👍 *Restaurant, café, cable TV, outdoor hot tub, bar, meeting room; no a/c, no smoking* ▭ *AE, DC, MC, V* ⊙ *Closed mid-Sept.–mid-May.*

RUTH GLACIER

Even the shortest flightseeing trips usually include a passage through the Great Gorge of the **Ruth Glacier,** one of the major glaciers flowing off Denali's south side. Bordered by gray granite walls and gigantic spires, this spectacular chasm is North America's deepest gorge.

Leaving the area, flightseers enter the immense, mountain-encircled glacial basins of Ruth Glacier's Don Sheldon Amphitheater. Among the enclosing peaks are some of the range's most rugged and descriptively named peaks, including Moose's Tooth and Rooster Comb.

$$ ✕🏨 **Denali Crow's Nest Log Cabins.** These individually crafted log cabins 1 mi north of the park entrance are on a forested hillside with river and mountain views. Each has two double beds and its own bath, and a 180-degree view of the park entrance area. The **Overlook Bar and Grill** is a full-service restaurant featuring Alaskan seafood and steaks; it claims to have the largest beer selection in northern Alaska, which includes a full selection of beers made by the Alaska Brewing Company. There's also a courtesy park shuttle from train. ✉ *Mile 238.5, Parks Hwy.* 📫 *Box 70, Denali Park 99755* ☎ *907/683–2723 or 888/917–8130* 🌐 *www.denalicrowsnest.com* ⟲ *39 rooms* 👍 *Restaurant, hot tub, bar, travel services; no a/c, no room phones, no room TVs* 💳 *MC, V* ⏲ *Closed Oct.–mid-May.*

$$$ 🏨 **Denali Cabins.** Cedar cabins built within the taiga forest have all the basic amenities (including TV and phone) and share hot tubs and barbecue grills at this complex along the highway 8 mi south of the park entrance. All units have private baths. Complimentary shuttle service to the park visitor center is provided. Stays at the lodge are packaged with a Denali Backcountry Adventure, which is a full-day narrated trip along the park road to Kantishna (with a rest stop and meal at Denali Backcountry Lodge), returning to the park entrance in the evening. The cost of that trip is $125 per person. ✉ *Mile 229, Parks Hwy.* 📫 *410 Denali St., Anchorage 99701* ☎ *907/644–9980 or 888/560–2489* 🌐 *www.denali-cabins.com* ⟲ *45 cabins* 👍 *Outdoor hot tubs, travel services; no a/c, no smoking* 💳 *MC, V* ⏲ *Closed mid-Sept.–mid-May* 🍽 *CP.*

$–$$$ 🏨 **Denali River Cabins and Cedars Lodge.** The cabins, nestled in forest and clustered along the glacially fed Nenana River, are next to McKinley Village Lodge, 6 mi south of the park entrance. A boardwalk connects the cedar-sided log cabins, all with double beds, and leads to spacious sun decks, as well as to the river. Cedars Lodge has standard, fully furnished hotel rooms. The management operates park excursions and a courtesy shuttle service to and from the train depot. ✉ *Mile 231.1, Parks Hwy.* 📫 *1 Doyon Place, Suite 300, Fairbanks 99701* ☎ *907/683–8000 in summer, 907/459–2121 in winter, 800/230–7275 year-round* 🌐 *www.denalirivercabins.com or www.seedenali.com* ⟲ *48 rooms, 54 cabins* 👍 *Restaurant, cable TV, sauna, bar; no a/c, no smoking* 💳 *AE, D, MC, V* ⏲ *Closed mid-Sept.–mid-May.*

$$ **Denali River View Inn.** This hotel sits atop a bluff overlooking the Nenana River, just north of the park entrance. Modern rooms—with a blue-and-beige color scheme, private baths, and a no-smoking policy—set above the highway rather than along it, offer a quieter experience. ✉ *Mile 238.4, Parks Hwy.* *Box 49, Denali Park 99755* ☎ *907/683–2663 or 866/683–2663* 🌐 *www.alaskan.com/denaliriverview* *12 rooms* *Cable TV; no a/c, no room phones, no smoking* *D, MC, V* *Closed mid-Sept.–mid-May.*

WORD OF MOUTH

"The Denali shuttle was great. We saw moose, caribou, bears, and Dall sheep. On the return, it was warmer and fewer animals were out. Definitely take the earliest shuttle." -Julie304

Sports, the Outdoors & Guided Tours

Flightseeing

One of the best ways to get a sense of the Alaska Range's rugged immensity, and also get some close-up views of Mt. McKinley and its neighboring giants, plus (if you choose) stand on a glacier without carrying gear and food, is to take a flightseeing tour of the park. Most flightseeing is done out of Talkeetna, a small end-of-the-road town between Anchorage and Denali. See "The High One" in this chapter for more information.

Guided Tours

In addition to exploring the park on your own, you can take free ranger-guided "discovery hikes" and learn more about the park's natural and human history. Rangers lead daily hikes throughout the summer. Ask about them at the visitor center.

Privately operated, narrated bus tours are available through **Denali Park Resorts** (☎ 907/276–7234 or 800/276–7234). The Tundra Wilderness Tour costs $90.75, lasts six to eight hours, and includes a boxed snack. The Natural History Tour lasts five hours and costs $60.30.

Kayaking & Rafting

Several privately owned raft and tour companies operate along the Parks Highway near the entrance to Denali, and they schedule daily rafting, both in the fairly placid areas on the Nenana and through the 10-mi-long Nenana River canyon, which contains some of the roughest white water in North America.

Alaska Raft Adventures books two-hour-long white-water and scenic raft trips along Nenana River through **Denali Park Resorts** (☎ 907/276–7234 or 800/276–7234 🌐 www.denaliparkresorts.com/rafting.shtml). **Denali Outdoor Center** (✉ Mile 238.5, Parks Hwy. Box 170, Denali Park 99755 ☎ 907/683–1925 or 888/303–1925 🌐 www.denalioutdoorcenter.com) takes visitors five years old and up, of all abilities, on scenic rafting trips on the Nenana River. It also leads more adventurous trips down the Nenana River Canyon's rapids in either rafts or inflatable kayaks. No river experience is necessary. The kayaks, called Duckies, are easy to get out

CLOSE UP

Alaska Through Our Readers' Eyes

QUESTION: "Okay, experts. What are your top Alaskan experiences?" –laslaff

Fodors.com Forum Users Weigh In (and overlap quite a bit!):

"A flightseeing trip. We did a short one over a glacier [on the Kenai Peninsula]. On second thought: the Kenai Fjords boat trip out of Seward. We lucked out with perfect weather and calm seas. I loved watching the Orca whales. Independence Mine was fascinating, so was the Pratt Museum in Homer." –dfrostnh

"One-way cruise into Seward; a Kenai Fjords boat tour; an overnight in Seward; train to Anchorage; one night in Talkeetna; two nights in Denali. Less is more here. Distances are vast, and it shouldn't be a marathon trip." –BudgetQueen

"The Alaska Marine Highway. It's a state-run system of ferry ships, which serve primarily the port towns in the Alaska Panhandle." –jorr

"Denali! Take the earliest bus trip you can in summer or early fall and you'll see the 'Big 5' animals in Alaska [Dall sheep, caribou, bears, moose, and wolves]. The Kenai Peninsula is also spectacular. Go to Seward and take a boat ride." –ShelleyWilma

"Here's my top-10 list:

- Bear viewing at McNeil River or Brooks Camp
- Denali flightseeing
- Kenai Fjords boat trip [out of Seward]
- Sunset drive on Turnagain Arm
- Hike Chilkoot Pass
- Bristol Bay fishing trip
- Prince William Sound kayaking or sailing trip
- Ruth Glacier spring skiing
- Follow Iditarod into the Bush or meet it at the finish line in Nome
- McCarthy/Kennicott Mine" –repete

of, stable, and self-bailing. The company also teaches white-water kayaking. All gear is provided, including full dry suits. Mountain-bike tours and rentals are also available, and there's a free local shuttle from hotels, lodges, AKRR depot, the Denali National Park visitor center, and elsewhere.

Denali Raft Adventures (☎ 907/683–2234 or 888/683–2234 ⊕ www.denaliraft.com) launches its rafts several times daily on 2- or 4-hour and all-day scenic and white-water raft trips on the Nenana River. Dry suits are provided. Guests under the age of 19 must have a release waiver signed by a parent or guardian. Contact the company for copies before the trip. Courtesy pickup at hotels and the train depot is available. **Nenana Raft Adventures** (☎ 907/683–7238 or 800/789–7238 ⊕ www.alaskaraft.com) runs a wide range of rafting trips along Nenana River, from white-water canyon rides to multiday adventures that begin within sight of the Nenana's "feeder" glaciers deep in the Alaska Range. The company, like others that operate on the Nenana, provides dry suits.

Mountain Biking

Mountain biking is allowed on the park's dirt road, and no permit is required for day trips. The first 15 mi of the road is paved. Beyond the

Savage River checkpoint the road is dirt and gravel and during the day is traversed by the park buses, which can make for a very dust-intensive experience. It can also be a bit sloppy if it's raining. Late night, when the midnight sun is shining and buses have ceased shuttling passengers for the day, can be a rewarding time to bike and view the park's wildlife. When biking on the road, you need to be very aware of your surroundings and observe park rules if you decide to get off the road. Off-road riding is forbidden, and some sensitive wildlife areas are closed to hiking. The Sable Pass area is always closed to off-road excursions on foot because of the high bear population, and other sites are posted due to denning activity or recent signs of carcass scavenging. **Denali Outdoor Center** (✉ Mile 238.5, Parks Hwy. ☎ 907/683–1925 or 888/303–1925 🌐 www.denalioutdoorcenter.com) rents mountain bikes by the hour or day, and conducts guided 2- to 2½-hour tours of the park, complete with bike, helmet, water bottle, and shuttle-van transport.

Mountaineering

Alaska Mountaineering School (☎ 907/733–1016 🌐 www.climbalaska.org) leads backpacking trips in Denali and elsewhere in the state, including the Brooks Range. It also conducts 6- and 12-day mountaineering courses, mountaineering expeditions to Denali and other peaks in the Alaska Range, and climbs for all levels of climbing expertise. **Mountain Trip** (☎ 907/243–0039 or 866/886–8747 🌐 www.mountaintrip.com) has been guiding climbing expeditions on Mt. McKinley and other Alaska Range peaks since 1976, making it the most senior of the guide companies to operate on the High One. Though the company emphasizes climber safety, it also has a high rate of success: in 2005, for example, nine of Mountain Trip's 11 McKinley expeditions made the summit (experience required).

6

Winter Sports

Snowshoers and skiers generally arrive with their own gear and park or camp at the Riley Creek campground at the park entrance. Dog-mushing can also be done with your own team, or you can contact one of the park concessionaires that run day or multiday trips: **Denali West Lodge** (☎ 888/607–5566 or 907/674–3112 🌐 www.denaliwest.com) and **Earthsong Lodge Dog Sled Adventures** (☎ 907/683–2863 🌐 www.earthsonglodge.com).

RICHARDSON HIGHWAY

The Richardson Highway stretches 364 mi, from Fairbanks to the ice-free port of Valdez. The Richardson takes travelers the final 98 mi from the official end of the Alaska Highway in Delta Junction to Fairbanks, but it's more than a mere connecting route. The first road built in Alaska has fantastic mountain views and leads to excellent river and lake fishing. Named after General Wilds P. Richardson, first president of the Alaska Road Commission, the highway evolved from a pack-train trail and dogsled route that mail carriers and gold seekers followed in the early 1900s to a two-lane asphalt highway in 1957. It's a four-lane, divided highway for the 23 mi from Fairbanks to Eielson Air Force Base.

Along the route from Fairbanks, you'll go through North Pole, home of the Santa Claus House gift shop, with its towering Santa silhouette, and the North Pole Coffee Roasting Company, which provides many Fairbanks-area restaurants with fresh-roasted coffee. The Richardson also links Fairbanks with Delta's farm country and the winter and summer recreation areas near Summit Lake in the Alaska Range. At Paxson, the Richardson takes travelers to the Denali Highway, a gravel road leading west through the Alaska Range to campgrounds and fishing in the Tangle Lakes area and, later, to Denali National Park & Preserve. Fifty-six miles south of the Denali Highway, the Richardson borders Wrangell–St. Elias National Park, the largest U.S. national park.

North Pole

15 *15 mi southeast of Fairbanks, 85 mi northwest of Delta Junction.*

It may be a featureless suburb of Fairbanks, but it does have a cool name and Christmas lives in North Pole all year long. Many of the street names maintain the theme, including Santa Claus Lane and St. Nicholas Drive. The prime attraction here is the **Santa Claus House Gift Shop** (⇨ Shopping, *below*), a must-see if you have young children.

Off the Richardson Highway just south of North Pole, **Chena Lakes Recreation Area** (✉ Mile 346.8, Richardson Hwy.) offers hiking, swimming, boating, camping, picnicking, dog mushing, and cross-country skiing. Created by the Army Corps of Engineers as part of the Chena River Flood-Control Project, it is now operated by the local government, the **Fairbanks North Star Borough** (☎ 907/488–1655 Parks and Recreation Department).

Shopping

The **Knotty Shop** (✉ Mile 332, 6565 Richardson Hwy., 32 mi south of Fairbanks ☎ 907/488–3014) has a large selection of Alaskan handicrafts as well as a mounted wildlife display and a yard full of spruce-burl sculptures, including a 6-foot mosquito and other wooden animals that photographers find hard to resist. The shop serves soft drinks and ice cream over a counter carved from spruce burl.

The **Santa Claus House Gift Shop** (✉ Mile 349, 101 St. Nicholas Dr., 14 mi south of Fairbanks ☎ 907/488–2200 or 800/588–4078 🌐 www.santaclaushouse.com) is hard to miss. Look for the giant Santa statue and the Christmas mural on the side of the building. The store has a variety of toys, gifts, and Alaskan handicrafts. Santa is often on duty to talk to children, and two reindeer are kept in a pen outside the store.

Sports & the Outdoors

FISHING Rainbow trout are not native to the Interior, but they are stocked in some lakes. **Birch Lake** (Mile 303.5), **Harding Lake** (Mile 321.4), and **Quartz Lake** (Mile 277.8), easily accessible from the Richardson Highway between Fairbanks and Delta Junction, are good trout-fishing spots. All have campgrounds and boat-launching areas. To catch migrating salmon in the fall, head to **Salcha River,** 41 mi southeast of Fairbanks on the Richardson Highway.

Delta Junction

16 *100 mi southeast of Fairbanks, 106 mi northwest of Tok, 266 mi north of Valdez.*

Delta Junction is the official end of the Alaska Highway, an agricultural center and home to a major part of the nation's missile defense system. In summer Delta becomes a bustling rest stop for road-weary tourists traveling the Alaska and Richardson highways. Delta is also known for its access to good fishing and its proximity to the Delta Bison Range. However, don't expect to see the elusive bison, as they roam free and generally avoid people.

ON THE DEFENSIVE

Fort Greely, which is 5 mi south toward Valdez, contains a growing number of underground silos with missiles that are part of the Ballistic Missile Defense System. The missiles are connected to tracking stations elsewhere and would be launched to try to shoot down enemy missiles in space if the United States is ever attacked in that manner.

Historic landmark **Rika's Roadhouse** (⇨ Where to Eat, *below*), part of Big Delta State Historical Park, is well worth a detour if you're nearby for the free tours of the beautifully restored and meticulously maintained grounds, gardens, and historic buildings. Try the delicious baked goods.

Where to Eat

\$–\$\$\$\$ ✕ **Pizza Bella.** Delicious pizzas and other Italian and American entrées compose the menu here. Italian scenic paintings and maps bring a slice of Italy to Alaska. ✉ *Mile 265, Richardson Hwy.* ☎ *907/895–4841 or 907/895–4524* ▭ *MC, V.*

★ **¢–\$** ✕ **Rika's Roadhouse.** On beautiful, well-maintained grounds with gardens and historic buildings, Rika's serves breakfast and lunch. The home-baked goods, including pies, muffins, cookies, sweet rolls, and breads, are delectable. ✉ *Mile 275, Richardson Hwy.* ☎ *907/895–4201* 🌐 *www.rikas.com* ▭ *AE, D, MC, V* ⊗ *Closed mid-Sept.–mid-May. No dinner.*

FORTYMILE COUNTRY

A trip through the Fortymile Country up the Taylor Highway will take you back in time more than a century—when gold was the lure that drew hardy travelers to Interior Alaska. It's still one of the few places to see active mining without leaving the road system.

The 160-mi **Taylor Highway** runs north from the Alaska Highway at Tetlin Junction, 12½ mi south of Delta Junction. It's a narrow rough-gravel road that winds along mountain ridges and through valleys of the Fortymile River. The road passes the tiny community of Chicken and ends in Eagle at the Yukon River. This is one of only three places in Alaska where the Yukon River can be reached by road. A cutoff just south of Eagle connects to the Canadian Top of the World Highway leading to

Dawson City in the Yukon Territory. This is the route many Alaskans take to Dawson City. ⚠ **The highway is not plowed in winter, so it is snowed shut from fall to spring.** Watch for road equipment.

Tok

⓱ *12 mi west of Tetlin Junction, 175 mi southwest of Dawson City.*

Loggers, miners, and hunting guides who live and work along Tok's surrounding streams or in the millions of acres of spruce forest nearby come here for supplies, at the junction of the Glenn Highway and the Alaska Highway. Each summer the city, with a resident population of fewer than 1,500, becomes temporary home to thousands of travelers, including those journeying up the Alaska Highway from the Lower 48.

After crossing into Alaska from the Yukon Territory on the Alaska Highway, the first vestiges of what passes for civilization in the Far North are found in the town of Tok. Here you'll find food, fuel, hotels, and a couple of restaurants, and the need to make a decision.

Staying on the Alaska Highway and heading roughly west will take you into the Interior and to Fairbanks, whereas heading south on the Tok Cutoff will aim you toward South Central Alaska and the population center of Anchorage. Or, you can make a huge loop tour, covering most of the paved highway in the state, taking in much of the terrific variety of landscapes and terrains that the 49th state has to offer. Head down the Tok Cutoff to the Richardson Highway (no one in Alaska uses the highway route numbers), and from there go south to Valdez. From there catch the ferry to Whittier, Cordova, or Seward, explore the Kenai and Anchorage, then head north on the Seward Highway to the parks, to Denali, Fairbanks, and beyond. Loop back to Tok and you've seen most of what can be seen from the road system.

BORDER CROSSING ALERT

Crossing into Interior Alaska from the Lower 48 or from the ferry terminals in Southeast requires border crossings into Canada and then into Alaska. Be very certain of all the requirements for crossing an international border, including restrictions on pets, firearms, and the need for adequate personal identification for every member of the party.

The **Tetlin National Wildlife Refuge Visitor Center** parallels the Alaska Highway for the first 65 highway mi after leaving Canada. This 730,000-acre refuge has most of the charismatic megafauna that visitors travel to Alaska to see, including black and grizzly bears, moose, Dall sheep, wolves, and caribou, as well as numerous bird species. The visitor center has a large deck outfitted with spotting scopes, and inside you'll find maps, wildlife displays, books and interpretive information. ✉ *Mile 1229, Alaska Hwy.* ☎ *907/883–5312* 🌐 *http://tetlin.fws.gov* 🎫 *Free* ⏲ *May 15–Sept. 15.*

To help with your planning, stop in at the **Tok Main Street Visitors Center** (✉ Mile 1314, Alaska Hwy. ☎ 907/883–5775), which has travel information covering the entire state, as well as wildlife and natural-history exhibits. The staff is quite helpful.

Where to Stay & Eat

$–$$$$ ✕ **Fast Eddy's Restaurant.** It's much better than the name would indicate: the chef makes his own noodles for chicken noodle soup, and the homemade hoagies and pizza are a welcome relief from the roadhouse hamburgers served by most Alaska Highway restaurants. It's open 6 AM–11 PM (but the soup is usually gone by 5). ✉ *Mile 1,313.3, Alaska Hwy.* ☎ *907/883–4411* ▭ *AE, D, MC, V.*

$–$$ ✕ **Gateway Salmon Bake & RV Park.** For highway travelers, Tok is the first stop in Alaska, and the Gateway is in turn the first stop in Tok. As an introduction to informal Alaska dining, it's tough to beat, with all-you-can-eat salmon, halibut, reindeer sausage, barbecue ribs, chicken, buffalo burgers, and salmon chowder. Seating is at picnic tables, either outdoors or under a covered pavilion. There's also a full-service RV park out back, and a very clean shower facility if you need to hose off the road dust from the long drive. ✉ *Mile 1,313.1, Alaska Hwy.* ☎ *907/883–5555* ▭ *D, MC, V.*

$$ **Westmark Tok.** Made up of a series of interconnected buildings, the hotel has been updated and has decent accommodations for this remote part of Alaska. The dining room serves standard fare, while the lounge makes a point of offering "Alaska's largest margaritas." The spacious dining room of this reliable, comfortable, and well-appointed hotel is a welcome respite when you are traveling the long stretches between civilization outposts along the Alaska Highway. ✉ *Junction of Alaska and Glenn Hwys.* *Box 130, 99780* ☎ *907/883–5174 or 800/544–0970* 🌐 *www.westmarkhotels.com* *92 rooms* *Restaurant, cable TV, bar, shop, some pets allowed* ▭ *AE, D, DC, MC, V* *Closed Oct.–May.*

6

Shopping

The **Burnt Paw** (✉ Junction of Alaska and Glenn Hwys. ☎ 907/883–4121 🌐 www.burntpawcabins.com) sells jade and ivory, Alaskan ceramics, crafts, paintings, smoked salmon—even sled-dog puppies. There are also a B&B on the premises and log cabins with traditional Alaska sod roofs. In Northway, south of Tok, **Naabia Niign** (✉ Mile 1264, Alaska Hwy. ☎ 907/778–2297) is a native-owned crafts gallery with an excellent selection of authentic, locally made birch baskets, beadwork items, and fur moccasins and gloves.

Chicken

18 *78 mi north of Tok, 109 mi west of Dawson City.*

Chicken was once in the heart of major gold-mining operations, and the remains of many of these works are visible along the highway. Here you'll find the Chicken Creek Café, Saloon and Gas: a country store, bar, liquor store, café, and gas station all in one. ■ TIP→ **Ask about tours of the old mining operations ($5) at the café, which hosts a salmon barbecue every day from 4 PM to 8 PM.** Be careful not to trespass on private property. Miners rarely have a sense of humor about trespassing.

ALASKA HIGHWAY HISTORY

It's hard to overestimate the importance of the Alaska Highway in the state's development history. Before World War II, there was no road connection between the Alaskan Interior and the rest of North America. Alaska's population center was in the coastal towns of the Southeast panhandle region, and most of the state's commerce was conducted along its waterways. Access to the Interior was via riverboat, until 1923 when the railroad connection from Seward through Anchorage and into Fairbanks was completed.

The onset of World War II changed everything. An overland route to the state was deemed a matter vital to national security in order to supply war material to the campaign in the Aleutians, and to fend off a potential invasion by Japan. In a feat of amazing engineering and construction prowess, the 1,500-mi-long route was carved out of the wilderness in eight months in 1942. The original road was crude but effective, and has been undergoing constant maintenance and upgrading ever since. Today the highway is easily traversed by every form of highway vehicle imaginable, from bicycles and motorcycles to the biggest, lumbering RVs known not so affectionately by locals as "road barns."

Sports, the Outdoors & Guided Tours

CANOEING The beautiful **Fortymile River** offers everything from a 38-mi run to a lengthy journey to the Yukon and then down to Eagle. Its waters range from easy Class I to serious Class IV (possibly Class V) stretches. Only experienced canoeists should attempt boating on this river, and rapids should be scouted beforehand. Several access points can be found off the Taylor Highway.

CanoeAlaska (☎ 907/883–2628 🌐 canoealaska.net) has been conducting guided canoe and raft trips on Interior Alaska rivers since 1980. Trips (mid-May–Labor Day) range from two to eight days on rivers that vary in difficulty and remoteness. Evening interpretive tours in the *Arctic Voyageur*, a replica of a 34-foot voyageur canoe, are offered on a lake. Multiday Voyageur trips, ACA-certified canoe instruction, and rentals to qualified paddlers are also available.

Eagle

⓳ *95 mi north of Chicken, 144 mi northwest of Dawson City.*

Eagle was once a seat of government and commerce for the Interior. An army post (Ft. Egbert) operated here until 1911, and territorial judge James Wickersham had his headquarters in Eagle until Fairbanks began to grow from its gold strike. The population peaked at 1,700 in 1898. Today it is fewer than 200.

The **Eagle Historical Society** (✉ 1st St. ☎ 907/547–2325 🌐 www.eagleak.org) has a two- to three-hour walking tour ($5) that visits seven museum buildings while regaling participants with tales of the famous people who have passed through this historic Yukon River border town. One daily tour begins at the courthouse at 9 AM, from Memorial Day to Labor Day.

YUKON TERRITORY

Gold! That's what called Canada's Yukon Territory to the world's attention with the Klondike Gold Rush of 1897–98. Although Yukon gold mining today is mainly in the hands of a few large companies that go almost unnoticed by the visitor, the territory's history is alive and thriving.

Though the international border divides Alaska from Yukon Territory, the Yukon River tends to unify the region. Early prospectors, miners, traders, and camp followers moved readily up and down the river with little regard to national boundaries. An earlier Alaska strike preceded the Klondike find by years, yet Circle was all but abandoned in the stampede to the creeks around Dawson City. Later gold discoveries in the Alaskan Fortymile Country, Nome, and Fairbanks reversed that flow across the border into Alaska.

6

Dawson City

20–23 *109 mi east of Chicken.*

Dawson City today forms the heart of the Yukon's gold-rush remembrances. Since the first swell of the gold rush more than 100 years ago, many of the original buildings have disappeared, victims of fire, flood, and weathering. But enough of them have been preserved and restored to give more than a glimpse of the city's onetime grandeur. In a period of three years up to the turn of the 20th century, Dawson was transformed into the largest, most refined city north of San Francisco and west of Winnipeg. It had grand buildings with running water, telephones, and electricity. The city's population, only about 1,500 now, numbered almost 30,000 in 1899.

Regular air service to Dawson is available from Fairbanks. You can also drive the Taylor Highway route, leaving the Alaska Highway at Tetlin Junction and winding through the Fortymile Country past the little communities of Chicken and Jack Wade Camp into Canada. The border is open 8 AM to 8 PM in summer. The Canadian section of the Taylor Highway is called Top of the World Highway. Broad views of range after range of tundra-covered mountains stretch in every direction. Travelers heading north on the Alaska Highway can turn north at Whitehorse to Dawson City, then rejoin the Alaska Highway by taking the Taylor Highway south. This adds about 100 mi to the trip.

20 **Diamond Tooth Gertie's Gambling Hall** (✉ Arctic Brotherhood Hall, Queen St. ☎ 867/993–5525), for adults 19 and over only, presents live entertainment and three different cancan shows three times a night, seven days a week. It is the only authentic, legal gambling establishment op-

Dawson City Museum **21**
Diamond Tooth Gertie's Gambling Hall **20**
Jack London's Cabin **23**
Robert Service's Cabin **22**

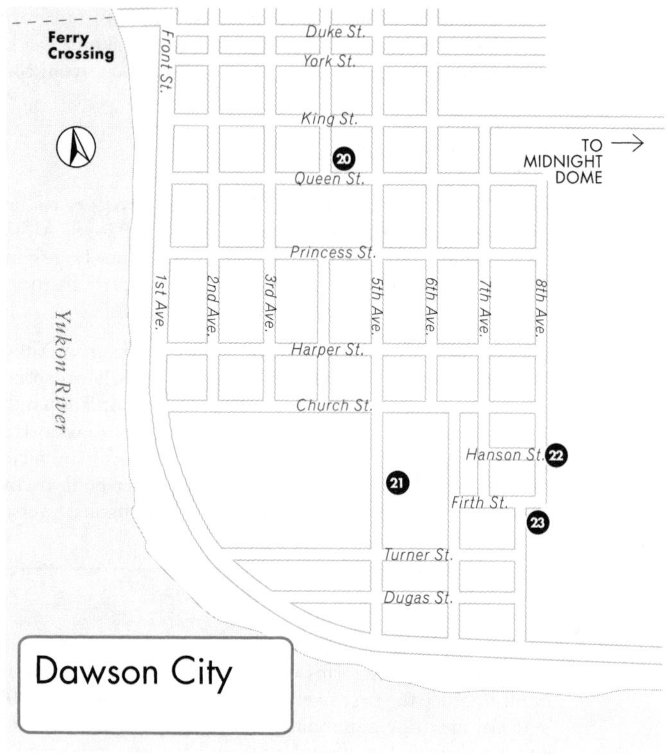

erating in all of the North. Yes, there really was a Diamond Tooth Gertie—Gertie Lovejoy, a prominent dance-hall queen who had a diamond between her two front teeth.

21 The **Dawson City Museum** houses a variety of gold-rush exhibits. You'll also find numerous relics in the Train Shelter next door, including trains from the Klondike Road Railroad that operated along the gold creeks. ✉ *Territorial Administration Bldg., 5th Ave.* ☎ *867/993–5291* C$7 ⏲ *Mid-May–Labor Day, daily 10–6.*

Parks Canada leads tours of **Bonanza Creek and *Gold Dredge Number 4,*** a wooden-hull gold dredge about 10 minutes outside town. The one-hour walk-through tour takes you into what's billed as "the largest wooden hulled, bucket line gold dredge in North America." There's also a short film about the site and the restoration of the dredge, and you can visit working gold mines in the area and pan for gold in Bonanza Creek. Exit the Klondike Highway at Km Marker 74. ✉ *Mile 7.8, Bonanza Creek Rd.* *Dredge #4 National Historic Site, P.O. Box 390, Dawson City, Yukon Territory YOB 1G0* ☎ *867/993–7200* 🌐 *www.pc.gc.ca* *C$5* ⏲ *June–mid-Sept., daily 10–4.*

Scholars still argue the precise details of the tenure of writers Robert Service (1874–1958) and Jack London (1876–1916) in Dawson City, but
no one disputes that between Service's poems and London's short stories, the two did more than anyone else to popularize and romanticize
the Yukon. Service lived in his Dawson cabin, but the Jack London cabin
is a reproduction, using some of the wood from his original wilderness
22 home that was found south of Dawson in the 1930s. **Robert Service's cabin**
(✉ 8th Ave. and Hanson St. ☎ 867/993–7237 🎫 C$5) is open for vis-
23 itors June through mid-September. **Jack London's cabin** (✉ 8th Ave. and
Firth St. ☎ 867/993–5575 🎫 C$2 ⌚ Mid-May–mid-Sept., daily 10–1
and 2–6) is literally a stone's throw from the Robert Service cabin. The
small museum contains photos, documents, and letters from London's
life and the gold-rush era. Half-hour talks are given at 11 and 2:15.

Where to Stay & Eat

$ ✕🏨 **Downtown Hotel.** A large collection of artwork from area artists, including mushing scenes, accents the hotel's early-1900s decorations, and all the rooms were renovated in 2002. The Jack London Grill ($–$$) is a best bet: go for the Canadian and American regional specialties, including daily appetizer, pasta, and prime-rib specials. The restaurant serves three meals a day and has an outside deck for summer dining. Suites have air-conditioning. ✉ *2nd Ave. and Queen St., Box 780, Y0B 1G0* ☎ *867/993–5346, 800/661–0514 reservations* 🌐 *www.downtown.yk.net* ⇨ *59 rooms, 5 suites* ☝ *Restaurant, cable TV, hot tub, bar, Internet, meeting room, airport shuttle* 💳 *AE, D, DC, MC, V.*

$–$$ 🏨 **Bombay Peggy's.** Named and fashioned after one of the last of Dawson's legal madams, Peggy's is done in elaborate Victorian gold-rush style, with heavy, plush draperies and rich color schemes. Bathrooms have claw-foot tubs and pedestal sinks, and the beds have elaborate headboards. In the evening, port and sherry and savory treats are served in the parlor, and for breakfast, croissants and coffee are available. The adjoining pub serves appetizers along with a large selection of single-malt scotches, and meals can be ordered for delivery by a nearby restaurant. ✉ *2nd Ave. and Princess St., Box 411, Y0B 1G0* ☎ *867/993–6969* 🌐 *www.bombaypeggys.com* ⇨ *3 rooms, 6 suites* ☝ *Fans, cable TV, in-room VCRs, Internet, airport shuttle; no smoking* 💳 *MC, V* 🍽 *CP.*

$ 🏨 **Eldorado Hotel.** The lobby of this hotel has gold rush–era decor. During the summer tourist season the staff dresses up in 1898-era garb. However, the modern rooms, some with kitchenettes, are outfitted with decidedly non-1898 amenities such as cable TV and remote controls. ✉ *3rd Ave. and Princess St., Box 338, Y0B 1G0* ☎ *867/993–5451, 800/764–3536 from Alaska* 🌐 *www.eldoradohotel.ca* ⇨ *52 rooms* ☝ *Dining room, some kitchenettes, cable TV, bar, laundry service, Internet, meeting room, airport shuttle; no a/c* 💳 *AE, D, DC, MC, V.*

$ 🏨 **Triple "J" Hotel.** Log cabins with kitchenettes, a central hotel, and a detached annex make up this clean, quiet compound next to Diamond Tooth Gertie's. All rooms have TVs, coffeemakers, phones, and private baths. ✉ *5th Ave. and Queen St., Box 359, Y0B 1G0* ☎ *867/993–5323 or 800/764–3555* 🌐 *www.triplejhotel.com* ⇨ *29 rooms, 18 cabins*

Restaurant, some kitchenettes, cable TV, bar, Internet, meeting room, airport shuttle ▭ *AE, DC, MC, V.*

$ **Westmark Dawson City.** This downtown two-story hotel is built around a central courtyard and is convenient to the sights. With its flocked wallpaper and lace curtains, the lobby recalls the days of the gold rush. While staying at the hotel enjoy a rare opportunity to have your photo taken with a genuine RCMP Mountie in Red Serge dress uniform. Rooms are decorated in soft blues and greens. ✉ *5th Ave. and Harper St., Box 420, Y0B 1G0* ☎ *867/993–5542, 800/544–0970 reservations* 🌐 *www.westmarkhotels.com* *133 rooms* *Dining room, bar, shop, laundry facilities, some pets allowed (fee); no a/c* ▭ *AE, DC, MC, V* ⏲ *Closed mid-Sept.–mid-May.*

Whitehorse

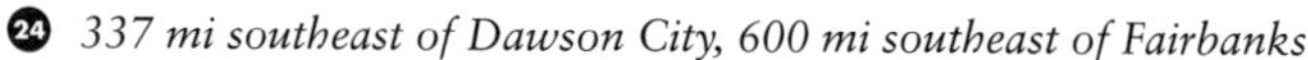

24 *337 mi southeast of Dawson City, 600 mi southeast of Fairbanks.*

Near the White Horse Rapids of the Yukon River, Whitehorse began as an encampment in the late 1890s. It was a logical layover point for gold rushers heading north along the Chilkoot Trail toward Dawson to seek their fortune. The next great population boom came during World War II with the building of the Alcan—the Alaska-Canada Highway. Today this city of more than 22,000 residents is Yukon's center of commerce, communication, and transportation and the seat of the territorial government.

Besides being a great starting point for explorations of other areas of the Yukon, the town itself has plenty of diversions and recreational opportunities. You can easily spend a day exploring its museums and cultural displays—research the Yukon's mining and development history, look into the backgrounds of the town's founders, learn about its indigenous First Nations people, and gain an appreciation of the Yukon Territory from prehistoric times up to the present. You can obtain a free three-day parking permit at **City Hall** (✉ 2121 2nd Ave. ☎ 867/668–8687).

The logical place to start touring Whitehorse is the **Yukon Visitor Information Centre,** housed in the block-long, pine-sided headquarters for Yukon Tourism. Anything to do with the Yukon can be found in the reception center. ✉ *100 Hanson St.* ☎ *867/667–3084* 🌐 *www.touryukon.com* ⏲ *May–Sept., daily 8–8; Oct.–Apr., weekdays 8:30–5.*

The lobby of the Yukon Territorial Government Building displays the **Yukon Permanent Art Collection,** works by Yukon artists depicting northern people and their culture. In addition to the collection on the premises, the brochure *Art Adventures on Yukon Time,* available at visitor reception centers throughout the Yukon, guides the way to artists' studios and provides locations of galleries and art shops. ✉ *2071 2nd Ave.* ☎ *867/667–5811* *Free* ⏲ *Weekdays 8:30–5.*

The **MacBride Museum** is your best general introduction to the spirit and heritage of the Yukon. More than 5,000 square feet of exhibits display natural history, geology, archaeology, First Nations, Mounties in the North, the gold rush, and the city of Whitehorse. Outdoor artifacts include Sam McGee's cabin—the same Sam McGee immortalized in

Robert Service's famous poem "The Cremation of Sam McGee"—the Whitehorse telegraph office, and various transportation vehicles. ✉ *1124 1st Ave. and Wood St.* ☎ *867/667–2709* 🌐 *www.macbridemuseum.com* 🎫 *C$5* 🕒 *Mid-May–Aug., daily 10–9; Sept., daily 10–5; Oct.–mid-May, Fri.–Sun. noon–5.*

The **Waterfront Walkway** along the Yukon River will take you past a few stops of interest. Your walk starts on the path along the river just east of the MacBride Museum entrance on 1st Avenue. Traveling upstream (south), you'll go by the old White Pass & Yukon Route Building, on Main Street.

The former Yukon Visitor Reception Centre at the Whitehorse Airport is the home of the **Yukon Beringia Interpretive Centre,** which presents the story of the Yukon during the Ice Age. Beringia is the name given to the large subcontinental landmass of eastern Siberia and Interior Alaska and the Yukon, which were linked by the Bering Land Bridge during the Ice Age. The center unfolds extensive information on the area's prehistory and pays tribute to the First Nations people and the miners who have contributed information and exhibits to the museum. The center displays large dioramas depicting the lives of animals in Ice Age Beringia and replicas of skeletons of the animals who lived there. ✉ *Mile 914, Alaska Hwy.* ☎ *867/667–8855* 🌐 *www.beringia.com* 🎫 *C$6* 🕒 *May and Sept., daily 9–6; June–Aug., daily 8:30–7 and by appointment.*

★ The **SS *Klondike,*** a national historic site, is dry-docked in Rotary Park. The 210-foot stern-wheeler was built in 1929, sank in 1936, and was rebuilt in 1937. In the days when the Yukon River was the transportation link between Whitehorse and Dawson City, the *Klondike* was the largest boat plying the river. ✉ *S. Access Rd. and 2nd Ave.* ☎ *867/667–4511* 🎫 *C$5, C$15 for families* 🕒 *May–Sept., daily 9–6.*

If you're in Whitehorse during late summer, it's possible to see the chinook (king) salmon, which hold one of nature's great endurance records: the longest fish migration in the world, which is more than 1,800 mi from the ocean to Whitehorse. The **Whitehorse Rapids Dam and Fish Ladder** has interpretive exhibits, display tanks of freshwater fish, and a platform for viewing the fish ladder. The best time to visit is August, when between 150 and 2,100 salmon (average count is 800) use the ladder to bypass the dam. ✉ *End of Nisutlin Dr.* ☎ *867/633–5965* 🎫 *Free* 🕒 *June–Labor Day, daily; hrs vary, so call ahead.*

Miles Canyon, a 10-minute drive south of Whitehorse, is both scenic and historic. Although the dam below it makes the canyon seem relatively tame, it was this perilous stretch of the Yukon River that determined the location of Whitehorse as the starting point for river travel north. In 1897 Jack London won the admiration—and cash—of fellow stampeders headed north to the Klondike goldfields because of his steady hand as pilot of hand-hewn wooden boats here. You can hike on trails along the canyon or take a two-hour cruise aboard the MV *Schwatka* and experience the canyon from the waters of Lake Schwatka, which obliterated the Whitehorse Rapids when the dam creating the lake was built in 1959. ✉ *Miles Canyon Rd., 2 mi south of Whitehorse* 📫 *68 Miles*

Canyon Rd., Yukon Territory ☎ 867/668–4716 🌐 www.yukon-wings.com/boatcruises.html 🎫 C$25 ⏲ Cruises depart early to mid-June at 2 PM, *mid-June to late Aug. at 2 and 6* PM, *late Aug.–Sept. at 2* PM.

At **Takhini Hot Springs,** off the Klondike Highway, there's swimming in the spring-warmed water (suits and towels are available for rent), horseback riding, areas for camping and picnicking, an outdoor climbing wall, and a "licensed" (beer and wine) restaurant. ✉ *Km 10, Takhini Hot Springs Rd., 17 mi north of Whitehorse* ☎ *867/633–2706* 🌐 *www.takhinihotsprings.yk.ca* 🎫 *C$7* ⏲ *May–Sept., daily 8* AM*–10* PM*; call for winter hrs.*

The **Canyon City Archaeological Dig** provides a glimpse into the past of the local First Nations people. Long before the area was developed by Western civilizations, the First Nations people used the Miles Canyon area as a seasonal fish camp. The Yukon Conservation Society conducts free tours of the area twice a day in summer; it also leads walks and hikes from short, child-friendly tours to challenging five- to six-hour scrambles on the nearby mountains. All the hikes are free and provide a great way to see the surrounding countryside with local naturalists. The society office houses a bookstore on Yukon history and wilderness and sells souvenirs, maps, and posters. ✉ *302 Hawkins St.* ☎ *867/668–5678* 🌐 *www.yukonconservation.org* 🎫 *Free* ⏲ *Tours July–late Aug., weekdays at 10 and 2.*

The **Yukon Wildlife Preserve** provides a fail-safe way of photographing rarely spotted animals in a natural setting. Animals roaming freely here include elk, caribou, mountain goats, musk ox, bison, mule deer, and Dall and Stone sheep. Two-hour tours can be arranged through Gray Line Yukon. ✉ *Gray Line Yukon, 208G Steele St.* ☎ *867/668–3225* 🌐 *www.yukonweb.com/tourism/westours* 🎫 *C$21* ⏲ *Tours mid-May–mid-Sept., daily.*

Where to Stay & Eat

$$$–$$$$ ✕ **The Cellar.** In the Edgewater Hotel in downtown Whitehorse, this intimate two-room spot—down some stairs, as the name implies—is touted by the locals as the place to go for special occasions. The "front" room is a tad less formal, with a bar and TV, while the back room, separated by an etched glass partition, is quieter. The menu is a combination of seafood and meat dishes and a tapas selection, complemented by a large wine list. Soups, salads, and homemade desserts are also available. ✉ *101 Main St.* ☎ *867/667–2572* 💳 *AE, DC, MC, V.*

$–$$$ ✕ **Klondike Rib & Salmon BBQ.** If you're in the mood for something completely different, this is the place. It's one of the very few places where you can order arctic char, caribou, and musk ox, as well as the more common barbecue specialties such as salmon, halibut, ribs, and chicken. It's open for lunch, but the game dishes are served only at dinner. It's a very popular spot with locals and tourists, so plan on a long wait on summer weekends. ✉ *2nd Ave and Steele St.* ☎ *867/667–7554* 💳 *MC, V* ⏲ *Closed mid-Sept.–mid-May.*

★ ¢ ✕ **The Chocolate Claim.** Choose from fresh-baked breads and pastries, homemade soups and sandwiches, salads, and quiches at this charming little deli. Artwork—ranging from paintings and pottery to rugs and quilts by local artists and artisans—is on display and for sale. On sunny days you can sit outside. Friday happy hour is from 5–7 PM, live music included. ✉ *305 Strickland St.* ☎ *867/667–2202* ▭ *MC, V* ⏲ *Closed Sun.*

$$ ✕ **Westmark Whitehorse Hotel and Conference Center.** You can catch a nightly Klondike vaudeville show, the Frantic Follies, in summer at this full-service, comfortable hotel in the heart of downtown. The carpeted lobby has low tables and plush chairs, an espresso bar, and a beautiful model of the Klondike riverboat. The restaurant serves pork chops, filet mignon, salmon, and low-calorie selections. ✉ *2nd Ave. and Wood St., Y1A 2E4* ☎ *867/393–9700, 800/544–0970 reservations* ⊕ *www.westmarkhotels.com* *180 rooms, 5 suites* *Restaurant, microwaves, cable TV with movies, in-room data ports, bar, shop, meeting rooms, some pets allowed; no a/c* ▭ *AE, MC, V.*

$–$$$ **High Country Inn.** At this downtown inn, you'll find tastefully appointed modern rooms. Deluxe suites come with kitchenettes. Public areas are cozy, and the location is close to the SS *Klondike* and the public swimming pool. There's a tour desk to help you plan your days. ✉ *4051 4th Ave., Y1A 1H1* ☎ *867/667–4471 or 800/554–4471* ⊕ *www.highcountryinn.yk.ca* *84 rooms, 18 suites* *Restaurant, some kitchenettes, cable TV, bar, Internet, meeting room, some pets allowed; no a/c in some rooms* ▭ *AE, D, MC, V.*

$ **Edgewater Hotel.** A comfortable, unpretentious bit of history in the downtown area, this corner hotel, first built during the 1898 gold rush, is in its third incarnation. The first two burned down, which might lead you to think that the place would be smoke-free, but there are some rooms for smokers. The restaurant and bar are first-rate, and the location, across the street from the Yukon River, is excellent. The small lobby is adorned with old photos of the hotel's predecessors, giving a feel for the gold-rush era. ✉ *101 Main St., Y1A 2A7* ☎ *867/667–2572 or 877/484–3334* ⊕ *www.edgewaterhotelwhitehorse.com* *30 rooms, 3 suites* *Restaurant, bar, meeting rooms, free parking, no-smoking rooms* ▭ *AE, DC, MC, V* *EP.*

6

Sports & the Outdoors

HIKING The **Kluane National Park and Reserve** (✉ Visitor Center, 119 Logan St., Haines Junction ☎ 867/634–7207), west of Whitehorse, has millions of acres for hiking. The **Yukon Conservation Society** (☎ 867/668–5678) leads hiking expeditions of varying lengths and degrees of difficulty.

SLED-DOG RACING Whitehorse and Fairbanks organize the **Yukon Quest International Sled-Dog Race** (☎ 867/668–4711) in February. The race's starting line alternates yearly between the two cities. This is one of the longest and toughest races in the North. See www.yukonquest.org.

INTERIOR ESSENTIALS

Transportation

BY AIR

For a city of its size, Fairbanks has good air connections to the rest of the world. The Fairbanks International Airport is home to more than 500 small aircraft and there is a good mix of jet service by major airlines and regional flights by commuter airlines. Alaska Airlines and Frontier Flying Service fly the Anchorage–Fairbanks route. Delta and Northwest Airlines offer seasonal nonstop service from Fairbanks to the Lower 48. Air North, based in Whitehorse, has direct, scheduled air service between Alaska and Canada, flying regular runs from Fairbanks and Juneau to the Yukon Territory towns of Dawson City and Whitehorse. **TIP→** ***See Smart Travel Tips, at the back of this book, for more airline information.***

Fairbanks-based commuter line Arctic Circle Air flies to Bush destinations. ERA Aviation flies to Whitehorse (and destinations elsewhere in the state) from Anchorage. Everts Air has charter flights

AIRPORT TRANSFERS There are hotel shuttles, rental cars, and taxis available at the Fairbanks airport.

Air North ☎ 800/764-0407, 800/661-0407 in Canada 🌐 www.flyairnorth.com. **Alaska Airlines** ☎ 800/252-7522 🌐 www.alaskaair.com. **Arctic Circle Air** ☎ 907//474-0112 🌐 www.arcticcircleair.com. **ERA Aviation** ☎ 907/243-6633 or 800/866-8394 🌐 www.flyera.com. **Everts Air Alaska** ☎ 907/450-2350 🌐 www.evertsair.com.

BY BUS

The most common bus run is between Fairbanks and Anchorage by way of Denali National Park & Preserve. However, you can take side trips by bus or van into the Yukon Territory. For more information about bus service throughout the Interior, contact Princess Tours. The Alaskon Express provides scheduled service between Whitehorse, Fairbanks, Valdez, Skagway, Denali National Park, Anchorage, and other communities en route. Haines is accessible from Skagway via water taxi.

The Alaska Park Connection provides regularly scheduled shuttle service between Seward, Anchorage, and Denali National Park mid-May to mid-September. Denali Overland Transportation serves Anchorage, Talkeetna, and Denali National Park with charter-bus and van service. Alaska/Yukon runs between Fairbanks, Denali, Anchorage, Talkeetna, Whitehorse, and Dawson City.

Fairbanks has a city bus system ($1.50 per ride). For information about schedules ask at the Fairbanks Convention and Visitors Bureau (⇨ Visitor Information).

Commuter Buses **Alaska Park Connection** ☎ 907/245-0200 or 800/208-0200 🌐 www.alaskatravel.com. **Alaska/Yukon Trails** ☎ 800/770-7275 🌐 www.alaskashuttle.com. **Alaskon Express** ☎ 907/451-6835 or 800/478-6388 🌐 www.graylineofalaska.com. **Denali Overland Transportation** ☎ 907/733-2384 or 800/651-5221 🌐 www.denalioverland.com.

City Bus **Fairbanks MACS Bus System** ☎ 907/459-1011 🌐 www.co.fairbanks.ak.us/transportation/.

BY CAR

If you choose to fly into Anchorage and drive to Fairbanks in a rental car, the George Parks Highway is the most direct route at 358 mi, and it provides easy access to Denali National Park. Another option is to take the Glenn and Richardson highways, which is 80 mi longer, but also has spectacular scenery. All of the roads are paved.

You need a car in the Interior, even if you're based in Fairbanks. The Steese Highway, the Dalton Highway, and the Taylor Highway (closed in winter) are mainly well-maintained gravel roads. However, summer rain can make them slick and dangerous. Rental car companies have varying policies on whether they allow travel on gravel roads.

If you are taking your time on the highway and going under the speed limit, be aware that ■ TIP→ **if there are more than five cars following you, state law requires that you pull over and allow them to pass.** This provision was placed into state law because of traffic delays along Alaska's two-lane highways created by lumbering motor homes.

Only one road connects Alaska to the Outside: the Alaska Highway. The highway starts in Dawson Creek, British Columbia, in Canada. It is paved but long, almost 1,500 mi to Fairbanks. Lots of people make this trek in the summer, so there are ample restaurants and motels along the way. Winter driving requires more planning, as many businesses and service stations shut down for the season. An alternative route through part of Canada is the Cassiar Highway, which leaves the Yellowhead Highway about 150 mi northwest of Prince Rupert and connects to the Alaska Highway just outside Watson Lake. The Cassiar is a more scenic drive but may have long sections of gravel road. Summer road construction somewhere along the Alaska Highway is a given.

ROAD CONDITIONS For road reports in Alaska call the State Department of Transportation in Fairbanks. Information about road conditions and construction is available by calling 511 in Alaska or going to 511.alaska.gov. There is also an online Road Weather Information System for checking on road conditions at www.dot.state.ak.us. For conditions in the Yukon Territory, call the Department of Community and Transportation Services.

Alaska State Department of Transportation ☎ 511 or 907/456-7623 🌐 www.511.gov or www.dot.state.ak.us. **Yukon Territory Department of Community and Transportation Services** ☎ 867/667-8215.

Rental Agencies **Alamo** ☎ 907/451-7368 🌐 www.alamo.com. **Avis** ☎ 907/474-0900, 800/478-2847 in Alaska, 800/331-1212 🌐 www.avisalaska.com. **Budget Rent-A-Car** ☎ 907/474-0855, 800/474-0855 in Alaska 🌐 www.budget.com. **Dollar Rent A Car** ☎ 907/451-4360, 800/800-4000 🌐 www.dollar.com. **Hertz** ☎ 907/452-4444, 907/456-4004, or 800/654-3131 🌐 www.hertz.com. **National Car Rental** ☎ 907/451-7368 or 907/451-8234. **Payless Car Rental** ☎ 907/474-0177 🌐 www.paylesscarrental.com.

BY TRAIN

Between late May and early September, daily passenger service runs between Anchorage and Fairbanks by way of Talkeetna and Denali National Park & Preserve. Standard railroad coach cars have access to dining, lounge, and dome cars, operated by the Alaska Railroad. There is no such thing as a poor seat. A panorama will unfold beyond your window, with scenes of alpine meadows and snowcapped peaks and the muddy rivers and taiga forests of the Interior.

If you're looking for a bit more luxury in your rail experience, ride in one of the two custom double-decked dome cars operated by the railroad. The railroad's "Gold Star" service includes access to an outdoor

CLOSE UP

Road-Tripping in Alaska

ALASKA'S HANDFUL OF STATE highways may only reach a fraction of the state, but many of these roads have been designated Scenic Byways, with high marks for beauty, archaeological and cultural significance, history and natural history, and recreational opportunities.

The Last Frontier wasn't even accessible by road until 1942 with the completion of the **Alaska Highway,** then known as the Alcan, a crooked, hastily built military road through Canada. It opened to only the hardiest of civilian travelers in 1948.

What follows is a list of the best roads for exploring the Alaska that not everyone gets to see. All are paved unless otherwise noted; roadside services and campgrounds are plentiful. Though all roads have official route numbers, everybody here calls them by their names.

GEORGE PARKS HIGHWAY

(358 mi, Wasilla to Fairbanks)

The two-lane "Parks" twists through two mountain ranges and over wild rivers on its spectacular north-south course. Along the way, vistas of Mount McKinley are best photographed from well-marked rest areas. The entrance to Denali National Park & Preserve is an easy 120 mi south of Fairbanks, at Milepost 237. From Anchorage, it's about 240 mi north (the first bit is on Hwy 1 out of the city). From backpackers to RV travelers, there's something for everyone in Denali's 6 million acres: backcountry camping, hiking, wildlife-watching, dog-mushing demonstrations, and infinite—yes, infinite—photo opportunities. Just outside the park you'll find white-water rafting on the roaring Nenana River, helicopter rides, gift shops, restaurants, and overnight accommodations. The Parks Highway also offers access to Denali State Park, with 48 mi of hiking trails and various recreational sites, including an interpretive wayside at Milepost 135.

RICHARDSON HIGHWAY

(364 mi, Fairbanks to Valdez)

Alaska's oldest highway, the Richardson passes through North Pole, Alaska, just 15 mi south of Fairbanks. Heading southbound, you may catch glimpses of the 800-mi trans-Alaska oil pipeline en route to its terminus in Valdez.

To the east, the snowcapped peaks of the Wrangell-St. Elias National Park & Preserve fill the horizon. Take some time at Mile 28 for an eyeful of Worthington Glacier near Thompson Pass (elevation 2,678 ft), perhaps the snowiest place in Alaska. (Even by August, there may be enough snow around for a snowball fight.) About 15 mi north of Valdez, Keystone Canyon is a 4-mi sweep of tumbling waterfalls and rock walls that are infamous as the site of a historic gunfight.

GLENN HIGHWAY AND TOK CUTOFF

(328 miles, Anchorage to Glennallen, Gakona Junction to Tok)

Long stretches of postcard beauty and sweet solitude mark this scenic drive from Anchorage, which heads north and east. About an hour northeast of Anchorage, walk the lush gardens of the Palmer Visitors Center & Museum. The Matanuska-Susitna (Mat-Su) Valley remains a productive farming region, and Palmer hosts the annual Alaska State Fair in late summer. The giant cabbage weigh-off is a favorite fair attraction, the current record-holder weighing in at 105.6 pounds. Visit the Musk Ox Farm at Mile 50 to see these descendants of prehistory and learn about their rare underwool called *qiviut*. Farther east, you'll see rest areas for photographing the massive Matanuska Glacier and the silty Matanuska River.

Fodor's Choice **SEWARD HIGHWAY** *(127 miles, Anchorage to Seward)*

Southbound from Anchorage, the Seward Highway shoulders the lush beauty of Turnagain Arm and Chugach National Forest as it heads toward the port of Seward. This drive is so outstanding that it was named an All-American Highway, the highest designation for a National Scenic Byway. Just minutes south of Anchorage, look for Dall sheep on the mountainsides; to the right, you may spy beluga whales, which look like bright flashes of white in the steel-gray Cook Inlet water.

Thirty-seven mi south of Anchorage, a spur road leads to the ski-resort town of Girdwood. In summer, guests can ride a tram up Mount Alyeska for superior views of the surrounding mountains, glaciers, and glittering water. About 10 mi down the highway is the turnoff for the Anton Anderson Tunnel, which crosses the neck of the Kenai Peninsula to Whittier.

Just north of Seward, signs show the way to Exit Glacier, one of the most accessible for visitors on foot. In Seward, go deep-sea fishing, take a trip on a Kenai Fjords cruise, and don't miss the Alaska SeaLife Center and its sea lions, seals, and puffins.

STERLING HIGHWAY
(143 miles, Seward Highway to Homer)

This well-traveled road south of Anchorage leads to pure paradise for sport anglers: the Kenai Peninsula, where the renowned Kenai and Russian rivers flow. A branch off the Seward Highway, the Sterling rolls west then south through several small communities that support the fishing frenzy. Guides will take you drifting or river rafting; or if deep water is your liking, you can book a salmon or halibut charter out of a seaside town, such as Anchor Point or Homer.

Get a taste of early Russian Alaska on the peninsula, too, through the shining domes of historic Russian Orthodox churches tucked away in Ninilchik and Kenai. The road ends in Homer, an appealing mix of commercial fishing town and arts enclave.

Be sure to pick up a copy of ***The Milepost*** (🌐 www.milepost.com) for expert road and planning advice.

The State of Alaska provides Alaska Traveler Information with road reports, animal alerts, and other advisories. (☎ Dial 511 in Alaska, dial 907/282-7577 outside of Alaska 🌐 511.alaska.gov)

To request a map of Alaska's highways, visit www.dot.state.ak.us/pop_request_map.shtml. And for more details, check out www.dot.state.ak.us/stwdplng/scenic/index.shtml.

–Tricia Brown

viewing platform and a 36-seat dining room. Holland America and Princess also have reserved luxury cars on each train, with domed windows, onboard guides, and meals. The tour companies offer a variety of packages, many with an overnight stay at Denali. The Alaska Railroad opened its new Fairbanks depot in 2005 off the Johansen Expressway, part of a continuing modernization effort for the full-service railroad, which is owned by the state of Alaska.

Alaska Railroad ☎ 907/456-4155 or 800/544-0552 ⊕ www.akrr.com. **Holland America Tours/Gray Line of Alaska** ☎ 907/456-7741 or 800/478-6388 ⊕ www.graylinealaska.com. **Princess Tours** ☎ 800/426-0500 ⊕ www.princesslodges.com.

Contacts & Resources

BANKS

Denali State Bank ✉ 119 N. Cushman St., Fairbanks ☎ 907/458-4236 ⊕ www.denalistatebank.com. **First National Bank Alaska** ✉ 800 Noble St., Fairbanks ☎ 907/459-5300 ⊕ www.fnbalaska.com. **KeyBank** ✉ 100 Cushman St., Fairbanks ☎ 907/459-3300 ⊕ www.key.com. **Mt. McKinley Bank** ✉ 530 4th Ave., Fairbanks ☎ 907/452-1751 ⊕ www.mtmckinleybank.com. **Northrim Bank** ✉ 714 4th Ave., Suite 100, Fairbanks ☎ 907/452-1260 ⊕ www.northrim.com. **Wells Fargo Bank** ✉ 613 Cushman St., Fairbanks ☎ 907/459-4300 ⊕ www.wellsfargo.com.

EMERGENCIES

Ambulance service is available in the Fairbanks area from local fire departments, which have different areas of jurisdiction. Make sure to pick up a copy of the "Help Along the Way" brochure at border crossings or visitor centers, which details emergency medical services for travelers.

Emergency Services **Police, emergency assistance** ☎ 911. **Alaska State Troopers** ☎ 907/895-4344 Delta Junction, 907/451-5100 Fairbanks, 907/832-5554 Nenana, 907/883-5111 Tok. **Royal Canadian Mounted Police** ☎ 250/782-5211 Dawson Creek, 867/667-5555 Whitehorse.

Hospitals & Clinics **Dawson City Nursing Station** ✉ 350 Church St., Dawson City, Yukon Territory, Canada ☎ 867/993-4444. **Fairbanks Clinic** ✉ 1919 Lathrop St., Fairbanks ☎ 907/452-1761 ⊕ www.fairbanksclinic.com. **Fairbanks Memorial Hospital** ✉ 1650 Cowles St., Fairbanks ☎ 907/452-8181. **Fairbanks Urgent Care Center** ✉ 1867 Airport Way, Fairbanks ☎ 907/452-2178. **General Hospital** ✉ Hospital Rd., Whitehorse, Yukon Territory, Canada ☎ 867/668-9444. **Public Health Clinic** ✉ 1314 Alaska Hwy., Tok ☎ 907/883-4101. **Tanana Valley Clinic 1st Care** ✉ 1001 Noble St., Fairbanks ☎ 907/459-3500 ⊕ www.tvcclinic.com.

24-Hour Pharmacy **Fairbanks Memorial Hospital** ✉ 1650 Cowles St., Fairbanks ☎ 907/452-8181.

INTERNET, MAIL & SHIPPING

Internet cafés range, roughly, from free with a purchase to $6 per hour. The Noel Wien Library has more than a dozen computers with high-speed access and has free Wi-Fi. The downtown post office on Barnette Street is open weekdays 10 to 6 and Saturday 10 to 2. If you want a "North Pole, Alaska" postmark, you can drop by the North Pole Branch during business hours, located appropriately at 325 South Santa Claus Lane in North Pole, 15 mi southeast of Fairbanks.

ALASKAPASS TIPS

The **AlaskaPass** allows unlimited travel on bus, ferry, and rail lines in Alaska, along with bus and ferry travel in British Columbia and the Yukon. Passes are available for 15 consecutive days of travel ($829), as well as for 8 days of travel in a 12-day period ($699) or 12 days of travel in a 21-day period ($849). There is a $75 booking fee. Most travelers book their entire itinerary in advance; if you don't have a car, there is usually room on ferries for those without prebookings. (☎ 206/463-6550 or 800/248-7598 🌐 www.alaskapass.com)

FedEx, DHL, and UPS all provide express package and document delivery services.

Internet Access **Blue Loon** ✉ Mile 353.5 Parks Hwy., Fairbanks ☎ 907/457-5666 🌐 www.theblueloon.com. **College Coffeehouse** ✉ 3677 College Rd., Fairbanks ☎ 907/374-0468 🌐 www.collegecoffeehousefairbanks.com. **Gulliver's Books** ✉ 3525 College Rd., Fairbanks ☎ 907/474-9574 🌐 http://gullivers-books.com. **Noel Wien Library** ✉ 1215 Cowles St., Fairbanks ☎ 907/459-1020 🌐 http://library.fnsb.lib.ak.us.

Mail **U.S. Postal Service** ✉ 315 Barnette St., Fairbanks ✉ 4024 Geist Rd. 🌐 www.usps.gov.

Overnight Services **DHL** ✉ 4415 Airport Way, Fairbanks ☎ 800/225-5345 🌐 www.dhl-usa.com/home/home.asp. **FedEx** ✉ 6059 Old Airport Way, Fairbanks ☎ 800/463-3339 🌐 www.fedex.com. **UPS** ✉ 1189 Van Horn Rd., Fairbanks ☎ 800/742-5877 🌐 www.ups.com.

MEDIA

Fairbanks has a daily newspaper, six local television stations, and a dozen radio stations offering everything from National Public Radio programming to a religious station that goes by the call letters KJNP for "King Jesus North Pole."

The moderately conservative *Fairbanks Daily News–Miner,* traces its history back to 1903, shortly after the founding of Fairbanks. It's the second-largest newspaper in the state.

RADIO

Nine of the commercial radio stations are owned by two companies. Clear Channel and New Northwest Broadcasters. Clear Channel also owns KTVF, Channel 11, the NBC-TV affiliate in Fairbanks. There are also CBS, Fox, and ABC affiliates and a Christian station.

On the AM-radio dial, KFAR 660 AM and KFBX 970 AM offer mostly conservative syndicated talk shows, while KCBF 820 AM carries ESPN sports, and KJNP 1170 AM is Christian talk and music.

On the FM side, public radio can be found at KUAC 89.9 FM, while KAIK 102.5 FM features country, KXLR 95.9 FM and KUWL 103.9 FM play oldies rock, KWLF 98.1 FM and KKED 104.7 FM offer today's hard rock, and KYSC 96.9 FM and KUWL 101.1 FM provide a blend of pop tunes.

VISITOR INFORMATION

Alaska Department of Fish and Game ✉ 1300 College Rd., Fairbanks ☎ 907/459-7207. **Alaska Public Lands Information Center** ✉ 250 Cushman St., Suite 1A, Fairbanks ☎ 907/456-0527 ⊕ www.nps.gov/aplic. **Delta Chamber of Commerce** ✉ Mile 1422, Alaska Hwy., Delta ☎ 907/895-5068. **Fairbanks Convention and Visitors Bureau** ✉ 550 1st Ave., Fairbanks ☎ 907/456-5774 or 800/327-5774 ⊕ www.explorefairbanks.com. **Klondike Visitors Association** ✉ Front and King Sts., Dawson City, Yukon Territory, Canada ☎ 867/993-5575. **Tok Main Street Visitors Center** ✉ Mile 1314, Alaska Hwy., Tok ☎ 907/883-5775. **Whitehorse Visitor Reception Centre** ✉ 100 Hanson St., Whitehorse, Yukon Territory, Canada Y1A 2C6 ☎ 867/667-3084.

The Bush

INCLUDING NOME, BARROW, PRUDHOE BAY & THE ALEUTIAN ISLANDS

Inuits dressed in native costumes walk the shoreline near Barrow.

WORD OF MOUTH

"If you want off-the-beaten-path Alaska, and if you can afford the time and airfare, I strongly suggest you investigate the Aleutian and Pribilof islands. Scenery, history, great people, and heaven on earth if you're a birder."

–John

www.fodors.com/forums

WELCOME TO THE BUSH

Lunchtime for this Alaskan grizzly

TOP REASONS TO GO

★ **Spend time in the company of bears:** The Alaska Peninsula has the world's largest concentration of brown bears, who congregate at salmon streams each summer.

★ **Native culture:** Native communities throughout Alaska are celebrating their cultural heritage. Many activities are being offered in the Bush, from blanket tossing to art exhibits.

★ **Go fishing:** The Bush offers some of the state's premier sportfishing for huge salmon and vibrant rainbow trout.

★ **The Land of the Midnight Sun:** All of Alaska has long hours of daylight in summer, but the sun is above the horizon 24 hours a day north of the Arctic Circle. In Barrow the sun doesn't set from May to August.

★ **Get outside like never before:** Alaska's Bush has many of the world's wildest and most remote parklands and refuges. You can spend days, or even weeks, enjoying the wilderness without other humans.

1 Southwest. This broad region ranges from the Kodiak Archipelago, in the northern Gulf of Alaska, to the Alaska Peninsula and Aleutian Island Chain, and inland to the Yukon-Kuskokwim Delta. It's Alaska's least-developed region, with dozens of small native villages and immense riches of wilderness, fish, and wildlife.

2 Northwest & the Arctic. Starting at the Seward Peninsula, this region sweeps north to the Beaufort Sea, and then across the state, where it encompasses Alaska's northernmost mountain chain, the Brooks Range, and the North Slope flatlands beyond those mountains. It's a land of extremes, juxtaposing Alaska's North Slope oil fields with thousands of miles of pristine wilderness in which caribou outnumber humans by more than 25 to 1.

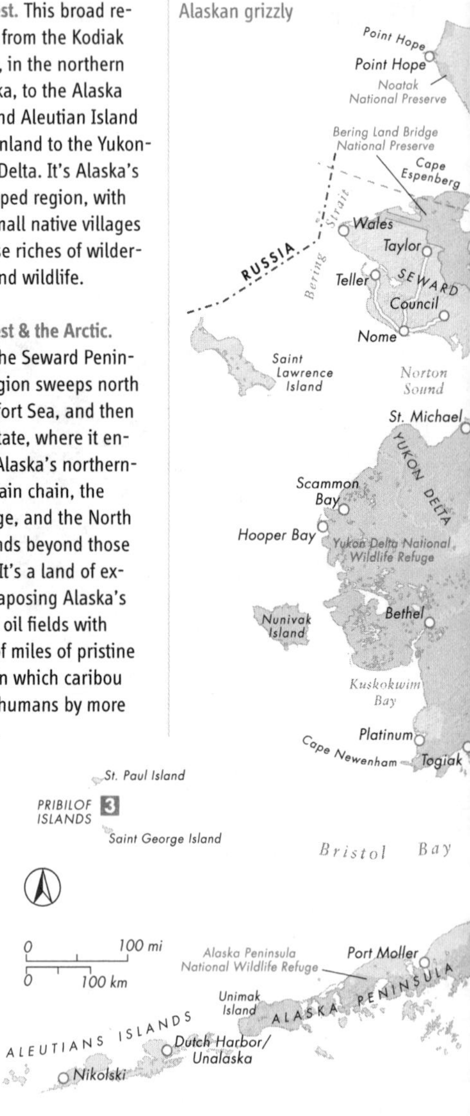

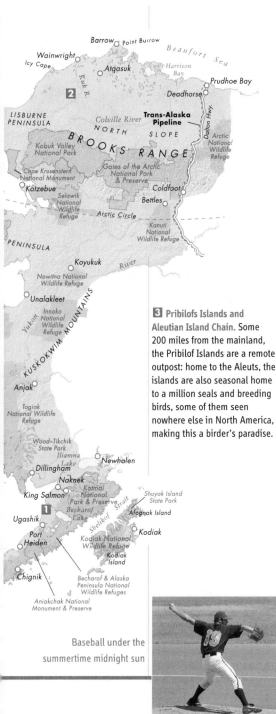

Barrow
Point Barrow
Beaufort Sea
Wainwright
Icy Cape
Atqasuk
Harrison Bay
Prudhoe Bay
Deadhorse
Kuk R.
2
LISBURNE PENINSULA
Colville River
Trans-Alaska Pipeline
Dalton Hwy.
NORTH SLOPE
BROOKS RANGE
Arctic National Wildlife Refuge
Kobuk Valley National Park
Gates of the Arctic National Park & Preserve
Cape Krusenstern National Monument
Kotzebue
Coldfoot
Selawik National Wildlife Refuge
Bettles
Arctic Circle
Kanuti National Wildlife Refuge
PENINSULA
Koyukuk
River
Nowitna National Wildlife Refuge
Unalakleet
Innoko National Wildlife Refuge
Yukon
KUSKOKWIM MOUNTAINS
Anjak
Togiak National Wildlife Refuge
Wood-Tikchik State Park
Iliamna Lake
Newhalen
Dillingham
Naknek
King Salmon
Katmai National Park & Preserve
Shuyak Island State Park
1
Becharof Lake
Shelikof Strait
Afognak Island
Ugashik
Kodiak
Port Heiden
Kodiak National Wildlife Refuge
Kodiak Island
Chignik
Becharof & Alaska Peninsula National Wildlife Refuges
Aniakchak National Monument & Preserve

3 Pribilofs Islands and Aleutian Island Chain. Some 200 miles from the mainland, the Pribilof Islands are a remote outpost: home to the Aleuts, the islands are also seasonal home to a million seals and breeding birds, some of them seen nowhere else in North America, making this a birder's paradise.

Baseball under the summertime midnight sun

GETTING ORIENTED

As much a lifestyle as a place, "the Bush" generally refers to all the areas beyond the road system. In other words: most of the state. Geographically it encompasses all of western Alaska, from the North Pacific to the Beaufort Sea. It also includes that part of Alaska's mainland which stretches north of the Arctic Circle. This is a region of immense wildness, with little industrial development beyond the North Slope's oil fields.

A blanket toss in Kotzebue

THE BUSH PLANNER

Making the Most of Your Time

Because of its immense size—the Bush comprises a third of the state—and the expense of transportation, it's best to give yourself at least a week and preferably more when exploring Alaska's rural regions. But even with a week or two you'll see no more than a small slice of Alaska's wildest and most remote parts.

If you're looking to go bear-viewing, bird-watching, sportfishing, or sea-kayaking, head to Southwest Alaska. Not only do Kodiak Island and the Alaska Peninsula have the world's densest populations of brown bears, they also present the best opportunities to watch bears in the wild, at designated viewing areas. Here too are the world's largest salmon runs. And few northern birding hot spots compare to the Pribilof Islands or the Yukon-Kuskokwim Delta. The region's vast expanses of shoreline present memorable opportunities for kayakers.

Turn your attention north for other wonders. Beyond the Arctic Circle in summer is the true Land of the Midnight Sun. These regions also boast premier native cultural tours. And the Arctic's mountain chain, the Brooks Range, presents opportunities for wilderness lovers to explore exciting wildlands. Here too is the only road to connect the Bush with Alaska's highway system: the Dalton Highway.

Timing

The best time to visit is from June through August, when the weather is mildest (though you should still anticipate cool, wet, and sometimes stormy weather), daylight hours are longest, and the wildlife is most abundant. Deciding when to visit depends on what you hope to experience. For instance, birding is often best in May and June, when migrants arrive in large numbers. The peak wildflower season is usually short, particularly in the Arctic, when most flowers may not blossom until mid-June and then go to seed by late July. Salmon runs vary from region to region, so it's best to do your homework before choosing dates. The shift to autumn's bright colors may begin in early to mid-August. And northern lights are "hidden" for most of the summer, because of the long daylight hours.

Getting Around

It's nearly impossible to travel to, and around, the Bush without taking an air taxi. Whether you're most interested in wilderness experiences, cultural tours, or village hopping, you'll likely do some flying. Still, certain areas can be reached by car or boat. The Dalton Highway (Haul Road) connects with the state's highway system and cuts across the Arctic. And for those with a flexible schedule and a desire to visit several of Alaska's remote coastal outposts, the Alaska State Ferry makes monthly trips April through October to Kodiak and Dutch Harbor/Unalaska.

Alaska State Ferry, Alaska Marine Highway System ✉ 6858 Glacier Hwy., Juneau 99801 ☎ 800/642–0066 🌐 www.ferryalaska.com

The Ultimate Wilderness

For those who love vast wilderness landscapes, few places left in North America can match the Brooks Range. Alaska's most northerly mountain chain stretches east–west across the state above the Arctic Circle. And, fortunately, most of this "ultimate wilderness" is protected by national parklands and the Arctic National Wildlife Refuge. These are places where you can go days, and even weeks, without seeing other people. These are the homelands of grizzlies, wolves, Dall sheep, caribou, moose, golden eagles, and numerous other mammals and birds. They are also the homelands of Athabascan Indians and Inupiat and Nunamiut Eskimos, who have lived here for centuries.

Arctic Treks (✉ Box 73452, Fairbanks 99707 ☎ 907/455–6522 🌐 www.arctictreksadventures.com) guides wilderness hikes and backpacking expeditions, sometimes combined with river trips, in both Gates of the Arctic and the Arctic National Wildlife Refuge. Contact **Sourdough Outfitters** (✉ Box 26066, Bettles Field 99726 ☎ 907/692–5252 ☞ 907/692–5557 🌐 www.sourdoughoutfitters.com) for summer backpacking and river trips (from family float trips to wild-rapid running and fishing expeditions) and winter dogsled trips in the Brooks Range.

About the Hotels & Restaurants

The dining options are few when traveling through Alaska's Bush. In most cases, reservations are not needed.

Lodging choices in the Bush are also limited. Rooms go fast during the summer season, so be sure to book several months ahead.

WHAT IT COSTS

	$$$$	$$$	$$	$	¢
Restaurants	over $25	$20–$25	$15–$20	$10–$15	under $10
Hotels	over $225	$175–$225	$125–$175	$75–$125	under $75

Restaurant prices are per person for a main course at dinner. Hotel prices are for two people in a standard double room in high season.

Getting Outside

The Bush presents some of Alaska's—and the world's—best opportunities to participate in backcountry adventures, from backpacking to sea-kayaking, camping, sportfishing, and wildlife-viewing.

CONTACTS

Alaska Department of Fish and Game ✉ Box 25526, Juneau 99802-5526 ☎ 907/465-4100 general information about fish and wildlife, 907/465-4180 sportfishing seasons and regulations, 907/465-2376 licenses 🌐 www.adfg.state.ak.us

Alaska State Parks Information ✉ 550 W. 7th Ave., Suite 1260, Anchorage 99501 ☎ 907/269-8400 🌐 www.alaskastateparks.org

Anchorage Alaska Public Lands Information Center ✉ 605 W. 4th Ave., Suite 105, Anchorage 99501 ☎ 866/869-6887 or 907/271-2737 🌐 www.nps.gov/aplic

Fairbanks Alaska Public Lands Information Center ✉ 250 Cushman St., Suite 1A, Fairbanks 99701 ☎ 866/869-6887 or 907/456-0527 🌐 www.nps.gov/aplic

U.S. Fish and Wildlife Service ✉ 1011 E. Tudor Rd., Anchorage 99503 ☎ 907/786-3309 🌐 www.r7.fws.gov

A GATHERING OF BEARS

Every summer, dozens of brown bears gather at McNeil River, on the Alaska Peninsula. And every year, hundreds of people are given the opportunity to spend time in the company of those bears and watch them fish, play, and nap.

Updated by Bill Sherwonit

ALASKANS CALL IT THE BUSH—those wild and lonely expanses of territory beyond cities, towns, highways, and railroad corridors, stretching from the Kodiak Archipelago, Alaska Peninsula, and Aleutian Islands in the south through the Yukon-Kuskokwim Delta and Seward Peninsula and into the northern High Arctic. It is a land where caribou roam and, in its northern regions, where the sun really does shine at midnight; in fact, it remains in the sky for several weeks in summer—and disappears altogether for weeks in winter. It is a land that knows the soft footsteps of the Eskimos and the Aleuts, the scratchings of those who search for oil and gold, and the ghosts of almost-forgotten battlefields of World War II.

It is a vast, misunderstood wonderland—bleak yet beautiful, harsh yet bountiful. If you visit the Arctic plains in summer, you'll see bright wildflowers growing from a sponge of rich green tundra dotted with pools of melting snow. In the long, dark Arctic winter, a painter's-blue kind of twilight rises from the ice and snowscapes at midday. Spring and fall are fleeting moments when the tundra awakens from its winter slumber or turns briefly brilliant with autumn colors.

The Arctic is separated by the Brooks Range from the rest of the state, and the Brooks Range—stretching as it does east–west across the state from Canada to the sea—is so grand that it contains several mountain systems. Each has its own particular character, ranging from pale, softly rounded limestone mountains in the east and west to the towering granite spires of the Arrigetch Peaks in the heart of the range. Large portions of the Brooks Range's middle and western sections are preserved within Gates of the Arctic National Park and neighboring Noatak National Preserve and its eastern reaches within the Arctic National Wildlife Refuge.

North of the Brooks Range, a great apron of land called the North Slope tilts gently until it slides under the Beaufort Sea and the Arctic Ocean. The vast sweep of this frozen tundra brightens each summer with yellow Arctic poppies and dozens of other wildflower species that pepper infinite stretches of landscape. Buried beneath the surface, permanently frozen ground known as permafrost has shifted and shaped this land for centuries, fragmenting it into giant polygons that make a fascinating pattern when viewed from the sky. It's on the edge of this land where America's largest oil field, Prudhoe Bay, was discovered in 1968. At its peak, more than 2 million barrels a day of North Slope crude from Prudhoe

STOMPING GROUNDS

Great herds of caribou—hundreds of thousands of them—move slowly across the tundra, feeding and fattening for the next winter and attempting to stay clear of wolves and grizzlies. On the Arctic Ocean's Beaufort Sea, polar bears, stained a light gold from the oil of seals they have killed, pose like monarchs on ice floes. One of Alaska's premier wildlands, the Arctic National Wildlife Refuge protects mountain and tundra landscape important to caribou, polar bears, grizzlies, wolves, and musk ox.

Japanese bombs in 1942, is one of America's busiest commercial-fishing ports. Deep-sea trawlers and factory ships venture from here into the stormy north Pacific Ocean and the Bering Sea for harvests of bottom fish, crab, and other catches. Unalaska, an ancient Aleut village, is Dutch Harbor's neighbor and home to one of the oldest Russian Orthodox churches in Alaska. North of the Aleutian chain, in the Bering Sea, the remote volcanic islands called the Pribilofs support immense populations of birds and sea mammals as well as two small Aleut communities, St. George and St. Paul.

Bush Alaskans have a deep affection for their often-raw land, which is difficult to explain to strangers. They talk of living "close to nature," a cliché, perhaps, until you realize that these Alaskans reside in the Bush all year long, adapting to brutal winter weather and isolation. They have accepted the Bush for what it is: dramatic, unforgiving, and glorious.

Exploring the Bush

Philosophically speaking, the Bush is more of a lifestyle than a location. Technically, it's a place in Alaska that can't be reached by road. A tour of the state's southwestern region can begin in Bethel, an important Bush outpost on the Yukon-Kuskokwim Delta, surrounded by the Yukon Delta National Wildlife Refuge; off the mainland coast is the undeveloped wilderness of Nunivak Island. Next is the Alaska Peninsula, which juts out between the Pacific Ocean and the Bering Sea; here are Katmai National Park & Preserve, Aniakchak National Monument & Preserve, and the Becharof and Alaska Peninsula National Wildlife refuges. To the southeast of the Alaska Peninsula is the Kodiak Archipelago, where you'll find the Kodiak National Wildlife Refuge and Shuyak Island State Park; the Aleutian Islands start where the peninsula ends and sweep southwest toward Japan.

The Pribilof Islands lie north of the Aleutians, 200 mi off Alaska's coast. Head north along the Bering Sea coast and you come to Nome, just below the Arctic Circle. North of Nome is the Bering Land Bridge National Preserve. Kotzebue, just above the circle, is a coastal Eskimo town surrounded by sea and tundra and a jumping-off place for several parklands: Kobuk Valley, Noatak, Cape Krusenstern, and Gates of the Arctic (though the last is more easily reached from the town of Bettles). Barrow, another Eskimo community, sits at the very top of the state, and is the northernmost town in the United States. Follow the Arctic coastline eastward and you reach Deadhorse, on Prudhoe Bay, the custodian to the region's important oil and gas reserves. And east of Prudhoe Bay is the Arctic National Wildlife Refuge.

SOUTHWEST

The Southwest region encompasses some of Alaska's most remote, inaccessible, and rugged land- and seascapes. Reaching from the Alaska Peninsula down through the Aleutian chain, it also includes many islands within the Bering Sea, among them the Pribilof Islands, as well as the Bristol Bay watershed, the Kodiak Archipelago, and the Yukon-Kuskokwim Delta. A place of enormous biological richness, it harbors many of North America's largest breeding populations of seabirds and waterfowl and also supports the world's densest population of brown bears and the world's greatest salmon runs. Given all this richness, it's no surprise to learn that Southwest Alaska has some of Alaska's premier parklands and refuges, from Katmai National Park to Aniakchak National Monument and the Kodiak National Wildlife Refuge. Here, too, are dozens of rural communities, most of them small native villages whose residents continue to engage in subsistence gathering.

Bethel

❶ *400 mi west of Anchorage.*

Spread out on the tundra along the Kuskokwim River, Bethel is a frontier town of about 6,400 residents, originally established by Moravian missionaries in the late 1800s. One of rural Alaska's most important trading centers, it is a hub for more than 50 native villages in a region roughly the size of the state of Oregon. The surrounding lowland tundra is a rich green in summer and turns fiery shades of red, orange, and yellow in autumn, when plants burst with blueberries, cranberries, blackberries, and salmonberries. Salmon, arctic grayling, and Dolly Varden trout fill the area's many lakes, ponds, and streams, providing excellent fishing just a few miles outside town. The wetlands are also important breeding grounds for many varieties of birds.

The town is also the northernmost freshwater port for oceangoing vessels. Among its businesses are radio and television stations, a theater, credit union, auto repair shop, car-rental agency, beauty/barber shop, video/DVD rental store, newspaper, two colleges (including a tribal college), and the largest Alaska Native Health Service field hospital in the state, which is contracted to the tribally owned Yukon-Kuskokwim Health Corporation.

Each year, on the last weekend in March, Bethel hosts a regional celebration called the Camai Dance Festival (in Yup'ik, *camai* means "hello"). Held in the local high school's gym, which is filled to capacity for the three-day event, this festival draws dance groups from dozens of villages (www.bethelarts.com).

TAKE NOTE

Many of the Bush communities have voted to be dry areas in order to fight alcohol-abuse problems affecting Alaska's native peoples. The sale and possession of alcohol is prohibited. Enforcement is strict, and bootlegging is a felony. Nome, of course, remains wet, with numerous lively saloons.

★ The **Yupiit Piciryarait (the People's way of living) Museum** emphasizes cultural education through native elders, while also showcasing artifacts and artwork of three native cultures: Dene Athabascan, Cup'ik, and Yup'ik. In its three galleries you'll find historic and prehistoric treasures: masks, statues, and carvings in ivory, baleen, and whalebone. Its permanent collection features past and present clothing styles plus numerous implements and tools used in traditional subsistence lifestyles of the people inhabiting the Yukon-Kuskokwim region. A small gift shop has locally made native artwork for sale, including water-grass baskets, wooden spirit masks, ivory-handle knives, grass and reindeer-beard dance fans, yo-yos, dolls, and seal-gut raincoats. ✉ *Museum, 420 Eddie Hoffman Hwy.* ☎ *907/543–1819 or 800/478–3521* 🌐 *www.avcp.org/services/CulturalCenter.html* *Free (donations requested)* ⏲ *Weekdays noon–5.*

Where to Stay & Eat

$–$$ ✕ **Shogun.** This rural café-style restaurant specializes in Chinese food, with daily lunch and dinner specials. It also serves Japanese and Italian dishes, plus American-style steaks and seafood. ✉ *320 Tundra Ave.* ☎ *907/543–2272* ▭ *MC, V.*

$–$$$ ✕ **Pacifica Guest House.** Three detached buildings make up this inn, which provides a quiet stay and Bush-savvy owners who provide insightful tips. Alaskan crafts and artwork adorn the modern rooms, some of which share a bath; others are full suites. The main building is fully wired for online access, complete with Internet café. Next door in a solarium, **Diane's Café** (¢–$2) serves Alaskan salmon, halibut, steaks, and roasts, as well as vegetarian and Mexican food. ✉ *1220 Hoffman Hwy., Box 1208, 99559* ☎ *907/543–4305* 🌐 *www.pacificaguesthouse.com* *30 rooms, 14 with bath* *Restaurant, Internet café, cable TV, library, meeting room; no a/c, no smoking* ▭ *AE, D, DC, MC, V.*

7

$$ **Bentley's Porter House B&B.** Hospitality is never in short supply at this two-story B&B in downtown Bethel. Rooms are decorated according to theme, including African, Southwestern United States, and English countryside. Several overlook the Kuskokwim River. Besides those in the main inn, rooms are available in a nearby smaller inn, made up of a duplex and two cottages. Rooms in the newer, smaller inn have their own baths; others share. ✉ *624 1st Ave., Box 529, 99559* ☎ *907/543–3552* *9 rooms with bath; 35 other rooms share 14 baths* *Cable TV, Internet, some pets allowed; no a/c, no smoking* ▭ *AE, D, DC, MC, V* 🍽 *BP.*

Shopping

BOOKSTORE The **Moravian Bookstore** (✉ 301 3rd Ave. ☎ 907/543–2474) stocks arts and crafts as well as books about religion and Eskimo culture. It is open Wednesday through Saturday noon–4.

OFF THE BEATEN PATH

NUNIVAK ISLAND – Due west of Bethel, and separated from the Yukon-Kuskokwim Delta by Etolin Strait, Nunivak Island is an important wildlife refuge. Part of the **Yukon Delta National Wildlife Refuge,** this site is noted for its large herd of reindeer, a transplanted herd of musk ox, and the Eskimo settlement of Mekoryuk.

For information on the island, contact the **U.S. Fish and Wildlife Service** (☎ 907/543–3151 🌐 www.r7.fws.gov) in Bethel. Visitors, lured by fine ivory carvings, masks, and items knit from qiviut (musk-ox) wool, should check with **ERA Aviation** (☎ 800/866–8394 🌐 www.flyera.com) about transport and accommodations, which are limited and far from deluxe.

Yukon Delta National Wildlife Refuge

❷ *Surrounds Bethel.*

At 20 million acres, Yukon Delta is the nation's largest wildlife refuge; nearly one-third of the area is water, in the form of lakes, sloughs, bogs, creeks, and rivers. The two most significant of these waters are the **Yukon** and **Kuskokwim** rivers, Alaska's two largest. As they flow toward the Bering Sea, these rivers carry huge amounts of sediment; over the millennia, the sediments have formed an immense delta that serves as critical breeding and rearing grounds for an estimated 100 million shorebirds and waterfowl.

Not all of the refuge is flat wetlands. North of the Yukon River are the Nulato Hills, site of the 1.3-million-acre **Andreafsky Wilderness area,** which includes both forks of the Andreafsky River, one of Alaska's specially designated Wild and Scenic Rivers. Rainbow trout, arctic char, and grayling flourish in upland rivers and creeks; pike, sheefish, and burbot thrive in lowland waters. These abundant waters are also spawning grounds to five species of Pacific salmon. Black and grizzly bears, moose, beavers, mink, and arctic foxes call this refuge home. Occasionally, wolves venture into the delta's flats from neighboring uplands.

Given the abundance of fish and wildlife, it's not surprising that the delta holds special importance to surrounding residents. Yup'ik Eskimos have lived here for thousands of years; despite modern encroachment, they continue their centuries-old subsistence lifestyle. Access is by boat or aircraft only, and, as in most of Alaska's other remote wildlands, visitor facilities are minimal. Refuge staff can provide tips on recreational opportunities and guides and outfitters who operate in the refuge. *Box 346, Bethel 99559* ☎ *907/543–3151* *www.r7.fws.gov.*

NESTING GROUNDS

More than 100 species of birds nest here, traveling from nearly every state and province in North America and from every continent that borders the Pacific Ocean. All of North America's cackling Canada geese and more than half the continent's population of black brant are born here. Other birds making the annual pilgrimage to the Yukon Delta refuge include emperor geese, tundra swans, gulls, jaegers, cranes, loons, snipe, sandpipers, and the rare bristle-thighed curlew.

Sports, the Outdoors & Guided Tours

Opportunities to observe wildlife abound at the Yukon Delta refuge. Given its abundance of lakes, ponds, streams, and wetlands, the other primary recreational activities are boating and birding. There's also substantial opportunity for sportfishing, especially for rainbow trout, salmon char, pike, grayling, and sheefish. Hiking and river-floating are possible in the uplands of the Andreafsky Wilderness area.

EXPERT LOCAL GUIDES **Kuskokwim Wilderness Adventures** (☎ 907/543–3900 www.kuskofish.com) offers camping, fishing, birding, photo trips, and more, led by local Jim McDonald.

Wood-Tikchik State Park

★ 3 *150 mi southeast of Bethel, 300 mi southwest of Anchorage.*

In the Bristol Bay region, Wood-Tikchik State Park—the nation's largest state park—is a water-based wildland despite its inland setting. Two separate groups of large, idyllic, interconnected lakes, some of which are up to 45 mi long, dominate the park. Grizzlies, caribou, porcupines, eagles, and loons inhabit the park's forests and tundra, but Wood-Tikchik is best known for its fish. Its lakes and streams are critical spawning habitat for five species of Pacific salmon; they also support healthy populations of rainbow trout, arctic char, arctic grayling, and northern pike. The abundance of fish attracts anglers from around the world. Boaters, including rafters and kayakers, also come to explore its expansive and pristine waterways.

Managed as a wild area, Wood-Tikchik has no maintained trails and few other visitor amenities. ■ TIP→ **Most of its campsites are primitive, and those who plan to explore the park should be experienced in backcountry travel and camping.** Access is by either boat or air. *Mid-May–Sept., Box 3022, Dillingham 99576* ☎ *907/842–2375* ✉ *Oct.–mid-May, 550 W. 7th Ave., Suite 1380, Anchorage 99501* ☎ *907/269–8698* 🌐 *www.alaskastateparks.org.*

Besides the many large lakes and streams that fill its 1.6 million acres, the park's landscape includes rugged mountains, glaciers, and vast expanses of tundra.

You can also travel from Dillingham, a town close to Wood-Tikchik, by boat or by air to view the walruses offshore on Round Island within **Walrus Islands State Game Sanctuary.** *Box 1030, Dillingham 99576-1030* ☎ *907/842–2334* 📠 *907/842–5514* 🌐 *www.wildlife.alaska.gov.*

Sports, the Outdoors & Guided Tours

Because it is largely a water-based region, Wood-Tikchik is most easily explored by boat, including canoe, kayak, or raft. The most popular fly-in float trip is the 90-mi journey from Lake Kulik to Aleknagik, a Yup'ik Eskimo village. Most people doing this trip arrange for drop-off and pick-up services with local guides in Dillingham. The lakes are large enough to behave like small inland seas in stormy weather, so boaters need to be cautious when winds are high. The water systems also present some of the world's best sportfishing opportunities for salmon and rainbow trout. Anglers come from around the world to stay at wilderness fishing lodges. Hiking is difficult, because of dense brush, except for the uppermost part of the park, where tundra makes on-land travel easier.

FISHING LODGES **Tikchik Narrows Lodge** (☎ 907/243–8450 🌐 www.tikchiklodge.com) is owned and managed by Bud Hodson, who has been a guide in the Wood-Tikchik region for more than 25 years. The lodge primarily caters to sportfishing enthusiasts who are also looking for comfortable housing and scrumptious gourmet-style meals at night—and who can afford

$6,600 for a week's stay, which includes guided fishing trips throughout the region. The lodge also rents kayaks and rafts and occasionally flies people into the park's most remote corners. If you're looking to reel one in, **Reel Wilderness Adventures** (☎ 800/726–8323 🌐 www.reelwilderness.com) offers an alternative to lodges, while emphasizing small groups, gourmet meals, and fly-fishing for rainbow trout and other species.

Katmai National Park & Preserve

★ ❹ *100 mi southeast of Wood-Tikchik, 290 mi southwest of Anchorage.*

Compared with Denali National Park, Katmai is much more remote and its visitor facilities are fewer and more rustic (except for those able to afford to stay at pricey wilderness lodges)—but therein lies part of the park's appeal. These 4-million acres offer up plenty of opportunities for wildlife viewing and an extraordinary perspective on the awesome power of volcanoes. In this wild, remote area at the northern end of the Alaska Peninsula, moose and almost 30 other species of mammals, including foxes, lynx, and wolves, share the landscape with bears fishing for salmon from stream banks, rivers, and along the coast. At the immensely popular **Brooks Falls and Camp,** you can see brown bears when the salmon are running in July and September. No special permits are required here, though there is a $10 day-use fee at Brooks. Bears are also common along the park's outer coast, where they graze on sedge flats, dig clams from the beach at low tide (quite a sight!), and fish for salmon. Ducks are common along the park's rivers, lakes, and outer coast, as are whistling swans, loons, grebes, gulls, and shorebirds. Bald eagles perch on rocky pinnacles by the sea. More than 40 species of songbirds alone can be seen during the short spring and summer season. Marine life abounds in the coastal area, with Steller's sea lions and hair seals hanging out on rock outcroppings.

From Brooks Lodge, a daily tour bus with a naturalist aboard makes the 23-mi trip through the park to the **Valley Overlook.** Hikers can walk the 1½-mi trail for a closer look at the pumice-covered valley floor. (Some consider the return climb strenuous.)

The Katmai area is one of Alaska's premier sportfishing regions. It's possible to fish for rainbow trout and salmon at the **Brooks River,** though seasonal closures have been put in place to prevent conflicts with bears, and only fly-fishing is permitted. For those who would like to venture farther into the park, seek out the two other backcountry lodges, **Grosvenor** and **Kulik,** set in prime sportfishing territory, or contact fishing-guide services based in King Salmon. A short walk up the Brooks River brings you to Brooks Falls, where salmon leaping a 6-foot-high cascade can be seen from two viewing platforms, one at the falls and another a short way below it (an access trail and boardwalk are separated from the river to avoid confrontations with bears). 📫 *National Park Service, Box 7, King Salmon 99613* ☎ *907/246–3305* 🌐 *www.nps.gov/katm.*

HALLO BAY BEAR LODGE

Bears also congregate in large numbers along the park's remote outer coast to fish for salmon at such places as Hallo Bay. Located at the northern end of the bay, this remote eco-friendly camp provides easy access to some of Alaska's best brown-bear viewing. The camp is reached by air taxi from Homer. Guests stay in rustic yet comfortable heated platform tents, and enjoy gourmet meals in an enclosed kitchen. The high price tag includes a round-trip flight from Homer, meals, lodging, and guide services. ☎ *888/235-2237* 🌐 *www.hallobay.com.*

No roads lead to the national park, at the base of the Alaska Peninsula. Planes wing from Anchorage along Cook Inlet, rimmed by the lofty, snowy peaks of the Alaska Range (check out www.alaskaair.com for fares and schedules). They land at **King Salmon,** near fish-famous Bristol Bay, where passengers transfer to smaller floatplanes for the 20-minute hop to **Naknek Lake** and Brooks Camp. Travel to Brooks from King Salmon is also possible by boat. You are required to check into the park ranger station, next to Brooks Lodge (see information below), for a mandatory bear talk.

7

Fodor'sChoice ★ At the northern end of the Alaska Peninsula, 200 mi southwest of Anchorage, **McNeil River State Game Sanctuary** was established in 1967 to protect the world's largest gathering of brown bears. Since then, it has earned a reputation as the finest bear-viewing locale in North America, and likely the world, the standard by which all others are measured. The main focus is **McNeil Falls,** where bears come to feed on chum salmon returning to spawn. During the peak of the chum run (July to mid-August) dozens of brown bears congregate at the falls. As many as 70 bears, including cubs, have been observed along the river in a single day and more than 100 bears have been identified within a single season. It's not only the number of bears that makes McNeil special; over the years, several of these bears have become highly accustomed to a human presence. They will play, eat, nap, and nurse cubs within 15 to 20 feet of the falls viewing pad—sometimes closer. This is not to say the bears are tame; these are still wild animals and the sanctuary staff makes sure that visitors behave in a non-threatening, non-intrusive way.

No more than 10 people a day, always accompanied by one or two state biologists, are allowed to visit bear-viewing sites from June 7 through August 25. Because demand is so high, an annual drawing is held in mid-March to determine permit winners. ■ TIP→ **Applications must be received by March 1 to be eligible.** Nearly all visitors fly into McNeil Sanctuary on floatplanes. Most arrange for air-taxi flights out of Homer, on the Kenai Peninsula. Once you are in the sanctuary, all travel is on foot. ✉ *Alaska Department of Fish and Game, Division of Wildlife Conservation, 333 Raspberry Rd., Anchorage 99518-1599* ☎ *907/267–2182* 🌐 *www.wc.adfg.state.ak.us/mcneil.*

Where to Stay

All of the four lodges below are on inholdings within Katmai National Park. Three are inland, and Katmai Wilderness Lodge is on the remote outer coast.

$$$$ Fodor'sChoice ★ **Brooks Lodge.** All the attractions of Katmai National Park are at this lodge's doorstep: fly-fishing for rainbow trout, lake trout, arctic grayling, and salmon; brown-bear viewing; and tours to the Valley of Ten Thousand Smokes. Accommodations are in detached modern cabins adorned with Alaskan artwork; they accommodate two to four people. All cabins have heat, electricity, and private toilet facilities. The cabins surround the main lodge, which has a spectacular view of aquamarine Naknek Lake; it has a circular stone fireplace and a dining area where buffet-style meals are served three times daily. Price includes airfare from Anchorage; special trips to the valley are extra. *Katmailand, 4125 Aircraft Dr., Anchorage 99502 907/243–5448 or 800/544–0551 www.katmailand.com/lodging/brooks.html 16 cabins Dining room, lake, boating, fishing, hiking, bar; no a/c, no room phones, no room TVs MC, V Closed mid-Sept.–May.*

$$$$ **Grosvenor Lodge.** Once you've arrived at this remote Katmai National Park lodge, reachable only by floatplane, you have access by motorboat to numerous rivers and streams filled with sport fish. The lodge can accommodate six people in three cabins; heated, with electricity, they share a separate bathhouse. The main lodge houses a kitchen, lounging area, and bar and has an excellent view of Grosvenor Lake. Three-, four-, and seven-night price packages include airfare from Anchorage, meals, lodging, and guiding. *Katmailand, 4125 Aircraft Dr., Anchorage 99502 907/243–5448 or 800/544–0551 www.katmailand.com/lodging/grosvenor.html 3 cabins with shared baths Dining room, lake, boating, fishing, bar, travel services; no a/c, no room phones, no room TVs MC, V Closed Oct.–May FAP.*

★ $$$$ **Katmai Wilderness Lodge.** Built on land owned by the Russian Orthodox Church, this rustic lodge straddles the rugged outer coast of Katmai National Park, along the shores of Kukak Bay. Mountains, coastal flats, and the waters of Shelikof Strait surround the modern log cabin–style lodge, where guests stay in private bedrooms with baths and gather to eat gourmet meals in the dining room or, if the weather is right, on outdoor decks. Recreational activities include bear-viewing, sea-kayaking, and fishing for halibut and salmon. You may stay from three nights to a week or more. Price includes a round-trip flight from Kodiak, meals, lodging, and guide services. *Box 4332, Kodiak 99615 800/488–8767 www.katmai-wilderness.com 7 rooms Dining room, boating, fishing, travel services; no a/c, no room phones, no room TVs No credit cards Closed Oct.–mid-May FAP.*

$$$$ **Kulik Lodge.** Positioned along the gin-clear Kulik River, between Nonvianuk and Kulik lakes, this remote wilderness lodge is reachable only by floatplane. It accommodates up to 28 anglers and is popular as a base for fly-out fishing to hot spots in the surrounding Katmai wilderness. Guests stay in two- or four-person cabins with electricity and private baths. In the evening, when fishing's done for the day, you gather in the spruce lodge, which has a large stone fireplace, dining area, and bar. Three-,

Continued on page 433

WELCOME TO BEAR COUNTRY

(top) Grizzly bears fishing in Katmai National Park (bottom) Polar bear

A 1,000-pound brown bear plows through the shallows of Pack Creek on Southeast Alaska's Admiralty Island, adroitly flipping a 20-pound salmon out of the current like an NFL lineman snapping a football. This bear, which stands over 8 feet tall when perched on his hind legs, can devour 50 pounds of food every day. And, when sprinting, he can reach speeds of 35 miles per hour. Governmentally speaking, Alaska is a democracy. But in the wilderness, the state is a monarchy—and the bear the undisputed king.

KING OF THE WILDERNESS

A Good Home

Thanks to its vast stretches of wilderness, Alaska is the only state that is home to healthy populations of all three North American ursine species. Polar bears (*Ursus maritimus*) don't venture south of the state's chilly Arctic coastline, while black bears (*Ursus americanus*) and brown bears (*Ursus arctos*; also known as grizzlies) live throughout the state's many refuges and parks. Bear populations are plentiful here: the Alaska Department of Fish and Game estimates that Alaska is home to roughly 100,000 to 200,000 black bears and 25,000 to 38,000 brown bears.

Watching a bear gorge on succulent salmon from a chilly creek; witnessing a mother bear wandering the shoreline in the early morning with two cubs trailing behind her—if you're lucky enough to catch such sights—and yes, viewing wildlife in Alaska does have to do with luck and timing—you can bet you won't be forgetting them anytime soon. However, as illustrated by *Grizzly Man*—a 2005 documentary by Werner Herzog about the troubled life and tragic death of Alaska bear activist Timothy Treadwell—Alaska's bears are wild, unpredictable creatures that should *never* be underestimated.

Safe Places to View Bears

Bear-viewing in Alaska has become an increasingly popular tourist activity—and one that is safely enjoyed by thousands of visitors using expert outdoor tour guides every year at such locations as **Denali National Park & Preserve** (⇨ Ch. 6), **Kodiak Island** (⇨ Ch. 7), **Katmai National Park's McNeil River State Game Sanctuary** (⇨ Ch. 7), **Admiralty Island's Pack Creek** (⇨ Ch. 3), **Anan Creek Wildlife Observatory** (⇨ Ch. 3), and **Fish Creek Wildlife Observation Site** (⇨ Ch. 3).

Keep in mind that your best bet is to hire an experienced guide and always to check in with rangers at the refuges or parks you plan to visit. It's never certain that you'll see a bear, though your chances increase dramatically if you're visiting one of the aforementioned premier viewing areas during summer salmon runs on a guided

Strolling black bear

BEAR OF THE NORTHERN REACHES

Along Alaska's icy northern coast roams the most majestic of all ursine species: the polar bear. Massive in stature (males can reach 1,700 pounds and 11 feet in height), polar bears are also cunning predators that prey chiefly on seals. With relatively short average life spans (15 to 20 years) and one of the slowest reproductive rates of any mammal on earth—females give birth to two cubs every two to five years—polar bear populations are especially vulnerable to human intrusion and, most recently, the continuing retreat of polar sea ice. These bears are worthy of the utmost respect: exercise special caution when traveling along the coastline, as they are known to be aggressive toward humans.

A Kodiak mama bear is followed by two young cubs.

tour or if you're traveling in Alaska's more remote backcountry regions. If it's the latter, the chances of an aggressive bear encounter are real but remote.

You should be very well prepared and well versed in safe travel and camping techniques, which include using bear-resistant food containers; traveling in large parties (chances of bear encounters increase exponentially if you're traveling alone); steering clear of forested areas, berry patches, and salmon runs; checking in with park rangers to find out about potential bear zones; and making noise to warn bears that humans are present.

Black Versus Brown

Despite their given names, black and brown bears have coloring ranging from black to dark blond. Size is the defining characteristic: male brown bears on Kodiak Island—home to the largest brown bear subspecies on Earth—can reach 1,700 pounds and stand 10 feet tall. Male black bears, by comparison, rarely exceed 600 pounds or stand taller than 6 feet. Brown bears have longer claws; wider faces; and a distinct shoulder hump. Brown bears are also more protective of their territory and less intimidated by human intrusion than black bears.

Black and brown bears feed on a diverse diet, the staples being salmon, berries, roots, carrion, and the occasional deer, moose, or caribou. Both species hibernate in winter, although bears in the southern coastal regions spend less time hibernating. In the wild, brown and black bears live for 20 to 30 years. Mature female brown and black bears produce a litter of one to four cubs every two years. And thanks to state and federal protections, Alaska's bear populations are holding steady.

THE SOFT SIDE OF TEDDY

Question: How did the bear—one of nature's largest, most fearsome creatures—become such a popular stuffed animal?

Answer: Because Theodore "Teddy" Roosevelt, former U.S. president, avid hunter, and all-around tough guy, refused to shoot a bear while hunting in Mississippi in 1902. Hence "Teddy's bear" was born. If Roosevelt were alive today, there's only one place he'd surely want to visit to see his beloved bears: Alaska.

A playful brown bear

THE BEAR FACTS: TIPS FOR STAYING SAFE

AVOID SURPRISE

Whenever possible, travel in open country, during daylight hours, and in groups. Make constant noise—talking or singing is preferable to carrying "bear bells"—and leave your dog at home. Most attacks occur when a bear is surprised at close quarters or feels threatened.

CAMP WITH CARE

Pitch your tent away from trails, streams with spawning salmon, berry patches, and other food sources. Avoid areas that have a rotten smell or where scavengers have gathered; these may indicate the presence of a nearby food cache, which a bear will aggressively defend.

BE BEAR AWARE

Keep your eyes open for the telltale signs of bears, such as fresh tracks, scat, matted vegetation, or partially consumed salmon.

ISOLATE YOUR FOOD SUPPLIES

Since bears are practically walking noses, it's imperative that you cook meals at least 100 yards from your tents and that you store food and other odorous items away from campsites. Hang food between trees or store it in bear-resistant food containers. Thoroughly clean your cooking area and utensils after each use. Store garbage in airtight containers—or burn it—and pack up the remains.

IF YOU ENCOUNTER A BEAR IN THE WILD

1 IDENTIFY YOURSELF. Talk to the bear in a steady, monotone voice. Don't yell. As for running: don't do it. Running has been known to trigger a bear's predatory instincts, and a bear can easily outrun you (remember, brown bears can run as fast as 35 mph). Back away slowly, and give the bear an escape route. Don't ever get between a mother and her cubs.

2 BIGGER IS BETTER. To increase your apparent size, raise your arms above your head wave them slowly. With two or more people, it helps to stand side by side. In a forested area it may be appropriate to climb a tree, but remember that black bears and young grizzlies are agile tree climbers.

3 AS A LAST RESORT, PLAY DEAD. If a bear charges and makes contact with you, fall to the ground, curl into a ball with your hands behind your neck, and remain passive. If you are wearing a pack, leave it on. Once a bear no longer feels threatened, it will usually end its attack. Wait for the bear to leave before you move. If such an attack persists for more than a few minutes–in other words, if the bear seems intent on actually harming you further–there's only one option: fight back with all of your might. Keep in mind that such worst-case scenarios are exceedingly rare.

In 2005, fewer than 12 bear maulings occurred; two were fatal.

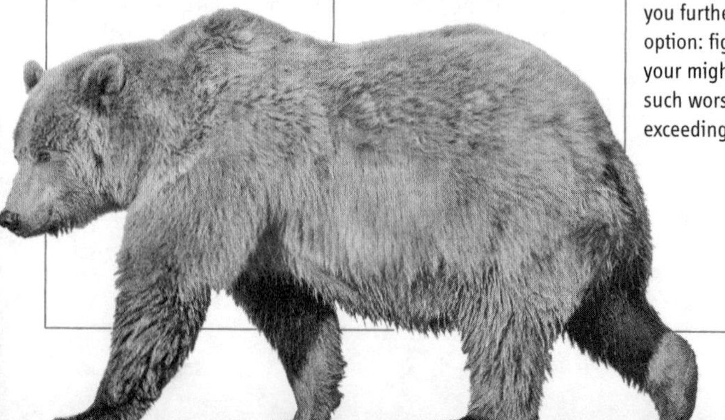

A grizzly bear strolls Katmai National Park's tidal flats.

four-, or seven-night packages include airfare from Anchorage, meals, lodging, and guiding. *Katmailand, 4125 Aircraft Dr., Anchorage 99502 907/243–5448 or 800/544–0551 www.katmailand.com/lodging/kulik.html 12 cabins Dining room, lake, boating, fishing, bar, travel services; no a/c, no room phones, no room TVs MC, V Closed mid-Oct.–May FAP.*

¢ **Brooks Campground.** This National Park Service campground is a short walk from Brooks Lodge, where campers can pay to eat and shower. Designated cooking and eating shelters, latrines, well water, and a storage cache to protect food from the ever-present brown bears are available. Reservations are required. *Portable toilets, drinking water, bear boxes, picnic tables, ranger station 60 sites Katmai National Park, Box 7, King Salmon 99613 907/246–3305, 800/365–2267 reservations www.nps.gov/katm $8 D, MC, V Closed mid-Sept.–May.*

Sports, the Outdoors & Guided Tours

The Katmai region offers an abundance of recreational opportunities, including sportfishing, bear-viewing, hiking through the Valley of 10,000 Smokes, river-running the Wild and Scenic Alagnak River and other clear-water streams, flightseeing, exploring the outer coast, and backpacking through remote and seldom-visited backcountry wilderness.

FLIGHTSEEING & WILDLIFE VIEWING **Emerald Air Service and Day Trips** (907/235–6993 www.emeraldairservice.com), in Homer, leads guided bear-viewing trips to remote reaches of Katmai National Park, including the seldom-visited outer coast. Though owners Chris and Ken Day specialize in day visits, they will also arrange overnight trips upon request. **Katmai Air Services** (907/246–3079 in King Salmon summer only, 800/544–0551 in Anchorage www.katmailand.com) can arrange flightseeing tours of the park and also does charter flights to Brooks Camp. **Katmailand** (4125 Aircraft Dr., Anchorage 99502 907/243–5448 or 800/544–0551 www.katmailand.com) assembles bear-viewing and fishing packages to Katmai National Park and also arranges trips to Katmai's Valley of 10,000 Smokes. **Lifetime Adventures** (800/952–8624 www.lifetimeadventures.net) organizes a variety of customized trips featuring small groups (8 people or less), from bear-watching to river-kayaking, mountain-biking, and hiking in the Valley of Smokes. **Northwind Aviation** (P.O. Box 646, Homer 99603 907/235–7482), in Homer, offers charter flights to Katmai's outer coast and McNeil River.

> **WORD OF MOUTH**
>
> "I just returned from day trip with Emerald Air Service. It was wonderful. We saw over 20 bears digging clams and grazing. A very informative trip observing how bears live instead of just taking pictures of them. This is a great company to go with."
>
> –Karenackermann

RIVER RUNNING & SPORTFISHING **Ouzel Expeditions** (800/825–8196 or 907/783–2216 www.ouzel.com) guides fishing and river-running trips down the Wild and Scenic

BELCHING GIANTS

The first visitors to the Katmai area arrived more than 4,000 years ago. Some evidence exists, in fact, that native Alaskan people inhabited Katmai's eastern edge for at least 6,000 years. On the morning of June 1, 1912, a 2,700-foot mountain called **Novarupta** erupted. The earth shook in violent tremors for five straight days. When the quakes subsided, rivers of white-hot ash poured into the valley. A foot of ash fell on Kodiak Island, 100 mi away. Winds carried the ash to eastern Canada and as far as Texas. While Novarupta was belching pumice and scorching ash, another explosion occurred 6 mi east. The mountaintop peak of **Mt. Katmai** collapsed, creating a chasm almost 3 mi long and 2 mi wide. The molten andesite that held up Mt. Katmai had rushed through newly created fissures to Novarupta and was spewed out. Sixty hours after the first thunderous blast, more than 7 cubic mi of volcanic material had been ejected, and the green valley lay under 700 feet of ash. Those who did live in this remote area fled; no one was killed.

By 1916 things had cooled off sufficiently to allow scientists to explore the area. A National Geographic expedition led by Dr. Robert F. Griggs reached the valley and found it full of steaming fumaroles (holes in the volcanic terrain that fume smoke), creating a decidedly moonlike landscape. The report on what Griggs dubbed the **Valley of Ten Thousand Smokes** inspired Congress in 1918 to declare the valley and the surrounding wilderness a national monument. Steam spouted in thousands of fountains from the smothered streams and springs beneath the ash and gave the valley its name. Although the steam has virtually stopped, an eerie sense of earth forces at work remains, and several nearby volcanoes still smolder.

The native peoples never returned to their traditional village sites, though many now live in other nearby communities. They are joined by sightseers, anglers, hikers, and other outdoors enthusiasts who migrate to the Katmai region each summer. Fish and wildlife are plentiful, and a few "smokes" still drift through the volcano-sculpted valley.

Alagnak River, which flows through Katmai National Park and is widely known as a rainbow-trout heaven.

Aniakchak National Monument & Preserve

❺ *100 mi southwest of Katmai National Park.*

Aniakchak, an extraordinary living volcano, rises to the south of Katmai. It has one of the largest calderas in the world, with a diameter averaging 6 mi across, and the small **Surprise Lake** is contained within it. Although Aniakchak last erupted in 1931, the explosion that formed the enormous crater occurred before history was written. Because the area is not glaciated, geologists place the blowup after the last Ice Age. It was literally a world-shaking event. To mark the volcano's significance, in 1980 Congress established the 586,000-acre Aniakchak National Monument & Preserve.

This is wild and forbidding country, with a climate that brews mist, clouds, and winds of great force much of the year. Although the **Aniakchak River** (which drains Surprise Lake) is floatable, it has stretches of Class III and IV white water navigable only by expert river runners, and you must travel through open ocean waters to reach the nearest community, Chignik Bay (or get picked up by plane, along the coast); this makes the run an ambitious undertaking. An alternate way to enjoy Aniakchak is to wait for a clear day and fly to it in a small plane that will land you on the caldera floor or on Surprise Lake. However you choose to see it, it's an unforgettable experience. But be aware that there are no trails, campgrounds, ranger stations, or other visitor facilities here; you must be prepared to be self-sufficient.

Aniakchak is remote and expensive to reach. The only easy access is by air, usually from the town of King Salmon. Thus, few people visit this spectacular place—and those who do are likely to have the caldera all to themselves. *Aniakchak National Monument and Preserve, Box 7, King Salmon 99613 ☎ 907/246–3305 www.nps.gov/ania.*

Sports, the Outdoors & Guided Tours

FLIGHTSEEING **Branch River Air** (☎ 907/246–3437 June–Sept., 907/248–3539 Oct.–May www.branchriverair.com), in King Salmon, offers charter flights and flightseeing and will also arrange fishing and bear-viewing trips.

RIVER RUNNING **Ouzel Expeditions** (☎ 800/825–8196 or 907/783–2216 www.ouzel.com) guides river-running trips down the Aniakchak River. Trips begin at Surprise Lake, within the caldera, and end at the coast, and feature white-water rafting and fishing for salmon, char, and rainbow trout.

Becharof & Alaska Peninsula National Wildlife Refuges

★ 6 *Adjacent to Aniakchak National Monument & Preserve, 250 to 450 mi southwest of Anchorage.*

Stretching along the southern edge of the Alaska Peninsula, these two refuges encompass nearly 6 million acres of towering mountains, glacial lakes, broad tundra valleys, and coastal fjords. Volcanoes dominate the landscape—14 in all, of which 9 are considered active. **Mt. Veniaminov** last erupted in 1993. Other glimpses of volcanic activity include **Gas Rocks,** where gases continually seep through cracks in granitic rocks, and **Ukrinek Marrs,** a crater that bears the marks of a violent eruption in 1977.

Aside from their rugged volcanic landscapes, these two refuges are best known for abundant wildlife. More than 220 species of resident and migratory wildlife seasonally inhabit the region, including 30 land and 11 marine mammals, nearly 150 varieties of birds, and 35 species of fish. Caribou, wolves, and moose roam the region's tundra; sea lions, seals, seabirds, and waterfowl thrive along the rocky shores; bald eagles and falcons nest on craggy cliffs above the coast. You'll find brown bears nearly everywhere, from coastal lowlands to high mountain ridges.

Becharof Lake, at 35 mi long and up to 15 mi wide, is the second-largest lake in Alaska (behind Lake Iliamna). Fed by two rivers and 14 major creeks, it serves as a nursery to the world's second-biggest run of salmon. **Ugashik Lakes** are known for their salmon and trophy grayling. The world-record grayling, nearly 5 pounds (most grayling weigh a pound or less), was caught at Ugashik Narrows in 1981.

Remote and rugged, with weather that is frequently stormy, the Becharof and Alaska Peninsula refuges draw mostly anglers and hunters; however, backpackers, river runners, and mountain climbers also occasionally visit. No visitor facilities are available here, and access is only by boat or plane. Most visitors begin their trips in King Salmon and use guides or outfitters. *Box 277, King Salmon 99613 907/246–3339 www.r7.fws.gov.*

Kodiak National Wildlife Refuge

7 *50 mi south of Katmai National Park, 300 mi southwest of Anchorage.*

The 1.9-million-acre Kodiak National Wildlife Refuge lies mostly on Kodiak Island and partly on neighboring Afognak and Uganik islands, in the Gulf of Alaska. All are part of the Kodiak Archipelago, separated from Alaska's mainland by the often stormy Shelikof Strait. Within the refuge are rugged mountains, tundra meadows and lowlands, thickly forested hills, lakes, marshes, and hundreds of miles of pristine coastland. No place in the refuge is more than 15 mi from the ocean. The weather here is generally wet and cool, and storms born in the North Pacific often bring heavy rains.

The world's largest carnivores (along with polar bears), Kodiak brown bears weigh only 1 pound at birth, but weigh up to 1,700 pounds when full grown.

Dozens of species of birds inhabit the refuge each spring and summer, including Aleutian terns, horned puffins, black oystercatchers, ravens, ptarmigan, and chickadees. At least 600 pairs of bald eagles live on the islands, nesting on shoreline cliffs and in tall trees. Seeing the Kodiak brown bears alone is worth the trip to this rugged country. When they emerge from their dens in spring, the bears feed on sedges and grasses, become fish eaters when salmon return in early summer, and depend heavily on Kodiak's berries in fall. Kodiak brown bears share the refuge with only a few other land mammals native to the archipelago: red foxes, river otters, short-tailed weasels, and tundra voles.

Five species of Pacific salmon—chums, kings, pinks, silvers, and sockeyes—return to Kodiak's waters each year in a series of runs that begin in May and last into October. Other resident species include rainbow trout, steelhead, Dolly Varden, and arctic char. The abundance of fish and bears makes the refuge popular with anglers, hunters, and wildlife watchers. Access is only by boat or plane. Refuge staff will provide lists of guides, outfitters, and air taxis. *1390 Buskin River Rd., Kodiak 99615 888/408–3514 or 907/487–2600 kodiak.fws.gov.*

Where to Stay

¢ **Kodiak Refuge Public-Use Cabins.** It's possible to rent one of seven recreation cabins (accessible by floatplane or boat) within the refuge for up to seven days (longer in the off-season). Set along the coast and on inland lakes, the cabins include bunks with mattresses, kerosene heaters, tables, and benches. Reservations are awarded through quarterly lotteries, held on the first of January, April, July, and October. The cabins on inland lakes are usually not accessible in winter. ✉ *1390 Buskin River Rd., Kodiak 99615* ☎ *907/487–2600* 🌐 *www.r7.fws.gov or kodiak.fws.gov/visiting.htm* *7 cabins* *Reservations essential* *No credit cards.*

Sports, the Outdoors & Guided Tours

BEAR-VIEWING & SPORTFISHING **Rohrer Bear Camp** (☎ 907/486–5835 🌐 www.sportfishingkodiak.com) guides both bear-viewers and visitors who come to Kodiak seeking the island's abundant sportfishing opportunities.

Shuyak Island State Park

8 *50 mi north of Kodiak Island.*

The 46,000-acre Shuyak Island State Park is one of the newest (and most overlooked) units in the state parks system. The park, at the northern end of the Kodiak Archipelago, is accessible only by plane or boat. Its rugged outer coastline is balanced by a more protected system of interconnected bays, channels, and passages that make the park a favorite with sea-kayakers. It also has excellent wildlife viewing, especially for seabirds and sea mammals, and top-notch sportfishing for salmon. Wildlife ranges from Sitka black-tailed deer and brown bears to sea otters, sea lions, bald eagles, puffins, and whales. The park has four public-use cabins but no developed campgrounds; limited hiking trails pass through old-growth coastal rain forest. ✉ *Alaska State Parks, Kodiak District Office, 1400 Abercrombie Dr., Kodiak 99615* ☎ *907/486–6339* 🌐 *www.alaskastateparks.org.*

Where to Stay

¢ **Alaska State Parks Cabins.** Alaska State Parks maintains four recreational public-use cabins on Shuyak Island. All are accessible by boat or plane only. The cabins may be rented for up to seven days and hold up to eight people. Each has a woodstove, propane lights, hot plate, four bunks, outside shower and wash area, cooking utensils, and pit toilets. You can make reservations up to six months in advance. ✉ *Alaska State Parks, Kodiak District Office, 1400 Abercrombie Dr., Kodiak 99615* ☎ *907/486–6339, 907/269–8400 DNR* *907/486–3320* *DNR Public Information Center, 550 W. 7th Ave., Suite 1260, Anchorage 99501* 🌐 *www.alaskastateparks.org* *4 cabins* *MC, V.*

¢ **Alaska State Parks Campgrounds.** The state has three road-accessible campgrounds (Ft. Abercrombie, Buskin River, and Pasagshak) on Kodiak Island, with a total of 48 tent sites. All have toilets, drinking water, and fishing; two have nearby hiking trails. Camping at Pasagshak is free; the campgrounds at Fort Abercrombie and Buskin River charge $10–$15 a night. Camping limits are 15 consecutive nights at Buskin River and Pasagshak, seven nights at Fort Abercrombie. *Portable toilets, drinking water, bear boxes, picnic tables* *48 tent sites* ✉ *Alaska State Parks, Kodiak District Office, 1400 Abercrombie Dr., Kodiak 99615* ☎ *907/486–6339* *907/486–3320* *Reservations not accepted* *$10* *No credit cards.*

Sports, the Outdoors & Guided Tours

For those new to the region or the sport of kayaking, companies based in Kodiak lead trips to local coastal areas, including Shuyak Island. Besides exploring the coastal land- and seascape, participants will have a chance to see a variety of birds and marine mammals, including whales.

SEA KAYAKING & WILDLIFE VIEWING **Mythos Expeditions** (☎ 907/486–5536 or 907/486–1771 🌐 www.thewildcoast.com) organizes trips both in the Kodiak area and along the Katmai coast. **Orcas Unlimited Charters of Kodiak** (☎ 907/654–1979 🌐 www.orcasunlimited.com) offers tours, wildlife viewing, and photography trips throughout the Kodiak Archipelago.

Aleutian Islands

The Aleutians begin 540 mi southwest of Anchorage and stretch more than 1,000 mi.

Separating the North Pacific Ocean from the Bering Sea, the Aleutian Islands (also called the Chain) stretch from the Alaska Peninsula in a southwesterly arc toward Japan. The distance from the point nearest the Alaska mainland, Unimak Island, to the most distant island, Attu, is more than 1,000 mi. This volcanic, treeless archipelago consists of about 20 large islands and several hundred smaller ones. The Aleutian Islands and surrounding coastal waters make up one of the most biologically rich areas in Alaska, harboring abundant seabird, marine mammal, and fish populations.

Before the Russians arrived in the mid-1700s, the islands were dotted with Aleut villages. Today's communities include **Nikolski,** on Umnak Island; **Atka,** on Atka Island; and **Cold Bay,** at the peninsula's tip. The hardy Aleuts work at commercial fishing or in canneries and as expert guides for those who hunt and fish. The settlements are quite small, and accommodations are scarce.

Visitors aren't allowed on Shemya Island, which has a remote U.S. Air Force base, without special permission. Because of downsizing, the military has closed its Adak operation, and the base's infrastructure provides the core infrastructure for what now is a small coastal community and commercial fishing port.

❾ **Unalaska/Dutch Harbor,** are by far the most populous destinations in the Aleutian Islands. Sometimes called "the Crossroads of the Aleutians," these twin cities are among Alaska's most remote communities. Usually referred to simply as Unalaska/Dutch Harbor; they're connected by a bridge that spans a narrow channel between Unalaska and Amaknak Islands. (Locals playfully call the span "The Bridge to the Other Side.") Despite the often-harsh weather—this region is known as the "Cradle of Storms" for good reason—the Aleut people and their ancestors have occupied these islands and others in the Aleutian Chain for up to thousands of years This is the region's tourism center. The Japanese bombed Dutch Harbor during World War II, and you can still see concrete bunkers, gun batteries, and a partially sunken ship left over from the war. In addition to military sites, you'll find a hotel and restaurants that rival those on Alaska's mainland, plus guided adventure tours.

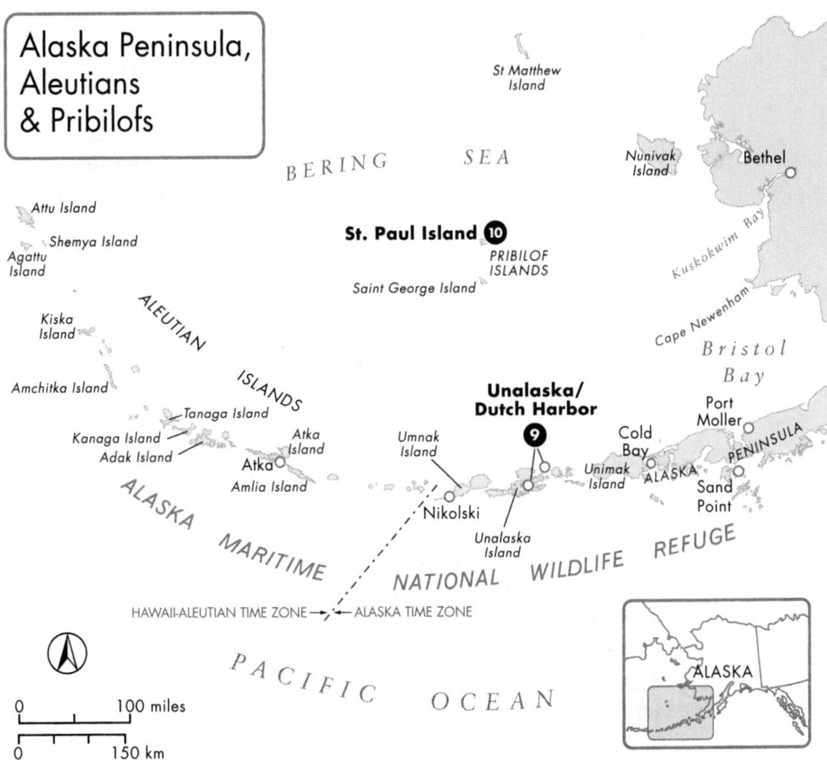

Where to Stay & Eat

★ $$$ **Grand Aleutian Hotel.** An airy three-story atrium lobby with a large stone fireplace conjures images of a Swiss chalet. Rooms have views of either Margaret Bay or Unalaska Bay. Each lushly carpeted, brightly lighted room is decorated with Alaskan artwork and is equipped with full bath, hair dryer, extra vanity and sink, and in-room coffeemaker. The Chart Room Restaurant and Lounge ($$–$$$$) specializes in Pacific Rim cuisine with locally caught seafood and features a seafood buffet every Wednesday night and an elaborate Sunday brunch, year-round. Barbecues are scheduled on Friday nights in summer, on the deck overlooking Margaret Bay. For more informal dining, there's the Margaret Bay Café. Guided activities include bird-watching, cultural tours, archaeological digs, marine wildlife tours, photography, and fishing. ✉ *498 Salmon Way, Box 921169, Dutch Harbor 99692-1169* ☎ *907/581–3844 or 866/581–3844* 🌐 *www.grandaleutian.com* *112 rooms, 2 suites* *2 restaurants, cable TV, fishing, bar, Internet, meeting rooms, airport shuttle, travel services, some pets allowed, no-smoking rooms; no a/c* 💳 *AE, D, DC, MC, V.*

$ **Grand Aleutian Hotel and Unisea Inn.** For travelers on a budget, this hotel on the water has clean, spartan rooms; try to book a room with a view of the small-boat harbor. Pizza, burgers, and sandwiches are served in the Unisea Inn Sports Bar and Grill ($–$$). Sit back and watch satellite broadcasts of spectator sports or try your hand at darts, pool, or video games. Local bands play Top 40 or country music. *185 Gilman Rd., Box 921169, Dutch Harbor 99692 907/581–1325, 866/581–3844 reservations 25 rooms Restaurant, cable TV, hair salon, sports bar, Internet, airport shuttle, travel services, no-smoking rooms; no a/c AE, D, DC, MC, V.*

TAKE THE HIGHWAY

The Alaska Marine Highway System, that is. This much-loved form of Alaskan transport is best known for its routes along the Inside Passage. In summer these ferries also depart from Homer, in South Central, and pass by Kodiak on the way to Dutch Harbor. What an unforgettable way to see Southwest's mysterious landscape (www.ferryalaska.com).

Sports, the Outdoors & Guided Tours

OUTDOOR ADVENTURING **Grand Aleutian Hotel Tours** (800/891–1194 www.grandaleutian.com) offers outdoors activities, ranging from birding to wildlife photography, halibut and salmon fishing, and tours of cultural sites; make arrangements through the hotel.

SPORTFISHING & BIRDING **Volcano Bay Adventures** (907/581–3414 www.volcano-bay.com) has a fish camp at seldom-visited Volcano Bay, with guided fishing for four species of salmon. The company will also lead bird-watching tours, upon request.

Pribilof Islands

200 mi north of the Aleutian Islands, 800 mi southwest of Anchorage.

The Pribilof Islands are misty, fog-bound breeding grounds of seabirds and northern fur seals. Five islets make up the Pribilof group, a tiny, green, treeless oasis with rippling belts of lush grass contrasting with red volcanic soil. In early summer seals come home from far Pacific waters to mate, and the larger islands, St. Paul and St. George, are overwhelmed with scenes of frenzied activity. The seals' barks and growls can roll out several miles to sea.

The islands are a 1,600-mi round-trip from Anchorage, over the massive snowy peaks of the Alaska Peninsula and past the rocky islands of the Aleutian chain. This was the supply route for U.S. forces during World War II, when Japan invaded Attu and Kiska islands toward the tip of the chain. During the Bering Sea leg of the flight, a playful pod of whales may be lurking below.

Wildlife watching is what brings nearly all visitors to the Pribilof Islands. Together, St. Paul and St. George islands are seasonal homes to nearly 1 million fur seals (about 80% of them on St. Paul) and nearly 250 species of birds. Some birds migrate here from as far away as Argentina, whereas others are year-round residents. Most spectacular of all is the islands' seabird population: each summer more than 2 million seabirds gather at traditional Pribilof nesting grounds; about 90% of them breed on St. George. The Pribilofs are also home to foxes; sea lions and whales are occasionally spotted off their shores.

For most travelers, it is much easier and more cost-efficient to participate in package tours that arrange air travel from Anchorage, lodging, ground transportation on the islands, and guided activities. If you are planning to visit here, be aware that guest accommodations in the Pribilofs are very limited.

10 Fodor'sChoice ★ At **St. Paul Island,** nature lovers can watch members of the largest northern fur-seal herd in the world and more than 180 varieties of birds. In town, you can visit with local residents; about 500 descendants of Aleut-Russians live here now, in the shadow of the old Russian Orthodox church and the vestiges of Aleut culture. **St. George Island** is home to nearly 2 million nesting seabirds, but it is much less frequently visited, because no organized tours go there and accommodations are limited.

Where to Stay & Eat

Of special interest to birders are the rare vagrant birds of native Asian species, such as the Siberian rubythroat and Eurasian skylark, sometimes blown here by winds.

$$ ✕ **Trident Sea Foods.** This cafeteria-style eatery—the island's only restaurant—serves fish processors as well as visitors to St. Paul Island. Plan your day carefully, because meals are served according to a strict schedule: breakfast 5–6:30, lunch noon–1, and dinner 5–6. ✉ *Downtown St. Paul, 2 blocks from King Eider Hotel* ☎ *907/546–2377* ▭ *No credit cards.*

$$$$ **King Eider Hotel.** More functional than luxurious, this rustic three-story clapboard hotel is filled in summer by tour groups. The original part of this historic landmark dates to the late 1800s; it's been expanded four times since. The hotel has simply furnished rooms, a TV room, reading lounge, and gift shop. If you are traveling on your own, make reservations months in advance, because most rooms are reserved for tours. ✉ *523 Tolstoi St., Box 88, St. Paul 99660* ☎ *907/546–2477, 907/278–2312, 877/424–5637 to make tour reservations* 🌐 *www.alaskabirding.com* *26 rooms, 5 shared baths* *Travel services; no a/c, no room phones, no room TVs, no smoking* ▭ *AE, MC, V.*

$$$$ **St. George Tanaq Hotel.** A national historic landmark, St. George Island's only hotel is a small, rustic building with a dark-wood interior and a mix of modern and vintage furniture. Originally built by the government to house visiting officials, the hotel can accommodate up to 18 guests and is within easy walking distance of fur-seal rookeries. Rooms are sparsely furnished with shared baths. The hotel's shared kitchen includes a stove, a refrigerator, and cooking utensils—necessary, since the island has no restaurant. ✉ *Downtown, Box 939, St. George 99591* ☎ *907/272–9886 or 907/859–2255* 🌐 *www.stgeorgetanaq.com* *10 rooms share 4 baths* *Dining room, cable TV; no a/c, no smoking* ▭ *MC, V.*

7

Sports, the Outdoors & Guided Tours

There is good reason that the Pribilofs are considered a birders' paradise: species seldom, if ever, seen elsewhere in North America may be observed here, including the "Asian vagrants" blown here by westerly winds. Birders can expect to find all manner of shorebirds, waterfowl, and seabirds, including puffins, murres, red- and black-legged kittiwakes, plovers—the list goes on and on. Tour guides will also show visitors the best places to view seals and whales.

BIRDING & SEAL WATCHING Contact **Tanadgusix Village Corporation of St. Paul Island** (✉ 4300 B St., Suite 402, Anchorage 99503 ☎ 907/278–2312 or 877/424–5637 ⊕ www.alaskabirding.com) for St. Paul Island tour information. The owners of **Wilderness Birding Adventures** (☎ 907/694–7442 ⊕ www.wildernessbirding.com) combine birding, hiking, and river rafting in their wilderness adventures.

NORTHWEST & THE ARCTIC

This is a largely roadless region of long, dark, sunless winters and short, bright summers, when the sun provides nearly three months of perpetual daylight in places like Barrow, but only shines around-the-clock for one or two days on points much farther south, just north of the Arctic Circle. It's the land of Eskimos and huge caribou herds and polar bears, a place where people still lead subsistence lifestyles and where native cultural traditions live on. It's also a place of gold rushes past and America's largest oil field as well as a region with many of Alaska's wildest and most remote parklands and one of the country's grandest refuges, the Arctic National Wildlife Refuge.

Nome

⓫ *540 mi northwest of Anchorage.*

More than a century has passed since a great stampede for gold put a speck of wilderness now called Nome on the Alaska map, but gold mining and noisy saloons are still mainstays in this frontier community of 3,700 people on the icy Bering Sea. Mainly a collection of ramshackle houses and low-slung commercial buildings, Nome looks like a vintage gold-mining camp or the neglected set of a Western movie—rawboned, rugged, and somewhat shabby. Cheerful hospitality and colorful history balance the town's somewhat unkempt appearance.

Only 165 mi from the coast of Siberia, Nome is considerably closer to Russia than to either Anchorage or Fairbanks. And though you'll find a local road system, to get to Nome you must either fly or mush a team of sled dogs.

For centuries before Nome gained fame as a gold-boom town, Inupiat Eskimos seasonally inhabited the area in hunting and fishing camps. The Inupiat traditionally led a nomadic lifestyle, moving with the seasons, so no permanent settlement was established at the site until gold was found by white Euro-American prospectors in the late 1890s, though

RICHES OF THE PAST

Nome's golden years began in 1898, when three prospectors–known as the Lucky Swedes–struck rich deposits on Anvil Creek, about 4 mi from what became Nome. Their discovery was followed by the formation of the Cape Nome Mining District. The following summer, even more gold was found on the beaches of Nome. Word spread quickly to the south, and when the Bering Sea ice parted the next spring, ships from Puget Sound (in the Seattle area) arrived in Nome with eager stampeders. An estimated 15,000 people landed in Nome between June and October of 1900, bringing the area's population to more than 20,000. Dozens of gold dredges were hauled into the region to extract the metal from Seward Peninsula sands and gravels; more than 40 are still standing, though most are no longer operable. Among the gold-rush luminaries were Wyatt Earp, the old gunfighter from the O.K. Corral, who mined the gold of Nome by opening a posh saloon; Tex Rickard, the boxing promoter, who operated another Nome saloon; and Rex Beach, the novelist.

The city of Nome was incorporated in 1901, making it Alaska's oldest first-class city, with the oldest continuous school district. The community's heyday lasted only two decades; by the early 1920s the bulk of the region's gold had been mined and only 820 or so people continued to live in Nome. Though the city's boom times ended long ago, gold mining has continued to the present, though nowadays the existing operations are small ones. Visitors are welcome to try their own luck; they can pick up a gold pan at one of Nome's stores and sift through the beach sands along a 2-mi stretch of shoreline east of Nome. Visitors can also contact the **Nome Convention and Visitors Bureau** (see below) for information on tours that feature gold panning.

Christian missionaries had introduced church missions to the region earlier in the century.

Besides being known for its gold-mining origins, Nome's fame is closely tied to the **historic Iditarod Trail.** Some portions of that route were used for centuries by Eskimos and Athabascan Indians residing in Alaska's northwest region. But the Iditarod Trail's heyday was during the Territory's gold-rush era, from the late 1800s through the mid-1920s. Primarily a winter pathway, the trail acted as a transportation and communication corridor that connected mining camps and other settlements. Actually a network of trails, the Iditarod (derived from the Athabascan Indian word *haiditarod,* meaning "a far, distant place") began at the ice-free port of Seward and ended in Nome. Including all its branches, the entire system measured more than 2,000 mi. Through the 1920s, thousands of people traveled the Iditarod Trail; most drove dog teams, but some rode on horse-drawn sleds. Others walked, snowshoed, or even bicycled, usually because they couldn't afford to own or rent a dog team.

Though Nome today is most closely associated with the Iditarod Trail Sled Dog Race, in the early 1900s it was also the site of Alaska's first organized mushing event, the All-Alaska Sweepstakes. From 1908 through 1917, the Nome Kennel Club annually staged a 408-mi sled-dog race from Nome to Candle and back. The race established the reputations of several early-20th-century mushers, including three-time winners Scotty Allan and Leonhard Seppala. Seppala, a Norwegian, would race dogs over a career that spanned 45 years; he would also be a heroic figure in the 1925 "Great Race of Mercy," in which a relay of mushers and their dog teams transported diphtheria anti-toxin serum to Nome to stop what could have been a disastrous outbreak of the disease, then commonly known as the "black death." The 1925 serum run is annually celebrated as part of the Iditarod race.

Besides its gold-discovering founders and famous mushers, Nome is also proud to be the hometown of General James H. Doolittle, the Tokyo raider of World War II. When Doolittle's bombers hit Japan in a daring raid in 1942, the headline in the *Nome Nugget* proudly announced: "NOME TOWN BOY MAKES GOOD!"

A network of 250 mi or so of gravel roads around the town leads to creeks and rivers for gold panning or fishing for trout, salmon, and arctic grayling. You can also see reindeer, bears, foxes, and moose in the wild on the back roads that once connected early mining camps and hamlets. Independent travelers with hardy vehicles should go exploring. **Alaska Cab Garage** (☎ 907/443–2335 or 907/443–2939) rents pickup trucks, Suburbans, minibuses, and vans, both two- and four-wheel drive. **Stampede Car Rentals** (☎ 907/443–3838 or 800/354–4606 🌐 www.aurorainnome.com) rents vans, pickup trucks, and SUVs. Since the sun stays up late in the summer months, drive to the top of **Anvil Mountain,** near Nome, for a panoramic view of the old gold town and the Bering Sea. Be sure to carry mosquito repellent.

For exploring downtown, stop at the **Nome Convention and Visitors Bureau** (✉ 301 Front St. ☎ 907/443–6624, 800/478–1901 in Alaska 📠 907/443–5832 🌐 www.nomealaska.org/vc) for a historic-walking-tour map, a city map, and information on local activities from flightseeing to bird-watching.

Nome's only museum, the **Carrie M. McClain Memorial Museum** showcases the history of the Nome gold rush, from the "Lucky Swedes" discovery in 1898 to Wyatt Earp's arrival in 1899 and the stampede of thousands of people into Nome in 1900. The museum also has exhibits about the Bering Strait Inupiat Eskimos, plus historic photos and stories about the Nome Kennel Club and its All-Alaska Sweepstakes. ✉ *223 Front St.* ☎ *907/443–6630* 🎫 *Free* 🕒 *June–early Sept., daily 9–5:30; early Sept.–May, Tues.–Fri. noon–6.*

Where to Stay & Eat

$–$$$$ ✕ **Milano's Pizzeria.** This Front Street restaurant has a casual but comfortable atmosphere and offers dine-in service as well as take-out. Besides pizzas with a wide assortment of toppings, the pizzeria features Japanese and Italian food. ✉ *110 W. Front St.* ☎ *907/443–2924* 💳 *MC, V.*

★ $–$$$ **Fat Freddie's.** This popular café-style eatery overlooking the Bering Sea serves New York steak and prime rib, plus its notable burgers and seafood. During the Iditarod, many mushers hang out here after completing their grueling trips across Alaska. If you're staying at the Nome Nugget Inn, you can enter directly from the hotel. *50 Front St. 907/443–5899 AE, D, MC, V.*

$–$$$ **Polar Café.** American diner food, from omelets to steak, fills the menu here. Locals like to linger over coffee, making it a good place to eavesdrop on residents discussing area issues, or just to gaze out at the Bering Sea. With its sea views, good prices, and friendly service, it's a great place for early-morning breakfast. *Next to seawall, 205 W. Front St. 907/443–5191 AE, MC, V.*

$$$$ **John Elmore's Grayling on a Fly.** At the site of an early 1900s gold-mining camp, this lodge (formerly known as Camp Bendeleben) sits along the clear-water Niukluk River, about 75 mi northeast of Nome. You can fish for arctic char, grayling, and four species of salmon; other outdoor activities include bird-watching and wildlife photography. The all-inclusive packages include transportation between the lodge and Nome. There is a three-night minimum and rates vary depending on the activities you choose to do. *In summer: Box 1045, Nome 99762 In winter: 9351 Abbott Loop Rd., Anchorage 99507 907/522–6663 www.grayling-on-a-fly.com 3 rooms Dining room, fishing; no a/c, no room phones, no room TVs No credit cards Closed Oct.–May.*

$ **Nome Nugget Inn.** The architecture and decor of the Nugget Inn combine every cliché of the Victorian gold-rush era. Authentic it's not, but fun it is. Outside, a signpost marks the mileage to various points, serious and silly, around the globe. Inside, frontier memorabilia abounds in the lobby and lounge. Rooms are small and clean but not nearly as atmospheric. Arctic tour groups stay here. Fat Freddie's restaurant is conveniently attached to the hotel. *Front St., Box 1470, 99762 907/443–4189 or 877/443–2323 47 rooms Restaurant, cable TV, bar, laundry service, Internet, some pets allowed, no-smoking rooms; no a/c AE, MC, V.*

WORD OF MOUTH

"The more I think about it, the more I like Nome. I think the attraction is that it's so different. I love looking off in the distance and knowing there's nothing but wilderness for hundreds of miles. I've never been anywhere with such a sense of the vast and the remote. The town is funky and friendly. It seems to have a real sense of humor about itself. It is a bit of a rough town, with more than its share of local bars and saloons, but it's also a funky place with lots of character. The Iditarod ends here every March—it's quite an event." —Julie304

¢ **Bureau of Land Management Campground.** BLM manages a free campground at Mile 40 of the Nome-Taylor Highway. The campground, which is a short walk from the highway, has six tent sites, toilet facilities, and nearby fishing. The maximum length of stay is 14 days. The campground has a pit toilet and fire rings for cooking, but the only water is in nearby

Salmon Lake and Pilgrim River; it must be boiled or otherwise treated. *Portable toilets, fire pits, swimming (lake) 6 tent sites Bureau of Land Management, Nome Field Office, Box 925, 99762 907/443–2177 in Nome, 907/474–2231 in Fairbanks, 907/267–1246 in Anchorage, or 800/478–1263 (Alaska only) www.ak.blm.gov Reservations not accepted No credit cards Closed Oct.–Apr.*

Shopping

Nome is one of the best places to buy ivory, because many of the Eskimo carvers from outlying villages come to Nome first to sell their wares to dealers. The **Arctic Trading Post** (Bering and Front Sts. 907/443–2686) has an extensive stock of authentic Eskimo ivory carvings and other Alaskan artwork, jewelry, and books. **Chukotka–Alaska** (514 Lomen 907/443–4128) sells both native Alaskan and Russian artwork and handicrafts as well as books, beads, and furs. The **Maruskiyas of Nome** (907/443–2955) on Front Street specializes in authentic native Alaskan artwork and handicrafts, including ivory, baleen, and jade sculptures, jewelry, dolls, and masks.

Sports, the Outdoors & Guided Tours

LOCAL TOURS **Alaska Airlines Vacations** (800/468–2248 www.alaskaair.com) arranges trips to Nome (such as the "Day in Nome" and "Adventure in Nome" packages), including air travel, hotels, and local tours. Visitors seeking to learn more about Nome and the surrounding region can join former Broadway showman Richard Beneville, who emphasizes Nome's gold rush and Inupiat history of the region in his **Nome Discovery Tours** (Box 2024, Nome 99762 907/443–2814). **Northern Alaska Tour Company** (P.O. Box 82991-W, Fairbanks 99708 800/474–1986 or 907/474–8600 www.alaskasarctic.com) arranges one-day cultural tours to Nome via Fairbanks or Anchorage.

SLED-DOG RACING The famed **Iditarod Trail Sled Dog Race**—the Olympics of sled-dog racing—reaches its culmination in Nome in mid-March. Racers start in Anchorage for a trip of nine days to two weeks. The arrival of the mushers heralds a winter carnival. For dates, starting times, and other information, contact the **Iditarod Trail Committee** (Box 870800, Wasilla 99687 907/376–5155 www.iditarod.com).

Bering Land Bridge National Preserve

12 *100 mi north of Nome.*

The frozen ash and lava of the 2.8-million-acre Bering Land Bridge National Preserve lie between Nome and Kotzebue, immediately south of the Arctic Circle. The Imuruk lava flow is the northernmost flow of major size in the United States, and the paired *maars* (clear volcanic lakes) are a geological rarity.

Of equal interest are the paleontological features of this preserve. Sealed into the permafrost are flora and fauna—bits of twigs and leaves, tiny insects, small mammals, even remnants of woolly mammoths—that flourished here when the Bering Land Bridge linked North America to what is now Russia. Early peoples wandered through this treeless landscape, perhaps following the musk ox, whose descendants still occupy this terrain. A remarkable 250 species of flowering plants thrive in this seemingly barren region, and there are tens of thousands of migrating birds. More than 100 species, including ducks, geese, swans, sandhill cranes, and various shorebirds and songbirds, come here from around the world each spring. You may hear the haunting call of loons on the many clear lakes and lagoons.

The Bering Land Bridge National Preserve has no trails, campgrounds, or other visitor facilities. Access is largely by air taxi, although there is a road north of Nome that passes within walking distance. *National Park Service, Box 220, Nome 99762* *907/443–2522 or 907/442–3890* *www.nps.gov/bela.*

Kotzebue

13 *170 mi northeast of Nome.*

Kotzebue, Alaska's largest Eskimo community, is home to around 3,000 residents. The large majority of its people are Inupiats, who have lived at this site for at least 600 years. Their ties to the region go back thousands of years. For most of that time, the Inupiat were a seminomadic people who followed caribou and other wildlife across the landscape. In addition to caribou, they depended on whales, seals, fish, moose, and a variety of berries and other plants. Besides being talented hunters, the Inupiat were—and still are—skilled craftsmen and artists, known for their rugged gear, ceremonial parkas, Eskimo dolls, caribou skin masks, birch-bark baskets, and whalebone and walrus-ivory carvings.

Built on a 3-mi-long spit of land that juts into Kotzebue Sound, this village lies 33 mi above the Arctic Circle, on Alaska's northwest coast. Before Europeans arrived in the region, the Inupiat name for this locale was Kikiktagruk; that was changed to Kotzebue after German explorer Otto von Kotezbue "discovered" the area in 1818 while sailing for Russia. Nowadays Kotzebue is the region's economic and political hub and headquarters for both the Northwest Arctic Borough and the NANA corporation, one of the 13 regional native corporations formed when Congress settled the Alaskan natives' aboriginal land claims in 1971. The region's other Eskimo villages are much smaller, with populations of 90 to 700 people.

Just as their ancestors did, modern Inupiats depend heavily on subsistence harvesting; household economies are generally a mix of hunting, fishing, gathering, and part-time seasonal jobs. Some residents also fish commercially. This region of the state has few employment opportunities outside of the government and corporation. The biggest private employer is the Red

WELCOME TO KOTZEBUE

Comprised of clusters of weather-bleached little houses and a few public buildings on the gravelly shore of Kotzebue Sound, this village provides you with a glimpse of the way Alaska's Eskimos live today. It was an ancient Eskimo trading center; now it is an example of the modern spirit nudging Alaska's native peoples into the state's mainstream culture without leaving their traditions behind.

Dog Mine. Located on NANA land, Red Dog has the world's largest deposit of zinc and is expected to produce ore for at least 50 years. Local government here, as in many Bush villages, is a blend of tribal government and a more modern borough system. Other facilities and programs include the Maniilaq Health Center, the Northwest Arctic District Correspondence Program, and the University of Alaska Chukchi Campus.

Kotzebue has long, cold winters and short, cool summers. The average low temperature in January is -12°F, and midsummer highs rarely go much higher than the 60s. "We have four seasons—June, July, August, and winter," a tour guide jests. But don't worry about the sometimes chilly weather—the local sightseeing company has snug, bright loaner parkas for visitors on package tours. And there's plenty of light to take in the village and surrounding landscape: the sun doesn't set for 36 days, from June into July. One of summer's highlights is the annual Northwest Native Trade Fair; held each year after the July 4th celebration, it features traditional native games, seal hook throwing contests, and an Eskimo buggy race.

The **NANA Regional Corporation** (Northwest Alaska Native Association; ☎ 907/442–3301 or 800/478–3301 ⊕ www.nana.com) has its headquarters in Kotzebue. It was NANA that built the **Living Museum of the Arctic** (☎ 907/265–4100 or 907/442–3301 ⊕ www.tour-arctic.com or www.nana.com) in 1977 and turned it into one of Alaska's top-rated museums. The museum features cultural and natural-history displays, as well as presentations by local residents. Bleachers face a stage where stories are told, and after the storytelling, a cultural slide show relates the wisdom of the elders, followed by traditional Eskimo singing and dancing and blanket tossing, in which audience members are invited to participate. It may look like a game, but the blanket toss was serious business in the early days, when Eskimo hunters were launched high in the air from blankets of walrus or seal hide to scan the seas for game. You may even be urged to take a turn on the bouncing blanket. The museum is open when tour groups are in town or by special arrangement. Admission to the museum is free, but a fee is charged for cultural programs. After attending programs at the museum, stop at the **Gift Shop** (☎ 907/442–2500 or 800/478–1110) in the Northwest Arctic Borough building. The store features native arts and crafts from throughout the Arctic region.

Fodor'sChoice ★

Additional information about Kotzebue and the surrounding region can be obtained through the **Northwest Arctic Borough** (Box 1110, Kotzebue 99752 ☎ 907/442–2500 or 800/478–1110)

If you're hiking the wildflower-carpeted tundra around Kotzebue, you are entering a "living museum" dedicated to **permafrost**, the permanently frozen ground that lies just a few inches below the spongy tundra. Even Kotzebue's 6,000-foot airport runway is built on permafrost—with a 6-inch insulating

GETTING TO KOTZEBUE

Alaska Airlines offers regular flights between Anchorage and Kotzebue. Check out www.alaskaair.com for more details.

layer between the frozen ground and the airfield surface to ensure that landings are smooth.

Kotzebue serves as a gateway for three exceptional national **wilderness areas:** Cape Krusenstern National Monument, Kobuk Valley National Park, and Noatak National Preserve. North and east of Kotzebue is the **Brooks Range,** one of Alaska's great mountain ranges. Stretching across the state, much of the range is protected by Gates of the Arctic National Park and Preserve and the Arctic National Wildlife Refuge.

Where to Stay & Eat

¢–$$$$ ✕ **Kotzebue Pizza House.** Although this cozy pizza parlor serves pizza and Chinese food, locals especially tout the burgers, which are said to be among the best in the state. ✉ *2nd Ave. and Bison St.* ☎ *907/442–3432* ▭ *AE, MC, V.*

$$$ ✕🏨 **Nullagvik Hotel.** This hotel overlooking Kotzebue Sound is built on pilings driven into the ground because the heat of the building would melt the underlying permafrost and cause the hotel to sink. Images of Eskimo life adorn the spacious, modern rooms. Public areas on the second and third floors provide picture-window views of the bay. Usually open only in the summer, the hotel's Niggivik Restaurant ($–$$$$) serves a variety of dishes, from reindeer sausage and sourdough pancakes to New York steak and fresh, locally harvested Arctic fish. ✉ *308 Shore Ave., Box 336, 99752* ☎ *907/442–3331* 🌐 *www.nullagvik.com* *75 rooms* *Restaurant, cable TV, meeting room, gift shop, travel services, some pets allowed, no-smoking rooms; no a/c* ▭ *AE, D, DC, MC, V.*

7

Cape Krusenstern National Monument

⓮ *10 mi north of Kotzebue.*

Just north of Kotzebue, the 560,000-acre Cape Krusenstern National Monument has important cultural and archaeological value. This is a coastal parkland, with an extraordinary series of beach ridges built up by storms over a period of at least 5,000 years. Almost every ridge—more than 100 in all—contains artifacts of different human occupants, representing every known Arctic Eskimo culture in North America. The present Eskimo occupants, whose culture dates back some 1,400 years, use the fish, seals, caribou, and birds of this region for food and raw materials much as their ancestors did. They are also closely involved in the archaeological digs in the park that are unearthing part of their own history.

Cape Krusenstern is a starkly beautiful Arctic land shaped by ice, wind, and sea. Its low, rolling gray-white hills scalloped with light-green tundra attract hikers and backpackers, and kayakers sometimes paddle its coastline. The monument is valuable also for human and historical reasons, and it should be experienced as a marvelous living museum. **■ TIP→ It's possible to camp in the park, but be mindful, as are the native people when they pitch their white canvas tents for summer fishing, that the shoreline is subject to fierce winds. Both grizzlies and polar bears patrol the beaches in search of food, so clean camping is a must.**

Check with the National Park Service in Kotzebue about hiring a local guide to the monument, which has no visitor facilities; it's accessible by air taxi and by boat from Kotzebue. *National Park Service, Box 1029, Kotzebue 99752* *907/442–3890* *www.nps.gov/cakr.*

Kobuk Valley National Park

15 *65 mi east of Kotzebue.*

Kobuk Valley National Park lies entirely north of the Arctic Circle, along the southern edge of the Brooks Range. Its 1.14 million acres contain remarkable inland deserts and the **Great Kobuk Sand Dunes** and are home to interesting relict (remnants of otherwise extinct) flora. The park is bisected by the west-flowing **Kobuk River,** a 347-mi-long stream born in the foothills of the western Brooks Range. The Kobuk, whose native name means "big river," has been a major transportation and trade route for centuries. Besides the Kobuk, this park contains two smaller streams that provide delightful river running, the Ambler and the Salmon. These brilliantly clear rivers are accessible by wheeled plane, and each provides a good week's worth of pleasure (if the weather cooperates).

Another place of special interest is the **Onion Portage.** Human occupation here dates back 12,500 years; herds of caribou that fed the Woodland Eskimo centuries ago are still hunted at Onion Portage by present-day Eskimo residents of the region.

Kobuk Valley National Park is, like most other Alaska parks, undeveloped wilderness with no visitor facilities. If you come prepared, it can be a good place for backpacking and river trips. In nearby Kotzebue, the National Park Service has a visitor center where staff can provide tips for travel into the park. The villages of Kobuk and Kiana both provide immediate take-off points and have air service. *National Park Service, Box 1029, Kotzebue 99752* *907/442–3890* *www.nps.gov/kova.*

Noatak National Preserve

16 *20 mi northeast of Kotzebue.*

Adjacent to Gates of the Arctic National Park and Preserve, the 6.5-million-acre Noatak National Preserve encompasses much of the basin of the **Noatak River.** This is the largest mountain-ringed river basin in the United States that is still relatively undeveloped; part of it is designated by the National Park Service as a Wild and Scenic River. Along its 425-mi course, this river carves out the "Grand Canyon of the Noatak," so-called by the NPS, which serves as a migration route between Arctic and sub-Arctic ecosystems. Its importance to wildlife and plants has resulted in this parkland's designation as an International Biosphere Reserve.

The Noatak River also serves as a natural highway for humans and offers particular pleasures to river runners, with inviting tundra to camp on and the Poktovik Mountains and the Igichuk Hills nearby for good hiking. Birding can be exceptional: horned grebes, gyrfalcons, golden eagles, parasitic jaegers, owls, terns, and loons are among the species you may see. You may also observe grizzly bears, Dall sheep, wolves, caribou, or lynx. As with other parks and preserves in this northwest corner of Alaska, no visitor facilities are available and you are expected to be self-sufficient. *National Park Service, Box 1029, Kotzebue 99752* *907/442–3890* *www.nps.gov/noat.*

Gates of the Arctic National Park & Preserve

★ 17 *180 mi east of Kotzebue.*

Gates of the Arctic National Park & Preserve is entirely north of the Arctic Circle, in the center of the Brooks Range; at 8.2 million acres, it's the size of four Yellowstones. This is parkland on a scale suitable to the country. It includes the **Endicott Mountains** to the east and the **Schwatka Mountains** to the southwest, with the **Arrigetch Peaks** in between. To the north lies a sampling of the Arctic foothills, with their colorful tilted sediments and pale green tundra. Lovely lakes are cupped in the mountains and in the tundra.

This landscape, the ultimate wilderness, captured the heart of Arctic explorer and conservationist Robert Marshall in the 1930s. Accompanied by local residents, Marshall explored much of the region now included within Gates and named many of its features, including Frigid Crag and Boreal Mountain, two peaks on either side of the North Fork Koyukuk River. These were the original "gates" for which the park is named.

Arrigetch is an Eskimo word meaning "fingers of a hand outstretched," which aptly describes the immensely steep and smooth granite peaks here.

Wildlife known to inhabit the park include barren-ground caribou, grizzlies, wolves, moose, Dall sheep, wolverines, and smaller mammals and birds. The communities of Bettles and Anaktuvuk Pass are access points for Gates of the Arctic, which has no developed trails, campgrounds, or other visitor facilities (though there is a wilderness lodge on private land within the park). You can fly into Bettles commercially and charter an air taxi into the park or hike directly out of Anaktuvuk Pass. The Park Service has rangers stationed in both Bettles and Anaktuvuk Pass, who can provide information for those entering the wilderness. *National Park Service, 201 1st Ave., Fairbanks 99701* *907/457–5752, 907/692–5494 (in Bettles), or 907/661–3520 (Anaktuvuk Pass)* *www.nps.gov/gaar.*

Where to Stay

★ $$$$ **Peace of Selby Wilderness.** On Selby/Narvak Lakes within Gates of the Arctic National Park, Peace of Selby is perfectly situated for wilderness adventures. Crafted from white spruce, the main lodge includes a kitchen, small library, bathroom, and loft. Meals, included with some rates, are cooked with fresh vegetables, fruits, and meats. If you want to rough it, you can bring along your sleeping bags and cook your own meals in one of four remote rustic log cabins, which can accommodate up to four people each. The owners also organize custom guided expeditions. Activities include hiking, fishing, wildlife-viewing and -photographing, river-floating, and flightseeing. *Box 86, Manley Hot Springs 99756 907/672–3206 www.alaskawilderness.net 1 room in lodge, 4 cabins Dining room, boating, fishing, hiking, cross-country skiing, library; no a/c, no room phones, no room TVs No credit cards Closed mid-Sept.–mid-June, except for specially arranged expeditions Mar.–Apr.*

Sports, the Outdoors & Guided Tours

OUTDOOR ADVENTURING **Arctic Treks** (Box 73452, Fairbanks 99707 907/455–6522 www.arctictreksadventures.com) guides wilderness hikes and backpacking expeditions, sometimes combined with river trips, in both Gates of the Arctic and the Arctic National Wildlife Refuge. Contact **Sourdough Outfitters** (Box 26066, Bettles Field 99726 907/692–5252 www.sourdoughoutfitters.com) for summer backpacking and river trips (from family float trips to wild-rapid running and fishing expeditions) and winter dogsled trips in the Brooks Range.

Barrow

18 *330 mi northeast of Kotzebue.*

The northernmost community in the United States, Barrow sits 1,300 mi south of the North Pole. The village is 10 mi south of the Beaufort Sea and Point Barrow, from which it takes its name. Point Barrow, in turn, was named in 1825 by British Capt. Beechey, who'd been ordered by the British navy to map the continent's northern coastline. Beechey wished to honor Sir John Barrow, a member of the British Admiralty. As is often the rule, the traditional indigenous name is much more locally relevant and reflects an aspect of the landscape. The region's Inupiat Eskimos knew the site as Ukpeagvik, or "place where owls are hunted." Even today, many snowy owls nest in the tundra outside Barrow each summer, though they're not hunted as they once were: they are now protected by federal law.

About 4,400 people inhabit Barrow today, making it easily the largest community on the North Slope. Nearly two-thirds of the residents are Inupiat Eskimos. Though they remain deeply rooted in their Inupiat heritage, Barrow's residents have adopted a modern lifestyle. Homes are heated by natural gas taken from nearby gas fields, and the community is served by most modern conveniences, including a public-radio station and cable TV and Internet access. The community recreation center has a gymnasium, racquetball courts, weight room, and sauna and hosts a variety of social events, from dances to basketball tournaments. In Barrow, as in much of Bush Alaska, basketball is the favored sport, played year-round by people of all ages.

Barrow is the economic and administrative center of the **North Slope Borough,** which encompasses more than 88,000 square mi, making it the world's largest municipal government (in terms of area). The village is also headquarters of the **Arctic Slope Regional Corporation,** formed in 1971 through the Alaska Native Claims Settlement Act (ANCSA), as well as the Ukpeagvik Inupiat Corporation, which economically and po-

BARROW'S RICHNESS IN SKY, EARTH & SEA

In recent years, increasing numbers of people have come to experience the local culture, wildlife, and far-north climatic extremes that define Barrow. This is truly the land of the midnight sun. From mid-May until August, the sun doesn't set for over 80 days. (Conversely, the sun disappears during the dead of winter from November through January—this is called the polar winter.) Despite the season's unending daylight, summertime temperatures can be brisk—you should even be prepared for snow flurries. Nevertheless, midsummer temperatures can occasionally reach the 60s and low 70s. Despite the region's abundant wetlands, Barrow—and the North Slope in general—has a desert climate, with annual precipitation averaging less than 10 inches.

Archaeological evidence from more than a dozen nearby ancient "dwelling mounds" suggests that people have inhabited this area for at least the past 1,500 years. A highlight of those mounds is **Mound 44,** where the frozen body of a 500-year-old Eskimo was discovered. Scientists have been studying her remains to learn more about Eskimo life and culture before encounters with outsiders. Described as members of the **Birnirk culture,** these early residents depended heavily on marine mammals, a tradition that continues to this day. Combining modern technology with traditional knowledge, Barrow's whaling crews annually hunt for the bowhead whales that migrate through Arctic waters each spring and fall. If the whalers are successful in their springtime hunts, they share muktuk—whale meat—with other members of the village and celebrate their good fortune with a festival called **Nalukataq.** Besides whales, residents depend on harvests of seals, walrus, caribou, waterfowl, grayling, and whitefish.

7

litically represents the community of Barrow. Several village councils are also headquartered in the town.

Non-natives established a presence at Barrow in the early 1880s, when the U.S. Army built a research station here. Drawn to the area by the Beaufort Sea's abundant whales, commercial whalers established the **Cape Smythe Whaling and Trading Station** in 1893; a cabin from that operation still stands, and is the oldest frame building in Alaska's Arctic. The station is now listed on the National Register of Historic Places (as are the Birnirk dwelling mounds).

By the early 1900s both a Presbyterian church and U.S. post office had been established. Recalling those days, an Inupiat elder named Alfred Hopson once recounted that the famed Norwegian explorer Vilhjalmur Stefansson used the church as a base for studies of local residents, including measurements of their head sizes. From then on, Stefansson was known locally as the "head measurer." Oil and gas exploration later brought more whites from the lower 48 to the area; even more came as schools and other government agencies took root in the region. Hopson, too, played a role in the area's development, as he funneled millions of dollars in tax revenues into road building, sanitation and water services, and heath-care services.

Barrow has opened its annual springtime whale festival to outsiders, and there are several historic sites, including a military installation, points of native cultural importance, and a famous crash site. The Barrow airport is where you'll find the **Will Rogers and Wiley Post Monument,** marking the 1935 crash of the American humorist and his pilot 15 mi south of town.

Drawn by both cultural and natural attractions, visitors in Barrow usually arrive on a one- or two-day tour with Alaska Airlines, the only national carrier serving the area. Packages include a bus tour of the town's dusty roads and major sights. ■ **TIP→ Though Barrow's residents invite visitors to attend their annual whale festival in the spring, summer is the ideal time to survey the town and its historic sites.**

Where to Stay & Eat

★ **$–$$$$** ✕ **Pepe's North of the Border.** The warmth of Pepe's will make you forget that you're in the middle of the Arctic tundra. Murals depicting Mexican village scenes highlight the Mission-style decor, and an extensive selection of Mexican dishes, from soft tacos to burritos and flautas, makes this restaurant a favorite of locals and visitors alike. The restaurant's menu is also spiced up with dishes that feature Alaskan seafood and, at the high end of things, steak and lobster. Dinner at Pepe's is surprisingly refined for being on the very fringe of civilization. ✉ *1204 Agvik St., next to Top of the World Hotel* ☎ *907/852–8200* ▭ *DC, MC, V.*

$$–$$$ ✕ **Ken's Restaurant.** Burgers, steaks, seafood, and Chinese food are the staples at this family restaurant, which has daily specials and the best prices in town. Breakfast is served throughout the day. ✉ *1721 Ogrook St., above airport terminal Bldg.* ☎ *907/852–8888* ▭ *MC, V.*

★ **$$$** 🏨 **Top of the World Hotel.** Built in 1974, this refurbished hotel on the shore of the Arctic Ocean has just about every imaginable modern convenience, including cable TV and Internet access. Still, it retains a frontier atmosphere; the lobby, for example, has one complete stuffed polar bear and the mounted head of another. You can mingle in the lobby or in front of the community television. Modern, spacious rooms have sitting areas; ask for a room with an ocean view. ✉ *1200 Agviq St., Box 189, 99723* ☎ *907/852–3900, 800/882–8478, 800/478–8520 in Alaska* *44 rooms* *Some refrigerators, cable TV, some in-room data ports, Internet; no a/c, no smoking* ▭ *AE, D, DC, MC, V.*

$ 🏨 **Barrow Airport Inn.** As the name suggests, this modern and well-appointed property is convenient to the airport (it's only two blocks away). ✉ *1815 Momegana St., Box 933, 99723* ☎ *907/852–2525 or 800/375–2527 in Alaska only* *15 rooms* *Some kitchenettes, microwaves, refrigerators, cable TV, Internet, travel services, no-smoking rooms; no a/c* ▭ *AE, DC, MC, V* *CP.*

Shopping

The AC Value Center, or, as it's known locally, **Stuaqpak** ("Big Store"; ✉ 4725 Ahkovak St. ☎ 907/852–6711 ⊕ www.alaskacommercial.com), is the largest store in town. Though it mainly sells groceries, the

CLOSE UP

The Pipeline Highway

STRETCHING 800 MI across the 49th state, the trans-Alaska pipeline is both an engineering marvel and a reminder of Alaska's economic dependence on oil and gas production. It begins at Prudhoe Bay, along the Arctic Ocean, and snakes its way south to the port town of Valdez, on the shores of Prince William Sound. Along the way, the pipeline carries crude oil across three mountain ranges, 34 major rivers—including the mighty Yukon—and hundreds of smaller creeks. Though much of it is buried, half of the pipeline runs aboveground, where it is held by 78,000 vertical supports. You can see sections along some of Alaska's major roadways, most notably the Dalton.

Plenty of hardy, adventurous visitors are choosing to "do the Dalton," a 414-mi gravel highway that connects Interior Alaska to the oilfields at Prudhoe Bay. Alaska's northernmost highway, the Dalton was built in the 1970s, during the state's oil-boom days, so that trucks could haul supplies to Prudhoe and pipeline construction camps in Alaska's northern reaches.

Thousands of 18-wheelers still drive the Dalton each year, but they now share it with sightseers, anglers, and other travelers. That doesn't mean the Dalton has become an easy drive. It's narrow, often winding, and has several steep grades. Sections may be heavily potholed, and its coarse gravel is easily kicked up into headlights and windshields by fast-moving trucks. Besides being tough on vehicles, the road has few visitor facilities. And with tow-truck charges of up to $5 per mi (both coming and going), a vehicle breakdown can cost hundreds of dollars even before repairs. Public access ends at Deadhorse.

The origins of the Haul Road and trans-Alaska pipeline can be traced to 1968, when oil companies announced the discovery of a major field at Prudhoe Bay. A lawsuit by environmental groups temporarily halted work on the proposed pipeline across Alaska, but congressional legislation authorizing its construction was signed into law in November 1973. Things moved quickly after that. Work on the Haul Road began the following April and was finished in five months. Forty-eight inches wide and up to 60 feet long, the first pipes were installed in March 1975; 27 months later, oil began moving down the pipeline and reached Valdez on July 28, 1977. Four days later, the *ARCO Juneau* headed south with the first tanker load of Prudhoe Bay crude.

Since it began operation, the pipeline has transported more than 14 billion barrels (approximately 600 billion gallons) of oil across Alaska. At its peak in 1988, 2.14 million barrels of oil flowed through the pipeline in a day's time. Nowadays the daily flow has sunk below 1 million barrels.

The main catastrophic event connected to the trans-Alaska pipeline project was the 1989 *Exxon Valdez* oil spill, in which 270,000 barrels of oil oozed from the damaged tanker into Prince William Sound. The aging pipeline presents many hazards to the environment. In early 2006, a leaking pipeline led to a spill of thousands of gallons of oil. Additional leaks discovered that summer led to temporary closures, diminishing the flow substantially for several weeks.

store also stocks Eskimo crafts made by locals, including furs, parkas, mukluks, and ceremonial masks.

Sports, the Outdoors & Guided Tours

CULTURAL TOURS From mid-May through September you can take an **Alaska Airlines Vacations** (☎ 800/468–2248 🌐 vacations.alaskaair.com/Alaska/Barrow/Barrow-Arctic-Tours.asp) package from Anchorage or Fairbanks to "the top of the world" and get a chance to learn about the natural and cultural history of the area. Year-round tours are organized through **Tundra Tours** (☎ 907/852–3900). Offered from mid-September through mid-May, the winter tours feature visits to a traditional hunting camp, the whaling station, the DEWS site, and opportunities to visit Point Barrow and watch northern lights. The summer program is highlighted by visits to local historic sites and opportunities to witness traditional cultural activities such as Eskimo dances, sewing demonstrations, and the blanket toss. In both winter and summer, visitors can purchase locally made Inupiat arts and crafts.

Prudhoe Bay

 *250 mi southeast of Barrow.*

Most towns have museums that chronicle local history and achievements. Deadhorse is the town anchoring life along Prudhoe Bay, but it could also serve as a museum dedicated to humankind's hunt for energy and its ability to adapt to harsh conditions.

The costly, much-publicized Arctic oil and gas project is complex and varied. One-day tours with the Arctic Caribou Inn explore the tundra terrain from oil pipes to sandpipers. Along with chances to spot caribou, wildflowers, and an unusual stand of willow trees at the edge of the Arctic Ocean, the field tour surveys oil wells, stations, and oil-company residential complexes—small cities themselves. Your guide will discuss the multimillion-dollar research programs aimed at preserving the region's ecology and point out special tundra vehicles known as Rollagons, whose great weight is distributed to diminish their impact on delicate terrain.

In the past, individual travelers rarely turned up in Deadhorse and Prudhoe Bay. But now that the Dalton Highway has been opened as far north as Deadhorse, adventurous independent travelers are finding their way north. Still, most people traveling to Deadhorse either work here or come on a tour with one of Alaska's airlines or bus-tour operators. And even those who travel here on their own must join a guided tour (arranged through the Arctic Caribou Inn) if they wish to cross the oil fields to get to the Arctic Ocean. You'll find no restaurants here, though meals can sometimes be arranged through the Prudhoe Bay Hotel.

Where to Stay

$$ **Arctic Caribou Inn.** Located near the end of the Haul Road, this simple hotel is open only from May through September. It is the center of visitor activity at Deadhorse during the summer months, with a cafeteria-style restaurant, gift shop, and visitor center, plus the only tours offered to nearby Prudhoe Bay. *Pouch 340111, Prudhoe Bay 99734*

877/659–2368 www.arcticcaribouinn.com 50 rooms Restaurant, shop AE, MC, V.

$$ **Prudhoe Bay Hotel.** Located near the end of the road at Deadhorse, this hotel is primarily intended for the workers employed in the Prudhoe Bay oil-field complex, but tourists are also welcome. Some of the rooms are bare-bones dormitory-style rooms, whereas others are slightly more upscale, with TVs and phones. All rooms share baths. The hotel includes a cafeteria/dining hall with specific hours for breakfast, lunch, and dinner; meals are buffet style. Food and drinks can be purchased from vending machines around the clock. The hotel is also just a short hop from Deadhorse's airport. *Pouch 340004, Prudhoe Bay 99734 907/659–2449 www.prudhoebayhotel.com 170 rooms Cafeteria, shop, car rental; no a/c, no phones in some rooms, no TV in some rooms AE, MC, V.*

ANOTHER SPILL

In early 2006 a punctured pipe leaked 200,000 gallons of crude oil across the Prudhoe Bay tundra. It was the North Slope's largest oil spill to date. For the sake of comparison, the 1989 *Exxon Valdez* disaster in South Central spilled 11 million gallons across that area's precious coastline.

Arctic National Wildlife Refuge

★ 20 *70 mi southeast of Prudhoe Bay.*

The 18-million-acre Arctic National Wildlife Refuge, lying wholly above the Arctic Circle, is administered by the U.S. Fish and Wildlife Service and contains the only protected Arctic coastal lands in the United States (and some of the very few protected in the world), as well as millions of acres of mountains and alpine tundra, in the easternmost portion of the Brooks Range.

This is the home of one of the greatest remaining groups of caribou in the world, the **Porcupine Caribou Herd.** The herd, numbering around 123,000, is unmindful of international boundaries and migrates back and forth across Arctic lands into Canada, flowing like a wide river across the expansive coastal plain, through U-shape valleys and alpine meadows, and over high mountain passes. The refuge's coastal areas also serve as critical denning grounds for polar bears, which spend most of their year on the Arctic Ocean's pack ice. Other residents here are grizzly bears, Dall sheep, wolves, musk ox, and dozens of varieties of birds, from snowy owls to geese and tiny songbirds. The refuge's northern areas host legions of breeding waterfowl and shorebirds each summer. As in many of Alaska's more remote parks and refuges, there are no roads here, and no developed trails, campgrounds, or other visitor facilities. This is a place to experience true wilderness—and to walk with care, for the plants are fragile and the ground can be soft and wet in summer. You can expect snow to sift over the land in almost any season and should anticipate subfreezing temperatures even in summer, particularly in the mountains. Many of the refuge's clear-flowing rivers are runnable, and tundra lakes are suitable for base camps (a Kaktovik or Fort Yukon air taxi can drop you off and pick you up). The hiking is worth it; upon scrambling up a ridge, you'll look out upon a wilderness that seems to stretch forever. ✉ *Refuge Manager, Arctic National Wildlife Refuge, 101 12th Ave., Room 236, Box 20, Fairbanks 99701* ☎ *907/456–0250 or 800/362–4546* 🌐 *arctic.fws.gov.*

Sports, the Outdoors & Guided Tours

EXPERT GUIDES **Arctic Treks** (☎ 907/455–6522 🌐 www.arctictreksadventures.com) guides wilderness hikes and backpacking expeditions in both Gates of the Arctic and the Arctic National Wildlife Refuge. The owners of **Wilderness Birding Adventures** (☎ 907/694–7442 🌐 www.wildernessbirding.com) are both experienced river runners and expert birders.

> **RAGING DEBATE**
>
> 2006 saw plenty of heated discussion about whether to open ANWR to drilling. Opponents, including many Interior native groups and countless environmentalists, vow to protect this great refuge. Supporters (including Ted Stevens) say that with responsible drilling will come an estimated 10 billion barrels of oil that will help to curb the country's dependence on foreign oil.

THE BUSH ESSENTIALS

Transportation

BY AIR

Alaska Airlines is among the major carriers serving Alaska from Seattle, and it flies within Alaska to most major communities. Peninsula Airways serves the communities on the Alaskan Peninsula, the Aleutian and Pribilof islands, and parts of the Interior and northwest.

Many Anchorage and Fairbanks air taxis serve the Bush in addition to Bush-based carriers such as Bering Air, which also offers local flightseeing tours and, weather and politics permitting, specially arranged charter flights to Provideniya, on the Siberian coast across the Bering Strait. Frontier Flying Service serves the Interior and the Bering and Arctic coasts. Wright Air Service flies throughout the Interior and Arctic Alaska.

Besides flights on those carriers, information about certified air-taxi operations is available from the Federal Aviation Administration. Individual parks and Alaska Public Lands Information centers also can supply lists of reputable air-taxi services. Make your reservations in advance, and plan for the unexpected; weather can delay a scheduled pickup for days.

ℹ **Alaska Airlines** ☎ 800/426-0333 🌐 www.alaskaair.com. **Alaska Public Lands Information Center** ✉ 250 Cushman St., Suite 1A, Fairbanks 99701 ☎ 866/869-6887 or 907/456-0527 🌐 www.nps.gov/aplic. **Bering Air** 📫 Box 1650, Nome 99762 ☎ 907/443-5464, 800/478-5422 in Alaska, 907/443-5620 Russian desk 🌐 www.beringair.com. **Federal Aviation Administration** ✉ Flight Standards District Office, 4510 W. International Airport Rd., Anchorage 99502-1088 ☎ 907/271-2000 🌐 www.faa.gov. **Frontier Flying Service** ✉ 5245 Airport Industrial Way, Fairbanks 99709 ☎ 907/450-7250, 800/478-6779 for reservations 🌐 www.frontierflying.com. **Peninsula Airways** ✉ 6100 Boeing Ave., Anchorage 99502 ☎ 907/243-2323 or 800/448-4226 🌐 www.penair.com. **Wright Air Service** ✉ 3842 University Ave. 📫 Box 60142, Fairbanks 99706 ☎ 907/474-0502, 800/478-0502 in Alaska 🌐 www.wrightair.net.

BY BOAT & FERRY

The Alaska Marine Highway System's ferries make summer trips to Kodiak, Dutch Harbor/Unalaska, and several other Bush communities in southwestern Alaska.

Alaska State Ferry ✉ Alaska Marine Highway System, 6858 Glacier Hwy., Juneau 99801 ☎ 800/642-0066 📠 907/277-4829 🌐 www.dot.state.ak.us/amhs.

BY BUS

There's no regular bus service between communities in the Bush, though some tour companies do offer motor coach tours along the Dalton Highway, between Fairbanks and Prudhoe Bay. *See* Tour Options, below.

BY CAR

The James W. Dalton Highway—formerly the construction road for the trans-Alaska pipeline—is Alaska's only highway to the High Arctic. Popularly known as the Haul Road, this 414-mi, all-gravel road begins about 73 mi north of Fairbanks, connecting with the Steese and Elliott highways to points south. Private vehicles may travel the entire length of the highway to Deadhorse. However, access to oil-company facilities and the shore of the Arctic Ocean is limited to commercial operators.

Vehicle services are limited along the highway. There are plans to add new facilities, but currently fuel, repairs, food, and lodging are available at only three places: the Yukon River crossing (Mile 56), Coldfoot (Mile 175), and Deadhorse (Mile 414). Motorists are cautioned not to expect assistance from truckers shuttling between Prudhoe Bay and Fairbanks. For Dalton Highway information, contact the Fairbanks office of the Alaska Public Lands Information Center.

Neither the Arctic and near-Arctic communities of Nome, Kotzebue, and Barrow nor Bethel, the Aleutian chain, nor the Pribilof Islands have highway connections to the rest of Alaska.

Alaska Public Lands Information Center ✉ 250 Cushman St., Suite 1A, Fairbanks 99701 ☎ 866/869-6887 or 907/456-0527 🌐 www.nps.gov/aplic.

Contacts & Resources

BANKS

Most small villages don't have bank offices, so visitors should bring money or, even better, traveler's checks and a major credit card; if possible, find out in advance what sort of payment tour companies, hotels, and restaurants accept. Certain hub communities do have bank services, as listed below.

Alaska USA Federal Credit Union 🌐 www.alaskausa.org has a branch in Bethel (Bethel Native Corporation Building, 907/543-2619). **Credit Union 1** ☎ 800/478-2222 🌐 www.cu1.org has a branch in Nome (110 Front St., 907/443-2737). **First National Bank Alaska** 🌐 www.fnbalaska.com has a branch in Bethel (700 Front St., 907/543-7650). **Wells Fargo** ☎ 800/869-3557 🌐 www.wellsfargo.com has branches in Barrow (1078 Kiogak St., 907/852-6200); Bethel (460 Ridgecrest Drive, 907/543-3875 and 830 River St., 800/869-3557); Kotzebue (360 Lagoon St., 907/442-3258); and Nome (109A Front St., 907/443-2223).

7

EMERGENCIES

DOCTORS & DENTISTS A statewide air-ambulance service operates through Alaska Regional Lifeflight in Anchorage.

Alaska Regional Lifeflight ☎ 800/478-9111 🌐 www.alaskaregional.com. **Maniilaq Health Center** ✉ Kotzebue ☎ 800/478-3321 🌐 www.maniilaq.org.

EMERGENCY SERVICES **Police** ☎ 907/852–0311 in Barrow, 907/543–3871 in Bethel, 907/442–3351 in Kotzebue, 907/443–5262 in Nome 🌐 www.kotzebuepolice.com, www.nomealaska.org in Nome. **State troopers** ☎ 907/852–3783 in Barrow, 907/543–2294 in Bethel, 800/789–3222, 907/442–3222 in Kotzebue, 907/443–5525 in Nome 🌐 www.dps.state.ak.us/ast.

HOSPITALS **Norton Sound Regional Hospital** ✉ Nome ☎ 907/443-3311 🌐 www.nortonsoundhealth.org. **Samuel Simmonds Memorial Hospital** ✉ Barrow ☎ 907/852-4611.

INTERNET, MAIL & SHIPPING

Few villages in the Bush have any sort of public Internet access, though some of the larger hub communities do, usually at the public library.

INTERNET ACCESS **Chukchi Consortium Library** ✉ 604 Third St., Kotzebue ☎ 907/442-2410. **City Library** ✉ 220 Front St., Nome ☎ 907/443-6628 🌐 www.nomealaska.org/library/index.html. **Pacifica Guest House** ✉ 1220 Hoffman Hwy., Bethel ☎ 907/543-4305 🌐 www.pacificaguesthouse.com. **Tuzzy Library** ✉ 5421 N. Star St., Arrow ☎ 907/852-1720 🌐 www.ilisagvik.cc.

MAIL & SHIPPING Most Alaskan communities, even small villages, have some sort of U.S. Postal Service office. Some larger Bush towns also have United Parcel Service (🌐 www.ups.com) and/or Federal Express (🌐 www.fedex.com) service. Check the Web sites for details.

U.S Postal Service 🌐 www.usps.gov branches: Barrow ✉ 3080 Eben Hobson St. ☎ 907/852-6800; Bethel ✉ 1484 Chief Eddie Hoffman Way ☎ 907/543-2525; Kotzebue ✉ 333 Shore Ave. ☎ 907/442-3291; Nome ✉ 113 E. Front St. ☎ 907/443-2401.

MEDIA

Even in the Bush, most communities have some form of cable or satellite TV, though they may receive a limited number of stations. Several regional hubs have locally produced public and/or commercial radio programs, plus locally published newspapers; several also are reached by the *Anchorage Daily News* and/or *Fairbanks Daily News-Miner.*

RADIO Barrow's lone radio station is **KBRW AM & FM** ☎ 907/852-6811, which broadcasts 24 hours a day, with programs in English and Inupiat Eskimo. Newspapers distributed here include the *Arctic Sounder, Anchorage Daily News*, and the *Fairbanks Daily News-Miner.*

NEWSPAPERS One of Bethel's two newspapers, the *Tundra Drums* (✉ 311 Willow St. ☎ 907/543-3551 🌐 www.alaskanewspapers.com) features stories from throughout the Yukon-Kuskokwim Delta region. Locally owned and operated, the *Delta Discovery* (☎ 907/543-4113 🌐 www.deltadiscovery.com) serves both the Y-K Delta and Bristol Bay regions. Bethel's public-radio station, KYUK 640 AM (☎ 907/543-3131 🌐 www.kyuk.org) has served the area for more than three decades.

Though published by the Anchorage-based Alaska Newspapers chain, *The Arctic Sounder* ☎ 907/442–2716 🌐 www.alaskanewspapers.com has staff based in Kotzebue.

Nome is home to Alaska's oldest newspaper, *The Nome Nugget* (☎ 907/443–5235 🌐 www.nomenugget.net), which has served Northwest Alaska nearly continuously since New Year's Day 1897. The town also has three radio stations: KNOM AM/FM 78, KICY AM 85, and KICY FM 100.

TOURS

Package tours are the most common way of traveling to Bush communities, where making your flight connections and having a room to sleep in at the end of the line are no small feats. Guided trips, or stays in wilderness lodges, can be arranged in many of the Bush's remote parklands and wildlife refuges. Independent travel, particularly for campers and hikers, can be highly rewarding, but it takes careful planning. During peak season—late May through Labor Day—planes, state ferries, hotels, and sportfishing lodges are likely to be crowded with travelers on organized tours. Booking well ahead is recommended; many Alaska travelers make their reservations a year in advance.

The type of tour you choose will determine how you get there. On air tours—which include travel to most Bush communities—you will fly to and from your destination. On bus tours to Deadhorse and Prudhoe Bay, you will travel at least one way by bus. Each type of tour has its own advantages: air travel is faster and gives you an aerial perspective of the Arctic; bus tours travel at a more leisurely pace and give you a ground-level view of sweeping tundra vistas. However, most Bush locales can be reached only by plane.

Most tours to Arctic towns and villages are short—one, two, or three days. These often can be combined with visits to other regions of the state. Packages may include stays at wilderness lodges.

The Bush is home to many native Alaskan groups, many of which are active in tourism. Often, local native corporations act as your hosts—running the tours, hotels, and attractions. Nome Tour and Marketing in Nome (book through Alaska Airlines Vacations) provides ground transportation, accommodations, and other services for visitors. The NANA Development Corporation provides ground transportation and accommodations in Kotzebue as well as at Prudhoe Bay in conjunction with bus tours. If you visit Barrow and stay at the Top of the World Hotel, Tundra Tours (book through Alaska Airlines Vacations), another native operation, will be your host. On Gambell Island (book through Alaska Village Tours), local residents also run all the ground operations.

Alaska Airlines Vacations Box 68900, Seattle, WA 98168 ☎ 800/468–2248 🌐 alaskaair.com. **Tundra Tours** ☎ 907/852–3900.

BUS & COMBO TOURS In the summer tourist season, tour operators run trips up the Dalton Highway out of Fairbanks and Anchorage. Travelers usually go one way by air, the other by motor coach. The route crosses the rugged Brooks Range, the Arctic Circle, and the Yukon River. It also brushes the edges

CLOSE UP

Visiting in Winter

ALTHOUGH MANY PEOPLE THINK visiting Alaska in the winter is insane, there are plenty of good reasons for doing so. It just takes a bit of attitude adjustment, an adventurous spirit, and proper clothing. The advantages and opportunities for adventure are manifold.

The northern lights (aurora borealis) are active all year long, but it has to get dark before you can enjoy them. On a clear night, away from city lights, these shimmering curtains of color in the sky are absolutely breathtaking. Weather and solar activity have to cooperate in order to make the aurora performances happen, but when they do, the results are astounding.

There are **fewer bugs** in the winter months; if you've visited Alaska during the summer and been subjected to hordes of mosquitoes, no-see-ums, and white socks, this alone might be enough to entice you to visit.

For a real Alaska winter experience, **dog mushing** is the ultimate. Spectators can watch sprint and long distance races all over the state, capped off by the Yukon Quest and Iditarod races in February and March. There are numerous outfits in the Interior and South Central that will train you to mush your own team for a day, an overnight, or an extended trip. Fodor's discusses dog mushing and surrounding competitions with the expectation and hope that all the animals are treated with care and respect.

Numerous opportunities exist in Alaska for both **downhill and cross-country skiing** adventures. You can charter a helicopter to go backcountry skiing in the Valdez area or visit one of the downhill areas near Anchorage, Fairbanks, or Juneau. You can also ski in the winter or summer by chartering a plane to a glacier in Denali National Park.

At Juneau, Eaglecrest is across from the city on the slopes of Douglas Island. Skiing is also done on the glaciers of the Juneau Ice Field, reached by helicopter. Turnagain Pass, 59 mi from Anchorage on the Seward Highway, is often trafficked with backcountry skiers and snowmobilers. Hilltop Ski Area and Alpenglow are small alpine ski areas within 10 mi of downtown Anchorage.

The **World Extreme Skiing Championships** are held at Valdez every April. Cross-country skiers will find many miles of groomed trails in Anchorage. Additional cross-country ski trails can be found around Fairbanks, Homer, and Palmer. Snowboarding has more than caught on in South Central Alaska, and boarders are welcome at all three Anchorage ski areas. Rentals are available at the various ski areas and outdoor equipment shops.

---

of Gates of the Arctic National Park and the Arctic National Wildlife Refuge. Holland America Tours/Gray Line of Alaska operates package tours that travel the Dalton Highway to Deadhorse. Princess Tours also runs tours along the Dalton Highway.

The Northern Alaska Tour Company conducts ecotours to the Arctic Circle, the Brooks Range, and Prudhoe Bay that emphasize natural and cultural history, wildlife, and geology. Groups are limited to 25 people on Arctic day tours and to 10 on Prudhoe Bay overnight trips. Some tours are completely ground-based; others include a mix of ground and air travel.

Holland American Tours/Gray Line of Alaska ⌧ 1980 S. Cushman, Fairbanks 99701 ☎ 907/451-6835, 800/887-7741 in Alaska, 800/544-2206 for reservations 🌐 www.graylineofalaska.com. **Northern Alaska Tour Company** Box 82991-W, Fairbanks 99708 ☎ 907/474-8600 or 800/474-1986 🌐 www.northernalaska.com. **Princess Tours** ⌧ 2815 2nd Ave., Suite 400, Seattle, WA 98121 ☎ 206/336-6000 in Seattle, 907/479-9660 in Fairbanks, 800/426-0442 reservations 🌐 www.princess.com.

PLANE Alaska Airlines Vacations packages air tours to Barrow and Nome. Local arrangements are taken care of by native ground operators. These trips are especially good for travelers who would otherwise move about independently. The Alaska Travel Industry Association can give tips on air travel and flightseeing opportunities throughout the Bush.

Alaska Airlines Vacations Box 68900, Seattle, WA 98168 ☎ 800/468-2248 🌐 www.alaskaair.com. **Alaska Travel Industry Association** ⌧ 2600 Cordova St., Suite 201, Anchorage 99503 ☎ 907/929-2200, 800/862-5275 for vacation planner 📠 907/561-5727 🌐 www.travelalaska.com.

VISITOR INFORMATION

Alaska Travel Industry Association ⌧ 2600 Cordova St., Suite 201, Anchorage 99503 ☎ 907/929-2200, 800/862-5275 for vacation planner 📠 907/561-5727 🌐 www.travelalaska.com. **Bethel Chamber of Commerce** Box 329, Bethel 99559 ☎ 907/543-2911 📠 907/543-2255 🌐 www.bethelakchamber.org. **City of Barrow** Box 629, Barrow 99723 ☎ 907/852-5211 📠 907/852-5871. **Nome Convention and Visitors Bureau** Box 240, Nome 99762 ☎ 907/443-6624, 800/478-1901 in Alaska 📠 907/443-5832 🌐 www.nomealaska.org. **Southwest Alaska Municipal Conference** ⌧ 3300 Arctic Blvd., Suite 203, Anchorage 99503 ☎ 907/562-7380 📠 907/562-0438 🌐 www.swamc.org. **Unalaska-Dutch Harbor Convention and Visitors Bureau** Box 545, Unalaska 99685 ☎ 907/581-2612 or 877/581-2612 📠 907/581-2613 🌐 www.unalaska.info.

7

UNDERSTANDING ALASKA

FISHING THE LAST FRONTIER: IN SEARCH OF HOLY WATER

AFTER THE FLOATPLANE ROARED off and the silence settled in, I found myself standing on a remote Southeast Alaska beach feeling vaguely lost and wondering aloud if we'd come too early for good fishing. From his seat on a log surrounded by yellow beach rye, my friend Tony Route fiddled with his fly rod. Without looking up, he shrugged and replied, "Maybe."

But who knew? We had come to discover—to explore a coastal stream that was little known and rarely fished. It was one more Alaska enigma, and the steelhead we hoped to find there—big, bright, sea-run rainbow trout that come and go with the tides—were the most mysterious game fish of all.

From that lonely Southeast stream to the Arctic's coastal plain, Alaska remains a startling composition of mass and isolation. From an angler's point of view, this is our continent's Amazon. The state's 375 million acres span several distinct climate zones, each with its own series of weathers and geographies through which 3,000 rivers and uncounted smaller streams collectively flow. Little-explored places and unfished waters still exist here.

Not many years ago, a commercial fisherman friend who worked Alaska's gulf coast shared stories of steelhead turning up in nets off the mouth of a particular stream. I later found the place on a map, but efforts to learn more about it and its fish turned up little. Like many other remote waters here the stream had not been thoroughly surveyed.

Weeks later, in mid-April, I paid a bush pilot to drop me off on a windswept beach near the stream. Once I started fishing, only a few casts were needed to answer the riddle for good: The waters, as untouched and unspoiled as when time began, were a steelhead fisherman's dream. I spent two long, lovely days catching and releasing hard-fighting, sea-run trout as long as my arm. When the time came to leave, I hiked back out to the beach, met my pilot and simply flew away.

To this day the stream's name and location remain my secret. I've never told a soul. And I've never been back.

Fish species here are hardly limited to coastal steelhead. There are five species of Pacific salmon that return each summer by the millions to natal rivers and rills. In the Kenai River alone, the state's most readily accessed and popular sportfishing river, more than 5 million sockeye salmon (locally called reds) returned to spawn in the summer of 2005.

The Kenai is also known for enormous king salmon: the official state sportfishing record, a 97-pound, 4-ounce monster, was pulled, lunging and flopping, from its glacial-tinted waters in 1985. Even so, more than a few hard-core anglers believe bigger kings remain, if not in the Kenai then somewhere else in Alaska. Indeed, a whopping 126-pounder was taken in 1949 from a commercial fish trap near Petersburg in Southeast.

Beyond sockeyes and kings, Alaska's streams and oceans are periodically darkened by silver (coho) salmon, pinks, and chums. Meanwhile, insect-sipping arctic grayling, set apart by their sail-like dorsal fins, dimple the surfaces of ponds and creeks from the Copper River Delta to the high Arctic. The planet's finest rainbow trout fishing is found here as well; in Southwest's Bristol Bay region, trout sometimes grow to a yard in length and weigh up to 20 pounds.

Dolly Varden, pink-spotted char related to eastern brook trout and named for a character in Dickens' *Barnaby Rudge,* are found throughout the state in such large numbers that prior to statehood in 1959, a jealous commercial salmon fishing industry had a bounty placed on their tails. In an effort to keep the ubiquitous Dollys from gobbling up too many young salmon, the program paid 2½ cents per tail and ended only after authorities realized that more trout, grayling, and salmon tails were being turned in than Dollys.

Northern pike weighing up to nearly 40 pounds are stalked in weedy muskeg ponds and river sloughs of the Interior, and sheefish (which bear a passing resemblance to the tropical tarpon) heavier than 50 pounds run in the rivers like the Kobuk and the Pah in the northwestern part of the state. Beyond all of these species, there are lake trout, whitefish, cutthroat trout, and a curious but tasty freshwater lingcod called burbot.

Those are the main freshwater fish and anadromous transients. The ocean along Alaska's 6,640 mi of coastline—a bouillabaisse of halibut, snapper, cod, mollusk, crab, and salmon sharks weighing 500 pounds or more—is quite another kettle of fish indeed.

Back on the beach in far-flung Southeast, Tony Route and I hauled our gear into a USDA Forest Service cabin set in a bench of hemlocks over a remote salt chuck (a sort of brackish lake, connected to the sea by a channel that floods and drains with the tides). Reserved months in advance for twenty-five bucks a night, the place came with a skiff, four bunks, and a woodstove. The place would be our steelhead fishing base camp for the days ahead.

That night, beneath the angular forms of Orion and the Big Dipper, our backs cold against the April darkness, faces warm and orange by the fire, we sipped peaty single-malt scotch from our camp cups and absorbed the solitude that defines wilderness Alaska. We kicked around our chances of finding steelhead, believing the odds for the next day were in our favor. And as it turned out, we were right. Tony would catch the first one, a respectable eight-pound fish. There would be others, and silver-sided Dolly Varden and cutthroat trout too, all hoodwinked by our flies in that tannic stream which flowed amber in the sunshine and black in the shade.

One afternoon something shocking happened. Tony had wandered alone to the salt chuck's outlet to catch and release some sea-run cutthroat trout. "Just little ones," he'd said. "Eight or 10 inches." He was wading navel-deep, casting in the tidal current, when a 10-ounce trout struck and struggled with all of its heart. The little cutthroat was splashing near Tony's rod tip, a skipping silver flash, when a shark struck. "Ripped the fish right off my hook," he said, his expression still faintly startled. Tony later surmised that he likely wasn't in any danger; the shark was a dogfish, a toothy fish-eater virtually harmless to humans. But the sight of it was enough for him to hastily rush out of the water and quit fishing for the day. "I'm sure it was four feet long," he said that night in the glow of the campfire, "Forty pounds, easy."

That's the way it is in Alaska. Sharks come with the territory, along with 800-pound grizzly bears and unpredictable weather. For anglers, the danger and mystery form a beguiling edge—this is extreme fishing, and exploring Southeast Alaska's temperate rain-forest streams for wild steelhead trout is on par with probing Amazon backwaters for peacock bass or casting Australia's coastal fringes for barramundi. Caribou still outnumber people here, and unsurveyed streams remain to be fished. To cast here on a wild river is to be, as the late Charles Kuralt once wrote, "alone in the universe."

–Ken Marsh

ALASKA AT A GLANCE

Fast Facts

Nicknames: Great Land, Land of the Midnight Sun, Last Frontier
Capital: Juneau
Motto: North to the Future
State song: *Alaska's Flag,* by Marie Drake
State bird: Willow Ptarmigan
State flower: Forget-Me-Not
State tree: Sitka spruce
Administrative divisions: 27 counties
Entered the Union: January 3, 1959, as the 49th state
Population: 640,000
Population density: 1.1 person per square mi
Median age: 34.2
Ethnic groups: White 69%; American Indian or Alaska native 13%; other 7%; Asian 4%; Latino 4%; black 3%
Religion: Unaffiliated 66%; Protestant 18%; Catholic 9%; other 4%; Mormon 3%

The really heroic people are not the ones who travel 10,000 miles by dog sled, but those who stay 10,000 days in one place.

–William Gordon, Episcopal Bishop of Alaska

Geography & Environment

Land area: 570,373 square mi, the largest state
Coastline: 6,640 mi (33,904 mi of shoreline, including all islands) along North Pacific Ocean, Bering Sea, Chukchi Sea, Arctic Ocean
Terrain: Rough, tundra-dominated coast, with grass-covered, treeless islands along the western edge; barren, mountainous inland, carved by more than 3,000 rivers and dotted by more than 3 million lakes; icebound and permanently frozen North Slope; highest point: Mt. McKinley, 20,320 feet (the tallest mountain in North America)
Islands: 1,800 named islands, largest is Kodiak (3,588 square mi)
Natural resources: Arable land, cod, crab, forests, halibut, herring, natural gas, petroleum, salmon, seals, shrimp
Natural hazards: Earthquakes, extreme cold, flooding, tsunami
Environmental issues: The effects of the 1989 *Exxon Valdez* spill are still being felt in the ecosystem; oil accidents continue to be a problem. Fish are monitored for mercury, heavy metals, dioxins, and pesticides from runoff. Cruise ships are tightly regulated for wastewater and air pollution.

There is much to be said against the climate on the coast of British Columbia and Alaska; yet, I believe that the scenery of one good day will compensate the tourists who will go there in increasing numbers.

–Franklin D. Roosevelt

Economy

GSP: 28.8 billion
Per capita income: $33,568
Unemployment: 7.1%
Workforce: 292,286; government 27%; trade, transportation, and utilities 21%; educational and health services 10%; leisure and hospitality 10%; professional and business services 8%; construction 5%; financial 4%; natural resource and mining 4%; other 5%; manufacturing 4%; information 2%

Major industries: Fishing, mining, oil, timber, tourism
Agricultural products: Crab, cod, dairy products, halibut, herring, potatoes, salmon, shrimp
Exports: $1 billion
Major export products: Petroleum and coal products 6%; lumber and wood products 6%; food products 4%; transportation equipment 3%; industrial machinery and computers 3%

Did You Know?

- Alaska is home to Mt. McKinley, the highest peak in North America, as well as 17 of the 20 of the highest mountains in the United States.

- Dog mushing, once the only way to get around in many areas, is now the state sport.

- With an estimated 100,000 glaciers, Alaska has more than anywhere else in the inhabited world. Five percent of the state, or 29,000 square mi, is covered by them.

- North America's strongest earthquake was recorded in Alaska on March 27, 1964, with a magnitude of 9.2. Alaska has approximately 5,000 earthquakes each year.

- The trans-Alaska pipeline moves oil from the North Slope of Alaska to Valdez, the northernmost ice-free port. The pipeline is 48 inches in diameter and moves oil at about 5½ mph, requiring just under six days to travel from Prudhoe Bay to the sea.

- Alaska is home to both the easternmost and westernmost points in the United States, due to the 180th meridian, which is the global dividing line between all eastern and western longitudes on the globe. Amatignak Island, at 179° west, is only 70 mi away from Semisopochnoi Island at 179° east.

NATIVE ALASKANS

THE HISTORY OF ALASKA'S NATIVE peoples—Eskimos, Indians, and Aleuts—is not unlike that of aboriginal people throughout Central and North America. After they had held domain over their land for thousands of years, their elaborate societies were besieged by a rapid onslaught of white settlers. Unable to stem the tide, the native peoples were forced into retreat.

The first European to visit Alaska—in 1728—was Vitus Bering, a Dane serving in the Russian navy. Bering died on his journey home, but survivors from that voyage returned to Russia with a rich booty of sea-otter furs, sparking a stampede that would crush the traditional lifestyles of Alaska's native peoples. The way was open for eager Russian fur traders who plundered Aleut territory along the Aleutian Islands.

Records indicate that the native population of the Aleutian chain dropped from perhaps 20,000 to about 2,500 in the first 50 years of Russian rule. Diseases took a heavy toll, but the more ruthless among the Russian frontiersmen were also responsible—killing Aleut leaders to discourage uprisings. Stories of brutality are common. One trader, Feodor Solovief, reportedly tied together 12 Aleuts and fired a musket ball through them to see how far it would penetrate. It stopped in the body of the ninth man.

In 1867 when the United States purchased Alaska, the native peoples were classified in the Treaty of Cession as "uncivilized tribes." To early tourists, they were little more than "those charming folk you take pictures of in their quaint villages."

Early missionaries and government teachers in Southeast Alaska ordered Indian totem poles destroyed, mistakenly believing them to be pagan symbols. Important works of art were lost. The totem poles of the Tlingit and Haida Indians were—and still are—simply the decorative record of outstanding events in the life of a family or clan.

The plight of the natives improved little as Alaska grew more prosperous by exploiting its great natural resources. A painful split between traditional and modern living developed—public health experts call it "a syndrome of grief." Under increasing pressure from this clash of cultures, alcoholism grew to epidemic levels, and the suicide rate of Alaskan natives climbed to twice that of Native Americans living on reservations in the continental United States. Still, by the 1960s, native groups were making major strides toward claiming overdue political clout. In 1966 native leaders from across the state gathered and organized the present Alaska Foundation of Natives. It was a fragile coalition of differing cultures, but the meeting was a significant move. With 16% of the state's population, a unified native voice was suddenly a political force to be reckoned with.

At the same time, Eskimo leaders founded the *Tundra Times* and selected Howard Rock, a quiet, articulate man from Point Hope village, as its editor. Rock, whose background was in art rather than journalism, quickly prodded natives to press their aboriginal land claims.

"The natives are reticent by nature, and time was passing them by," the Eskimo editor said. "At first, it was kind of discouraging. Nothing happened. And then, one by one, the native leaders started speaking up."

The *Tundra Times* helped file the first suit for native land claims. More lawsuits followed, and soon the whole state was tied up in litigation. Oil companies, hungry to build a pipeline from the newly discovered giant oil field at Prudhoe Bay to Valdez, on Alaska's southern coast, soon realized they could not get federal construction permits until the native land claims were settled.

In 1971 the natives won a spectacular settlement in Congress: 40 million acres of land and almost $1 billion in cash. The settlement has not been a cure-all for the many problems of Alaska's natives. Poverty is still widespread, as little of the land-claims money (allocated mostly to 13 regional, for-profit native corporations by Congress) has trickled down to the village level. But the settlement has given many a sense of dignity and purpose. Several villages in the Arctic have voted themselves dry (prohibiting alcohol) to combat drinking problems.

Today, the fundamental issue is whether the natives will be allowed by the larger Alaskan society to pursue their own future, says Byron Mallott, former chief operating officer of Sealaska Corp., the regional native corporation for Southeast Alaska.

"In one way, Alaska is truly the last frontier," Mallott says. "Will the final chapter of the total and unremitting decimation of our nation's Native American people be written in Alaska—or will, with the benefit of the lesson of history, Alaska be the place where native peoples finally are able to become a part of the overall society with their pride, strength, and ethnicity intact?" There are, he adds, few guideposts to suggest the answer.

Most of Alaska's natives still reside in widely scattered communities spread across the ½-million square mi of Alaska. Unlike the Native Americans of the Lower 48 states, the Alaskan natives have never been restricted to reservations. Many villages remain isolated, the preference of traditional villagers; others have plunged into modern life with mixed results. Recently, Alaska's native peoples have become more enterprising in the tourist business. No longer content to let out-of-state tour operators have all the business, they are now starting to take charge of tours in their communities.

The various native peoples tend to group in well-defined regions. Here is a brief look at the different native cultures and their locations.

Eskimos. Most of Alaska's more than 40,000 Eskimos are found in scattered settlements along the Bering Sea and Arctic Ocean coasts, the deltas of the lower Yukon and Kuskokwim rivers in western Alaska, and on remote islands in the Bering Sea such as St. Lawrence, Nunivak, and Little Diomede. The principal Arctic and sub-Arctic Eskimo communities include Barrow, Kotzebue, Nome, Gambell, Savoonga, Point Hope, Wainwright, and Shishmaref.

The Eskimos are divided into two linguistic groups: the Inupiat of the Far North and the Yup'ik, who reside mostly along the coastal regions of the west. The Yup'ik share the same dialect as the Eskimos of Siberia. Both groups are famed for their hunting and fishing skills. They are also noted craftspeople, carving animals and creating jewelry from native materials.

Indians. Alaska has four major Indian cultures: Tlingit, Haida, Athabascan, and Tsimshian.

Once among North America's most powerful tribes, the **Tlingits** (pronounced *klink*-its) are found mostly throughout coastal Southeast Alaska. They number about 13,000 and live in cities such as Juneau, Ketchikan, and Sitka and in villages from Hoonah, near Juneau, to Klukwan, near Haines.

The Tlingits developed a highly sophisticated culture and fought hard against Russian incursions. Social status among early Tlingits depended on elaborate feasts called potlatches. Heads of families and clans vied in giving away vast quantities of valuable goods, their generosity so extravagant at times that the hosts fell into a form of ancient bankruptcy. There are still potlatches for important occasions, such as funerals, but they are greatly scaled down from earlier times.

Haidas are also found mainly in Southeast Alaska, as well as in British Columbia. They number only about 1,000 in Alaska. Their principal community is Hydaburg on Prince of Wales Island, near Ketchikan. The Queen Charlotte Islands of British Columbia are another Haida center. Historically, the Haidas were far-ranging voyagers and traders. Some historians credit the artistic Haidas with originating totem carving among Alaska's natives.

Most of Alaska's 7,000 or so **Athabascan** Indians are found in the villages of Alaska's vast Interior, including Fort Yukon, Stevens Village, Beaver, Chalkyitsik, and Minto, near Fairbanks. Other Athabascans are scattered from the Kenai Peninsula–Cook Inlet area, near Anchorage, to the Copper River area near Cordova. Linguistically, the Athabascans are related to the Navajo and Apache of the American Southwest. They were driven out of Canada by Cree tribes more than 700 years ago.

The ancestral home of the **Tsimshian** (pronounced *sim*-shee-ann) Indians was British Columbia, but Tsimshian historians say their forebears roamed through much of southeastern Alaska fishing, hunting, and trading long before the arrival of the white man. The 1,000 or so Tsimshians of Alaska settled in 1887 on Annette Island, near Ketchikan, when a dissident Church of England lay missionary, William Duncan, led them out of British Columbia to escape religious persecution. The town of Metlakatla on Annette Island is their principal community. Their artwork includes wood carvings, from totem poles to ceremonial masks.

Aleuts. With their villages on the Aleutian Islands, curving between Siberia and Alaska like broken beads, the Aleuts (pronounced al-ee-*oots*) were first in the path of early explorers and ruthless fur traders. There are about 7,000 Aleuts in Alaska today, their principal communities being Dutch Harbor/Unalaska, Akutan, Nikolski, and Atka in the Aleutians and St. Paul and St. George in the Pribilof Islands. Grass basketry, classed by museums as some of the best in the world, is the principal art of the Aleuts. Finely woven baskets from Attu, at the tip of the Aleutian chain—where villages were destroyed in American–Japanese combat during World War II and never rebuilt—are difficult-to-obtain treasures.

–Stanton H. Patty

THE CHARACTER OF ALASKA

IF YOU'RE CONSIDERING a cruise to Alaska, chances are you're already enchanted by the imagery associated with the 49th American state. After all, "The Great Land," a loose translation of the Aleut word *Alyeska,* boasts the highest mountain in North America—Mt. McKinley (also called Denali)—as well as 17 of the 20 highest peaks in the United States. There are more bald eagles here than anywhere else, more totem poles, thousands of glaciers, king-size salmon, and humongous halibut.

There is nothing ordinary about this land—or the people who call it home. The people of Alaska embody a spirit of adventure, self-sufficiency, and independence. Status in Alaska is measured by longevity. The greatest honor, and the title of "sourdough," is reserved for those who have spent the most time in Alaska. In the gold-rush days, prospectors and pioneers carried a stash of sourdough starter so that they could always whip up a batch of bread in short order. The old-timers became known as sourdoughs, beginning the tradition.

If your mountains are skyscrapers and wildlife means mostly pigeons, Alaska is the place to satisfy your craving for space. Room to roam is something Alaska has in abundance. Alaska is the largest state in the Union; its 570,373 square mi equal one-fifth the land mass of the Lower 48. A popular postcard shows Alaska superimposed on a map of the United States: it stretches nearly from sea to shining sea.

Geography alone makes Alaska an ideal cruise destination. Except for those in and around Haines and Skagway in the north, there are no roads linking the towns along the Panhandle. In fact, Juneau is the only state capital in the United States that cannot be reached over land. You fly in or you sail in, but you don't drive in. On a typical seven-day itinerary you'll visit up to four ports of call and one or two scenic bays or fjords. And the nature of ship travel is perfectly suited to discovering what Alaska is all about. From the deck of a cruise ship, you can come face to face with a glacier. From the dining room, you can watch a full moon rise over a snow-striped mountain. And you can enjoy it all in the lap of luxury.

The natural beauty of Alaska is hard to overstate. As you prepare for your cruise, consider these facts about Alaska's grandeur: the Inside Passage, the traditional route north to Alaska, stretches 1,000 mi from Puget Sound, Washington, in the south, to Skagway, Alaska, in the north. From there, the Gulf of Alaska arcs for another 500 mi from east to west. Alaska has thousands of glaciers. Among the most famous ones that cruise passengers visit are LeConte outside Petersburg, the southernmost calving glacier in North America, and Hubbard at Yakutat Bay in the Gulf of Alaska, 6 mi wide and 76 mi long to its source. There are 12 tidewater glaciers in Glacier Bay National Park and Preserve and another 16 glaciers in College Fjord off Prince William Sound. The Malaspina Glacier, at the entrance to Yakutat Bay, is bigger than the state of Rhode Island. Tongass National Forest, which spans great stretches of the Inside Passage, is the largest national forest in the United States. Wrangell–St. Elias National Park, a UNESCO World Heritage Site east of Anchorage and bordering the Gulf of Alaska, is the largest national park in the United States—six times the size of Yellowstone.

In such broad expanses of land, airplanes have become as common as taxis in New York. The bush plane in particular holds a special place in Alaskan folklore: this was the machine that opened the wilderness and that provides the only access to remote communities to this day. Lake Hood, near the airport in Anchorage, is the world's largest and busiest seaplane base; if you have time, be sure to stop by to watch the brightly painted Cessnas and De Havilland Beavers coming and going hourly. Anchorage pays special tribute to the bush pilots of the past in two museums, the Alaska Aviation Heritage Museum and the Reeve Aviation Picture Museum. Even today, the bush pilot is a revered figure, and many Alaskans agree that there are few better ways to appreciate the wonder of the land than from the window of a Cessna.

Mere numbers cannot capture the effect of Alaska on the human spirit. First-time visitors will catch their breath at first sight of a glacier and gawk at Anchorage's Ship Creek during the annual salmon run, when the water is so thick with fish it seems you could wade in and pluck one out.

Wildlife is everywhere in Alaska. Southeast Alaska has more brown bears than the rest of the United States combined. And Alaska ranks number one in bald eagles. Bird-watchers will have a field day looking for them perched high in the treetops—or atop telephone poles—all along the Inside Passage. In fact, eagles are so numerous here you'll have to remind yourself that they remain a threatened species. There's even an eagle hospital, the Alaska Raptor Rehabilitation Center in Sitka, where injured eagles and other birds of prey are nursed back to health.

You may also come across whales during your cruise. If so, your captain may cut the ship's engines so as not to disturb them and to allow you some time to observe them. The state has 15 species of whales. On a small-ship cruise, you may find yourself close enough to a gushing waterfall to fill a pitcher with the cool, mineral-rich glacial runoff. And don't be surprised if you see a bear foraging on the shoreline. Such are the simple pleasures of an Alaskan cruise: calving glaciers, sea lions and seals, and sensational sunsets—at midnight.

In addition to glaciers and wildlife, there's an exciting frontier history to discover. Scientists estimate that the first people arrived in Alaska some 15,000 years ago, when they migrated across the Bering Land Bridge from Asia. (Some expedition ships sail from Alaska to the Russian Far East, allowing you to follow the migration pattern in reverse.) The earliest evidence of human habitation along the Inside Passage can be found in Wrangell, where petroglyphs—mysterious markings carved into rocks and boulders on the beach—are thought to be at least 8,000 years old.

Alaska's indigenous people belong to one of four groups: Aleuts, Athabascans, Eskimos, and Northwest Coast Indians. The Aleuts live on the Aleutian Islands. Athabascans populate the Interior, and Eskimos inhabit the Arctic regions of the Far North. The native Alaskans you are most likely to meet during your cruise are the Tlingit, Haida, or Tsimshian people of the Inside Passage.

The Tlingit are responsible for Alaska's famous totem carvings. Totem poles tell the story of a great event, identify members of the same clan, and honor great leaders. The best place to see totem poles is Saxman Native Village in Ketchikan. The original totems at the Totem Heritage Center are the oldest authentic poles in Alaska, some dating back about 200 years. Today you can still see native artisans at work on totem poles in Ketchikan, Haines, and Sitka. Miniature totem reproductions are among the most popular souvenirs in Alaska, but ceremonial masks, decorative paddles, and woven baskets also make great gifts. These and other native crafts are sold throughout the Inside Passage. Before you buy, look for the silver hand label, which guarantees authenticity.

Buying local crafts is just one way for cruise passengers to appreciate the local culture. Native Alaskans are often happy to show you around. In Juneau, Ketchikan, and Sitka, you can book a sightseeing tour with a native point of view. Performances of native dance and traditional storytelling entertain visitors in Juneau, Sitka, and Haines. Ask about these aboard your ship or at the visitor information office near the pier.

In the footsteps of native Alaskans came European explorers. The first was Vitus Bering, who "discovered" Alaska and later claimed it for Russia in 1741. The Russians made Kodiak their capital before moving the seat of government to Sitka in 1808. Next came British and Spanish explorers. Cook Inlet in Anchorage is named for British explorer Captain Cook. One member of Cook's expedition was George Vancouver, namesake of the Canadian port city where most Alaska cruises begin or end. Ketchikan sits on an island named after a Spaniard, the Count of Revillagigedo, viceroy of New Spain and a proponent of Spanish exploration of Alaska. Wrangell Island, at the southern end of the Inside Passage, is the only Alaskan port of call to have flown three flags—Russian, British, and finally American.

The connection with Europe is echoed in the nicknames given to some of Alaska's port cities. Valdez is often referred to as Alaska's Little Switzerland for the mountains that ring the city. Petersburg is Alaska's Little Norway, so named after its first non-native settlers. The town's residents still celebrate their Scandinavian heritage every May in a festival of Norwegian song and dance. If you are lucky enough to visit Petersburg on your cruise (only the smallest ships and ferries call here), you may be treated to a performance at the Sons of Norway Hall—followed by a Norwegian smorgasbord.

Russia sold Alaska to the United States in 1867 for $7.2 million, or about 2¢ an acre. Secretary of State William H. Seward, who orchestrated the purchase, was publicly ridiculed for his "folly." But opinions changed when word got out that gold had been discovered in the Far North; the news set off a stampede of legendary proportion. The gold rush, perhaps the most colorful episode in Alaska's storied history, reached a fever pitch during the winter of 1897–98. Some say up to 100,000 men headed for the goldfields. More conservative estimates put the number as low as 30,000. In either case, the Klondike Gold Rush put Alaska on the map, as gold-crazed prospectors, con men, and assorted other characters headed up the Inside Passage.

Anyone cruising Alaska should pick up a copy of *The Call of the Wild,* Jack London's classic novel based on his personal experiences in the Yukon. And if you're wondering what to watch, make it the Walt Disney adaptation of London's *White Fang*; it was filmed on location in Haines.

If you're an aficionado of gold-rush history, choose a cruise that includes a call at Skagway, the gateway to the Klondike of a century ago. As you sail the Lynn Canal, the natural channel that connects Skagway with the rest of the Inside Passage, keep in mind that you are following the same route and traveling in the same manner (albeit a bit more luxuriously) as the original prospectors. Once ashore, you'll hear the story of Frank Reid (the good guy) and Jefferson Randolph "Soapy" Smith (the bad guy), who shot it out for control of Skagway. You'll hear how Superintendent Samuel Steele of the Canadian Mounted Police called Skagway "the roughest place on earth." And you'll learn how, after the gold rush died down, Skagway became the birthplace of Alaska's tourism industry. Today the town looks much as it did in the early 1900s. The entire downtown area is a National Historic District, part of Klondike Gold Rush National Historic Park. Be sure to take a ride on the vintage parlor cars of the White Pass & Yukon Railway. It's one of the few chances cruise passengers have to venture deep into the mountains—just as prospectors traveled over the treacherous White Pass. From the cars of the train, you can still see the "Trail of '98," a footpath worn permanently into the mountainside.

Few establishments evoke the spirit of the frontier like the local saloon, and, depending on your itinerary, you'll have the opportunity to visit two of Alaska's most famous ones. Near the cruise-ship docks in Skagway is the Red Onion Saloon. To step inside is to return to 1898, when the saloon was founded; the bartender still serves drinks on the original mahogany bar. In Juneau, the Red Dog Saloon has been a favorite local watering hole since early in the last century. In fact, Wyatt Earp's six-shooter still hangs on the wall. It's said he left it here while just passing through.

Like Wyatt Earp, you, too, will just be passing through. But, as you are about to discover, cruising is a great way to see "The Great Land." Spend as much time as you can in Alaska. Bring plenty of film or videotape, don't forget a rain slicker, and do try everything. Go hiking and fishing. Ride the railroads, book a salmon bake, scope for eagles. Think big—and be sure to buy a souvenir totem pole.

ALASKA: A GEOLOGIC STORY

MOST PEOPLE KNOW ABOUT ALASKA'S oil and gold. But did you know that the state has a desert? That camels once roamed here? That there's a fault line nearly twice as long as the San Andreas Fault? That the largest earthquake ever to hit North America struck Alaska in 1964 and affected the entire planet? That the state has 80 potentially active volcanoes and approximately 100,000 glaciers?

All these physical wonders are geological in origin and are in addition to a North Slope oil supply that accounts for 25% of U.S. production and more than 10% of U.S. consumption, as well as caches of gold that fueled more than 20 rushes.

Glaciers

Nearly all visitors will have at least one encounter with a glacier (with 29,000 square mi of them, they're hard to miss). Courtesy of the Pleistocene Ice Age, high-latitude location, and abundant moisture from the North Pacific, Alaska has approximately 100,000 of these large sheets of ice. The vast majority are in the southern and southeastern parts of the state, as these are the areas with the most moisture. How much moisture? Portions of the Chugach Mountains can gather 600 inches of snow each year, an amount that is comparable, in rain, to the annual precipitation in Seattle. In north-central Alaska, the Brooks Range contains a glacial field of approximately 280 square mi. Although small by Alaskan standards, it is larger than all the glacial fields in the rest of the United States combined, which comprise approximately 230 square mi.

There are alpine or valley glaciers, those that form high in mountain valleys and travel to lower elevations. Alaska harbors several of the great alpine glaciers in the world, found in the high country of the Alaska Range, the Talkeetna, Wrangell, Chugach, St. Elias, and Coast mountains. Some, such as the Bering Glacier, come tantalizingly close to the water. At more than 100 mi in length, and with an area of more than 2,250 square mi, the Bering is the longest and largest Alaskan glacier, its seclusion guarded by Cape St. Elias and the stormy waters of the Gulf of Alaska. Also impressive are the Hubbard, its imposing terminus dominating the head of isolated Yakutat Bay; and the Columbia, foreboding and threatening, calving icebergs that tack in line like Nelson's fleet across the mouth of Valdez Arm.

The Malaspina Glacier is an unusual piedmont glacier. Formed by the coalescence of several glaciers, this 850-square-mi mass is lobate, or fan-shape, and occupies a benchland on the northwest side of Yakutat Bay. So much of the Alaska Range, Wrangell, Chugach, St. Elias, and Coast mountains are covered by glacial ice that it is often more appropriate to talk about ice fields than individual glaciers.

Then there are the great tidewater glaciers of Prince William Sound and southeastern Alaska. Alpine glaciers that come right to the water's edge, they creak, moan, thunder, and calve off great bergs and little bergeys. The world's longest is the previously mentioned Hubbard Glacier, which, because it stretches more than 70 mi from its head in Canada to its terminus in Yakutat Bay, is both an alpine and a tidewater glacier. Sixteen tidewater glaciers can be found in Glacier Bay National Park, 20 in Prince William Sound. Some are advancing, some retreating. Hubbard has not only advanced in recent years but has surged. In 1986, a surge by Hubbard blocked the Russell Fjord at the upper end of Yakutat Bay, turning it into Russell Lake. Later that year, the portion of the glacier acting as a dam in front of Russell Lake gave way, violently releasing the backed-up water to an elevation of 83 feet above sea level. That's pretty impressive when you stop to think that the Russell Fjord is normally at sea level. Surging glaciers can move downhill hundreds of feet per day. The Hubbard's greatest surge was in September 1899, when it advanced ½ mi into the bay in just five minutes, courtesy of an earthquake.

Glaciologists are interested in knowing more about how glaciers, especially tidewater glaciers, advance and retreat. The Columbia Glacier, both an alpine and a tidewater glacier like the Hubbard, in Prince William Sound is approximately 40 mi long, covers more than 400 square mi, and flows to sea level from 10,000- to 12,000-foot peaks in the Chugach Range. Its width at the terminus can be as much as 4 mi; its ice thickness can reach 900 feet (on average 300 feet above the water and 600 feet below). It is also only 8 mi from the shipping lanes traveled by oil tankers leaving the Alaska pipeline terminal at Valdez. Columbia has been receding since the early 1980s, sending berg after berg into Prince William Sound and into the shipping lanes to Valdez, and now that it's receding, it has the potential to calve even more bergs. Although a shallow sill, or shoal, of underwater glacial deposits keeps icebergs more than 100 feet thick from entering Prince William Sound, some big bergs still make it to the shipping lanes. Columbia's calving took its toll just after midnight on March 29, 1989, when Captain Hazlewood of the *Exxon Valdez* steered too far east while trying to avoid bergs in Valdez Arm and ran aground on Bligh Reef.

You can see many glaciers from the Alaska Marine Highway. The tidewater glaciers of Glacier Bay and the Malaspina and Hubbard glaciers in Yakutat Bay are best seen by boat or ship. Sailing into Valdez Arm, you may see more of the Columbia Glacier than you want—it's often coming to see you in the form of scores of bergs and bergeys, forcing you east toward Bligh Reef. Once you are safely ashore in Valdez it's time to look at valley glaciers. You can access either the Valdez or Worthington Glacier by road. If in the Matanuska Valley, go see the Matanuska Glacier. If on the Kenai Peninsula, try either the Exit or Portage Glacier. If you are visiting Juneau, the Mendenhall Glacier is on the outskirts of town.

Volcanoes

More than 80 volcanoes in Alaska are potentially active. Novarupta, Pavlof, Augustine, Redoubt, and Spurr are Alaskan volcanoes that are part of the "Ring of Fire," the volcanic rim of the Pacific. From Mt. Wrangell at 144° west longitude in Southeast Alaska to Cape Wrangell at 173° east longitude at the tip of the Aleutian archipelago, southern Alaska exists, to paraphrase historian Will Durant, by volcanic decree . . . subject to change.

Anchorage (and the greater Cook Inlet area) is a great place to watch volcanoes erupt. Augustine, Redoubt, and Spurr volcanoes have put on shows up and down the Cook Inlet; the Mt. Spurr eruption of August 1992 temporarily stopped air travel into and out of Anchorage. The most violent Alaskan eruption? The 2½-day eruption of Novarupta in 1912 in what is now Katmai National Park. The 2.5 cubic mi of ash deposited there has left an Alaskan legacy: the surreal Valley of Ten Thousand Smokes.

Earthquake Country

The length of a fault system and whether or not the fault is straight over great distances are of interest to geologists. Fault length is related to earthquake magnitude. Generally speaking, the longer a fault, the greater the potential magnitude. Impressed by the 600-mi length of California's San Andreas? The onshore portion of the Denali Fault System is more than 1,000 mi long. Numerous long faults around the world move horizontally. This produces some interesting results if the fault trace is not straight. A fault system such as the Denali has a large component of horizontal movement (called strike-slip motion): crustal blocks on either side move past each other, rather than up or down. If a strike-slip fault bends, one of two situations results: a gap or hole in the crust (usually filled by volcanic outbreaks and/or sediments sloughing into the hole) or a compression of the bend, resulting in vertical uplift (mountains). Which condition occurs is a function of fault motion, whether into or out of the bend. South of Fairbanks, the Denali Fault System changes trend, from northwest–southeast to northeast–southwest. The sense of horizontal motion is into the bend, resulting in vertical uplift. What mountain just happens to be in the vicinity? Mt. McKinley, at 20,320 feet the tallest mountain in North America. Moreover, its relief (difference in elevation between the base and top of the mountain), at 18,000 feet, is unsurpassed. Mt. Everest is more than 29,000 feet, but "only" 11,000 feet above the Tibetan Plateau, which forms its base.

With such big faults, it's no wonder geologists look at Alaska as big earthquake country. Seward, Valdez, Whittier, and Anchorage are just some of the more prominent names associated with the Good Friday Earthquake of 1964. Upgraded in 1977 to magnitude 9.2, the Good Friday quake is the largest on record for North America. Fifteen to thirty seconds is not unusual for ground motion in a big, destructive earthquake; Alaskans shook for three to four minutes during the Good Friday quake. The epicenter was about 6 mi east of College Fjord in Prince William Sound, some 70 mi east of Anchorage. Vertical deformation (uplift or down-dropping of the land) affected an area of 100,000 square mi. By the time the shaking had stopped, the area of Latouche Island had moved 60 feet to the southeast and portions of the Montague Island area were uplifted by as much as 30 feet. The area of Portage was down-dropped by approximately 10 feet. The largest tsunami (often misnamed a tidal wave) that hit Hilo, Hawaii, checked in at 12½ feet; the largest at Crescent City, California, was 13 feet; and in Chenega, Alaska, native residents were never sure what rose from the sea to smite them . . . just that it was 90 feet tall. The entire planet was affected: the area in which the quake was felt by people is estimated at 500,000 square mi—South Africa checked in to report that groundwater was sloshing around in wells.

Geologists generally describe tsunamis with respect to displacement on a fault underwater. They use the more general term "seismic sea wave" when other things, such as submarine landslides, cause enormous waves. The 90-foot seismic sea wave that hit Chenega was topped by the 220-foot wave reported from the Valdez Arm area. But a few years earlier in southeastern Alaska, on the evening of July 9, 1958, an earthquake in the Yakutat area dumped an enormous landslide into the head of Lituya Bay. The result was a seiche, or splash wave, that traveled 1,740 feet up the opposite mountainside.

Impressed yet? In the last century the average recurrence interval for Alaskan earthquakes in excess of 8.0 on the Richter Scale was 10 years. The recurrence interval for earthquakes over 7.0 is just over a year. Never mind California—Alaska is the most seismically active state in the Union. Volcanic hazard? Well, Pavlof has averaged an eruption every 6 years over the last 240.

Desert

And now about that desert. The North Slope of Alaska is 80,000 square mi of frozen, windswept desert where Inupiat Eskimos live. It's a desert from the climatological perspective that the North Slope receives less than 10 inches of precipitation each year. If you go around the west end of the Brooks Range, you can even find sand dunes—Great Kobuk, Little Kobuk, and Hunt River sand-dune fields. Temperatures during the short, cool summers are usually between 30°F and 40°F. Temperatures during the winter can average –20°F. In winter, the Arctic Ocean moderates temperatures on the North Slope, but there is nothing to moderate the wind.

Rocks & Minerals

The first people to come into the country came across the Bering Land Bridge from Asia, between 10,000 and 40,000 years ago. The Bering Land Bridge was a product of the Pleistocene epoch—the Great Ice Age—which lowered the sea level enough for the bridge to form. At the start of the Mesozoic era (beginning about 245 million years before the present), sandstones and conglomerates deposited in a warm, shallow sea marked the beginning of Prudhoe Bay. That abundant organic matter is now abundant oil under the North Slope. Also during the Mesozoic era, oil-bearing shales were deposited in the Cook Inlet, home of Alaska's first oil boom; copper and silver deposits were formed in what is now the Copper River country; Cretaceous swamps in South Central Alaska became the Matanuska coalfield; and gold was emplaced around present-day Fairbanks and near Nome on the Seward Peninsula.

The oldest rocks in Alaska are of Precambrian age (the "Time Before Life") and are in southwestern Alaska. They have been dated at 2 billion years of age, nearly half the age of the earth. Rocks 1 billion years old have been identified in the area of the Brooks Range south to the Yukon River. Interestingly, the 1-billion-year-old rocks are native; the 2-billion-year-old rocks are expatriates. In fact, southern and southeastern Alaska are composed of a mosaic or quilt of microplates, all much smaller than continent size. Some terranes (blocks or fragments of the Earth's crust that may vary in age, geologic character, or site of origin) arrived in Alaska from as far south as the equator.

Certain Alaskan rocks tell a tale of warm climates and seas. Evidence? Hike the Holitna River basin in Southwest Alaska and look for fossil remains of the many trilobites (those now-extinct three-lobe marine arthropods that scavenged the bottoms of warm, shallow, Cambrian seas—parents, if you don't know what they look like, ask your children). The central interior of Alaska evidently was never covered by ice but was instead a cool steppe land roamed by mammoths, bison, horses, saber-toothed cats, and camels. Yes, camels.

A Geologic Wonder

Alaska's stunning expanse incorporates fire and ice, wind and rain, volcano, glacier, windswept tundra, towering rain forest, and mist-shrouded island. Its geologic story covers a great deal of time and distance and has produced (and is producing) some of the most exquisite land anywhere. In the north, the rocks tell a story of relative stability—geological homebodies born and raised. In the south, the patchwork terrains tell a tale of far-traveled immigrants coming into the country. Geological processes that have produced, and are still producing, both homebodies and expatriates create a land in constant flux. But the majesty of the land: that is the unchanging legacy of Alaska.

–Dr. Charles Lane

BOOKS & MOVIES

Books

Alaska has long been a setting for tales of heroes, great journeys, and people's epic struggle with nature. Novels with rich descriptions of the state's people, wildlife, and landscapes include Ivan Doig's *The Sea Runners* (Penguin), an adventure set in 1853, when Alaska still belonged to Russia; *Athabasca* (out of print), an Alistair MacLean thriller set around the trans-Alaska pipeline; and *Sitka* (Signet), by the popular chronicler of the American frontier, Louis L'Amour. *Alaska* (Random House), by James Michener, is a weighty historical novel about the state from prehistoric to modern times.

Alaskan authors have written a number of mystery novels about their state. Among the best are Sue Henry's *Murder on the Iditarod Trail* (Avon); John Straley's *The Woman Who Married a Bear* (Signet), about the adventures of private eye Cecil Younger; and Dana Stabenow's *A Cold-Blooded Business* (Berkley Books), whose hero is Aleut private investigator Kate Shugak.

Alaska has produced an even more significant collection of high-quality nonfiction literature. John McPhee's *Coming into the Country* (Noonday Press) is considered by some to be the most insightful book ever written about Alaska. Joe McGinniss, in *Going to Extremes* (Plume), presents a provocative outsider's portrait of Alaska's varied communities, people, and landscapes. Velma Wallis's best-selling *Two Old Women: An Alaska Legend of Betrayal, Courage and Survival* (Epicenter Press) recounts a traditional native Alaskan story.

For lovers of adventure, Art Davidson's *Minus 148 Degrees: The First Winter Ascent of Mt. McKinley* (The Mountaineers Books) describes the harrowing survival story of mountaineers caught in a ferocious storm on North America's highest peak. John Krakauer's *Into the Wild* (Anchor) wonderfully constructs the life and death of a young man who died in the Alaskan wilderness while on a personal vision quest. *Fish Camp: Life on an Alaskan Shore* (Counterpoint Press), by Nancy Lord, describes the natural and cultural history of the place where she and her partner have fished for salmon for the past two decades. Former Alaska poet laureate John Haines has written several books of poetry and essays. Among his best is the essay collection *The Stars, the Snow, the Fire* (Graywolf Press), which recounts 25 years in Alaska's wilderness. Another compelling collection of essays with natural-history themes is Sherry Simpson's *The Way Winter Comes: Alaska Stories* (Sasquatch Books). One anthology of special note is Wayne Mergler's *The Last New Land: Stories of Alaska Past and Present* (Alaska Northwest Books), a wide-ranging collection of poems, short stories, and essays about Alaska; another is Bill Sherwonit's *Denali: A Literary Anthology* (The Mountaineers Books), which presents a century's worth of published stories about Mt. McKinley, North America's highest mountain, and the surrounding wilderness.

Movies

The Last Frontier has also inspired a number of filmmakers, many offering family fare. *White Fang* (1991), based on the Jack London novel, is a Walt Disney production about the life of a wild wolf dog and the hardships prospectors faced during the Klondike gold rush. The movie set is now a tourist destination in Haines. The animated family film *Balto* (1995) tells the story of one of the canine heroes in Alaska's 1925 Great Race of Mercy, in which mushers and dog teams carry diphtheria serum to Nome to stop an outbreak of the deadly disease. More pooches star in the family comedy *Snow Dogs* (2002), in which Cuba Gooding Jr. plays a Miami dentist who inherits a team of huskies. Another popular family flick is *Alaska* (1996) in which two teens set out to rescue their bush pilot dad from the wilderness.

A number of action-adventure pictures have also taken place in Alaska. *Runaway Train* (1985), a thriller starring Jon Voight, was filmed south of Anchorage; the scenery and ending are equally dramatic. *On Deadly Ground* (1994) stars Steven Seagal as an oil-company troubleshooter who rebels after discovering his employers are exploiting the land and its native peoples. A portion of *Star Trek VI* (1991) was filmed on the Knik Glacier, northeast of Anchorage. *Limbo* (1999), set in Southeast Alaska, is a frontier drama that centers on a commercial fisherman who has become afraid of the sea. In *The Edge* (1997) Anthony Hopkins and Alec Baldwin have a great deal to be afraid of while lost in the Alaskan wilderness. *Insomnia* (2002), starring Al Pacino and Robin Williams, sees two Los Angeles detectives sent to Alaska to investigate a murder.

In August 2005, Werner Herzog's highly anticipated movie *Grizzly Man* opened in theaters, telling the fascinating and ultimately sordid story of Timothy Treadwell, a zany nature lover and actor who lived among Alaska's grizzly bears (and who was found, along with his girlfriend, mauled to death in 2003). Herzog uses Treadwell's original footage of bears as well as dozens of interviews with family members and friends.

SMART TRAVEL TIPS

AIR TRAVEL

Alaska Airlines is the flagship carrier to Alaska, with year-round service from Seattle to Anchorage, Fairbanks, Juneau, Ketchikan, and Sitka. In addition, the airline has nonstop flights linking Anchorage with Chicago, Denver, Las Vegas, Los Angeles, Portland, and Vancouver. Alaska Airlines and its subsidiary, Horizon Air, fly to many other North American cities from their Seattle hub, with nonstop connecting flights to Boston, Dallas, Denver, Washington, D.C., Miami, Newark, Orlando, San Diego, and San Francisco. Continental, Delta, and United have year-round flights to Anchorage from Seattle. Other year-round nonstop flights to Anchorage are aboard USAirways from Phoenix and Las Vegas, Northwest from Minneapolis–St. Paul, Delta from Salt Lake City, and United from Denver and San Francisco. Hawaiian Vacations has year-round charters between Anchorage and Honolulu, and seasonal service between Anchorage and Maui or Fairbanks and Maui.

Several airlines provide summer-only nonstop Anchorage flights from Lower 48 cities: Alaska Airlines from Phoenix; American from Dallas and Chicago; Continental from Houston; Delta from Atlanta, Cincinnati, and Los Angeles; Frontier from Denver; Northwest from Detroit; and United from Chicago, San Francisco, and Vancouver. Sun Country Airlines has seasonal charters connecting Anchorage with Minneapolis–St. Paul. To Fairbanks, Delta has summer-only nonstop flights from Salt Lake City, and Northwest has nonstop flights from Minneapolis–St. Paul.

Average travel time (nonstop flights only) is 3½ hours from Seattle to Anchorage, 6 hours from Chicago, 7 hours from Dallas, and 5 hours from Los Angeles. Travel times from other destinations depend on your connection, since you'll need to route through other cities. Many of the low-fare flights out of Anchorage depart around 1 AM, so be sure you are at the airport on the correct day when flying just after midnight.

WITHIN ALASKA

Air travel within Alaska can be quite expensive, particularly to Bush destinations where flying is the only option. A round-trip flight between Anchorage and Dutch Harbor typically costs more than $800—more than a flight from Anchorage to Hong Kong! Quick flights between Anchorage, Fairbanks, and Juneau are more reasonable—a typical Anchorage-to-Fairbanks or Anchorage-to-Juneau flight will cost $100–$200 one way.

The workhorses of the north are the six-passenger Beavers, most of which were built in the 1950s and are still flying. The cost of an air-taxi flight between towns or backcountry locations depends upon distance and the type of plane used, the number of people in your group, the length of the flight in each direction (including the time the pilot flies back after dropping you off), and the destination. Typical hourly rates are approximately $515 for a Beaver, with room for up to six people and gear; or $310 for a Cessna 185, with room for three people and gear.

Small planes have played a legendary part in the state's history: Bush pilots helped explore Alaska and have been responsible for many dramatic rescue missions. But be aware that small planes cannot transport more than a limited amount of gear and cannot fly safely in poor weather. Your drop-off and pickup flights are subject to delays, which are sometimes counted in days, not hours. When traveling in remote areas, be sure to carry extra food. Although most villages have general stores, fresh produce tends to be expensive and sometimes unavailable. Note also that some items are not allowed on commercial aircraft. This includes camp-stove fuel and the so-called "bear mace" (pepper spray) sold in camping-goods stores.

Contact the following airlines for flights within Alaska: Bering Air for flights from Nome or Kotzebue to smaller communities of the Far North; Era Aviation for flights from Anchorage to Cordova, Homer, Iliamna, Kenai, Kodiak, Valdez, and 17 western Alaska villages; and Frontier Flying Service for flights from Anchorage to Fairbanks, Bethel, and many Bush villages. Contact Warbelow's Air Ventures and Larry's Flying Service for flights out of Fairbanks to Interior destinations. Peninsula Airways (PenAir), based in Anchorage, covers southwestern Alaska, including Aniak, Dutch Harbor, McGrath, Dillingham, King Salmon, Sand Point, St. Paul, and St. George. Wings of Alaska serves several Southeast Alaska towns, including Juneau, Skagway, Haines, and Gustavus.

To and From Alaska **Alaska Airlines** ☎ 800/252-7522 or 206/433-3100 🌐 www.alaskaair.com. **American Airlines** ☎ 800/433-7300 🌐 www.aa.com. **Continental Airlines** ☎ 800/523-3273 for U.S. and Mexico reservations, 800/231-0856 for international reservations 🌐 www.continental.com. **Delta Airlines** ☎ 800/221-1212 for U.S. reservations, 800/241-4141 for international reservations 🌐 www.delta.com. **Frontier Airlines** ☎ 800/432-1359 for U.S. reservations 🌐 www.frontierairlines.com. **Hawaiian Vacations** ☎ 907/261-2700 or 800/770-2700 🌐 www.hawaiianvacations.com. **Northwest Airlines** ☎ 800/225-2525 for U.S. reservations, 800/447-4747 for international destinations 🌐 www.nwa.com. **Sun Country Airlines** ☎ 800/359-6786 🌐 www.suncountry.com. **United Airlines** ☎ 800/864-8331 for U.S. reservations, 800/538-2929 for international reservations 🌐 www.united.com. **USAirways** ☎ 800/428-4322 for U.S. and Canada reservations, 800/622-1015 for international reservations 🌐 www.usairways.com.

Within Alaska **Bering Air** ☎ 907/443-5464 or 800/478-5422 Nome reservations, 907/442-3943 or 800/478-3943 Kotzebue reservations 🌐 www.beringair.com. **Era Aviation** ☎ 907/266-8394 or 800/866-8394 🌐 www.eraaviation.com. **Frontier Flying Service** ☎ 907/450-7200 or 800/478-6779 🌐 www.frontierflying.com. **Larry's Flying Service** ☎ 907/474-9169 🌐 www.larrysflying.com. **PenAir** ☎ 907/243-2323 or 800/448-4226 🌐 www.penair.com. **Warbelow's Air Ventures** ☎ 907/474-0518 or 800/478-0812 🌐 www.warbelows.com. **Wings of Alaska** ☎ 907/789-0790 🌐 www.wingsofalaska.com.

CHECK-IN & BOARDING

Double-check your flight times, especially if you made your reservations far in advance. Airlines change their schedules, and alerts may not reach you. This is especially important if you're taking smaller, charter flights or Bush planes, the schedules of which are greatly affected by weather conditions.

Always **bring a government-issued photo I.D. to the airport** (even when it's not required, a passport is best), and **arrive early.** Check-in usually at least an hour before domestic flights and two to three hours for international flights. But many airlines have more stringent advance check-in requirements at some busy airports. The TSA estimates the waiting time for security at most major airports and publishes the information on its Web site. Note that if you aren't at the gate at least 10 minutes before your flight is scheduled to take off (sometimes earlier), you won't be allowed to board.

Minimize the time spent standing in line. Buy an e-ticket, check in at an electronic kiosk, or—even better—check in on your airline's Web site before you leave home. These days, most domestic airline tickets are electronic; international tickets may be either electronic or paper. Also, pack light and limit carry-on items to only the essentials.

You usually pay a surcharge (up to $50) to get a paper ticket, and its sole advantage is that it may be easier to endorse over to another airline if your flight is cancelled and the airline with which you booked can't accommodate you on another flight. With an e-ticket, the only thing you receive is an e-mailed receipt citing your itinerary and reservation and ticket numbers. Be sure to carry this with you as you'll need it to get past security. If you lose you receipt, though, you can simply print out another copy or ask the airline to do it for you at check-in.

Particularly during busy travel seasons and around holiday periods, if a flight is oversold, the gate agent will usually ask for volunteers and will offer some sort of compensation if you are willing to take a different flight. **Know your rights.** If you are bumped from a flight *involuntarily*, the airline must give you some kind of compensation if an alternate flight can't be found within one hour. If your flight is delayed because of something within the airline's control (so bad weather doesn't count), then the airline has a responsibility to get you to your destination on the same day, even if they have to book you on another airline and in an upgraded class if necessary. Read your airline's Contract of Carriage; it's usually buried somewhere on the airline's Web site.

Be prepared to quickly adjust your plans by programming a few numbers into your cell: your airline, an airport hotel or two, your destination hotel, your car service, and/or your travel agent.

CUTTING COSTS

The least expensive airfares to Alaska are often priced for round-trip travel and must usually be purchased in advance. Airlines generally allow you to change your return date for a fee; most low-fare tickets, however, are nonrefundable. It's always good to **comparison shop.** Web sites and travel agents can have different arrangements with the airlines and offer different prices for exactly the same flight and day. Certain Web sites have tracking features that will e-mail you immediately when good deals are posted. Other people prefer to stick with one or two frequent-flier programs, racking up free trips and accumulating perks that can make trips easier. On some airlines, perks include a special reservations number, early boarding, access to upgrades, and more roomy economy-class seating.

Check early and often. Start looking for cheap fares up to a year in advance, and keep looking until you see something you can live with; you never know when a good deal may pop up. That said, **jump on the good deals.** Waiting even a few minutes might mean paying more. For most people, saving money is more important than flexibility, so the more affordable nonrefundable tickets work. Just remember that you'll pay dearly (often as much as $100) if you must change your travel plans. Check on prices for departures at different times of the day and to and from alternate airports, and look for departures on Tuesday, Wednesday, and Thursday, typically the cheapest days to travel. Remember to **weigh your options,** though. A cheaper flight might have a long layover rather than being nonstop, or landing at a secondary airport might substantially increase your ground transportation costs.

Note that many airline Web sites—and most ads—show prices *without* taxes and surcharges. Don't buy until you know the full price. Government taxes add up quickly. Also **watch those ticketing fees.** Surcharges are usually added when you buy your ticket anywhere but on an airline's own Web site. (By the way, that includes on the phone–even if you call the airline directly—and for paper tickets regardless of how you book).

Alaska Airlines and some other carriers have specials to and from Alaska. These generally allow only a maximum one-week stay but sometimes cost less than half the going rate. In general, prices are lowest when booked at least two weeks ahead, but Web fares often pop up with lower rates.

Online Consolidators **AirlineConsolidator.com** www.airlineconsolidator.com; for international tickets. **Best Fares** www.bestfares.com; $59.90 annual membership. **Cheap Tickets** www.cheaptickets.com. **Expedia** www.expedia.com. **Hotwire** www.hotwire.com is a discounter. **lastminute.com** www.lastminute.com specializes in last-minute travel; the main site is for the UK, but it has a link to a U.S. site. **Luxury Link** www.luxurylink.com has auctions (surprisingly good deals) as well as offers at the high-end side of travel. **Onetravel.com** www.onetravel.com. **Orbitz** www.orbitz.com. **Priceline.com** www.priceline.com is a discounter that also allows bidding. **Travel.com** www.travel.com allows you to compare its rates with those of other booking engines. **Travelocity** www.travelocity.com charges a booking fee for airline tickets but promises good problem resolution.

ENJOYING THE FLIGHT

Get the seat you want. Avoid those on the aisle directly across from the lavatories. Most frequent fliers say those are even worse than the seats that don't recline (e.g., those in the back row and those in front of a bulkhead). For more legroom, you can request emergency-aisle seats, but only do so if you're capable of moving the 35- to 60-pound airplane exit door—a Federal Aviation Administration requirement of passengers in these seats. Seats behind a bulkhead also offer more legroom, but they don't have under-seat storage. Often, you can pick a seat when you buy your ticket on an airline's Web site. But it's not always a guarantee, particularly if the airline changes the plane after you book your ticket; check back before you leave. SeatGuru.com has more information about specific seat configurations, which vary by aircraft.

Fewer airlines are providing free food for passengers in economy class. **Don't go hungry.** If you're scheduled to fly during meal times, verify if your airline offers anything to eat; even when it does, be prepared to pay. If you have dietary concerns, request special meals. These can be vegetarian, low-cholesterol, or kosher, for example.

Ask the airline about its children's menus, activities, and fares. On some lines infants and toddlers fly for free if they sit on a parent's lap, and older children fly for half price in their own seats. Also inquire about policies involving car seats; having one may limit where you can sit. While you're at it, ask about seatbelt extenders for car seats. And note that you can't count on a flight attendant to automatically produce an extender; you may have to inquire about it again when you board.

All flights to and within Alaska are smoke-free, including charter flights and flights into the Bush. Many scheduled flights to Bush communities are on small planes, most of which seat 6 to 15 passengers. Turbulence is not uncommon, which at times can leave you white-knuckled and green in the face. Fortunately, most flights are uneventful, though the scenery below makes them memorable.

HOW TO COMPLAIN

If your baggage goes astray or your flight goes awry, complain right away. Most carriers require that you **file a claim immediately.** The Aviation Consumer Protection Division of the Department of Transportation publishes *Fly-Rights,* which discusses airlines and consumer issues and is available online. You can also find articles and information on mytravelrights.com, the Web site of the nonprofit Consumer Travel Rights Center.

Airline Complaints **Office of Aviation Enforcement and Proceedings** (Aviation Consumer Protection Division) ☎ 202/366-2220 🌐 airconsumer.ost.dot.gov. **Federal Aviation Administration Consumer Hotline** ☎ 866/835-5322 🌐 www.faa.gov.

AIRPORTS

Anchorage's Ted Stevens International Airport is Alaska's main hub. There are also major airports ("major" meaning that they serve more than just Bush planes) in Fairbanks, Juneau, and Ketchikan; the Fairbanks airport is the largest of the three—Juneau and Ketchikan are very small and don't have many facilities or gates.

Vancouver, in Canada, is the starting point for some Alaskan cruises that make their first stop in Ketchikan, Alaska's southernmost town. Unless you're flying from the West Coast or manage to get a nonstop flight, chances are you'll spend some time in Seattle's international airport (known locally as Sea-Tac), waiting for a connection.

You won't find much in terms of entertainment in Ted Stevens, Sea-Tac, or Vancouver's airport, so if you have really long layovers at any of the three, consider taking a taxi into the city. Ted Stevens is only 6 mi from downtown Anchorage; Seattle's downtown area is 14 mi from the airport, and if you don't get stuck in Seattle's notorious rush-hour traffic, you can get there in 20 minutes. It can take 30 to 45 minutes to get to downtown Vancouver from the airport, so it's probably inadvisable unless you're stuck for hours.

There are no departure taxes for travel within the United States. Vancouver's airport does have a departure tax of C$5 for flights within British Columbia and the Yukon or C$10 to U.S. destinations, payable before you board your flight at automatic ticket machines or staffed booths.

Airports **Airline and Airport Links.com** 🌐 www.airlineandairportlinks.com has links to many of the world's airlines and airports. **Fairbanks International Airport** (FAI) 🌐 www.dot.state.ak.us/faiiap. **Juneau International Airport** (JNU) ☎ 907/789-9539 Alaska Airlines flight info 🌐 www.juneau.org/airport. **Ketchikan Airport** (KTN) ☎ 907/225-6800 🌐 www.borough.ketchikan.ak.us/airport/airport.htm. **Seattle-Tacoma International Airport** (SEA) ☎ 206/431-4444 🌐 www.portseattle.org/seatac. **Ted Stevens Anchorage International Airport** (ANC) ☎ 907/266-2525 🌐 www.dot.state.ak.us/anc. **Vancouver International Airport** (YVR) ☎ 604/303-3603 🌐 www.yvr.ca.

Airline Security Issues **Transportation Security Administration** 🌐 www.tsa.gov/public has answers for almost every question that might come up.

BOAT & FERRY TRAVEL

If you are looking for a casual alternative to a luxury cruise, **travel as Alaskans do, aboard the ferries of the Alaska Marine Highway System.** The ferries may not have the same facilities as the big cruise ships, but they do meander through some of the most beautiful parts of the state. You won't be completely without entertainment, either. Forest Service naturalists ride the larger ferries in summer, providing a running commentary on sights. In addition, the Arts-on-Board Program presents educators and entertainers on selected summer routes.

Most long-haul ferries have cabins with private bathrooms; be sure to book ahead if you want to reserve one. If you don't get a cabin, you'll have to settle for a reclining seat. Most ships also have spaces where passengers can roll out their sleeping bags or even pitch tents. All long-haul ferries have cafeterias with hot meal service (not included in the ticket price), along with concession stands and vending machines. Almost all ships have showers that are either free or cost a nominal fee.

The Alaska Marine Highway ferries provide service to much of the state. The Inside Passage route, which stretches from Bellingham, Washington (or Prince Rupert, British Columbia) all the way up to Skagway and Haines, is the most popular, mimicking the route of most major cruise lines. The Bellingham-to-Ketchikan trip, the longest leg, takes roughly 37 hours. (The trip from Prince Rupert to Ketchikan takes six hours; BC Ferries provide service from Vancouver to Prince Rupert.) Other trips along the Inside Passage take from three to eight hours.

Sporadic summer service across the Gulf of Alaska from either Prince Rupert, Ketchikan, or Juneau links the Southeast with South Central Alaska destinations (trips usual end in Whittier, about 60 mi south of Anchorage). There is further service to limited ports in South Central Alaska, as well as connecting service to the Southwest from Whittier and Homer to Kodiak and Port Lions, respectively. Southwest ferries can take you all the way to Dutch Harbor.

Two high-speed catamarans can cut travel time in half. The *MV Fairweather* is based in Juneau and serves Haines, Skagway, and Sitka. In summer, the *MV Chenega*, based in Cordova, serves the Prince William Sound, with stops in Valdez and Whittier. In the fall and winter, its route changes, serving either the same route as the *Fairweather* or Ketchikan to Juneau via Wrangell and Petersburg.

The Inter-Island Ferry Authority connects Southeast Alaska's Prince of Wales Island with the towns of Ketchikan, Wrangell, and Petersburg. Note that although major ports like Juneau and Ketchikan will likely have daily departures, service to smaller towns is much more sporadic—one departure per week in some cases. Request a copy of a printed schedule over the phone, or download it from the Internet at www.ferryalaska.com.

CUTTING COSTS

The AlaskaPass allows unlimited travel on bus, ferry, and rail lines in Alaska, along with bus and ferry travel in British Columbia and the Yukon. Passes are available for 15 consecutive days of travel ($829), as well as for 8 days of travel in a 12-day period ($699) or 12 days of travel in a 21-day period ($849). There is a $75 booking fee. Most travelers book their entire itinerary in advance; if you don't have a car, there is usually room on ferries for those without prebookings.

AlaskaPass 206/463-6550 or 800/248-7598 www.alaskapass.com.

FARES & SCHEDULES

Make reservations for ferry travel by calling the Alaska Marine Highway System. Online reservations are also available. They will mail the tickets, or you can pick them up from the ferry office at your starting point. Book as far in advance as possible for summertime travel, especially if you have a vehicle. You should also book ahead for the Bellingham–Ketchikan journey.

The Bellingham-to-Ketchikan route costs roughly $230 one way in summer. Shorter trips cost anywhere from $30 to $140 one way; for example, Petersburg to Sitka will cost around $40, while Ketchikan to Skagway will cost roughly $140 one way. Note that there are surcharges for vehicles, motorcycles, bicycles, and kayaks. Renting cabins will also increase the fare significantly.

PAYING

You can pay for ferry travel by cash, credit card (American Express, Discover, MasterCard, or Visa), cashier's check, money order, certified check, or personal check from an Alaskan bank.

Boat & Ferry Information **Alaska Marine Highway** 907/465-3941 or 800/642-0066 www.ferryalaska.com. **B.C. Ferries** 250/386-3431 or 888/223-3779 www.bcferries.bc.ca. **Inter-Island Ferry Authority** 907/826-4848 or 866/308-4848 www.interislandferry.com.

BUSINESS HOURS

Most Alaskan stores are open weekdays from 9 AM to 5 PM, though many have longer hours and remain open on weekends. Larger towns have at least one convenience store that stays open 24 hours a day. In small Bush villages, the general store may be open just a few hours per day and closed on Sunday, whereas in larger cities the grocery stores remain open 24 hours a day, seven days a week.

BANKS & OFFICES

Banks and credit unions are typically open weekdays 10–5, and some have limited Saturday hours, particularly in Anchorage, Fairbanks, and Juneau. Most government and other offices are open weekdays 9–5, though some close at 4:30.

GAS STATIONS

Many Alaskan gas stations remain open until 10 PM, and in the larger towns and cities, some stay open 24 hours a day. Most are also open on weekends, particularly along the main highways. In the smallest villages gas may be available only on weekdays, but these settlements typically have only a few miles of roads.

MUSEUMS & SIGHTS

Hours of sights and attractions are denoted in the book by the clock icon, ⏲. Museums in smaller Southeast Alaska towns typically open whenever a cruise ship or ferry is in port, even if it is late on a Sunday evening. *See* specific town descriptions for more information.

PHARMACIES

Pharmacy hours vary across Alaska, but most local hospitals have a pharmacy that provides service at any hour.

SHOPS

Alaskan gift shops are typically open weekdays or whenever cruise ships are in port. Gift shops in Anchorage are generally open year-round, but in other towns many places close in October and reopen in May.

BUS TRAVEL

Traveling by bus in Alaska can sometimes be more economical than traveling by train or by air, but don't count on it being your main mode of travel. Always confirm your trip via phone, as schedules often change at the last minute. Smoking is prohibited on all Alaska buses or vans. Contact individual companies for schedules.

Greyhound Lines of Canada serves Vancouver, with service as far north as Whitehorse in the Canadian Yukon. Two companies provide onward bus service into South Central and Interior Alaska from Whitehorse. Alaska Direct Bus Lines operates year-round van service connecting Anchorage and Fairbanks with Glennallen, Delta Junction, Skagway, and Tok in Alaska, along with Whitehorse in the Yukon. Alaska/Yukon Trails provides year-round bus service between Anchorage and Fairbanks, plus seasonal service connecting Fairbanks with Dawson City in the Yukon.

Denali Overland Transportation has frequent van service in the summer between Anchorage, Talkeetna, and Denali National Park & Preserve. The Alaska Park Connection has summertime bus service between Seward and Anchorage, continuing north to Denali. Homer Stage Line provides year-round service between Anchorage and Homer, plus summertime service connecting Seward with Anchorage and Homer.

Quick Shuttle bus service runs between Vancouver and Seattle. Green Tortoise buses provide a casual alternative way to travel north, with funky classic buses that are popular with young backpackers.

CUTTING COSTS

The AlaskaPass allows unlimited travel on ferry, rail lines, and Holland America buses (Whitehorse to Fairbanks only) in Alaska and the Yukon (*see* Cutting Costs *in* Boat & Ferry Travel).

PAYING

Accepted forms of payment vary among the bus companies, but all accept MasterCard, Visa, and traveler's checks.

RESERVATIONS

Many bus lines—particularly those heading to Denali—either require reservations or strongly recommend them.

Bus Information **Alaska Direct Bus Lines** ☎ 907/277-6652 or 800/770-6652. **Alaska Park Connection** ☎ 907/245-0200 or 800/266-8625 🌐 www.alaskacoach.com. **Alaska/Yukon Trails** ☎ 907/457-2034 or 800/770-7275 🌐 www.alaskashuttle.com. **Denali Overland Transportation** ☎ 907/733-2384 or 800/651-5221 🌐 www.denalioverland.com. **Green Tortoise** ☎ 415/956-7500 or 800/867-8647 🌐 www.greentortoise.com. **Greyhound Lines of Canada** ☎ 604/482-8747 or 800/661-8747 🌐 www.greyhound.ca. **Homer Stage Line** ☎ 907/235-7090 or 907/399-1847 🌐 www.homerstageline.com. **Quick Shuttle** ☎ 604/244-3744 or 800/665-2122 🌐 www.quickcoach.com.

CAMERAS & PHOTOGRAPHY

Alaska is one of the world's premier spots for nature photography. Because of the high latitude, the light remains at a low angle for many hours during summer days, creating extraordinary photographic conditions.

Digital cameras are increasingly used by both amateurs and professional photographers, and the proliferation of Internet cafés has made it possible to e-mail digital photos to friends easily as you travel. Larger towns generally have at least one business where you can transfer these photos to CDs or output them as prints. Serious photographers often carry a laptop computer or an iPod to download and store images. If you're shooting digital, be sure to bring extra rechargeable batteries (and a charger), along with additional memory cards.

Photographers who shoot with film will find that an ISO 200-speed print film is sufficient for most purposes, though ISO 400 is better for low-light situations and action shots. Many professional photographers shoot color slides, using Fuji's Sensia II or Velvia, along with Kodak's Ektachrome 100SW.

A zoom lens covering 28 mm–105 mm is adequate for most Alaskan scenes, but longer telephoto lenses (200 mm and up) are useful for wildlife photos. A tripod is essential in dimly lighted situations and highly recommended for photographing wildlife with a telephoto lens.

Not everyone in Alaska appreciates being photographed, particularly in smaller native villages. Ask for permission before taking a photograph. Many museums do not allow flash or tripods, and photography is restricted or prohibited inside Russian Orthodox churches and certain native cemeteries.

The *Kodak Guide to Shooting Great Travel Pictures* (available at bookstores everywhere) is loaded with tips.

Photo Help Kodak Information Center www.kodak.com.

EQUIPMENT PRECAUTIONS

A plastic bag or umbrella will help keep your camera dry during wet weather. Winter travelers may need to contend with extremely cold conditions, which can greatly reduce battery life, fog lenses, and even cause complete mechanical failure. Be sure to pack extra batteries for your camera, especially when heading into remote areas. Lens fogging can be lessened by storing the camera and lenses in a cool place.

Don't pack film or equipment in checked luggage, where it is much more susceptible to damage. X-ray machines used to view checked luggage are extremely powerful and therefore are likely to ruin your film. Try to ask for hand inspection of film, which becomes clouded after repeated exposure to airport X-ray machines, and keep videotapes and computer disks away from metal detectors. Always keep film, tape, and computer disks out of the sun. Carry an extra supply of batteries, and be prepared to turn on your camera, camcorder, or laptop to prove to airport security personnel that the device is real.

CAR RENTAL

Rental cars are available in most Alaska towns. In Anchorage and other major destinations, expect to pay around \$55–\$75 a day or \$300 (and up) a week for an economy or compact car with automatic transmission and unlimited mileage. Some of the locally owned companies offer lower rates for older cars. Rates can be substantially higher for larger vehicles, four-wheel drives, SUVs, and vans. In small towns, particularly those off the road system in Southeast Alaska or the Bush, rental rates are higher. Also note that vehicles in these remote towns are typically several years old, and some would rate as "beaters." **Reserve well ahead for the summer season, particularly for the popular minivans and SUVs.** A 10% state tax is tacked on to all car rentals in Alaska, plus any local taxes.

In Alaska you must be 21 to rent a car, and rates may be higher if you're under 25. When picking up a car, non-U.S. residents will need a reservation voucher, a passport, a driver's license (written in English), and a travel policy that covers each driver.

Request car seats and extras such as GPS when you book, and make sure that a confirmed reservation guarantees you a car. Agencies sometimes overbook, particularly for busy weekends and holiday periods. Rates are sometimes—but not always—better if you book in advance or reserve through a rental agency's Web site.

CUTTING COSTS

Discount travel Web sites such as Travelocity.com can help with finding the lowest rates for Alaska's larger cities. Be sure to ask in advance about discounts if you have a AAA or Costco card, or are over age 50.

Really weigh your options. Find out if a credit card you carry or organization or frequent-renter program to which you belong has a discount program. And check that such discounts really are the best deal. You can often do better with special weekend or weekly rates offered by a rental agency. (And even if you only want to rent for five or six days, ask if you can get the weekly rate; it may very well be cheaper than the daily rate for that period of time.)

Price local car-rental companies as well as the majors. Also investigate wholesalers, which don't own fleets but rent in bulk from those that do and often offer better rates (note you must usually pay for such rentals before leaving home). Consider adding a car rental onto your air/hotel vacation package; the cost will often be cheaper than if you had rented the car separately on your own.

Beware of hidden charges. Those great rental rates may not be so great when you add in taxes, surcharges, cancellation penalties, taxes, drop-off charges (if you're planning to pick up the car in one city and leave it in another), and surcharges (for being under or over a certain age, for additional drivers, or for driving over state or country borders or out of a specific radius from your point of rental).

Note that airport rental offices often add supplementary surcharges that you may avoid by renting from an agency whose office is just off airport property. Don't buy the tank of gas that's in the car when you rent it unless you plan to do a lot of driving. Avoid hefty refueling fees by filling the tank at a station well away from the rental agency (those nearby are often more expensive) just before you turn in the car.

Automobile Associations **American Automobile Association** (AAA) ☎ 315/797-5000 🌐 www.aaa.com; most contact with the organization is through state and regional members. **National Automobile Club** ☎ 650/294-7000 🌐 www.thenac.com; membership is open to California residents only.

Local Agencies **Arctic Rent-A-Car** ☎ 800/478-8696, 907/561-2990 in Anchorage, 907/479-8044 in Fairbanks 🌐 www.arcticrentacar.com. **Denali Car Rental** ☎ 907/276-1230, 800/757-1230 in Anchorage. **U-Save Auto Rental** ☎ 907/272-8728 or 800/254-8728 in Anchorage, 907/479-7060 or 877/979-7060 in Fairbanks 🌐 www.usaveak.com.

Major Agencies **Alamo** ☎ 800/462-5266 🌐 www.alamo.com. **Avis** ☎ 800/230-4898 🌐 www.avis.com. **Budget** ☎ 800/527-0700 🌐 www.budget.com. **Hertz** ☎ 800/654-3131 🌐 www.hertz.com. **National Car Rental** ☎ 800/227-7368 🌐 www.nationalcar.com.

INSURANCE

Everyone who rents a car wonders about whether the insurance that the rental companies offer is worth the expense. No one—not even us—has a simple answer. It all depends on how much regular insurance you have, how comfortable you are with risk, and whether or not money is an issue. That said, keep in mind that Alaskan roads can be treacherous and gravelly. Also, moose routinely cross the throughways in just about every region.

If you own a car and carry comprehensive car insurance for both collision and liability, your personal auto insurance will probably cover a rental, but read your policy's fine print to be sure. If you don't have auto insurance, then you should probably buy the collision- or loss-damage waiver (CDW or LDW) from the rental company. This eliminates your liability for damage to the car. Some credit cards offer CDW coverage, but it's usually supplemental to your own insurance and rarely covers SUVs, minivans, luxury models and the like. If your coverage is secondary, you may still be liable for loss-of-use costs from the car-rental company (again, read the fine print). But no credit-card insurance is valid unless you use that card for *all* transactions, from reserving to paying the final bill.

You may also be offered supplemental liability coverage; the car-rental company is required to carry a minimal level of liability coverage that covers all renters, but it's rarely enough to cover claims in a really serious accident if you're at fault. Your own auto insurance policy will protect you if you own a car; if you don't, you have to decide if you are willing to take the risk.

U.S. rental companies sell CDWs and LDWs for about $15 to $25 a day; supplemental liability is usually over $10 a day. The car-rental company may offer you all sorts of other policies, but they're rarely worth the cost. Personal accident insurance, which is basic hospitalization coverage, is an especially egregious rip-off if you already have health insurance.

Note that you can decline the insurance from the rental company and purchase it through a third-party provider such as Travel Guard (www.travelguard.com)—$9 per day for $35,000 of coverage. That's sometimes just under half the price of the CDW offered by some car-rental companies. Also, Diners Club offers primary CDW coverage on all rentals reserved and paid for with the card. This means that Diners Club's company—not your own car insurance—pays in case of an accident. It *doesn't* mean your car-insurance company won't raise your rates once it discovers you had an accident.

CAR TRAVEL

Driving to Alaska is a popular alternative to flying or cruising, especially for RVers, but you'll need to **set aside plenty of time.** Though journeying through Canada on the Alaska Highway can be exciting, the trek from the Lower 48 states is a long one. It's a seven-day trip from Seattle to Anchorage or Fairbanks, covering close to 2,500 mi. From Bellingham, Washington, and the Canadian ports of Prince Rupert and Stewart, you can link up with ferry service along the Marine Highway to reach southeastern Alaska.

The Alaska Highway begins at Dawson Creek, British Columbia, and stretches 1,442 mi through Canada's Yukon to Delta Junction; it enters Alaska at Tok. The two-lane highway is paved for its entire length and is open year-round. Highway services are available about every 50 to 100 mi (sometimes at shorter intervals).

The rest of the state's roads are found almost exclusively in the South Central and Interior regions. They lie mainly between Anchorage, Fairbanks, and the Canadian border. Only one highway extends north of Fairbanks, and a couple run south of Anchorage to the Kenai Peninsula. These roads vary from four-lane freeways to nameless two-lane gravel roads. The Glenn Highway begins at Tok and travels south to Anchorage. The Richardson Highway parallels the Alaska pipeline from Fairbanks south to the port city of Valdez.

The Seward Highway heads south from Anchorage through the Kenai Mountains to Seward, with the Sterling Highway branch heading southwest to Kenai and Homer. The George Parks Highway connects Anchorage and Fairbanks, passing Denali National Park en route. The Steese Highway runs northwest of Fairbanks to the gold-rush town of Circle. The Dalton Highway begins at the end of the Elliott Highway, 73 mi north of Fairbanks, and leads 414 mi to Deadhorse, the supply center for the Prudhoe Bay oil fields. This gravel truck route presents unique challenges; **contact the Alaska Public Lands Information centers** (*see* Visitor Information *below*) in Fairbanks, Tok, or Anchorage if you plan to drive the Dalton Highway.

If you plan extensive driving in Alaska, join an automobile club such as AAA that offers towing and other benefits. Because of the long distances involved, you should seriously consider a plan (such as AAA Plus) that extends towing benefits to 100 mi in any direction. *The Milepost,* available in bookstores or from Morris Communications, is a mile-by-mile guide to sights and services along Alaska's highways. It is indispensable.

The Milepost ☎ 907/272-6070 or 800/726-4707 🌐 www.themilepost.com.

GASOLINE

Gas prices in the Anchorage area are comparable with those in the Lower 48, but expect to pay more elsewhere, for example Juneau or Ketchikan, and far more in remote areas, particularly small villages off the road network, where fuel must be flown in. Fuel prices in Canada along the Alaska

Highway are also very high. Most gas stations take Visa and MasterCard, and many also accept other credit cards and debit cards. Most gas stations are self-serve.

ROAD CONDITIONS

If you are planning to drive to Alaska, come armed with patience. Road construction sometimes creates long delays on the Canadian side of the border, so don't plan a tight schedule. Also, frost damage creates dips in the road that require slower driving.

Driving in Alaska is much less rigorous than it used to be, although it still presents some unusual obstacles. Moose often wander onto roads and highways. If you come across one while you're driving, it's best to **stop your car, pull off the road, and wait for the moose to cross.** Be especially vigilant when driving at dusk or at night, since moose can be active at all hours. In addition, keep your eyes open for other moose in the area, since a mother will often cross the road followed by one or two calves.

Flying gravel is a hazard along the Alaska and Dalton highways, especially in summer. A bug screen will help keep gravel and kamikaze insects off the windshield, but few travelers use them. Some travelers use clear, hard plastic guards to cover their headlights. (These are inexpensive and are available from garage or service stations along the major access routes.) Don't cover headlights with cardboard or plywood, because you'll need your lights often, even in daytime, as dust is thrown up by traffic passing in both directions. (Headlights must be used at all times on the Seward Highway south of Anchorage.)

Unless you plan to undertake one of the remote highways (especially the Dalton Highway to Prudhoe Bay), you won't need any special equipment. But be sure that the equipment you do have is in working condition, from tires and spare to brakes and engine. Carrying spare fuses, spark plugs, jumper cables, a flashlight with extra batteries, a tool kit, and an extra fan belt is recommended.

If you get stuck on any kind of road, be careful about pulling off; the shoulder can be soft. In summer it stays light late, and though traffic is also light, one of Alaska's many good Samaritans is likely to stop to help and send for aid (which may be many miles away). In winter, pack emergency equipment—a shovel, tire chains, high-energy food, and extra clothing and blankets. Never head out onto unplowed roads unless you are prepared to walk back.

Cellular phones are an excellent idea for travel in Alaska, particularly on the main roads, but check with your service provider for coverage. AAA members may also want to upgrade to the "Plus" policy, which allows for towing of up to 100 mi if you break down. Road maps are available at gas stations and grocery stores throughout Alaska.

RULES OF THE ROAD

Alaska honors valid driver's licenses from any state or country, and the speed limit on most state highways is 55 mph, but much of the Parks Highway (between Wasilla and Fairbanks) and the Seward Highway (between Anchorage and Seward) is 65 mph. Unless otherwise posted, you may make a right turn on a red light after coming to a complete stop. Seat belts are required on all passengers in Alaska, and children under age five must be in child safety seats. State troopers rigorously enforce speed limits along the main highways.

State law requires that slow-moving vehicles pull off the road at the first opportunity if leading more than five cars. This is particularly true on the highway between Anchorage and Seward, where RV drivers have a bad reputation for not pulling over. Alaskans don't take kindly to being held up en route to their favorite Kenai River fishing spot.

There is no cell-phone ban in Alaska and you are not required to use a hands-free set while driving.

RVS

The secret to a successful RV trip to Alaska is preparation. Expect to drive on more gravel and rougher roads than you're accustomed to. **Batten down everything**; tighten every nut and bolt in and out of sight, and don't leave anything to bounce around inside. Travel light, and your tires and suspension system will take less of a beating. Protect your headlights and the grille area in front of the radiator. Make sure you carry adequate insurance to cover the replacement of your windshield.

Most of Alaska's public campgrounds accommodate trailers, but hookups are available only in private RV parks. Water can be found at most stopping points, but it may be limited for trailer use. Think twice before deciding to drive an RV or pull a trailer during the spring thaw. The rough roadbed can be a trial.

RV Rentals & RV Tours **ABC Motorhome Rentals** ☎ 907/279-2000 or 800/421-7456 🌐 www.abcmotorhome.com. **Alaska Motorhome Rentals** ☎ 907/258-7109 or 800/254-9929 🌐 www.alaskarv.com. **Alaska Superior RV** ☎ 907/561-7723 or 800/764-4625 🌐 www.goalaska.com. **Clippership Motorhome Rentals** ☎ 907/562-7051 or 800/421-3456 🌐 www.clippershiprv.com. **Fantasy RV Tours** ☎ 970/642-4562 or 800/952-8496 🌐 www.fantasyrvtours.com. **GoNorth RV Camper Rental** ☎ 907/479-7272 or 866/236-7272 🌐 www.gonorthalaska.com. **Great Alaskan Holidays** ☎ 907/248-7777 or 888/225-2752 🌐 www.greatalaskanholidays.com.

CRUISE TRAVEL

Flip to Chapter 2: Cruising in Alaska for information about cruises and our favorite voyages.

EATING OUT

Alaska is best known for its seafood, particularly such stars as king salmon, halibut, king crab, and shrimp. Anchorage and Juneau have superb restaurants specializing in fresh seafood, but you will also find seafood on the menu in virtually any coastal Alaskan town. The open-air salmon bakes in Juneau, Tok, Denali National Park & Preserve, and Fairbanks serve excellent, all-you-can-eat grilled salmon and halibut. Anchorage has the greatest diversity of restaurants, including classy steak houses, noisy brewpubs, authentic Thai and Mexican eateries, and a wide variety of other ethnic places.

Was the service stellar or not up to snuff? Did the food give you shivers of delight or leave you cold? Did the prices and portions make you happy or sad? Rate restaurants and write your own reviews in Travel Ratings or start a discussion about your favorite places in Travel Talk on www.fodors.com. Your comments might even appear in our books. Be a Fodor's correspondent!

MEALS & MEALTIMES

Alaskan restaurants typically serve breakfast until 10 or 11, lunch from 11 to 2, and dinner starting around 4. Unless otherwise noted, the restaurants listed in this guide are open daily for lunch and dinner.

PAYING

Credit cards are widely accepted in resort restaurants and in many restaurants in major towns like Anchorage. Many small towns only have a one or two eateries; some establishments may not take credit cards. For guidelines on tipping *see* Tipping, *below.*

WHAT IT COSTS

CATEGORY	COST*
$$$$	over $25
$$$	$20–$25
$$	$15–$20
$	$10–$15
¢	under 10

**Prices are per person for a main course, excluding drinks, service, and tax.*

RESERVATIONS & DRESS

Alaska is a casual place—the cruise ship is probably the only place you'll encounter formal wear. Some of the pricier lodges may have dress codes for dinner. We mention dress only when men are required to wear a jacket or a jacket and tie.

During summer high season, you should make reservations when possible, especially in the Southeast. We only mention specifically when reservations are essential or when they are not accepted. For popular restaurants, book as far ahead as you can (often 30 days), and reconfirm as soon as you arrive.

WINES, BEER & SPIRITS

Alcohol is sold at liquor stores in most Alaskan towns and cities along the road system, as well as in settlements along the Inside Passage. Alcoholism is a devastating problem in native villages, and because of this many of these Bush communities are "dry" (no alcohol allowed) or "damp" (limited amounts allowed for personal use, but alcohol cannot be sold). Be sure to check the rules before flying into a Bush community with alcohol, or you might find yourself charged with illegally importing it.

Alaska's many excellent microbrews include Glacier BrewHouse, Silver Gulch, Sleeping Lady, Kodiak Brewery, and Moose's Tooth. The state's best-known beer, Alaskan Amber, is made by Alaskan Brewing Company in Juneau. Anchorage is home to several popular brewpubs, and their beers are sold in local liquor stores. Homer Brewing Company in the town of Homer sells its beers in local bars or in take-away bottles. You'll also find brewpubs in Fairbanks, Haines, Skagway, and Wasilla.

ECOTOURISM

Concern for the environment has spawned a worldwide movement called ecotourism, or green tourism. Ecotourists aim to travel responsibly, taking care to conserve the environment and respect indigenous populations. The Alaska Wilderness Recreation and Tourism Association includes many of the state's wilderness-dependent businesses and promotes eco-friendly activities across the state. For information about environmental concerns peculiar to Alaska as well as a list of resources and ecotour operators, *see* Chapter 1.

The **Alaska Wilderness Recreation and Tourism Association** 907/258-3171 www.awrta.org. **The International Ecotourism Society** www.ecotourism.org.

GAY & LESBIAN TRAVEL

Alaska is a politically conservative state, and openly gay and lesbian travelers may not be well accepted in some towns. Although Fairbanks and Juneau both have active gay and lesbian communities, Anchorage is the real center for Alaska, with a Gay and Lesbian Community Center and two gay bars (Mad Myrna's and the Raven), along with gay-oriented travel agencies, stores, and a theater company (Out North Contemporary Art House). For gay and lesbian information, Identity Inc. produces a monthly magazine, operates a gay and lesbian help line, and runs the above-mentioned community center.

Gay- & Lesbian-Friendly Travel Agencies **Different Roads Travel** 760/325-6964 or 800/429-8747 (Ext. 14) lgernert@tzell.com. **Skylink Travel and Tour/Flying Dutchmen Travel** 707/546-9888 or 800/225-5759; serving lesbian travelers.

Gay & Lesbian Resources **Identity Inc.** 907/929-4528 www.identityinc.org.

HEALTH

During the summer months Alaska is infamous for its sometimes dense clouds of mosquitoes and other biting insects. They are generally the worst in Interior Alaska but can be an annoyance throughout the state. **Be sure to bring mosquito repellent with DEET!** Also occasionally used (but less effective) is the Avon product Skin So Soft. Mosquito coils may be of some help if you are camping or staying in remote cabins. Head nets are sold in local sporting-goods stores and are a wise purchase if you plan to spend extended time outdoors, particularly in the Interior or on Kodiak Island.

Other problems that may afflict outdoors adventurers are: sunburn (always bring sunscreen with you on outings, even if the temperature is cool), snow blindness (sunglasses are essential for visits to glaciers), and altitude sickness.

HOLIDAYS

In addition to the standard nationwide holidays, Alaska also celebrates two statewide holidays: Alaska Day (October 18), celebrating the transfer of the state's ownership from Russia to the United States, and Seward's Day (last Monday in March), which marks the signing of the treaty that authorized the transfer. Although these are not major holidays, some businesses may be closed, particularly in Sitka.

INSURANCE

What kind of coverage do you honestly need? Do you even need trip insurance at all? Take a deep breath and read on.

We believe that comprehensive trip insurance is especially valuable if you're booking a very expensive or complicated trip (particularly to an isolated region) or if you're booking far in advance. Who knows what could happen six months down the road? But whether or not you get insurance has more to do with how comfortable you are assuming all that risk yourself.

Comprehensive travel policies typically cover trip-cancellation and interruption, letting you cancel or cut your trip short because of a personal emergency, illness, or, in some cases, acts of terrorism in your destination. Such policies also cover evacuation and medical care. Some also cover you for trip delays because of bad weather or mechanical problems as well as for lost or delayed baggage. Another type of coverage to look for is financial default—that is, when your trip is disrupted because a tour operator, airline, or cruise line goes out of business. Generally you must buy this when you book your trip or shortly thereafter, and it's only available to you if your operator isn't on a list of excluded companies.

Expect comprehensive travel insurance policies to cost about 4% to 7% of the total price of your trip (it's more like 12% if you're over age 70). A medical-only policy may or may not be cheaper than a comprehensive policy. Always read the fine print of your policy to make sure that you are covered for the risks that are of the most concern to you. Compare several policies to make sure you're getting the best price and range of coverage available.

Insurance Comparison Sites **Insure My Trip.com** www.insuremytrip.com. **Square Mouth.com** www.quotetravelinsurance.com.

Comprehensive Travel Insurers **Access America** 800/729-6021 www.accessamerica.com. **CSA Travel Protection** 800/873-9855 www.csatravelprotection.com. **HTH Worldwide** 610/254-8700 or 888/243-2358 www.hthworldwide.com. **Travelex Insurance** 888/457-4602 www.travelex-insurance.com. **Travel Guard International** 715/345-0505 or 800/826-4919 www.travelguard.com. **Travel Insured International** 800/243-3174 www.travelinsured.com.

Medical-Only Insurers **Wallach & Company** 800/237-6615 or 504/687-3166 www.wallach.com. **International Medical Group** 800/628-4664 www.imglobal.com. **International SOS** 215/942-8000 or 713/521-7611 www.internationalsos.com.

FOR INTERNATIONAL TRAVELERS

CURRENCY

The dollar is the basic unit of U.S. currency. It has 100 cents. Coins are the penny (1¢); the nickel (5¢), dime (10¢), quarter (25¢), and half-dollar (50¢); and the very rare golden $1 coin and even rarer silver $1. Bills are denominated $1, $5, $10, $20, $50, and $100, all mostly green and identical in size; designs and background tints vary. You may come across a $2 bill, but the chances are slim.

DRIVING

Driving in the United States is on the right. Speed limits are posted in miles per hour along roads and highways (usually between 55 mph and 70 mph). Watch for lower limits in small towns and on back roads (usually 30 mph to 40 mph). Most states require front-seat passengers to wear seat belts; many states require children to sit in the back seat and to wear seat belts. In major cities, rush hour is between 7 and 10 AM; afternoon rush hour is between 4 and 7 PM. To encourage carpooling, some freeways have special lanes for so-called high-occupancy vehicles (HOV)—cars carrying more than one passenger—ordinarily marked with a diamond.

Highways are well paved. Interstate highways—limited-access, multilane highways whose numbers are prefixed by "I–"—are the fastest routes. Interstates with three-digit numbers encircle urban areas, which may have other limited-access expressways, freeways, and parkways as well. Tolls may be levied on limited-access highways. So-called U.S. highways and state highways are not necessarily limited-access but may have several lanes.

Gas stations are plentiful. Most stay open late (24 hours along large highways and in big cities), except in rural areas, where Sunday hours are limited and where you may drive long stretches without a refueling opportunity. Along larger highways, roadside stops with restrooms, fast-food restaurants, and sundries stores are well spaced. State police and tow trucks patrol major highways and lend assistance. If your car breaks down on an interstate, pull onto the shoulder and wait for help, or have your passengers wait while you walk to an emergency phone (available in most states). If you carry a cell phone, dial *55, noting your location on the small green roadside mileage markers.

ELECTRICITY

The U.S. standard is AC, 110 volts/60 cycles. Plugs have two flat pins set parallel to each other.

EMBASSIES

Australia ☎ 202/797-3000 🌐 www.austemb.org. **United Kingdom** ☎ 202/588-7800 🌐 www.britainusa.com. **Canada** ☎ 202/682-1740 🌐 www.canadianembassy.org.

EMERGENCIES

For police, fire, or ambulance dial 911 (0 in rural areas).

HOLIDAYS

Major national holidays are New Year's Day (Jan. 1); Martin Luther King Day (3rd Mon. in Jan.); Presidents' Day (3rd Mon. in Feb.); Memorial Day (last Mon. in May); Independence Day (July 4); Labor Day (1st Mon. in Sept.); Columbus Day (2nd Mon. in Oct.); Thanksgiving Day (4th Thurs. in Nov.); Christmas Eve and Christmas Day (Dec. 24 and 25); and New Year's Eve (Dec. 31).

MAIL

You can buy stamps and aerograms and send letters and parcels in post offices. Stamp-dispensing machines can occasionally be found in airports, bus and train stations, office buildings, drugstores, and the like. U.S. mail boxes are stout, dark blue, steel bins at strategic locations in major cities; pickup schedules are posted inside the bin (pull down the handle to see them). Parcels more than 1 pound must be mailed at a post office or at a private mailing center.

Within the United States, a first-class letter weighing 1 ounce or less costs 39¢, and each additional ounce costs 24¢; postcards cost 24¢. A 1-ounce airmail letter to most countries costs 84¢, an airmail postcard costs 75¢; to Canada and Mexico, a 1-ounce letter costs 63¢, a postcard 55¢. An aerogram—a single sheet of lightweight blue paper that folds into its own envelope, stamped for overseas airmail—costs 75¢ regardless of its destination.

To receive mail on the road, have it sent c/o General Delivery at your destination's main post office (use the correct five-digit ZIP code). You must pick up mail in person within 30 days and show a driver's license or passport.

DHL ☎ 800/225-5345 🌐 www.dhl.com. **Federal Express** ☎ 800/463-3339 🌐 www.fedex.com. **Mail Boxes, Etc.** (The UPS Store) ☎ 800/789-4623 🌐 www.mbe.com. **United States Postal Service** 🌐 www.usps.com.

PASSPORTS & VISAS

Visitor visas aren't necessary for citizens of Australia, Canada, the United Kingdom, as well as for most citizens of European Union countries if you're coming for tourism and staying for fewer than 90 days. If you require a visa, the cost is $100 and, depending on where you live, the waiting time can be substantial. Apply for a visa at the U.S. consulate in your place of residence; look at the U.S. State Department's special Visa Web site for further information. *See* Passports & Visas, below, for more information.

Visa Information Destination USA 🌐 www.unitedstatesvisas.gov.

PHONES

All U.S. telephone numbers consist of a three-digit area code and a seven-digit local number. Within many local calling areas, you dial only the seven-digit number; in others, you must dial "1" first and then the area code. To call between area-code regions, dial "1" then all 10 digits; the same goes for calls to numbers prefixed by "800," "888," "866," and "877"—all toll free. For calls to numbers preceded by "900" you must pay—usually dearly.

For international calls, dial "011" followed by the country code and the local number. For help, dial "0" and ask for an overseas operator. The country code is 61 for Australia, 64 for New Zealand, 44 for the United Kingdom. Calling Canada is the same as calling within the United States. Most phone books list country codes and U.S. area codes. The country code for the United States is 1.

For operator assistance, dial "0." To obtain someone's phone number, call directory assistance at 555–1212 or occasionally 411 (free at many public phones). You can reverse the charges on a long-distance call by calling "collect"; dial "0" instead of "1" before the 10-digit number.

At pay phones, instructions often are posted. Usually you insert coins in a slot (usually 25¢–50¢ for local calls) and wait for a steady tone before dialing. When you call long-distance, the operator tells you how much to insert; prepaid phone cards, widely available in various denominations, can be used from any phone. Follow the directions to activate the card (there is usually an access number and then an activation code for the card), then dial your number.

The United States has several GSM (Global System for Mobile Communications) networks, so multiband mobile phones from most countries (except for Japan) work here. Unfortunately, it's almost impossible to buy a pay-as-you-go mobile SIM card in the U.S.—which allows you to avoid roaming charges—without a phone. That said, cell phones with pay-as-you-go plans are available for well under $100. The cheapest ones with decent national coverage are the GoPhone from Cingular and Virgin Mobile, which only offers pay-as-you-go service.

Cell Phone Contacts **Cingular** ☎ 888/333-6651 🌐 www.cingular.com. **Virgin Mobile** ☎ No phone 🌐 www.virginmobileusa.com.

LODGING

Off-season hotel rates are often much lower, but most travelers prefer to visit Alaska in the summer, when days are long and temperatures are mild. Shoulder-season (May and September) travelers may find somewhat lower rates, but some businesses and attractions may be closed. Camping is always an option, particularly if you enjoy the great outdoors. Travelers willing to sleep in bunks may want to check out the state's many hostels, some of which have family rooms.

Did the hotel look as good in real life as it did in the photos? Did you sleep like a baby, or were the walls paper thin? Did you get your money's worth? Rate hotels and write your own reviews in Travel Ratings or start a discussion about your favorite places in Travel Talk on www.fodors.com. Your comments might even appear in our books.

For hotels:

WHAT IT COSTS

CATEGORY	ANCHORAGE
$$$$	over $250
$$$	$200–$250
$$	$150–$200
$	$100–$150
¢	under $100

CATEGORY	ELSEWHERE IN ALASKA
$$$$	over $225
$$$	$175–$225
$$	$125–$175
$	$75–$125
¢	under $75

**All prices are for a standard double room in high season, excluding tax and service.*

Most hotels and other lodgings require you to give your credit card details before they will confirm your reservation. If you don't feel comfortable e-mailing this information, ask if you can fax it (some places even prefer faxes). However you book, get confirmation in writing and have a copy of it handy when you check in. If you book through an online travel agent, discounter, or wholesaler, you might even want to confirm your reservation with the hotel before leaving home—just to be sure everything was processed correctly.

Be sure you understand the hotel's cancellation policy. Some places allow you to cancel without any kind of penalty—even if you prepaid to secure a discounted rate—if you cancel at least 24 hours in advance. Others require you to cancel a week in advance or penalize you for the cost of one night. Small inns and B&Bs are most likely to require you to cancel far in advance. Most hotels allow children under a certain age to stay in their parents' room at no extra charge, but others charge for them as extra adults; find out the cutoff age for discounts.

Assume that hotels operate on the European Plan (**EP,** no meals) unless we specify that they use the Breakfast Plan (**BP,** with full breakfast), Continental Plan (**CP,** Continental breakfast), Full American Plan (**FAP,** all meals), Modified American Plan (**MAP,** breakfast and dinner) or are **all-inclusive** (all meals and most activities).

BED & BREAKFASTS

Bed-and-breakfasts are common across Alaska and provide a fine way to learn about the area you're in while staying with a local. Nearly every Alaskan town has at least one B&B, and dozens of choices are available in the larger cities. At last count, Anchorage had more than 175 B&Bs, including modest suburban apartments, elaborate showcase homes with dramatic vistas, and everything in between.

Reservation Services **Alaska Private Lodgings/Stay with a Friend** ☎ 907/235-2148 🌐 www.alaskabandb.com. **Alaska's Mat-Su Bed & Breakfast Association** 🌐 www.alaskabnbhosts.com. **Anchorage Alaska Bed & Breakfast Association** ☎ 907/272-5909 or 888/584-5147 🌐 www.anchorage-bnb.com. **Bed & Breakfast Association of Alaska** 🌐 www.alaskabba.com. **Bed & Breakfast Association of Alaska INNside Passage Chapter** 🌐 www.accommodations-alaska.com. **Bed & Breakfast.com** ☎ 512/322-2710 or 800/462-2632 🌐 www.bedandbreakfast.com **Bed & Breakfast Inns Online** ☎ 615/868-1946 or 800/215-7365 🌐 www.bbonline.com. **BnB Finder.com** ☎ 212/432-7693 or 888/547-8226 🌐 www.bnbfinder.com. **Fairbanks Association of Bed & Breakfasts** 🌐 www.ptialaska.net/~fabb. **Kenai Peninsula Bed & Breakfast Association** ☎ 907/776-8883 or 866/436-2266 🌐 www.kenaipeninsulabba.com.

CAMPING & CABINS

Camping in Alaska needn't be a daunting experience: think of it as camping elsewhere in the Lower 48, except that the mosquitoes are worse and there's a greater likelihood of a nighttime bear visit. Some newcomers to bear country are uneasy sleeping in a tent, but encounters are rare. **Store food inside your vehicle or in bear-safe containers** where it's less likely to tempt bears. The midnight sun can also keep tent campers awake. Whether you're in a tent or an RV, you'll need warm bedding, insect repellent, rain protection, and tight containers for food storage.

Public campgrounds in Alaska are operated by the U.S. Forest Service, State Division of Parks and Outdoor Recreation, National Park Service, and Bureau of Land Management. Of the national parks, only Denali has developed car-camping facilities, and these campsites fill quickly. Several other Alaskan national parks have walk-in campgrounds, and all parks allow backcountry camping. In addition to the public campgrounds, private RV parks can be found in Alaska's larger towns. For more information, *see* Chapter 1.

Both the U.S. Forest Service and the Bureau of Land Management operate rustic cabins that provide a bit more shelter to those interested in backcountry stays. Some can be reached by hiking in from populated areas, but others require a short plane ride to reach. Advance reservations are a must, especially for hike-in cabins. The Alaska Public Lands Information Center's Web site has information on all cabins, and reservations for any of the Forest Service cabins can be made through ReserveUSA.

Alaska Public Lands Information Centers 🌐 www.nps.gov/aplic/cabins. **ReserveUSA** ☎ 877/444-6777 🌐 www.reserveusa.com.

HOME EXCHANGES

With a direct home exchange, you stay in someone else's home while they stay in yours. Some outfits also deal with vacation homes, so you're not actually staying in someone's full-time residence, just their vacant weekend place.

Exchange Clubs **HomeLink International** ☎ 800/638-3841 🌐 www.homelink.org; $80 yearly for Web-only membership; $125 with Web access and two directories. **Home Exchange.com** ☎ 800/877-8723 🌐 www.homeexchange.com $59.95 for a 1-year online listing. **Intervac U.S.** ☎ 800/756-4663 🌐 www.intervacus.com; $78.88 for Web-only membership; $126 includes Web access and a catalog.

HOSTELS

Hostels offer barebones lodging at low, low prices—often in shared dorm rooms with shared baths—to people of all ages, though the primary market is young travelers, especially students. Most hostels serve breakfast; dinner and/or shared cooking facilities may also be available. In some hostels, you aren't allowed to be in your room during the day, and there may be a curfew at night. Nevertheless, hostels provide a sense of community, with public rooms where travelers often gather to share stories. Many hostels are affiliated with Hostelling International (HI), an umbrella group of hostel associations with some 4,500 member properties in more than 70 countries. Other hostels are completely independent and may be nothing more than a really cheap hotel.

Membership in any HI association, open to travelers of all ages, allows you to stay in HI-affiliated hostels at member rates. One-year membership is about $28 for adults; hostels charge about $10–$30 per night. Members have priority if the hostel is full; they're also eligible for discounts around the world, even on rail and bus travel in some countries.

Official Hostelling International hostels can be found in Ketchikan and Sitka. Many other Alaskan hostels are not affiliated with HI, including ones in Anchorage, Denali, Fairbanks, Girdwood, Haines, Homer, Juneau, McCarthy, Petersburg, Seward, Skagway, Slana, Sterling, Talkeetna, Tok, and Wrangell. Most of these are only open seasonally, but hostels in Anchorage, Fairbanks, Girdwood, Homer, Juneau, Skagway, and Talkeetna provide year-round lodging. Hostels.com has contact information for all Alaskan hostels.

Hostels.com www.hostels.com. **Hostelling International–USA** 301/495-1240 www.hiusa.org.

HOTELS

Weigh all your options (we can't say this enough). Join "frequent guest" programs. You may get preferential treatment in room choice and/or upgrades in your favorite chains. Check general travel sites and hotel Web sites as not all chains are represented on all travel sites. Always research or inquire about special packages and corporate rates. If you prefer to book by phone, note you can sometimes get a better price if call the hotel's local toll-free number (if one is available) rather than the central reservations number.

If your destination's high season is December through April and you're trying to book, say, in late April, you might save considerably by changing your dates by a week or two. Note, though, that many properties charge peak-season rates for your entire stay even if your travel dates straddle peak and nonpeak seasons. High-end chains catering to businesspeople are often busy only on weekdays and often drop rates dramatically on weekends to fill up rooms. **Ask when rates go down.**

Watch out for hidden costs, including resort fees, energy surcharges, and "convenience" fees for such things as unlimited local phone service you won't use and a free newspaper—possibly written in a language you can't read. Always verify whether local hotel taxes are or are not included in the rates you are quoted, so that you'll know the real price of your stay. In some places, taxes can add 20% or more to your bill. If you're traveling overseas **look for price guarantees,** which protect you against a falling dollar. With your rate locked in, you won't pay more, even if the price goes up in the local currency.

Alaskan motels and hotels are similar in quality to those in the Lower 48 states. Most Alaskan motels are independent, but you'll find the familiar chains (including Best Western, Comfort Inn, Days Inn, Hampton Inn, Hilton, Holiday Inn, Marriott, Motel 6, Super 8, and Sheraton) in Anchorage. Westmark Hotels is a regional chain, owned by cruise-tour operator Holland America Westours, with 15 locations, including hotels in Anchorage, Fairbanks, Kenai, Kodiak, Sitka, and Valdez in Alaska, plus Beaver Creek and Whitehorse in Canada's Yukon Territory. Princess Tours owns a luxury hotel in Fairbanks and lodges outside Denali National Park, near Denali State Park, near Wrangell–St. Elias National Park, and on the Kenai

Peninsula. All hotels listed have private bath unless otherwise noted.

Discount Hotel Rooms **Accommodations Express** ☎ 800/444-7666 or 800/277-1064. **Hotels.com** ☎ 800/219-4606 or 800/364-0291 🌐 www.hotels.com. **Quikbook** ☎ 800/789-9887 🌐 www.quikbook.com. **Turbotrip.com** ☎ 800/473-7829 🌐 w3.turbotrip.com.

WILDERNESS LODGES

To really get away from it all, book a remote lodge with rustic accommodations in the middle of breathtaking Alaskan wilderness. Some of the most popular are in the river drainages of Bristol Bay, in Southeast Alaska, and along the Susitna River north of Anchorage. Most of these lodges place a heavy emphasis on fishing; a stay generally includes daily guided fishing trips as well as all meals. They can be astronomically expensive (daily rates of $250–$900 per person), so if you're not interested in fishing, you won't want to seek these out. Lodges in and near Denali National Park emphasize the great outdoors, and some even include wintertime dogsledding. Activities focus on hiking, rafting, flightseeing, horseback-riding, and natural-history walks. For getting deep into the wilderness, these lodges are an excellent alternative to the hotels and cabins outside the park entrance. For some of our favorite lodges, *see* Chapter 1.

MONEY MATTERS

Because of its off-the-beaten-path location, Alaska has always been an expensive travel destination. Major roads link Anchorage with Fairbanks and other cities and towns in South Central and Interior Alaska, but most other parts of the state are accessible only by air or water. This is even true of Alaska's state capital, Juneau. Costs in Anchorage and Fairbanks are only slightly higher than for Lower 48 cities, and you will find discount chain stores, but as you head to more remote parts of the state, prices escalate. In Bush communities food, lodging, and transportation costs can be far higher than in Anchorage, since nearly everything must be brought in by air.

Prices throughout this guide are given for adults. Substantially reduced fees are almost always available for children, students, and senior citizens. For information on taxes, *see* Taxes.

CREDIT CARDS

Throughout this guide, the following abbreviations are used: **AE,** American Express; **D,** Discover; **DC,** Diners Club; **MC,** MasterCard; and **V,** Visa.

It's a good idea to inform your credit-card company before you travel, especially if you're going abroad and don't travel internationally very often. Otherwise, the credit-card company might put a hold on your card owing to unusual activity—not a good thing halfway through your trip. Record all your credit-card numbers—as well as the phone numbers to call in the if your cards are lost or stolen—in a safe place so you're prepared should something go wrong. Both MasterCard and Visa have general numbers you can call (collect if you're abroad) if your card is lost, but you're better off calling the number of your issuing bank since MasterCard and Visa usually just transfer you to your bank; your bank's number is usually printed on your card.

Reporting Lost Cards **American Express** ☎ 800/992-3404 in the U.S. or 336/393-1111 collect from abroad 🌐 www.americanexpress.com. **Diners Club** ☎ 800/234-6377 in the U.S. or 303/799-1504 collect from abroad 🌐 www.dinersclub.com. **Discover** ☎ 800/347-2683 in the U.S. or 801/902-3100 collect from abroad 🌐 www.discovercard.com. **MasterCard** ☎ 800/622-7747 in the U.S. or 636/722-7111 collect from abroad 🌐 www.mastercard.com. **Visa** ☎ 800/847-2911 in the U.S. or 410/581-9994 collect from abroad 🌐 www.visa.com.

TRAVELER'S CHECKS & CARDS

Some consider this the currency of the cave man, and it's true that fewer establishments accept traveler's checks these days. Nevertheless, they're a cheap and secure way to carry extra money, particularly on trips to urban areas. Both Citibank (under the Visa brand) and American Express issue traveler's checks in the United States, but Amex is better known and more widely accepted; you can also avoid hefty surcharges by cashing Amex checks at Amex offices. Whatever you do, keep track of all the serial numbers in case the checks are lost or stolen. Traveler's checks issued by banks are still generally accepted in Alaska, especially in large resorts or lodges; however, you shouldn't rely on them in smaller towns.

American Express now offers a stored-value card called a Travelers Cheque Card, which you can use wherever American Express credit cards are accepted, including ATMs. The card can carry a minimum of $300 and a maximum of $2,700, and it's a very safe way to carry your funds. Although you can get replacement funds in 24 hours if your card is lost or stolen, it doesn't really strike us as a very good deal. In addition to a high initial cost ($14.95 to set up the card, plus $5 each time you "reload"), you still have to pay a 2% fee for each purchase in a foreign currency (similar to that of any credit card). Further, each time you use the card in an ATM you pay a transaction fee of $2.50 on top of the 2% transaction fee for the conversion—add it all up and it can be considerably more than you would pay for simply using your own ATM card. Regular traveler's checks are just as secure and cost less.

American Express ☎ 888/412-6945 in the U.S., 801/945-9450 collect outside of the U.S. to add value or speak to customer service 🌐 www.americanexpress.com.

PACKING

Why do some people travel with a convoy of suitcases the size of large-screen TVs and yet never have a thing to wear? How do others pack a toaster-oven-size duffle with a week's worth of outfits *and* supplies for every possible contingency? We realize that packing is a matter of style—a very personal thing—but there's a lot to be said for traveling light. The tips in this section will help you win the battle of the bulging bag.

Make a list. In a recent Fodor's survey, 29% of respondents said they make lists (and often pack) at least a week before a trip. Lists can be used at least twice—once to pack and once to repack at the end of your trip. You'll also have a record of the contents of your suitcase, just in case it disappears in transit.

Think it through. What's the weather like? Is this a business trip or a cruise or resort vacation? Going abroad? In some places and/or sights, traditions of dress may be more or less conservative than you're used to. As your itinerary comes together, jot activities down and note possible outfits next to each (don't forget those shoes and accessories).

Edit your wardrobe. Plan to wear everything twice (better yet, thrice) and to do laundry along the way. Stick to one basic look—urban chic, sporty casual, etc. Build around one or two neutrals and an accent (e.g., black, white, and olive green). Women can freshen looks by changing scarves or jewelry. For a week's trip, you can look smashing with three bottoms, four or five tops, a sweater, and a jacket you can wear alone or over the sweater.

Be practical. Put comfortable shoes at the top of your list. (Did we need to tell you this?) Pack items that are lightweight, wrinkle resistant, compact, and washable. (Or this?) Try a simple wrinkling test: Intentionally fold a piece of fabric between your fingers for a couple minutes. If it refuses to crease, it will probably come out of your suitcase looking fresh. That said, if you stack and then roll your clothes when packing, they'll wrinkle less.

Check weight and size limitations. In the United States you may be charged extra for checked bags weighing more than 50 pounds. Abroad some airlines don't allow you to check bags weighing more than 60 to 70 pounds, or they charge outrageous fees for every pound your luggage is over. Carry-on size limitations can be stringent, too.

Check carry-on restrictions. Research restrictions with the TSA. Rules vary abroad, so check them with your airline if your traveling overseas on a foreign carrier. Consider packing all but essentials (travel documents, prescription meds, wallet) in checked luggage. This leads to a "pack only what you can afford to lose" approach that might help you streamline.

Lock it up. If you must pack valuables, use TSA-approved locks (about $10) that can be unlocked by all U.S. security personnel.

Tag it. Always put tags on your luggage with some kind of contact information; use your business address if you don't want people to know your home address. Put the same information (and a copy of your itinerary) inside your luggage, too.

Rethink valuables. On U.S. flights, airlines are only liable for about $2,800 per person for bags. On international flights, the liability limit is around $635 per bag. But items like computers, cameras, and jewelry aren't covered, and as gadgetry regularly goes on and off the list of carry-on no-no's, you can't count on keeping things safe by keeping them close. Although comprehensive travel policies may cover luggage, the liability limit is often a pittance. Your homeowner's policy may cover you sufficiently when you travel—or not.

Report problems immediately. If your bags—or things in them—are damaged or go astray, file a written claim with your airline *before you leave the airport*. If the airline is at fault, it may give you money for essentials until your luggage arrives. Most lost bags are found within 48 hours, so alert the airline to your whereabouts for two or three days. If your bag was opened for security reasons in the United States and something is missing, file a claim with the TSA.

WHAT YOU'LL NEED IN ALASKA

Not all of Alaska has the fierce winters that are usually associated with the state. Winter in the Southeast and South Central coastal regions is relatively mild—Chicago and Minneapolis experience harsher weather than Juneau. It's a different story in the Interior, where temperatures in the subzero range and biting winds keep most visitors indoors.

The best way to keep warm under colder conditions is to **wear layers of clothing, starting with thermal underwear and socks.** The outermost layer should be lightweight, windproof, rainproof, and hooded. Down jackets (and sleeping bags) have the disadvantage of becoming soggy when wet; the newer synthetics (particularly wind-block fabrics) are the materials of choice. Footgear needs to be sturdy, and if you're going into the backcountry, be sure it's waterproof. Rubber boots are often a necessity in coastal areas. When wearing snow boots, be certain they are not too tight. Restricting your circulation will only make you colder.

Summer travelers should pack plenty of layers, too. Although Alaskan summers are mild, temperatures can vary greatly through the course of a day, and you may be happy that you brought that extra sweater or jacket when the sun goes down.

Wherever you go in Alaska (and especially in the Southeast), **be prepared for rain.** To keep yourself dry, pack a collapsible umbrella or bring a rain slicker, as sudden storms are common. UVA/UVB sunscreen, insect repellent, and sunglasses are necessities. A pair of binoculars will help you track any wildlife you encounter.

Befitting the frontier image, dress is mostly casual day and night. Bring along one outfit that is appropriate for "dress-up," if you enjoy doing so, though it's not necessary.

PASSPORTS & VISAS

As of December 31, 2006, all U.S and Canadian citizens will need passports to cross the border between the two countries **by air or by sea.** Check your itinerary carefully and make sure that you bring a passport if your travel plans require air or sea border crossings.

U.S. and Canadian citizens may still cross the border **by land** without a passport until December 31, 2007, at which time passports will be required for that type of crossing as well. If you decide not to carry your passport and you plan to cross the border, be sure that you bring two forms of identification, such as a driver's license, social security card or birth certificate.

Citizens of all other countries need passports and possibly visas to travel to the United States and Canada.

Note that parents traveling with small children should bring photocopies of their children's birth certificates to avoid any problems.

SAFETY

Alaska does have a high crime rate, but that doesn't mean it's unsafe for tourists. Distribute your cash, credit cards, I.D.s, and other valuables between a deep front pocket, an inside jacket or vest pocket, and a hidden money pouch. Don't reach for the money pouch once you're in public.

WOMEN'S SAFETY

Women are generally safe in Alaska, but sexual assaults do occur at an alarming rate, so a little extra caution is in order when traveling alone. Common sense is enough of a safeguard in most cases: don't hike in secluded areas alone, be sure to keep your hotel room door locked, don't accept drinks from strangers, and take cabs if you're returning to your hotel late at night. Some of the out-in-the-middle-of-nowhere work towns can resemble frontier towns a little *too* much, and women may experience unwanted attention (catcalls and the like).

In addition to following the bear safety rules listed below, women who are camping during their menstrual cycle should take extra care in how they dispose of feminine hygiene products—seal them tightly in plastic bags and store them in bear-proof containers.

OUTDOOR SAFETY

Alaska is big, wild, and not particularly forgiving, so travelers lacking outdoor experience need to take precautions when venturing away from the beaten path. If you lack backcountry skills or feel uncomfortable handling yourself if a bear should approach, hire a guide, go on guided group tours, or join a class at the National Outdoor Leadership School, which is based in Palmer (one hour north of Anchorage).

Education **National Outdoor Leadership School** ☎ 907/745-4047 ⊕ www.nols.edu.

BEARS

For an in-depth look at bears, turn to *Welcome to Bear Country* in Chapter 7. If you're lucky—and careful—the sight of one of these magnificent creatures in the wild can be a highlight of your visit. By respecting bears and exercising care in bear country, neither you nor the bear will suffer from the experience. Remember that bears don't like surprises. Make your presence known by talking, singing, rattling a can full of gravel, or tying a bell to your pack, especially when terrain or vegetation obscures views. Travel with a group, which is noisier and easier for bears to detect. If possible, walk with the wind at your back so your scent will warn bears of your presence. And avoid bushy, low-visibility areas whenever possible.

Give bears the right-of-way—lots of it—especially sows with cubs. Don't camp on animal trails; they're likely to be used by bears. If you come across a carcass of an animal or detect its odor, avoid the area entirely; it's likely a bear's food cache. Store all food and garbage away from your campsite in airtight or specially designed bear-proof containers. The Park Service supplies these for hikers in Denali and Glacier Bay national parks and requires that backcountry travelers use them. If a bear approaches you while you are fishing, stop. If you have a fish on your line, cut your line.

If you do encounter a bear at close range, don't panic, and, above all, don't run. You can't outrun a bear, and by fleeing you could trigger a chase response from the bear. Talk in a normal voice to help identify yourself as a human. If traveling with others, stand close together to "increase your size." If the bear charges, it could be a bluff; as terrifying as this may sound, the experts advise standing your ground. If a brown bear actually touches you, then drop to the ground and play dead, either flat on your stomach or curled in a ball with your hands behind your neck. If you don't move, a brown bear will typically break off its attack once it feels the threat is gone. If you are attacked by a black bear, you are probably better off fighting back with rocks, sticks, or anything else you find, since black bears are more likely to attack a person intentionally. Polar bears can be found in remote parts of the Arctic, but tourists are highly unlikely to encounter them in summer.

For more information on bears, ask for the brochure "Bear Facts: The Essentials for Traveling in Bear Country" from any of the Alaska Public Lands offices. Bear safety information is also available on the Internet at 🌐 www.state.ak.us/adfg.

SHOPPING

The best buys in Alaska are products of local materials made by native peoples and other artists and craftspeople living in the state. Before you buy, **make sure the local crafts are genuine.** The state has adopted two symbols that guarantee the authenticity of crafts made by Alaskans. A silver hand symbol indicates the item was made by one of Alaska's native peoples. A polar bear verifies the item was "Made in Alaska." If some items with these tags seem more expensive than you expected, examine them closely and you'll probably find that they are handmade, one-of-a-kind pieces. Keep in mind, also, that not all native artisans use these symbols.

Although these symbols are designed to ensure authentic Alaskan and native-made products, it doesn't mean that items lacking them are not authentic. This applies in particular to native artists who may or may not go through the necessary paperwork to obtain the silver hand labels. They often come to town and sell items directly to shop owners for cash. It pays to shop around, ask questions, and learn about the different types of native crafts from around the state. For more information about native crafts, check out *Made in Alaska* in Chapter 3.

Some Alaskan shops sell carved items made in Southeast Asia, primarily Bali, and not all of these crafts are labeled as such. When some clerks are asked about these items' origins, they may say, "We got it in Anchorage." Unfortunately, this may just mean that they picked it up at the Anchorage airport after the items were flown in from Asia. Before buying something—particularly an expensive piece—ask questions to make sure it is authentic. You can protect yourself by visiting a number of shops first to learn the differences between Alaskan handcrafted items and those that are mass-produced.

Carved walrus ivory pieces are sold in many Alaskan shops. Some of these are pieces of raw ivory carved by native Alaskan artists, and others are fossilized ivory, which can be legally used by other carvers. Although walrus ivory is legal to own in the United States, transporting it through other countries—including Canada—requires a permit from Convention on International Trade in Endangered Species (CITES).

ℹ Authenticity & Permits **Alaska State Council on the Arts** ☎ 907/269-6610 or 888/278-7424 🌐 www.eed.state.ak.us/aksca. **Convention on Trade in Endangered Species (CITES)** 🌐 www.cites.org. **Made in Alaska** 🌐 www.madeinalaska.org.

SMART SOUVENIRS

Authentic native art is always worth looking over, even if you cannot afford the finest pieces. Alaska has an abundance of artists whose works fill local galleries. Some, such as Rie Muñoz and Barbara Lavalle, are nationally known, but you should also check out prints by Ray Troll and Evon Zerbetz in Ketchikan, unique and colorful pins by William Spear in Juneau, and the paintings of Nancy Yaki and Erik Behnke in Homer. Several towns are known for their galleries, most notably Homer, but also Sitka, Juneau, Haines, and Ketchikan. Be sure to look for items made from musk-ox wool (qiviut) in Anchorage and Palmer, along with birch syrup from Kahiltna Birchworks (🌐 www.alaskabirchsyrup.com); it's sold in many Alaskan gift shops and at the Anchorage Saturday and Sunday Markets.

TAXES

Alaska does not impose a state sales tax, but individual cities and boroughs have their own taxes. (Anchorage has no sales tax.)

City taxes, and an additional hotel tax, are often applied to your hotel bill. Rates are variable, generally ranging from 2%–6%.

You won't have to pay any departure taxes if you're flying within the United States. Vancouver's airport has a departure tax of C$5 for flights within British Columbia and the Yukon or C$10 to U.S. destinations, payable before you board your flight at automatic ticket machines or staffed booths.

TIME

Nearly all of Alaska lies within the Alaska time zone, 20 hours behind Sydney, 9 hours behind London, 4 hours behind New York City, 3 hours behind Chicago, and 1 hour behind Los Angeles and western Canada. The nearly unpopulated Aleutian Islands are in the same time zone as Hawaii, 5 hours behind the East Coast.

TIPPING

In addition to tipping waiters and waitresses, taxi drivers, and baggage handlers, tipping others who provide personalized services is common in Alaska. Tour-bus drivers who offer a particularly informative trip generally receive a tip from passengers at the end of the tour. A small amount left in your hotel room is also much appreciated by the cleaning staff. Fishing guides are commonly tipped around 10% by their clients, particularly if the guide helped them land a big one. In addition, gratuities may also be given to pilots following a particularly good flightseeing or bear-viewing trip, but the amount is up to your own discretion.

TOURS & PACKAGES

GUIDED TOURS

Guided tours are a good option when you don't want to do it all yourself. You travel along with a group (sometimes large, sometimes small), stay in prebooked hotels, eat with your fellow travelers (sometimes included in the price of your tour, sometimes not), and follow a schedule. But not all guided tours are a "If This is Tuesday, It Must Be Belgium" kind of experience. A knowledgeable guide can take you places that you might never discover on your own, and you may be pushed to see more than you would have otherwise. Tours aren't for everyone, but they can be just the thing for trips to places where making travel arrangements is difficult or time-consuming (particularly when you don't speak the language). Whenever you book a guided tour, find out what's included and what isn't. A "land-only" tour includes all your travel (by bus, in most cases) in the destination, but not necessarily your flights to or even within it. Also, in most cases, prices in tour brochures don't include fees and taxes. And remember that you'll be expected to tip your guide (in cash) at the end of the tour.

Recommended Generalists **Abercrombie & Kent** ☎ 630/954–2944 or 800/554–7016 www.abercrombiekent.com. **Collette Vacations** ☎ 401/728–9000 or 800/340–5158 www.collettevacations.com. **Gadabout Tours** ☎ 760/325–5556 or 800/952–5068 www.gadabouttours.com. **Globus** ☎ 303/797–2800 or 866/755–8581 www.globusjourneys.com. **Maupintour** ☎ 800/255–4266 www.maupintour.com. **Tauck World Discovery** ☎ 203/899–6500 or 800/788–7885 www.tauck.com. **Trafalgar Tours** ☎ 212/689–8977 or 866/544–4434 www.trafalgartours.com.

Bike Tours **Alaska Backcountry Bike Tours** ☎ 907/746–5018 or 866/354–2453 www.mountainbikealaska.com. **Backroads** ☎ 510/527–1555 or 800/462–2848 www.backroads.com.

Bird-Watching Tours **Alaska Birding and Wildlife Tours** ☎ 877/424–5637 www.alaskabirding.com. **Victor Emanuel Nature Tours** ☎ 512/328–5221 or 800/328–8368 www.ventbird.com. **Wilderness Birding Adventures** ☎ 907/694–7442 www.wildernessbirding.com. **Wings Birding Tours** ☎ 520/320–9868 or 888/293–6443 www.wingsbirds.com.

Canoeing, Kayaking & Rafting **Above and Beyond Alaska** ☎ 907/364–2333 www.beyondak.com. **Alaska Discovery** ☎ 907/780–6226 or 800/586–1911 www.akdiscovery.com. **Alaska Outdoor Adventures** ☎ 907/472–2534 or 877/472–2534 www.akadventures.com. **Alaska Wildland Adventures** ☎ 907/783–2928 or 800/334–8730 www.alaskawildland.com. **Anadyr Adventures** ☎ 907/835–2814 or 800/865–2925 www.anadyradventures.com. **Chugach Adventure Guides** ☎ 907/783–2004 or 877/783–2004 www.alaskanrafting.com. **James Henry River Journeys** ☎ 415/868–1836 or 800/786–1830 www.riverjourneys.com. **Nova** ☎ 907/745–5753 or 800/746–5753 www.novalaska.com. **OARS** ☎ 209/736–4677 or 800/346–6277 www.oars.com. **REI Adventures** ☎ 253/437–1100 or 800/622–2236

🌐 www.rei.com. **TrekAmerica** ☎ 973/983-1144 or 800/221-0596 🌐 www.trekamerica.com.

Dogsledding Tours **Chugach Express Dog Sled Tours** ☎ 907/783-2266 🌐 www.chugachexpress.com. **Godwin Glacier Dog Sled Tours** ☎ 907/224-8239 or 888/989-8239 🌐 www.alaskadogsled.com. **IdidaRide Sled Dog Tours** ☎ 907/224-8607 or 800/478-3139 🌐 www.ididaride.com. **Plettner Sled Dog Kennels** ☎ 907/892-6944 or 877/892-6944 🌐 www.plettner-kennels.com. **Sourdough Outfitters** ☎ 907/692-5252 🌐 www.sourdoughoutfitters.com.

Heli-skiing **Chugach Adventure Guides** ☎ 907/783-2004 or 877/783-2004 🌐 www.chugachpowderguides.com. **Valdez Heli-Camps** ☎ 907/783-3243 in Anchorage, 907/783-3513 in Valdez 🌐 www.valdezhelicamps.com. **Valdez Heli-Ski Guides** ☎ 907/835-4528 🌐 www.valdezheliskiguides.com.

Hiking **Alaskan Gourmet Adventures** ☎ 907/346-1087 🌐 www.hikealaska.com. **Alaska Two-Legged Tours** ☎ 907/317-4813 or 877/252-5344 🌐 www.twoleggedtours.com. **Mountain Travel-Sobek** ☎ 510/594-6000 or 888/687-6235 🌐 www.mtsobek.com. **Sourdough Outfitters** (⇨ Dogsledding).

Learning Vacations **Earthwatch Institute** ☎ 978/461-0081 or 800/776-0188 🌐 www.earthwatch.org. **National Audubon Society** ☎ 212/979-3000 or 800/967-7425 🌐 www.audubon.org. **Natural Habitat Adventures** ☎ 303/449-3711 or 800/543-8917 🌐 www.nathab.com. **Nature Expeditions International** ☎ 954/693-8852 or 800/869-0639 🌐 www.naturexp.com. **Naturequest** ☎ 949/499-9561 or 800/369-3033 🌐 www.naturequesttours.com. **Oceanic Society Expeditions** ☎ 415/441-1106 or 800/326-7491 🌐 www.oceanic-society.org. **Sierra Club** ☎ 415/977-5522 🌐 www.sierraclub.org. **Smithsonian Journeys** ☎ 202/357-4700 or 877/338-8687 🌐 www.smithsonianjourneys.org.

Native Tours **Alexander's River Adventure** ☎ 907/474-3924 🌐 http://fairbanks-alaska.com/alexander.htm. **Cape Fox Tours** ☎ 907/225-4846 🌐 www.capefoxtours.com. **Goldbelt Tours** ☎ 907/789-4183 or 800/478-3610 🌐 www.goldbelttours.com. **Northern Alaska Tour Company** ☎ 907/474-8600 or 800/474-1986 🌐 www.northernalaska.com. **Sitka Tours** ☎ 907/747-2954 or 888/270-8687 🌐 www.sitkatribe.org.

Natural History Tours **Alaska Two-Legged Tours** (⇨ Hiking). **Alaska Wildland Adventures** (⇨ Canoeing, Kayaking & Rafting). **Camp Denali** ☎ 907/683-2290 🌐 www.campdenali.com. **Great Alaska Adventure Lodge** ☎ 907/262-4515 or 800/544-2261 🌐 www.greatalaska.com. **Hallo Bay Wilderness Camp** ☎ 907/235-2237 🌐 www.hallobay.com. **Walrus Islands Expeditions** ☎ 907/235-9349 🌐 www.alaskawalrusisland.com. **Wilderness Birding Adventures** (⇨ Bird-Watching).

Photography Tours **Alaska Birding and Wildlife Tours** (⇨ Bird-Watching). **Camp Denali** (⇨ Natural History). **Dolphin Charters** ☎ 510/527-9622 or 800/472-9942 🌐 www.dolphincharters.com. **Hallo Bay Wilderness Camp** (⇨ Natural History). **Joseph Van Os Photo Safaris** ☎ 206/463-5383 🌐 www.photosafaris.com. **Naturally Wild Photo Adventures** ☎ 740/774-6243 🌐 www.naturallywild.net.

Sportfishing Tours **Alaska River Adventures** ☎ 907/595-2000 or 888/836-9027 🌐 www.alaskariveradventures.com. **Alaska Wildland Adventures** (⇨ Canoeing, Kayaking & Rafting). **Fishing International** ☎ 707/542-4242 or 800/950-4242 🌐 www.fishinginternational.com. **Great Alaska Adventure Lodge** (⇨ Natural History). **Rod & Reel Adventures** ☎ 541/349-0777 or 800/356-6982 🌐 www.rodreeladventures.com. **Sport Fishing Alaska** ☎ 907/344-8674 or 888/552-8674 🌐 www.alaskatripplanners.com.

Wilderness Adventures **Alaska Mountain Guides** ☎ 907/766-3366 or 800/766-3396 🌐 www.alaskamountainguides.com. **Alaska Mountaineering School** ☎ 907/733-1016 🌐 www.climbalaska.org. **Brooks Range Aviation** ☎ 907/692-5444 or 800/692-5443 🌐 www.brooksrange.com. **Regal Air** ☎ 907/243-8535 🌐 www.regal-air.com. **Rust's Flying Service** ☎ 907/243-1595 or 800/544-2299 🌐 www.flyrusts.com. **Sourdough Outfitters** (⇨ Dogsledding).

VACATION PACKAGES

Packages *are not* guided tours. Packages combine airfare, accommodations, and perhaps a rental car or other extras (theater tickets, guided excursions, boat trips, reserved entry to popular museums, transit passes), but they let you do your own thing. During busy periods, packages may be your only option because flights and rooms may be otherwise sold out. Packages will definitely save you time. They can also save you money, particularly in peak seasons, but—and this is a really big "but"—you should price each part of the package separately to be sure. And be aware that prices advertised on Web sites and in newspapers rarely include service charges or taxes, which can up your costs by hundreds of dollars.

Note that local tourism boards can provide information about lesser-known and small-niche operators that sell packages to just a few destinations. And don't always assume that you can get the best deal by booking everything yourself. Some packages and cruises are sold only through travel agents.

Each year consumers are stranded or lose their money when packagers—even large ones with excellent reputations—go out of business. How can you protect yourself? First, always pay with a credit card; if you have a problem, your credit-card company may help you resolve it. Second, buy trip insurance that covers default. Third, choose a company that belongs to the United States Tour Operators Association, whose members must set aside funds ($1 million) to cover defaults. Finally choose a company that also participates in the Tour Operator Program of the American Society of Travel Agents (ASTA), which will act as mediator in any disputes. You can also check on the tour operator's reputation among travelers by posting an inquiry on one of the Fodors.com forums.

Organizations **American Society of Travel Agents** (ASTA) ☎ 703/739-2782 or 800/965-2782 24-hr hotline 🌐 www.astanet.com. **United States Tour Operators Association** (USTOA) ☎ 212/599-6599 🌐 www.ustoa.com.

Package Tours **Alaska Airlines Vacations** ☎ 800/468-2248 🌐 www.alaskaair.com. **Alaska Bound** ☎ 231/439-3000 or 888/252-7527 🌐 www.alaskabound.com. **Alaska Tour & Travel** ☎ 907/245-0200 or 800/208-0200 🌐 www.alaskatravel.com. **Alaska Tours** ☎ 907/277-3000 🌐 www.alaskatours.com. **Gray Line of Alaska** ☎ 206/281-3535 or 800/544-2206 🌐 www.graylinealaska.com. **Homer Travel & Tours** ☎ 907/235-7751 or 800/478-7751 🌐 www.alaskahomertravel.com. **Juneau Guide** ☎ 907/789-3772 or 888/658-6328 🌐 www.juneaubb.com. **Knightly Tours** ☎ 206/938-8567 or 800/426-2123 🌐 www.knightlytours.com. **Princess Alaska Tours** ☎ 800/426-0500 🌐 www.princesslodges.com. **See Alaska Tours** ☎ 907/278-5704 🌐 www.alaskatours.net. **Viking Travel** ☎ 907/772-3818 or 800/327-2571 🌐 www.alaskaferry.com.

TRAIN TRAVEL

The state-owned Alaska Railroad has service connecting Seward, Anchorage, Denali National Park, and Fairbanks, as well as additional service connecting Anchorage and Whittier. The Alaska Railroad also offers a variety of package tours that range from one-day Denali excursions to 10-day tours, which include many excursions along the way between Anchorage and Fairbanks.

Traveling by train isn't as economical as traveling by bus, but it is a wonderful way to go; the scenery along the way is spectacular. Some cars have narration, and food is available on board in the dining car and at the café. Some private tour companies that offer a more glitzy trip between Anchorage and Fairbanks hook their luxury railcars to the train.

Travel aboard the Alaska Railroad is leisurely: Anchorage to Seward ($62 one way) takes four hours, Anchorage to Denali ($100–$130) takes a little over seven hours, and Anchorage to Fairbanks ($150–$185) takes about 12 hours. The trip to Whittier takes a little over two hours and costs $55 one way (but only $68 round-trip).

Except for the Seward–Anchorage leg, all service operates year-round. Trains run daily in summer; service is reduced from September to late May. Dining cars are available on all trains.

Gray Line of Alaska offers three-day package tours that include luxury train travel from Anchorage to Fairbanks or vice versa. You can opt for one-way or round-trip travel. All packages include at least a day of exploring in Denali National Park.

For a scenic and historic trip between Skagway and Fraser, British Columbia, take the White Pass & Yukon Route, which follows the treacherous path taken by prospectors during the Klondike gold rush of 1897–98. The trip to Fraser takes two hours and costs $72 one way. If you want to continue on to Whitehorse, the capital of the Yukon Territory, you can catch a bus at Fraser's train terminal. A combo rail/bus ticket costs $99 one way. The entire trip takes five hours. A shorter excursion that only goes as far as the White Pass Summit is also available daily. It takes three hours round-trip, and there are usually three departures daily from Skagway starting at around 8:15 am. The fare is $95 round-trip.

Note that smoking is not permitted on trains.

CUTTING COSTS

The AlaskaPass allows unlimited travel on bus, ferry, and rail lines in Alaska; *see* Cutting Costs *in* Boat & Ferry Travel.

For a less expensive alternative, ride one of the public dome cars, owned and operated by the railroad. Seating in the public cars is unassigned, and passengers take turns under the observation dome. The railroad's public cars are a great place to meet resident Alaskans.

FARES & SCHEDULES

Tickets can be purchased in advance over the phone using a credit card. If your reservation is a month or more ahead of time, the company will mail you the ticket; otherwise travelers can pick them up at the departure station. Travel agents also sell tickets for travel aboard the Alaska Railroad.

All rail lines post up-to-date schedules on their Web sites. Trains usually leave on time, so be sure to arrive at the station at least 15 minutes prior to departure to ensure that you make it aboard.

Train Information **Alaska Railroad** ☎ 907/265-2494 in Anchorage, 907/458-6025 in Fairbanks, 800/544-0552 🌐 www.alaskarailroad.com. **Gray Line Alaska** ☎ 907/277-5581 in Anchorage, 907/451-6835 in Fairbanks, 888/452-1737 🌐 www.graylinealaska.com. **White Pass & Yukon Route** ☎ 907/983-2217 or 800/343-7373 🌐 www.whitepassrailroad.com.

PAYING

Cash, Discover, MasterCard, and Visa are accepted on all train lines.

RESERVATIONS

Advance reservations are highly recommended for midsummer train travel, particularly between Seward and Anchorage and between Anchorage and Denali National Park & Preserve. The White Pass Summit excursion offered on the White Pass & Yukon Route rail is a very popular shore excursion for cruise passengers, so advance reservations for this trip are strongly recommended.

TRAVEL AGENCIES

If you use an agent—brick-and-mortar or virtual—you'll pay a fee for the service. And know that the service you get from some online agents isn't comprehensive. For example, Expedia or Travelocity don't search for prices on budget airlines like JetBlue, Southwest, or small foreign carriers. That said, some agents (online or not) *do* have access to fares that are difficult to find otherwise, and the savings can more than make up for any surcharge.

A knowledgeable brick-and-mortar travel agent can be a godsend if you're booking a cruise, a package trip that's not available to you directly, an air pass, or a complicated itinerary including several overseas flights. What's more, travel agents that specialize in a destination may have exclusive access to certain deals and insider information on things such as charter flights. Agents who specialize in types of travelers (senior citizens, gays and lesbians, naturists) or types of trips (cruises, luxury travel, safaris) can also be invaluable.

Alaska is the land of the package tour, but it doesn't have to be that way. Travel agents can be good resources for people who want to avoid the package-tour experience, but aren't quite comfortable going it on their own. A travel agent can help with complicated itineraries, secure reservations, and offer discounts, without committing you to a rigid tour during which you rarely have an opportunity to get off the bus or the boat. That said, it's worth pricing a trip on your own using Web sites and online consolidators before you consult an agent. Although travel agents can in many cases keep the costs of an Alaska vacation down, they don't always offer the best prices.

Travel agents are found in all of Alaska's cities and larger towns, and some of the state's larger travel agencies are listed below.

Agent Resources **American Society of Travel Agents** ☎ 703/739–2782 🌐 www.travelsense.org.

Online Agents **Expedia** 🌐 www.expedia.com. **Onetravel.com** 🌐 www.onetravel.com. **Orbitz** 🌐 www.orbitz.com. **Priceline.com** 🌐 www.priceline.com. **Travelocity** 🌐 www.travelocity.com.

Alaska Travel Agencies **Alaska Tours** ☎ 907/277–3000 or 866/317–3325 🌐 www.alaskatours.com. **Easy Travel** ☎ 907/562–3279 or 800/383–3279 🌐 www.easytravel.nu. **Explore Tours** ☎ 907/786-0192 or 800/523–7405 🌐 www.exploretours.com. **Homer Travel & Tours** ☎ 907/235–7751 or 800/478-7751 🌐 www.alaskahomertravel.com. **USTravel** ☎ 907/561–2434 or 800/478–2434 🌐 www.ustravelak.com. **Viking Travel** ☎ 907/772–3818 or 800/327–2571 🌐 www.alaskaferry.com.

VISITOR INFORMATION & HELPFUL WEB SITES

The Alaska Travel Industry Association (a partnership between the state and private businesses) publishes the *Alaska Vacation Planner,* a free, comprehensive information source for statewide travel year-round. Alaska's regional tourism councils distribute vacation planners highlighting their local attractions.

Get details on Alaska's vast public lands from Alaska Public Lands Information centers in Ketchikan, Tok, Anchorage, and Fairbanks.

Statewide Information **Alaska Department of Fish and Game** ☎ 907/465–4112, 907/465–4180 sportfishing seasons and regulations, 907/465–2376 license information 🌐 www.state.ak.us/adfg. **Alaska Division of Parks** ☎ 907/269–8400 Anchorage, 907/451–2705 Fairbanks 🌐 www.alaskastateparks.org. **Alaska Public Lands Information Center** ☎ 907/271–2737 in Anchorage, 907/456–0527 in Fairbanks, 907/228–6234 in Ketchikan, 907/883–5667 in Tok 🌐 www.nps.gov/aplic. **Alaska Travel Industry Association** ☎ 907/929–2200 or 800/862–5275 to order Alaska Vacation Planners 🌐 www.travelalaska.com.

Regional Information **Kenai Peninsula Tourism Marketing Council** ☎ 907/262–5229 or 800/535-3624 🌐 www.kenaipeninsula.org. **Southeast Alaska Discovery Center** ☎ 907/228–6220 🌐 www.fs.fed.us/r10/tongass/districts/discoverycenter. **Southwest Alaska Municipal Conference** ☎ 907/562–7380 🌐 www.southwestalaska.com.

City Information **Anchorage** 🌐 www.anchorage.net. **Cordova** 🌐 www.cordovachamber.com. **Fairbanks** 🌐 www.explorefairbanks.com. **Haines** 🌐 www.haines.ak.us. **Homer** 🌐 www.homeralaska.org. **Juneau** 🌐 www.traveljuneau.com. **Ketchikan** 🌐 www.visit-ketchikan.com. **Kodiak** 🌐 www.kodiak.org. **Matanuska-Susitna Valley** 🌐 www.alaskavisit.com. **Nome** 🌐 www.nomealaska.org. **Petersburg** 🌐 www.petersburg.org. **Prince of Wales Island** 🌐 www.princeofwalescoc.org. **Seward** 🌐 www.sewardak.org. **Sitka** 🌐 www.sitka.org. **Skagway** 🌐 www.skagway.com. **Soldotna** 🌐 www.soldotnachamber.com. **Talkeetna** 🌐 www.talkeetna-chamber.com. **Unalaska/Dutch Harbor** 🌐 www.unalaska.info. **Valdez** 🌐 www.valdezalaska.org. **Whittier** 🌐 www.whittieralaska.com. **Wrangell** 🌐 www.wrangellchamber.org. **Yakutat** 🌐 www.yakutatalaska.com.

British Columbia & Yukon **Tourism British Columbia** ☎ 604/435–5622 or 800/435–5622 🌐 www.hellobc.com. **Tourism Yukon** ☎ 867/667-5340 or 800/789–8566 🌐 www.touryukon.com.

WEB SITES

We're really proud of our Web site: Fodors.com is a great place to begin any journey. Scan Travel Wire for suggested itineraries, travel deals, restaurant and hotel openings, and other up-to-the-minute info. Check out Booking to research prices and book plane tickets, hotel rooms, rental cars, and vacation packages. Head to Talk for on-the-ground pointers from travelers who frequent our message boards. You can also link to loads of other travel-related resources.

After your trip, be sure to rate the places you visited and share your experiences and travel tips with us and other Fodorites in Travel Ratings and Talk on www.fodors.com.

All About Alaska **Alaska.com** 🌐 www.alaska.com is a subsidiary of *The Anchorage Daily News* and has travel features, photo galleries, and a service that allows you to order a variety of brochures and e-newsletters. **Alaska Department of Fish and Game** 🌐 www.adfg.state.ak.us has tips on wildlife viewing and news on conservation issues and efforts. ***Alaska Magazine*** 🌐 www.alaskamagazine.

com posts some of its feature stories online, and maintains an extensive statewide events calendar. **Alaska Native Heritage Center** 🌐 www.alaskanative.net has information on Alaska's native tribes, as well as links to other cultural and tourism Web sites. **Alaska Natural History Association** 🌐 www.alaskanha.org has links to sites with information on the state's public lands, national parks, forests, and wildlife refuges, as well as an online bookstore where you can find maps and books about the Alaskan experience.

Time Zones **Timeanddate.com** 🌐 www.timeanddate.com/worldclock can help you figure out the correct time anywhere in the world.

Weather **Accuweather.com** 🌐 www.accuweather.com is an independent weather-forecasting service with especially good coverage of hurricanes. **Weather.com** 🌐 www.weather.com is the Web site for the Weather Channel.

INDEX

B

PHOTO CREDITS

Cover Photo *(Tracy Arm, Fords Terror Wilderness, Tongass Forest, Inside Passage): John Hyde.* 5, *Stephen Frink Collection/Alamy.* 7, *Photodisc.* 10, *Mark Newman/age fotostock.* 11 (left), *Frank Lukasseck/age fotostock.* 11 (right), *Morales/age fotostock.* 12, *True North Images/age fotostock.* 13, *Richard Cummins/viestiphoto.com.* 16, *Photodisc.* 17 (left), *Stuart Westmorland/age fotostock.* 17 (right), *Bill Terry/viestiphoto.com.* 19, *Liane Cary/age fotostock.* 20, *Robert Winslow/viestiphoto.com.* 21 (left), *Photodisc.* 21 (right), *John W. Warden/age fotostock.* 24 (left), *James Prout/age fotostock.* 24 (top center), *James Gritz/Alamy.* 24 (bottom center), *Bill Terry/viestiphoto.com.* 24 (top right), *Don Johnston/Alamy.* 24 (bottom right), *Danita Delimont/Alamy.* 25 (top left), *Ron Niebrugge/Alamy.* 25 (bottom left and center), *Patrick Frischknecht/age fotostock.* 25 (right), *Kevin Schafer/age fotostock.* 26, *Leo Keeler/Alamy.* 27 (left), *Henry Ausloos/age fotostock.* 27 (right), *Bill Terry/viestiphoto.com.* 28 (left), *Dennis Frates/Alamy.* 28 (top center), *Kevin Schafer/age fotostock.* 28 (bottom center), *Lydie Gigerichova/age fotostock.* 28 (top right), *Tracy Ferrero/Alamy.* 28 (bottom right), *Richard Cummins/viestiphoto.com.* 29 (top left), *Mark Newman/age fotostock.* 29 (bottom left), *Steven J. Kazlowski/Alamy.* 29 (top center), *Michael S. Nolan/age fotostock.* 29 (bottom center), *Lise Dumont/Alamy.* 29 (right), *Brian Durell/age fotostock.* 30, *Frank Siteman/age fotostock.* 31 (left), *Dorothy Keeler/Alamy.* 31 (center), *Christina Krutz/age fotostock.* 31 (right), *Michael S. Nolan/age fotostock.* **Chapter 1: Sports & Wilderness Adventures:** 33, *True North Images/age fotostock.* 34, *Alaska Stock LLC/Alamy.* 46, *Ron Niebrugge/Alamy.* 53, *Bill Montagne/bushplanes.com.* 55, *Mitch Diamond/Alamy.* 58, *Alaska Stock LLC/Alamy.* 63, *Danita Delimont/Alamy.* 67, *Alaska Stock LLC/Alamy.* 73 (top), *Stephen Frink Collection/Alamy.* 73 (bottom), *ImageState/Alamy.* 74 (top), *Andoni Canela/age fotostock.* 74 (bottom), *Pieter Folkens.* 75 (top), *William Wu.* 75 (bottom), *Pieter Folkens.* 76 (top), *Michael S. Nolan/age fotostock.* 76 (bottom), *Pieter Folkens.* **Chapter 2: Cruising in Alaska:** 81, *American Safari Cruises.* **Chapter 3: Southeast Alaska:** 113, *Liane Cary/age fotostock.* 114 (top), *Richard Cummins/viestiphoto.com.* 114 (bottom), *Alaska Stock LLC/Alamy.* 151, *Bryan & Cherry Alexander Photography/Alamy.* 152 (left), *Jeff Greenberg/age fotostock.* 152 (right), *Robert Mitchell/viestiphoto.com.* 153 (left), *Sitka National Historical Park.* 153 (right), *Tracy Ferrero/Alamy.* 154-155 (all), *Alaska State Museum, Juneau.* 197, *University of Washington Libraries. Special Collections Division, Alaska Photograph Collection, UW7326.* 198 (top), *University of Washington Libraries. Special Collections Division, Eric A. Hegg Photograph Collection. PH Coll 274, Hegg20a.* 198 (bottom), *Alaska and Polar Regions Collections, Elmer E. Rasmuson Library, University of Alaska Fairbanks. 199, P277-001-009, Alaska State Library, James Wickersham / State Historic Sites Collection.* 201 (top left), *Pep Roig/Alamy.* 201 (bottom left), *Alaska Stock LLC/Alamy.* 201 (right), *Christian Racich.* **Chapter 4: Anchorage:** 209, *Greg Vaughn/*

Alamy. 210 (top), *David Sanger Photography/Alamy.* 210 (bottom), *Ken Graham/age fotostock.* 211 (top), *Anchorage Museum of History and Art.* 211 (bottom), *David Sanger Photography/Alamy.* 213, *Richard Cummins/viestiphoto.com.* 244 (top), *Ronald Johansen.* 244 (bottom), *Alaska Bounty.* 245 (top), *William Wu.* 245 (bottom), *Alaska Brewing Company.* 246, *Alaska Bounty.* **Chapter 5: South Central Alaska:** 259, *John Schwieder.* 260 (top), *David Sanger Photography/Alamy.* 260 (bottom), *Chris A. Crumley/Alamy.* 261 (top), *Alaska Stock LLC/Alamy.* 261 (bottom), *Renaud Visage/age fotostock.* 262, *Ron Niebrugge/Alamy.* 292, *Don B. Stevenson/Alamy.* 293, *Robert Mitchell/viestiphoto.com.* 295 (top), *Alaska Stock LLC/Alamy.* 295 (bottom), *Renaud Visage/age fotostock.* **Chapter 6: The Interior and Denali National Park & Preserve:** 333, *Papilio/Alamy.* 334, *Arco Images/Alamy.* 335, *Stuart Westmorland/age fotostock.* 359, *JTB Photo/Alamy.* 375, *Brett Baunton/Alamy.* 376, *Ross Geredien/viestiphoto.com.* 376-377, *Alissa Crandall/Corbis.* 377 (bottom), *John Schwieder/Alamy.* 378 (top), *Library of Congress Prints and Photographs Division.* 378 (bottom), *Bill Montagne/bushplanes.com.* **Chapter 7: The Bush:** 413, *Peter Arnold, Inc./Alamy.* 414, *Mark Hambllin/age fotostock.* 415 (left), *Goldpanners.* 415 (right), *Alaska Stock LLC/Alamy.* 416, *Steven J. Kazlowski/Alamy.* 429 (top), *Juan Carlos Muñoz/age fotostock.* 429 (bottom), *Morales/age fotostock.* 430 (top), *Michael S. Nolan/age fotostock.* 430 (bottom), *Morales/age fotostock.* 431 (top), *Peter Arnold, Inc./Alamy.* 431 (bottom), *SuperStock/age fotostock.* 432, *Mark Hamblin/age fotostock.* **Color Section:** *Self-propelled exploration in the waters of Prince William Sound: True North Images/age fotostock. Hiking in Glacier Bay National Park & Preserve: Larry Carver/viestiphoto.com. Colorful autumn tundra in Denali National Park & Preserve: Joe Englander/viestiphoto.com. A bull moose enjoying Alaskan waters: Bill Terry/viestiphoto.com. Bald Eagle, Alaska Raptor Center in Sitka: Glenn W. Swan/viestiphoto.com. Mt. McKinley: Photodisc. Grizzly bear: Steve Kaufman/age fotostock. Prince William Sound: Larry Carver/viestiphoto.com. Prince William Sound's Steller sea lions: Photodisc. Humpback whale: Michael S. Nolan/age fotostock. Hiker, Chugach State Park: True North Images/age fotostock. Caribou: Frank Krahmer/age fotostock. Totem pole, Alaska Native Heritage Center in Anchorage: Richard Cummins/viestiphoto.com. Bald eagle: Bill Terry/viestiphoto.com.*

NOTES

NOTES

NOTES

ABOUT OUR WRITERS

Jim Altieri moved to Fairbanks for the same reason as many other people move there: experimental music. Jim is the programmer for John Luther Adams's *The Place Where You Go to Listen* in the UAF Museum of the North. He has released several CDs of original work. Jim wrote about the midnight sun and the Klondike Gold Rush for this edition.

Former Fodor's editor **Carissa Bluestone** traded steady paychecks for the freelance life and the East Coast for the Pacific Northwest. In addition to updating and editing Fodor's guides, she works for several Seattle-based organizations. She updated Smart Travel Tips for this edition.

During more than 20 years in Alaska, **Tricia Brown** wrote numerous nonfiction books about the state, among them *The World-Famous Alaska Highway: A Guide to the Alcan and Other Wilderness Roads of the North*. She is also the author of three children's books, including the critically acclaimed *Children of the Midnight Sun*. Tricia contributed her road-tripping expertise to this book.

Dermot Cole is the author of five Alaska history books and is a longtime columnist for the Fairbanks *Daily News-Miner.* He and his wife have three children and live in the hills north of Fairbanks. They enjoy traveling, skiing, hiking, and exploring the wonders of Alaska. Dermot updated the Interior chapter this year.

A native Seattleite and lifelong fan of all things outdoors, **Nick Horton** has always been infatuated with the 49th state. Nick, who writes about travel, the outdoors, and politics for a variety of magazines, is an avid cyclist who counts a 1,200-mile Alaskan bicycle trip among his most memorable journeys. He updated the Southeast chapter and wrote original close-up pieces about bears, whales, glaciers, and Alaska's native crafts for this edition.

Ken Marsh is the former outdoors editor and executive editor of *Alaska* magazine. A lifelong Alaskan, he has explored all regions of the state. Ken's articles have appeared in many national outdoors magazines, and he is the author of *Breakfast at Trout's Place: The Seasons of an Alaska Fly-fisher.* He makes his home in Anchorage. He updated the Anchorage and Sports & Wilderness Adventures chapters this year.

A Midwesterner who moved to Alaska in 1984, **Tom Reale** has traveled extensively throughout the state, writing about it and about wilderness adventures for a variety of publications. He and his wife hunt, fish, camp, backpack, ski, and hike at every opportunity. Tom updated the South Central chapter of this book.

An Anchorage resident since 1982, nature and travel writer **Bill Sherwonit** has contributed stories about Alaska to a wide variety of newspapers, magazines, journals, and books and is the author of 10 books about Alaska. He also teaches classes and workshops about nature and travel/adventure writing. For this edition Bill updated the Bush chapter and the Denali section of Chapter 6.